Treasury of the True Dharma Eye
Dōgen's *Shōbōgenzō*

Treasury of the True Dharma Eye
Dōgen's *Shōbōgenzō*

Volume I

The Seventy-five-Chapter Compilation

Part 1

Chapters 1–15

An annotated translation
by the Sōtō Zen Text Project

Sōtōshū Shūmuchō
Tokyo

University of Hawai'i Press
Honolulu

© 2023 by Sōtōshū Shūmuchō
The Administrative Headquarters of Sōtō Zen Buddhism
All rights reserved.
Printed in China

Treasury of the True Dharma Eye: Dōgen's *Shōbōgenzō*
Volume I: The Seventy-five-Chapter Compilation, Part 1, Chapters 1-15

Published in Japan by Sōtōshū Shūmuchō, Tokyo
ISBN: 978-4-911061-00-8

Published for the rest of the world by University of Hawai'i Press, Honolulu

Library of Congress Cataloging-in-Publication Data

Names: Dōgen, 1200–1253, author. | Sōtō Zen Text Project, translator.

Title: Treasury of the true dharma eye : Dōgen's Shōbōgenzō / an
annotated translation by the Sōtō Zen Text Project.

Other titles: Shōbō genzō. English

Description: Honolulu : University of Hawai'i Press, [2024] | Published in
Japan by Sōtōshū Shūmuchō, 2023. | Includes bibliographical
references and index. | Contents: v. 1. The seventy-five-chapter
compilation, part 1, chapters 1–15

Identifiers: LCCN 2024004760 (print) | LCCN 2024004761 (ebook) | ISBN
9780824899172 (v. 1 ; paperback) | ISBN 9780824899189 (v. 2 ; paperback)
| ISBN 9780824899196 (v. 3 ; paperback) | ISBN 9780824899202 (v. 4 ;
paperback) | ISBN 9780824899219 (v. 5 ; paperback) | ISBN 9780824899226
(v. 6 ; paperback) | ISBN 9780824899233 (v. 7 ; paperback) | ISBN
9780824899240 (v. 8 ; paperback) | ISBN 9780824899257 (paperback) | ISBN
9798880700264 (v. 1 ; pdf) | ISBN 9798880700271 (v. 2 ; pdf) | ISBN
9798880700288 (v. 3 ; pdf) | ISBN 9798880700295 (v. 4 ; pdf) | ISBN
9798880700301 (v. 5 ; pdf) | ISBN 9798880700318 (v. 6 ; pdf) | ISBN
9798880700325 (v. 7 ; pdf) | ISBN 9798880700332 (v. 8 ; pdf)

Subjects: LCSH: Sōtōshū—Doctrines—Early works to 1800.

Classification: LCC BQ9449.D653 E5 2024 (print) | LCC BQ9449.D653 (ebook)
| DDC 294.3/85—dc23/eng/20240318

LC record available at https://lccn.loc.gov/2024004760
LC ebook record available at https://lccn.loc.gov/2024004761

Cover art: Eihei Dōgen Zenji Gyōjōzu scroll, courtesy of Rev. Ōtani Tetsuo
Cover design by Urs App

University of Hawai'i Press books are printed on acid-free paper and meet the
guidelines for permanence and durability of the Council on Library Resources.
Printer-ready copy has been provided by Sōtōshū Shūmuchō

CONTENTS

VOLUME I

THE SEVENTY-FIVE-CHAPTER COMPILATION

PART 1

Foreword (Hattori Shūsei) iii

Preface (Ishii Seijun) v

About the Translation vii

Conventions viii

Abbreviations x

Introduction to the Seventy-five-Chapter *Shōbōgenzō* 1

1. The Realized Kōan *Genjō kōan* 現成公案 3

2. Mahā-prajñā-pāramitā *Maka hannya haramitsu* 摩訶般若波羅蜜 17

3. Buddha Nature *Busshō* 佛性 29

4. Studying the Way with Body and Mind *Shinjin gakudō* 身心學道 ..119

5. This Mind Itself Is the Buddha *Soku shin ze butsu* 即心是佛 145

6. Deportment of the Practicing Buddha *Gyōbutsu iigi* 行佛威儀 161

7. One Bright Pearl *Ikka myōju* 一顆明珠 209

8. The Mind Cannot Be Got *Shin fukatoku* 心不可得 227

9. The Old Buddha Mind *Kobutsushin* 古佛心 239

10. Great Awakening *Daigo* 大悟 255

11. Principles of Seated Meditation *Zazen gi* 坐禪儀 275

12. Needle of Seated Meditation *Zazen shin* 坐禪箴 285

13. Ocean Seal Samādhi *Kaiin zanmai* 海印三 325

14. Sky Flowers *Kūge* 空華 347

15. Radiance *Kōmyō* 光明 373

FOREWORD

ON THE OCCASION OF THE PUBLICATION
OF THE ENGLISH TRANSLATION OF THE *SHŌBŌGENZŌ*

The Sōtō Zen Text Project, launched by the Sōtōshū in 1995, has previously published translations of the *Soto School Scriptures for Daily Services and Practice*, the *Standard Observances of the Soto School*, and the *Record of the Transmission of Illumination*. Now, it is bringing out the long-awaited translation of Zen Master Dōgen's *Treasury of the True Dharma Eye*. We would like to express our deepest gratitude to all those involved in this project of translating the Sōtō Zen scriptures.

We hope that readers of this book will study it for the sake of Buddhism and strive in their daily lives to practice in harmony with the teachings of Zen Master Dōgen. As we welcome this publication, it is our hope that, as followers of the Sōtōshū, we may spread its teachings widely among family and friends, with a heart of great compassion and mercy and the aspiration to liberate all sentient beings.

Hattori Shūsei

Chairperson, Sōtō Zen Text Project
President, Administrative Headquarters of Sōtō Zen Buddhism

March 2023

英語翻訳版『正法眼蔵』発刊に寄せて

曹洞宗では、1997年に宗典経典翻訳事業を発足し、爾来『曹洞宗日課勤行聖典』、『曹洞宗行持規範』、『伝光録』を翻訳、出版してまいりました。この度、その発刊を待ち望まれていた曹洞宗の根本宗典である道元禅師の『正法眼蔵』の翻訳がなされ、出版する運びとなりました。

曹洞宗宗典経典翻訳事業に関わった全ての人に対して、甚深の謝意を表する次第であります。

皆様には、本書を学ぶのにあたり、仏道のために学ぶ心をもって、道元禅師のみ教えと常に共にありつつ、日々の行持に励まれますことを祈念いたします。

また、曹洞宗の法孫として大慈大悲の心、広度衆生の願いを胸に、有縁の方々に普及されますことを冀い発刊のご挨拶といたします。

2023年3月吉日
曹洞宗宗典経典翻訳事業会長
曹洞宗宗務総長
服部秀世

PREFACE

In 1995, the Sōtō Zen Text Project began the work of translating the scriptures of the Sōtō School. Since then, the results of this work have steadily appeared, beginning with the publication of the *Soto School Scriptures for Daily Services and Practice* in August 2001, followed by the *Standard Observances of the Soto School* in January 2010, and the *Record of the Transmission of Illumination* in November 2017.

The present English translation of Zen Master Dōgen's *Shōbōgenzō* is a major achievement, representing the culmination of the committee's work. The road to publication has not been smooth: due to the number of volumes and the difficulty of the contents, the original plan had to be considerably extended. That it has now come to fruition is a testament to the tireless efforts of the project members and staff involved in the translation and editorial processes.

Translation, of course, necessarily involves interpretation; and, particularly in the case of the *Shōbōgenzō*, for which there are no definitive interpretations even in Japanese, how to render it into other languages without altering its nuances has been a major issue. Hence, in previous translations, there has been a tendency to introduce much personal interpretation. Here, this issue has been largely resolved through the project team's careful consideration of the translation equivalents.

Particularly noteworthy is the copious annotation. In his *Shōbōgenzō*, Dōgen quotes the words of the Chinese ancestral masters and adds his own interpretations, often completely subverting the meaning of the source Chinese. Indeed, such semantic development was one of Dōgen's intentions in composing the *Shōbōgenzō* in Japanese. Without resolving this tiered structure into a single voice, the English style of this translation remains faithful to the source text and makes use of the annotation to clarify the divergent elements in the original. This technique, which provides the reader with a maximum amount of information on the text, is a unique feature of the translation.

From long ago, the forerunners of Sōtō scholarship have commented that the text of the *Shōbōgenzō* displays various aspects in accordance with the ability of its readers. This is an expression of the fact that, while difficult to understand, the world of the *Shōbōgenzō* opens up in various ways according to the reader's abilities at the present moment. This work, while in one sense "definitive," offers us a translation that reveals this essential character of the original without restricting the reader to a single view.

I would like to express my appreciation once again for the efforts of all those involved in the translation project. I am confident that this translation will contribute greatly to the global development of Sōtō Zen.

Ishii Seijun
Chair of the Translation and Editorial Committee, Sōtō Zen Text Project
November 17, 2022, at the Soto Zen Buddhism North America 100th Anniversary Jukai-e

『正法眼蔵』英訳の刊行によせて

本宗典編纂委員会が立ち上がり、宗典の翻訳を開始したのは1995年のことであった。その成果は、2001年8月に刊行された『曹洞宗日課勤行聖典』に始まり、2010年1月の『曹洞宗行持軌範』、そして2017年11月『伝光録』と、着実に発表されてきた。

このたび、道元禅師の仮字『正法眼蔵』英訳が完成し刊行されたことは、その集大成にも位置する大きな成果であるといえよう。とはいえ、刊行への道のりは平坦ではなかった。原典の巻数の多さと内容の難解さから、当初の計画を大幅に延長しながら進められてきたのである。それがここに成ったことは、翻訳編集にたずさわってこられた編集員と担当職員のたゆみなき努力の賜に他ならない。

「翻訳」には、もとより解釈が入り込まざるを得ないものではあるが、こと仮字『正法眼蔵』に関しては、日本語においてさえも確定的解釈が存在しない状況において、そのニュアンスを変えずに他言語に展開してゆくことは、大いなる課題であった。それゆえ、従来の翻訳に私的解釈が大きく入り込んでしまう傾向が存在していたのでえある。

このたびの英訳では、プロジェクトチームが訳語を綿密に検討することにより、この問題はほぼ解決されている。さらに特筆すべきは重厚な注記である。道元禅師は、仮字『正法眼蔵』において、中国祖師の言葉を引用しながら、それに対して独自の解釈を付す。それは、原典の中国語の意味を完全に覆していることも少なくない。まさにこのような意味的展開が、道元禅師が仮字『正法眼蔵』を和文で著された意図の一つであったといえる。その段階構造を、一元的に翻訳文に繰り込むことをせず、翻訳は原文に忠実に行い、相違点を注記において明確化するという手法を用いて、最大限の情報を与えてくれるのが、この翻訳の特徴といえるであろう。

いにしえより、曹洞宗学の先達は、仮字『正法眼蔵』と向き合うとき、その本文が、読む側の力量に合わせてさまざまな様相を見せるものであると評されていた。これは、難解ながらも、読み手の、その時（而今）の力量に伴って、さまざまに『正法眼蔵』の世界が広がることを表現したものといえよう。このたびの翻訳は、まさに、そのような、「確定的」でありながらも、読み手を縛り付けない、原典の本質を発揮する翻訳を提供しているといえるであろう。

ここに改めて翻訳事業関係各位のご努力に感謝申し上げたい。そしてそれが大きく曹洞禅の世界的展開に寄与することを確信している。

2022年11月17日北アメリカ国際布教100周年記念授戒会にて記す
石井清純

About the Translation

This translation of Dōgen's *Shōbōgenzō* is a product of the Sōtō Zen Text Project (Sōtōshū Shūten Kyōten Hon'yaku Jigyō 曹洞宗宗典経典翻訳事業). Founded in 1995 under the auspices of the International Department (Kokusaika 国際課) of the Administrative Headquarters of Sōtō Zen Buddhism (Sōtōshū Shūmuchō 曹洞宗宗務庁), the Sōtō Zen Text Project brings together a team of scholars to produce English translations of the foundational texts of the Japanese Sōtō Zen School. In addition to translations of the ritual and liturgical texts of the School, the Project has previously published *Record of the Transmission of Illumination* (Tokyo: 2017; revised edition Honolulu: 2021), an annotated English version of the *Denkōroku* 傳光錄, by Keizan Jōkin 瑩山紹瑾 (1264–1325), founder of the Sōjiji Monastery 總持寺.

The aim of the Sōtō Zen Text Project is to provide English-language materials for the study of Sōtō Zen texts. In keeping with this aim, the present translation of the *Shōbōgenzō* places emphasis on the linguistic characteristics of the original text — its vocabulary and grammar, rhetorical devices and textual sources. The English of the translation is intended, in so far as it is linguistically realistic, to provide a reflection of Dōgen's Japanese style — a style that is idiosyncratic and notoriously difficult, brimming with cryptic remark and baffling logic, obscure allusion and witty word play. Hence, a faithful English reflection of Dōgen's style will also tend to be odd and difficult, often almost impossible to understand or appreciate without extensive annotation. The present translation tries to provide such annotation, but it remains a guiding principle of the work that this English-language *Shōbōgenzō* should be as challenging to the reader as the Japanese version has always been.

Contributions to this translation were made by Carl Bielefeldt, William M. Bodiford, T. Griffith Foulk, and the late Stanley Weinstein. Sarah J. Horton served as copy editor; Urs App provided technical assistance and page layout. Carl Bielefeldt served as editor and, as such, expresses here our deep appreciation to the numerous friends of the Project, both within and beyond the Sōtō School, who have supported and contributed to this work over so many years.

Carl Bielefeldt
Editor

viii

CONVENTIONS

This publication is an annotated translation, in seven volumes, of one hundred three texts of Dōgen's Japanese *Shōbōgenzō,* plus an additional volume containing an introduction, supplementary notes, appendices, and list of works cited. The translation is based on the edition of the *Shōbōgenzō* published in Kawamura Kōdō 河村孝道, ed., *Dōgen zenji zenshū* 道元禅師全集, vols. 1-2 (Tokyo: Shunjūsha, 1991, 1993), cited herein as DZZ.1 and DZZ.2; volume and page numbers of this edition are noted in braces at the corresponding locations in the translation.

The Japanese text accompanying the translation here follows the punctuation and *kanazukai* of the Kawamura edition; for ease of reference to premodern sources, Kawamura's modern Japanese kanji have been replaced with traditional forms. Also, for ease of reference, the sections into which the texts of the Kawamura edition are divided have been assigned numbers in square brackets by the translators. The translation of Kawamura's longer sections is sometimes broken into separate paragraphs, and transitions to new topics between sections are sometimes marked by a string of asterisks.

Though primarily written in Japanese, the *Shōbōgenzō* includes many passages of Chinese, ranging from long quotations of texts to short phrases inserted into the Japanese sentences. Since this inclusion of Chinese is a prominent linguistic feature of the original texts, the translation seeks to indicate such passages by the use of oblique font. The reader is warned that, given the ubiquity in the Japanese language of expressions adopted from Chinese, the identification of the shorter phrases as Chinese, rather than Japanese, is often rather arbitrary.

Much of the *Shōbōgenzō* is devoted to comment on material in other texts. The translation uses quotation marks to indicate terms and passages on which Dōgen is commenting. Here, again, the reader is warned that the distinction between use and mention can often be difficult to draw.

Sanskrit, Chinese, and Japanese terms appearing in the *Oxford English Dictionary* (3rd edition) are considered to have been adopted into English; other such terms are treated as foreign words and rendered in italics. Romanization of all such terms, whether treated as foreign or English, is given with diacritics.

With some exceptions, Chinese transliterations of Sanskrit terms are rendered as romanized Sanskrit. Indic proper nouns, whether transliterated or translated in the Chinese, are rendered as their presumed originals where possible; the reader is warned that some such reconstructions are unattested and speculative.

The proper noun "Zen" is used in reference to (a) the tradition that Dōgen calls the "buddhas and ancestors," and (b) the Japanese instantiation of that tradition; the Chinese name "Chan" is used in reference to the Chinese instantiation of the tradition.

Romanized readings of the Japanese text given in the notes follow wherever possible the ruby in Kawamura's text; readings not provided by Kawamura are based on *Zengaku daijiten* 禅学大辞典 (1978) and/or Katō Shūkō 加藤宗厚, *Shōbōgenzō yōgo sakuin* 正法眼藏用語索引 (1962).

Citations of T (*Taishō shinshū daizōkyō* 大正新脩大藏經) are from the *SAT Daizōkyō Text Database* (https://21dzk.l.u-tokyo.ac.jp/SAT). Citations of ZZ (*Dainihon zokuzōkyō* 大日本續藏經) are from the *CBETA Hanwen dazangjing* 漢文大藏經 (http://tripitaka.cbeta.org). Citations of KR are from *Kanripo* 漢リポ *Kanseki Repository* (https://www.kanripo.org).

The Kawamura edition provides colophons from several sources, some following the relevant chapter, some in the head notes of the chapter, some in the collation notes (*honbun kōi* 本文校異) for that chapter in the end matter of DZZ.1 and DZZ.2. For the convenience of the reader, this translation collects these colophons (and occasionally others omitted by Kawamura) at the end of each chapter. Colophons without attribution are assumed to have been written by Dōgen.

ABBREVIATIONS

C   Chinese language

DZZ   *Dōgen zenji zenshū* 道元禅師全集, Kagamishima Genryū 鏡島元隆 et al., compilers. 7 vols. Tokyo: Shunjūsha, 1988–1993.

ESST   *Eihei Shōbōgenzō shūsho taisei* 永平正法眼藏蒐書大成, Kawamura Kōdō 河村孝道, ed. 27 vols. Tokyo: Taishūkan Shoten, 1974-1982.

J   Japanese language

KR   Kanseki Repository (Kanseki Ripo 漢籍リポ). Online: https://www.kanripo.org

M   *Dai kanwa jiten* 大漢和辞典, Morohashi Tetsuji 諸橋轍次, ed. 13 vols. (plus 2-vol. supplement). Tokyo: Taishūkan Shoten, 1955-1960.

S   Sanskrit

SCZ   *Shōbōgenzō chūkai zensho* 正法眼藏註解全書, Jinbo Nyoten 神保如天 and Andō Bun'ei 安藤文英, eds. 11 vols. Reprint Tokyo: Nihon Bussho Kankōkai, 1956-1957.

SZ   *Sōtōshū zensho* 曹洞宗全書. 20 vols. Tokyo: Kōmeisha, 1929-1938.

T   *Taishō shinshū daizōkyō* 大正新脩大藏經, Takakusu Junjirō 高楠順次郎 and Watanabe Kaikyoku 渡邊海旭, eds. 100 vols. Tokyo: Daizōkyōkai, 1924–1935.

ZT   *Zengaku taikei* 禪學大系. 8 vols. Tokyo: Kokusho Kankōkai, 1952 (orig. publ. 1910-11).

ZTS   *Zengaku tenseki sōkan* 禅学典籍叢刊, Yanagida Seizan 柳田聖山 and Shiina Kōyū 椎名宏雄, eds. 12 vols. Kyoto: Rinsen Shoten, 1999-2001.

ZZ   *Dainihon zokuzōkyō* 大日本續藏經. 150 vols. Kyoto: Bussho Kankōkai, 1905-1912.

Introduction to

The Seventy-five-Chapter *Shōbōgenzō*

Among the several compilations of Dōgen's Japanese *Shōbōgenzō* texts, the seventy-five-chapter *Shōbōgenzō* (*Nanajūgokan bon Shōbōgenzō* 七十五卷本正法眼藏) has long been considered the one closest to its author's own vision of the work, containing as it does the most polished versions of texts, most of which are found in draft form elsewhere, in the sixty-chapter compilation and twenty-eight-text *Himitsu* 秘密 collection. Although it contains chapters originally dating from all periods of Dōgen's teaching career, it is thought to represent the fruit of editorial work in its author's later years. Thus, its seventy-five texts are often taken together with the twelve-chapter compilation as preserving the eighty-seven chapters Dōgen had intended for his *Shōbōgenzō* at the time of his death. The seventy-five-chapter *Shōbōgenzō* was the basis for the earliest commentary, the *Shōbōgenzō kikigaki shō* 正法眼藏聞書抄, completed in 1308, by Dōgen's followers Senne 詮慧 and Kyōgō 經豪.

In addition to the inclusion of its chapters in other compilations, the seventy-five-chapter *Shōbōgenzō* has been preserved in many manuscript witnesses, of which three are perhaps the most often cited: (a) the Kenkon'in 乾坤院 manuscript of 1488, based on an earlier copy dated 1430; (b) the Shōbōji 正法寺 manuscript of 1512, from a 1472 copy of a manuscript dated 1333; and (c) the Ryūmonji 龍門寺 manuscript of 1547, from a 1430 copy of the same 1333 manuscript. It is the last of these that serves as the text for the modern edition that is translated here below.

TREASURY OF THE TRUE DHARMA EYE
NUMBER 1

The Realized Kōan
Genjō kōan

現成公案

The Realized Kōan

Genjō kōan

Introduction

This brief essay was composed in the autumn of 1233, probably at its author's newly opened monastery, Kōshōji, in Fukakusa, just south of the imperial capital of Heiankyō (modern Kyoto). It represents the first text in both the seventy-five and sixty-chapter compilations of the *Shōbōgenzō* and number 3 in the ninety-five-chapter Honzan edition. The work bears an unusual colophon stating that it was presented to a lay disciple, Yō Kōshū 楊光秀 (or Yanagi Mitsuhide), apparently an official at the government office in Chikuzen 筑前, in present-day Kyushu, about whom little is known.

The title theme of the essay is an expression occurring frequently in Zen literature, where it originally carried the juridical sense of a legal matter or case (*kōan* 公案) in which the finding or verdict is settled or is immediately apparent (*genjō* 現成). Its use in Zen is thought to derive from a saying attributed to the Tang-dynasty figure Chen Zunsu 陳尊宿, who, upon seeing a monk approaching, said, "Yours is a settled case, but I spare you the thirty blows." The expression (or variants of it) occur frequently in Dōgen's writing. It came to be used as a technical term in Sōtō tradition to express the direct manifestation of ultimate truth in the phenomenal world.

The essay is a much-celebrated statement on Buddhist religious practice, most famously described here as the study of the self, in which one forgets the self, sloughs off body and mind, and is verified by all things. Such practice, we are told, has no end: it is the practitioner's natural environment, like water to a fish or the sky to a bird. It is like the wind that is always blowing, even as we fan ourselves.

正法眼藏第一
Treasury of the True Dharma Eye
Number 1
現成公案
The Realized Kōan

[01:1] {1:2}

諸法の佛法なる時節、すなはち迷悟あり、修行あり、生あり、死あり、諸佛あり、衆生あり。

At times when the dharmas are the buddha dharma, just then there are delusion and awakening; there is practice; there is birth; there is death; there are buddhas; there are living beings.[1]

[01:2]

萬法ともにわれにあらざる時節、まどひなく、さとりなく、諸佛なく、衆生なく、生なく、滅なし。

At times when all the myriad dharmas are not self, there is no delusion; there is no awakening; there are no buddhas; there are no living beings; there is no arising; there is no cessation.[2]

[01:3]

佛道もとより豊倹より跳出せるゆえに、生滅あり、迷悟あり、生佛あり。しかもかくのごとくなりといへども、花は愛惜にちり、草は棄嫌におふるのみなり。

Because, from the start, the way of the buddhas has jumped out from abundance and scarcity, there are arising and ceasing, there are delusion and awakening, there are living beings and buddhas.[3] And yet, while this

---

1 **Realized Kōan** (*genjō kōan* 現成公案): Also written 見成公案. From a saying attributed to the Tang-dynasty figure Venerable Chen 陳尊宿 (also known as Muzhou 睦州 or Daoming 道明; dates unknown); see Supplementary Notes.

At times when the dharmas are the buddha dharma (*shohō no buppō naru jisetsu* 諸法の佛法なる時節): Probably to be taken in the sense "when everything is seen in terms of the Buddhist teachings."

2 **At times when all the myriad dharmas are not self** (*manbō tomo ni ware ni arazaru jisetsu* 萬法ともにわれにあらざる時節): Probably to be taken in the sense, "when everything is seen to be empty of independent existence."

3 **Because, from the start, the way of the buddhas has jumped out from abundance and scarcity** (*butsudō motoyori hōken yori chōshutsu seru yue ni* 佛道もとより豊倹より

6   DŌGEN'S *SHŌBŌGENZŌ* VOLUME I

may be so, it is simply "flowers falling when we cherish them, weeds growing when we despise them."[4]

[01:4]

自己をはこびて萬法を修證するを迷とす、萬法すすみて自己を修證するはさとりなり。

Bringing the self to practice and verify the myriad dharmas represents delusion; the myriad dharmas proceeding to practice and verify the self is awakening.[5]

[01:5]

迷を大悟するは諸佛なり、悟に大迷なるは衆生なり。さらに悟上に得悟する漢あり、迷中又迷の漢あり。

Those who greatly awaken to delusion are the buddhas; those who are greatly deluded about awakening are the living beings. Moreover, there are people who attain awakening on top of awakening, and there are people who are *further deluded within their delusion.*[6]

[01:6] {1:3}

諸佛のまさしく諸佛なるときは、自己は諸佛なりと覺知することをもちいず。しかあれども證佛なり、佛を證しもてゆく。

When the buddhas are truly the buddhas, they make no use of perceiving that they themselves are buddhas. Nevertheless, they are verified buddhas; they go on verifying buddhahood.[7]

跳出せるゆえに): Presumably, meaning that the way of the buddhas transcends the affirmation and negation of the previous two sentences.

4 **"flowers falling when we cherish them, weeds growing when we despise them"** (*hana wa aijaku ni chiri, kusa wa kiken ni ouru* 花は愛惜にちり、草は棄嫌におふる): A Japanese reworking of a saying attributed to Chan Master Jing of Niutou 牛頭精禪師 (dates unknown) (see *Tiansheng guangdeng lu* 天聖廣燈錄, ZZ.135:860b6-7):

> 間、如何是和尚家風。師云、華從愛惜落、草逐棄嫌生。
> Someone asked, "What is the Reverend's house style?"
> The Master said, "Flowers fall from my love for them; weeds grow from my hatred of them."

Dōgen also quotes this line in his *Eihei kōroku* 永平廣錄 (DZZ.3:36, no. 51).

5 **the myriad dharmas proceeding to practice and verify the self** (*manbō susumite jiko o shushō suru* 萬法すすみて自己を修證する): This phrase could also be read "to practice and verify the self while the myriad dharmas advance."

6 **further deluded within their delusion** (*meichū u mei* 迷中又迷): An expression in Chinese that occurs several times in the *Shōbōgenzō*; perhaps reflecting the *Dahui Pujue chanshi yulu* 大慧普覺禪師語錄 at T.1998A.47:893a21.

7 **they are verified buddhas** (*shōbutsu nari* 證佛なり): Or "they verify buddhahood"; an expression occurring several times in the *Shōbōgenzō*, usually as a verb-object compound.

1. The Realized Kōan *Genjō kōan* 現成公案

[01:7]

身心を擧して色を見取し、身心を擧して聲を聽取するに、したしく會取すれども、かがみにかげをやどすがごとくにあらず、水と月とのごとくにあらず。一方を證するときは一方はくらし。

When we take up body and mind and see forms, when we take up body and mind and hear sounds, although we understand them intimately, it is not like the reflection in a mirror, not like the water and the moon: when one side is verified, the other side is obscure.[8]

[01:8]

佛道をならふといふは、自己をならふなり。自己をならふといふは、自己をわするるなり。自己をわするるといふは、萬法に證せらるるなり。萬法に證せらるるといふは、自己の身心および他己の身心をして脱落せしむるなり。悟迹の休歇なるあり、休歇なる悟迹を長長出ならしむ。

To study the way of the buddhas is to study oneself. To study oneself is to forget oneself. To forget oneself is to be verified by the myriad dharmas. To be verified by the myriad dharmas is to slough off one's own body and mind and the body and mind of others. There is an ending to the traces of awakening; and the traces of awakening that are ended are brought out for a long, long time.[9]

[01:9]

人、はじめて法をもとむるとき、はるかに法の邊際を離却せり。法、すでにおのれに正傳するとき、すみやかに本分人なり。

---

8 **We take up body and mind and see forms** (*shinjin o ko shite shiki o kenshu shi* 身心を擧して色を見取し): Most interpreters take this phrase to mean, "we (or perhaps the buddhas) see with the entire body and mind." Hence, they read the passage as describing a non-dualistic apprehension in which there is no opposition between the object and its reflection in the mirror or the water. It is also possible, however, to take the phrase to mean simply, "we see using the body and mind," and to understand the passage as describing ordinary, biased perception, in contrast to the undistorted reflection of the mirror or the water. See Supplementary Notes, s.v. "Body and mind."

when one side is verified, the other side is obscure (*ippō o shō suru toki wa ippō wa kurashi* 一方を證するときは一方はくらし): Perhaps to be taken as a description of a non-dualistic perception, in which the object (moon) and the subject (water) are both complete in themselves.

9 **the traces of awakening that are ended are brought out for a long, long time** (*kyūkatsu naru goshaku o chōchō shutsu narashimu* 休歇なる悟迹を長長出ならしむ): A difficult passage typically taken to mean that the traces of having ended the traces of awakening continue forever. In his use here of the unusual expression *chōchō shutsu* 長長出, Dōgen may have had in mind the saying by Changsha Jingcen 長沙景岑 (dates unknown), alluded to in *Shōbōgenzō kenbutsu* 正法眼藏見佛, that "You can't get out [the eye of the śramaṇa] for a long, long time" (*chōchō shutsu futoku* 長長出不得); see Supplementary Notes, s.v. "All the worlds in the ten directions are the single eye of the śramaṇa."

8 DŌGEN'S *SHŌBŌGENZŌ* VOLUME I

People, when they first seek the dharma, remove themselves far from the borders of the dharma. The dharma, when it has been directly transmitted to one, is immediately the person of the original lot.[10]

[01:10]

人、舟にのりてゆくに、目をめぐらしてきしをみれば、きしのうつるとあやまる。　目をしたしく舟につくれば、舟のすすむをしるがごとく、身心を亂想して萬法を辨肯するには、自心自性は常住なるかとあやまる。もし行李をしたしくして箇裡に歸すれば、萬法のわれにあらぬ道理あきらけし。

When people ride in a boat, if they turn their eyes and gaze at the shore, they make the mistake of thinking that the shore is moving. When they fix their eyes more closely on the boat, they understand that it is the boat that is advancing. Similarly, in confirming the myriad dharmas with a confused conception of body and mind, we make the mistake of thinking that our own mind and our own nature are eternally abiding. If we become intimate with our conduct and return here, the principle that the myriad dharmas are not self is clear.[11]

[01:11]

たき木、はいとなる、さらにかへりてたき木となるべきにあらず。しかあるを、灰はのち、薪はさきと見取すべからず。しるべし、薪は薪の法位に住して、さきあり、のちあり。前後ありといへども、前後際斷せり。灰は灰の法位にありて、のちあり、さきあり。かのたき木、はいとなりぬるのち、さらにたき木とならざるがごとく、人のしぬるのち、さらに生とならず。しかあるを、生の死になるといはざるは、佛法のさだまれるならひなり、このゆえに不生といふ。死の生にならざる、法輪のさだまれる佛轉なり、このゆえに不滅といふ。生も一時のくらいなり、死も一時のくらいなり。たとへば冬と春とのごとし。冬の春となるとおもはず、春の夏となるといはぬなり。

Firewood becomes ashes, and it is not possible for it to return again to firewood. However, we should not take the view that the ashes are after and the firewood is before. We should know that firewood occupies the dharma position of firewood, and has a before and has an after.[12] Al-

---

10 **person of the original lot** (*honbun nin* 本分人): An expression, occurring several times in Chan literature, for one who has realized his or her true nature, or fundamental lot in life. The translation of this sentence seeks to preserve the syntactical parallel with the preceding sentence, such that "the dharma" (*hō* 法) is read as the grammatical subject of both verbs here. Perhaps more naturally, we may read, "When the dharma has been transmitted to one, one is immediately the 'person of the original lot.'"

11 **If we become intimate with our conduct and return here** (*moshi anri o shitashiku shite kori ni ki sureba* もし行李をしたしくして箇裡に歸すれば): I.e., when we attend closely to our actions in the place where we are.

12 **firewood occupies the dharma position of firewood** (*takigi wa takigi no hōi ni jū shite* 薪は薪の法位に住して): Drawing on the common Buddhist teaching that each

1. The Realized Kōan *Genjō kōan* 現成公案

though it may have a before and after, before and after are cut off.[13] The ashes occupy the dharma position of ashes, and have an after and have a before. Just as that firewood does not become firewood again after it has been reduced to ashes, after people die they do not come to life again. However, it is an established practice of the buddha dharma not to speak of life becoming death; therefore, we say, "not arising." It is an established buddha-turning of the dharma wheel that death does not become life; therefore, we say, "not ceasing."[14] Life is one position in time, and death is one position in time. It is, for example, like winter and spring: we do not think that winter becomes spring; we do not say that spring becomes summer.

[01:12] {1:4}

人の、さとりをうる、水に月のやどるがごとし。月ぬれず、水やぶれず。ひろくおほきなるひかりにてあれど、尺寸の水にやどり、全月も彌天も、くさの露にもやどり、一滴の水にもやどる。さとりの、人をやぶらざること、月の、水をうがたざるがごとし。人の、さとりを罣礙せざること、滴露の、天月を罣礙せざるがごとし。ふかきことは、たかき分量なるべし。時節の長短は、大水・小水を檢點し、天月の廣狹を辨取すべし。

A person's attaining of awakening is like the moon residing in the water. The moon does not get wet, and the water is not disturbed. Although its illumination is wide and great, it resides in water of a foot or an inch. Even the whole moon and all the heavens reside in the dew on a blade of grass or reside in a single drop of water. Awakening's not disturbing the person is like the moon's not boring into the water; the person's not obstructing the awakening is like the dewdrop's not obstructing the heavens or the moon. The depth must be a measure of the height.[15] The

---

dharma exists in its own moment, or temporal position, without changing into something else. Allusion to a passage in the *Lotus Sūtra* that can be read "The dharmas abide in their dharma positions." See Supplementary Notes, s.v. "Dharmas abide in their dharma positions."

13 **before and after are cut off** (*zengo saidan* 前後際斷): A common idiom, found in the prajñā-pāramitā literature; see Supplementary Notes, s.v. "Before and after cut off."

14 **"not arising"** (*fushō* 不生); **"not ceasing"** (*fumetsu* 不滅): A standard pair in many Mahāyāna texts expressing the doctrine that all dharmas are empty and, hence, neither arise nor cease. Dōgen here is conflating "arising and ceasing" (*shōmetsu* 生滅) with "life and death" (*shōji* 生死).

an established buddha-turning of the dharma wheel (*hōrin no sadamareru butten* 法輪のさだまれる佛轉): A play with the standard phrase, the "buddha turns the dharma wheel" (*butten hōrin* 佛轉法輪).

15 **The depth must be a measure of the height** (*fukaki koto wa, takaki bunryō naru beshi* ふかきことは、たかき分量なるべし): Likely meaning that the depth of one's awakening is a function of the loftiness of the dharma that inspired it.

10 DŌGEN'S *SHŌBŌGENZŌ* VOLUME I

length of time must be determined by whether the water is large or small, must be appraised by the breadth of the heavens or the moon.[16]

[01:13]
身心に、法いまだ參飽せざるには、法すでにたれりとおぼゆ。法もし身心に充足すれば、ひとかたはたらずとおぼゆるなり。たとへば、船にのりて山なき海中にいでて四方をみるに、ただまろにのみみゆ。さらにことなる相、みゆることなし。しかあれど、この大海、まろなるにあらず、方なるにあらず、のこれる海德、つくすべからざるなり。宮殿のごとし、瓔珞のごとし。ただわがまなこのおよぶところ、しばらくまろにみゆるのみなり。かれがごとく、萬法もまたしかあり。塵中・格外、おほく様子を帶せりといへども、參學眼力のおよぶばかりを、見取・會取するなり。萬法の家風をきかんには、方圓とみゆるよりほかに、のこりの海德・山德おほくきわまりなく、よもの世界あることをしるべし。かたはらのみかくのごとくあるにあらず、直下も一滴もしかある、としるべし。

When, in our body and mind, we have yet to study our fill of the dharma, we feel that the dharma is already sufficient; if the dharma is replete in body and mind, we feel that it is insufficient in some respect. For example, when we board a boat, go out into the middle of the ocean where no mountains are in sight, and look around in the four directions, all we see is a circle. We do not see any different shapes. Nevertheless, the great ocean is not round, nor is it square, and the remaining virtues of the ocean can hardly be exhausted.[17] It is like a palace; it is like a jeweled necklace.[18] It is just that, for the moment, the part our eyes can reach appears circular.

Like that, so are the myriad dharmas. Amidst the dust and beyond its bounds are included many forms, but we see and understand only what is reached by the strength of the eye of study.[19] If we wish to perceive the

---

16 **The length of time** (*jisetsu no chōtan* 時節の長短): Likely the time of (or until) awakening.

17 **virtues of the ocean** (*kaitoku* 海德): Buddhist texts sometimes attribute eight virtues to the ocean: that it is vast and deep; that its tides are regular; that it does not retain corpses; that it contains precious substances; that it collects the five rivers; that it absorbs precipitation without increase or decrease; that it contains great fish; and that it is a single saltiness throughout. (See, e.g., *Fo shuo hai ba de jing* 佛説海八德經, T.35.1:819a19-b7.)

18 **It is like a palace; it is like a jeweled necklace** (*gūden no gotoshi, yōraku no gotoshi* 宮殿のごとし、瓔珞のごとし): Likely reflecting the Buddhist teaching, found especially in Yogācāra literature, known as "the four views of water" (*issui shiken* 一水四見): devas see water as jewels (or jeweled ground), humans as water, pretas ("hungry ghosts") as pus and blood, fish as a dwelling.

19 **Amidst the dust and beyond its bounds** (*jinchū kakugai* 塵中格外): Perhaps to be taken as the mundane world of the six sense objects (or "dusts") and the higher realm of the buddha dharma. See Supplementary Notes, s.v. "Dust."

1. The Realized Kōan *Genjō kōan* 現成公案   11

house styles of the myriad dharmas, in addition to seeing the square and the round, we should realize that there are worlds in the four directions in which the remaining virtues of the ocean and virtues of the mountains are numerous and boundless.[20] We should realize that it is not that this is so only beside us: it is so right here as well, in a single drop as well.[21]

[01:14] {1:5}

魚、水を行くに、ゆけども水のきはなく、鳥、そらをとぶに、とぶといへどもそらのきはなし。しかあれども、うを・鳥、いまだむかしよりみづ・そらをはなれず。ただ用大のときは使大なり、要小のときは使小なり。かくのごとくして、頭頭に邊際をつくさずといふことなく、處處に踏翻せずといふことなしといへども、鳥、もしそらをいづれば、たちまちに死す、魚、もし水をいづれば、たちまちに死す。以水爲命しりぬべし、以空爲命しりぬべし。以鳥爲命あり、以魚爲命あり。以命爲鳥なるべし、以命爲魚なるべし。このほかさらに進歩あるべし。修證あり、その壽者命者あること、かくのごとし。

When a fish moves in water, however far it goes, the water has no boundaries; when a bird flies in the sky, fly as it may, the sky has no boundaries. However, from long ago, fish and birds have never been separated from the water and the sky.[22] It is just that, when their function is great, their use is great; when their need is small, their use is small.[23] In this way, while none of them fails to reach its limits, and nowhere do

---

only what is reached by the strength of the eye of study (*sangaku gan riki no oyobu bakari* 參學眼力のおよぶばかり): I.e., only those objects that the vision gained through our practice is capable of perceiving. The expression "eye of study" (*sangaku gen* 參學眼) occurs with some frequency in the *Shōbōgenzō*.

20 **house styles of the myriad dharmas** (*manbō no kafū* 萬法の家風): The expression "house style" (*kafū* 家風) usually refers to the teaching styles of the various "houses," or lineages, of Zen. Dōgen may be using it here simply as a playful way of saying "what things are like," but it is possible that the "dharmas" here are not only the "things" of this world, but also the myriad "teachings" of the various schools of Buddhism.

the square and the round (*hōen* 方圓): These terms, while here of course reflecting Dōgen's point that the ocean is neither square nor round, are also used as Buddhist technical terms for "partial" and "complete" teachings respectively — i.e., teachings that utilize expedient devices (*hōben* 方便; S. *upāya*) and teachings that directly reveal the highest truth.

21 **it is not that this is so only beside us** (*katawara nomi kaku no gotoku aru ni arazu* かたはらのみかくのごとくあるにあらず): The term *katawara* かたはら (literally, one's "side") may be taken to mean one's "surroundings" — as opposed to the following *jikige* 直下 ("right here"), meaning "at our very feet" or, perhaps, "we ourselves."

22 **from long ago** (*mukashi yori* むかしより): Probably best taken in the sense "from the start" (*moto yori* もとより).

23 **when their function is great** (*yōdai no toki* 用大のとき): "Great function" (*daiyū* 大用; also read *daiyō*) is a common term in Zen literature for the activities of the awakened master; see Supplementary Notes, s.v. "Manifestation of the great function."

12   DŌGEN'S *SHŌBŌGENZŌ* VOLUME I

they fail to overturn it, if the bird were to leave the sky, it would quickly die, and if the fish were to leave the water, it would quickly die.[24] We should know that they *take water as life*; we should know that they *take the sky as life*.[25] There is *taking the bird as life*; there is *taking the fish as life*. It should be *taking life as the bird*; it should be *taking life as the fish*. Other than these, there should be further steps forward.[26] That there are practice and verification, and that they have those with lifespans, those with lives, are like this.[27]

[01:15]

しかあるを、水をきわめ、そらをきわめてのち、水・そらをゆかんと擬する鳥魚あらんは、水にもそらにも、みちをうべからず、ところをうべからず。このところをうれば、この行李したがひて現成公案す。このみちをうれば、この行李したがひて現成公案なり。このみち、このところ、大にあらず小にあらず、自にあらず他にあらず、さきよりあるにあらず、いま現ずるにあらざるがゆえに、かくのごとくあるなり。しかあるがごとく、人もし佛道を修證するに、得一法通一法なり、遇一行修一行なり。これにところあり、みち通達せるによりて、しらるるきはのしるからざるは、このしることの、佛法の究盡と同生し同參するがゆえに、しかあるなり。

Nevertheless, if there were birds or fish that thought to go through the water or sky after reaching the limits of the water or sky, they could get no way, could get no place, to do so in either water or sky. When we get this place, our actions accordingly realize the kōan; when we get this

---

24 **none of them fails to reach its limits, and nowhere do they fail to overturn it** (*zuzu ni henzai o tsukusazu to iu koto naku, shosho ni tōhon sezu to iu koto nashi* 頭頭に邊際をつくさずといふことなく、處處に踏飜せずといふことなし): A loose translation of a passage more literally read, "for each of them, there is no case in which it fails to exhaust the boundaries; in each place, there is no case in which they fail to kick over." The verb *tōhon* 踏飜, rendered here as "overturn" (as in tipping over a boat), is used in Chan texts to express the "great function" — as in phrases like "kick over the great oceans, jump over Mount Sumeru" (*tōhon daikai tekitō shumi* 踏翻大海趯倒須彌).

25 **We should know that they take water as life** (*i sui i myō shirinu beshi* 以水爲命しりぬべし): The saying that fish (and dragons) "take water as life" occurs in several Chan sources. The grammatical subject of the verb "should know" (*shirinu beshi* しりぬべし) here is unexpressed and could also be taken as "they" (i.e., "the fish must have known"), a reading suggesting that Dōgen was recalling a line by Hongzhi Zhengjue 宏智正覺 (1091-1157) (*Hongzhi chanshi guanglu* 宏智禪師廣錄, T.2001.48:25c23):

龍魚未知水爲命。
Dragons and fish don't know that water is life.

26 **there should be further steps forward** (*sara ni shinpo aru beshi* さらに進歩あるべし): I.e., there must be other permutations of the phrase; see Supplementary Notes, s.v. "Stepping forward and stepping back."

27 **That there are practice and verification, and that they have those with lifespans, those with lives, are like this** (*shushō ari, sono jusha myōsha aru koto, kaku no gotoshi* 修證あり、その壽者命者あること、かくのごとし): I.e., Buddhist practice and verification are to living beings as water is to fish or the sky is to birds.

1. The Realized Kōan. *Genjō kōan* 現成公案 13

way, our actions accordingly are the realized kōan.[28] This way and this place are neither great nor small, are neither self nor other; it is not that they existed before, nor that they appear now. Hence, they exist like this.[29] In this way, when a person practices and verifies the way of the buddhas, it is *to get one dharma is to penetrate one dharma; to meet one practice is to cultivate one practice.*[30] Since, in this, the place exists, and the way penetrates [everywhere], the fact that the known limits are not conspicuous is so because this knowing is born together with and studies together with the exhaustive investigation of the buddha dharma.[31]

[01:16] {1:6}

得處かならず自己の知見となりて、慮知にしられんずるとならふことなかれ。證究すみやかに現成すといへども、密有かならずしも見成にあらず。見成これ何必なり。

Do not think that finding one's place will necessarily become one's own knowledge and be understood by thinking.[32] While ultimate verification may be realized suddenly, what is intimately ours is not necessarily realized; what is realized is, "why necessarily so?"[33]

---

28 **When we get this place, our actions accordingly realize the kōan** (*kono tokoro o ureba, kono anri shitagaite genjō kōan su* このところをうれば、この行李したがひて現成公案す*):* "Realize the kōan" renders Dōgen's novel verbal form *genjō kōan su* 現成公案す, which might be understood, "manifests, or expresses, 'the realized kōan.'"

29 **This way and this place** (*kono michi kono tokoro* このみちこのところ): "This place" could also be read in apposition to "this way": "this way, this place."

they exist like this (*kaku no gotoku aru nari* かくのごとくあるなり): The sense of "like this" is unclear; perhaps, "in a way that enables them to be the loci for the expression of the realized kōan."

30 **To get one dharma is to penetrate one dharma; to meet one practice is to cultivate one practice** (*toku ippō tsū ippō nari, gū ichigyō shu ichigyō nari* 得一法通一法なり、遇一行修一行なり): Dōgen gives these two phrases in Chinese, as if quoting some text; but there is no known source. "Dharma" here likely refers to "teaching": one thoroughly understands each Buddhist teaching one learns.

31 **the fact that the known limits are not conspicuous is so because this knowing is born together with and studies together with the exhaustive investigation of the buddha dharma** (*shiraruru kiwa no shirukazaru wa, kono shiru koto no, buppō no gūjin to dōshō shi dōsan suru ga yue ni, shika aru nari* しらるるきはのしるからざるは、このしることの、佛法の究盡と同生し同参するがゆえに、しかあるなり): Perhaps meaning something like, "the limits of this place and this way are not obvious to the practitioner because they are experienced as the practice itself." Dōgen often uses the expressions *dōshō* 同生 ("arises together" or "lives together") and *dōsan* 同参 ("studies together") to express identity or equivalence.

32 **finding one's place** (*tokusho* 得處): Taken here as the Chinese version of Dōgen's earlier Japanese *tokoro o uru* ところをうる, though it could as well be read as "what one gets."

33 **what is intimately ours is not necessarily realized** (*mitsu'u kanarazushimo genjō*

14 DŌGEN'S *SHŌBŌGENZŌ* VOLUME I

* * * * *

[01:17]

麻浴山寶徹禪師、あふぎをつかふちなみに、僧きたりてとふ、風性常住、
無處不周なり、なにをもてかさらに和尚あふぎをつかふ。師云く、なんぢ
ただ風性常住をしれりとも、いまだところとしていたらずといふことなき
道理をしらず、と。僧曰く、いかならんかこれ無處不周底の道理。とき
に、師、あふぎをつかふのみなり。僧、禮拜す。

Chan Master Baoche of Mount Mayu was fanning himself when a
monk came and asked, "*The nature of the wind is constant, and there's
no place it does not circulate*; why does the Reverend fan himself?"[34]

The Master said, "You only understand that '*the nature of the wind is
constant*'; you still don't understand the principle that there's no place
it doesn't reach."

The monk said, "What is the principle of '*there's no place it does not
circulate*'?"

The Master at this point just fanned himself.

The monk bowed.

[01:18]

佛法の證驗、正傳の活路、それかくのごとし。常住なればあふぎをつかふ
べからず、つかはぬおりも風をきくべきといふは、常住をもしらず、風性
をもしらぬなり。風性は常住なるがゆえに、佛家の風は、大地の黄金なる
を現成せしめ、長河の蘇酪を參熟せり。

The proof of the buddha dharma, the life-saving path directly transmitted, is like this. To say that, since it is constant, he need not fan himself,
and that, even when he does not fan himself, he should feel the wind,
is not to understand "constant" and not to understand "the nature of the
wind." Because the nature of the wind is constant, the wind of the house

---

ni arazu 密有かならずしも見成にあらず): "What is intimately ours" (or, perhaps, "private being") renders *mitsu'u* 密有, a term not found elsewhere in the *Shōbōgenzō* and
not common in the Buddhist literature; typically taken as a reference to our innermost
reality.

what is realized is, "why necessarily so?" (*genjō kore ka hitsu nari* 見成これ何必
なり): "Why necessarily so?" (*ka hitsu* 何必) is a fixed expression in Chinese used to
question (or challenge) a statement; perhaps meaning here that what is realized in "ultimate verification" is not a previously unrealized reality but a questioning of previous
understanding.

34 **Chan Master Baoche of Mount Mayu** (*Mayokuzan Hōtetsu zenji* 麻浴山寶徹禪
師): Dates unknown; a follower of Mazu Daoyi 馬祖道一 (709-788). Mount Mayu 麻
浴山 is in present-day Shanxi province. Dōgen here recounts, largely in Japanese, a
conversation found, e.g., at *Zongmen tongyao ji* 宗門統要集, ZTS.1:54d4-7; and *shinji
Shōbōgenzō* 眞字正法眼藏, DZZ.5:194, case 123.

1. The Realized Kōan *Genjō kōan* 現成公案   15

of the buddhas has revealed the whole earth to be golden and prepared the butter of the Long River.[35]

正法眼藏現成公案第一
Treasury of the True Dharma Eye
The Realized Kōan
Number 1

[Ryūmonji MS:]
これは、天福元年中秋のころ、かきて鎮西の俗弟子楊光秀にあたふ
This was written on the mid-autumn day, first year of Tenpuku [20 September 1233], and given to the lay disciple Yō Kōshū of Chinzei[36]

建長壬子拾勒
Compiled and ordered in the senior water year of the rat, [fourth year of] Kenchō [1252][37]

于時永享二秊正月吉日、校了
Proofed. Auspicious [first] day of the first month, second year of Eikyō [25 January 1430][38]

天文丁未二月念三日書
Copied on the twenty-third day of the second month, junior fire year of the sheep, [the sixteenth year of] Tenbun [14 March 1547][39]

---

35 **revealed the whole earth to be golden and prepared the butter of the Long River** (*daichi no ōgon naru o genjō seshime, chōga no soraku o sanjuku seri* 大地の黄金なるを現成せしめ、長河の蘇酪を參熟せヲ): Taking *soraku* 蘇酪 as a variant of *soraku* 酥酪, a form of processed milk, variously described as "butter," "yogurt," "curd cheese," etc. "The Long River" refers to the Milky Way. The phrase reflects an expression used in reference to the powers of the advanced bodhisattva, "to churn the Long River into butter and turn the whole earth into gold" (*kaku Chōga i soraku, hen daichi i ōgon* 攪長河爲酥酪、變大地爲黄金).

36 The Tōunji 洞雲寺 MS shares an identical colophon.

mid-autumn day (*chūshū* 中秋): I.e., the Harvest Moon Festival, on the fifteenth of the eighth lunar month.

lay disciple Yō Kōshū of Chinzei (*Chinzei no zoku deshi Yō Kōshū* 鎮西の俗弟子楊光秀): A name that might also be read Yanagi Mitsuhide 楊光秀. The identity of this individual is unknown; presumably, an official at Chinzei 鎮西, the government office of Dazaifu 太宰府, in Chikuzen 筑前, in present-day Kyushu.

37 It has been speculated that this colophon, written in 1252, presumably by Dōgen himself, may have indicated completion of his work on the seventy-five-chapter *Shōbō-genzō*.

38 Copyist unknown.

39 By Tessō Hōken 喆囱芳賢 (d. 1551), copyist of the Ryūmonji 龍門寺 MS.

TREASURY OF THE TRUE DHARMA EYE
NUMBER 2

Mahā-prajñā-pāramitā
Maka hannya haramitsu
摩訶般若波羅蜜

Mahā-prajñā-pāramitā
Maka hannya haramitsu

INTRODUCTION

Based on its colophon, this brief text represents the earliest dated work found in traditional editions of the *Shōbōgenzō*. It appears as number 2 in both the sixty- and seventy-five-chapter compilations, as well as in the ninety-five-chapter Honzan edition. It is said to have been composed during the summer retreat of 1233, at the Kannon Dōriin (i.e., Kōshō-ji), Dōgen's quarters at Fukakusa, just south of the imperial capital of Heiankyō (modern Kyoto).

We do not know who might have kept that 1233 retreat with Dōgen. He had been back from China for six years at this point, but it had been only three years since he left the Zen monastery of Kenninji 建仁寺, in Heiankyō, to make his own way as an independent teacher. We know that the Chinese monk Jiyuan 寂圓 (J. Jakuen) had already joined him, but his most important disciple, Ejō, would not arrive until the following year. Thus, it is not clear for whom and to what end this work was written.

Unlike Dōgen's "Bendōwa," 辦道話 of 1231, and the majority of *Shōbōgenzō* texts that were to come, the "Maka hannya haramitsu" chapter does not yet address the stories and sayings of the Chinese Chan masters. Apart from a brief comment on a single poem by Dōgen's recently deceased Chinese master, Rujing 如淨, the essay is devoted entirely to its title theme of the "perfection of wisdom" (prajñā-pāramitā), opening with an interpretation of the *Heart Sūtra* (*Mohe bore boluomiduo xin jing* 摩訶般若波羅蜜多心經), the most popular of the prajñā-pāramitā texts, and then proceeding to quotations from the massive *Da bore boluomiduo jing* 大般若波羅蜜多經, Xuanzang's 玄奘 translation of the *Mahā-prajñā-pāramitā-sūtra*, in six hundred fascicles. Although Dōgen does not introduce here the rich allusions to Chan literature that mark his mature writing, we can already see in some of his comments a taste for the novel readings of Chinese passages that would become a hallmark of his style.

正法眼藏第二
Treasury of the True Dharma Eye
Number 2
摩訶般若波羅蜜
Mahā-prajñā-pāramitā

[02:1] {1:8}

觀自在菩薩の行深般若波羅蜜多時は、渾身の照見五蘊皆空なり。五蘊は色・受・想・行・識なり、五枚の般若なり。照見、これ般若なり。この宗旨の開演現成するにいはく、色即是空なり、空即是色なり。色是色なり、空即空なり。百草なり、萬象なり。般若波羅蜜十二枚、これ十二入なり。また十八枚の般若あり、眼・耳・鼻・舌・身・意、色・聲・香・味・觸・法、および眼・耳・鼻・舌・身・意識等なり。また四枚の般若あり、苦・集・滅・道なり。また六枚の般若あり、布施・淨戒・安忍・精進・静慮・般若なり。また一枚の般若波羅蜜、而今現成せり、阿耨多羅三藐三菩提なり。また般若波羅蜜三枚あり、過去・現在・未來なり。また般若六枚あり、地・水・火・風・空・識なり。また四枚の般若、よのつねにおこなはる、行・住・坐・臥なり。

"When Bodhisattva Avalokiteśvara practiced the deep prajñā-pāramitā," it was his whole body *"perceiving that the five aggregates are all empty."*[1] The five aggregates are form, sensation, perception, formations, and consciousness; they are prajñā in five pieces.[2] "Perceiving" is prajñā. When the exposition of this essential point appears, it is said, *"form*

---

1 **"When Bodhisattva Avalokiteśvara practiced the deep prajñā-pāramitā"** (*Kanjizai bosatsu no gyō jin hannya haranitta ji* 觀自在菩薩の行深般若波羅蜜多時): The opening paragraph here is devoted to comments on the *Heart Sūtra* (*Bore boluomiduo xin jing* 般若波羅蜜多心經). This first sentence represents Dōgen's variation, in mixed Chinese and Japanese, on the first sentence of the *Sūtra* (T.251.8:848c6-7):

觀自在菩薩行深般若波羅蜜多時、照見五蘊皆空。

When Bodhisattva Avalokiteśvara practiced the deep prajñā-pāramitā, he perceived that the five aggregates were all empty.

See Supplementary Notes, s.v. "Four elements and five aggregates."

2 **they are prajñā in five pieces** (*gomai no hannya nari* 五枚の般若なり): I.e., each of the five aggregates is an instance of wisdom. Cf. the *Heart Sūtra* here (*Bore boluomiduo xin jing* 般若波羅蜜多心經, T.251.8:848c10):

是故空中、無色、無受想行識。

Therefore, in emptiness, there is no form, no sensation, perception, formations or consciousness.

20 DŌGEN'S *SHŌBŌGENZŌ* VOLUME I

is itself emptiness; emptiness is itself form."[3] *Form is form; emptiness is itself emptiness.* They are the hundred grasses; they are the myriad forms.[4] Twelve pieces of prajñā-pāramitā — these are the twelve entrances.[5] Again, there is prajñā in eighteen pieces: the eye, ear, nose, tongue, body, and mind; form, sound, smell, taste, touch, and dharma; the consciousnesses of seeing, hearing, smelling, tasting, touching, and knowing.[6] Again, there is prajñā in four pieces: suffering, its arising, its cessation, and the path.[7] Again, there is prajñā in six pieces: giving, morality, patience, vigor, meditation, and prajñā.[8] Again, the prajñā in one

---

3 **When the exposition of this essential point appears, it is said** (*kono shūshi no kaien genjō suru ni iwaku* この宗旨の開演現成するにいわく): Taking *shūshi no kaien* 宗旨の 開演 as the subject of *genjō suru* 現成する. The antecedent of "this" (*kono* この) here is uncertain. Perhaps, the phrase is to be understood simply as, "in explaining its teaching on wisdom, it is said [in the *Sūtra*]."

"form is itself emptiness; emptiness is itself form" (*shiki soku ze kū nari, kū soku ze shiki nari* 色即是空なり、空即是色なり): Quoting from the famous passage in the *Heart Sūtra*; see Supplementary Notes, s.v. "Form is itself emptiness; emptiness is itself form."

4 **"They are the hundred grasses; they are the myriad forms"** (*hyakusō nari, banzō nari* 百草なり、萬象なり): Or perhaps "it is"; the translation takes the unexpressed subject here to be "form" and "emptiness," but it might as well be the immediately preceding "emptiness." "The hundred grasses" (*hyakusō* 百草) and "the myriad forms" (*banzō* 萬象) are two common expressions for all things in the world; see Supplementary Notes, s.v. "Myriad forms."

5 **twelve entrances** (*jūni nyū* 十二入): Synonymous with the "twelve spheres" (or "bases"; S. *āyatana*): i.e., the six sense organs (*kon* 根; S. *indriya*) and their objects (*kyō* 境; S. *viṣaya*).

6 **prajñā in eighteen pieces** (*jūhachi mai no hannya* 十八枚の般若): The list here corresponds to the eighteen constituents (*jūhachi kai* 十八界; S. *dhātu*), involved in cognition: the six sense organs, their objects, and the corresponding consciousnesses. This and the preceding sentence reflect the *Heart Sūtra* (*Bore boluomiduo xin jing* 般若波羅 蜜多心經) at T.251.8:848c10-12:

無眼耳鼻舌身意。無色聲香味觸法。無眼界。乃至無意識界。

There is no eye, ear, nose, tongue, body or mind. There is no form, sound, smell, taste, touch or dharma. There is no eye constituent, and so on until, there is no mental consciousness constituent.

7 **prajñā in four pieces** (*shimai no hannya* 四枚の般若): I.e., the Buddhist four sacred truths.

8 **prajñā in six pieces** (*rokumai no hannya* 六枚の般若): I.e., the six perfections (*rokudo* 六度; S. *ṣaṭ-pāramitā*) of the bodhisattva: perfection of giving (*dando* 檀度; S. *dāna-pāramitā*), perfection of morality (*kaido* 戒度; S. *śīla-pāramitā*), perfection of patience (*nindo* 忍度; S. *kṣānti-pāramitā*), perfection of vigor (*shōjindo* 精進度; S. *vīrya-pāramitā*), perfection of meditation (*zendo* 禪度; S. *dhyāna-pāramitā*), and perfection of wisdom (*chido* 智度; S. *prajñā-pāramitā*).

2. Mahā-prajñā-pāramitā *Maka hannya haramitsu* 摩訶般若波羅蜜 21

piece has been realized in the present: it is *anuttara-samyak-sambodhi.*[9] Again, there are three pieces of prajñā-pāramitā: the past, present, and future. Again, there are six-pieces of prajñā: earth, water, fire, wind, space, and consciousness.[10] Again, the prajñā in four pieces is the walking, standing, sitting, and reclining performed in everyday life.[11]

* * * * *

[02:2] {1:9}

釋迦牟尼如來會中有一苾蒭。竊作是念、我應敬禮甚深般若波羅蜜多。此中雖無諸法生滅、而有戒蘊・定蘊・慧蘊・解脫蘊・解脫知見蘊施設可得、亦有預流果・一來果・不還果・阿羅漢果施設可得、亦有獨覺菩提施設可得、亦有無上正等菩提施設可得、亦有佛法僧寶施設可得、亦有轉妙法輪・度有情類施設可得。佛知其念、告苾蒭言、如是如是、甚深般若波羅蜜、微妙難測。

There was a bhikṣu in the assembly of Tathāgata Śākyamuni who thought to himself,[12]

I should honor and pay obeisance to the most profound prajñā-pāramitā. Although in it, there are no dharmas that arise or cease, still it can be postulated that there are the morality aggregate, concentration aggregate, wisdom aggregate, liberation aggregate, and knowledge of liberation aggregate.[13] Again, it can be postulated

---

9 **the prajñā in one piece has been realized in the present** (*ichimai no hannya haramitsu, nikon genjō seri* 一枚の般若波羅蜜、而今現成せり): Probably, to be understood simply as, "the single prajñā-pāramitā has been expressed here [in the *Heart Sūtra*]," in reference to the line at T.251.8:848c16-17:

三世諸佛、依般若波羅蜜多故、得阿耨多羅三藐三菩提。

The buddhas of the three times, by relying on prajñā-pāramitā, attain *anuttara-samyak-sambodhi.*

anuttara-samyak-sambodhi (*anokutara sanmyaku sanbodai* 阿耨多羅三藐三菩提): I.e., "unsurpassed, perfect awakening," the supreme wisdom of a buddha.

10 **six pieces of prajñā** (*hannya rokumai* 般若六枚): I.e., the six elements (*rokudai* 六大; S. *mahābhūta*) of Buddhist cosmology: earth, water, fire, wind, space, and consciousness.

11 **prajñā in four pieces** (*shimai no hannya* 四枚の般若): I.e., the four deportments (*iigi* [or *igi*] 威儀; S. *īryāpatha*) of the body: walking, standing, sitting, and reclining (*gyōjūzaga* 行住坐臥). See Supplementary Notes, s.v. "Deportment."

12 **There was a bhikṣu** (*ichi bissū* 一苾蒭): This entire section is a quotation from the *Great Perfection of Wisdom Sūtra* (*Da bore boluomiduo jing* 大般若波羅蜜多經, T.220.6:480b17-26).

13 **morality aggregate, concentration aggregate, wisdom aggregate, liberation aggregate, and knowledge of liberation aggregate** (*kai un jō un e un gedatsu un gedatsu chiken un* 戒蘊・定蘊・慧蘊・解脫蘊・解脫知見蘊): The so-called "undefiled five aggregates" (*muro goun* 無漏五蘊) attributed to an awakened one, also treated as the "five-part dharma body" (*gobun hosshin* 五分法身) of a buddha. For an earlier meaning

*that there are the fruit of the stream-entrant, the fruit of the once-re-
turner, the fruit of the nonreturner, and the fruit of the arhat.[14] Again,
it can be postulated that there is the bodhi of the solitary awakened
one; and again, it can be postulated that there is the unsurpassed,
perfect bodhi.[15] Again, it can be postulated that there are the treasures of buddha, dharma, and saṃgha.[16] Again, it can be postulated
that there are turning the wheel of the wondrous dharma and delivering sentient beings.*

*The Buddha, knowing his thoughts, addressed the bhikṣu, saying,
"Rightly so, rightly so. The most profound prajñā-pāramitā is subtle
and wondrous, difficult to fathom."*

[02:3]

而今の一苾蒭の竊作念は、諸法を敬禮するところに、雖無生滅の般若、こ
れ敬禮なり。この正當敬禮時、ちなみに施設可得の般若現成せり、いはゆ
る戒・定・慧、乃至度有情類等なり。これを無といふ。無の施設、かくの
ごとく可得なり。これ甚深微妙難測の般若波羅蜜なり。

Where the bhikṣu here thinks to himself to honor and pay obeisance to
the dharmas, the prajñā of "although there are no arising and ceasing" —
this is "honoring and paying obeisance."[17] At the very time that he hon-
ors and pays obeisance, the prajñā of "it can be postulated" is realized
— that is, the "morality," "concentration," and "wisdom," down to "de-

---

of "five aggregates" (*goun* 五蘊), see Supplementary Notes, s.v. "Four elements and five
aggregates."

14   **The fruit of the stream-entrant, the fruit of the once-returner, the fruit of the
nonreturner, and the fruit of the arhat** (*yoru ka ichirai ka fugen ka arakan ka* 預流
果・一來果・不還果・阿羅漢果): I.e., the four stages, or "fruits" (S. *phala*), on the traditional Buddhist path to nirvāṇa.

15   **bodhi of the solitary awakened one** (*dokkaku bodai* 獨覺菩提): I.e., the awakening
of a *pratyeka-buddha*.

the unsurpassed, perfect bodhi (*mujō shōtō bodai* 無上正等菩提): I.e, the full awakening of a buddha; S. *anuttara-samyak-saṃbodhi*.

16   **the treasures of buddha, dharma, and saṃgha** (*buppōsōbō* 佛法僧寶): I.e., the
"**three treasures**" (*sanbō* 三寶; S. *tri-ratna*), traditional symbol of the Buddhist religion.

17   **Where the bhikṣu here thinks to himself to honor and pay obeisance to the
dharmas** (*nikon no ichi bissū no setsu sanen wa, shohō o kyōrai suru tokoro ni* 而今の
一苾蒭の竊作念は、諸法を敬禮するところに): This entire passage is an exercise in
reorganizing the semantic units in the sūtra quotation. Here, honor is paid to the dharmas,
rather than to prajñā; and it is prajñā, rather than the dharmas, that is without arising and
ceasing.

2. Mahā-prajñā-pāramitā *Maka hannya haramitsu* 摩訶般若波羅蜜 23

livering sentient beings."[18] This is called "there are no."[19] In this way, the "postulation" "there are no" "can be."[20] This is "the prajñā-pāramitā," "most profound," "subtle and wondrous, difficult to fathom."[21]

[02:4]

天帝釋問具壽善現言、大德、若菩薩摩訶薩、欲學甚深般若波羅蜜多、當如何學。善現答言、憍尸迦、若菩薩摩訶薩、欲學甚深般若波羅蜜多、當如虛空學。

> Deva Lord Śakra asked Elder Subhūti, "Most Virtuous One, if a bodhisattva-mahāsattva wishes to study the most profound prajñā-pāramitā, how should he study it?"[22]
>
> Subhūti replied, "Kauśika, if a bodhisattva-mahāsattva wishes to study the most profound prajñā-pāramitā, he should study it as if it were empty space."

[02:5] {1:10}

しかあれば、學般若これ虛空なり、虛空は學般若なり。

Thus, to study prajñā is empty space; empty space is to study prajñā.

---

18 **the prajñā of "it can be postulated" is realized** (*sesetsu katoku no hannya genjō seri* 施設可得の般若現成せり): Or, perhaps, "the prajñā that 'can be postulated' . . . ." Likely meaning something like, "the wisdom that recognizes that [although ultimately 'there are no dharmas,' the entire list of dharmas that follow here in the sūtra] 'can be postulated' [i.e., conventionally proposed]" — such wisdom is realized in the act of "honoring and paying obeisance" to the dharmas.

19 **This is called "there are no"** (*kore o mu to iu* これを無といふ): I.e., the list of dharmas, from "the morality aggregate" down to "delivering sentient beings," is characterized by the bhikṣu as "there are no dharmas that arise or cease."

20 **In this way, the "postulation" "there are no" "can be"** (*mu no sesetsu kaku no gotoku katoku nari* 無の施設かくのごとく可得なり): The translation struggles here to retain something of Dōgen's play with the terms of the sūtra passage. Here, he has split the predicate "can be postulated" (*sesetsu katoku* 施設可得) and made the term *mu* 無 ("there are no," in the phrase "there are no dharmas") the "designation" that "can be" in this way.

21 **This is "the prajñā-pāramitā," "most profound," "subtle and wondrous, difficult to fathom"** (*kore jinjin mimyō nansoku no hannya haramitsu nari* これ甚深微妙難測の般若波羅蜜なり): Variation on the last line of the sūtra quotation above.

22 **Deva Lord Śakra asked Elder Subhūti** (*Ten Taishaku mon guju Zengen* 天帝釋問具壽善現): Continuing to quote from the *Da bore boluomiduo jing* 大般若波羅蜜多經, T.220.6:480b28-c2. "Deva Lord Śakra" (*Ten Taishaku* 天帝釋) is the god Indra, also addressed here as Kauśika (*Kyōshika* 憍尸迦); "Elder Subhūti" (*guju Zengen* 具壽善現) is Buddha Śākyamuni's disciple.

24 DŌGEN'S *SHŌBŌGENZŌ* VOLUME I

[02:6]

天帝釋復白佛言、世尊、若善男子善女人等、於此所説甚深般若波羅蜜多、
受持讀誦、如理思惟、爲他演説、我當云何而爲守護。唯願世尊、垂哀示
教。爾時具壽善現、謂天帝釋言、憍尸迦、汝見有法可守護不。天帝釋言、
不也。大德、我不見有法是可守護。善現言、憍尸迦、若善男子善女人等、
作如是説、甚深般若波羅蜜多、即爲守護。若善男子善女人等、作如所説、
甚深般若波羅蜜多、常不遠離。當知、一切人非人等、伺求其便、欲爲損
害、終不能得。憍尸迦、若欲守護、作如所説、甚深般若波羅蜜多、諸菩薩
者、無異爲欲守護虚空。

Deva Lord Śakra further addressed the Buddha saying,[23] "World-Honored
One, if good men and good women receive and keep, read and recite,
correctly reflect on, and preach for the benefit of others the most profound
prajñā-pāramitā spoken of here, in what way should I protect it? I beg the
World-Honored One to extend his compassion and instruct me."

At that time, Elder Subhūti said to Deva Lord Śakra, "Kauśika, do you
see any dharma that should be protected?"

Deva Lord Śakra replied, "No, Most Virtuous One, I do not see any
dharma that should be protected."

Subhūti said, "Kauśika, if good men and good women speak like this,
the most profound prajñā-pāramitā will itself be their protection. If
good men and good women speak like this, the most profound prajñā-pāramitā will never be distant. This you should know: whatever
humans or non-humans might look for the chance to harm it, in the
end they will be unable to do so. Kauśika, if you wish to protect it,
you should do so in accordance with what has been said: for the bodhisattvas, [wishing to protect] the most profound prajñā-pāramitā is no
different from wishing to protect empty space."

[02:7] {1:11}

しるべし、受持・讀誦・如理思惟、すなはち守護般若なり。欲守護は、受
持・読誦等なり。

We should know that "receiving and keeping, reading and reciting,
correctly reflecting on," are themselves protecting prajñā. "Wishing to
protect" is "receiving and keeping, reading and reciting," and so on.

* * * * *

---

23 **Deva Lord Śakra further addressed the Buddha** (*Ten Taishaku fuku byaku Butsu*
天帝釋復白佛): Continuing the quotation from the *Da bore boluomiduo jing* 大般若波
羅蜜多經, T.220.6:480c2-15.

2. Mahā-prajñā-pāramitā *Maka hannya haramitsu* 摩訶般若波羅蜜　　25

[02:8]

先師古佛云、渾身似口掛虚空、不問東西南北風、一等爲他談般若、滴丁東
了滴丁東。

> My former master, the Old Buddha, said,[24]
>
> Its whole body, like a mouth, hanging in empty space,
> Without asking if the winds are from north, south, east, or west,
> Equally, for them, it talks of prajñā:
> Di dingdong liao di dingdong.[25]

[02:9]

これ佛祖嫡嫡の談般若なり。渾身般若なり、渾他般若なり。渾自般若な
り、渾東西南北般若なり。

This is the "talking of prajñā" of successor after successor of buddhas
and ancestors. It is the prajñā of "the whole body"; it is the prajñā of the
whole "other"; it is the prajñā of the whole self; it is the prajñā of the
whole "north, south, east, or west."[26]

* * * * *

---

24 **My former master, the Old Buddha** (*senshi kobutsu* 先師古佛): I.e., Dōgen's
teacher, Tiantong Rujing 天童如淨 (1162-1227). The verse quoted here, entitled "Ode
to the Wind Chime" ("Fengling song" 風鈴頌), is cited elsewhere in Dōgen's writings.
His source for it is uncertain: it can be found in the *Rujing heshang yulu* 如淨和尚語錄
(T.2002A.48:132b15-16), but that record of Rujing's sayings did not reach Dōgen until
the eighth month of 1242, well after the date of our text here.

25 **Equally, for them, it talks of prajñā** (*ittō i ta dan hannya* 一等爲他談般若): The
translation takes the word *ta* 他 here as a third person plural pronoun referring to "the
winds"; it could also be read "others," and indeed, in his comment below, Dōgen reads it
as "other" (in contrast to "self"). In the *Rujing heshang yulu*, this line appears as "equally, with them, it talks of prajñā" (*ittō yo kyo dan hannya* 一等與渠談般若) — a version
that suggests the chime and the winds are talking together. This latter version is closer to
the text cited at *Eihei kōroku* 永平廣錄, DZZ.4:220. In his *Hōkyōki* 寶慶記 (DZZ.7:40),
Dōgen records Rujing's appreciation of his interpretation of the verse.

Di dingdong liao di dingdong (*teki teitō ryō teki teitō* 滴丁東了滴丁東): An onomato-
poetic representation of the sound of the wind chime, here read in modern Mandarin. A
premodern Japanese reading (*chi chintsun ryan chi chintsun* ちちんつんりゃんちちん
つん) is recorded at *Maka hannya haramitsu monge* 摩訶般若波羅蜜聞解, SCZ.1:165.

26 **the whole "other"** (*konta hannya* 渾他般若): The translation here obscures Dōgen's
play with Rujing's verse, which extends the adjective "whole" (*kon* 渾) from the expression "whole body" (*konjin* 渾身) in the first line to other terms in the verse. Here, the
English "other" renders *ta* 他 (translated in the verse as "them"), to which Dōgen adds
the contrasting "whole self" (*konko* 渾己).

26 DŌGEN'S *SHŌBŌGENZŌ* VOLUME I

[02:10]

釋迦牟尼佛言、舍利子、是諸有情、於此般若波羅蜜多、應如佛住供養禮
敬。思惟般若波羅蜜多、應如供養禮敬佛薄伽梵。所以者何。般若波羅蜜
多、不異佛薄伽梵、佛薄伽梵、不異般若波羅蜜多。般若波羅蜜多、即是佛
薄伽梵、佛薄伽梵、即是般若波羅蜜多。何以故。舍利子、一切如來應正等
覺、皆由般若波羅蜜多得出現故。舍利子、一切菩薩摩訶薩・獨覺・阿羅
漢・不還・一來・預流等、皆由般若波羅蜜多得出現故。舍利子、一切世間
十善業道・四靜慮・四無色定・五神通、皆由般若波羅蜜多得出現故。

Buddha Śākyamuni said,[27]

> Śariputra, these sentient beings should make offerings, honor, and
> pay obeisance to this prajñā-pāramitā as if a buddha dwelt there.
> When they reflect upon the prajñā-pāramitā, they should do so as
> if they were making offerings, honoring, and paying obeisance to a
> buddha, a *bhagavat*. What is the reason? The prajñā-pāramitā is no
> different from a buddha, a *bhagavat*; a buddha, a *bhagavat*, is no
> different from the prajñā-pāramitā. The prajñā-pāramitā is identical
> with a buddha, a *bhagavat*; a buddha, a *bhagavat*, is identical
> with the prajñā-pāramitā. Why is this so? Because, Śariputra,
> all the tathāgatas, the worthy ones, the perfectly awakened ones
> appear owing to the prajñā-pāramitā.[28] Because, Śariputra, all the
> *bodhisattvas-mahāsattvas, pratyeka-buddhas*, arhats, nonreturners,
> once-returners, and stream-entrants appear owing to the prajñā-
> pāramitā. Because, Śariputra, the way of the ten virtuous deeds, the
> four tranquil contemplations, the four formless concentrations, and
> the five spiritual powers, in all worlds, appear owing to the prajñā-
> pāramitā.[29]

[02:11] {1:12}

しかあればすなはち、佛薄伽梵は般若波羅蜜多なり、般若波羅蜜多は是れ
諸法なり。この諸法は空相なり、不生不滅なり、不垢不淨、不增不減な
り。この般若波羅蜜多の現成せるは、佛薄伽梵の現成せるなり。問取すべ

---

27 **Buddha Śākyamuni** (*Shakamuni butsu* 釋迦牟尼佛): Quoting again from the *Da
bore boluomiduo jing* 大般若波羅蜜多經 (T.220.5:925a8-20).

28 **the tathāgatas, the worthy ones, the perfectly awakened ones** (*nyorai ō shōtōgaku*
如來應正等覺): Three standard epithets of the buddhas. "The worthy ones" translates *ō* 應
(abbreviation of *ōgu* 應供, "worthy of reverence"); i.e., "arhats."

29 **way of the ten virtuous deeds** (*jūzengōdō* 十善業道): Here, the sūtra begins a list
of standard Buddhist spiritual practices: "the ten virtuous deeds," or wholesome actions
(*zengōdō* 善業道; S. *kuśala-karma-patha*); "the four tranquil contemplations," or meditations (*jōryo* 靜慮; S. *dhyāna*); "the four formless concentrations," or formless absorptions (*mushiki jō* 無色定; S. *ārūpya-samāpatti*), and "the five spiritual powers," or
higher knowledges (*jinzū* 神通; S. *abhijñā*). For the last, see Supplementary Notes, s.v.
"Spiritual powers."

2. Mahā-prajñā-pāramitā *Maka hannya haramitsu* 摩訶般若波羅蜜 27

し、參取すべし。供養禮敬する、これ佛薄伽梵に奉覲承事するなり、奉覲承事の佛薄伽梵なり。

Thus, a buddha, a *bhagavat*, is the prajñā-pāramitā. The prajñā-pāramitā is the dharmas. "These dharmas are marked by emptiness; they do not arise or cease; they are not sullied or pure; they do not increase or decrease."[30] When this prajñā-pāramitā appears, a buddha, a *bhagavat*, appears. We should question him; we should study with him. To "make offerings, do obeisance, and honor" is to attend and serve the buddha, the *bhagavat*. Attending and serving is a buddha, a *bhagavat*.[31]

正法眼藏摩訶般若波羅蜜第二
Treasury of the True Dharma Eye
Mahā-prajñā-pāramitā
Number 2

[Ryūmonji MS:]

爾時天福元年夏安居日、在觀音導利院示衆
Presented to the assembly at Kannon Dōri Cloister; on a day of the summer retreat, in the first year of Tenpuku [1233][32]

永享二季正月書、校了
Proofed. Copied in the first month, second year of Eikyō [25 January-22 February 1430][33]

---

30 **"These dharmas are marked by emptiness; they do not arise or cease; they are not sullied or pure; they do not increase or decrease"** (*kono shohō wa kūsō nari, fushō fumetsu nari, fuku fujō fuzō fugen nari* この諸法は空相なり、不生不滅なり、不垢不淨不增不減なり): Dōgen here gives a Japanese rendering of a line from the *Heart Sūtra* (*Bore boluomiduo xin jing* 般若波羅蜜多心經, T.251.8:848c9-10).

31 **Attending and serving is a buddha, a *bhagavat*** (*bugon shōji butsu bagabon nari* 奉覲承事佛薄伽梵なり): Following the punctuation in Kawamura's text; the passage might also be parsed, "To make offerings, do obeisance, and honor is to attend and serve the buddha, the *bhagavat*; is to be a buddha, a *bhagavat*, who attends and serves."

32 The Tōunji 洞雲寺 MS shares an identical colophon.

day of the summer retreat (*ge ango no hi* 夏安居日): Dates of the summer retreat vary; a common practice put it from the fifteenth of the fourth month through the fifteenth of the seventh month; in 1233, this would correspond to 25 May through 21 August.

33 Copyist unknown.

28 DŌGEN'S *SHŌBŌGENZŌ* VOLUME I

[Tōunji MS:]

寛元二年甲辰春三月二十一日、侍越宇吉峰精舎侍司書寫之。懷奘
*Copied this while serving in the acolyte's office, Kippō Vihāra, Etsuu;
twenty-first day of the third month, spring of the senior wood year of
the dragon, second year of Kangen [29 April 1244]. Ejō*

嘉慶三年正月十三日、在永平寺衆寮奉書寫之。宗吾
*Copied this as a memorial offering while in the common quarters of
Eihei Monastery; thirteenth day, first month, third year of Kakyō
[9 February 1389]. Sōgo*[34]

---

34 **Sōgo** 宗吾: 1343-1406, ninth abbot of Eiheiji.

TREASURY OF THE TRUE DHARMA EYE

NUMBER 3

Buddha Nature
Busshō
佛性

Buddha Nature

Bussho

Introduction

Dōgen's essay on buddha nature is one of the most celebrated texts in the *Shōbōgenzō*. It was composed in the autumn of 1241, at Kōshōji, the monastery Dōgen had established five years earlier on the southern outskirts of the imperial capital at Heiankyō. The work appears as number 3 in both the sixty- and seventy-five-chapter compilations of the *Shōbōgenzō*, and as number 22 in the Honzan edition; it is also extant in a holograph manuscript by Dōgen's disciple Ejō dated 1243.

The concept of buddha nature, one of the most widely discussed topics in East Asian Buddhism, was subject to a wide range of interpretations. In his opening remarks, Dōgen dismisses several of the most common views: that buddha nature is the potential to become a buddha, that it is the activity of cognition within us, or that it is a universal self pervading the world. Rather, he says, buddha nature is existence itself — not an abstract principle of being, but the actual occurrence of things, or, as he puts it simply at the end of his essay, "fences, walls, tiles, and pebbles."

Like the majority of the representative texts of the *Shōbōgenzō*, Dōgen's essay takes the form of commentary on thematically related passages from the Chinese Chan literature. His readings of these passages can be highly idiosyncratic and often depend on linguistic play with the grammar and syntax of his Chinese quotations — a feature famously exemplified at the beginning of our text, where Dōgen transforms a statement in the *Nirvāṇa Sūtra* that beings all have buddha nature to the claim that all beings are buddha nature. Similar play is found throughout the essay and makes this text one of the most demanding, for both translator and reader, in the *Shōbōgenzō*.

正法眼藏第三
Treasury of the True Dharma Eye
Number 3
佛性
Buddha Nature

[03:1] {1:14}

釋迦牟尼佛言、一切衆生、悉有佛·生。如來常住、無有變易。

Buddha Śākyamuni said, "All living beings in their entirety have buddha nature. The Tathāgata always abides, without any change."[1]

[03:2]

これ、われらが大師釋尊の師子吼の轉法輪なりといへども、一切諸佛、一切祖師の、頂顎眼睛なり。參學しきたること、すでに二千一百九十年＜當日本仁治二年辛丑歳＞、正嫡わづかに五十代＜至先師天童淨和尚＞、西天二十八代、代代住持しきたり、東地二十三世、世世住持しきたる。十方の佛祖、ともに住持せり。

Though it is said that this is turning the dharma wheel of the lion's roar of Great Master Śākya, the Honored One, it is the crown of the head and the eyes of all the buddhas, all the ancestral masters.[2] Its study has come down for two thousand, one hundred ninety years (to this, the

---

1 **Buddha Śākyamuni** (*Shakamuni butsu* 釋迦牟尼佛): From the Northern text of the *Nirvāṇa Sūtra* (*Da banniepan jing* 大般涅槃經, T.374.12:522c24). The initial phrase, "all living beings in their entirety have buddha nature," appears thirteen times in that text and represents one its key doctrinal assertions. The second phrase, "the Tathāgata always abides, without any change," also appears seven times in the *Nirvāṇa Sūtra*. The two phrases are only juxtaposed in two places: T.374.12:522c24 (quoted here by Dōgen) and T.374.12:574c24-28.

"All living beings in their entirety have buddha nature" (*issai shujō, shitsu u busshō* 一切衆生、悉有佛性): Or, more simply, "all living beings have buddha nature." The term *shitsu* 悉, rendered here as "in their entirety," functions simply as an emphatic adverb meaning "each and every," "without exception," etc.; the English here represents an attempt to facilitate translation of Dōgen's play with this term below (see Note 7). See Supplementary Notes, s.v. "All living beings in their entirety have buddha nature," for a parable from the *Nirvāṇa Sūtra* that explains the meaning of the saying.

2 **turning the dharma wheel of the lion's roar** (*shishi ku no ten bōrin* 師子吼の轉法輪): Mixing two standard metaphors for the preaching of the dharma. The passage cited here from the *Nirvāṇa Sūtra* is presented in the sūtra as "the lion's roar."

Great Master, Śākya, the Honored One (*daishi Shakuson* 大師釋尊): An epithet for the Buddha combining a standard East Asian reference to Śākyamuni as "world honored" (*seson* 世尊) with the honorific title "Great Master" (*daishi* 大師) awarded to prominent clerics.

32 DŌGEN'S *SHŌBŌGENZŌ* VOLUME I

junior metal year of the ox, the second year of the Japanese Ninji [era]),
through merely fifty generations of direct descent (to my former master, Reverend Jing of Tiantong).[3] Through twenty-eight generations in
Sindh in the West, it has been maintained in generation after generation;
through twenty-three descendants in the Land of the East, it has been
maintained by descendant after descendant.[4] The buddhas and ancestors
of the ten directions have all maintained it.

[03:3]
世尊道の一切衆生悉有佛性は、その宗旨いかむ。是什麼物恁麼來の道、轉
法輪なり。あるひは衆生といひ、有情といひ、群生といひ、群類といふ。
悉有の言は、衆生なり、群有なり。すなはち悉有は佛性なり、悉有の一悉
を衆生といふ。正當恁麼時は、衆生の内外すなはち佛性の悉有なり。單傳
する皮肉骨髓のみにあらず、汝得吾皮肉骨髓なるがゆえに。しるべし、い
ま佛性に悉有せらるる有は、有無の有にあらず。悉有は佛語なり、佛舌な
り、佛祖眼睛なり、衲僧鼻孔なり。悉有の言、さらに始有にあらず、本有
にあらず、妙有等にあらず。いはんや緣有・妄有ならんや。心境・性相等
にかかはれず。しかあればすなはち、衆生悉有の依正、しかしながら業增
上力にあらず、妄緣起にあらず、法爾にあらず、神通修證にあらず。衆生
の悉有、それ業增上および緣起法爾等ならんには、諸聖の證道および諸佛
の菩提、佛祖の眼睛も、業增上力および緣起法爾なるべし。しかあらざる
なり。　盡界はすべて客塵なし、直下さらに第二人あらず、直截根源人未
識、忙忙業識幾時休なるがゆえに。　妄緣起の有にあらず、徧界不曾藏の
ゆえに。徧界不曾藏といふは、かならずしも滿界是有といふにあらざる
なり。徧界我有は、外道の邪見なり。本有の有にあらず、亙古亙今のゆえ
に。始起の有にあらず、不受一塵のゆえに。條條の有にあらず、合取のゆ
えに。無始有の有にあらず、是什麼物恁麼來のゆえに。始起有の有にあら
ず、吾常心是道のゆえに。まさにしるべし、悉有中に衆生快便難逢なり。
悉有を會取することかくのごとくなれば、悉有それ透體脱落なり。

3　**two thousand, one hundred ninety years (to this, the junior metal year of the ox,
the second year of the Japanese Ninji [era])** (*nisen ippyaku kyūjū nen* [*tō nihon Ninji
ninen shin-chū sai*] 二千一百九十年＜當日本仁治二年辛丑歳＞): Parentheses here are
in the original text. The second year of the Ninji 仁治 era (1240-1243) corresponds to
1241 CE of the Gregorian calendar, 2190 years from 949 BCE, the date traditionally
used in East Asia for the *parinirvāṇa* of Buddha Śākyamuni.

my former master, the Reverend Jing of Tiantong (*senshi Tendō Jō oshō* 先師天童淨
和尚): I.e., Dōgen's Chinese teacher, Tiantong Rujing 天童如淨 (1162-1227), to whom
he regularly refers as "my former (or "late") master." Again, the parentheses are in the
original.

4　**twenty-eight generations in Sindh in the West** (*Saiten nijūhachi dai* 西天二十八
代); **twenty-three generations in the Land of the East** (*Tōchi nijūsan se* 東地二十三
世): I.e., the twenty-eight members in the traditional lineage of ancestors in India, from
Śākyamuni's disciple Mahākāśyapa to Bodhidharma; and the twenty-three ancestors in
the Chinese Chan lineage leading from Bodhidharma to Rujing 如淨. (The total of "fifty
generations" mentioned here reflects the fact that Bodhidharma is counted as both the
twenty-eighth ancestor in the Indian succession and the first ancestor of the Chinese
succession.)

3. Buddha Nature *Busshō* 佛性

33

What is the essential point of the World-Honored One's saying, "*All living beings in their entirety have buddha nature*"? It is turning the dharma wheel of the saying, "*What thing is it that comes like this?*"[5] One speaks of "living beings," or "sentient beings," or "the multitude of beings," or "the multitude of types."[6] The words "in their entirety have" refer to living beings, the multitude of beings.[7] That is, the "entirety of beings" is buddha nature; one entirety of the "entirety of beings" is called "living beings."[8] At this very moment, the interior and exterior of living beings is the "entirety of beings" of buddha nature. This is not only the skin, flesh, bones, and marrow uniquely transmitted; for *you've gotten my skin, flesh, bones, and marrow.*[9]

---

5 **turning the dharma wheel of the saying, "What thing is it that comes like this?"** (*ze jūmo butsu inmo rai no dō, ten bōrin* 是什麼物恁麼來の道、轉法輪): I.e., a Buddhist teaching equivalent to the famous question put to Nanyue Huairang 南嶽懷讓 (677-744) by the Sixth Ancestor, Huineng 慧能, in a dialogue recorded in Dōgen's *shinji Shōbōgenzō* 眞字正法眼藏 (DZZ.5:178, case 101) and often cited elsewhere in his writing; see Supplementary Notes, s.v. "What thing is it that comes like this?"

6 **"sentient beings"** (*ujō* 有情); **"the multitude of beings"** (*gunjō* 群生); **"the multitude of types"** (*gunrui* 群類): Terms regularly used as synonyms for "living beings," as is "the multitude of beings" (*gun'u* 群有) in the following sentence.

7 **The words "in their entirety have"** (*shitsu'u no gon* 悉有の言): Or "the words 'the entirety of beings.'" Dōgen here begins play with a neologism created from the adverb *shitsu* 悉 and the verb *u* 有 in the phrase *shitsu u busshō* 悉有佛性, translated in the quotation as "in their entirety have buddha nature." The play relies on the fact that the term *u* 有 means both "to have" and "to exist" and is regularly used in philosophical discourse as a noun for "being" or "beings." The resultant expression might also be rendered "all existents" or, more simply, "everything" (the singular, "entirety of being," is less likely with *shitsu* 悉).

8 **one entirety of the "entirety of beings"** (*shitsuu no isshitsu* 悉有の一悉): Presumably the point is that "living beings' represent but one type within the "entirety of beings" — with, perhaps, the added suggestion that any one type is in some sense one with the entire set.

9 **skin, flesh, bones, and marrow** (*hi niku kotsu zui* 皮肉骨髓): An expression, very common in Dōgen's writings for the essence or truth or entirety of something or someone, as handed down in Zen tradition; from the famous story of Bodhidharma's testing of four disciples, to whom he said of each in turn that he (or, in one case, she) had gotten his skin, flesh, bones, and marrow. See Supplementary Notes, s.v. "Skin, flesh, bones, and marrow."

for you've gotten my skin, flesh, bones, and marrow (*nyo toku go hi niku kotsu zui naru ga yue ni* 汝得吾皮肉骨髓なるがゆえに): Quoting Bodhidharma's statement, "you've gotten" to each of his four disciples. Presumably, the implication here is that the statement concerns not just Bodhidharma's "single transmission" to the Second Ancestor, Huike 慧可, but the affirmation of buddha nature in all beings (as proposed, e.g., at *Shōbōgenzō keiteki* 正法眼藏啓迪 2:185).

34 DŌGEN'S *SHŌBŌGENZŌ* VOLUME I

We should realize that the being that is here made the "entirety of beings" by buddha nature is not the being of being and non-being.[10] The
"entirety of beings" is the word of the buddha, the tongue of the buddha, the eyes of the buddhas and ancestors, the nose of the patch-robed
monk. Furthermore, the term "entirety of beings" is not initial being,
not original being, not wondrous being, and the like; how much less is it
conditioned being or deluded being.[11] It has nothing to do with the likes
of mind and object, nature and mark.[12] Therefore, the secondary and
primary recompense of the "entirety of beings" of living beings is not
by any means the generative power of karma, not deluded conditioned
arising, not of its own accord, not the practice and verification of spiritual powers.[13] Were the "entirety of beings" of living beings generated
by karma, or conditioned arising, or of its own accord, the verification of
the way of the sages as well as the bodhi of the buddhas and the eyes of

---

10 **the being that is here made the "entirety of beings" by buddha nature** (*ima
busshō ni shitsuu seraruru u* いま佛性に悉有せらるる有): An odd locution, presumably
meaning something like, "the term 'being' in the expression 'entirety of beings' that is
here being identified with buddha nature."

11 **initial being** (*shi'u* 始有); **original being** (*hon'u* 本有); **wondrous being** (*myō'u*
妙有); **conditioned being** (*en'u* 緣有); **deluded being** (*mō'u* 妄有): A series of terms
expressing modes of existence discussed in Buddhist thought. The first, "initial being"
(*shi'u* 始有), while not itself particularly common, is here contrasted with the familiar
"original being" (*hon'u* 本有), a term used to express the fundamental reality from which
the phenomenal world emerges. The expression "wondrous being" (*myō'u* 妙有) is probably best known in the phrase "true emptiness and wondrous being" (*shinkū myō'u* 眞空
妙有), where it expresses the ultimate emptiness of phenomena. The term "conditioned
being" (*en'u* 緣有) suggests that which exists as a result of conditions — i.e., the conditioned dharmas of dependent origination (*engi* 緣起; S. *pratīya-samutpāda*); "deluded
being" (*mō'u* 妄有) suggests that which exists as a result of deluded thoughts — i.e., the
false objects of our misguided discrimination (*funbetsu* 分別; S. *vikalpa*).

12 **nature and mark** (*shōsō* 性相): A standard Buddhist dichotomy between what a
thing is in itself (S. *svabhāva*) and its phenomenal characteristics (S. *lakṣana*).

13 **secondary and primary recompense** (*eshō* 依正): A standard Buddhist term for
the results of past karma reflected respectively in the circumstances into which one is
born and the mental and physical makeup of the person; see Supplementary Notes, s.v.
"Secondary and primary recompense." Here, perhaps to be understood as "the quality of
the experience" of living beings as the "entirety of beings."

the generative power of karma (*gō zōjō riki* 業增上力): I.e., the power of karma to
produce phenomena; S. *adhipati*.

deluded conditioned origination (*mō engi* 妄緣起): An unusual expression, probably
indicating phenomena that arise as a result of deluded thoughts. Given the apparent
distinction, above, between "conditioned being" and "deluded being," one is tempted to
parse the expression "deluded or conditioned origination."

of its own accord (*hōni* 法爾): A loose translation of a fairly common Buddhist term
meaning something like "the thing itself," "the dharma as it is in itself," etc.

3. Buddha Nature *Busshō* 佛性   35

the buddhas and ancestors would also be the generative power of karma, conditioned arising, and of its own accord. And this is not the case.

In all the worlds, there is no adventitious dust at all; right here, there is no second person beyond this.[14] For "*the root source is directly cut, but people have not noticed; the busy, busy karmic consciousness, when will it rest?*"[15] It is not the being of deluded conditioned arising; for "*in the realms everywhere, it has never been hidden.*"[16] To say that "*in the realms everywhere, it has never been hidden*" is not necessarily to say that *what fills the realms is being*: [the notion] that *the realms everywhere are my being* is a false view of other paths.[17] It is not the being of original being; for it is throughout the past and throughout the pres-

---

14 **adventitious dust** (*kyakujin* 客塵): The spiritual defilements (*bonnō* 煩惱; S. *kleśa*) understood as extrinsic (S. *agantuka*) to the mind; see Supplementary Notes, s.v. "Dust."

there is no second person (*daini nin arazu* 第二人あらず): A common expression in Zen texts, likely used here in the sense "this is all there is." The expression also appears in Dōgen's "Bendōwa" 辨道話; the version here seems to reflect the *Fozhao chanshi zoudui lu* 佛照禪師奏對錄 (*Guzunsu yulu* 古尊宿語錄, ZZ.118:823a7): *jikige kō mu daini nin* 直下更無第二人.

15 **For "the root source is directly cut, but people have not noticed; the busy, busy karmic consciousness, when will it rest?"** (*jiki setsu kongen jin mishiki, bōbō gosshiki kiji kyū naru ga yue ni* 直截根源人未識、忙忙業識幾時休なるがゆえに): Dōgen inserts here two lines in Chinese found in the *Yuanwu Foguo chanshi yulu* 圓悟佛果禪師語錄 (T.1997.47:744b8). The translation therefore takes the final *yue ni* ゆえに rendered as "for," to govern both lines — a reading that makes them an intriguing explanation of the preceding claim that the "entirety of beings" is a single, undefiled buddha nature. A somewhat less satisfying reading would limit the scope of "for" to the first clause: "the root source is directly cut, but people have not noticed; for the busy, busy karmic consciousness, when will it rest?"

"the root source is directly cut" (*jiki setsu kongen* 直截根源): Recalling a line from the famous poem *Zhengdao ge* 證道歌, attributed to the early Chan figure Yongjia Xuanjue 永嘉玄覺 (d. 723) (T.2014.48:395c21-22):

直截根源佛所印。摘葉尋枝我不能。

Directly cutting off the root source — this is sealed by the Buddha;
Plucking at the leaves and searching the branches — this I can't do.

the busy, busy karmic consciousness (*bōbō gosshiki* 忙忙業識): An idiomatic expression in Zen texts, sometimes in reverse order (*gosshiki bōbō* 業識忙忙). The term "karmic consciousness" (*gosshiki* 業識; also read *gōshiki*) may be understood either as the consciousness that arises from past karma or the consciousness that produces future karma; see Supplementary Notes, s.v. "Karmic consciousness."

16 **"in the realms everywhere, it has never been hidden"** (*henkai fu zō zō* 徧界不曾藏): A popular saying, found in the *shinji Shōbōgenzō* 眞字正法眼藏 (DZZ.5:157-158, case 58), attributed to Chan Master Shishuang Qingzhu 石霜慶諸 (807-888); see Supplementary Notes, s.v. "In the realms everywhere, it has never been hidden."

17 **what fills the realms is being** (*man kai ze u* 滿界是有): An odd locution, put in Chinese syntax, presumably meaning something like "being is the stuff of the cosmos."

36 DŌGEN'S *SHŌBŌGENZŌ* VOLUME I

ent.[18] It is not the being of initial arising; for it *"does not admit a single dust mote."*[19] It is not the being of individual instances; for it combines them. It is not the being of beginningless being; for *"What thing is it that comes like this?"*[20] It is not the being of initially arising being; for *"my usual mind is the way."*[21] We should realize that, within the "entirety of beings," *living beings cannot readily be met.*[22] When the understanding of the "entirety of beings" is like this, the "entirety of beings" is passing through the body and sloughing it off.[23]

---

the realms everywhere are my being (*henkai ga u* 徧界我有): Or "I exist in the realms everywhere," or "the realms everywhere belong to me." Another phrase in Chinese syntax, thought to express the notion in Indian thought that the self (S. ātman) is co-extensive with reality (S. *brahman*).

18 **throughout the past and throughout the present** (*gōko gōkon* 亙古亙今; also written 亘古亘今). A common idiom for extension throughout all history.

19 **"does not admit a single dust mote"** (*fuju ichijin* 不受一塵): From a line attributed to Weishan Lingyou 潙山靈祐 (771-853) (*Jingde chuandeng lu* 景德傳燈錄, T.2076.51:265a1-2):

實際理地不受一塵。萬行門中不捨一法。

The ground of principle at the limit of reality does not admit a single dust mote;
Those within the gate of the myriad practices, do not discard a single dharma.

20 **"What thing is it that comes like this?"** (*ze jūmo butsu inmo rai* 是什麼物恁麼來): See above, Note 5. Here, presumably, the point is that the "entirety of beings" actually appears and is, therefore, not merely some eternal being.

21 **It is not the being of initially arising being; for "my usual mind is the way"** (*shiki u no u ni arazu, go jō shin ze dō no yue ni* 始起有の有にあらず、吾常心是道のゆえに): The expression "initially arising being" (*shikiu* 始起有) is an unusual one; it may mean simply "a kind of being that comes into existence," or, on the analogy of the common term "initial awakening" (*shikaku* 始覺), it may suggest "a kind of being that one acquires upon awakening." The expression "my usual mind is the way" (*go jō shin ze dō* 吾常心是道) is likely a variant of a famous saying attributed to Nanquan Puyuan 南泉普願 (748-835): "Ordinary mind is the way" (*byōjō shin ze dō* 平常心是道). (Recorded in the *shinji Shōbōgenzō* 眞字正法眼藏, DZZ.5:134, case 19; and see Supplementary Notes, s.v., "Ordinary mind is the way." Some MS witnesses of our text give Nanquan's version. Presumably, Dōgen wants to contrast change implied by "initially arising being" with the constancy (*jō* 常) of the "usual mind."

22 **living beings cannot readily be met** (*shujō kaiben nanbō* 衆生快便難逢): Perhaps meaning that (since the "entirety of beings" is equated with "living beings") one does not easily encounter living beings in the "entirety of beings." The phrase rendered here "cannot readily be met" (*kaiben nanbō* 快便難逢) is an idiomatic Chinese expression, used often in Zen texts but not elsewhere in the *Shōbōgenzō*.

23 **passing through the body and sloughing it off** (*tōtai datsuraku* 透體脫落): Or, perhaps, simply, "thoroughly sloughing off." Generally taken to mean that the "entirety of beings" itself is liberation. The expression translated "passing through the body" (*tōtai* 透體) is not common and does not appear elsewhere in Dōgen's writings. The term "slough off" (*datsuraku* 脫落) is best known from the expression "body and mind

3. Buddha Nature *Busshō* 佛性

[03:4] {1:15}

佛性の言をききて、學者おほく先尼外道の我のごとく邪計せり。それ人に
あはず、自己にあはず、師をみざるゆえなり。いたづらに風火の動著する
心意識を、佛性の覺知・覺了とおもへり。たれかいふし、佛性に覺知・覺
了ありと。覺者・知者は、たとひ諸佛なりとも、佛性は覺知・覺了にあら
ざるなり。いはんや諸佛を覺者・知者といふ覺知は、なんだちが云云の
邪解を覺知とせず、風火の動静を覺知とするにあらず。ただ一兩の佛面祖
面、これ覺知なり。

Many students, hearing the term "buddha nature," have falsely reckoned that it is like the "I" in the other path of Śreṇika.[24] This is because
they have not met a person, they have not met themselves, they have
not seen a teacher.[25] They have foolishly thought that the mind, mentation, and consciousness moved by wind and fire are the perception
and comprehension of buddha nature.[26] Who said that buddha nature has
perception and comprehension?[27] While those who perceive and those
who know may be buddhas, buddha nature is not perception and comprehension.[28] Much less does the perception with which one refers to
the buddhas as perceivers and knowers represent the perception in the

---

sloughed off" (*shinjin datsuraku* 身心脱落) that Dōgen attributes to his master, Rujing
如淨; see Supplementary Notes, s.v. "Slough off," and "Body and mind sloughed off."

24 **other path of Śreṇika** (*Senni gedō* 先尼外道): Or "Śreṇika, of an other path." I.e.,
the non-Buddhist view expressed to the Buddha by the *tīrthika* Śreṇika, who held that
the self (S. ātman) is constant and pervades all space. Dōgen refers to this position in
several texts of the *Shōbōgenzō*; his source is likely the *Nirvāṇa Sūtra* (*Da banniepan
jing* 大般涅槃經, T.374.12:594a16ff).

25 **they have not met a person** (*hito ni awazu* 人にあはず): I.e., a "real" person; probably akin to the expression "that person" (*sono hito* その人) used in reference to a significant spiritual figure (as seen below, section 26: "If the Sixth Ancestor is 'that person'").

26 **mind, mentation, and consciousness moved by wind and fire** (*fūka no dōjaku suru
shin i shiki* 風火の動著する心意識): An unusual expression not repeated elsewhere in
Dōgen's writings; probably meaning something like "mental processes as a function of
physical life." The expression "wind and fire" is regularly used to indicate the physical
basis of life. Its use here doubtless anticipates the saying of Chan Master Changsha Jingcen 長沙景岑 that Dōgen will introduce below, section 77.

27 **perception and comprehension** (*kakuchi kakuryō* 覺知覺了): An unusual combination, not encountered elsewhere in the *Shōbōgenzō*. "Perception" here renders the
compound expression *kakuchi* 覺知, which Dōgen will take apart below into its component glyphs *kaku* 覺 ("sensing," "perceiving") and *chi* 知 ("knowing"), as in the common
expression "seeing, hearing, perceiving, and knowing" (*ken mon kaku chi* 見聞覺知).
The translation of the compound *kakuryō* 覺了 as "comprehension" takes the element
ryō 了 as "understanding"; some would read it as a particle of completed action (Chinese
le 了), though this seems somewhat unlikely in our context.

28 **those who perceive and those who know** (*kakusha chisha* 覺者知者): Dōgen has
here divided the compound *kakuchi* 覺知 into two terms, used for "the perceiver" and
"the knower," respectively.

DŌGEN'S *SHŌBŌGENZŌ* VOLUME I

misunderstandings you talk on about, the perception of the motion and rest of wind and fire.[29] Just one or two faces of the buddhas and faces of the ancestors — this is perception.[30]

[03:5] {1:16}

往往に古老先德、あるひは西天に往還し、あるひは人天を化導する、漢唐より宋朝にいたるまで、稲麻竹葦のごとくなる、おほく風火の動著を佛性の知覺とおもへる、あはれむべし、學道轉疏なるによりて、いまの失誤あり。いま佛道の晩學初心、しかあるべからず。たとひ覺知を學習すとも、覺知は動著にあらざるなり。たとひ動著を學習すとも、動著は恁麼にあらざるなり。もし眞箇の動著を會取することあらば、眞箇の覺知・覺了を會取すべきなり。佛之與性、達彼達此なり。佛性かならず悉有なり、悉有は佛性なるがゆえに。悉有は百雜碎にあらず、悉有は一條鐵にあらず。拈拳頭なるがゆえに大小にあらず。すでに佛性といふ、諸聖と齊肩なるべからず、佛性と齊肩すべからず。

There have frequently been ancient elders and prior worthies who have gone to Sindh in the West and back or have guided humans and devas; from the Han and Tang through the court of the Song, they are like "rice, hemp, bamboo, and reeds."[31] It is pitiful that many of them have thought that the movements of wind and fire are the perception of buddha nature. It is because they are estranged from the study of the way that they make this mistake.[32] Late students and beginners in the way of the buddhas today should not be like this. We may study perception, but perception is not movements; we may study movements, but movements are not like this.[33] If one has an understanding of true movement, one will understand true perception and comprehension.

---

29 **the misunderstandings you talk on about** (*nandachi ga unnun no jage* なんだちが云云の邪解): Dōgen here addresses his imagined opponents directly, in a rather dismissive second person plural. To "talk on" loosely renders *unnun* 云云, somewhat akin to the English "blah blah."

30 **one or two faces of the buddhas and faces of the ancestors** (*ichiryō no butsumen somen* 一兩の佛面祖面): Perhaps suggesting "actual historical instances of buddhas and ancestors"; see Supplementary Notes, s.v. "Buddha faces, ancestor faces."

31 **"rice, hemp, bamboo, and reeds"** (*tō ma chiku i* 稲麻竹葦): I.e., they are dense and profuse; a simile from Kumārajīva's translation of the *Lotus Sūtra*; see Supplementary Notes.

32 **estranged from the study of the way** (*gakudō tenso* 學道轉疏): Or "the study of the way is remote [from them]"; as, e.g., in the saying of Mazu Daoyi 馬祖道一 (709-788) (*Guzunsu yulu* 古尊宿語錄, ZZ.118:159b14):

若向外馳求轉疏轉遠。

If you run around seeking it outside, you get more remote and distant from it.

33 **movements are not like this** (*dōjaku wa inmo ni arazaru nari* 動著は恁麼にあらざるなり): The antecedent of "this" is likely "the movements of wind and fire" identified with "the knowing and perceiving of buddha nature."

3. Buddha Nature *Busshō* 佛性　　　39

With "buddha" and "nature," to master that one is to master this one.[34] Buddha nature is always the "entirety of beings"; for the "entirety of beings" is buddha nature. The "entirety of beings" is not a hundred fragments; the "entirety of beings" is not one strip of iron.[35] Since it is raising a fist, it is not large or small.[36] Given that we are calling it "buddha nature," it should not be of equal stature to the sages; it should not be made of equal stature to buddha nature.[37]

[03:6]

ある一類おもはく、佛性は草木の種子のごとし。法雨のうるほひしきりにうるほすとき、芽茎生長し、枝葉華果、もすことあり、果實さらに種子をはらめり。かくのごとく見解する、凡夫の情量なり。たとひかくのごとく見解すとも、種子および華果、ともに條條の赤心なりと參究すべし。果裏に種子あり、種子みえざれども根茎等を生ず。あつめざれどもそこばくの枝條大圍となれる、内外の論にあらず、古今の時に不空なり。しかあれば、たとひ凡夫の見解に一任すとも、根茎枝葉、みな同生し同死し、同悉有なる佛性なるべし。

There is one type that thinks buddha nature is like the seed of grasses and trees. When the rain of the dharma continually waters it, it sprouts and grows, the branches, leaves, flowers, and fruits flourish, and the fruits contain further seeds.[38] To hold this kind of view is the sentiment

---

34　**With "buddha" and "nature," to master that one is to master this one** (*butsu shi yo shō, tatsu bi tatsu shi* 佛之與性、達彼達此): I.e., to understand one is to understand the other; a sentence in Chinese syntax employing a linguistic pattern often found in Zen texts: e.g., "the buddha and the way" (*fo zhi yu dao* 佛之與道), "the buddha and the dharma" (*fo zhi yu fa* 佛之與法), etc.

35　**a hundred fragments** (*hyaku zassui* 百雜碎): A common Chan idiom for the multiplicity of phenomena. For other meanings and examples of usage, see Supplementary Notes, s.v. "A hundred fragments."

one strip of iron (*ichijō tetsu* 一條鐵): A common Chan idiom for the unity of phenomena, as in the saying, "one strip of iron for ten thousand miles" (*banri ichijō tetsu* 萬里一條鐵); see Supplementary Notes.

36　**raising a fist** (*nen kentō* 拈拳頭): The raising of the fist is a common Chan gesture expressing what is beyond language and discrimination; see Supplementary Notes, s.v. "Fist."

37　**it should not be of equal stature to the sages** (*shoshō to seiken naru bekarazu* 諸聖と齊肩なるべからず): The sense here is likely that, while we call the "entirety of beings" buddha nature, it should not be thought of as the spiritual state of the advanced Buddhist adepts. The following "it should not be made of equal stature to buddha nature" (*busshō to seiken su bekarazu* 佛性と齊肩すべからず) might be taken to mean that the "entirety of beings," being the entirety, is beyond compare.

38　**When the rain of the dharma continually waters it** (*hō'u no uruoi shikiri ni uruosu toki* 法雨のうるほひしきりにうるほすとき): "Dharma rain" (*hō'u* 法雨; S. *dharma-varṣa*) is a common metaphor for the Buddhist teachings; see Supplementary Notes. The Japanese *uruoi* here should probably be read as the grammatical subject: literally, "when the watering of the rain of the dharma repeatedly waters."

40 DŌGEN'S *SHŌBŌGENZŌ* VOLUME I

of common people.[39] Even if one holds this kind of view, we should investigate that the seeds and the flowers and fruits are bare mind in each instance.[40] Within the fruit is the seed; though the seed cannot be seen, it generates the roots and trunks and the rest. Though not assembled, that they become the many twigs, branches, and great trunk is not an issue of inside or outside, and is not empty in past or present.[41] Therefore, even if we accept the view of common people, the root, trunk, branches, and leaves are all born together, die together, and are buddha nature that is the "entirety of beings" together.[42]

* * * * *

[03:7] {1:17}

佛言、欲知佛性義、當觀時節因緣。時節若至、佛性現前。

The Buddha said, "If you wish to know the meaning of 'buddha nature,' you should observe the conditions of the time. If the time arrives, buddha nature appears."[43]

39　**the sentiment of common people** (*bonbu no jōryō* 凡夫の情量): I.e., the thinking of ordinary people. The term translated "sentiment" (*jōryō* 情量) is a common compound in Buddhist texts, usually parsed as the "calculations" (*ryō* 量) of a mind governed by emotional attachments (*jō* 情). In Buddhist usage, "commoners" (*bonbu* 凡夫; S. *pṛthagjana*) are those not yet advanced on the Buddhist path, in contrast to "sages" (or "nobles"; *shō* 聖; S. ārya).

40　**bare mind in each instance** (*jōjō no sekishin* 條條の赤心): Perhaps derived from the more common expression "bare mind in pieces (*sekishin henpen* 赤心片片); see Supplementary Notes, s.v. "Bare mind in pieces." A "bare (or red) mind" (*chixin* 赤心) is a common Chinese idiom for a sincere, or straightforward, mind (or heart); here, commonly interpreted as the buddha mind (*busshin* 佛心), equivalent to buddha nature.

41　**though not assembled** (*atsumezaredomo* あつめざれども): Presumably, the sense is "though no one (or nothing) puts them together."

is not an issue of inside or outside, and is not empty in past or present (*naige no ron ni arazu, kokon no toki ni fukū nari* 内外の論にあらず、古今の時に不空なり): Presumably, meaning something like, "[the development of the tree] is not the result of internal or external causes but is nevertheless true throughout history."

42　**are all born together, die together, and are buddha nature that is the "entirety of beings" together** (*mina dōshō shi dōshi shi, dōshitsu'u naru busshō naru beshi* み な同生し同死し、同悉有なる佛性なるべし): Or, perhaps, "are all buddha nature, with which they are born together, die together, and are the 'entirety of beings' together." The expressions "same birth" (*dōshō* 同生) and "same death" (*dōshi* 同死) are elsewhere used in Dōgen's writings to indicate the identity or co-extension of two things.

43　**The Buddha** (*butsu* 佛): Although both sentences here are attributed to the Buddha, only the first is a saying that, according to some Chan sources, comes from a sūtra. Modern scholars identify that sūtra as the *Nirvāṇa Sūtra* (*Da banniepan jing* 大般涅槃經). The second sentence does not correspond perfectly to any extant source but is typical of comments that Baizhang Huaihai 百丈懷海 (749-814) and other Chan masters attached

3. Buddha Nature *Bisshō* 佛性　　41

[03:8]

いま佛性義をしらんとおもはばといふは、ただ知のみにあらず、行ぜんと
おもはば、證せんとおもはば、とたんとおもはばとも、わすれんとおもは
ばともいふなり。かの説・行・證・亡・錯・不錯等も、しかしながら時節
の因縁なり。時節の因縁を觀ずるには、時節の因縁をもて觀ずるなり。
拂子・拄杖等をもて相觀するなり。さらに有漏智・無漏智、本覺・始覺、
無覺・正覺等の智をもちいるには、觀ぜられざるなり。

This "*if you wish to know the meaning of buddha nature*" is not just
about knowing: it means also "if you wish to practice it," "if you wish
to verify it," "if you wish to preach it," "if you wish to forget it." That
preaching, practicing, verifying, forgetting, mistaking, and not mistaking are, all of them, "the conditions of the time." In "observing the conditions of the time," one observes them using the conditions of the time;
one observes their marks using the whisk, the staff, and so on.[44] They
cannot be observed using in addition the wisdoms of contaminated wisdom, uncontaminated wisdom, original awakening, initial awakening,
non-awakening, right awakening, and the like.[45]

---

to the sūtra saying that precedes it. For details, see Supplementary Notes, s.v. "If you
wish to know the meaning of 'buddha nature,' you should observe the conditions of the
time."

"you should observe the conditions of the time" (*tō kan jisetsu innen* 當觀時節因緣):
Perhaps a variant of the line from the *Nirvāṇa Sūtra*. In a Buddhist context, the term translated as "observe" (*kan* 觀; "to see," "regard," "contemplate," etc.) often (though not always) indicates a contemplative practice. The expression *jisetsu innen* 時節因緣, translated here as "the conditions of the time," typically in the sense "the actual circumstances
of the particular occasion," occurs often in Chan texts. For examples, see Supplementary
Notes, s.v. "If you wish to know the meaning of 'buddha nature,' you should observe the
conditions of the time."

44　**the whisk, the staff, and so on** (*hossu shujō tō* 拂子拄杖等): I.e., the concrete
objects of (or, perhaps, their use by) the Chan teacher. The whisk (*hossu* 拂子) is a cer-
emonial fly-whisk, often held by the master during lectures and other rituals; the staff
(*shujō* 拄杖) is a walking stick, often carried by the master when he "ascends to the hall"
(*jōdō* 上堂; i.e., presides over a formal convocation). See Supplementary Notes, s.v.
"Whisk," "Staff."

45　**contaminated wisdom, uncontaminated wisdom, original awakening, initial
awakening, non-awakening, right awakening, and the like** (*uro chi muro chi hongaku
shikaku mukaku shōkaku tō* 有漏智無漏智本覺始覺無覺正覺等): A list of terms for various sorts of knowledge discussed in Buddhist texts. "Contaminated wisdom" (*uro chi*
有漏智; S. *sāsrava-jñāna*) and "uncontaminated wisdom" (*muro chi* 無漏智; S. *anāsra-
va-jñāna*) refer respectively to knowledge defiled or undefiled by the mental "afflictions"
(*bonnō* 煩惱; S. *kleśa*). The former is characteristic of the spiritual "commoner" (*bonbu*
凡夫; S. *pṛthagjana*); the latter, of the spiritual "noble" (*shō* 聖; S. *ārya*), or "sage." The
pair "original awakening" (*hongaku* 本覺) and "initial awakening" (*shikaku* 始覺) distinguishes between the *bodhi* inherent in buddha nature and the *bodhi* attained at the end of
the bodhisattva path. "Non-awakening" (*mukaku* 無覺; "without awakening") plays on
the sense of *kaku* 覺 as both "perception" and "awakening": it is used in reference both

42　DŌGEN'S *SHŌBŌGENZŌ* VOLUME I

[03:9]

當觀といふは、能觀・所觀にかかはれず、正觀・邪觀等に準すべきにあらず、これ當觀なり。當觀なるがゆえに不自觀なり、不他觀なり。時節因緣聻なり、超越因緣なり。佛性聻なり、脱體佛性なり。佛佛聻なり、性性聻なり。

[The meaning of] "should observe" has nothing to do with the observer or what is observed; it should not be gauged by such [notions] as right observation or false observation: it is "should observe."[46] Because it is "should observe," it is not one's own observing, it is not another's observing.[47] It is the very "conditions of the time" themselves; it transcends conditions.[48] It is buddha nature itself; it is buddha nature with body stripped.[49] It is buddha after buddha themselves; it is nature after nature themselves.

---

to insentience and to a mental state free from ordinary perception, as in Zen sayings such as "the awakening of non-awakening — this is called the true awakening" (*mukaku shi kaku ze myō shin kaku* 無覺之覺是名眞覺), or "right awakening is without awakening; true emptiness is not empty" (*shōkaku mukaku shinkū fukū* 正覺無覺眞空不空). "Right awakening" (*shōkaku* 正覺) is a standard translation of Sanskrit *saṃbodhi* or *samyak-saṃbodhi*, often translated "perfect enlightenment."

46　**"should observe"** (*tōkan* 當觀): Dōgen has here created a neologism from the predicate in the clause "you should observe the conditions of the time" (*tōkan jisetsu innen* 當觀時節因緣). The translation loses the play with the element *tō* 當, which functions in the quotation simply as a deontic modal ("should," "ought to," etc.) but also has among its uses such meanings as "now," "at that very time," "immediately," "just then," etc. Hence, the sense of *tōkan* here is typically understood as "observing right now," "immediately observing," etc.

47　**it is not one's own observing, it is not another's observing** (*fujikan nari, futakan nari* 不自觀なり、不他觀なり): This could also be parsed "it is not observing the self, it is not observing the other."

48　**the very "conditions of the time" themselves** (*jisetsu innen nii* 時節因緣聻): Here and in the parallel constructions that follow, the translation attempts to capture something of the use of the colloquial final particle *nii* 聻 (sometimes read *ni*), which has the primary function of an emphatic or a device for calling the hearer's attention to the preceding, somewhat akin to an English final "right?" In Dōgen's use here, it is usually interpreted to mark off what precedes it as "X itself," "X just as it is," "nothing but X," etc.

it transcends conditions (*chōotsu innen nari* 超越因緣なり): Or, possibly, "it is the traditions transcended."

49　**buddha nature with body stripped** (*dattai busshō* 脱體佛性): Or "the fully exposed buddha nature." The term *dattai* 脱體, translated rather literally here as "body stripped," can indicate a state of liberation; but, in Chan texts, it often carries the sense "to reveal all," or, as we might say, "to say it as it is" — hence, "the very thing itself," "the 'naked' thing." See Supplementary Notes, s.v. "Body stripped."

3. Buddha Nature *Busshō* 佛性

43

[03:10]

時節若至の道を、古今のやから往注におもはく、佛性の現前する時節の
向後にあらんずるをまつなりとおもへり。かくのごとく修行しゆくとこ
ろに、自然に佛性現前の時節にあふ。時節いたらざれば、參師問法するに
も、辨道功夫するにも、現前せずといふ。恁麼見取して、いたづらに紅塵
にかへり、むなしく雲漢をまぼる。かくのごとくのたぐひ、おそらくは
天然外道の流類なり。いはゆる欲知佛性義は、たとへば當知佛性義といふ
なり。當觀時節因緣といふは、當知時節因緣といふなり。いはゆる佛性
をしらんとおもはば、しるべし、時節因緣これなり。時節若至といふは、
すでに時節いたれり、なにの疑著すべきところかあらんとなり。疑著時節
さもあらばあれ、還我佛性來なり。しるべし、時節若至は、十二時中不空
過なり。若至は既至といふがごとし。時節若至すれば、佛性不至なり。
しかあればすなはち、時節すでにいたれば、これ佛性の現前なり。あるひ
は其理自彰なり。おほよそ時節の若至せざる時節いまだあらず、佛性の現
前せざる佛性あらざるなり。

A bunch in the past and present have frequently thought the words
"if the time arrives" mean that one awaits a time later when buddha nature might appear. "Continuing to practice in this way," they say, "one
encounters the time when buddha nature appears naturally; if the time
does not arrive, even though one studies with a teacher and asks about
the dharma, even though one makes concentrated effort in pursuit of
the way, it will not appear."[50] Taking such a view, they return in vain to
the red dust, they stare vacantly at the Milky Way.[51] Types like this are
doubtless followers of an other path of natural occurrence.[52]

---

50 **"one encounters the time when buddha nature appears naturally"** (*jinen ni
busshō genzen no jisetsu ni au* 自然に佛性現前の時節にあふ): Or "one naturally encounters the time when buddha nature appears."

51 **red dust** (*kōjin* 紅塵): I.e., the secular world. The sense of this common Chinese
expression is said to derive from the dust kicked up by the bustle of the city streets.

stare vacantly at the Milky Way (*munashiku unkan o maboru* むなしく雲漢をまぼ
る): Or, by extension, "at the sky." "To gaze at the Milky Way" (*mu shi yunkan* 目視雲
漢) is a fairly common expression for idleness. The unusual verb *maboru* here is best
understood as *mimamoru* 見守る.

52 **An other path of natural occurrence** (*tennen gedō* 天然外道): Seemingly synonymous with the more familiar *jinen gedō* 自然外道; non-Buddhist religion holding
the view that things exist or arise of themselves, rather than as the result of causes and
conditions. A fairly common pejorative in Dōgen's writings.

44   DŌGEN'S *SHŌBŌGENZŌ* VOLUME I

To say, "*if you wish to know the meaning of buddha nature*" is saying, for example, "*you should know the meaning of buddha nature.*"[53] To say "*you should observe the conditions of the time*" is to say, "*you should know the conditions of the time.*" If you wish to know what is called "buddha nature," you should know that it is precisely "the conditions of the time."[54] To say, "if the time arrives," means "the time has already arrived; what is there to doubt?"[55] Let doubting the time be as it may, *return buddha nature to me.*[56] We should realize that "if the time arrives" is "*not passing the twelve times in vain.*"[57] "If it arrives" is like saying, "it has arrived." If it were "if the time arrives," buddha nature would not

---

53 **"you should know the meaning of buddha nature"** (*tōchi busshō gi* 當知佛性 義): Here and in the following sentence, Dōgen seems again to be playing with the modal auxiliary "should" (*tō* 當) in its additional meaning of "now," etc., as above (see Note 46). Hence, these sentences might be interpreted as follows: "To say 'if you wish to know the meaning of buddha nature' is to say, for example, 'you know right now the meaning of buddha nature.' To say 'just observe the conditions of the time' is to say 'you know right now the conditions of the time.'"

54 **you should know that it is precisely "the conditions of the time"** (*shiru beshi, jisetsu innen kore nari* しるべし、時節因緣これなり): Or, more literally, "you should know that 'the conditions of the time' are it."

55 **"The time has already arrived"** (*sude ni jisetsu itareri* すでに時節いたれり): Dōgen is here giving a vernacular reading of Baizhang's comment, "once the time has arrived..." (*jisetsu ki shi* 時節既至), as that appears in the *Jingde chuandeng lu* 景德傳 燈錄; for a translation of the relevant passage in that text, see Supplementary Notes, s.v. "If you wish to know the meaning of 'buddha nature,' you should observe the conditions of the time."

"what is there to doubt?" (*nani no gijaku su beki tokoro ka aran* なにの疑著すべきと ころかあらん): Possibly a Japanese variant of the common Chinese idiom "who could doubt it?" (*you shui yi zhao* 有誰疑著).

56 **return buddha nature to me** (*gen ga busshō rai* 還我佛性來): Or, more colloquially, "give me back buddha nature." The Chinese imperative construction here, *huan wo ... lai* 還我 ... 來 ("give me back ..."), is a fairly common challenge in Chan texts, in such expressions as "give me back the buddha dharma" (*huan wo fofa lai* 還 我佛法來); "give me back the lion's roar" (*huan wo shizi hou rai* 還我師子吼來); "give me back your original face" (*huan wo benlai mianmu lai* 還我本來面目來); etc. Dōgen uses the construction (or the closely similar *gen go ... rai* 還吾 ... 來) elsewhere in the *Shōbōgenzō*, in phrases like "return the bright mirror to me" (*gen ga myōkyō rai* 還我 明鏡來), "return the fragments [of the mirror] to me" (*gen go saihen rai* 還吾碎片來) ("Shōbōgenzō kokyō" 正法眼藏古鏡, DZZ.1:227); "return concentrated effort to me" (*gen go kufū rai* 還吾功夫來) ("Shōbōgenzō hakujushi" 正法眼藏柏樹子, DZZ.1:440).

57 **"not passing the twelve times in vain"** (*jūni ji chū fukū ka* 十二時中不空過): I.e., "not wasting the day [waiting for the time to arrive]." The "twelve times" (*jūni ji* 十二時) are the twenty-four hours of the day figured traditionally in two-hour divisions. The use of this expression here may be a reflection of a conversation recorded in Dōgen's *shinji Shōbōgenzō* 眞字正法眼藏 (DZZ.5:260, case 261):

雲門因僧問、十二時中如何即得不空過。師曰、向什麼處著此一問。

3. Buddha Nature *Busshō* 佛性   45

arrive; therefore, since the time has already arrived, this is the appearance of buddha nature.[58] Or "its principle will appear of itself."[59] In sum, there has never been a time when the time does not arrive, nor a buddha nature that does not appear.[60]

* * * * *

[03:11] {1:18}

第十二祖馬鳴尊者、十三祖のために佛性海をとくにいはく、山河大地、皆依建立、三昧六通、由茲發現。

The Twelfth Ancestor, Venerable Aśvaghoṣa, in teaching the ocean of buddha nature to the Thirteenth Ancestor, said,[61]

The mountains, rivers, and the whole earth
Are all constructed dependent upon it;
Samādhi and the six powers
Appear from here.[62]

Once a monk asked Yunmen, "How can we not pass the twelve times in vain?" The Master said, "Where do you ask this question?"

58 **If it were "if the time arrives," buddha nature would not arrive** (*jisetsu nyaku shi sureba, busshō fushi nari* 時節若至すれば、佛性不至なり): The translation interprets the argument to be that, if we take the phrase "if the time arrives" literally, it implies that buddha nature is not yet present — hence, the need to read the phrase as "since the time has already arrived."

59 **"its principle will appear of itself"** (*go ri ji shō* 其理自彰): Or, perhaps, "its principle will be self-evident." Taken from a variant of Baizhang's saying; see above, Note 43.

60 **a time when the time does not arrive** (*jisetsu no nyaku shi sezaru jisetsu* 時節の若至せざる時節): The translation fails to capture the play with the expression *nyaku shi* 若至 ("if [the time] arrives") treated as a compound verb; a literal translation would yield the grotesque, "a time when the time does not 'if it arrives.'"

61 **The Twelfth Ancestor, Venerable Aśvaghoṣa** (*daijūni so Memyō sonja* 第十二祖馬鳴尊者): The famous second-century Buddhist author; his biography as the twelfth Zen ancestor can be found in the *Jingde chuandeng lu* 景德傳燈錄 (T.2076.51:209c1ff). His verse on the "ocean of the nature" for the Thirteenth Ancestor, Kapimala, occurs at T.2076.51:209c20-21.

ocean of buddha nature (*busshō kai* 佛性海): I.e., buddha nature likened to an ocean; a term not common in Dōgen's lexicon: elsewhere in the *Shōbōgenzō*, it receives only passing notice in the "Kaiin zanmai" 海印三昧 chapter (DZZ.1:125). In the *Jingde chuandeng lu* 景德傳燈錄 version of this episode (T.2076.51:209c19-20), Aśvaghoṣa's teaching is said to be on the "ocean of the nature" (*shōkai* 性海), a more familiar East Asian Buddhist term for the ultimate realm of suchness.

62 **Samādhi and the six powers** (*zanmai rokuzū* 三昧六通): Or "the samādhis and the six powers." I.e., states of extreme mental concentration and the standard list of six paranormal powers said to be attainable through their cultivation: physical powers, paranormal vision, paranormal hearing, mind reading, recollection of past lives, and

46 DŌGEN'S *SHŌBŌGENZŌ* VOLUME I

[03:12]

しかあれば、この山河大地、みな佛性海なり。皆依建立といふは、建立せ
る正當恁麼時、これ山河大地なり。すでに皆依建立といふ、しるべし、
佛性海のかたちはかくのごとし。さらに内外中間にかかはるべきにあら
ず。恁麼ならば、山河をみるは佛性をみるなり、佛性をみるは驢腮馬觜を
みるなり。皆依は全依なり、依全なりと、會取し、不會取するなり。三昧
六通、由茲發現。しるべし、諸三昧の發現・未現、おなじく皆依佛性な
り。全六通の由茲・不由茲、ともに皆依佛性なり。六神通はただ阿笈摩教
にいふ六神通にあらず。六といふは、前三三後三三を六神通波羅蜜とい
ふ。しかあれば、六神通は明明百草頭、明明佛祖意なりと參究することな
かれ。六神通に滞累せしむといへども、佛性海の朝宗に罣礙するものな
り。

Thus, these "mountains, rivers, and the whole earth" are all the ocean
of buddha nature. To say that they "*are all constructed dependent upon
it*" means that the very time they are constructed is the "mountains, rivers, and the whole earth." Since it is said that they "*are all constructed
dependent upon it,*" we should realize that such is the shape of the ocean
of buddha nature; it has nothing beyond this to do with inside, outside,
or in between.[63] If such is the case, to see the mountains and rivers is
to see buddha nature; to see buddha nature is to see an ass's jaw and a
horse's muzzle.[64] "All . . . dependent," we understand — and we do not
understand — as "wholly dependent," as "dependent on the whole."[65]
"*Samādhi and the six powers appear from here*": we should realize that
the "appearance" and the non-appearance of the samādhis are equally
"all dependent" on buddha nature; the "from here" — and the not "from
here" — of the whole of the six powers are both "*all dependent*" on

---

knowledge of the exhaustion of the mental contaminants (*rojin* 漏盡; S. *āsraya-kṣaya*);
see Supplementary Notes, s.v. "Spiritual powers."

63 **such is the shape of the ocean of buddha nature** (*busshō kai no katachi wa kaku
no gotoshi* 佛性海のかたちはかくのごとし): Presumably, the antecedent of "such" here
is "the mountains, rivers, and the whole earth."

64 **an ass's jaw and a horse's muzzle** (*rosai bashi* 驢腮馬觜): A Chinese colloquial
expression, appearing often in Chan texts, for "this and that," "every sort of thing," etc.

65 **"All . . . dependent," we understand — and we do not understand — as "wholly
dependent," as "dependent on the whole"** (*kai e wa zen'e nari, ezen nari to, eshu shi,
fueshu suru nari* 皆依は全依なり、依全なりと、會取し、不會取するなり): Dōgen is
here playing with the Chinese grammar, taking the adverb-verb combination *kai e* 皆
依 ("all dependent") as if it were a compound expression and then substituting *zen* 全
("complete," "total," "perfect," etc.) for *kai* 皆; presumably, the results are intended to
convey the sense that each thing is dependent on the whole [ocean of buddha nature].
The implication of the playful remark that we both understand and do not understand this
is ambiguous; it is often taken to suggest that this is true whether or not we understand it.

3. Buddha Nature *Busshō* 佛性　　47

buddha nature.[66] The six spiritual powers are not just the six spiritual powers spoken of in the teachings of the āgamas: "six" means that *"three three in front, three three in back"* are the *pāramitā* of the six spiritual powers.[67] Therefore, do not investigate the six spiritual powers as being "perfectly clear, the tips of the hundred grasses; perfectly clear, the intention of the buddhas and ancestors."[68] Although they may be constrict-

---

66　**the "from here" — and the "not from here" — of the whole of the six powers** (*zen rokuzū no yūji fuyūji* 全六通の由茲不由茲): The awkward translation tries to retain something of Dōgen's play here again with the Chinese passage, in which he takes the prepositional phrase translated "from here" (*yū ji* 由茲) as a verbal nominative ("deriving from here," "depending on here," etc.); like the structure, the sense seems to parallel the preceding clause and to be something like, "whether or not we take the complete six powers as arising from or not arising from buddha nature, they are dependent on it."

67　**the teachings of the** āgamas (*agyūma kyō* 阿笈摩教): I.e., the teachings of the non-Mahāyāna sūtras of the Buddhist canon (more commonly transliterated as *agon* 阿含); for Dōgen, equivalent to the teachings of the Small Vehicle. Dōgen doubtless has in mind here the standard Buddhist list of powers given above, Note 62. In his "Shōbōgenzō jinzū" 正法眼藏神通 (DZZ.1:394), Dōgen identifies this list with what he calls there the "small spiritual powers" discussed in the traditional Buddhist texts, in contrast to the "great spiritual powers" discussed in Chan texts:

二乗外道經師論師等は、小神通をならふ、大神通をならはず。諸佛は大神通を住特す、大神通を相傳す、これ佛神通なり....また五通六通みな小神通なり。

The two vehicles, the other paths, the sūtra masters and treatise masters, and the like, learn the small spiritual powers; they do not learn the great spiritual powers. The buddhas maintain the great spiritual powers; they transmit the great spiritual powers. These are the spiritual powers of a buddha. . . . Further, the five powers or six powers are all small spiritual powers.

"three three in front, three three in back" (*zen sansan go sansan* 前三三後三三): Or, perhaps, "three and three of the former, three and three of the latter." Dōgen is clearly playing here with the number six, but the exact sense of this Zen expression is uncertain. The source appears in several Chan collections as well as in Dōgen's *shinji Shōbōgenzō* 眞字正法眼藏 (DZZ.5:194-195, case 127); see Supplementary Notes, s.v. "Three three in front, three three in back."

the *pāramitā* of the six spiritual powers (*roku jinzū haramitsu* 六神通波羅蜜): Or "the six spiritual power *pāramitās*." I.e., the perfection of the six paranormal powers, or the paranormal powers as the six perfections of the bodhisattva. The paranormal powers are not typically listed among the six *pāramitās*, or "perfections"; rather, Dōgen seems here to be playing with the coincidence that both the powers and perfections are listed as six in number.

68　**do not investigate the six spiritual powers as being "perfectly clear, the tips of the hundred grasses; perfectly clear, the intention of the buddhas and ancestors"** (*roku jinzū wa meimei hyaku sōtō, meimei busso i nari to sankyū suru koto nakare* 六神通は明明百草頭、明明佛祖意なりと參究することなかれ): Variant of a saying best known from a conversation between the famous Layman Pang Yun 龐蘊居士 (740?-808) and his daughter, Lingzhao 靈照, found in several Chan sources as well as Dōgen's *shinji Shōbōgenzō* 眞字正法眼藏 (DZZ.5:168, case 88); see Supplementary Notes, s.v. "Perfectly clear, the tips of the hundred grasses." The surprising imperative "do not

48 DŌGEN'S *SHŌBŌGENZŌ* VOLUME I

ed by the six spiritual powers, they are obstructions in the flow to the source in the ocean of buddha nature.[69]

* * * * *

[03:13] {1:19}

五祖大滿禪師、蘄州黃梅人也。無父而生。童兒得道。乃栽松道者也。初在蘄州西山栽松、遇四祖出遊。告道者、吾欲傳法與汝、汝已年邁。若待汝再來、吾尚遲汝。師諾。遂往周氏家女托生。因抛濁港中。神物護持、七日不損。因收養矣。至七歲爲童子。於黃梅路上逢四祖大醫禪師。祖見師、雖是小兒、骨相奇秀、異乎常童。祖見問曰、汝何姓。師答曰、姓即有、不是常姓。祖曰、是何姓。師答曰、是佛性。祖曰、汝無佛性。師答曰、佛性空故、所以言無。祖識其法器、俾侍者至其家、於父母所乞令出家。父母以宿緣故、殊無難色捨爲弟子。 後付正法眼藏。居黃梅東山、大振玄風。

The Fifth Ancestor, Chan Master Daman, was from Huangmei in Qizhou.[70] *He was born without a father and gained the way as a child; he was actually the Pine-Planting Practitioner.*[71] *First, when he was re-*

---

investigate as" (*to sankyū suru koto nakare* と參究することなかれ) is perhaps best taken here to mean "there is no need to investigate as" — i.e., to add a "higher" interpretation to what is already "three three in front, three three in back."

69 **Although they may be constricted by the six spiritual powers, they are obstructions in the flow to the source in the ocean of buddha nature** (*roku jinzū ni tairui seshimu to iedomo, busshō kai no chōsō ni keige suru mono nari* 六神通に滯累せしむといへども、佛性海の朝宗に罣礙するものなり): A tentative translation of an odd sentence, taken to mean that, even though defined as the six spiritual powers, the powers belong to the ocean of buddha nature. The expression *keige suru mono* 罣礙するもの, translated here as "obstructions," should probably be taken as something like "that which identifies with," in keeping with Dōgen's recurrent use of the passive form *keige seraru* in the sense "to be identified with" (given the active mood of the predicate, the particle *ni* に is taken here as a locative, rather than an instrumental). The expression *chōsō* 朝宗, translated loosely here as "flow to the source," has the primary sense "to attend court" but is regularly used for rivers flowing into the ocean.

70 **The Fifth Ancestor, Chan Master Daman** (*goso Daiman zenji* 五祖大滿禪師): I.e., the fifth ancestor of Chan in China, Daman Hongren 大滿弘忍 (602-675). Huangmei 黃梅 was located in Qizhou 蘄州, modern Hubei. Dōgen's source for this story is unknown. Elements of his account (without mention of Hongren's rebirth) can be found in several texts — e.g., at *Jianzhong Jingguo xudeng lu* 建中靖國續燈錄 (ZZ.136:46b3-11); *Jingde chuandeng lu* 景德傳燈錄 (T.2076.51:222b10-14). A version including the rebirth story does appear in *Chanzong songgu lianzhu tongji* 禪宗頌古聯珠通集 (ZZ.115:74a2-9).

71 **He was born without a father** (*mu fu ni shō* 無父而生): As is explained below, he simply used the womb of the Zhou woman to take rebirth.

gained the way as a child (*dōji tokudō* 童兒得道): The term "gained the way" (*tokudō* 得道) can refer either to the spiritual attainment of awakening or to the ritual admission into the Buddhist order.

the Pine-Planting Practitioner (*sai shō dōsha* 栽松道者): I.e., he was the reincarnation

3. Buddha Nature *Busshō* 佛性

49

siding on Mount Xi in Qizhou planting pines, he encountered the Fourth Ancestor on an outing there.[72]

[The Fourth Ancestor] addressed the Practitioner, "I want to transmit the dharma to you, but your years are already full. If you wait till you come again, I'll wait for you."[73]

The Master agreed. Thereafter, he went to a woman of the Zhou Clan for rebirth. Upon being thrown into a dirty waterway, he was protected by spiritual forces and was unharmed for seven days. And so, [his mother] took him up and raised him. As a boy of seven, he met the Fourth Ancestor, Chan Master Dayi, on the road in Huangmei. The Ancestor saw that, although he was a child, the Master's physiognomy was remarkably fine, different from that of an ordinary child.

Seeing this, the Ancestor asked, "What's your surname?"

The Master answered, "I have a surname, but it's not an ordinary surname."

The Ancestor said, "What is this surname?"

The Master answered, "It's Buddha Nature."[74]

The Ancestor said, "You have no buddha nature."[75]

The Master replied, "It's because buddha nature is empty that you say I have none."

The Ancestor, recognizing that he was a vessel of the dharma, had his acolyte go to his house and beg his parents to permit him to leave

---

of the practitioner who, as the story tells us, had planted pines in his previous life. The term *dōsha* 道者 ("person of the way") may refer to any Buddhist (or Daoist) practitioner or, in particular, to a Buddhist acolyte.

72 **Mount Xi in Qizhou** (*Kishū Seizan* 蘄州西山): I.e., Mount Shuangfeng 雙峰山, known as the West Mountain (Xishan 西山), in contrast to the Fifth Ancestor's East Mountain (Dongshan 東山).

Fourth Ancestor (*shiso* 四祖): I.e., Dayi Daoxin 大醫道信 (580-651), the fourth ancestor of Chan in China, who resided at Huangmei 黃梅.

73 **"If you wait till you come again"** (*nyaku tai nyo sai rai* 若待汝再來): I.e., when you return in your next life.

74 **"It's Buddha Nature"** (*ze busshō* 是佛性): The boy's answer plays on the close semantic relationship between the homophonous Chinese glyphs for "surname" (*xing* 姓) and "nature" (*xing* 性). The graph for "surname" is regularly used in Buddhist texts to translate the Sanskrit *gotra* ("clan") and, hence, appears in reference both to the "clan" of Buddha Śākyamuni and, metaphorically, to the "clan," or "lineage," of the bodhisattvas who seek to become buddhas.

75 **"You have no buddha nature"** (*nyo mu busshō* 汝無佛性): Or, more colloquially, "you don't have a buddha nature"; a fairly common retort in Chan texts. The translation seeks to facilitate Dōgen's play with "no buddha nature" (*mu busshō* 無佛性) below. In scholastic Buddhism, the lack of buddha nature makes one an *icchantika* (*issendai* 一闡提), someone without the potential to achieve the perfect awakening of a buddha.

50 DŌGEN'S *SHŌBŌGENZŌ* VOLUME I

home.[76] *Because of the karma of his previous life, his parents had no objection whatsoever and relinquished him to become a disciple. Later, he transmitted the treasury of the true dharma eye. [The Master] resided on Mount Dong in Huangmei, where he greatly wielded the dark style.*[77]

[03:14] {1:20}

しかあればすなはち、祖師の道取を參究するに、四祖いはく汝何姓は、その宗旨あり。むかしは何國人の人あり、何姓の姓あり。なんぢは何姓と爲說するなり。たとへば吾亦如是、汝亦如是と道取するがごとし。

Thus, in investigating the saying of the Ancestral Master, there is an essential point to the Fourth Ancestor's saying, "What's your surname?"[78] In ancient times, there was a person from the Land of What, who had the surname What.[79] He is saying to him, "You're of the What family." It is like saying, "*I'm also like this, you're also like this.*"[80]

[03:15]

五祖いはく、姓即有、不是常姓。いはゆるは、有即姓は常姓にあらず、常姓は即有に不是なり。

The Fifth Ancestor said, "*I have a surname, but it's not an ordinary surname.*" That is, the surname Being Itself is not "an ordinary surname"; "an ordinary surname" is "not right" for what is itself being.[81]

---

76 **his parents** (*bumo* 父母): At this point in the story, Hongren seems to have acquired a father.

77 **Dongshan at Huangmei** (Ōbai Tōzan 黄梅東山): I.e., the eastern peak at Mount Huangmei. The community of Daoxin 道信 and Hongren 弘忍 became known as the "East Mountain teachings" (*Dongshan famen* 東山法門).

78 **"What's your surname?"** (*nyo ka shō* 汝何姓): Dōgen begins here a play with the terms in the quotation. First up is a Chinese version of the old Abbott and Costello joke, "Who's on first?" The game puns on the Chinese interrogative *he* 何 ("what"), also used as a family name.

79 **Person from the Land of What** (*Gakokunin* 何國人): Or "a person of He." Reference to a dialogue found in the *Jingde chuandeng lu* 景德傳燈錄 (T.2076.51:433a9-10) and elsewhere; the version in the *Liandeng huiyao* 聯燈會要 (ZZ.136:927a13-14) reads:

泗州大聖或問、師何姓。師云、姓何。或云、何國人。師云、何國人。

Dasheng of Sizhou would be asked, "Master, what [*he*] is your surname?"
The Master would answer, "My surname is He ['What']."
Or he would be asked, "What land are you from?"
The Master answered, "I'm from the Land of He ['What']."

80 **"I'm also like this, you're also like this"** (*go yaku nyo ze, nyo yaku nyo ze* 吾亦如是、汝亦如是): From the words of the Sixth Ancestor, Huineng 慧能, in the dialogue with Nanyue Huairang 南嶽懷讓 alluded to above, section 3; see above, Note 5, and Supplementary Notes, s.v. "You're also like this, I'm also like this."

81 **the surname Being Itself is not "an ordinary surname"** (*u soku shō wa joshō ni arazu* 有即姓は常姓にあらず): The translation struggles in vain to capture a bit of this complicated word game. Dōgen has here reversed the order of the three glyphs *shō soku*

3. Buddha Nature *Busshō* 佛性   51

[03:16]

四祖いはく是何姓は、何は是なり、是を何しきたれり、これ姓なり。何
ならしむるは是のゆえなり、是ならしむるは何の能なり。姓は是也何也
なり。これを蒿湯にも點ず、茶湯にも點ず、家常の茶飯ともするなり。

The Fourth Ancestor's saying, "What is this surname?" means "what"
is "this"; he has "what-ed" "this" — this is his "surname."[82] For what
makes it "what" is "this"; making it "this" is the function of "what."[83] His
"surname" is both "this" and "what." We serve this also in an artemisia

---

u 姓即有 in the Fifth Ancestor's "I have a surname, but," in the process, opening up the
possibility of play with the meanings of *u* 有 as both "have" and "be" (see above, Note
7), and of redoing the function of *soku* 即 from the concessive ("I may have a surname,
but . . .") to an emphatic copula ("is precisely," "is itself"). The resulting phrase, *u soku
shō* 有即姓, can be read in several ways: e.g., as here, "the surname Being Itself"; or
"Being is itself my surname"; or "the surname I Have Itself"; or "I Have is itself my
surname."

an ordinary surname is "not right" for what is itself being (*jōshō wa sokuu ni fuze
nari* 常姓は即有に不是なり): Further play with the the Chinese terms in the Fifth Ancestor's answer. The translation assumes that here Dōgen has taken the glyphs *soku u* 即
有 ("I do have, but") as a compound term with a sense, presumably, of something like
"precisely being," "being itself," etc., and has treated the negative copula *fuze* 不是 ("it's
not") as the adjectival "not correct," "not appropriate," etc. To the extent that we take
"surname" (*shō* 姓) as a play on "nature" (*shō* 性) in this dialogue, we can read "ordinary
surname" (*jōshō* 常姓) as "constant nature" (*jōshō* 常性), and understand Dōgen's point
to be that being has no permanent nature

82   **"what" is "this"** (*ga wa ze nari* 何は是なり): Or "'what' is 'right.'" Continuing
his play with the interrogative "what," Dōgen here reads the question, "what is this
[surname]?" as a declarative sentence. The translation obscures the pun on the graph, *ze*
是, rendered here as "this" (from the Fourth Ancestor's question, "What is this name?")
and as "right" in the preceding remark by Dōgen, "An ordinary surname is 'not right' for
what is itself being."

he has "what-ed" "this" (*ze o ga shikitareri* 是を何しきたれり): Here, the interrogative "what" is treated as a transitive verb presumably the meaning is "to make 'what' of
'this,'" "to take 'this' as 'what.'" A common interpretation takes "what" here to represent
the ultimate mystery of things, and "this" to stand for the immediate presence of things;
hence, to "what" "this" is to see the mystery in the presence.

this is his "surname" (*kore shō nari* これ姓なり): The antecedent of "this" here is unclear; possibly the act of "what-ing" "this."

83   **For what makes it "what" is "this"; making it "this" is the function of "what"**
(*ga narashimuru wa ze no yue nari, ze narashimuru wa ga no nō nari* 何ならしむるは
是のゆえなり、是ならしむるは何の能なり): If we follow the common interpretation,
the causatives here would convey the reciprocal relationship between the "what" of the
ultimate mystery and the "this" of the immediate presence: it is the immediate realm of
things that reveals the ultimate; it is the ultimate realm that expresses itself as things.

DŌGEN'S *SHŌBŌGENZŌ* VOLUME I

brew; we serve it also as in a tea brew; we even make it our everyday tea and rice.[84]

[03:17] {1:21}

五祖いはく是佛性。いはくの宗旨は、是は佛性なりとなり。何のゆえに佛なるなり。是は何姓のみに究取しきたらんや、是すでに不是のとき佛性なり。しかあればすなはち、是は何なり、佛なりといへども、脱落しきたり、透脱しきたるに、かならず姓なり。その姓すなはち周なり。しかあれども、父にうけず、祖にうけず、母氏に相似ならず、傍觀に齊肩ならんや。

The Fifth Ancestor said, "It's buddha nature." The essential point of what he says is that "it's" is "buddha nature."[85] Because of "what," it is buddha.[86] Has "it's" been exhaustively investigated only in the surname "What"?[87] When "it's" was [said to be] "it's not," it was "buddha nature."[88] Therefore, while "it's" is "what" and is buddha, when they have been sloughed off and have been transcended, it is necessarily his "surname."[89] That surname is Zhou.[90] Nevertheless, he does not get it from

---

84 **We serve this in an artemisia brew** (*kore o kōtō ni mo tenzu* これを蒿湯にも點ず): Or, perhaps, "he [i.e., the Fourth Ancestor (?)] serves it"; here and in the following two clauses, the grammatical subject is unexpressed. The antecedent of "this" (*kore* これ) is unclear; presumably, his "name." "Artemisia tea" (*kōtō* 蒿湯) is likely a suffusion of mugwort (or wormwood) taken for medicinal purposes.

everyday tea and rice (*kajō no sahan* 家常の茶飯): Japanese version of a fairly common expression, in both Zen texts and Dōgen's writings, for the "daily fare" of the home, or "normal practice"; well known in a saying of Furong Daokai 芙蓉道楷 (1043-1118), found in the *shinji Shōbōgenzō* 眞字正法眼藏 (DZZ.5:202, case 143) and often cited by Dōgen; see Supplementary Notes.

85 **"it's" is "buddha nature"** (*ze wa busshō nari* 是は佛性なり): Or "'this' is buddha nature." Continuing the play with the graph *ze* 是, here translated as "it's" in Hongren's remark, "It's buddha nature."

86 **Because of "what," it is buddha** (*ga no yue ni butsu naru nari* 何のゆえに佛なるなり): Or "because of 'what' is it buddha?"

87 **Has "it's" been exhaustively investigated only in the surname "What?"** (*ze wa ga shō nomi ni kyūshu shikitaranya* 是は何姓のみに究取しきたらんや): I.e., is the term *ze* 是 ("it's") being treated in this conversation only as the name "What"?

88 **When "it's" was [said to be] "it's not," it was "buddha nature"** (*ze sude ni fuze no toki busshō nari* 是すでに不是のとき佛性なり): I.e., when Hongren said, "it's not [an ordinary surname]," the negation of "it's" (*ze* 是), "it's not" (*fu ze* 不是), also indicated buddha nature.

89 **When they have been sloughed off and have been transcended, it is necessarily his "surname"** (*datsuraku shikitari, tōdatsu shikitaru ni, kanarazu shō nari* 脱落しきたり、透脱しきたるに、かならず姓なり): Taken to mean that, although "it's" can be identified with "what" or "buddha," when it is freed from these higher abstractions, it is Hongren's actual name. See Supplementary Notes, s.v. "Slough off."

90 **That surname is Zhou** (*sono shō sunawachi Shū nari* その姓すなはち周なり): According to his biography (e.g., *Jingde chuandeng lu* 景德傳燈錄, T.2076.51:222c6),

3. Buddha Nature *Busshō* 佛性 53

his father; he does not get it from his ancestors; he does not resemble his mother's family; how could he be of equal stature to bystanders?[91]

[03:18]

四祖いはく汝無佛性。いはゆる道取は、汝はたれにあらず、汝に一任すれ
ども、無佛性なりと開演するなり。しるべし、學すべし、いまはいかなる
時節にして無佛性なるぞ。佛頭にして無佛性なるか、佛向上にして無佛性
なるか。七通を逼塞することなかれ、八達を摸索することなかれ。無佛性
は一時の三昧なりと修習することもあり。佛性成佛のとき、無佛性なる
か、佛性發心のとき、無佛性なるかと問取すべし、道取すべし。露柱を
しても問取せしむべし、露柱にも問取すべし、佛性をしても問取せしむべ
し。

The Fourth Ancestor said, "*You have no buddha nature.*" This saying proclaims, "Although I allow that 'you' are 'you' and not another, you are 'no buddha nature.'"[92] We should know, we should study, what time it is now such that he is "no buddha nature"[93] Is it at the head of buddha that he is "no buddha nature"? Is it beyond the buddha that he is "no buddha nature"?[94] Do not block up the seven penetrations; do not grope for the eight masteries.[95] There are instances when "no buddha nature"

Hongren's family name was Zhou 周 (a common surname, with the meaning "all-embracing"); and see above, section 13, for the identification of his mother's clan as Zhou.

91 **how could he be of equal stature to bystanders?** (*bōkan ni seiken naranya* 傍観に齊肩ならんや): I.e., how could the Fifth Ancestor be compared with others?

92 **"Although I allow that 'you' are 'you' and not another"** (*nyo wa tare ni arazu, nyo ni ichinin suredomo* 汝はたれにあらず、汝に一任すれども): A tentative translation of an odd locution, literally something like, "you are not someone; although entrusting [this] to you . . . "); taken here to mean, "acknowledging your identity as 'you.'" The verb *ichinin su* 一任 (translated here "allowing") occurs often in Dōgen's writings in the sense, common in Chan texts, "to leave entirely to . . . ."

you are "no buddha nature" (*mu busshō nari* 無佛性なり): Or, less awkwardly, "you are without buddha nature." Here and in the remainder of his discussion of this topic, Dōgen treats the phrase *mu busshō* 無佛性 ("having no buddha nature," "lacking buddha nature") as a single semantic unit.

93 **what time it is now** (*ima wa ikanaru jisetsu ni shite* いまはいかなる時節にして): Perhaps recalling the earlier discussion of the phrase "if the time arrives."

94 **the head of the buddha** (*buttō* 佛頭): An unusual expression, not occurring elsewhere in Dōgen's writings; possibly a variant of the more common *butchō* 佛頂 ("buddha's 'crown,' or 'topknot'"; S. *buddhōṣṇīṣa*), often used metaphorically as the very pinnacle of awakening; perhaps to be taken here to indicate the attainment of buddhahood.

beyond the buddha (*butsu kōjō* 佛向上): A common expression in Chan texts and Dōgen's writings; see Supplementary Notes, s.v. "Beyond the buddha."

95 **block up the seven penetrations** (*shittsū o hissaku su* 七通を逼塞す); **grope for the eight masteries** (*hattatsu o mosaku su* 八達を摸索す): The "seven penetrations and eight masteries" (*shittsū hattatsu* 七通八達), or "seven passes and eight arrivals," is a

54 DŌGEN'S *SHŌBŌGENZŌ* VOLUME I

is also studied as a momentary samādhi.[96] When buddha nature attains buddhahood, is this "no buddha nature"? When buddha nature brings forth the mind [of bodhi], is this "no buddha nature"?[97] We should ask this; we should say it. We should make the pillars ask it; we should ask it to the pillars.[98] We should make buddha nature ask it.

[03:19]
しかあればすなはち、無佛性の道、はるかに四祖の祖室よりきこゆるものなり。黄梅に見聞し、趙州に流通し、大潙に擧揚す。無佛性の道、かならず精進すべし、趑趄することなかれ。無佛性たどりぬべしといへども、何なる標準あり、汝なる時節あり、是なる投機あり、周なる同姓あり、直趣なり。

Thus, the words "no buddha nature" are something heard far beyond the ancestral room of the Fourth Ancestor.[99] They are seen and heard in Huangmei; they circulate to Zhaozhou; they are raised by Dawei.[100] The words "no buddha nature," we should pursue with vigor; do not falter or

---

common expression in Dōgen's writings and earlier Chan texts for "thorough understanding," or "complete mastery."

96 **studied as a momentary samādhi** (*ichiji no zanmai nari to shujū su* 一時の三昧なりと修習す): The term "samādhi" here should probably be understood in its common usage in reference to any spiritual practice or experience, rather than to a psychological state of extreme concentration. Some interpreters take *ichiji no zanmai* 一時の三昧 as indicating "samādhi in each moment"; the translation takes it simply as a temporary state, or experience (in contrast to a general condition), of which the following two questions here would be examples.

97 **buddha nature attains buddhahood** (*busshō jōbutsu* 佛性成佛); **buddha nature brings forth the mind** (*busshō hosshin* 佛性發心): I.e. at the end and at the beginning of the bodhisattva path, respectively. The questions may presuppose the common notion that the "buddha nature" refers to the potential to undertake and complete the bodhisattva's quest for buddhahood.

98 **We should make the pillars ask it; we should ask it to the pillars** (*rochū o shitemo monshu seshimu beshi, rochū ni mo monshu su beshi* 露柱をしても問取せしむべし、露柱にも問取すべし): The term *rochū* 露柱 ("exposed column") refers to the free-standing pillars of monastic buildings, appearing often in Chan conversations as symbols of the objective world. Dōgen here reflects a saying attributed to the famous Tang-dynasty Chan master Shitou Xiqian 石頭希遷 (700-790) recorded in the *shinji Shōbōgenzō* 眞字正法眼藏 (DZZ.5:148, case 41); see Supplementary Notes, s.v. "Pillars and lanterns."

99 **ancestral room** (*soshitsu* 祖室): A common expression in Chan for the "inner recesses" of the tradition handed down from master to disciple.

100 **Huangmei** (Ōbai 黄梅); **Zhaozhou** (*Jōshū* 趙州); **Dawei** (*Daii* 大潙): Reference to famous Chan masters who use the expression "no buddha nature." "Huangmei" indicates the Fourth Ancestor, Daoxin, himself; "Zhaozhou" and "Dawei" refer to Zhaozhou Congshen 趙州從諗 (778-897) and Weishan Lingyou 潙山靈祐, respectively, both of whom will be quoted below.

3. Buddha Nature *Busshō* 佛性　　　　55

hesitate.[101] Though we may well have lost our bearings in "no buddha nature," we have "what" as the standard, "you" as the time, "this" as the accord, "Zhou" as the same name; and we advance directly.[102]

[03:20]

五祖いはく佛性空故、所以言無。あきらかに道取す、空は無にあらず。佛性空を道取するに、半斤といはず、八兩といはず、無と言取するなり。空なるゆえに空といはず、無なるゆえに無といはず、佛性空なるゆえに無といふ。しかあれば、無の片片は空を道取する標榜なり、空は無を道取する力量なり。いはゆるの空は、色即是空の空にあらず。色即是空といふは、色を強爲して空とするにあらず、空をわかちて色を作家せるにあらず、空是空の空なるべし。空是空の空といふは、空裏一片石なり。しかあればすなはち、佛性無と佛性空と佛性有と、四祖・五祖、問取道取。

The Fifth Ancestor said, "*It's because buddha nature is empty that you say I have none.*" He says it clearly: being "empty" is not "having none."[103] In saying "buddha nature is empty," without calling it "half

---

101　**pursue with vigor** (*shōjin su* 精進す): Presumably meaning "make effort to understand." The term *shōjin* 精進, commonly used for the virtue of "zeal," or "exertion," does not typically occur as a transitive verb.

102　**Though we may well have lost our bearings in "no buddha nature"** (*mu busshō tadorinu beshi to iedomo* 無佛性たどりぬべしといへども): Taking the verb *tadoru* here in the sense *tomadoi* 戸惑 ("lose one's way," "grope about," etc.).

we have "what" as the standard (*ga naru hyōjun ari* 何なる標準あり): The first in a list of four terms in Dōgen's preceding discussion of the dialogue. The term *hyōjun* 標準 occurs fairly often in Dōgen's writings in the sense of a "marker" or "norm"; akin to *hyōkaku* 標格.

"you" as the time (*nyo naru jisetsu* 汝なる時節): It is unclear what "time" is referred to here: the most likely candidate is the "time" in the question of the preceding section: "what time it is now that he is 'no buddha nature.'"

"this" as the accord (*ze naru tōki* 是なる投機): The term *ze* 是 ("this") has also appeared above as "it's" in Hongren's statement, "it's buddha nature." The word "accord" here translates *tōki* 投機, a term often indicating a perfect "fit," or "match," perhaps especially between master and disciple; here, perhaps the accord between "what" and "this."

"Zhou" as the same name (*Shū naru dōshō* 周なる同姓): Some MS witnesses give the more familiar expression *dōshō* 同生 ("the same birth," "born together"). "Zhou" 周 ("all-embracing") is Hongren's family name (see, above, Note 90), here apparently shared with "no buddha nature."

we advance directly (*jikishu* 直趣): The implication seems to be that, though "no buddha nature" may be confusing, given the guidance of the terms in the dialogue listed, we can immediately understand it. The expression, "advance directly" here may reflect the words, quoted elsewhere in Dōgen's writings, "advance directly to unsurpassed bodhi" (*jikishu mujō bodai* 直趣無上菩提).

103　**being "empty" is not "having none"** (*kū wa mu ni arazu* 空は無にあらず): Or, as more commonly read, "emptiness is not non-existence." Here and in the following discussion, the translation aims to retain something of the language of the Fifth Ancestor's

56 DŌGEN'S *SHŌBŌGENZŌ* VOLUME I

a catty," without calling it "eight tael," he says he "has none."[104] He does not say it is "empty" because it is emptiness; he does not say he "has none" because it is non-existence: he says he "has none" because it is the "emptiness of buddha nature."[105] Therefore, the pieces of his "having none" are the signposts of his saying it is "empty"; it's being "empty" is the power to say "I have none."[106] This "emptiness" is not the "emptiness" of *form is itself emptiness*."[107] "*Form is itself emptiness*" does not mean that "form" is forced into "emptiness"; it does not mean that "emptiness" has been divided up to author "form": it is the "emptiness" of "emptiness is emptiness."[108] The "emptiness" of "emptiness is

---

remark with which Dōgen is playing. Hence, the translation of the graph *mu* 無, (the "no" of Daoxin's "no buddha nature") which might well be taken here in the abstract sense of "nothingness" or "non-existence," keeps to the original sense "to have none." An alternative, more metaphysical translation of this passage might read as follows:

> The Fifth Ancestor said, "It's because buddha nature is empty that you say I have none." This says it clearly: "emptiness" is not "non-existence." In speaking of "the emptiness of buddha nature," he does not call it "a half catty"; he does not call it "eight tael": he calls it "non-existent." He does not call it "empty" because it is emptiness; he does not call it "non-existent" because it is non-existence: he calls it "non-existent" because it is the "emptiness of buddha nature." Therefore, the pieces of "non-existence" are the signposts of his saying it is "empty"; "emptiness" is the power to say it is "non-existent."

104 **"half a catty"** (*han kin* 半斤); **"eight tael"** (*hachi ryō* 八兩): A tael (C. *liang* 兩) is a unit of weight (varying throughout history) equal to 1/16 catty (C. *jin* 斤); hence, eight tael equal a half catty. Although Dōgen's use here could be taken to mean simply "without calling it this or that," the point may be "without saying that *kū* 空 ("emptiness") equals *mu* 無 ("non-existence").

105 **"emptiness of buddha nature"** (*busshō kū* 佛性空): Or "buddha nature is empty." The translation assumes that here and below Dōgen is treating the glyph *kū* 空 ("empty") in the Fifth Ancestor's remark, no longer as a predicate adjective, but as a noun modified by *busshō* 佛性 ("buddha nature"). The influential *Shōbōgenzō monge* 正法眼藏開解 (SCZ.3:125) interprets this sentence to mean that the use of *kū* 空 and *mu* 無 here are not the "emptiness" taught in the two [non-Mahāyāna] vehicles (*nijō no kū* 二乘の空) or the "non-existence" of annihilation in non-Buddhist thought (*gedō no mu* 外道の無) but "non-existence" as the ultimate meaning of buddha nature (*busshō no daiichi gi no mu* 佛性の第一義の無).

106 **the pieces of his "having none" are the signposts of his saying it is "empty"** (*mu no henpen wa kū o dōshū suru hyōbō nari* 無の片片は空を道取する標榜なり): An odd locution that might be taken to mean something like, "the individual instances of [the use of] *mu* are the markers of what he means by saying '[buddha nature is] empty.'" The following clause would then seem to say, "what he means by 'empty' is what enables him to say that [buddha nature] 'does not exist.'"

107 **"Form is itself emptiness"** (*shiki soku ze kū* 色即是空): The famous formula of the perfection of wisdom literature, known especially from the *Heart Sūtra*; see Supplementary Notes, s.v. "Form is itself emptiness; emptiness is itself form."

108 **divided up to author "form"** (*wakachite shiki o soka seru* わかちて色を作家せ

3. Buddha Nature *Busshō* 佛性   57

emptiness" is "a single stone in space."[109] Therefore, the "non-existence of buddha nature," the "emptiness of buddha nature," the "existence of buddha nature" — this is what the Fourth Ancestor and the Fifth Ancestor are asking about and talking about.

* * * * *

[03:21] {1:22}

震旦第六祖曹溪山大鑑禪師、そのかみ黄梅山に參ぜしはじめ、五祖とふ、なんぢいづれのところよりかきたれる。六祖いはく、嶺南人なり。五祖いはく、きたりてなにごとをかもとむる。六祖いはく、作佛をもとむ。五祖いはく、嶺南人無佛性、いかにしてか作佛せん。

When the Sixth Ancestor of Cīnasthāna, Chan Master Dajian of Mount Caoxi, first consulted at Mount Huangmei, the Fifth Ancestor asked, "Where have you come from?"[110]

The Sixth Ancestor said, "I'm a person of Lingnan."[111]

る): I.e., "form" has been constructed from parts [of "emptiness"]. The term *soka* 作家 (commonly read *sakke*) derives from the Chinese *zuojia* 作家, an author or poet and, in Chan usage, an accomplished master; here put in a verbal form seen elsewhere in the *Shōbōgenzō*.

109 **"a single stone in space"** (*kūri ippen seki* 空裏一片石): Usually understood to indicate the complete identity of "form" and "emptiness." The word "space" here translates the term *kū* 空, the same graph used for "emptiness." Likely a variant of a saying by Shishuang Qingzhu 石霜慶諸 (*Jingde chuandeng lu*, T.2076.51:320c26-28).

> 僧問、如何是西來意。師曰、空中一片石。僧禮拜。師曰、會麼。曰、不會。師曰、賴汝不會。若會即打破爾頭。
> A monk asked, "What is the intention of coming from the west?"
> The Master said, "A single stone in space."
> The monk bowed. The Master said, "Do you understand?"
> He said, "I don't understand."
> The Master said, "I trust you don't understand. If you understood, it [or, perhaps, I] would bust your head."

110 **the Sixth Ancestor of Cīnasthāna, Chan Master Dajian of Mount Caoxi** (*Shintan dairokuso Sōkeizan Daikan zenji* 震旦第六祖曹溪山大鑑禪師): I.e., Huineng 慧能, who would become the Sixth Ancestor; Chan Master Dajian 大鑑禪師 is a posthumous title. Mount Caoxi 曹溪山, in present-day Guangdong, is the site of his temple, the Baolinsi 寶林寺. The term *Shintan* 震旦 (C. *Zhendan*) represents the Chinese transliteration of a Sanskrit name for China, "Cīnasthāna" ("Land of the Qin"). Dōgen here begins retelling in Japanese the famous story of the first encounter between the Fifth and Sixth Ancestors, as found, for example, in the *Jingde chuandeng lu* 景德傳燈錄, T.2076.51:222c10-13. The conversation between the two masters is continued below, following Dōgen's comments on this section.

111 **"a person of Lingnan"** (*Reinan nin* 嶺南人): "Lingnan" is a term for the region "south of the peaks" — i.e., the area of present-day Guangdong and other Southeastern provinces. In Tang times, it was considered a semi-barbaric border region, beyond the pale of Han civilization.

DŌGEN'S *SHŌBŌGENZŌ* VOLUME I

The Fifth Ancestor said, "What did you come here for?"

The Sixth Ancestor said, "I want to become a buddha."

The Fifth Ancestor said, "*A person of Lingnan has no buddha nature. How can you become a buddha?*"

[03:22]

この嶺南人無佛性といふ、嶺南人は佛性なしといふにあらず、嶺南人は佛性ありといふにあらず、嶺南人無佛性となり。いかにしてか作佛せんといふは、いかなる作佛をか期するといふなり。

This "a person of Lingnan has no buddha nature" does not mean that a person of Lingnan does not have buddha nature; it does not mean that a person of Lingnan has buddha nature: it is the "*no buddha nature of the person of Lingnan.*"[112] "How can you become a buddha?" means "what kind of becoming a buddha are you expecting?"

[03:23]

おほよそ佛性の道理、あきらむる先達すくなし。諸阿笈摩教および經論師のしるべきにあらず。佛祖の兒孫のみ單傳するなり。佛性の道理は、佛性は成佛よりさきに具足せるにあらず、成佛よりのちに具足するなり。佛性かならず成佛と同參するなり。この道理、よくよく參究功夫すべし、三二十年も功夫參學すべし。十聖三賢のあきらむるところにあらず。衆生有佛性、衆生無佛性と道取する、この道理なり。成佛已來に具足する法なりと參學する、正的なり。かくのごとく學せざるは、佛法にあらざるべし。かくのごとく學せずば、佛法あへて今日にいたるべからず。もしこの道理あきらめざるには、成佛をあきらめず、見聞せざるなり。

Generally speaking, there are few predecessors who have clarified the principle of buddha nature. The masters of the teachings of the āgamas and the sūtras and treatises could not be expected to know it; only descendants of the buddhas and ancestors uniquely transmit it. The principle of buddha nature is that one is not endowed with buddha nature before attaining buddhahood: one is endowed with it after attaining buddhahood. It is buddha nature always studies together with attaining buddhahood.[113] This principle, we should fully investigate and make concentrated effort on; we should make concentrated effort on and investigate it for twenty or thirty years. It is not something clarified by the ten sages and three

---

112 **"no buddha nature of the person of Lingnan"** (*Reinan nin mu busshō* 嶺南人無佛性): Dōgen simply repeats here the Chinese of Hungren's remark; the translation assumes that he wants us to read the declarative sentence as a single nominal expression.

113 **It is buddha nature always studies together with attaining buddhahood** (*busshō kanarazu jōbutsu to dōsan suru nari* 佛性かならず成佛と同參するなり): The term *dōsan* 同參 ("to study, or practice, together"), occurring frequently in the *Shōbōgenzō*, is regularly used in reference to fellow students; here, it suggests that buddha nature and the attainment of buddhahood occur together within spiritual practice.

3. Buddha Nature *Busshō* 佛性   59

worthies.[114] To say, "*living beings have buddha nature,*" "*living beings have no buddha nature,*" is this principle. To study this as the dharma that one is endowed [with buddha nature] after attaining buddhahood is right on the mark. If it is not studied in this way, it would not be the buddha dharma; if it had not been studied in this way, the buddha dharma would not have reached us today. Those who have not clarified this principle have not clarified, have not seen or heard of, attaining buddhahood.

[03:24] {1:23}

このゆえに、五祖は向他道するに、嶺南人無佛性と爲道するなり。見佛聞法の最初に、難得難聞なるは衆生無佛性なり。或從知識、或從經卷するに、きくことのよろこぶべきは衆生無佛性なり。一切衆生無佛性を見聞・覺知に參飽せざるものは、佛性いまだ見聞・覺知せざるなり。六祖、もはら作佛をもとむるに、五祖、よく六祖を作佛せしむるに、他の道取なし、善巧なし。ただ嶺南人無佛性といふ。しるべし、無佛性の道取・聞取、これ作佛の直道なりといふことを。しかあれば、無佛性の正當恁麼時、すなはち作佛なり。無佛性いまだ見聞せず、道取せざるは、いまだ作佛せざるなり。

Therefore, the Fifth Ancestor said to him, "*A person of Lingnan has no buddha nature.*" When one first sees the buddha and hears the dharma, what is difficult to acquire, difficult to hear, is that "*living beings have no buddha nature*"; *whether from a wise friend, whether from a sūtra scroll,* what is a joy to hear is that "*living beings have no buddha nature.*"[115] Those who have not studied their fill of seeing, hearing, perceiving, and knowing that "*all living beings have no buddha nature*" have not yet seen, heard, perceived, or known buddha nature.[116] When the Sixth Ancestor sought solely to "become a buddha," the Fifth Ancestor, in order to make a buddha of the Sixth Ancestor, had no other words, no other ingenious device: he just said, "*A person of Lingnan has no*

---

114 **ten sages and three worthies** (*jisshō sanken* 十聖三賢): Also read *jisshō sangen*. A common Buddhist technical term in reference to the traditional path of the bodhisattva: the ten stages, or "grounds" (*chi* 地, S. *bhūmi*), of the sage, or "noble" (*shō* 聖; S. *ārya*) — i.e., those on the advanced levels of the path — and the three types of "worthy" (*ken* 賢; S. *bhadra*) — i.e., those on the level just preceding the ārya. Also written *sanken jisshō* 三賢十聖.

115 **whether from a wise friend, whether from a sūtra scroll** (*waku jū chishiki waku jū kyōkan* 或從知識或從經卷): A fixed phrase in Chinese syntax occurring often in Dōgen's writings; see Supplementary Notes.

116 **Those who have not studied their fill of seeing, hearing, perceiving, and knowing** (*ken mon kaku chi ni sanpō sezaru mono* 見聞覺知に參飽せざるもの): I.e., "those who have not fully understood the experience." The expression *ken mon kaku chi* 見聞覺知 ("seeing, hearing, perceiving, and knowing") is a common idiom for cognition; the term *sanpō* 參飽 ("studied their fill") is a somewhat unusual expression, occurring several times in the *Shōbōgenzō*, that suggests one who is "satiated" or "surfeited" with Buddhist study.

60   DŌGEN'S *SHŌBŌGENZŌ* VOLUME I

buddha nature." We should recognize the fact that speaking and hearing of "no buddha nature" — this is the direct path to "becoming a buddha." Therefore, the very time of "no buddha nature" is just then "becoming a buddha." Those who have not yet seen or heard, who have not yet spoken of, "no buddha nature" have not yet "become a buddha."

[03:25]

六祖いはく、人有南北なりとも、佛性無南北なり。この道取を擧して、句裏を功夫すべし。南北の言、まさに赤心に照顧すべし。六祖道得の句に宗旨あり。いはゆる、人は作佛すとも、佛性は作佛すべからずといふ一隅の搆得あり。六祖これをしるやいなや。

The Sixth Ancestor said, "People may have north and south, but *buddha nature has no north or south.*"[117]

We should take up this saying and make concentrated effort on what is within its lines. We should reflect with bare mind on the words "north and south."[118] There is an essential point in the line spoken by the Sixth Ancestor: it captures one corner of [the fact that], though "people" may "become a buddha," buddha nature ought not "become a buddha."[119] Did the Sixth Ancestor know this or not?[120]

[03:26]

四祖・五祖の道取する無佛性の道得、はるかに導礙の力量ある一隅をうけて、迦葉佛および釋迦牟尼佛等の諸佛は、作佛し轉法するに、悉有佛性と道取する力量あるなり。悉有の有、なんぞ無無の無に嗣法せざらん。しかあれば、無佛性の語、はるかに四祖五祖の室よりきこゆるなり。このとき、六祖その人ならば、この無佛性の語を功夫すべきなり。有無の無はしばらくおく、いかならんかこれ佛性と問取すべし、なにものかこれ佛性とたづぬべし。いまの人も、佛性とききぬれば、さらにいかなるかこれ佛性と問取せず、佛性の有無等の義をいふがごとし、これ倉卒なり。しかあれば、諸無の無は、無佛性の無に學すべし。六祖の道取する人有南北、佛性無南北の道、ひさしく再三撈摝すべし、まさに撈波子に力量あるべきな

---

117   **The Sixth Ancestor said** (*rokuso iwaku* 六祖いはく): The text here returns to the conversation between the two ancestors begun in section 21.

118   **reflect with bare mind** (*sekishin ni shōko* 赤心に照顧): See above, Note 40.

119   **it captures one corner** (*ichigū no kōtoku ari* 一隅の搆得あり): A tentative translation of a somewhat unusual expression. The term *kōtoku* 搆得 (rendered here "capture") has the basic meaning "being able to pull in" or "hold back" something; it occurs in Chan texts with a sense "to grasp" (i.e., "understand"), akin to *kōtoku* 覯得. The term will appear again below, in the sense, probably, "to catch." The expression *ichigū* 一隅 ("one corner") suggests something partial.

120   **Did the Sixth Ancestor know this or not?** (*rokuso kore o shiru ya ina ya* 六祖これをしるやいなや): The implication seems to be that the Sixth Ancestor may not have understood the significance of his own saying. Although he is often critical of Chan masters' words, it is hard to find doubts about the famous Sixth Ancestor, Huineng, in Dōgen's writings; such doubts seem to recur in the section following.

3. Buddha Nature *Bisshō* 佛性   61

り。六祖の道取する人有南北、佛性無南北の道、しづかに拈放すべし。おろかなるやからおもはくは、人間には質礙すれば南北あれども、佛性は虚融にして南北の論におよばずと六祖は道取せりけるか、と推度するは、無分の愚蒙なるべし。この邪解を拋却して、直須勤學すべし。

When they become buddhas and turn the dharma, Buddha Kāśyapa and Buddha Śākyamuni, and the rest of the buddhas have the power to say, "in their entirety have buddha nature," by receiving from afar one corner, with the power to delimit them, the words "no buddha nature" spoken by the Fourth Ancestor and Fifth Ancestor.[121] How could the "have" of "in their entirety have" not inherit the dharma of the "have no" of "no no"?[122] Therefore, the words "no buddha nature" are heard from the distant rooms of the Fourth Ancestor and Fifth Ancestor.

---

121 **When they become buddhas and turn the dharma** (*sabutsu shi tenbō suru ni* 作佛し轉法するに): The expression "turn the dharma" (*tenbō* 轉法) is a common expression for the buddhas' teaching, equivalent to "turn the wheel of dharma" (*tenbōrin* 轉法輪).

Buddha Kāśyapa and Buddha Śākyamuni, and the rest of the buddhas (*Kashō butsu oyobi Shakamuni butsu tō no shobutsu* 迦葉佛および釋迦牟尼佛等の諸佛): The Buddha Kāśyapa is the sixth of the seven buddhas of the past (*kako shichi butsu* 過去七佛), of which Śākyamuni is the last; see Supplementary Notes, s.v. "Seven buddhas."

"in their entirety have buddha nature" (*shitsu u busshō* 悉有佛性): Or, in Dōgen's reading, "the entirety of beings is buddha nature." From the quotation of the *Nirvāṇa Sūtra* in section 1, above.

receiving from afar one corner, with the power to delimit them (*haruka ni gaige no rikiryō aru ichigū o ukete* はるかに導礙の力量ある一隅をうけて): An awkward attempt to render an odd expression probably meaning something like "receiving from [an historical] distance one feature [of the two ancestors' words] that defines [those words]." The term *gaige* 導礙 ("obstruction," "impediment"), translated here "to delimit," is regularly used by Dōgen in the sense "to identify," "to define"; synonymous with *keige* 罣礙.

122 **How could the "have" of "in their entirety have" not inherit the dharma of the "have no" of "no no"?** (*shitsu u no u, nanzo mu mu no mu ni shihō sezaran* 悉有の有、なんぞ無無の無に嗣法せざらん): The translation takes the sentence to mean that the term "have" (*u* 有, or "being") in the *Nirvāṇa Sūtra*'s expression "in their entirety have" (*shitsu u* 悉有, or "entirety of being") is consonant with the term "have no" (*mu* 無, or "no") in the Fourth Ancestor's saying "you have no buddha nature" (*nyo mu busshō* 汝無佛性) and the Fifth Ancestor's saying "a person of Lingnan has no buddha nature" (*Reinan nin mu busshō* 嶺南人無佛性). Alternatively, the expression rendered clumsily here as "the 'no' of 'no no'" (*mu mu no mu* 無無の無) could be taken simply as a double negation ("the 'no' that negates 'no'") and, hence, the logical equivalent of the assertion in the *Nirvāṇa Sūtra* passage. Some readers take this "no no" to mean "total, or absolute, non-being." The wording may reflect an ambiguous phrase attributed to Huineng's disciple Bianyan Xiaoliao 區檐曉了 (dates unknown) (*Jingde chuandeng lu* 景德傳燈錄, T.2076.51:237c7): *mu mu shi mu* 無無之無, which might be rendered variously as "the negation that negates negation," "the non-being that is not non-being," "the nothing that lacks nothing," etc.

At this point, if the Sixth Ancestor is that person, he should make concentrated effort on the words "no buddha nature."[123] Leaving aside the "have no" of "having" or "having no," he should ask, "What is it that is buddha nature?"[124] He should inquire, "What thing is it that is buddha nature?" People today as well, once they have heard "buddha nature," without going on to ask what it is that is buddha nature, seem to talk about the meaning of having and not having of buddha nature. This is precipitate. Therefore, we should study the "no" of the various "nos" in the "no" of "no buddha nature."[125] The words spoken by the Sixth Ancestor, "*People have north and south; buddha nature has no north and south*," we should long "scoop up two or three times"; there should be power in the scoop.[126] We should quietly take up and let go of the words spoken by the Sixth Ancestor: "*People have north and south; buddha nature has no north and south*."[127] The foolish think that the Sixth Ancestor might have been saying that, since humans are obstructed by materiality, they have north and south, but buddha nature, being vacant and pervasive, is beyond discussion of north and south.[128] Those who speculate

---

The expression "inherit the dharma" (*shihō* 嗣法) is a standard term referring to the reception, or "inheritance," of the teaching of a master; here used metaphorically to suggest that the buddhas' teachings "inherit" the teachings of the two Chan ancestors — an historical reversal seen elsewhere in the *Shōbōgenzō* (e.g., at the opening of "Shōbōgenzō kobutsushin" 正法眼藏古佛心, DZZ.1:87).

123   **if the Sixth Ancestor is that person** (*rokuso sono hito naraba* 六祖その人ならば): The expression *sono hito* その人, translated here "that person," occurs several times in the *Shōbōgenzō* in the sense "a real person," "a person with real understanding"; here, perhaps "a person worthy to be called the Sixth Ancestor." The implication seems to be that the Sixth Ancestor's response here was inadequate; and, indeed, this phrase could be translated as a past subjunctive: "had the Sixth Ancestor been that person."

124   **the "have no" of "having" or "having no"** (*u mu no mu* 有無の無): Or "being" of "being" and "non-being." Here, again, the translation struggles with the several uses of the terms *u* 有 and *mu* 無.

125   **study the "no" of the various "nos" in the "no" of "no buddha nature"** (*shomu no mu wa, mu busshō no mu ni gaku su* 諸無の無は、無佛性の無に學す): Probably meaning something like "the use of the term 'no' (*mu* 無; or 'has no') in the phrase 'has no buddha nature' provides the key to the meaning of the term in other contexts."

126   **"scoop up two or three times"** (*saisan rōroku* 再三撈摝): Reflecting a verse found in the *Shi xuantan* 十玄談, by Tong'an Changcha 同安常察 (dates unknown); see Supplementary Notes.

127   **take up and let go of** (*nenpō su* 拈放す): Perhaps meaning something like "to examine [the words] without clinging to them"; presumably, continuing the imagery of the preceeding "scoop up" and expressing what we might call the practice of linguistic "catch and release."

128   **obstructed by materiality** (*zetsuge su* 質礙す): A Buddhist technical term for the inability of two physical objects to occupy the same space at the same time, here treated as a verbal form.

3. Buddha Nature *Busshō* 佛性

like this must be indiscriminate simpletons. They should discard this false understanding and study with diligence.

* * * * *

[03:27] {1:24}

六祖示門人行昌云、無常者即佛性也、有常者即善悪一切諸法分別心也。

The Sixth Ancestor addressed his follower Xing Chang, saying, "'Impermanence' is buddha nature. 'Permanence' is the mind that discriminates all dharmas, good and bad.'[129]

[03:28]

いはゆる六祖道の無常は、外道二乗等の測度にあらず。二乗外道の鼻祖鼻末、それ無常なりといふとも、かれら窮盡すべからざるなり。しかあれば、無常のみづから無常を説著・行著・證著せんは、みな無常なるべし。今以現自身得度者、即現自身而爲説法なり、これ佛性なり。さらに或現長法身、或現短法身なるべし。常聖これ無常なり、常凡これ無常なり。常凡聖ならんは、佛性なるべからず。小量の愚見なるべし、測度の管見なるべし。佛者小量身也、性者小量年也。このゆえに六祖道取す、無常者佛性也。

The "impermanence" spoken of by the Sixth Ancestor is not what is calculated by the likes of other paths and the two vehicles. The two vehicles and the other paths, from first founder to final follower, may say that

---

129 **The Sixth Ancestor addressed his follower Xing Chang** (*Rokuso shi monjin Gyōshō* 六祖示門人行昌): From the *Jingde chuandeng lu* 景德傳燈録, T.2076.51:239a2-3. Xing Chang 行昌 is the lay name of the monk Jiangxi Zhiche 江西志徹 (dates unknown). According to tradition, he was sent by followers of the Northern School master Shenxiu 神秀 (d. 706) to assassinate Huineng. When his blade failed three times to injure the ancestor, Xing Chang repented, took the precepts, and eventually became a disciple of the Sixth Ancestor. The saying quoted here comes from a conversation between the two about the doctrine of permanence in the *Nirvāṇa Sūtra* (at *Jingde chuandeng lu* 景德傳燈録, T.2076.51:239a1ff).

弟子嘗覽涅槃經。未曉常無常義。乞和尚慈悲略爲宣説。祖曰無常者即佛性也。有常者即善悪一切諸法分別心也。曰和尚所説大違經文也。祖曰吾傳佛心印。安敢違於佛經。

[Xing Chang said,] "Your disciple has read the *Nirvāṇa Sūtra*, but I still don't understand its doctrines of permanence and impermanence. I beg the Reverend in his compassion briefly to explain it for me."
The Ancestor said, "'Impermanence' means buddha nature. 'Permanence' means the mind that discriminates all the dharmas good and bad."
[Xing Chang] said, "The Reverend's explanation is very different from the text of the sūtra."
The Ancestor said, "I transmit the buddha mind seal. How could it differ from the sūtras of the buddhas?"

64 DŌGEN'S *SHŌBŌGENZŌ* VOLUME I

is impermanence, but they could not exhaust it.[130] Therefore, impermanence itself preaching, practicing, and verifying impermanence — they should all be impermanent. *Now, if there are those who attain deliverance by its manifesting its own body, then it manifests its own body and preaches the dharma to them* — this is buddha nature.[131] Going further, there should be, *it may manifest a long dharma body, it may manifest a short dharma body.*[132] The permanent sage is impermanent; the permanent common person is impermanent; were there to be permanent common people or sages, it would not be buddha nature. It would be a small, stupid view; it would be a calculating, narrow view, [such that] *the buddha is a small body; the nature is a small activity.*[133] Hence, the Sixth Ancestor said, *"'Impermanence' is buddha nature."*

---

130 **other paths and the two vehicles, from first founder to final follower** (*nijō gedō no biso bimatsu* 二乘外道の鼻祖鼻末): Or, perhaps, "other paths and the two vehicles [may say] from first to last." The odd expression *biso bimatsu* 鼻祖鼻末, loosely translated here as "first founder to final ancestor," plays on the word *biso*, "founding ancestor" (literally, "nose ancestor," from the notion that the foetus develops from the nose); some read the expression here to mean "the founder and the descendants"; others take it simply as "beginning and end." The term "two vehicles" (*nijō* 二乘) refers to the non-Mahāyāna Buddhists of the *śrāvaka-yāna* (*shōmon jō* 聲聞乘) and *pratyeka-buddha-yāna* (*engaku jō* 緣覺乘); a common term of dismissal in Dōgen's writings.

131 **Now, if there are those who attain deliverance by its manifesting its own body, then it manifests its own body and preaches the dharma to them** (*kon i gen jishin tokudo sha, soku gen jishin ni i seppō* 今以現自身得度者、即現自身而爲説法): A sentence in Chinese that plays on the famous passage in the *Lotus Sūtra* describing the thirty-three manifestations of Bodhisattva Avalokiteśvara (*Kannon* 觀音); see Supplementary Notes, s.v. "Manifesting a body to preach the dharma." The grammatical subject is unexpressed; in the sūtra, it is clearly the Bodhisattva; here, presumably, the "buddha nature." The implication of the introductory adverb "now" (*kon* 今) here is unclear.

132 **long dharma body** (*chō hosshin* 長法身); **short dharma body** (*tan hossin* 短法身): Again, a sentence in Chinese reflecting Zen usage seen in sayings such as "the long one is a long dharma body; the short one is a short dharma body" (*chōsha chō hosshin tansha tan hosshin* 長者長法身短者短法身); i.e., whether long or short, it is the dharma body of the buddha.

133 **permanent sage** (*jōshō* 常聖); **permanent common person** (*jōbon* 常凡): Unusual expressions, not appearing elsewhere in the *Shōbōgenzō*, likely introduced here in expansion of the thought of the previous sentence: the ostensibly permanent dharma body of the spiritually advanced "sage" is impermanent, appearing variously as "long" and "short"; similarly one's seemingly permanent status as spiritual "commoner" is impermanent.

the buddha is a small body; the nature is a small activity (*butsu sha shōryō shin ya, shō sha shōryō sa ya* 佛者小量身也、性者小量作也): Dōgen here switches to Chinese for a sentence undoubtedly intended to convey the consequences of the "small, stupid view" (*shōryō no guken* 小量の愚見) of permanence: that, under such a view, buddha nature would be reduced to something trivial in both substance and function.

3. Buddha Nature *Busshō* 佛性　65

[03:29] {1:25}

常者未轉なり。未轉といふは、たとひ能斷と變ずとも、たとひ所斷と化すれども、かならずしも去來の蹤跡にかかはれず。ゆえに常なり。

"Permanence" means it is unconverted.[134] "Unconverted" means that, even though it may change by eradicating, even though it may transform by being the eradicated, this does not necessarily have anything to do with the traces of coming and going.[135] Therefore, it is "permanent."

[03:30]

しかあれば、草木叢林の無常なる、すなはち佛性なり。人物身心の無常なる、これ佛性なり。國土山河の無常なる、これ佛性なるによりてなり。阿耨多羅三藐三菩提、これ佛性なるがゆえに無常なり。大般涅槃、これ無常なるがゆえに佛性なり。もろもろの二乘の小見および經論師の三藏等は、この六祖の道を驚疑怖畏すべし。もし驚疑せんことは、魔外の類なり。

Therefore, that the grasses, trees, thickets, and groves are impermanent is itself buddha nature; that the body and mind of human beings are impermanent — this is buddha nature. That the lands, mountains, and rivers are impermanent — this is because they are buddha nature.[136]

134　**"Permanence" means it is unconverted** (*jō sha miten nari* 常者未轉なり): A difficult section, variously interpreted. Dōgen is here presumably commenting on the Sixth Ancestor's definition of "permanence": "'permanence' is the mind that discriminates all the dharmas, good and bad." Some readers take the term *miten* 未轉 here to mean simply "unchanging"; the translation "unconverted" treats it as a reference to the mental state prior to the "conversion of the basis" *tenne* 轉依; S. *āśraya-parivṛtti*), a technical term for the transformation of consciousness from defiled ignorance to undefiled knowledge; i.e., the state of the spiritual commoner's "mind that discriminates."

135　**change by eradicating** (*nōdan to henzu* 能斷と變ず); **transform by being eradicated** (*shodan to kesu* 所斷と化す): Dōgen splits the common word for "change" (*henka* 變化) into two verbs, translated here as "change" and "transform." The translation takes the term "eradicating" (*nōdan* 能斷) as referring to the wisdom that removes the two obstacles to bodhi: the afflictive obstacles (*bonnō shō* 煩惱障; S. *kleśāvaraṇa*) and the cognitive obstacles (*shochi shō* 所知障; S. *jñeyāvaraṇa*); "eradicated" (*shodan* 所斷) refers to the obstacles to be removed. On this reading, the clause might be paraphrased, "even though it [i.e., the discriminating mind that is unconverted] might be converted and achieve wisdom . . . ."

the traces of coming and going (*korai no shōseki* 去來の蹤跡): Typically, used in reference to the ordinary ups and downs of rebirth in saṃsāra; here, perhaps especially life among "all dharmas, good and bad."

136　**lands, mountains, and rivers** (*kokudo senga* 國土山河): An unusual combination; Dōgen seems here to be combining two common expressions often occurring together: "lands in the ten directions" (*jippō kokudo* 十方國土) and "mountains, rivers, and the whole earth" (*senga daichi* 山河大地), as, e.g., in a passage in the *Zongjing lu* 宗鏡錄 (T.2016.48:946c15-16):

十方國土、山河大地、石壁瓦礫、虛空與非空、有情無情、草木叢林、通爲一身。

66 DŌGEN'S *SHŌBŌGENZŌ* VOLUME I

Anuttara-samyak-sambodhi, because it is buddha nature, is impermanent; great *parinirvāṇa*, because it is impermanent, is buddha nature. All those with the small views of the two vehicles and *trepiṭakas* who are sūtra and treatise masters should be "alarmed, dubious, and frightened" at these words of the Sixth Ancestor.[137] If they are alarmed and dubious, they are grouped with Māra and other paths.[138]

* * * * *

[03:31]

第十四祖龍樹尊者、梵云那伽閼剌樹那、唐云龍樹亦龍勝、亦云龍猛。西天竺國人也。至南天竺國。彼國之人、多信福業。尊者爲説妙法。聞者遞相謂曰、人有福業、世間第一。徒言佛性、誰能覩之。尊者曰、汝欲見佛性、先須除我慢。彼人曰、佛性大耶小耶。尊者曰、佛性非大非小、非廣非狭、無福無報、不死・不生。彼聞理勝、悉廻初心。尊者復於座上現自在身、如滿月輪。一切衆會、唯聞法音、不覩師相。

The Fourteenth Ancestor, Venerable Nāgārjuna, is called Nāgārjuna in the language of the brahmans; in the language of the Tang, he is called Longshu or Longsheng or, again, Longmeng.[139] *He was from*

The lands in the ten directions, the mountains, rivers, and the whole earth, stones, walls, tiles, and pebbles, empty space and what is not space, the sentient and the insentient, grass, trees, thickets, and groves — all together make one body.

137 *trepiṭakas* **who are sūtra and treatise masters** (*kyōronji no sanzō tō* 經論師の 三藏等): The term "*trepiṭaka*" (*sanzō* 三藏) is used as an honorific for scholars of the Buddhist canon.

"alarmed, dubious, and frightened" (*kyōgi fui* 驚疑怖畏): Borrowing an expression found in the *Lotus Sūtra* (*Miaofa lianhua jing* 妙法蓮華經, T.262.9:31c19-21):

藥王、若有菩薩聞是法華經驚疑怖畏、當知是為新發意菩薩。若聲聞人聞是經驚疑怖畏、當知是為增上慢者。

[Buddha Śākyamuni said,] "Medicine King, if there are bodhisattvas who, upon hearing this *Lotus Sūtra*, are alarmed, dubious, or frightened, you should know that they are bodhisattvas who have newly produced the aspiration [for bodhi]. If there are *śrāvakas* who, upon hearing this sūtra, are alarmed, dubious, or frightened, you should know that they are the arrogant ones.

138 **Māra and other paths** (*mage* 魔外): A contraction of *tenma gedō* 天魔外道 ("Deva Māra and the other paths"). Māra, lord of the sixth heaven (S. *deva-loka*) of the realm of desire (S. *kāma-loka*), is "the evil one" (S. *pāpīyān*) who seeks to obstruct Buddhist awakening.

139 **The Fourteenth Ancestor, Venerable Nāgārjuna** (*daijūshi so Ryūju sonja* 第十四祖龍樹尊者): The early Mahāyāna philosopher thought to have lived in the second to third centuries CE, famed as the founder of the Madhyamaka school of thought; traditionally considered the fourteenth ancestor in the Indian lineage of Zen. The exact source of this quotation is unclear; a somewhat similar passage appears in the *Jingde chuandeng lu* 景德傳燈錄 (T.2076.51:210a29-b15); a more distant version can be found in the *Zongjing lu* 宗鏡錄 (T.2016.48:938b13-27).

3. Buddha Nature *Busshō* 佛性   67

a land of West Sindhu.[140] *He went to a land of South Sindhu, where many of the people of the land believed in meritorious deeds.*

When the Venerable preached the wondrous dharma to them, the listeners said to each other, "For people to have meritorious deeds is the foremost thing in the world. He talks futilely of buddha nature, but who can see it?"

The Venerable said, "If you want to see buddha nature, first you must eliminate self-conceit."[141]

Those people said, "Is buddha nature large or small?"

The Venerable said, "Buddha nature is neither large nor small, neither broad nor narrow; it is without merit and without recompense; it does not die and is not born."

Hearing the excellence of this principle, they all converted to the beginner's mind.[142] *The Venerable, further, at his seat, manifested his body of freedom, like the disk of the full moon.*[143] *All the assembly merely heard the sound of the dharma but did not see the form of the Master.*[144]

Longshu (*Ryūju* 龍樹); **Longsheng** (*Ryūshō* 龍勝); **Longmeng** (*Ryūmyō* 龍猛): Representing variant intepretations by Chinese translators of the etymology of the Sanskrit *nāgārjuna* (meaning roughly "dragon tree," "dragon victory," and "dragon ferocity," respectively). The first form, favored by the early translator Kumārajīva, is the most popular in East Asia.

140   **a land of West Sindhu** (*Saitenjiku koku* 西天竺國): The toponym *Saitenjiku* 西天竺 is ambiguous: it typically refers to "India to the west [of China]," but in the context here seems to indicate "western India." Although there is little reliable information on Nāgārjuna's life, most legendary biographies identify him with south India.

141   **"self-conceit"** (*gaman* 我慢): Though regularly used simply to mean "pride," in technical terms, *gaman* represents one member of a standard list of seven conceits (*shichi man* 七慢), referring especially to the conceit that one has an enduring self (S. *asmimāna*).

142   **converted to the beginner's mind** (*e shoshin* 廻初心): Or "turned to the first thought [of bodhi]." See Supplementary Notes, s.v. "Beginner's mind."

143   **body of freedom** (*jizai shin* 自在身): Or "autonomous body"; the body of a spiritual adept with the paranormal powers of physical transformation.

144   **did not see the form of the Master** (*futo shi sō* 不覩師相): Or, more simply, "did not see the Master." The glyph *sō* 相 ("form"), referring here simply to Nāgārjuna's physical appearance, will figure prominently in the following discussion. The term is multivalent: in addition to its common meanings of "aspect," "shape," "appearance," etc., it is used in Buddhist discourse for the identifying feature, or "sign" (S. *nimitta*) by which an epistemological object is recognized, and for the thirty-two "marks" (S. *lakṣana*), or attributes, said to adorn the body of a buddha. In what follows here, the English "form" will be used for *sō* 相, while "shape" will render the closely related *gyō* 形.

68   DŌGEN'S *SHŌBŌGENZŌ* VOLUME I

[03:32] {1:26}

於彼衆中、有長者子迦那提婆、謂衆會曰、識此相否。衆會曰、而今我等
目所未見、耳所未聞、心無所識、身無所住。提婆曰、此是尊者現佛性相、
以示我等。何以知之。蓋以無相三昧、形如滿月。佛性之義、廓然虛明。
言訖輪相即隱。復居本座、而説偈言、身現圓月相、以表諸佛體、説法無其
形、用辯非聲色。

In that assembly was Kāṇadeva, the son of a rich man. He said to the
assembly, "Do you know this form or not?"[145]

The assembly said, "Now, our eyes haven't seen it, our ears haven't
heard it, our minds know nothing of it, our bodies have no abode for
it.[146]

Kāṇadeva said, "This is the Venerable's manifesting the form of bud-
dha nature to show it to us. How do we know it? Because the signless
samādhi has a shape like the full moon.[147] The meaning of buddha
nature is wide open, spacious and clear."[148]

As soon as he had finished speaking, the disk form then vanished,
and [Nārgārjuna] was once again at his seat. Then, he recited a gāthā,
which said,

---

145 **Kāṇadeva** (*Kanadaiba* 迦那提婆): I.e., the famous Madhyamaka author Āryadeva,
considered Nārgājuna's leading disciple and regarded in Zen tradition as the fifteenth ancestor. The sobriquet Kāṇadeva ("one-eyed deva") derives from the story that Āryadeva
offered one of his eyes to (in Chinese accounts) an image of Maheśvara.

146 **"our ears haven't heard it"** (*ni shomimon* 耳所未聞): More literally, "not something heard by the ear"; an odd claim, not found in other sources, that seems to contradict
the earlier report that the assembly did in fact hear the dharma.

"our bodies have no abode for it" (*shin mu shojū* 身無所住): Or, perhaps, "not something accommodated by our bodies." A tentative translation of another rather odd claim
not found in other sources. Perhaps meaning something like, "we can't feel it."

147 **"the signless samādhi"** (*musō zanmai* 無相三昧): The translation of *musō* 無相
as "signless" here loses the play on the glyph *sō* 相 (otherwise rendered here "form").
The *musō zanmai* 無相三昧 (S. *animitta-samādhi*) is a member of a standard Buddhist
list of concentrations known as "the three samādhis" (*san zanmai* 三三昧): sometimes
rendered "empty" (*kū* 空), "signless" (*musō* 無相), and "wishless" (*mugan* 無願); in this
list, *musō* refers to the absence of an identifying feature, or "sign" (S. *nimitta*) by which
the object of meditation is recognized. The term *musō* 無相 is also used to describe the
body of the buddha as "without marks" — in particular, to be "empty" of the thirty-two
"marks" (S. *lakṣana*), or attributes, said to adorn the body of a buddha; more generally,
to be beyond all attribution.

148 **"wide open, spacious and clear"** (*kakunen komei* 廓然虛明): A loose translation.
The term *kakunen* 廓然 has the sense of vast, open expanse; *komei* 虛明 suggests something as clear and bright as the empty sky.

3. Buddha Nature *Busshō* 佛性 69

My body manifests a round moon form,
Showing by which the body of the buddhas.[149]
My preaching of the dharma lacks any shape;
The explanations are not sound or form.[150]

[03:33] {1:27}
しるべし、眞箇の用辨は聲色の即現にあらず。眞箇の説法は無其形なり。
尊者かつてひろく佛性を爲説する、不可數量なり。いまはしばらく一隅を
略擧するなり。

We should realize that true "explanations" are not "then it manifests"
"sound and form."[151] True "preaching of the dharma" "lacks any shape."
The Venerable's teachings on buddha nature are innumerable; here, for a
time, we briefly take up one corner of them.[152]

---

149 **"Showing by which the body of the buddhas"** (*i hyō shobutsu tai* 以表諸佛體):
Here and below, the translation makes a "theological" choice to take the plural marker
sho 諸 here to govern only *butsu* 佛; the expression could also be translated "the buddha
bodies" (*sho buttai*). The awkward phrase "showing by which" (*i hyō* 以表; "use it to
show") here seeks to establish a form of English that can reflect Dōgen's play with these
words below.

150 **"The explanations are not sound or form"** (*yōben hi shōshiki* 用辨非聲色): I.e.,
"my teachings are not what is heard or seen." The term *yōben* 用辨 (also written 用
辨) suggests "verbal clarifications" — i.e., explanations of the dharma. The expression
shōshiki 聲色 ("sound and form") is regularly used as shorthand for what is experienced
through the physical senses, as in the Zen expression, "beyond sound and form" (*shōshiki gai* 聲色外); this sense of "form" as the object of sight should not be confused with
the "form" used to render the glyph *sō* 相 ("appearance") in the expression "round moon
form" (*engetsu sō* 圓月相).

The *Jingde chuandeng lu* 景德傳燈錄 version of this story concludes here (at
T.2076.51:210b15) with the report:

彼衆聞偈頓悟無生、咸願出家以求解脱。

Hearing this gāthā, the assembly suddenly understood the unborn; and together they
vowed to leave home in order to pursue liberation.

151 **true "explanations" are not "then it manifests" "sound and form"** (*shinko no
yōben wa shōshiki no sokugen ni arazu* 眞箇の用辨は聲色の即現にあらず): Or, more
simply, "true explanation is not the appearance of sound and form." The awkward translation tries to preserve something of Dōgen's play with the words *soku gen* 即現 ("then
it manifests"), from his earlier line, "Now, if there are those who attain deliverance by
its manifesting its own body, then it manifests its own body and preaches the dharma to
them."

152 **briefly take up one corner** (*ichigū o ryakuko suru* 一隅を略擧する): I.e., give
a partial, summary account. Possibly, reflecting the well-known saying of Confucius
(*Lunyu* 論語 7, KR.1h0005.004.2a-b):

舉一隅不以三隅反、則不復也。

If I take up one corner, and he cannot come back with the other three, I don't do it
again.

70　　DŌGEN'S *SHŌBŌGENZŌ* VOLUME I

[03:34]

汝欲見佛性、先須除我慢。この爲説の宗旨、すごさず辦肯すべし。見はなきにあらず、その見これ除我慢なり。我もひとつにあらず、慢も多般なり、除法また萬差なるべし。しかあれども、これらみな見佛性なり。眼見目観に習ふべし。

　"If you want to see buddha nature, first you must eliminate self-conceit." We should confirm the essential point of this teaching without overlooking it. It is not that there is no "seeing"; but that seeing is itself "eliminating self-conceit." The "self" is not one, "conceit" is of many types, and the method of "eliminating" it must also be of myriad variations. Nevertheless, they are all "seeing buddha nature." We should learn this in the eye's seeing what the eye sees.[153]

[03:35]

佛性非大非小等の道取、よのつねの凡夫・二乗に例諸することなかれ。偏枯に佛性は廣大ならんとのみおもへる、邪念をたくはへきたるなり。大にあらず小にあらざらん正當恁麼時の道取に罣礙せられん道理、いま聽取するがごとく思量すべきなり。思量なる聽取を使得するがゆえに。

　Do not exemplify the saying, *"buddha nature is neither large nor small,"* and so on, in [the understandings of] common people and the two vehicles.[154] Thinking lopsidedly only that it means buddha nature must be vast is harboring false thoughts.[155] The principle delimited by the saying at this very time that it is not large and it is not small, we should think of just as we hear it here; for we make use of hearing that is our thinking.[156]

153　**We should learn this in the eye's seeing what the eye sees** (*gen ken moku to ni narau beshi* 眼見目観に習うべし): A tentative translation of a rather obscure sentence, perhaps meaning something like, "we should take 'seeing buddha nature' as our ordinary seeing." The unusual phrase *gen ken moku to* 眼見目観, which could be rendered simply "the eye's seeing," recalls the assembly's statement that "our eyes haven't seen" (*moku shomiken* 目所未見) the full moon; it simply creates two ways of saying "the eye sees," by splitting the compound terms "eye" (*ganmoku* 眼目) and "see" (*kento* 見観).

154　**Do not exemplify** (*reisho suru koto nakare* 例諸することなかれ): A somewhat odd use of a Chinese idiom meaning "to take as example or instance" — as in the phrase, "to take one instance" (*ko ichi reisho* 舉一例諸).

155　**lopsidedly** (*henko ni* 偏枯に): Adverbial form of a term, literally "half crippled," regularly used for one-sided or partial understandings, as in the expression "a lopsided view" (*kenjo henko* 見處偏枯; or *kenge hinko* 見解偏枯).

156　**The principle delimited by the saying at this very time that it is not large and it is not small, we should think of just as we hear it here** (*dai ni arazu shō ni arazaran shōtō inmo ji no dōshu ni keige seraren dōri, ima chōshu suru ga gotoku shiryō su beki nari* 大にあらず小にあらざらん正當恁麼時の道取に罣礙せられん道理、いま聽取するがごとく思量すべきなり): A rather convoluted sentence that might be restated, "what is meant at this point in the story by [Nāgārjuna's] saying [that buddha nature is] not large or small should be understood simply by attending to what we hear it saying [i.e., what it

3. Buddha Nature *Busshō* 佛性　　71

[03:36]

しばらく尊者の道著する偈を聞取つべし。いはゆる身現圓月相、以表諸佛
體なり。すでに諸佛體を以表しきたれる身現なるがゆえに、圓月相なり。
しかあれば、一切の長短・方圓、この身現に學習すべし。身と現とに轉疏
なるは、圓月相にくらきのみにあらず、諸佛體にあらざるなり。愚者おも
はく、尊者かりに化身を現ぜるを圓月相といふとおもふは、佛道を相承せ
ざる黨類の邪念なり。いづれのところのいづれのときか、非身の他現なら
ん。まさにしるべし、このとき尊者は高座せるのみなり。身現の儀は、
いまのたれ人も坐せるがごとくありしなり。この身、これ圓月相現なり。
身現は方圓にあらず、有無にあらず、隠顯にあらず、八萬四千蘊にあら
ず、ただ身現なり。圓月相といふ、這裏是甚麼處在、説細説麤月なり。こ
の身現は先須除我慢なるがゆえに龍樹にあらず、諸佛體なり。以表するが
ゆえに諸佛體を透脱す。しかあるがゆえに佛邊にかかはれず。佛性の、滿
月を形如する虚明ありとも、圓月相を排列するにあらず。いはんや用辨も
聲色にあらず、身現も色心にあらず、蘊處界にあらず。蘊處界に一似なり
といへども、以表なり、諸佛體なり。これ説法蘊なり、それ無其形なり。
無其形さらに無相三昧なるとき、身現なり。一衆いま圓月相を望見すとい
へども、目所未見なるは、説法蘊の轉機なり、現自在身の非聲色なり。
即隠・即現は、輪相の進歩・退歩なり。復於座上、現自在身の正當恁麼時
は、一切衆會、唯聞法音するなり、不覩師相なるなり。

We should listen for a while to the gāthā spoken by the Venerable:

> *My body manifests a round moon form,*
> *Showing by which the body of the buddhas.*

It is "the round moon form" because it is the "body manifesting,"
"showing by which" "the body of the buddhas."[157] Therefore, we should
study all long and short, square and round, in this "body manifesting."
For the "body" and its "manifesting" to be alienated from each other is

---

actually says]" (that is, we should take the words literally as "not large and not small," rather
than imagining that they indicate an enormous expanse). On the idiosyncratic use of *keige* 罣
礙 ("to obstruct"), translated here by the passive "delimited," see above, Note 8.

for we make use of hearing that is thinking (*shiryō naru chōshu o shitoku suru ga yue
ni* 思量なる聽取を使得するがゆえに): An obscure remark that might be taken to mean
that hearing [the principle expressed here] is itself (or involves?) a kind of thinking.
Elsewhere, as well, Dōgen uses the colloquial *shitoku* 使得 (commonly, "to be O.K.," "to
work") as a transitive verb in the sense "to use" or "to be able to use."

157 **the "body manifesting," "showing by which" "the body of the buddhas."** (*sude
ni shobuttai o ihyō shikitareru shingen* すでに諸佛體を以表しきたれる身現): Here and
below, the translation seeks to preserve Dōgen's use as nominal compounds the neolo-
gisms, "body manifesting" (*shingen* 身現) and "showing by which" (*ihyō* 以表) from
Nāgārjuna's lines, "My body manifests a round moon form, showing by which the body
of the buddhas." Like the English "manifest," the verb *gen* 現 in the compound *shingen*
身現 ("body manifests") can be used both transitively and intransitively (i.e., "body appears"). The emphasis here, as suggested by the following sentence, should probably be
on the word *en* 圓 ("round"), which also has the senses "perfect," "complete": i.e., it is
"round" because it is the perfect embodiment of the ultimate body of the buddhas.

72 DŌGEN'S *SHŌBŌGENZŌ* VOLUME I

not only to be in the dark about "the round moon shape"; it is not "the body of the buddhas."[158] The thinking of fools who think that a transformation body temporarily manifested by the Venerable is what is meant by "a round moon form" is the false thought of a bunch that has not inherited the way of the buddhas.[159] Where and when would it be another manifestation that is not his body?[160]

We should realize that, at this time, it was just the Venerable assuming the high seat: the appearance that his body manifested was like anyone's sitting now.[161] This body — this is the manifestation of the "round moon form." The "body manifesting" is not square or round; it is not being or non-being; it is not hidden or apparent; it is not an aggregate of eighty-four thousand: it is just the "body manifesting."[162] The "round moon form" is the moon of "*where are we here that we're talking of*

---

158 **For the "body" and its "manifesting" to be alienated from each other** (*shin to gen to ni tenso naru wa* 身と現とに轉疏なるは): Dōgen here takes apart his new compound *shingen* 身現 ("body manifesting"). "Alienated" translates *tenso* 轉疏 ("to turn away from"), as in the expression *tenso ten'on* 轉疏轉遠 ("to grow estranged, to grow distant"). The phrase may be taken to mean, "to think that the body and the manifestation of the body are distinct."

be in the dark about "the round moon form" (*engetsu sō ni kuraki* 圓月相にくらき): The translation seeks to preserve what may be intended as a pun on the term *kuraki* くらき, commonly used in the sense "ignorant" or "oblivious" but bearing the primary sense "dark."

159 **transformation body** (*keshin* 化身): I.e., an apparitional body manifest by a buddha or bodhisattva; a term regularly used to translate the Sanskrit *nirmāṇa-kāya*.

a bunch that has not inherited the way of the buddhas (*butsudō o sōjō sezaru tōrui* 佛道を相承せざる黨類): I.e., those without authentic transmission of the dharma. Dōgen uses the term *tōrui* 黨類 ("confederates"; also written 儻類) elsewhere, as here, in a dismissive sense.

160 **Where and when would it be another manifestation that is not his body?** (*izure no tokoro no izure no toki ka hi shin no ta gen naran* いづれのところのいづれのときか非身の他現ならん): A peculiar phrase that might also be read, "where and when would what is not his body manifest another?" However it is to be read, the point, as suggested by the following sentence, is presumably that the "full moon form" *is* Nāgārjuna's body.

161 **assuming the high seat** (*kōza seru* 高座せる): "The high seat" is a standard term for the place or office of Buddhist preaching, here put in verbal form.

162 **not hidden or apparent** (*onken ni arazu* 隱顯にあらず): The word "hidden" translates *on* 隱, rendered as "vanished" in the line in the quotation, "As soon as he had finished speaking, the disk form vanished."

an aggregate of eighty-four thousand (*hachiman shisen un* 八萬四千蘊): The numeral 84,000 is a standard expression for an extremely large number; "aggregate" renders *un* 蘊, a standard translation of the Sanskrit *skandha*. Here, likely indicating the buddha's dharma body (*hosshin* 法身), comprised of the 84,000 teachings of the aggregate of dharmas (*hō'un* 法蘊; S. *dharma-skandha*).

3. Buddha Nature *Busshō* 佛性

73

fine and talking of rough?"[163] Since this "body manifesting" is "*first you must eliminate self-conceit*," it is not Nāgārjuna: it is the "body of the buddhas." Since it "shows by which," it transcends the "body of the buddhas."[164] Therefore, it has nothing to do with the confines of the buddha.[165]

Though buddha nature has a "spacious clarity" that takes a "shape like" "the full moon," it is not the case that it lines up with the "round moon form," let alone that its "explanations" are "sound or sight," or its "body manifesting" is form and mind, or the aggregates, spheres, and constituents.[166] Even if we say it completely resembles the aggregates,

---

163 "**where are we here that we're talking of fine and talking of rough?**" (*shari ze jinmo shozai setsu sai setsu so* 這裏是甚麼處在説細説麤): A fixed rhetorical question, variants of which occur several times in the *Shōbōgenzō*. The force of the question is usually something like, "Where do you think we are, that we're talking about such trivial dualities?" Perhaps best known from the retort of the monk Puhua 普化 (dates unknown), when charged with being rough by Linji Yixuan 臨濟義玄 (d. 866) (*Linji lu* 臨濟錄, T.1985.47:503b5-6; recorded also at *shinji Shōbōgenzō* 眞字正法眼藏, DZZ.5:174, case 96):

這裏是什麼所在、説麤説細。
Where are we here that we're talking of rough and talking of fine?

An identical remark is attributed to Huangbo Xiyun 黄檗希運 (dates unknown) in the *Biyan lu* 碧巖錄 (T.2003.48:152c9-10; quoted by Dōgen in the first chapter of his "Shōbōgenzo gyōji" 正法眼藏行持).

164 **Since it "shows by which," it transcends the "body of the buddhas"** (*ihyō suru ga yue ni shobutsu tai o tōdatsu su* 以表するがゆえに諸佛體を透脱す): Here again Dōgen plays with the expression "showing by which" (*ihyō* 以表) from Nāgārjuna's verse. Presumably, the argument is that, since the "body manifesting" is said to reveal the "body of the buddhas," it must transcend that body.

165 **confines of the buddha** (*buppen* 佛邊): A term that can imply either "the limits of" or "the vicinity of the buddha," it appears with some frequency in Zen texts, often in a dismissive sense, as in "to fall into the confines of the buddha" (*raku buppen* 落佛邊 — as opposed to the "unlimited" [*muhen* 無邊] buddha body) or "what is within the confines of the buddha" (*buppen ji* 佛邊事 — as opposed to "what lies beyond the buddha" [*butsu kōjō ji* 佛向上事]).

166 **has a "spacious clarity" that takes a "shape like" "the full moon"** (*mangetsu o gyōnyo suru komei ari* 滿月を形如する虚明あり): Dōgen is here again playing with the language of the quotation, in Kāṇadeva's statement, "because the signless samādhi has a shape like the full moon. The meaning of buddha nature is wide open, spacious and clear," treating "spacious and clear" (*komei* 虚明) as a noun modified by the novel verb "to shape like" (*gyōnyo su* 形如す).

it is not the case that it lines up with the "round moon form" (*engetsu sō o hairetsu suru ni arazu* 圓月相を排列するにあらず): I.e., it cannot be associated with the visible shape of the full moon.

form and mind (*shiki shin* 色心): I.e., the material and mental realms; "form" here renders *shiki* 色 (S. *rūpa*), standing for the objects of the eye or, more broadly, the physical senses.

74 DŌGEN'S *SHŌBŌGENZŌ* VOLUME I

bases, and constituents, it is "showing by which"; it is "the body of the buddhas." It is the preaching of the aggregate of dharmas; and that is "without any shape."[167] When "without any shape" is further the "signless samādhi," it is "the body manifesting." Even if we say the entire assembly was here gazing upon a "round moon form," it is something "our eyes haven't seen"; for it is the turning point of the preaching of the aggregate of dharmas; it is the "not sound or form" of "manifesting his body of freedom."[168] "Then vanished" and "then manifest" are the stepping forward and stepping back of the form of the disk.[169] The very moment when, *"at his seat, he manifested his body of freedom"* is *"all the assembly merely hearing the sound of the dharma,"* is "not seeing the Master's form."

[03:37] {1:28}

尊者の嫡嗣迦那提婆尊者、あきらかに満月相を識此し、圓月相を識此し、身現を識此し、諸佛性を識此し、諸佛體を識此せり。入室瀉瓶の衆たとひおほしといへども、提婆と齊肩ならざるべし。提婆は半座の尊なり、衆會の導師なり、全座の分座なり。正法眼藏無上大法を正傳せること、靈山に摩訶迦葉尊者の座元なりしがごとし。龍樹未廻心のさき、外道の法にありしときの弟子おほかりしかども、みな謝遣しきたれり。龍樹すでに佛祖となれりしときは、ひとり提婆を付法の正嫡として、大法眼藏を正傳す。こ

---

aggregates, spheres, and constituents (*un jo kai* 蘊處界): Three common terms used in Buddhist writing to account for the psychophysical organism and its world: (a) the five *skandhas* (*goun* 五蘊): form (*shiki* 色; S. *rūpa*), sensation (*ju* 受; S. *vedanā*), perception (*sō* 想; S. *samjñā*), formations (*gyō* 行; S. *samskāra*), and consciousness (*shiki* 識; S. *vijñāna*); (b) the twelve āyatanas (*jūni sho* 十二處): i.e., the six sense faculties (*kon* 根; S. *indriya*) and their objects (*kyō* 境; S. *viṣaya*); and (c) the eighteen *dhātus* (*jūhachi kai* 十八界): the six sense faculties, six sense objects, and six consciousnesses (*shiki* 識; S. *vijñāna*). See Supplementary Notes, s.v. "Four elements and five aggregates."

167 **preaching of the aggregate of dharmas** (*setsu hōun* 説法蘊): The "aggregate of dharmas" (S. *dharma-skandha*) is a standard reference to the collection of the Buddhist teachings; here, no doubt, playing on the term "aggregate" (*un* 蘊) and indicating the manifestation of the body as a teaching.

168 **the "not sound or form" of "manifesting his body of freedom"** (*gen jizai shin no hi shō shiki* 現自在身の非聲色): An awkward attempt to retain Dōgen's playful nominative use of *hishōshiki* 非聲色 ("not sound or form"), from the final line of Nāgārjuna's verse: "The explanations are not sound or form" (*yōben hi shōshiki* 用辯非聲色).

169 **"Then vanished" and "then manifest" are the stepping forward and stepping back of the form of the disk** (*soku on soku gen wa, rinsō no shinpo taiho nari* 即隱即現は、輪相の進步退步なり): "Then vanished and then manifest" (*soku on soku gen* 即隱即現) continues Dōgen's play with "then it manifests" (see above, Note 151), adding "then vanished" from the line in the quotation, "As soon as he had finished speaking, the disk form then vanished." "Stepping forward and stepping back" (*shinpo taiho* 進步退步) is an expression occurring regularly in Dōgen's writings; it can refer simply to all the ordinary movements of the agent, or more specifically, to motion forward and back. Here, perhaps, it represents the manifesting and vanishing of the disk form. See Supplementary Notes, s.v. "Stepping forward and stepping back."

3. Buddha Nature *Busshō* 佛性

れ無上佛道の單傳なり。しかあるに、僭偽の邪群、ままに自稱すらく、われらも龍樹大士の法嗣なり。論をつくり義をあつむる、おほく龍樹の手をかれり。龍樹の造にあらず。むかしすてられし群徒の、人天を惑亂するなり。佛弟子はひとすぢに、提婆の所傳にあらざらんは、龍樹の道にあらずとしるべきなり。これ正信得及なり。しかあるに、偽なりとしりながら稟受するものおほかり。謗大般若の衆生の愚蒙、あはれみかなしむべし。

The Venerable's legitimate heir. Venerable Kāṇadeva, clearly "knew this" full moon form, "knew this" round moon form, "knew this" body manifesting, "knew this" nature of the buddhas, "knew this" body of the buddhas.[170] Though there may have been many who entered the room and drained the jug, they could not have been of equal stature with Kāṇadeva.[171] Kāṇadeva was a venerable with a co-seat, a leader of the assembly, a shared seat with the whole seat.[172] His direct transmission of the treasury of the true dharma eye, the unsurpassed great dharma, was like Venerable Mahākāśyapa's being the prime seat on Vulture Peak.[173]

---

170 **"knew this"** (*shiki shi shi* 識此し): Dōgen has here created a new verb, "to know this," from Kāṇadeva's question to the assembly, "Do you know this form or not?" (*shiki shi sō hi* 識此相否).

nature of the buddhas (*shobutsu shō* 諸佛性): Like the parallel expression "body of the buddhas," this expression could also be read as a plural: "buddha natures" (*shobusshō*); see above, Note 149.

171 **entered the room and drained the jug** (*nisshitsu shabyō* 入室瀉瓶): To "enter the room" is a standard term for study with a Zen master; to "drain the jug" is to receive the teachings of the master, from the image of draining the contents of one jar into another.

172 **a venerable with a co-seat** (*hanza no son* 半座の尊): I.e., an elder honored by sharing the "seat" of the master. The rite of sharing the seat is best known from the story in the *Lotus Sūtra* (*Miaofa lianhua jing* 妙法蓮華經, T.262.9:33c5-8) of Buddha Prabhūtaratna's sharing the seat in his stūpa with Buddha Śākyamuni.

a shared seat with the whole seat (*zenza no bunza* 全座の分座): The "shared seat" here is probably synonymous with "co-seat"; in the Zen monastery, it represents one function of the head monk, or "head seat" (*shuso* 首座), standing in for the abbot. Dōgen's playful expression probably means something like, "a co-teacher who was a whole teacher."

173 **treasury of the true dharma eye, the unsurpassed great dharma** (*shōbōgenzō mujō daihō* 正法眼藏無上大法): An unusual description of the content of Zen transmission, appearing elsewhere in the *Shōbōgenzō*; the more common form is "treasury of the true dharma eye, the wondrous mind of nirvāṇa" (*shōbōgenzō nehan myōshin* 正法眼藏涅槃妙心); see Supplementary Notes, s.v "Treasury of the true dharma eye."

like Venerable Mahākāśyapa's being the prime seat on Vulture Peak (*Ryōzen ni Makakashō sonja no zagen narishi ga gotoshi* 靈山に摩訶迦葉尊者の座元なりしがごとし): Reference to Śākyamuni's disciple, considered the First Ancestor of the Zen lineage. Vulture Peak (*Ryōzen* 靈山; S. Gṛdhrakūṭa) is the site in Magadha of the legendary first transmission of Zen from Śākyamuni to Mahākāśyapa. "Prime seat" (*zagen* 座元; also read *zogen*) is ordinarily a term for someone who has served as head monk in a monastery; here perhaps merely a reference to Mahākāśyapa's position as the inheritor of Śākyamuni's dharma.

76 DŌGEN'S *SHŌBŌGENZŌ* VOLUME I

Prior to Nāgārjuna's conversion, he had many disciples from the time he followed the teachings of an other path; but he sent them all away.[174] Once Nāgārjuna became a buddha and ancestor, he directly transmitted the treasury of the great dharma eye solely to Kāṇadeva as the direct descendant of the bequest of the dharma. This was the unique transmission of the unsurpassed way of the buddhas.[175] Nevertheless, a false bunch of usurpers willfully claimed of themselves, "We are also the dharma heirs of Bodhisattva Nāgārjuna." They made treatises and put together doctrines, many of which they ascribed to Nāgārjuna's hand.[176] They are not Nāgārjuna's works; they are [works of] the previously abandoned bunch deluding and confusing humans and devas. Disciples of the Buddha should know without doubt that what was not transmitted to Kāṇadeva is not the word of Nāgārjuna; this is believing correctly.[177] Nevertheless, there are many who accept them knowing they are apocryphal. How pitiful, how sad, the simpletons among living beings who disparage the great prajñā.

[03:38] {1:29}

迦那提婆尊者、ちなみに龍樹尊者の身現をさして、衆會につげていはく、此是尊者現佛性相、以示我等、何以知之、蓋以無相三昧、形如滿月、佛性之義、廓然虛明なり。

174　**Prior to Nāgārjuna's conversion** (*Ryūju mi kaishin* 龍樹未廻心): According to his hagiographies, before he converted to Buddhism, Nāgārjuna was a student of Brahmanical texts, no doubt the "other path" (*gedō* 外道) mentioned here.

175　**unique transmission** (*tanden* 單傳): While this term need not imply an exclusive dharma transmission to a single disciple, given the context here, it seems clear that Dōgen takes Kāṇadeva as Nāgārjuna's sole legitimate heir.

176　**They made treatises and put together doctrines, many of which they ascribed to Nāgārjuna's hand** (*ron o tsukuri, gi o atsumuru, ooku Ryūju no te o kareri* 論をつくり、義をあつむる、おほく龍樹の手をかれり): Or, perhaps, "many of which are borrowed from Nāgārjuna"; the expression *te o karu* 手をかる ("borrow a hand"), while most commonly meaning simply "to get help," may here include the sense of the "hand" of an author. The term *gi* 義, translated here as "doctrines," might also mean "teachings" or "works of interpretation." It is not clear what works Dōgen may have had in mind here.

177　**should know without doubt** (*hitosuji ni . . . shiru beki nari* ひとすぢに . . . しるべきなり): Taking *hitosuji ni* in the sense "single-mindedly"; it might also mean here "as one" (i.e., "all [disciples of the buddha], as a single group").

this is believing correctly (*kore shō shin toku gyū nari* これ正信得及なり): The form *shin toku gyū* (literally, "faith can reach it") is a common Chinese idiom for "to believe," as in expressions like *xu shi xin de ji* 須是信得及 ("believe it") or *huan xin di ji* 還信得及麼 ("can you believe it?").

3. Buddha Nature *Busshō* 佛性

Venerable Kāṇadeva then pointed out Venerable Nāgārjuna's body manifesting and admonished the assembly, saying,[178]

> This Venerable's manifesting the form of buddha nature to show it to us. How do we know it? Because the signless samādhi has a shape like the full moon. The meaning of buddha nature is wide open, spacious and clear.

[03:39]

いま天上・人間、大千法界に流布せる佛法を見聞せる前後の皮袋、たれか道取せる、身現相は佛性なりと。三千界には、ただ提婆尊者のみ道取せるなり。餘者はただ、佛性は眼見・耳聞・心識等にあらず、とのみ道取するなり。身現は佛性なり、としらざるゆえに道取せざるなり。祖師のおしむにあらざれども、眼耳ふさがれて見聞することあたはざるなり。身識いまだおこらずして、了別することあたはざるなり。無相三昧の形如満月なるを望見し禮拝するに、目未所覩なり。佛性之義、廓然虚明なり。

Among the prior and later skin bags who have seen and heard the buddha dharma that has now spread among devas and humans and throughout the dharma realms of the great chiliocosm, who else has said that the form of the body manifesting is buddha nature?[179] In the great chiliocosm, only Venerable Kāṇadeva has said it. The others say only that buddha nature is not something the eye sees or the ear hears or the mind knows; they have not said it because they do not know that the body manifesting is buddha nature. It is not that the Ancestral Master begrudged [teaching them], but they close their eyes and ears and cannot see or hear him. Never having known it with their bodies, they cannot discern it.[180] While gazing upon and bowing to the fact that the signless samādhi has a "shape like the full moon," their eyes haven't seen it.[181] It is "*the meaning of buddha nature, wide open, spacious and clear.*"

---

178 **Venerable Kāṇadeva** (*Kanadaiba sonja* 迦那提婆尊者): This passage simply repeats the earlier quotation of Kāṇadeva, with an introduction in Japanese.

179 **prior and later skin bags** (*zengo no hitai* 前後の皮袋): I.e., "Buddhist teachers throughout history." For the meaning of the metaphor and other examples of its usage, see Supplementary Notes, s.v. "Bag of skin."

180 **Never having known it with their bodies, they cannot discern it** (*shinshiki imada okorazushite, ryōbetsu suru koto atawazaru nari* 身識いまだおこらずして、了別することあたはざるなり): In the expression translated "known with their bodies" (*shinshiki* 身識), Dōgen has created a new term by substituting "body" (*shin* 身) for "mind" (*shin* 心) in the preceding expression "the mind knows." The word *ryōbetsu* 了別 ("discern") is a standard Buddhist term used variously for "cognition," "perception," "comprehension," etc.

181 **their eyes haven't seen it** (*moku mishoto* 目未所覩): Variation on the assembly's description of buddha nature as "our eyes haven't seen it" (*moku shomiken* 目所未見).

[03:40] {1:30}

しかあれば、身現の説佛性なる、虚明なり、廓然なり。説佛性の身現な
る、以表諸佛體なり。いづれの一佛二佛か、この以表を佛體せざらん。
佛體は身現なり、身現なる佛性あり。四大五蘊と道取し會取する佛量祖量
も、かへりて身現の造次なり。すでに諸佛體といふ、蘊處界のかくのごと
くなるなり。一切の功德、この功德なり。佛功德は、この身現の窮盡し、
囊括するなり。一切無量無邊の功德の往來は、この身現の一造次なり。

Therefore, that the body manifesting is the preaching of buddha nature
is "a spacious clarity," is "a wide openness"; that the preaching of dharma nature is the body manifesting is "*showing by which the body of the
buddhas*." Which one buddha or two buddhas does not "buddha body"
this "showing by which"?[182] The buddha body is the body manifesting,
has a buddha nature that is the body manifesting. Even the measure of a
buddha or the measure of an ancestor that speaks of and understands it
as the four elements and five aggregates is, nevertheless, the hasty act of
the body manifesting.[183] Since they are called "the body of the buddhas,"

---

182 **does not "buddha body" this "showing by which"** (*kono ihyō o buttai sezaran*
この以表を佛體せざらん): An ugly attempt to capture an odd locution that continues
the earlier play on "showing by which" as a noun and treats the noun "buddha body"
(*buttai* 佛體) as a verb. The meaning is probably something like, "[is there any buddha
that] does not embody the act of showing the buddha body?" or, perhaps, "[is there any
buddha that] does not show himself as the buddha body?"

183 **the measure of a buddha or the measure of an ancestor** (*butsuryō soryō* 佛量
祖量): Though not particularly common in Zen texts, the term *butsuryō* 佛量 appears
several times in Dōgen writings, often in a sense traditionally interpreted as "the thinking of a buddha" (*hotoke no shiryō* 佛の思量) or "the power of a buddha" (*hotoke no
rikiryō* 佛の力量); see Supplementary Notes, s.v. "Measure of the buddha." The unusual
term *soryō* 祖量 is no doubt employed to reflect the common compound "buddhas and
ancestors" (*busso* 佛祖); see Supplementary Notes, s.v. "Buddhas and ancestors." The
specific reference here is likely to a saying on the four elements and five aggregates
by the famous Tang-dynasty Chan master Zhaozhou Congshen 趙州從諗, which Dōgen
quotes in his *shinji Shōbōgenzō* 眞字正法眼藏 (DZZ.5:270, case 88) and elsewhere. See
Supplementary Notes, s.v. "Four elements and five aggregates."

the hasty act of the body manifesting (*shingen no zōji* 身現の造次): Or, perhaps "a
fleeting occurrence of the body manifesting." Here and in the following "single hasty
act" (*ichi zōji* 一造次), the translation seeks to reflect the common use of the term *zōji* 造
次 in the sense of something done "in haste," "on the spot," something done "rashly" or
"haphazardly"; the term can also mean (and is more often interpreted here to mean) "a
short time," "a while," "momentary," "transitory," etc. Elsewhere Dōgen uses the term
in a pejorative sense when he accuses a monk of "wild, hasty acts" (*araarashiki zōji* あ
らあらしき造次) ("Shōbōgenzō shin fukatoku" 正法眼藏心不可得, DZZ.1:86) and in a
positive sense when he quotes the saying "the hasty [or transient] mind is the way" (*zōji
shin kore dō* 造次心これ道) (*Himitsu* MS of "Shōbōgenzō shin fukatoku" 正法眼藏心
不可得, DZZ.2:509).

3. Buddha Nature *Busshō* 佛性

the aggregates, bases, and constituents are like this.[184] All their virtues are this virtue.[185] The virtues of a buddha complete and envelop this body manifesting; the comings and goings of all his incalculable, limitless virtues are a single hasty act of this body manifesting.[186]

[03:41]

しかあるに龍樹・提婆師資よりのち、三國の諸方にある前代後代、ままに佛學する人物、いまだ龍樹・提婆のごとく道取せず。いくばくの經師・論師等か、佛祖の道を蹉過する。大宋國むかしよりこの因縁を畫せんとするに、身に畫し、心に畫し、空に畫し、壁に畫することあたはず、いたづらに筆頭に畫するに、法座上に如鏡なる一輪相を圖して、いま龍樹の身現圓月相とせり。すでに數百歳の霜華も開落して、人眼の金屑をなさんとすれども、あやまるといふ人なし。あはれむべし、萬事の蹉跎たることかくのごときなる。もし身現圓月相は一輪相なりと會取せば、眞箇の畫餅一枚なり。弄他せん、笑也笑殺人なるべし。かなしむべし、大宋一國の在家・出家、いづれの一箇も龍樹のことばをきかず、しらず、提婆の道を通ぜず、みざること。いはんや身現に親切ならんや。圓月にくらし、滿月を虧闕せり。これ稽古のおろそかなるなり、慕古いたらざるなり。古佛・新佛、さらに眞箇の身現にあふて、畫餅を賞翫することなかれ。

Neverthess, following the master and disciple Nāgārjuna and Kāṇadeva, in prior and later generations throughout all quarters in the three countries, people who have occasionally studied Buddhism, have never said anything like Nāgārjuna and Kāṇadeva.[187] How many sūtra masters and treatise masters have missed the words of the buddhas and

---

184 **Since they are called "the body of the buddhas," the aggregates, bases, and constituents are like this** (*sude ni shobutsu tai to iu, un sho kai no kaku no gotoku naru nari* すでに諸佛體といふ、蘊處界のかくのごとくなるなり): Recalling Dōgen's earlier remark, "even if we say [the body manifesting] completely resembles the aggregates, fields, and constituents, it is 'showing by which'; it is 'the body of the buddhas.'" Presumably the antecedent of "like this" is "the hasty act of the body manifesting."

185 **All their virtues are this virtue** (*issai no kudoku, kono kudoku nari* 一切の功德、この功德なり): Or, perhaps, "all virtues are this virtue"; the translation supplies the pronoun "their," taking as the antecedent "the aggregates, fields, and constituents." The antecedent of "this" is again presumably "the hasty act of the body manifesting." The term *kudoku* 功德, rather like the English "virtue," can carry a sense both of (a) a "quality," or "attribute" (especially a positive quality) (S. *guṇa*), and (b) a moral property, state, or action — in the Buddhist context, "good karma," or "merit" (S. *puṇya*); the former sense is the likelier one in this passage.

186 **are a single hasty act of this body manifesting** (*kono shingen no ichi zōji nari* この身現の一造次なり): Or, perhaps, "are each a single hasty act of this body manifesting."

187 **prior and later generations throughout all quarters in the three countries** (*sangoku no shohō ni aru zendai kōdai* 三國の諸方にある前代後代): I.e., heads of the monastic establishments of India, China, and Japan.

80 DŌGEN'S *SHŌBŌGENZŌ* VOLUME I

ancestors?[188] In the Land of the Great Song, from long ago, in trying to paint this episode, being unable to paint it on their bodies, paint it on their minds, paint it on the sky, paint it on a wall, they have pointlessly painted it with a brush, depicting on a dharma seat the form of a disk that is like a mirror and taking it as this [scene of] Nāgārjuna's body manifesting a round moon form.[189] Already for hundreds of years of frost and flowers blossoming and falling, although they would have formed gold dust in people's eyes, no one has said they are wrong.[190] What a pity that everything has gone amiss like this.[191]

If we understand the body manifesting a round moon form to be the form of a disk, it is a real painted cake.[192] To play around with that —

---

people who have occasionally studied Buddhism (*mama ni butsugaku suru ninmotsu* ままに佛學する人物): Taking *mama* as 間間 ("on occasion," "now and then"); likely a sarcastic reference to the insufficient study of the "prior and later generations."

188   **missed the words of the buddhas and ancestors** (*busso no dō o shaka suru* 佛祖の道を蹉過する): Or "missed the way of the buddhas and ancestors." The translation takes the term *dō* 道 here in the sense of "speech," referring specifically to the words of Nāgārjuna and Kāṇadeva; it could also be taken as "path." The term *shaka* 蹉過 (also read *saka*) occurs often in Dōgen's writing; it has the sense "to pass by," "to miss [an opportunity]," "to overlook [a passage in a text]."

189   **paint it on their bodies** (*shin ni ga shi* 身に畫し): Here, and in the following "paint it on their bodies, paint it on their minds, paint it on the sky, paint it on a wall," the translation treats the particle *ni* as a locative marker, whereas in the subsequent "painted it with a brush tip," it is taken as an instrumental. The more radically consistent version would read "paint it with their bodies," etc. The phrase "paint it on the sky" (*kū ni ga shi* 空に畫し) could also be taken as "paint it on space," or "paint it on emptiness."

on a dharma seat (*hōza jō* 法座上): The *hōza* 法座 is the seat of the teacher at an assembly.

190   **Already for hundreds of years of frost and flowers blossoming and falling** (*sude ni sūhyaku sai no sōke mo kairaku shite* すでに數百歳の霜華も開落して): The expression "frost and flowers" (*sōke* 霜華, more often read *sōka*) is a common literary expression for autumn and spring — hence, a year. Since Dōgen has here modified the expression with the term "years" (*sai* 歳), this use seems somewhat redundant; given the predicate "blossom and fall" (*kairaku* 開落), which would seem to apply only to flowers, it may be that he is playing on the other poetic meaning of *sōke*, "frost flowers."

although they would have formed gold dust in people's eyes (*ningen no kinsetsu o nasan to suredomo* 人眼の金屑をなさんとすれども): From the common proverb, found in Buddhist texts, "gold dust may be precious, but it blinds when it gets in the eyes" (*kinsetsu sui ki raku gen jō ei* 金屑雖貴落眼成翳).

191   **that everything has gone amiss like this** (*banji no sada taru koto kaku no gotoki naru* 萬事の蹉跎たることかくのごときなる): More literally, "that [people] have stumbled over the myriad things"; the predicate *sada* 蹉跎 means to "lose one's footing," "to be tripped up," etc.

192   **a real painted cake** (*shinko no gabyō ichimai* 眞箇の畫餅一枚): Dōgen is playing here on both the round shape of the image and, more profoundly, on the well-known

3. Buddha Nature *Busshō* 佛性　　　81

what a laugh![193] How sad that not a single one among the householders
and renunciants in the entire Land of the Great Song has heard or known
Nāgārjuna's words, has penetrated or seen Kāṇadeva's saying — much
less has been intimate with the body manifesting. They are in the dark
about the round moon; they have made the full moon wane.[194] This is
neglect of investigating the ancient; it is lack of admiration for the ancients.[195] Old buddhas and new buddhas, going on to meet the real body
manifesting, do not enjoy the painted cake![196]

[03:42] {1:31}

しるべし、身現圓月相の相を畫せんには、法座上に身現相あるべし。揚眉
瞬目、それ端直なるべし。皮肉骨髓正法眼藏、かならず兀坐すべきなり。
破顔微笑、つたはるべし、作佛作祖するがゆえに。この畫いまだ月相なら
ざるには、形如なし、説法せず、聲色なし、用辨なきなり。もし身現をも
とめば、圓月相を圖すべし。圓月相を圖せば、圓月相を圖すべし、身現圓
月相なるがゆえに。圓月相を畫せんとき、滿月相を圖すべし、滿月相を現
ずべし。しかあるを、身現を畫せず、圓月を畫せず、滿月相を畫せず、
諸佛體を圖せず、以表を體せず、説法を圖せず、いたづらに畫餅一枚を圖
す、用作什麼。これを急著眼看せん、たれか直至如今飽不飢ならん。月は
圓形なり、圓は身現なり。圓を學するに、一枚錢のごとく學することなか
れ、一枚餅に相似することなかれ。身相圓月身なり、形如滿月形なり。
一枚錢・一枚餅は、圓に學習すべし。

Chan proverb that "a painted cake can't satisfy hunger" (*gabyō fukajū ki* 畫餅不可充飢);
see Supplementary Notes, s.v. "A painted cake can't satisfy hunger," for the source of
that saying. The attributive modifier "real" (*shinko no* 眞箇の) here probably carries the
colloquial emphatic sense (as in, e.g., "a real fool"), a sense seen again below, section 44:
"The bunch like this are real beasts" (*kaku no gotoku no yakara wa shinko ze chikushō
nari* かくのごとくのやからは眞箇是畜生なり).

193　**To play around with that — what a laugh!** (*rō ta sen, shō ya shōsatsu nin naru
beshi* 弄他せん、笑也笑殺人なるべし): The antecedent of "that" is likely the "painted
cake" (or, perhaps, the painted disk). "What a laugh" is a loose translation of a Chinese
phrase meaning something like, "laugh, it's laughable." The idiom *shōsatsu nin* 笑殺人
should probably be understood as "make people laugh," with the verb *satsu* 殺 ("to kill")
taken with *shō* 笑 ("to laugh") as an intensive.

194　**made the full moon wane** (*mangetsu o kiketsu seri* 滿月を虧闕せり): Dōgen has
here artfully made a transitive verb of the "waning" of the moon.

195　**investigating the ancient** (*keiko* 稽古; **admiration for the ancients** (*boko* 慕古):
Two fixed expressions from Chinese literature for the knowledge and appreciation of classical tradition as guide; both occur with great frequency in Dōgen's writing — often, as
here, in laments over the decline of Buddhist tradition.

196　**Old buddhas and new buddhas** (*kobutsu shinbutsu* 古佛新佛): Terms of ambiguous reference. They may be taken simply to mean "Buddhists of past and present"
(some would take them in a more "theological" sense to indicate "Buddhists, who are
at once buddhas by nature and practicing buddhas"). Though the terms appear together
elsewhere in Dōgen's work, it is unusual to find them used, as here, in direct address;
it is unclear whether Dōgen is addressing his own audience or the "householders and
renunciants" of the Song. See Supplementary Notes, s.v. "Old buddha."

82   DŌGEN'S *SHŌBŌGENZŌ* VOLUME I

We should know that, in painting the "body manifesting a round moon form," it should have the form of the body manifesting on the dharma seat. *Raising the eyebrows and blinking the eyes* should be authentic.[197] The skin, flesh, bones, and marrow, the treasury of the true dharma eye, should always be sitting fixedly.[198] It should convey *breaking into a smile*; for it is making a buddha, making an ancestor.[199] Where this painting fails to achieve the moon form, it has no "shape like," is not "preaching the dharma," has no "sound or sight," has no "explanations."[200]

---

197 **Raising the eyebrows and blinking the eye should be authentic** (*yōbi shunmoku, sore tanjiki naru beshi* 揚眉瞬目、それ端直なるべし): The expression "raising the eyebrows and blinking the eyes" (*yōbi shunmoku* 揚眉瞬目), occurring several times in the *Shōbōgenzō*, is a set phrase used in Zen texts to represent the ordinary actions through which Buddhism is expressed; see Supplementary Notes, s.v. "Raise the eyebrows and blink the eyes." The English "authentic" is a loose translation of *tanjiki* 端直, a term usually meaning "upright and straightforward"; here, presumably, used less as an ethical than as an aesthetic quality: "true to life," "realistically portrayed."

198 **The skin, flesh, bones, and marrow, the treasury of the true dharma eye, should always be sitting fixedly** (*hi niku kotsu zui shōbōgenzō, kanarazu gotsuza su beki nari* 皮肉骨髓正法眼藏、かならず兀坐すべきなり): The grammatical relationship between "the skin, flesh, bones, and marrow" and "the treasury of the true dharma eye" is unclear; the translation treats them in apposition, as two ways of expressing the Zen tradition. See Supplementary Notes, s.v. "Skin, flesh, bones, and marrow," "Treasury of the true dharma eye." The term *gotsuza* 兀坐 (C. *wuzuo*), translated here as "sitting fixedly," is regularly used in reference to seated meditation, or zazen 坐禪, and occurs frequently in Dōgen's work; see Supplementary Notes, s.v. "Sit fixedly." The sense of this sentence seems to be that the Zen tradition should be depicted [as "the shape of the body manifested"] seated in meditation.

199 **It should convey breaking into a smile** (*hagan mishō tsutawaru beshi* 破顔微笑つたはるべし): A reference to the famous story of the first transmission of Zen from Śākyamuni to Mahākāśyapa, which Dōgen records in his *shinji Shōbōgenzō* 眞字正法眼藏 (DZZ.5:258, case 253); see Supplementary Notes, s.v. "Break into a smile."

making a buddha, making an ancestor (*sabutsu saso suru* 作佛作祖する): Or "becoming a buddha, becoming an ancestor." The translation assumes that the diction of this passage reflects the famous episode, much treasured by Dōgen, involving Mazu Daoyi 馬祖道一 and his teacher, Nanyue Huairang 南嶽懷讓 (*Jingde chuandeng lu*, T.2076.51:240c20):

大德坐禪圖什麼。一日、圖作佛。

[Nanyue asked,] "Most Virtuous One, what are you figuring to do, sitting there in meditation?"
Daoyi said, "I'm figuring to make a buddha."

See Supplementary Notes, s.v. "Nanyue polishes a tile."

200 **it has no "shape like"** (*gyōnyo nashi* 形如なし): Dōgen has here created a nominal compound from Kāṇadeva's statement, "because the signless samādhi has a shape like the full moon" (*gyō nyo mangetsu* 形如滿月). The three subsequent characteristics in this sentence ("preaching the dharma," "sound or sight," and "explanations") are taken from Nāgārjuna's verse.

3. Buddha Nature *Bosshō* 佛性

If we seek the body manifesting, we should depict the "round moon form."[201] If we are depicting the round moon form, we should depict the round moon form; for [it says,] "My body manifests the round moon form." When we would paint the round moon form, we should depict the form of the full moon, we should manifest the form of the full moon.[202] But without painting the body manifesting, without painting the round moon, without painting the form of the full moon, without depicting the body of the buddhas, without embodying the "showing by which," without depicting the preaching of the dharma, just pointlessly to depict a painted cake — what good is that?[203] To look at it, who would be satisfied as I am now and not hungry?[204] The moon is a round shape; "round" is the body manifesting: when you study "round," do not study it in something like a coin; do not liken it to a cake.[205] The form of the body

---

201 **If we seek the body manifesting, we should depict the "round moon form"** (*moshi shingen o motomeba, engetsu sō o zu su beshi* もし身現をもとめば、圓月相を圖すべし): The English "depict" for the verb *zu* 圖 masks what may be a significant ambiguity in Dōgen's use of the term here and throughout this passage: in addition to its sense "to draw," "to picture," etc., the term has the meaning "to plan for," "to anticipate," "to 'figure' on doing or getting," etc., as in the expression "figuring to make a buddha" (*zu sabutsu* 圖作佛). In this latter sense, then, the sentence could be rendered, "if we seek to get (or get at) the body manifesting, we should figure to make a round (or perfect) moon." This additional connotation of the verb *zu* as the intention to become awakened reminds us that the other key terms in our passage here can also be taken in "nonvisual" senses masked by the translation — *en* 圓 ("round," in "the round moon") as "perfect"; *man* 滿 ("full," in "the full moon") as "complete" — and encourages us to read the passage as something more than art criticism.

202 **we should manifest the form of the full moon** (*mangetsu sō o genzu beshi* 滿月相を現ずべし): Dōgen has here borrowed the verb "manifest" from "the body manifesting"; it is unclear whether the manifestation occurs in the painting or the artist (or both).

203 **without embodying the "showing by which"** (*ihyō o tai sezu* 以表を體せず): Another awkward attempt to render Dōgen's playful use of *ihyō* 以表 as a noun (see above, Note 157).

204 **who would be satisfied as I am now and not hungry?** (*tare ka jikishi nyokon hō fuki naran* たれか直至如今飽不飢ならん): Dōgen is here playing on the painted cake that "doesn't satisfy one's hunger," borrowing a common saying in Chan texts that suggests satiation with the dharma. The expression is also written 直至如今飽不饑; a frequent variant, also found in the *Shōbōgenzō*, is *jikishi nyokon hōshōshō* 直至如今飽餉餉 ("I've been completely full right up till now").

205 **The moon is a round shape; "round" is the body manifesting** (*tsuki wa engyō nari, en wa shingen nari* 月は圓形なり、圓は身現なり): If we read the glyph *en* 圓 here as "perfect" rather than "round," this passage might be paraphrased, "The round moon represents the shape of perfection; what Nāgārjuna manifests is this perfection. Do not think that the word 'round' here simply means something round, like a coin or a cake."

84 DŌGEN'S *SHŌBŌGENZŌ* VOLUME I

is the body of the round moon; its "shape like" is the shape of the full moon.[206] The coin and the cake, we should study in "round."[207]

[03:43]

予、雲遊のそのかみ、大宋國にいたる。嘉定十六年癸未秋のころ、はじめて阿育王山廣利禪寺にいたる。西廊の壁間に、西天東地三十三祖の變相を畫せるをみる。このとき領覽なし。のちに寶慶元年乙酉夏安居のなかにかさねていたるに、西蜀の成桂知客と廊下を行歩するついでに、予、知客にとふ、這箇是什麼變相。知客いはく、龍樹身現圓月相。かく道取する顔色に鼻孔なし、聲裏に語句なし。予いはく、眞箇是一枚畫餅相似。ときに知客大笑すといへども、笑裏無刀、破畫餅不得なり。すなはち知客と予と、舍利殿および六殊勝地等にいたるあひだ、數番擧揚すれども、疑著するにもおよばず。おのづから下語する僧侶も、おほく都不是なり。予いはく、堂頭にとふてみん。ときに堂頭は大光和尚なり。知客いはく、他無鼻孔對不得、如何得知。ゆえに光老にとはず。恁麼道取すれども、桂兄も會すべからず。聞説する皮袋も道取せるなし。前後の粥飯頭、みるにあやしまず、あらためなをさず。又、畫することうべからざらん法は、すべて畫せざるべし。畫すべくは端直に畫すべし。しかあるに身現の圓月相なる、かつて畫せるなきなり。

In the past, during my wanderings, I reached the Land of the Great Song. In the autumn of the junior water year of the sheep, the sixteenth year of Jiading, I went to the Guangli Chan Monastery on Mount Ayuwang.[208] On the wall of the west corridor, I saw painted illustrations of the thirty-three ancestors of Sindh in the West and the Land of the East.[209] At the time, I had no grasp of them.

---

206 **The form of the body is the body of the round moon; its "shape like" is the shape of the full moon** (*shinsō engetsu shin nari, gyō nyo mangetsu gyō nari* 身相圓月身なり、形如滿月形なり): This sentence might also be parsed, "The round moon of the form of the body is the body [manifested]; the 'shape like the full moon' is the shape [of that body]."

207 **The coin and the cake, we should study in "round"** (*ichimai sen ichimai byō wa, en ni gakushū su beshi* 一枚錢一枚餅は、圓に學習すべし) I.e., "we should understand the roundness of the coin and cake through the meaning of "round" in "the round moon."

208 **autumn of the junior water year of the sheep, the sixteenth year of Jiading** (*Katei jūroku nen kimi shū* 嘉定十六年癸未秋): I.e., 1223, the tenth stem, eighth branch of the sexagenary calendar; the Jiading era of the Song Emperor Ningzong 寧宗, lasting from 1208 to 1225. The autumn date would have been within just a few months of Dōgen's arrival at Mount Tiantong.

Guangli Chan Monastery on Mount Ayuwang (*Aikuōzan Kōri zenji* 阿育王山廣利禪寺): I.e., the monastery better known as Ayuwangsi 阿育王寺. Mount Ayuwang ("King Aśoka Mountain") is located in present-day Zhejiang, just west of Mount Tiantong. The monastery there is said to have been founded in the fifth century; in Dōgen's day, it was famous for its relic of the Buddha and was ranked among the "five mountains" (*gozan* 五山), the leading Chan institutions supposed to have been recognized by the Southern Song court.

209 **the thirty-three ancestors of Sindh in the West and the Land of the East** (*Saiten Tōchi sanjūsan so* 西天東地三十三祖): I.e., the Zen ancestral lineage of India and China through the Sixth Ancestor, Huineng 慧能.

3. Buddha Nature *Busshō* 佛性   85

Later, when I went again during the summer retreat of the junior wood year of the rooster, the first year of Baoqing, while walking in the corridor with Guest Prefect Cheng Gui of Western Shu, I asked the Guest Prefect, "*What is this portrait?*"[210]

The Guest Prefect said, "*Nāgārjuna's body manifesting the round moon form.*" He spoke like this with no nose on his face, no words in his voice.[211]

I said, "*This really looks like a painted cake.*" Whereupon, the guest prefect gave a great laugh, but *in the laugh there was no blade, and he could not break the painted cake.*[212]

While the guest prefect and I were going to the *śarīra* hall and the six outstanding sites, I raised this with him several times, but he never even had doubts about it.[213] Most of the monks who volunteered comments were also completely wrong.

I said, "Let's ask the Head of Hall." At the time, the head of hall was Reverend Daguang.[214]

---

210 **the summer retreat of the junior wood year of the rooster, the first year of Baoqing** (*Hōkyō gannen itsuyū ge ango* 寶慶元年乙酉夏安居): I.e., 1225, second stem, tenth branch of the sexagenary calendar; the Baoqing era of the Emperor Lizong 理宗, covering 1225-1228. Dates of the summer retreat vary; a common practice put it from the fifteenth of the fourth lunar month to the fifteenth of the seventh month. This event would have taken place just prior to the start of Dōgen's study with Tiantong Rujing 天童如淨.

Guest Prefect Cheng Gui of Western Shu (*Seishoku no Jōkei shika* 西蜀の成桂知客): A figure otherwise unknown. The "guest prefect" (*shika* 知客) is the monastic officer in charge of visitors. "Western Shu" is the name of an ancient kingdom in present-day Sichuan; probably used here simply to indicate the Sichuan region.

211 **no nose on his face, no words in his voice** (*ganshiki ni bikū nashi, shōri ni goku nashi* 顔色に鼻孔なし、聲裏に語句なし): Probably meaning something like, "his facial expression showed he had no substance and his tone of voice revealed he had nothing to say"; see Supplementary Notes, s.v. "Nose."

212 **in the laugh there was no blade, and he could not break the painted cake** (*shōri mu tō, ha gabyō futoku* 笑裏無刀、破畫餅不得): Or "in the laugh there was no blade that could cut the painted cake"; the translation of the verb *ha* 破 as "break" takes it in the sense, "to attack a problem" or "to solve a case." The "blade" (*tō* 刀) is a metaphor for the insight that informs a Zen master's laugh (or words) and is intended to cut off a disciple's deluded thinking. Dōgen will use the idiom again below. The kōan that is the *locus classicus* of this idiom is recorded in Dōgen's *shinji Shōbōgenzō* 眞字正法眼藏 (DZZ.5:258, case 253); see Supplementary Notes, s.v. "A blade within the laugh."

213 **the *śarīra* hall and the six outstanding sites** (*shari den oyobi roku shushō chi tō* 舍利殿および六殊勝地等): I.e., the hall at Ayuwang enshrining its famous relic of the Buddha and six famous sites (unidentified) at the monastery.

214 **head of hall** (*dōchō* 堂頭): I.e. the abbot.

Reverend Daguang (*Daikō oshō* 大光和尚): His biography is unknown.

86   DŌGEN'S *SHŌBŌGENZŌ* VOLUME I

The guest prefect said, "*He has no nose and couldn't answer. What could he know?*"

So, we did not ask Old Daguang. Though he talked like this, Elder Brother Cheng Gui also did not understand; and the skin bags who were listening also had nothing to say. Prior and later heads of meals had seen it without having doubts about it or correcting it.[215] Again, a dharma that cannot be painted should not be painted at all; what is to be painted, should be painted authentically.[216] Nevertheless, that the body manifesting is the round moon form has never been painted.

[03:44] {1:32}

おほよそ佛性は、いまの慮知念覺ならんと見解することさめざるによりて、有佛性の道にも、無佛性の道にも、通達の端を失せるがごとくなり、道取すべきと學習するもまれなり。しるべし、この疏忽は廢せるによりてなり。諸方の粥飯頭、すべて佛性といふ道得を、一生いはずしてやみぬるもあるなり。あるひはいふ、聽教のともがら佛性を談ず、參禪の雲衲はいふべからず。かくのごとくのやからは、眞箇是畜生なり。なにといふ魔黨の、わが佛如來の道にまじはりけがさんとするぞ。聽教といふことの佛道にあるか、參禪といふことの佛道にあるか。いまだ聽教・參禪といふこと、佛道にはなしとしるべし。

In sum, because they have not awakened from the view that buddha nature is our present thinking and perceiving, they seem to have lost the point from which to penetrate either the words "have buddha nature" or the words "have no buddha nature," and even those who study that we should speak of them are rare.[217] We should realize that this neglect is due to a decline. Among the heads of meals in all quarters, there are even

215   **Prior and later heads of meals** (*zengo no shukuhantō* 前後の粥飯頭): I.e., "abbots one after another." The use of the term "head of meals" in reference to the abbot is sometimes said to reflect his ranking in the order of the meal service. Among the previous abbots of Mount Ayuwang was Dahui Zonggao 大慧宗杲 (1089-1163), arguably the most famous Chan monk of the Southern Song and a figure that Dōgen would come to criticize in his later writings.

216   **a dharma that cannot be painted** (*ga suru koto u bekarazaran hō* 畫することうべからざらん法): The glyph *hō* 法 ("dharma") can be understood as "thing" or, perhaps more likely here, as "teaching."

what is be painted, should be painted authentically (*ga subeku wa tanjiki ni ga su beshi* 畫すべくは端直に畫すべし): For this sense of *tanjiki* 端直 ("authentic"), see above, Note 197.

217   **because they have not awakened** (*samezaru ni yorite* さめざるによりて): The subject is unexpressed; presumably, the "heads of meals" discussed in the preceding paragraph and below.

thinking and perceiving (*ryo chi nen kaku* 慮知念覺): A loose translation of terms for cognitive functions not commonly found as a set in Buddhist literature but appearing several times in the *Shōbōgenzō*, where they seem to stand collectively for the ordinary operations of consciousness. The translation takes them as two compound expressions (the first of which does occur elsewhere in the *Shōbōgenzō* in reference to the thinking

3. Buddha Nature *Busshō* 佛性　　　　87

those who have spent their entire lives without ever speaking of buddha nature.[218] Or they say, "those who listen to the teachings talk of buddha nature; those robed in clouds who study Zen shouldn't speak of it."[219] The lot like this are really beasts.[220] What minions of Māra are these that have infiltrated our way of the buddhas, the tathāgatas, and seek to defile it? Is there something called "listening to the teachings" in the way of the buddhas? Is there something called "studying Zen" in the way of the buddhas? We should realize that there has never been anything called "listening to the teachings" or "studying Zen" in the way of the buddhas.

* * * * *

[03:45] {1:33}
杭州鹽官縣斎安國師は、馬祖下の尊宿なり。ちなみに衆にしめしていはく、一切衆生有佛性。

　National Teacher Qian of Yanguang District in Hangzhou was a venerable under Mazu.[221] On one occasion, he addressed the assembly saying, *"All living beings have buddha nature."*

---

mind); as individual terms, they might be rendered "considering, knowing, thinking, and perceiving." See Supplementary Notes.

lost the point from which to penetrate (*tsūdatsu no tan o shisseru* 通達の端を失せる): Taking *tan* 端 in the sense "beginning" (or, perhaps, "first premise").

218　**there are even those who have spent their entire lives without ever speaking of buddha nature** (*subete busshō to iu dōtoku o, isshō iwazu shite yaminuru mo aru nari* すべて佛性といふ道得を、一生いはずしてやみぬるもあるなり): In his "Shōbōgenzō sesshin sesshō" 正法眼藏説心説性 (DZZ.1:450), Dōgen returns to this theme, in a criticism of the former abbot of Mount Ayuwang, Dahui Zonggao 大慧宗杲, for warning against talking about buddha nature.

219　**"those who listen to the teachings"** (*chōkyō no tomogara* 聴教のともがら); **"those robed in clouds who study Zen"** (*sanzen no unnō* 參禪の雲衲): I.e., those who know Buddhism only from books vs. monks who engage in the practice of Zen. "Robed in clouds" (*unnō* 雲衲) is a literary term for the itinerant monk; synonymous with *unsui* 雲水 ("clouds and water"). In his "Shōbōgenzō butsudō" 正法眼藏佛道 (DZZ.1:472ff), Dōgen engages in an extended critique of those who distinguish Zen from the "way of the buddhas" (*butsudō* 佛道).

220　**The lot like this are really beasts** (*kaku no gotoku no yakara wa shinko ze chikushō nari* かくのごとくのやからは眞箇是畜生なり): An expression attributed to Tiantong Rujing 天童如淨 in "Shōbōgenzō senjō" 正法眼藏洗淨, in criticism there of monastics who grow out their hair; see also Rujing's words in the *Hōkyō ki* 寶慶記, DZZ.7:14, number 9.

221　**National Teacher Qian of Yanguang District in Hangzhou** (*Kōshū Enkan ken Seian kokushi* 杭州鹽官縣斎安國師): I.e., Yanguang Qian 鹽官齋安 (d. 842), disciple of the famed master Mazu Daoyi 馬祖道一. His saying here and that of Dawei quoted below come from a story found in the *Liandeng huiyao* 聯燈會要 (ZZ.136:542a10-b1) and *Zongmen tongyao ji* 宗門統要集 (ZTS.1:88b2-c2), as well in Dōgen's own *shinji Shōbōgenzō* 眞字正法眼藏 (DZZ.5:188, case 115).

88　DŌGEN'S *SHŌBŌGENZŌ* VOLUME I

[03:46]

いはゆる一切衆生の言、すみやかに參究すべし。一切衆生、その業道依正
ひとつにあらず、その見まちまちなり。凡夫・外道・三乘・五乘等、おの
おのなるべし。いま佛道にいふ一切衆生は、有心者みな衆生なり、心是衆
生なるがゆえに。無心者おなじく衆生なるべし、衆生是心なるがゆえに。
しかあれば、心みなこれ衆生なり、衆生みなこれ有佛性なり。草木國土、
これ心なり、心なるがゆえに衆生なり、衆生なるがゆえに有佛性なり。
日月星辰これ心なり、心なるがゆえに衆生なり、衆生なるがゆえに有佛性
なり。國師の道取する有佛性、それかくのごとし。もしかくのごとくにあ
らずは、佛道に道取する有佛性にあらざるなり。いま國師の道取する宗旨
は、一切衆生有佛性のみなり。さらに衆生にあらざらんは、有佛性にあら
ざるべし。しばらく國師にとふべし、一切諸佛有佛性也無。かくのごとく
問取し試驗すべきなり。一切衆生即佛性といはず、一切衆生有佛性といふ
と參學すべし。有佛性の有、まさに脱落すべし。脱落は一條鐵なり、一條
鐵は鳥道なり。しかあれば、一切佛性有衆生なり。これその道理は、衆生
を説透するのみにあらず、佛性をも説透するなり。國師たとひ會得を道得
に承當せずとも、承當の期なきにあらず。今日の道得、いたづらに宗旨な
きにあらず。又、自己に具する道理、いまだかならずしもみづから會取せ
ざれども、四大五陰もあり、皮肉骨髓もあり。しかあるがごとく、道取も
一生に道取することもあり、道取にかかれる生生もあり。

We should quickly investigate the words "all living beings." The deeds
and paths, secondary and primary recompense, of "all living beings" are
not the same, and their views are various.[222] They will variously be a
common person, a follower of an other path, or on the three vehicles or
five vehicles, and so on.[223] In "all living beings" spoken of here on the
way of the buddhas, those with mind are all living beings; for mind is
living beings.[224] Those without mind are similarly living beings; for liv-

---

222　**deeds and paths, secondary and primary recompense** (*gō dō eshō* 業道依正): I.e.,
karma and its consequences. "Deeds" (*gō* 業) translates the standard Buddhist term for "karma"; "paths" (*dō* 道) here refers to the "destinies" (*shu* 趣), or "births" (S. *gati*), of saṃsāra:
deva, human, animal, ghost, and dweller in hell (to which is added in some lists titan). For the
expression "secondary and primary recompense" (*eshō* 依正), see above, Note 13.

223　**three vehicles or five vehicles** (*sanjō gojō* 三乘五乘): I.e., the vehicles of the *śrāvaka* (*shōmon* 聲聞), the *pratyeka-buddha* (*engaku* 緣覺), and bodhisattva (*bosatsu* 菩
薩). The "five vehicles" adds the vehicles of humans (*nin* 人) and devas (*ten* 天) to the
three vehicles. See Supplementary Notes, s.v. "Three vehicles."

224　**"all living beings" spoken of here on the way of the buddhas** (*ima butsudō ni
iu issai shujō* いま佛道にいふ一切衆生): Beginning with this phrase, Dōgen introduces
what seems to represent an exploration of the term "living beings" in the light of famous
lines, popularly (though wrongly) attributed to the *Huayan jing* 華嚴經, discussed in
"Shōbōgenzō sangai yui shin" 正法眼藏三界唯心 (DZZ.1:443ff):

三界唯一心、心外無別法。心佛及衆生、是三無差別。

The three realms are only one mind;
Outside the mind, there's no other dharma.
The mind, the buddha, and living beings —
These three are without distinction.

3. Buddha Nature *Busshō* 佛性   89

ing beings are mind.[225] Therefore, all minds are living beings, and living beings all "have buddha nature." The grasses, trees, and lands are mind; because they are mind, they are living beings; because they are living beings, they "have buddha nature." The sun, moon, and stars are mind; because they are mind, they are living beings; because they are living beings, they "have buddha nature."[226]

[The words] "have buddha nature" said by the National Teacher are like this. If they were not like this, they would not be the "having buddha nature" said on the way of the buddhas.[227] The essential point of what the National Teacher says here is only that "*all living beings have buddha nature*"; to take this further, those who are not living beings would not "have buddha nature."[228] Let us for the moment ask the National Teacher, "*Do all buddhas have buddha nature?*" We should ask him and test him like this. We should study [the fact] that he does not say, "*all living beings are buddha nature*"; he says, "*all living beings have buddha nature.*" The "have" of "have buddha nature," he should slough off.[229] Sloughing it off is one strip of iron; one strip of iron is the path of the

---

See Supplementary Notes, s.v. "The three realms are only mind."

225 **those with mind** (*u shin sha* 有心者); **Those without mind** (*mu shin sha* 無心者): The term *ushin* 有心 ("having mind" or "having thought") is a standard reference to "conscious" or "sentient" beings; the term *mushin* 無心 ("having no mind"), while famously used in Chan as description of a spontaneous state free from discrimination or intention, is probably used here simply to mean the "non-conscious," or "insentient," phenomena ("grass and trees," etc.) that Dōgen will go on to invoke.

226 **sun, moon, and stars** (*nichigetsu seishin* 日月星辰): A common generic expression in Buddhist texts for the "celestial bodies"; occurs often in Dōgen's writings, not infrequently together with the expression "the mountains, rivers, and the whole earth" — a combination likely reflecting an exchange recorded in the *shinji Shōbōgenzō* 眞字正法眼藏; see Supplementary Notes, s.v. "Sun, moon, and stars."

227 **"having buddha nature" said on the way of the buddhas** (*butsudō ni dōshu suru u busshō* 佛道に道取する有佛性): I.e., what is meant by "having buddha nature" in Buddhist discourse.

228 **those who are not living beings would not "have buddha nature"** (*shujō ni arazaran wa, u busshō ni arazaru beshi* 衆生にあらざらんは、有佛性にあらざるべし): I.e., if we interpret the National Teacher's remark to mean that only sentient beings have buddha nature, it would follow that other beings would not have it. The logic is obscured by the Japanese syntax of the preceding clause, in which "only" (*nomi*) governs the entire Chinese phrase "all living beings have buddha nature."

229 **The "have" of "have buddha nature," he should slough off** (*u busshō no u, masa ni datsuraku su beshi* 有佛性の有、まさに脱落すべし): I.e., he should get rid of the verb "to have" in this saying; the result would be a phrase, *issai shujō busshō* 一切衆生佛性, that could be read "all living beings are buddha nature." The subject here is unexpressed and could as well be taken as "we" (the readers) rather than "he" (the speaker); but Dōgen is clearly taking Qian to task in his comments here.

90   DŌGEN'S *SHŌBŌGENZŌ* VOLUME I

bird.[230] Therefore, *all buddha natures have living beings*. The principle of this not only explains thoroughly living beings but explains thoroughly buddha nature.[231] Although the National Teacher may not have acceded to a saying of this understanding, this is not to say that he will have no opportunity to accede to it.[232] Today's saying is not without an essential point. Again, though he himself may not necessarily yet understand the principle with which he is endowed, he has the four elements and five aggregates, he has the skin, flesh, bones, and marrow.[233] In this way, in saying something, there is saying something one's whole lifetime, there are lifetimes after lifetimes contingent on a saying.[234]

* * * * *

[03:47] {1:34}

大潙山大圓禪師、あるとき衆にしめしていはく、一切衆生無佛性。

Chan Master Dayuan of Mount Dawei once addressed the assembly, saying, "*All living beings have no buddha nature*."[235]

---

230   **Sloughing it off is one strip of iron; one strip of iron is the path of the bird** (*datsuraku wa ichijō tetsu nari, ichijō tetsu wa chōdō nari* 脱落は一條鐵なり、一條鐵 は鳥道なり): For the verb "slough off" (*datsuraku* 脱落), see above, Note 23. For "one strip of iron" (*ichijō tetsu* 一條鐵), see above, Note 35. "The path of the bird" (*chōdō* 鳥 道) is a favorite expression of Dongshan Liangjie 洞山良价 (807-869) that occurs several times in Dōgen's writings; generally taken to imply a way that follows no route and leaves no traces. See Supplementary Notes, s.v. "Dongshan's three roads."

231   **explains thoroughly** (*settō su* 説透す): An unusual term not found elsewhere in Dōgen's writings. The translation takes the element *tō* 透 in the sense "completely penetrate"; the combination is regularly interpreted to mean "explain and transcend."

232   **may not have acceded to a saying of this understanding** (*etoku o dōtoku ni jōtō sezu* 會得を道得に承當せず): An odd locution probably meaning "did not know how to express this understanding." The verb *jōtō* 承當, quite common in Dōgen's writing, seems typically to mean "to succeed (to an office)," "to accept" (or "to understand" a teaching).

233   **he has the four elements and five aggregates, he has the skin, flesh, bones, and marrow** (*shidai goon mo ari, hi niku kotsu zui mo ari* 四大五陰もあり、皮肉骨髓もあ り): I.e., (while he may not understand the meaning of his buddha nature,) he has it by reason of his having the elements and aggregates, the skin, flesh, bones, and marrow. The translation takes the subject here to be "the National Teacher," but the sentence could also be read with the pronoun "we" or "one." See Supplementary Notes, s.v. "Four elements and five aggregates," "Skin, flesh, bones, and marrow."

234   **there are lifetimes after lifetimes contingent on a saying** (*dōshu ni kakareru shōshō mo ari* 道取にかかれる生生もあり): Perhaps best interpreted to mean "some sayings may take lifetimes."

235   **Chan Master Dayuan of Mount Dawei** (*Daiisan Daien zenji* 大潙山大圓禪師): I.e., Weishan Lingyou 潙山靈祐, disciple of Baizhang Huihai 百丈懷海. Chan Master Dayuan is an honorific posthumous title. Mount Dawei (also known as Weishan 潙山) is

3. Buddha Nature *Busshō* 佛性　　91

[03:48]
これをきく人天のなかに、よろこぶ大機あり、驚疑のたぐひなきにあらず。釋尊説道は、一切衆生悉有佛性なり。大潙の説道は、一切衆生無佛性なり。有無の言理、はるかにことなるべし、道得の當不うたがひぬべし。しかあれども、一切衆生無佛性のみ佛道に長なり。鹽官有佛性の道、たとひ古佛とともに一隻の手をいだすににたりとも、なほこれ一條挂杖両人昇なるべし。

Among the humans and devas hearing this, there are those of great capacities who rejoice and no lack of those who are alarmed and dubious. What Śākya, the Honored One, says is "*all living beings in their entirety have buddha nature*"; what Dawei says is "*all livings beings have no buddha nature.*" There is a big difference between the meanings of "have" and "have no," and which saying is correct must have been doubted. Nevertheless, "*all living beings have no buddha nature*" is superior on the way of the buddhas.[236] Yanguan's saying, "have buddha nature," while it seems to extend a hand with the Old Buddha, is still *one staff borne by two people.*[237]

[03:49]
いま、大潙はしかあらず、一條挂杖呑両人なるべし。いはんや國師は馬祖の子なり、大潙は馬祖の孫なり。しかあれども、法孫は師翁の道に老大なり、法子は師父の道に年少なり。いま大潙道の理致は、一切衆生無佛性を理致とせり。いまだ曠然繩墨外といはず。自家屋裏の經典、かくのごとくの受持あり。さらに摸索すべし、一切衆生なにとしてか佛性ならん、佛性あらん。もし佛性あるは、これ魔黨なるべし。魔子一枚を將來して、一切衆生にかさねんとす。佛性これ佛性なれば、衆生これ衆生なり。衆生もとより佛性を具足せるにあらず。たとひ具せんともとむとも、佛性はじめてきたるべきにあらざる宗旨なり。張公喫酒李公醉といふことなかれ。もしおのづから佛性あらんは、さらに衆生にあらず。すでに衆生あらんは、つひに佛性にあらず。

---

in present-day Hunan province. Dōgen here returns to the story of the two monks who studied with Yanguan and Dawei; see above, Note 221.

236　**superior on the way of the buddhas** (*bussudō ni chō nari* 佛道に長なり): I.e., "is the superior expression of Buddhism"; the phrase could also be read "superior as a Buddhist saying."

237　**Yanguan's saying, "have buddha nature"** (*Enkan u busshō no dō* 鹽官有佛性の道): I.e., the saying of Yanguang Qian 鹽官齋安 quoted above, section 45.

extend a hand with the Old Buddha (*kobutsu to tomo ni isseki no te o idasu* 古佛とともに一隻の手をいだす): I.e., offer a teaching together with Buddha Śākyamuni. "To extend a hand" (*shutsu isseki shū* 出一隻手) is a common idiom for teaching.

one staff borne by two people (*ichijō shujō ryōnin yo* 一條挂杖両人昇): I.e., "they are simply saying the same thing." An idiomatic expression in Chinese syntax indicating "two statements with the same purport," or, as we might say, "a distinction without a difference"; seemingly synonymous with the variant "two people leaning on one staff" (*ichijō shujō ryōnin fu* 一條挂杖両人扶). See Supplementary Notes, s.v. "Staff."

92 DŌGEN'S *SHŌBŌGENZŌ* VOLUME I

But here, Dawei is not like that: he is *one staff swallowing up two people*.[238] Moreover, the National Teacher is the child of Mazu, while Dawei is the grandchild of Mazu.[239] Nevertheless, the dharma grandchild is an elder in the way of his master's father, while the dharma child is a youth in the way of his master father.[240] What Dawei says here by way of explication is "all living beings have no buddha nature."[241] He has not said that it is a vastness beyond the line of ink.[242] He has this way of receiving and keeping a scripture within his own house.[243] We should grope further: how could all living beings be buddha nature or have buddha nature?[244] Any that have buddha nature must be minions of Māra; they

---

238 **one staff swallowing up two people** (*ichi jō shujō don ryōnin* 一條拄杖吞兩人): Likely meaning that Dawei's saying outdoes both Śākyamuni and Yanguan.

239 **the National Teacher is the child of Mazu, while Dawei is the grandchild of Mazu** (*koku shi wa Baso no ko nari, Daii wa Baso no mago nari* 國師は馬祖の子なり、大潙は馬祖の孫なり): As Dōgen mentions above, Yuanguan was a direct student of Mazu Daoyi 馬祖道一 (see above, Note 221). Dawei's teacher, Baizhang Huihai 百丈懷海, was also a disciple of Mazu.

240 **the dharma grandchild is an elder in the way of his master's father, while the dharma child is a youth in the way of his master father** (*hasson* [more often read *hōson*] *wa shiō no dō ni rōdai nari, hossu wa shifu no dō ni nenshō nari* 法孫は師翁の道に老大なり、法子は師父の道に年少なり): I.e., the grandson, Dawei, is a veteran of Mazu's tradition, while the son, Yuanguan, is still a beginner. The term *shiō* 師翁 ("master's old man"; also read *suō*) is used in reference to the teacher of one's teacher; *shifu* 師父 ("master father") is a term for master, understood as "master and father" or "fatherly master."

241 **What Dawei says here by way of explication** (*ima Daii dō no richi* いま大潙道の理致): A loose translation of a sentence that seems to say, more literally, "In regard to Dawei's explication, he takes 'all living beings have no buddha nature' as his explication." The term *richi* 理致, translated here as "explication," has the sense "presentation of the theory"; it is often used in Chan to indicate the use of Buddhist texts and doctrines in teaching.

242 **vastness beyond the line of ink** (*kōzen jōboku gai* 曠然繩墨外): A line from a comment made by Yuanwu Keqin 圜悟克勤 (1063-1135) on a kōan involving Shitou Xiqian 石頭希遷 (710–790) and the latter's dharma heir Yaoshan Weiyan 藥山惟儼 (751-834); for the full context, see Supplementary Notes, s.v. "Vastness beyond the line of ink." An "ink line" (*jōboku* 繩墨) is a carpenter's guide, similar to a "chalk line." The expression "vastness beyond the line of ink" suggests a realm free from norms. It does not occur elsewhere in Dōgen's writing.

243 **scripture within his own house** (*jike okuri no kyōten* 自家屋裏の經典): This phrase could be taken to mean "a tradition within Dawei's school"; more often it is read in a metaphorical sense, as "the authority of his own experience."

244 **We should grope further** (*sara ni mosaku su beshi* さらに摸索すべし): I.e., "we should extend our exploration [of this saying]"; *mosaku* 摸索 is a common idiom meaning "to search for," as in the expression *mosaku fu jaku* 摸索不著, "to grope for it without touching it."

3. Buddha Nature *Busshō* 佛性   93

bring in a son of Māra and try to pile him on "all living beings."[245] As buddha nature is buddha nature, so living beings are living beings. The essential point is that living beings are not endowed from the start with buddha nature; and even though they seek to provide themselves with it, buddha nature will not newly arrive. Do not say that, when *Mr. Chang drinks wine, Mr. Li gets drunk.*[246] Where there is inherently buddha nature, that is not a living being; where there is already a living being, that will not eventually be buddha nature.

[03:50] {1:35}

このゆえに百丈いはく、説衆生有佛性. 亦謗佛法僧。説衆生無佛性、亦謗佛法僧。しかあればすなはち、有佛性といひ、無佛性といふ、ともに謗となる。謗となるといふとも、道取せざるべきにはあらず。且問儞大潙・百丈、しばらくきくべし、謗はすなはちなきにあらず、佛性は説得すやいまだしや。たとひ説得せば、説著を罣礙せん。説著あらば聞著と同參なるべし。また大潙にむかひていふべし、一切衆生無佛性は、たとひ道得すといふとも、一切佛性無衆生といはず、一切佛性無佛性といはず、いはんや一切諸佛無佛性は、夢也未見在なり。試擧看。

Hence, Baizhang said, "*To talk of living beings having buddha nature is to denigrate the buddha, dharma, and saṃgha; to talk of living beings having no buddha nature is to denigrate the buddha, dharma, and saṃgha.*"[247]

---

245 **they bring in a son of Māra and try to pile him on "all living beings"** (*Masu ichimai o shōrai shite, issai shujō ni kasanen. to su* 魔子一枚を將來して、一切衆生にかさねんとす): The demonic "sons of Māra" (*masu* 魔子) appear elsewhere in the *Shōbōgenzō* in pejorative reference to what Dōgen considers heretical types, in contrast to "sons of the Buddha" (*busshi* 佛子). Here, there seems to be the additional sense that buddha nature itself is a demonic (i.e., anti-Buddhist) notion smuggled into the Buddhist concept of "all living beings." The translation ignores Dōgen's playful use of the numeric classifier *ichimai* 一枚, used for flat objects, in the expression *masu ichimai* 魔子一枚 (literally, "one sheet of Māra son").

246 **when Mr. Chang drinks wine, Mr. Li gets drunk** (*Chō kō kisshū Ri kō sui* 張公喫酒李公醉): A familiar idiom in Chan texts, generally taken to mean that two things, while distinct, are in some sense one. The common surnames "Chang and Li" regularly occur as examples of "everyman." Dōgen's admonition here can be taken as a warning simply not to collapse the two concepts of "living beings" and "buddha nature"; or, more pointedly, as a warning not to think that what the living being does will bring about buddha nature.

247 **Baizhang** (*Hyakujō* 百丈): I.e. Dawei's teacher, Baizhang Huihai 百丈懷海. His saying can be found at *Tiansheng guangdeng lu* 天聖廣燈錄, ZZ.135:670a18-b1:

説衆生有佛、亦謗佛法僧。説衆生無佛性、亦謗佛法僧。若言有佛性、名執著謗。若言無佛性、名虛妄謗。如云説佛性有、則增益謗。説佛性無、則損減謗。説佛性亦有亦無、則相違謗。説佛性非有非無、則戲論謗。

To talk of living beings having buddha nature is to denigrate the buddha, dharma, and saṃgha; to talk of living beings having no buddha nature is to denigrate the buddha, dharma, and saṃgha. If we say they have buddha nature, this is called the

94　　　DŌGEN'S *SHŌBŌGENZŌ* VOLUME I

Thus, both saying "have buddha nature" and saying "have no buddha nature" become denigration. Though we say they become denigration, this does not mean one should not say them. Now, let us ask you, Dawei and Baizhang: we should ask a bit, it is not that there is no denigration, but have you talked of buddha nature or not? If you have talked of it, it delimits the talk; and where there is talking, it should "study together" with hearing.[248] Again, we should say to Dawei: you may be able to say, *"all living beings have no buddha nature,"* but you do not say, *"all buddha natures have no living being"*; you do not say, *"all buddha natures have no buddha nature."* Not to mention that you *have never seen even in your dreams "all buddhas have no buddha nature."* Try taking this up.[249]

* * * * *

[03:51]

百丈山大智禪師、示衆云、佛是最上乘、是上上智、是佛道立此人、是佛有佛性、是導師、是使得無所礙風、是無礙慧。於後能使得因果、福智自由。是作車運載因果。處於生不被生之所留、處於死不被死之所礙、處於五陰如門開、不被五陰礙。去住自由、出入無難。若能恁麼、不論階梯勝劣、乃至蟻子之身、但能恁麼、盡是淨妙國土、不可思議。

　　Chan Master Dazhi of Mount Baizhang addressed the assembly saying,[250]

　　　Buddha is the supreme vehicle, is the highest wisdom, is this person established by the way of the buddhas, is a buddha having buddha

---

denigration of grasping; if we say they have no buddha nature, this is called the denigration of vacuousness. If we say buddha nature exists, that is the denigration of reification; if we say buddha nature does not exist, that is the denigration of nihilism; if we say buddha nature both exists and does not exist, that is the denigration of contradiction; if we say buddha nature neither exists nor does not exist, that is the denigration of conceptual proliferation.

248　**If you have talked of it, it delimits the talk; and where there is talking, it should "study together" with hearing** (*tatoi settoku seba, setsujaku o keige sen. Setsujaku araba, monjaku to dōsan naru beshi* たとひ説得せば、説著を罣礙せん。説著あらば、聞著と同參なるべし): A difficult passage, perhaps meaning something like, "if you have expressed it, this is buddha nature expressing itself; and if it can express itself, it can hear itself." For the idiosyncratic use of *keige* 罣礙 ("delimit"), see above, Note 8. For the use of *dōsan* 同參 ("study together with"), see above, Note 113.

249　**Try taking this up** (*shi ko kan* 試擧看): I.e., "what do you have to say?"; a Chan master's frequent challenge, here presumably directed at Dawei (and perhaps also Baizhang).

250　**Chan Master Dazhi of Mount Baizhang** (*Hyakujōzan Daichi zenji* 百丈山大智禪師): I.e., Baizhang Huaihai 百丈懷海. Dazhi chanshi 大智禪師 is his title; Mount Baizhang 百丈山 is in Hongzhou 洪州, modern Jiangxi province. The passage can be found in the *Tiansheng guangdeng lu* 天聖廣燈錄 (ZZ.135:167b10-16).

3. Buddha Nature *Busshō* 佛性

nature.[251] *[One such as this] is a guiding teacher, is making use of an unobstructed style, is unobstructed wisdom. Henceforth, one can make use of cause and effect, and is free in merit and wisdom; one becomes the cart that carries cause and effect* [252] *In life, one is unarrested by life; in death, one is unobstructed by death. In the five aggregates, like a gate opening, one is unobstructed by the five aggregates: one goes and stays freely, leaves and enters without difficulty. If one can be like this, there is no issue of rank or stage, superiority or inferiority, even down to the body of an ant; if one is simply like this, everything is the pure and wondrous land, inconceivable.*

[03:52] {1:36}

これすなはち百丈の道處なり。いはゆる五蘊は、いまの不壞身なり。いまの造次は、門開なり、不被五陰礙なり。生を使得するに生にとどめられず、死を使得するに死にさへられず。いたづらに生を愛することなかれ、みだりに死を恐怖することなかれ。すでに佛性の處在なり、動著し厭却するは外道なり。現前の衆緣と認ずるは、使得無礙風なり。これ最上乗なる是佛なり。この是佛の處在、すなはち淨妙國土なり。

251　**Buddha is the supreme vehicle** (*butsu ze saijō jō* 佛是最上乗): The translation of this sentence reflects the traditional Japanese reading of the Chinese passage, witnessed already in the fifteenth-century Kenkon'in manuscript of the *Shōbōgenzō* (ESST.1:116b5-6), as a series of characterizations of "buddha" (*butsu* 佛), each introduced by the copula *ze* 是 ("buddha is . . . ."). The passage could, however, be parsed differently; and, indeed, it would seem that Dōgen's quotation may itself have altered the sense of the Chinese: in its original context, "buddha" should probably not be read as the grammatical subject here; rather the passage is describing those who have "seen their own buddha nature" (*ken jiko busshō* 見自己佛性) (ZZ.135:167b6ff); of such people, it is said (ZZ.135:167b9-11):

是屬然燈後佛。是最上乗。最上上智。是佛道上立。此人是佛。有佛性。

They belong among the buddhas after Dīpaṃkara [i.e., those aware of their buddha nature]. This is the supreme vehicle, the highest wisdom. They are established on the way of the buddhas. These people are buddhas; they have buddha nature.

is a buddha having buddha nature (*ze butsu u busshō* 是佛有佛性): Following the reading at ESST.1:116b6: *kore butsu u busshō nari* 是レ佛有佛性ナリ; a more obvious reading would yield, "this buddha has buddha nature."

252　**free in merit and wisdom** (*fukuchi jiyū* 福智自由): I.e., one freely manifests the two desiderata of the bodhisattva ideal of perfect awakening: an infinite store of merit (S. *puṇya*) and complete knowledge (S. *jñāna*).

one becomes the cart that carries cause and effect (*ze sa sha unsai inga* 是作車運載因果): The exact significance is uncertain; and, while not normally read in this way, it may be that "cart" and "carry" should be understood in apposition respectively to "cause" and "effect": i.e., the vehicle (cause) that conveys one to the goal (effect) — an interpretation that might yield something like, "it forms the cart and the conveyance, the cause and effect."

96 DŌGEN'S *SHŌBŌGENZŌ* VOLUME I

This is Baizhang's statement. The "five aggregates" are the present body that "won't be destroyed"; the present hasty act is "a gate opening," is "unobstructed by the five aggregates."[253] In making use of life, one is not arrested by life; in making use of death, one is not obstructed by death. Do not futilely love life; do not irrationally fear death. Since they are the locus of buddha nature, to be moved by them or to reject them is an other path. To recognize the conditions right before one is "*making use of the unobstructed style.*" This is "this buddha" that is "the supreme vehicle."[254] The location of "this buddha" is "the pure and wondrous land."

* * * * *

[03:53]

黃檗在南泉茶堂内坐。南泉問黃檗、定慧等學、明見佛性、此理如何。黃檗曰、十二時中不依倚一物始得。南泉云、莫便是長老見處麼。黃檗曰、不敢。南泉云、漿水錢且致、草鞋錢教什麼人還。黃檗便休。

Huangbo was sitting in Nanquan's tea hall.[255] Nanquan asked Huangbo, "'Studying meditation and wisdom equally, one clearly sees buddha nature' — what about this principle?"[256]

---

253 **the present body that "won't be destroyed"** (*ima no fue shin* いまの不壞身): Likely an allusion to Zhaozhou's saying that the "nature that won't be destroyed" is "the four elements and the five aggregates." See above, Note 183.

the present hasty act (*ima no zōji* いまの造次): I.e., the everyday act (here, presumably, of the "present body"); for this notion, see above, Note 183.

254 **This is "this buddha" that is "the supreme vehicle"** (*kore saijō jō naru ze butsu nari* これ最上乗なる是佛なり): Dōgen appears here to be switching the word order of Baizhang's first phrase, "Buddha is the supreme vehicle" (*butsu ze saijō jō* 佛是最上乘), such that the copula "is" (*ze* 是) in "buddha is" now modifies "buddha" in "this buddha." Alternatively, he may be borrowing *ze butsu* 是佛 from Baizhang's line, "is a buddha having buddha nature" (or "this buddha has buddha nature"; *ze butsu u busshō* 是佛有佛性).

255 **Huangbo was sitting in Nanquan's tea hall** (*Ōbaku zai Nansen sadō nai za* 黃檗在南泉茶堂内坐): "Huangbo" refers to the famous monk Huangbo Xiyun 黃檗希運, disciple of Baizhang Huaihai; "Nanquan" is Nanquan Puyuan 南泉普願, disciple of Mazu Daoyi 馬祖道一. The "tea hall" (*sadō* 茶堂) is the abbot's private reception room. The conversation can be found in the *Tiansheng guangdeng lu* 天聖廣燈錄 (ZZ.135:658b14-18); a variant occurs in the *Jingde chuandeng lu* 景德傳燈錄 (T.2076.51:257c25-28).

256 **"'Studying meditation and wisdom equally, one clearly sees buddha nature'"** (*jō e tō gaku, myōken busshō* 定慧等學、明見佛性): From a teaching of the *Nirvāṇa Sūtra* (*Da banniepan jing* 大般涅槃經, T.374.12:547a1216):

善男子、十住菩薩智慧力多三昧力少、是故不得明見佛性。聲聞緣覺三昧力多智慧力少、以是因緣不見佛性。諸佛世尊定慧等故、明見佛性。了了無礙如觀掌中菴摩勒果。

3. Buddha Nature *Busshō* 佛性

Huangbo said, "You only achieve it when you don't rely on a single thing throughout the twelve times."[257]

Nanquan said, "Isn't this the Elder's viewpoint?"

Huangbo said, "Not at all."[258]

Nanquan said, "Leaving aside the money for the rice water, whom can I get to pay back the money for the straw sandals?"[259]

Huangbo desisted.

[03:54] {1:37}

いはゆる定慧等學の宗旨は、定學の慧學をさへざれば、等學するところに明見佛性のあるにはあらず、明見佛性のところに、定慧等學の學あるなり。此理如何と道取するなり。たとへば、明見佛性はたれが所作なるぞと道取せんもおなじかるべし。佛性等學、明見佛性、此理如何、と道取せんも道得なり。

The essential point of "meditation and wisdom studied equally" is not that, since studying meditation does not interfere with studying wisdom, we "clearly see buddha nature" where they are studied equally: it is that, where we "clearly see buddha nature," we have a study that is "meditation and wisdom studied equally." He says, "what about this principle?" This is like saying, for example, "by whom is 'clearly seeing buddha nature' done"? Another saying would also be, "*When buddha and nature are studied equally, one clearly sees buddha nature — what about this principle?*"[260]

Good son, the bodhisattvas on the ten stages are strong in wisdom and weak in samādhi and, because of this, cannot clearly see buddha nature. The *śrāvakas* and *pratyeka-buddhas* are strong in samādhi and weak in wisdom and, for this reason, cannot see buddha nature. The buddhas, the World-Honored Ones, are equal in meditation and wisdom and, therefore, clearly see buddha nature, with complete clarity, like a betel nut in the palm of the hand.

257 **"throughout the twelve times"** (*jūni ji chū* 十二時中): I.e., "twenty-four hours a day"; see above, Note 57.

258 **"Not at all"** (*fukan* 不敢): As Dōgen explains below, section 57, a colloquial expression of modest acknowledgement of a compliment; short for *fukan tō* 不敢當.

259 **"the money for the rice water"** (*shōsui sen* 漿水錢); **"the money for the straw sandals"** (*sōai sen* 草鞋錢): I.e., the cost of Huangbo's board and travels respectively. The term *shōsui* 漿水 refers to the water in which rice has been cooked (what we might call "rice slops") that can be taken as a thin rice gruel.

260 **"buddha and nature are studied equally"** (*busshō tōgaku* 佛性等學): The translation retains the original grammatical structure "A B studied equally"; but, given the preceding question about the agent, the phrase might also be read, "when buddha nature studies equally."

98   DŌGEN'S *SHŌBŌGENZŌ* VOLUME I

[03:55]

黄檗いはく、十二時中不依倚一物、といふ宗旨は、十二時中たとひ十二時中に處在せりとも、不依倚なり。不依倚一物、これ十二時中なるがゆえに佛性明見なり。この十二時中、いづれの時節到來なりとかせん、いづれの國土なりとかせん。いまいふ十二時は、人間の十二時なるべきか、他那裏に十二時のあるか、白銀世界の十二時のしばらくきたれるか。たとひ此土なりとも、たとひ他界なりとも、不依倚なり。すでに十二時中なり、不依倚なるべし。

Huangbo says, "*You don't rely on a single thing throughout the twelve times.*" The essential point of this is that, although "throughout the twelve times" is located "thoughout the twelve times," it is "not relying": because "not relying on a single thing" is "throughout the twelve times," it is the "clear seeing" of buddha nature.[261] This "throughout the twelve times" — in which time does it arrive? In which land? This "twelve times" — is it the twelve times among humans? Are there twelve times over there?[262] Have the twelve times of the silver world come to us for a while?[263] Whether it is this land, whether it is other worlds, it is "not relying."[264] Since it is "throughout the twelve times," it must be "not relying."

---

261 **because "not relying on a single thing" is "throughout the twelve times," it is the "clear seeing" of buddha nature** (*fuei ichimotsu, kore jūni ji chū naru ga yue ni busshō myōken nari* 不依倚一物、これ十二時中なるがゆえに佛性明見なり): I.e., "because 'not relying' is [the nature of] the twenty-four hours a day." The phrase *busshō myō ken* 佛性明見 (rendered here "the clear seeing of buddha nature") could also be read "buddha nature is clearly seen" or "buddha nature clearly sees."

262 **Are there twelve times over there?** (*ta nari ni jūni ji no aru ka* 他那裏に十二時のあるか): Dōgen uses here a colloquial term for "there," "in that place"— presumably here, indicating a place other than the human realm.

263 **the silver world** (*byakugon sekai* 白銀世界): A pure realm sometimes associated with Bodhisattva Samantabhadra (Puxian pusa 普賢菩薩); known in Chan perhaps especially from a line in a verse by Shoushan Xingnian 首山省念 (926-993) (*Jingde chuandeng lu* 景德傳燈錄, T.2076.51:305a3-4):

白銀世界金色身、情與非情共一眞。

The silver world and the golden body,
Sentient and insentient share a single truth.

264 **this land** (*shido* 此土); **other worlds** (*takai* 他界): Terms of ambiguous referent. Depending on context, *shido* 此土 ("this land") can indicate (a) the Sahā world (*shaba sekai* 娑婆世界), the world of Buddha Śākyamuni; (b) the human realm (*ningen* 人間), as opposed to other realms of saṃsāra; or (c) China (or East Asia), as opposed to India. Similarly, *takai* 他界 ("other worlds") can refer to (a) other buddha lands, or (b) other realms of saṃsāra; it can also be translated in the singular, as a reference (much like the English "the other world") to (c) the world of the dead, of spirits, etc.

3. Buddha Nature *Busshō* 佛性

99

[03:56]

莫便是長老見處麼といふは、これを見處とはいふまじや、といふがごとし。長老見處麼と道取すとも、自己なるべしと回頭すべからず。自己に的當なりとも黄檗にあらず、黄檗かならずしも自己のみにあらず。長老見處は露回回なるがゆえに。

"*Isn't this the Elder's viewpoint?*" is like saying, "Aren't you saying this is your viewpoint?" Though he says, "is it the Elder's viewpoint?" he should not turn his head, thinking it must refer to himself.[265] It may be accurate of himself, but it is not Huangbo, and Huangbo is not necessarily merely himself; for the "Elder's viewpoint" is everywhere exposed.[266]

[03:57]

黄檗いはく、不敢。この言は、宋土に、おのれにある能を問取せらるるには、能を能といはんとても、不敢といふなり。しかあれば、不敢の道は不敢にあらず。この道得はこの道取なること、はかるべきにあらず。長老見處たとひ長老なりとも、長老見處たとひ黄檗なりとも、道取するには不敢なるべし。一頭水牯牛出來道吽吽なるべし。かくのごとく道取するは道取なり。道取する宗旨、さらに又道取なる道取、こころみて道取してみるべし。

Huangbo said, "*Not at all.*" Regarding this term: in the Land of the Song, when asked about one's own ability, even while saying an ability is one's ability, one says, "not at all." Therefore, saying "*not at all*" does not mean "not at all," and we should not reckon that this saying is saying that. The "Elder's viewpoint" may be that of an elder, the "Elder's viewpoint" may be that of Huangbo; but in speaking of it, he should say, "not at all." He should be *a water buffalo coming up and saying, "moo, moo.*"[267] Saying it like this is saying it. The essential point of what he is saying, we should try to say by another saying that also says it.

---

265 **he should not turn his head, thinking it must refer to himself** (*jiko naru beshi to kaitō su bekarazu* 自己なるべしと回頭すべからず): I.e., Huangbo should not respond with the assumption that Nanquan is referring to him by the expression "the elder."

266 **It may be accurate of himself, but it is not Huangbo, and Huangbo is not necessarily merely himself** (*jiko ni tekitō nari to mo Ōbaku ni arazu, Ōbaku kanarazushimo jiko nomi ni arazu* 自己に的當なりとも黄檗にあらず、黄檗かならずしも自己のみにあらず): A rather obscure passage, perhaps to be interpreted, "It may be that it is accurate to say that Huangbo's statement is 'the Elder's viewpoint,' but 'the Elder' here does not refer to Huangbo, nor does 'Huangbo' here necessarily refer merely to Huangbo."

for the "Elder's viewpoint" is "everywhere exposed" (*chōrō kenjo wa rokaikai naru ga yue ni* 長老見處は露回回なるがゆえに): A tentative translation. The term *rokaikai* 露回回, rendered here rather loosely as "everywhere exposed," represents a variant of the somewhat more common *rokeikai* 露迴迴; subject to two lines of interpretation: (a) "clearly visible" (taking *kaikai* 回回 in the sense "brilliant"); (b) "visible far and wide" (taking *kaikai* as "distant").

267 **He should be a water buffalo coming up and saying, "moo, moo"** (*ittō suikogyū*

100 DŌGEN'S *SHŌBŌGENZŌ* VOLUME I

[03:58] {1:38}

南泉いはく、漿水錢且致、草鞋錢教什麼人還。いはゆるは、こんづのあた
ひはしばらくおく、草鞋のあたひは、たれをしてかかへさしめん、とな
り。この道取の意旨、ひさしく生生をつくして參究すべし。漿水錢、いか
なればかしばらく不管なる、留心勤學すべし。草鞋錢、なにとしてか管得
する。行脚の年月にいくばくの草鞋をか踏破しきたれるとなり。いまいふ
べし、若不還錢、未著草鞋。またいふべし、兩三鞴。この道得なるべし、
この宗旨なるべし。

Nanquan said, "*Leaving aside the money for the rice water, whom can
I get to pay back the money for the straw sandals?*" What he is saying is,
"Putting aside for the moment the cost of your rice water, whom can I
get to return the cost of your sandals?"[268] The meaning of this saying, we
should investigate for a long time, exhausting life after life. We should
take heed and diligently study why he is not for the moment concerned
about the "money for the rice water," and why he is concerned about
the "money for the straw sandals." [The question is,] how many straw
sandals has he worn out in his years of pilgimage?[269] He should say, "*If I
hadn't returned the money, I wouldn't have put on the straw sandals.*"[270]
Or he should say, "Two or three pair." This should be his saying; this
should be his essential point.

[03:59]

黃檗便休。これは休するなり。不肯せられて休し、不肯にて休するにあら
ず。本色衲子、しかあらず。しるべし、休裏有道は、笑裏有刀のごとくな
り。これ佛性明見の粥足飯足なり。

"*Huangbo desisted.*" This means he "desisted"; it does not mean that,
not being affirmed, he desisted, or, not affirming, he desisted.[271] A patch-

---

shutsurai dō un'un naru beshi 一頭水牯牛出來道吽吽なるべし): Dōgen here slips into
Chinese for this phrase. The sense would seem to be that it is as natural for Huangbo to
say "not at all" as it is for the water buffalo to say "moo, moo." Chan masters themselves
regularly respond by saying "moo, moo" (*un'un* 吽吽); and Nanquan famously predicted
that in a hundred years he would be water buffalo; see Supplementary Notes, s.v. "Water
buffalo."

268 **What he is saying** (*iwayuru wa* いはゆるは): Dōgen is here simply translating the
Chinese into the vernacular.

269 **years of pilgimage** (*angya no nengetsu* 行脚の年月): Literally, "months and years
of traveling on foot." The term *angya* 行脚 is regularly used for the peregrinations of the
Zen monk in search of the dharma.

270 **"If I hadn't returned the money, I wouldn't have put on the straw sandals"**
(*nyaku fu gen sen, mijaku sōai* 若不還錢、未著草鞋): Dōgen puts this remark into Chinese. The tense of the first clause is unexpressed; it might also be translated, "if I weren't
going to return the money."

271 **not being affirmed, he desisted, or, not affirming, he desisted** (*fukō serarete kyū
shi, fukō nite kyū su* 不肯せられて休し、不肯にて休す): I.e., he stopped because his

3. Buddha Nature *Busshō* 佛性   101

robed one of true colors is not like that.[272] We should realize that there is speech within desisting, like the blade within the laugh.[273] This is *the gruel is enough, the rice is enough,* of buddha nature clearly seen.[274]

[03:60]

この因縁を挙して、潙山、仰山にとふていはく、莫是黄檗搆得他南泉不得麼。仰山いはく、不然、須知黄檗有陷虎之機。潙山云、子見處、得恁麼長。

Raising this episode, Weishan asked Yangshan, *"Doesn't this mean that Huangbo couldn't catch that Nanquan?"*[275]

Yangshan said, *"Not so. You should realize that Huangbo has the ability to trap a tiger."*[276]

Weishan said, *"Your viewpoint is so superior."*

---

words were not approved by Nanquan, or he stopped because he did not himself approve Nanquan's words.

272 **A patch-robed one of true colors** (*honjiki nossu* 本色衲子): I.e., an authentic Zen monk. The translation "of true colors" represents a playful rendering of the term *honjiki* 本色: while the graph *shiki* 色 is used for "color," in this case, the sense is probably more like "authentic type." The term *nossu* 衲子 ("patch-robed one") is synonymous with *nassō* [or *nōsō*] 衲僧 ("patch-robed monk").

273 **blade within the laugh** (*shōri u tō* 笑裏有刀): See above, Note 212.

274 **This is the gruel is enough, the rice is enough, of buddha nature clearly seen** (*kore busshō myōken no shuku soku han soku nari* これ佛性明見の粥足飯足なり): Or "of buddha nature seeing clearly." The expression "the gruel is enough, the rice is enough" (*shuku soku han soku* 粥足飯足) is a fairly common Zen idiom, occurring several times in Dōgen's writings, meaning that the monk's meals are sufficient and suggesting, by metaphorical extension, that the monk's practice is replete.

275 **Weishan asked Yangshan** (*Isan Kyōzan ni tōte iwaku* 潙山仰山にとふていはく): Dōgen here quotes the passage that immediately follows the story of Huangbo and Nanquan in the *Tiansheng guangdeng lu* 天聖廣燈錄 (ZZ.135:658b18-22). "Weishan" 潙山 has appeared several times above; see, e.g., Note 235. "Yangshan" refers to Weishan's disciple Yangshan Huiji 仰山慧寂 (803-887). Together, the two monks are treated by later histories as the founders of the so-called Weiyang 潙仰 lineage of Chan.

"Huangbo couldn't catch that Nanquan" (*Ōbaku kōtoku ta Nansen futoku* 黄檗搆得他南泉不得): For the predicate "catch" (*kōtoku* 搆得), see above, Note 119.

276 **"the ability to trap a tiger"** (*kan ko shi ki* 陷虎之機): A fixed expression in Zen texts for a superior type. The term "trap" *kan* 陷 (variant 陷) here connotes especially use of a pit for catching animals.

102 DŌGEN'S *SHŌBŌGENZŌ* VOLUME I

[03:61] {1:39}

大潙の道は、そのかみ黄檗は南泉を搆不得なりやといふ。仰山いはく、黄檗は陥虎の機あり。すでに陥虎することあらば、拶虎頭なるべし。陥虎拶虎異類中行。明見佛性也開一隻眼。佛性明見也失一隻眼。速道速道。佛性見處、得恁麼長なり。このゆえに、半物・全物これ不依倚なり。百千物、不依倚なり、百千時、不依倚なり。このゆえにいはく、籮籠一枚、時中十二、依倚不依倚、如葛藤倚樹。天中及全天、後頭未有語なり。

Dawei's words say, "At that time, Huangbo could not catch Nan-quan."[277] Weishan says, "Huangbo has the ability to trap a tiger." If he has trapped the tiger, he should pet the tiger's head.

> *Trapping a tiger and petting the tiger,*
> *He moves among different types.*[278]
> *In clearly seeing buddha nature,*
> *He opens one eye;*
> *In the clear seeing of buddha nature,*
> *He loses one eye.*[279]
> *Speak! Speak!*
> *The viewpoint of buddha nature*
> *Is "so superior."*[280]

Therefore, a half thing or a whole thing is "not relying"; a hundred thousand things are "not relying"; a hundred thousand times are "not relying." Therefore, we say,

---

277 **Dawei's words** (*Daii no dō* 大潙の道): This and the following sentence represent simply Dōgen's rendering of the Chinese quotation into Japanese.

278 **Trapping a tiger and petting the tiger, he moves among different types** (*kan ko chiku ko irui chū gyō* 陥虎拶虎異類中行): Dōgen here and in the following sentence shifts to balanced parallel Chinese phrases, in the style of traditional Chan comment. The expression "move among different types" (*irui chū gyō* 異類中行) is a fixed expression, occurring several times in the *Shōbōgenzō*, suggesting life as a dumb beast, as well as the salvific activities of the buddhas and bodhisattvas among the beasts; it is associated especially with a comment by Nanquan Puyuan 南泉普願, quoted in Dōgen's *shinji Shōbōgenzō* 眞字正法眼藏 (DZZ.5:154-156, case 57). See Supplementary Notes, s.v., "Move among different types," "A head of three feet and a neck of two inches."

279 **In the clear seeing of buddha nature, he loses one eye** (*busshō myōken ya shitsu isseki gen* 佛性明見也失一隻眼): Here, again, the phrase *busshō myō ken* 佛性明見 ("the clear seeing of buddha nature") could also be read "when buddha nature is clearly seen" or "when buddha nature clearly sees." (See, above, Note 257.) "To lose an eye" (*shitsu isseki gen* 失一隻眼) is used in reference to the experience of awakening; see Supplementary Notes, s.v. "Eye," "All the worlds in the ten directions are the single eye of the śramaṇa."

280 **The viewpoint of buddha nature** (*busshō kenjo* 佛性見處): A phrase likely meaning "the buddha nature's own viewpoint," though it could also be read "[his (Huang-bo's?)] buddha nature viewpoint."

3. Buddha Nature *Busshō* 佛性   103

A single snare,
Throughout times twelve.[281]
Relying and not relying,
Like tangled vines rely on a tree[282]
Throughout the heavens and the whole of heaven;
Afterwards, he had no words.[283]

---

281 **A single snare, throughout times twelve** (*rarō ichimai, ji chū jūni* 籮籠一枚、時中十二): A loose translation of the term *rarō* 籮籠 ("nets and cages," for catching and holding birds and fish; also written 羅籠), used very commonly in Zen, and in Dōgen's writings, for spiritual or cognitive "traps." See Supplementary Notes, s.v. "Nets and cages." "Throughout times twelve" reflects the text's reversal of the syntax of Huangbo's saying. Here, again, to the end of this section, Dōgen has shifted into Chinese parallel construction.

282 **Relying and not relying, like tangled vines relying on a tree** (*ei fuei, nyo kattō i ju* 依倚不依倚、如葛藤倚樹): Again, a loose translation for the term *kattō* 葛藤, an expression composed of two terms denoting twining plants — the former often used for the arrowroot; the latter, for wisteria; see Supplementary Notes, s.v. "Tangled vines." The phrase "like tangled vines relying on a tree" represents a variation on the more common expression, "like vines relying on a tree" (*nyo tō i ju* 如藤倚樹), perhaps simply expanded here to achieve the requisite five glyphs to the line. See Supplementary Notes, s.v. "Like vines relying on a tree."

283 **Throughout the heavens and the whole of heaven** (*tenchū gyū zenten* 天中及全天): A tentative translation. The term *tenchū* 天中 ("throughout the heavens") is a common expression, usually meaning "among the devas" (i.e., the beings of the Buddhist "heavens"). The word *zenten* 全天 ("the whole of heaven") is less common and does not appear elsewhere in the *Shōbōgenzō*; taken here to mean "all of heaven" or "all the heavens."

Afterwards, he had no words (*gotō mi u go* 後頭未有語): No doubt an allusion to Huangbo's "desisting"; likely reflecting another remark by Huangbo that occurs in the *Tiansheng guangdeng lu* 天聖廣燈錄 soon after the passage Dōgen has been examining here. Note that, in this passage (ZZ.135:659a6-13), Huangbo is also seen "desisting," as well as using the expression, akin to that in our text, "patch-robed monk of true colors."

一日五人新到、同時相看。四人禮拜。一人不禮拜、以手畫一圓相而立。師云、還知道好隻獵犬廢。云尋羚羊氣來。師云、羚什無氣、汝向什麼處尋。云尋羚羊蹤。來師云、羚羊無蹤。汝向什麼處尋。云與麼則死羚羊也。師便休。來日昇座退、問昨日尋羚羊僧出來。其僧便出。師云、老僧昨日後頭未有語在。作麼生。其僧無語。師云、將謂本色衲僧、元來是羲學沙門。

One day, five people newly arrived came to see [Huangbo] together. Four of them bowed. One did not bow but drew a circle with his hand and stood there.
The Master said, "Do you know a good hunting dog?"
The monk said, "He seeks the antelope's scent."
The Master said, "If the antelope has no scent, where does he seek it?"
The monk said, "He seeks the antelope's tracks."
The Master said, "If the antelope has no track, where does he seek it?"
He said, "That's a dead antelope."
The Master desisted.
The next day, as he was retiring from his lecture, he called out the monk he had asked about seeking the antelope. The monk came out.

104 DŌGEN'S *SHŌBŌGENZŌ* VOLUME I

* * * * *

[03:62]

趙州眞際大師に、ある僧とふ、狗子還有佛性也無。

A monk asked Great Master Zhenji of Zhaozhou, "*Does even a dog have buddha nature?*"[284]

[03:63]

この問の意趣、あきらむべし。狗子とはいぬなり。かれに佛性あるべしと問取せず、なかるべしと問取するにあらず。これは、鐵漢また學道するかと問取するなり。あやまりて毒手にあふうらみふかしといへども、三十年よりこのかた、さらに半箇の聖人をみる風流なり。

We should be clear about the meaning of this question. [The word] *gouzi* means "dog."[285] He is not asking whether it has buddha nature; he is not asking whether it does not have buddha nature: he is asking whether the man of iron also studies the way.[286] Although he may deeply regret having inadvertently encountered a poison hand, it is in the style of seeing half a sage after thirty years.[287]

The Master said, "Since yesterday, this old monk has had no words. How about it?" The monk had no words.
The Master said, "He was supposed to be a patch-robed monk of true colors, but from the beginning he was a "*śramaṇa* who studies doctrine."

284 **Great Master Zhenji of Zhaozhou** (*Jōshū Shinsai daishi* 趙州眞際大師): I.e., the famous Tang-dynasty Chan master Zhaozhou Congshen 趙州從諗.

"Does even a dog have buddha nature?" (*kushi gen u busshō ya mu* 狗子還有佛性也無): One of the most famous kōans, appearing throughout Chan and Zen literature, perhaps most prominently as the first case in the popular kōan collection *Wumen guan* 無門關 (T.2005.48:292c20-21). Recorded in Dōgen's *shinji Shōbōgenzō* 眞字正法眼藏 (DZZ.5:188, case 114); the source for this version is thought to be the *Congrong lu* 從容錄 (T.2004.48:238b25-c1), the kōan collection based on the verses of Hongzhi Zhengjue 宏智正覺 (1091-1157).

285 **[The word] *gouzi* means "dog"** (*kushi to wa inu nari* 狗子とはいぬなり): Dōgen is here simply explaining what must have been a Chinese word unfamiliar to his Japanese audience.

286 **whether the man of iron also studies the way** (*tekkan mata gakudō suru ka* 鐵漢また學道するか): Dōgen plays here with the first line of a verse attributed to Li Zunxu 李遵勗 (988-1038):

學道須是鐵漢。

To study the way one should be a man of iron.

See Supplementary Notes, s.v. "Man of iron."

287 **Although he may deeply regret having inadvertently encountered a poison hand** (*ayamarite dokushu ni au urami fukashi to iedomo* あやまりて毒手にあふうらみふかしといへども): The "poison hand" is an idiom referring to the stringent methods of the Chan teacher. The unexpressed subject here is no doubt the monk who asked the question.

3. Buddha Nature *Busshō* 佛性   105

[03:64]

趙州いはく、無。この道をききて、習學すべき方路あり。佛性の自稱する無も怎麼道なるべし、狗子の自稱する無も怎麼道なるべし、傍觀者の喚作の無も怎麼道なるべし。その無、わづかに消石の日あるべし。

Zhaozhou said, "No."

There is a route we should study when we hear this saying. The "no" that buddha nature calls itself should also be such a saying; the "no" that the dog calls itself should also be such a saying; the "no" by which the onlooker calls it should also be such a saying. There will be a day when this "no" fairly erases the stone.[288]

---

it is in the style of seeing half a sage after thirty years (*sanjū nen yori kono kata, sara ni hanko no shōnin o miru fūryū nari* 三十年よりこのかた、さらに半箇の聖人をみる風流なり): Likely in praise of the monk for his willingness to face Zhaozhou. Allusion to a story about the Chan monk Sanping Yizhong 三平義忠 (781-872) facing the arrow of the former hunter Shigong Huizang 石鞏慧藏 (dates unknown) (*Jingde chuandeng lu* 景德傳燈錄, T.2076.51:316b20-25):

初參石鞏。石鞏常張弓架箭以待學徒。師詣法席。鞏曰、看箭。師乃撥開胸云、此是殺人箭。活人箭又作麼生。鞏乃扣弓絃三下。師便作禮。鞏云、三十年一張弓兩隻箭。只謝得半箇聖人。遂拗折弓箭。

[Yizhong] first visited Shigong. Shigong always kept his bow drawn and an arrow set, waiting for a student. When the Master [Yizhong] approached the dharma seat, Gong said, "See the arrow."
The Master exposed his breast and said, "That's an arrow that kills people. How about the arrow that revives people?"
Gong twanged his bow string three times. The Master bowed. Gong said, "For thirty years, a single bow with a pair of arrows. I only hit half a sage." Then, he broke his bow and arrow.

Some versions of the *Jingde chuandeng lu* record a simpler variant.

師乃披襟當之。石鞏曰、三十年張弓架箭。只射得半箇漢。

The Master exposed his breast as a target.
Shigong said, "For thirty years, I drew my bow and set an arrow. I only hit half a man."

288 **There will be a day when this "no" fairly erases the stone** (*sono mu wazuka ni shōshaku no hi aru beshi* その無わづかに消石の日あるべし): A tentative translation, taking *wazuka ni* わづかに ("fairly") in the sense "virtually" and *hi* 日 as "day" (rather than "sun"). This does not appear to be a common expression and does not appear elsewhere in Dōgen's writings; perhaps meaning that, in the presence of this "no," all things are dissolved.

106 DŌGEN'S *SHŌBŌGENZŌ* VOLUME I

[03:65]

僧いはく、一切衆生、皆有佛性、狗子爲甚麼無。

The monk said, "*All living beings have buddha nature. Why doesn't the dog have it?*"[289]

[03:66] {1:40}

いはゆる宗旨は、一切衆生無ならば、佛性も無なるべし、狗子も無なるべしといふ、その宗旨作麼生となり。狗子佛性、なにとして無をまつことあらん。

The essential point of what he says is that, if "all living beings" are "no," "buddha nature" must also be "no," "the dog" must also be "no" — what about this point?[290] Why should the buddha nature of the dog depend on "no"?

[03:67]

趙州いはく、爲他有業識在。この道旨は、爲他有は業識なり、業識有、爲他有なりとも、狗子無、佛性無なり。業識いまだ狗子を會せず、狗子いかでか佛性にあはん。たとひ雙放雙收すとも、なほこれ業識の始終なり。

Zhaozhou said, "*Because it has karmic consciousness.*"[291]

The meaning of these words is that, while "because it has" is "karmic consciousness," and "*having karmic consciousness*" *is* "*because it has*," the "*no*" *of the dog is the* "*no*" *of buddha nature.*[292] Karmic conscious-

---

289 **"Why doesn't the dog have it?"** (*kushi i jinmo mu* 狗子爲甚麼無): The translation masks the word "no" (*mu* 無) central to Dōgen's comment below; to better follow that comment, the monk's question here might be put, "Why is it 'no' in the case of the dog?"

290 **if "all living beings" are "no"** (*issai shujō mu naraba* 一切衆生無ならば): The translation seeks to reflect Dōgen's emphasis on Zhaozhou's "no" as "the 'no' buddha nature calls itself," "the 'no' the dog calls itself." In this passage, he seems to be assigning that "no" to each of the nouns in the monk's question: "all living beings," "buddha nature," and "the dog." Thus, he interprets the monk as asking, in effect, when "no" applies equally to "living beings" and "buddha nature," obviously it applies to "the dog"; so why say "no" in the case of the dog? Alternative readings could take the term *mu* 無 here (a) as "lacking" ("if all living beings have no [buddha nature] . . . ."), or (b) as "non-existent" ("if all living beings are non-existent . . . .").

291 **"Because it has karmic consciousness"** (*i ta u gosshiki zai* 爲他有業識在): For the term "karmic consciousness" (*gosshiki* 業識), see above, Note 15: "the busy, busy karmic consciousness." In Buddhist usage, of course, all sentient beings have karmic consciousness.

292 **"because it has" is "karmic consciousness," and "having karmic consciousness" is "because it has"** (*i ta u wa gosshiki nari, gosshiki u, i ta u nari* 爲他有は業識なり、業識有、爲他有なり): Dōgen is here playing with the terms in Zhaozhou's answer, treating the first three words, "because it has" (*i ta u* 爲他有) as a single nominal expression identified with "karmic consciousness." Part of the play depends on the fact that the words happen to include the graphs for the term *ita* 爲他 ("for the other," "for the sake

3. Buddha Nature *Busshō* 佛性

ness does not understand the dog; so how could the dog meet buddha nature?[293] Whether we disperse the pair or collect the pair, it is still karmic consciousness from beginning to end.[294]

[03:68]

趙州有僧問、狗子還有佛性也無。

Zhaozhou was asked by a monk, "Does the dog have buddha nature?"[295]

[03:69]

この問取は、この僧、搆得趙州の道理なるべし。しかあれば、佛性の道取・問取は、佛祖の家常茶飯なり。

The reason for this question must be for this monk to catch Zhaozhou. Thus, talking about and asking about buddha nature is the everyday tea and rice of the buddhas and ancestors.[296]

[03:70]

趙州いはく、有。

Zhaozhou said, "Yes."[297]

[03:71]

この有の様子は、教家の論師等の有にあらず、有部の論有にあらざるなり。すすみて佛有を學すべし。佛有は趙州有なり、趙州有は狗子有なり、狗子有は佛性有なり。

---

of others"; S. *parārtha*); hence, the phrase could be rendered "being for others is karmic consciousness, and having karmic consciousness is being for others."

293 **Karmic consciousness does not understand the dog; so how could the dog meet buddha nature?** (*gosshiki imada kushi o e sezu, kushi ikade ka busshō ni awan* 業識いまだ狗子を會せず、狗子いかでか佛性にあはん): Likely meaning that, since "karmic consciousness," "the dog," and "buddha nature" are all "no," they do not understand or meet each other; possibly a play on the graph *e* 會, which has the sense both "to understand" and "to meet."

294 **Whether we disperse the pair or collect the pair** (*tatoi sōhō sōshū su tomo* たとひ雙放雙収すとも): Probably to be understood, "whether we take [the dog and buddha nature] as two or take them as one."

295 **Zhaozhou was asked by a monk** (*Jōshū u sō mon* 趙州有僧問): Dōgen is continuing his quotation from the same passage. In both the *shinji Shōbōgenzō* 眞字正法眼藏 and *Congrong lu* 從容録 texts, this part of the passage actually occurs prior to the part quoted above.

296 **everyday tea and rice** (*kajō sahan* 家常茶飯): I.e., normal practice; see above Note 84. No doubt directed at those "beasts," criticized above, section 44, who say that Zen students should not talk about buddha nature.

297 **Zhaozhou said, "Yes"** (*Jōshū iwaku, u* 趙州いはく、有): Or "it has." Dōgen will again play here with the multivalence of the glyph *u* 有 ("to have," "to exist," "being," etc.; see above, Note 7).

108 DŌGEN'S *SHŌBŌGENZŌ* VOLUME I

The status of this "yes" is not the "existence" of the treatise masters of the teaching houses, not the "existence" discussed by the Existence School.[298] We should go on to study the Buddha's "yes." The Buddha's "yes" is Zhaozhou's "yes"; Zhaozhou's "yes" is the "yes" of the dog; the "yes" of the dog is the "yes" of buddha nature.[299]

[03:72]

僧いはく、既有、爲甚麼却撞入這皮袋。

The monk said, *"Given it has it, why does it force entry into this bag of skin?"*[300]

[03:73]

この僧の道得は、今有なるか、古有なるか、既有なるかと問取するに、既有は諸有に相似せりといふとも、既有は孤明なり。既有は撞入すべきか、撞入すべからざるか。撞入這皮袋の行履、いたづらに蹉過の功夫あらず。

In this monk's saying, in asking whether it is present having, past having, or "already having," though we may say "already having" resembles the various [other types of] having, "already having" shines alone.[301] Should "already having" "force entry" or should it not "force

---

298 **not the "existence" of the treatise masters of the teaching houses, not the "existence" discussed by the Existence School** (*kyōke no ronji tō no u ni arazu, ubu no ron u ni arazaru nari* 教家の論師等の有にあらず、有部の論有にあらざるなり): Taking Zhaozhou's "yes" (*u* 有) now as "exist." "Teaching houses" (*kyōke* 教家) refers to those styles of Buddhism that emphasize scriptural study. The "Existence School" (*ubu* 有部) refers to the Buddhist philosophical school known as Sarvāstivāda (*Setsu issai ubu* 説一切有部), which held the position that dharmas were real entities (S. *dravya*) existing through past, present, and future.

299 **Buddha's "yes"** (*butsu u* 佛有): Or "buddha's existence"; similarly, mutatis mutandis, for the remainder of the sentence.

300 **"force entry into this bag of skin"** (*tōnyū sha hitai* 撞入這皮袋): I.e., "enter this dog body"; see Supplementary Notes, s.v. "Bag of skin." The unexpressed grammatical subject is "buddha nature." The English "force entry" renders a compound term, *tōnyū* 撞入, that suggests something like, "ram (or stab) into and enter"; the translation here is intended to facilitate Dōgen's remarks on the second element (*nyū* 入, "enter") in his comments below.

301 **present having** (*kon u* 今有); **past having** (*ko u* 古有); **"already having"** (*ki u* 既有): Dōgen here treats the adverb and verb, *ki u* 既有 ("since it already has"), of the monk's question as the nominal expression "already having" (or "already being"), in parallel with "past having" and "present having." The adverb *ki* 既 is a marker of both temporal and logical senses of completion: "already," "previously," etc.; and "since," "given that," etc.

"already having" shines alone (*ki u wa komyō nari* 既有は孤明なり): I.e., "already having" stands out from the other types of having. The term *komyō* 孤明, while common throughout Buddhist literature, does not appear elsewhere in the *Shōbōgenzō*; it is typically parsed as "shines by itself."

3. Buddha Nature *Busshō* 佛性　　109

entry"? There is no concentrated effort that idly overlooks the conduct of "forcing entry into this bag of skin."[302]

[03:74] {1:41}

趙州いはく、爲他知而故犯。

Zhaozhou said, "*Because it knowingly commits an intentional crime.*"

[03:75]

この語は、世俗の言語として、ひさしく途中に流布せりといへども、いまは趙州の道得なり。いふところは、しりてことさらおかす、となり。この道得は、疑著せざらん、すくなかるべし。いま一字の入、あきらめがたしといへども、入之一字も不用得なり。いはんや欲識庵中不死人、豈離只今這皮袋なり。不死人はたとひ阿誰なりとも、いづれのときか皮袋に莫離なる。故犯はかならずしも入皮袋にあらず、撞入這皮袋かならずしも知而故犯にあらず。知而のゆえに故犯あるべきなり。しるべし、この故犯すなはち脱體の行履を覆藏せるならん。これ撞入と説著するなり。脱體の行履、その正當覆藏のとき、自己にも覆藏し、他人にも覆藏す。しかもかくのごとくなりといへども、いまだのがれずといふことなかれ、驢前馬後漢。いはんや、雲居高祖いはく、たとひ佛法邊事を學得する、はやくこれ錯用心了也。

These words may have long circulated in the world as a secular expression, but here they are Zhaozhou's saying.[303] What they say is that, knowing, it intentionally transgressed.[304] Not a few must have had doubts about this saying. The word "entry" here may be difficult to clarify, but "the word 'enter,' you can't use."[305] Still more, "*If you wish to know the deathless one within the hut, how could it be apart from this present bag*

302　**There is no concentrated effort that idly overlooks the conduct of "forcing entry into this bag of skin"** (*tōnyū sha hitai no anri, itazura ni shaka no kufu arazu* 撞入這皮袋の行履、いたづらに蹉過の功夫あらで): A tentative translation of an ambiguous sentence, perhaps meaning something like, "in making concentrated effort, one should not idly miss this conduct of 'forcing entry into this bag of skin.'" The effort in question is likely the study of the conduct (rather than the conduct itself).

303　**These words may have long circulated in the world as a secular expression** (*kono go wa, sezoku no gongo toshite, hisashiku tochū ni rufu seri to iedomo* この語は、世俗の言語として、ひさしく途中に流布せりといへども): I.e, the phrase "knowingly to commit an intentional crime" (*zhi er gu fan* 知而故犯) is a common expression in Chinese.

304　**knowing, it intentionally transgressed** (*shirite kotosara okasu* しりてことさらをかす): Dōgen is here simply explaining the Chinese phrase.

305　**The word "entry" here** (*ima ichiji no nyū* いま一字の入): Dōgen is here referring back to the monk's question, "why does it still force entry into this bag of skin?"

"the word 'enter,' you can't use" (*nyū no ichiji mo fuyōtoku nari* 入之一字も不用得なり): Allusion to a conversation involving Yangshan Huiji 仰山慧寂 and the magistrate Lu Xisheng 陸希聲 (d. 895), found at *shinji Shōbōgenzō* 眞字正法眼藏, DZZ.5:200, case 139; see Supplementary Notes, s.v. "The one word 'enter.'"

110 DŌGEN'S *SHŌBŌGENZŌ* VOLUME I

of skin?"[306] Whoever the "undying person" is, when would it leave the bag of skin?

"Committing an intentional crime" is not necessarily "entering the bag of skin"; "*forcing entry into this bag of skin*" is not necessarily "*knowingly committing an intentional crime*": because it is "knowingly," there must be "the commission of an intentional crime."[307] We should realize that this "commission of an intentional crime" may have covered and concealed the conduct of the body stripped.[308] This is spoken of as "forcing entry." The conduct of the body cast off, at the very time it is covered and concealed, is covered and concealed in self and covered and concealed in others. Nevertheless, though this may be the case, do not say it has not escaped — "*the guy ahead of the ass and behind the horse.*"[309] Moreover, as the Eminent Ancestor Yunju says, "Studying the marginal matters of the buddha dharma, you've already misused your mind."[310]

306 **"If you wish to know the deathless one within the hut, how could it be apart from this present bag of skin?"** (*yoku shiki an chū fushi nin, ki ri shikon sha hitai* 欲識庵中不死人、豈離只今這皮袋): Closing lines from the *Caoan ge* 草庵歌, by Shitou Xiqian 石頭希遷; see Supplementary Notes, s.v. "*Reverend Shitou's Song of the Thatched Hut.*"

307 **because it is "knowingly," there must be "the commission of an intentional crime"** (*chi ni no yue ni ko bon aru beki nari* 知而のゆえに故犯あるべきなり): I.e., it is "knowingly" that makes it an "intentional crime." Dōgen here creates a new term from the two graphs translated "knowingly" (*chi ni* 知而 ["knows, but"]); presumably meaning that life in the "bag of skin" (commission of an "intentional crime") depends on states of consciousness ("knowingly").

308 **this "commission of an intentional crime" may have covered and concealed the conduct of the body stripped** (*kono ko han sunawachi dattai no anri o fukuzō seru naran* この故犯すなはち脱體の行履を覆藏せるならん): For "the body stripped" (*dattai* 脱體), see above, Note 49. Presumably, the sense here is that our karmically determined body conceals the fact that we are liberated.

309 **"the guy ahead of the ass and behind the horse"** (*ro zen ba go kan* 驢前馬後漢): I.e., an ordinary workman, probably to be taken here as descriptive of the one of whom it is (wrongly) said he "has not escaped." A colloquial expression best known from the words of Muzhou Daozong 睦州道蹤 (Venerable Chen 陳尊宿, dates unknown) (*Jingde chuandeng lu* 景德傳燈錄, T.2076.51:291c15-16):

師問新到僧、什麼處來。僧瞪目視之。師云、驢前馬後漢。僧云、請師鑒。師云。驢前馬後漢、道將一向來。無對。

The Master questioned a newly arrived monk, "Where did you come from?"
The monk stared at him.
The Master said, "A guy ahead of the ass and behind the horse."
The monk said, "Could the Master give an example?"
The Master said, "A guy ahead of the ass and behind the horse. Tell me something serious."
[The monk] did not respond.

310 **the Eminent Ancestor Yunju says** (*Ungo kōso iwaku* 雲居高祖いはく): I.e., Yunju Daoying 雲居道膺 (d. 902), prominent disciple of Dongshan Liangjie 洞山良价. His saying, here put in Japanese, comes from a lecture found at *Liandeng huiyao* 聯燈會要,

3. Buddha Nature *Busshō* 佛性　　　111

[03:76]

しかあれば、半枚學佛法邊事、ひさしくあやまりきたること日深月深なり
といへども、これ這皮袋に撞入する狗子なるべし。知而故犯なりとも有佛
性なるべし。

Thus, although the days and months are long during which we have
been mistaken in our half a "study of the marginal matters of the buddha dharma," this is the dog forcing entry into this bag of skin. While
it is "knowingly committing an intentional crime," it is "having buddha
nature."

* * * * *

[03:77]

長沙景岑和尚の會に、竺尚書とふ、蚯蚓斬爲兩段、兩頭俱動。未審、佛性
在阿那箇頭。師云、莫妄想。書云、爭奈動何。師云、只是風火未散。

In the community of Reverend Changsha Jingcen, Minister Zhu asked,

*"When you cut a worm in two pieces, the two both move. I don't un-
derstand, in which one is buddha nature?"*[311]

The Master said, "Don't have deluded ideas."

The Minister said, "What do you make of their moving?"

The Master said, "It's just that the wind and fire haven't dispersed."[312]

ZZ.136:797a15:

示衆云、汝等直饒學得佛法邊事。早是錯用心了也。

Addressing the assembly, he said, "If you study the marginal matters of the buddha
dharma, you've already misused your mind."

Though Kawamura's edition makes a section break after this quotation, it is probably
best understood as the lead-in to Dōgen's comment in the following section, to the effect
that, although we have long been misusing our minds on the margins of Buddhism, we
are still like the dog with the buddha nature in its bag of skin.

311　**Reverend Changsha Jingcen** (*Chōsha Keishin oshō* 長沙景岑和尚): Dates unknown; a disciple of Nanquan Puyuan 南泉普願. Minister Zhu (*Chiku shōsho* 竺尚書)
is otherwise unknown; the government title *shōsho* 尚書 indicates that he was head of
the Department of State Affairs (*shangshu sheng* 尚書省) in the Tang government. This
exchange is found in several sources, including Dōgen's *shinji Shōbōgenzō* 眞字正法眼
藏 (DZZ.5:136, case 20).

312　**"wind and fire haven't dispersed"** (*fūka misan* 風火未散): The expression "wind
and fire" is likely shorthand for the "four elements" (*shidai* 四大; S. *catvāri-mahā-
būtāni*): earth (*chi* 地), water (*sui* 水), fire (*ka* 火), and wind (*fū* 風). Regularly used in
reference to the life of the physical body. See Supplementary Notes, s.v. "Four elements
and five aggregates."

112   DŌGEN'S *SHŌBŌGENZŌ* VOLUME I

[03:78] {1:42}

いま尚書いはくの蚯蚓斬爲兩段は、未斬時は一段なりと決定するか。佛祖の家常に不恁麼なり。蚯蚓もとより一段にあらず、蚯蚓きれて兩段にあらず。一・兩の道取、まさに功夫參學すべし。兩頭倶動といふ兩頭は、未斬よりさきを一頭とせるか、佛向上を一頭とせるか。兩頭の語、たとひ尚書の會・不會にかかはるべからず、語話をすつることなかれ。きれたる兩段は一頭にして、さらに一頭のあるか。その動といふに倶動といふ、定動智拔ともに動なるべきなり。

The Minister says here "*cut a worm in two pieces*": is it certain that, before it is cut, it is one piece? In the everyday life of the buddhas and ancestors, this is not so: from the beginning, the worm is not one piece, nor is it two pieces when one cuts it. We should make concentrated effort and study the words "one" and "two." Does "the two" in his saying "the two both move" mean that he has taken what they were before they are cut as one? Or that he has taken what lies beyond the buddha as one?[313] Whether or not the Minister understands or does not understand the words "the two," do not discard his words. Is it that, while the two cut pieces are one, there is a further one?[314] In speaking of the movement, he says "both move": "*concentration moves them and wisdom uproots them*" should both be this "movement."[315]

---

313   **beyond the buddha** (*butsu kōjō* 佛向上): See above, Note 94. Presumably, the question here is, are we talking simply about an uncut worm or a higher oneness?

314   **Is it that, while the two cut pieces are one, there is a further one?** (*kiretaru ryōdan wa ittō ni shite, sara ni ittō no aru ka* きれたる兩段は一頭にして、さらに一頭のあるか): Probably meaning, "is there one thing beyond the one thing that was cut?"

315   **"concentration moves them and wisdom uproots them" should both be this "movement"** (*jō dō chi batsu tomo ni dō naru beki nari* 定動智拔ともに動なるべきなり): Identifying the movement of the bifurcated worm with the twin Buddhist practices of meditation and wisdom. Based on a passage in the *Nirvāṇa Sūtra* (*Da banniepan jing* 大般涅槃經, T.347.12:548b4-8).

善男子、菩薩摩訶薩具足二法能大利益。一者定、二者智。善男子、如刈菅草、執急則斷。菩薩摩訶薩修是二法、亦復如是。善男子、如拔堅木、先以手動後則易出。菩薩定慧亦復如是。先以定動後以智拔。

Good man, the bodhisattva mahāsattva is equipped with two methods that are highly beneficial: one is concentration; the other is wisdom. Good man, it is like cutting sedge: you grasp them firmly, then you cut them. The bodhisattva mahāsattva's practice of these two methods is like this. Good man, it is like uprooting an unyielding tree: first you move it with your hands, then it will easily come out. The bodhisattva's practice of meditation and wisdom is like this: first he moves [the afflictions] with meditation, then he uproots them with wisdom.

3. Buddha Nature *Busshō* 佛性　　113

[03:79]

未審、佛性在阿那箇頭。この道得は審細にすべし。佛性斬爲兩段、未審蚯
蚓在阿那箇頭といふべし。兩頭倶動、佛性在阿那箇頭といふは、倶動なら
ば、佛性の所在に不堪なりといふか。倶動なれば、動はともに動ずといふ
とも、佛性の所在は、そのなかにいづれなるべきぞといふか。

"*I don't understand, in which one is buddha nature?*" This saying, we
should examine in detail. He should say, "*When buddha nature is cut in
two pieces, I don't understand, in which one is the worm?*"[316] In saying,
"*the two both move; in which one is buddha nature?*" is he saying that,
if both move, they are unfit as the location of buddha nature? Or is he
saying that, since both move, the movement moves in both, but which of
them should be the location of buddha nature?

[03:80]

師いはく、莫妄想、この宗旨は、作麼生なるべきぞ。妄想することなか
れ、といふなり。しかあれば、兩頭倶動するに妄想なし、妄想にあらずと
いふか、ただ佛性は妄想なしといふか。佛性の論におよばず、兩頭の論に
およばず、ただ妄想なしと道取するか、とも參究すべし。

"The Master said, '*Don't have deluded ideas.*'" What should we make
of his point here? He says, "Do not have deluded ideas."[317] So, is he
saying that, "when the two both move," they have no deluded ideas,
are not deluded ideas?[318] Or is he just saying that buddha nature has no
deluded ideas? Or, without bothering to discuss buddha nature or discuss
"the two," is he just saying that there are no deluded ideas. We should
investigate all these [possibilities].

316　**"I don't understand"** (*mishin* 未審): The translation follows the Kawamura text
here. Other versions give a different order of these sentences:

> 未審、佛性在阿那箇頭。佛性斬爲兩段、未審蚯蚓在阿那箇頭といふべし。この
> 道得は審細にすへし。
>
> "I don't understand, in which one is buddha nature?" He should say, "When buddha
> nature is cut in two pieces, I don't understand, in which one is the worm?" This say-
> ing, we should examine in detail.

317　**He says, "Do not have deluded ideas"** (*mōsō suru koto nakare, to iu nari* 妄想
することなかれ、といふなり): Dōgen here simply renders Changsha's Chinese into
Japanese.

318　**they have no deluded ideas, are not deluded ideas** (*mōsō nashi, mōsō ni arazu* 妄
想なし、妄想にあらず): The exact sense is uncertain. The translation assumes that the
unexpressed grammatical subject of both clauses is "the two" (or perhaps their movement); i.e., that Changsha's "don't have deluded ideas" is not an imperative directed at
the Minister but a property of "the two both moving."

114   DŌGEN'S *SHŌBŌGENZŌ* VOLUME I

[03:81]

動ずるはいかがせん、といふは、動ずればさらに佛性一枚をかさぬべしと
道取するか、動ずれば佛性にあらざらんと道看するか。

"What do you make of their moving?"[319] Is this saying that, since
they are moving, there must be another layer of buddha nature on top of
them?[320] Or is it trying to say that, since they are moving, they are not
buddha nature?[321]

[03:82] {1:43}

風火未散といふは、佛性を出現せしむるなるべし。佛性なりとやせん、風
火なりとやせん。佛性と風火と、倶出すといふべからず、一出・一不出と
いふべからず、風火すなはち佛性といふべからず。ゆえに長沙は、蚯蚓に
有佛性、といはず、蚯蚓無佛性、といはず、ただ、莫妄想、と道取す、風
火未散、と道取す。佛性の活計は、長沙の道を卜度すべし。風火未散、と
いふ言語、しづかに功夫すべし。未散、といふは、いかなる道理かある。
風火のあつまれりけるが、散ずべき期いまだしきと道取するに、未散とい
ふか、しかあるべからざるなり。風火未散は、ほとけ、法をとく。未散風
火は、法、ほとけをとく。たとへば、一音の法をとく時節到來なり。説法
の一音なる、到來の時節なり。法は一音なり、一音の法なるゆえに。

To say "*the wind and fire haven't dispersed*" must be to make buddha
nature appear. Should we take it as buddha nature? Should we take it
as wind and fire? We should not say that buddha nature and wind and
fire both emerge; we should not say that one emerges and one does not
emerge; we should not say that the wind and fire are themselves buddha nature. Therefore, Changsha does not say that *the worm has buddha
nature*; he does not say that *the worm has no buddha nature*. He simply
says, "*Don't have deluded ideas*"; he says, "*the wind and fire haven't
dispersed.*" We should calculate the way of life of buddha nature by the
saying of Changsha; we should quietly make concentrated effort on the
words "*the wind and fire haven't dispersed.*"[322] What is the reasoning behind his saying "not dispersed"? Does "not dispersed" mean he is saying
that the wind and fire have been collected and have not yet reached the
point when they will be dispersed? This cannot be the case. "*The wind*

---

319 **"What do you make of their moving?"** (*dō zuru wa ikaga sen* 動ずるはいかがせ
ん): Dōgen here puts the Minister's question into Japanese.

320 **since they are moving, there must be another layer of buddha nature on top of
them** (*dō zureba sara ni busshō ichimai o kasanu beshi* 動ずればさらに佛性一枚をか
さぬべし): This could also be read, "since they are moving, we should add another layer
of buddha nature on top of them."

321 **"Is it trying to say"** (*dōkan suru ka* 道看するか): Following the Kawamura text's
dōkan 道看 ("try to say"); other versions give *dōjaku* 道著 ("say") here.

322 **the way of life of buddha nature** (*busshō no kakkei* 佛性の活計): Or "the livelihood of buddha nature." The term *kakkei* 活計 is a colloquial expression for one's way
of "making a living," often applied to the Zen master's activities.

3. Buddha Nature *Busshō* 佛性

and fire haven't dispersed" is buddha preaching the dharma; "the undispersed wind and fire" is the dharma preaching buddha. It is like the arrival of the time when a single sound preaches the dharma; it is the time of the arrival of the single sound that is the preaching of the dharma. The dharma is a single sound; for it is the dharma of a single sound.[323]

[03:83]

又、佛性は生のときのみにありて、死のときはなかるべしとおもふ、もとも少聞薄解なり。生のときも有佛性なり、無佛性なり。死のときも有佛性なり、無佛性なり。風火の散・未散を論することあらば、佛性の散・不散なるべし。たとひ散のときも佛性有なるべし、佛性無なるべし。たとひ未散のときも有佛性なるべし、無佛性なるべし。しかあるを、佛性は動・不動によりて在・不在し、識・不識によりて神・不神なり、知・不知に性・不性なるべき、と邪執せるは、外道なり。無始劫來は、癡人おほく識神を認じて、佛性とせり、本來人とせる、笑殺人なり。さらに佛性を道取するに、拕泥滞水なるべきにあらざれども、牆壁瓦礫なり。向上に道取するとき、作麼生ならんかこれ佛性。還委悉麼。三頭八臂。

Moreover, to think that buddha nature exists only at the time of birth and not at the time of death is [a case of] little learning and slight understanding. The time of birth is "has buddha nature," is "has no buddha nature"; the time of death is also "has buddha nature," is "has no buddha nature." If we discuss the dispersal and non-dispersal of the wind and fire, it would be the dispersal and non-dispersal of buddha nature. The time that it disperses must be buddha nature existing, must be buddha nature not existing; the time that it has not dispersed must be "having buddha nature," must be "having no buddha nature."[324] Despite this, to cling mistakenly to [the views that] buddha nature is present or not present depending on whether something is moving or not moving, or it is spirit or is not spirit depending on whether something is conscious or not conscious, or it is the nature or is not the nature depending on whether something is knowing or not knowing — these are other paths. "From beginningless kalpas," that "the deluded," "acknowledging the knowing

---

323 **The dharma is a single sound; for it is the dharma of a single sound** (*hō wa itton nari, itton no hō naru yue ni* 法は一音なり、一音の法なるゆえに): The adverb *yue ni* ("for") could also be taken as governing the preceding sentence — a reading that would yield, "For the dharma is a single sound; a single sound is the dharma." The notion that dharma is a single sound derives from the common claim that the Buddha speaks with a single voice, while his audience understands him in varied ways; see, e.g., the *Vimalakīrti Sūtra* (*Weimojie suoshuo jing* 維摩詰所説經. T.475.14:538a2):

佛以一音演説法。衆生隨類各得解。

The Buddha preaches the dharma with a single sound;
Living beings each understand it according to his or her type.

324 **buddha nature existing** (*busshō u* 佛性有); **buddha nature not existing** (*busshō mu* 佛性無): Dōgen has here simply reversed the phrases *u busshō* 有佛性 ("have buddha nature") and *mu busshō* 無佛性 ("have no buddha nature").

116 DŌGEN'S *SHŌBŌGENZŌ* VOLUME I

spirit," have taken it as buddha nature, have taken it as "the original person" — what a laugh![325]

To say something further about buddha nature, although we need not be dragged through the mud and drenched with water, it is "fences, walls, tiles, and pebbles."[326] When we say something beyond this, what is buddha nature? *Is everything clear?*[327] *Three heads and eight arms.*[328]

{1:44}

正法眼藏佛性第三
Treasury of the True Dharma Eye
Buddha Nature
Number 3

[Ryūmonji MS:]

爾時仁治二年辛丑十月十四日、在雍州觀音導利興聖寶林寺示衆
Presented to the assembly at Kannon Dōri Kōshō Hōrin Monastery, Yōshū; fourteenth day, tenth month, of the junior metal year of the ox, the second year of Ninji [18 November 1241][329]

---

325 **"From beginningless kalpas"** (*mushi kō rai* 無始劫來): This sentence reflects the verse by Changsha Jingcen 長沙景岑 for Minister Zhu, commenting on the worm conversation quoted in section 76, above.

學道之人不識眞、祇爲從前認識神。無始劫來生死本、癡人喚作本來人。

That people who study the way do not know the truth;
Is just because from the past they have acknowledged the knowing spirit.
The root of birth and death from beginningless kalpas,
The deluded call the original person.

326 **dragged through the mud and drenched with water** (*dadei taisui* 拖泥滯水): Reading *taisui* 滯水 as the more common *taisui* 帶水. An idiomatic expression for being "sullied" by words and concepts; see Supplementary Notes, s.v. "Dragged through the mud and drenched with water." Here, Dōgen seems to be saying, "while there is no need to teach more about this matter."

"fences, walls, tiles, and pebbles" (*shō heki ga ryaku* 牆壁瓦礫): An expression, appearing frequently in Dōgen's writing, for the inanimate world of objects. Best known from a saying attributed to Nanyang Huizhong 南陽慧忠 (d. 775); see Supplementary Notes.

327 **Is everything clear?** (*gen ishitsu mo* 還委悉麼): A fixed Chinese phrase often used by Chan masters but not appearing elsewhere in the *Shōbōgenzō*.

328 **Three heads and eight arms** (*sanzu happi* 三頭八臂): A fixed expression, used in reference to certain wrathful forms of Buddhist divinities. See Supplementary Notes, s.v. "Three heads and eight arms."

329 The Tōunji 洞雲寺 MS shares an identical colophon.

3. Buddha Nature *Busshō* 佛性 117

天文丁未二月廿四日書焉、挍了

*Proofed. Copied on the twenty-fourth day, second month, junior fire
year of the sheep, [sixteenth year of] Tenbun [15 March 1547][330]*

[Tōunji MS:]

于時弘長元年辛酉夏安居日、在越州吉田郡吉祥山永平寺、以先師御草本書
寫之、彼本、所所散散或書消或書入或被書直、仍今挍合書寫之也。
小師比丘＜二代和尚御名＞

*Copied my late master's draft at Eihei Monastery, Kichijōzan, Yoshida
District, Esshū; on a day of the summer retreat,
junior metal year of the rooster, first year of Kōchō [1261].[331]
That text was riddled here and there with overwrites, inserted phrases,
and rewritten passages; hence, I collated and copied it.
The disciple, Bhikṣu (name of the venerable of the second generation)[332]*

建治三年夏安居日、書寫之。寬海

*Copied this on a day of the summer retreat, third year of Kenji [1277].
Kankai[333]*

嘉慶三年正月廿日、在永平寺衆寮奉書寫之。宗吾

*Copied this as a memorial offering in the common quarters of Eihei
Monastery; twentieth day of the first month, third year of Kakyō [16
February 1389]. Sōgo[334]*

---

330 By Tessō Hōken 喆岗芳賢 (d. 1551), copyist of the Ryūmonji 龍門寺 MS.

331 **my late master's draft** (*senshi gosōhon* 先師御草本): I.e., a draft MS by Ejō's master, Dōgen.

day of the summer retreat (*ge ango no hi* 夏安居日): Dates of the summer retreat vary; a common practice put it from the fifteenth of the fourth lunar month through the fifteenth of the seventh month; in 1251, this would have corresponded to 15 May through 12 August.

332 **The disciple, Bhikṣu (name of the venerable of the second generation)** (*shōshi biku* [*Nidai oshō gomei*] 小師比丘＜二代和尚御名＞): I.e., Ejō; the phrase in parentheses is in the original.

333 This colophon is also attested in the Rurikōji 瑠璃光寺 MS in 83 chapters.

day of the summer retreat (*ge ango no hi* 夏安居日): If the the common practice of holding the retreat from the fifteenth of the fourth lunar month through the fifteenth of the seventh month was followed, in 1277, it would have been held 18 May through 15 August.

Kankai 寬海 (d.u.).

334 **Sōgo** 宗吾 (1343-1406).

DŌGEN'S *SHŌBŌGENZŌ* VOLUME I

[Ejō MS:][335]

同四年癸卯正月十九日書寫之。懷奘

Copied this on the nineteenth day, first month, of the senior water year of the tiger, the fourth year of the same [Ninji era] [9 February 1243]. Ejō

爾時仁治二年辛丑十月十四日、在雍州觀音導利興聖寶林寺示衆
再治御本之奧書也

Presented to the assembly at Kannon Dōri Kōshō Hōrin Monastery, Yōshū; fourteenth day, tenth month, of the junior metal year of the ox, the second year of Ninji [18 November 1241] Corrected colophon to his holograph[336]

正嘉二年戊午四月廿五日、以再治御本交合了

Collated his corrected holograph, twenty-fifth day, fourth month, senior earth year of the horse, the second year of Shōka [29 May 1258]

---

335 **Ejō MS**: The following three colophons by Ejō are preserved in the so-called "Sozanbon Busshō" 祖本佛性 MS, a copy of the text in Ejō's own hand owned by Eiheiji 永平寺 (ESST.27:690a-b).

336 **his holograph** (*gohon* 御本): Here and in the following entry, the reference is to Dōgen's holograph MS.

TREASURY OF THE TRUE DHARMA EYE

NUMBER 4

Studying the Way with Body and Mind
Shinjin gakudō
身心學道

Studying the Way with Body and Mind

Shinjin gakudō

INTRODUCTION

This work was written at Kōshōji in the autumn of 1242, during one of the most productive periods in Dōgen's literary career. It appears as number 37 in the Honzan edition of the *Shōbōgenzō* and as number 4 in both the sixty- and seventy-five-chapter compilations.

Dōgen explains the title of his essay at the outset: "studying the way" means to study the way of the buddhas — which, for him, means not simply to learn what the Buddha taught but to put into practice what all the buddhas practice. For purposes of discussion, he says, we can divide such study into two: studying with the body and studying with the mind. He then divides his essay into roughly equal parts, focused on each of these two in turn.

Elsewhere (in the twenty-eight-text *Shōbōgenzō* version of the "Butsu kōjō ji" 佛向上事 chapter), Dōgen defines studying with the mind as "clarifying the buddha mind" and studying with the body as "pursuing the way in seated meditation, practicing buddhahood without seeking to make a buddha." But in our essay here, body and mind are expanded well beyond the mind and body of the individual student of the way. "Mind" is "fences, walls, tiles, and pebbles"; "the mountains, rivers, and the whole earth, the sun, moon, and stars." "Body" is "all the worlds in the ten directions"; "birth and death, coming and going." Studying ourselves as such bodies and minds is studying the way with body and mind.

正法眼藏第四

Treasury of the True Dharma Eye
Number 4

身心學道

Studying the Way with Body and Mind

[04:1] {1:45}

佛道は、不道を擬するに不得なり、不學を擬するに轉遠なり。

The way of the buddhas: should we think not to speak of it, we cannot; should we think not to study it, we grow distant from it.[1]

[04:2]

南嶽大慧禪師のいはく、修證はなきにあらず、染汚することえじ。

Chan Master Dahui of Nanyue said, "It's not that it lacks practice and verification, but it can't be defiled by them."[2]

[04:3]

佛道を學せざれば、すなはち外道・闡提等の道に墮在す。このゆえに、前佛後佛かならず佛道を修行するなり。

When we do not study the way of the buddhas, we fall into the ways

---

1 **should we think not to speak of it, we cannot; should we think not to study it, we grow distant from it** (*fudō o gi suru ni futoku nari, fugaku o gi suru ni ten'on nari* 不道を擬するに不得なり、不學を擬するに轉遠なり): A tentative translation of a sentence variously interpreted. Dōgen appears here to have split the term *gakudō* 學道 ("studying the way") in his title and negated both its component glyphs. The translation treats the two resulting negatives, *fudō* 不道 and *fugaku* 不學, as verbs, rendered here respectively as "not to speak of [the way of the buddhas]" and "not to study [the way of the buddhas]"; the first term is often interpreted "to deny [the way of the buddhas]." The negative *futoku* 不得 (rendered here "cannot") is ambiguous: it could mean that, if we fail to speak of (or if we deny) the way of the buddhas, we cannot attain it; or, perhaps more interestingly, that, though we might attempt not to speak of the way of the buddhas, we cannot but do so. However exactly we are to interpret this sentence, it should probably be read as an introductory comment on the quotation that follows: that the way of the buddhas is something that must be put into practice.

2 **Chan Master Dahui of Nanyue** (*Nangaku Daie zenji* 南嶽大慧禪師): I.e., Nanyue Huairang 南嶽懷讓 (677-744). His saying here occurs in a famous dialogue, recorded in the *shinji Shōbōgenzō* 眞字正法眼藏 (DZZ.5:178, case 101) and cited throughout the *Shōbōgenzō*, with the Sixth Ancestor, Huineng 慧能; see Supplementary Notes, s.v. "What thing is it that comes like this?"

122 DŌGEN'S *SHŌBŌGENZŌ* VOLUME I

of other paths and the *icchantika*.[3] It is for this reason that prior buddhas and later buddhas invariably practice the way of the buddhas.

[04:4]

佛道を學習するに、しばらくふたつあり。いはゆる心をもて學し、身をもて學するなり。心をもて學するとは、あらゆる諸心をもて學するなり。その諸心といふは、質多心・汗栗駄心・矣栗駄心等なり。又、感應道交して、菩提心をおこしてのち、佛祖の大道に歸依し、發菩提心の行李を習學するなり。たとひいまだ眞實の菩提心おこらずといふとも、さきに菩提心をおこせりし佛祖の法をならふべし。これ發菩提心なり、赤心片片なり、古佛心なり、平常心なり、三界一心なり。

In studying the way of the buddhas, [we may say] for the time being there are two [approaches]: studying with the mind and studying with the body.[4] "Studying with the mind" means to study with all the various minds. These "various minds" mean the mind of *citta*, the mind of *hṛdaya*, the mind of *vṛddha* [?], and the like.[5] Again, with the interaction

---

3 **The ways of other paths and the *icchantika*** (*gedō senda tō no dō* 外道闡提等の道): I.e., non-Buddhist religions and those incapable of attaining the Buddhist goal of liberation from saṃsāra. The sense of the head word *dō* 道 ("ways") here is unclear — it is redundant if modified by *gedō* 外道 ("non-Buddhist ways") and seemingly inappropriate in reference to the *icchantika*, who would not normally be said to have their own "way."

4 **for the time being there are two approaches** (*shibaraku futatsu ari* しばらくふたつあり): I.e., for purposes of our discussion here, let us say there are two. Dōgen repeats this twofold division of study in the so-called *Himitsu Shōbōgenzō* text of the "Butsu kōjō ji" 佛向上事 (DZZ.2:572):

佛道をならうに、しばらく二の樣子あり。いはゆる、こころしてならひ、身してならふなり。

In studying the way of the buddhas, [we may say] for the time being there are two forms: to study with the mind, and to study with the body.

He goes on there to define "studying with the mind" as "clarifying the buddha mind" (*busshin o akiramuru* 佛心をあきらむる), and "studying with the body" as "pursuing the way in seated meditation, practicing buddhahood without seeking to make a buddha (*zazen bendō suru tokoro ni, sabutsu wo motomezaru gyōbutsu* 坐禪辨道するところに、作佛をもとめざる行佛).

5 **the mind of *citta*, the mind of *hṛdaya*, the mind of *vṛddha*** (*chitta shin karida shin irida shin* 質多心・汗栗駄心・矣栗駄心): These three types of mind are thought to have been borrowed from a passage in the *Mohe zhiguan* 摩訶止觀 (T.1911.46:4a20-23), in which Zhiyi 智顗 (538-597) defines three Sanskrit terms rendered by the Chinese glyph *xin* 心 ("mind"):

質多者天竺音、此方言心、即慮知之心也。天竺又稱汙栗駄、此方稱是草木之心也。又稱矣栗駄、此方是積聚精要者爲心也。

Zhiduo 質多 [S. *citta*] is the pronunciation of Sindhu; here, we say *xin* 心 — i.e., the thinking "mind." In Sindhu, they also speak of *wulituo* 汙栗駄 [S. *hṛdaya*], which here is called [*xin* 心 in the sense] the "heart" [or "core"] of grasses and trees. They also speak of *yilituo* 矣栗駄 [S. *vṛddha* (?)], which here is [*xin* 心 in the sense] the "heart" [or "pith"] of accumulated spiritual essence.

4. Studying the Way with Body and Mind *Shinjin gakudō* 身心學道 123

of feeling and response, after we have brought forth the mind of bodhi, we take refuge in the great way of the buddhas and ancestors and train in the observances of bringing forth the mind of bodhi.[6] Even if the true mind of bodhi has not yet been brought forth, we should study the dharma of the buddhas and ancestors who previously brought forth the mind of bodhi. This is bringing forth the mind of bodhi; it is the bare mind in pieces; it is the old buddha mind; it is the ordinary mind; it is the three realms are one mind.[7]

[04:5] {1:46}

これらの心を放下して學道するあり、拈擧して學道するあり。このとき、思量して學道す、不思量して學道す。あるひは金襴衣を正傳し、金襴衣を稟受す。あるひは汝得吾髓あり、三拜依位而立あり。碓米傳衣する以心學心あり。剃髮染衣、すなはち回心なり、明心なり。踰城し入山する、出一心入一心なり。山の所入なる、思量箇不思量底なり。世の所捨なる、非思量なり。これを眼睛に團しきたること二三斛、これを業識に弄しきたること千萬端なり。かくのごとく學道するに、有功に賞おのづからきたり、有

The Sanskrit original of Zhiyi's third term here is uncertain: some scholars have suggested *vṛddha* ("expanded," "developed"), while others take *yilituo* 矣栗馱 simply as an alternative transliteration of *hṛdaya*, here treated as a separate Sanskrit term. These three terms are also introduced in the "Hotsu bodai shin" 發菩提心 chapter of the twelve-chapter *Shōbōgenzō*.

6 **interaction of feeling and response** (*kannō dōkō* 感應道交): A fixed expression for the communication between a devotee and a deity; the devotee's feeling evokes a response from the deity and vice versa. Dōgen's reliance on the expression here (as also in his "Hotsu bodai shin" 發菩提心 chapter) no doubt reflects Zhiyi's use of it to explain bringing forth the mind of bodhi (at *Mohe zhiguan* 摩訶止觀, T.1911.46:4c13-15):

> 問、行者自發心他教發心。答、自他共離皆不可。但是感應道交而論發心耳。
> Question: Do practitioners bring forth the mind by themselves, or are they caused to bring forth the mind by another?
> Answer: It cannot happen apart from self and other together. Only when feeling and response interact can we speak of bringing forth the mind.

mind of bodhi (*bodai shin* 菩提心): I.e., the bodhisattva's aspiration to attain the unsurpassed, perfect bodhi of a buddha; S. *bodhi-citta*. See Supplementary Notes, s.v. "Bring forth the mind." The translation of *shin* 心 as "mind" (rather than the more common "thought") reflects its place here in the discussion of "studying with the mind."

observances of bringing forth the mind of bodhi (*hotsu bodai shin no anri* 發菩提心の行李): The exact meaning here is unclear; perhaps "observances that express one's bringing forth the mind of bodhi."

7 **bare mind in pieces** (*sekishin henpen* 赤心片片); **old buddha mind** (*kobutsushin* 古佛心); **ordinary mind** (*byōjō shin* 平常心): Dōgen here introduces three popular Chan expressions that use the term "mind," which he will discuss below. See Supplementary Notes, s.v. "Bare mind in pieces," "Old buddha."

three realms are one mind (*sangai isshin* 三界一心): An uncommon variant of the common Buddhist expressions "the three realms are only one mind" (*sangai yui isshin* 三界唯一心) or "the three realms are only mind" (*sangai yui shin* 三界唯心). See Supplementary Notes, s.v. "The three realms are only mind."

124   DŌGEN'S *SHŌBŌGENZŌ* VOLUME I

賞に功いまだいたらざれども、ひそかに佛祖の鼻孔をかりて出氣せしめ、
驢馬の脚蹄を拈じて印證せしむる、すなはち萬古の榜樣なり。

There is casting away these minds and studying the way; there is taking them up and studying the way. At this time, one thinks and studies
the way; one does not think and studies the way.[8] Some directly transmit
the golden brocade robe and receive the golden brocade robe.[9] Or there
is *"you've gotten my marrow,"* and there is *"making three bows and
standing in place."*[10] There is the study of the mind by means of the mind
that pounds the rice and transmits the robe.[11] To shave the head and dye
the robe is to turn the mind, is to illumine the mind.[12] To leap the wall
and enter the mountains is to exit one mind and enter one mind.[13] That

---

8   **one thinks and studies the way; one does not think and studies the way** (*shiryō
shite gakudō su, fushiryō shite gakudō su* 思量して學道す、不思量して學道す): Allusion to the words, much cited by Dōgen, of Yaoshan Weiyan 藥山惟儼 (751-834);
recorded in Dōgen's *shinji Shōbōgenzō* 眞字正法眼藏 (DZZ.5:196, case 129). See Supplementary Notes, s.v. "Yaoshan's not thinking."

9   **directly transmit the golden brocade robe** (*kinran'e o shōden shi* 金襴衣を正傳
し): Allusion to the legend that Buddha Śākyamuni gave his robe to the First Ancestor
of Zen, Mahākāśyapa, to keep for the coming buddha, Maitreya. (See, e.g., *Tiansheng
guangdeng lu* 天聖廣燈錄, ZZ.135:612a1-4.)

10   **"you've gotten my marrow'"** (*nyo toku go zui* 汝得吾髓); **"making three bows
and standing in place"** (*sanpai e i ni ryū* 三拜依位而立): Allusion to the famous story
of Bodhidharma's testing of his disciples, in which the First Ancestor said to Huike 慧可
that he had gotten his marrow. The version of the story that Dōgen quotes in his "Shōbōgenzō kattō" 正法眼藏葛藤 chapter says that Huike demonstrated his understanding by
"making three bows and standing in place" (*sanpai e i ni ryū* 三拜依位而立). See Supplementary Notes, s.v. "Skin, flesh, bones, and marrow."

11   **study of the mind by means of the mind that pounds the rice and transmits the
robe** (*tai bei den e suru i shin gaku shin* 碓米傳衣する以心學心): "To pound the rice and
transmit the robe" (*tai bei den e* 碓米傳衣) alludes to the biography of Huineng 慧能,
who worked pounding rice at the Fifth Ancestor's monastery before receiving the transmission of Bodhidharma's robe as a token of his recognition as the Sixth Ancestor. (See,
e.g., *Jingde chuandeng lu* 景德傳燈錄, T.2076.51:222c6-223b5; Dōgen's four-character
phrase here does not seem to be common and does not appear elsewhere in his writing.)
"Study the mind by means of the mind" (*i shin gaku shin* 以心學心), another unusual
expression not appearing elsewhere in the *Shōbōgenzō*, is apparently Dōgen's play on
the well-known Chan expression, "transmit the mind by the mind" (*i shin den shin* 以
心傳心).

12   **shave the head and dye the robe** (*tei hatsu zen e* 剃髮染衣): A standard expression
for joining the Buddhist clerical order.

turn the mind (*kaishin* 回心); **illumine the mind** (*myōshin* 明心): The former expression can mean simply to "change one's mind" but is commonly used, as here, in the
sense of spiritual "conversion"; the latter expression, while most often encountered as
the nominative "bright mind," or "lucid mind," is here clearly a verb-object construction.

13   **leap the wall and enter the mountains** (*yujō shi nissan suru* 踰城し入する): Allusion to the legend of Prince Siddhārtha's departure from the palace in search of libera-

4. Studying the Way with Body and Mind *Shinjin gakudō* 身心學道   125

the mountains are entered is "*thinking of not thinking*"; that the world is abandoned is "nonthinking."[14] Having balled this up as one's eye is two or three bushels; having played with this as karmic consciousness is a thousand or ten thousand lengths.[15] In studying the way like this, whether the reward naturally comes from the effort, or the effort has yet to reach the reward, secretly to borrow the nose of the buddhas and ancestors and exhale through it; to take up the hoofs of a donkey and validate with them — these are a model ten thousand ages old.[16]

---

tion; by extension, to leave home and become a renunciant.

exit one mind and enter one mind (*shutsu isshin nyū isshin* 出一心入一心): This could be understood simply to mean that, by leaving home, one moves from one state of mind to another. More likely, given that "the three realms are one mind," both the household life and the life of renunciation occur "within" the one mind.

14 **"thinking of not thinking"** (*shiryō ko fushiryōtei* 思量箇不思量底); **"nonthinking"** (*hishiryō* 非思量): See above, Note 8.

15 **Having balled this up as one's eye is two or three bushels; having played with this as karmic consciousness is a thousand or ten thousand lengths** (*kore o ganzei ni dan shikitaru koto nisan koku, kore o gosshiki ni rō shikitaru koto senman tan nari* これを眼睛に團しきたること二三斛、これを業識に弄しきたること千萬端なり): A sentence subject to varied interpretation. The antecedents of the two pronouns "this" (*kore*) are not clear. Somewhat as in English, the "eye" (*ganzei* 眼睛) typically indicates (a) what is essential or central, and (b) (spiritual) vision, or insight; hence, to "ball up as (or in) one's eye" suggests to "see as something really is." See Supplementary Notes, s.v. "Eye." To "play with karmic consciousness" (*rō gosshiki* 弄業識) is a common expression in Zen literature for being caught up in ordinary, deluded thoughts; some readers follow that negative sense here, but others see our sentence as a playful affirmation of karmic consciousness. See Supplementary Notes, s.v. "Karmic consciousness." "Two or three bushels" (*nisan koku* 二三斛) renders the dry measure *koku* 斛, typically figured at five pecks (*to* 斗); "a thousand or ten thousand lengths" (*senman tan* 千萬端) refers to *tan* 端, a measurement for bolts of cloth, the exact dimensions varying in different periods. A possible interpretation of the two clauses might be something like, "when seen with the eye of wisdom, these [the mountains entered and the world abandoned (?)] are just a bit; when experienced with our ordinary consciousness, they are a lot."

16 **whether the reward naturally comes from the effort, or the effort has yet to reach the reward** (*ukō ni shō onozukara kitari, ushō ni kō imada itarazaredomo* 有功に賞おのづからきたり、有賞に功いまだいたらざれども): Presumably, meaning, "whether or not one has reaped the rewards of his or her Buddhist practice." Dōgen here plays with the term *ukō* 有功 ("effort").

nose of the buddhas and ancestors (*busso no bikū* 佛祖の鼻孔): The term *bikū* 鼻孔 refers both to the nose and the nostrils; often used in Chan texts to indicate (a) the person, especially (b) that which is essential to the person, or (c) the very essence or identity of someone or something. A term occurring frequently in the *Shōbōgenzō*; see Supplementary Notes, s.v. "Nose." To borrow and cause this nose to exhale presumably means to practice just as the buddhas and ancestors do.

hoofs of a donkey (*roba no kyakutei* 驢馬の脚蹄): Likely reflecting a saying of Huanglong Huinan 黃龍慧南 (1002-1069) on which Dōgen comments in the *Eihei kōroku* 永平廣錄 (DZZ.4:8, no. 420). The version recorded in the *Jiatai pudeng lu* 嘉泰

[04:6]

しばらく山河大地・日月星辰、これ心なり。この正當恁麼時、いかなる保任か現前する。山河大地といふは、山河はたとへば山水なり、大地は此處のみにあらず。山もおほかるべし、大須彌・小須彌あり。横に處せるあり、豎に處せるあり。三千界あり、無量國あり。色にかかるあり、空にかかるあり。河もさらにおほかるべし、天河あり、地河あり、四大河あり、無熱池あり。北俱盧洲には四阿耨達池あり、海あり、池あり。地はかならずしも土にあらず、土かならずしも地にあらず。土地もあるべし、心地もあるべし、寶地もあるべし。萬般なりといふとも、地なかるべからず、空を地とせる世界もあるべきなり。日月星辰は、人天の所見不同あるべし、諸類の所見おなじからず。恁麼なるがゆえに、一心の所見、これ一齊なるなり。これらすでに心なり。内なりとやせん、外なりとやせん、來なりとやせん、去なりとやせん。生時は一點を増するか、増せざるか。死には一塵をさるか、さらざるか。この生死および生死の見、いづれのところにおかんとかする。向來はただこれ心の一念二念なり。一念二念は一山河大地なり、二山河大地なり。山河大地等、これ有無にあらざれば、大・小にあらず、得・不得にあらず、識・不識にあらず、通・不通にあらず、悟・不悟に變ぜず。

For now, [let us say that] the mountains, rivers, and the whole earth, the sun, moon, and stars — these are mind.[17] At this very time, taking on what [form] does it appear before us?[18] When we say, "the mountains, rivers, and the whole earth," the "mountains and rivers," for example, are mountains and waters; and "the whole earth" is not merely this place.[19]

普燈錄 (ZZ.137:302c24) reads:

> 舉手問僧、我手何似佛手。垂足曰、我腳何似驢腳。
>
> Raising his hand, he asked a monk, "Why is my hand like a buddha's hand?" Stretching out his leg, he said, "Why is my foot like a donkey's foot?"

To take up and cause these hoofs to seal and verify presumably means to use one's own feet to tread the path of the buddhas and ancestors.

model ten thousand ages old (*banko no bōyō* 萬古の榜樣): I.e., an ancient examplar [of studying the way of the buddhas].

17 mountains, rivers, and the whole earth, the sun, moon, and stars (*senga daichi nichigetsu seishin* 河大地・日月星辰): Common expressions for heaven and earth, appearing frequently in Dōgen's writings; likely reflecting an exchange recorded in the *shinji Shōbōgenzō* 眞字正法眼藏 (DZZ.5:212, case 168). See Supplementary Notes, s.v. "Sun, moon, and stars."

18 taking on what [form] does it appear before us? (*ikanaru hōnin ka genzen suru* いかなる保任か現前する): A tentative translation of a phrase difficult to interpret; taken here to mean "how does the mind appear [when it is mountains, etc.]?" The grammatical subject, *hōnin* 保任 (also read *honin*), a term appearing often in the *Shōbōgenzō*, generally means "to maintain" or "to preserve," "to take responsibility for" or "to be entrusted with"; here, perhaps, "to make one's own."

19 "mountains and rivers," for example, are mountains and waters (*senga wa tatoeba sansui nari* 河はたとへば水なり): Perhaps the point is that mountains and rivers as the mind are the actual physical landscape of the world around us.

4. Studying the Way with Body and Mind *Shinjin gakudō* 身心學道 127

The mountains, too, should be many: there are great Sumerus and small Sumerus; they are situated horizontally; they are situated vertically.[20] There are the three chiliocosms; there are incalculable countries.[21] There are some hanging on form; there are some hanging in emptiness.[22]

And rivers must also be still more numerous: there is the River of Heaven; there are rivers of earth; there are the four great rivers; there is Heatless Lake.[23] On the continent of Uttarakuru, there are four Anavatapta Lakes; there are seas; there are lakes.[24]

Ground is not necessarily soil; soil is not necessarily ground.[25] There must be soil ground; there must be mind ground; there must be jeweled ground.[26] Although they are of myriad types, they must not lack

---

20 **great Sumerus and small Sumerus** (*dai Shumi shō Shumi* 大須彌・小須彌): "Sumeru" is the name of the mountain at the center of a world system in Buddhist cosmology. "Great" and "small" here may reflect the size of the world system.

21 **three chiliocosms** (*sanzenkai* 三千界): Abbreviation of *sanzen daisen sekai* 三千大千世界 ("great threefold thousandfold worlds"), equal to one billion Sumeru world systems.

incalculable countries (*muryō koku* 無量國): Given the context here, this could be taken as a reference to the innumerable buddha lands (*bukkoku* 佛國).

22 **There are some hanging on form; there are some hanging in emptiness** (*shiki ni kakaru ari, kū ni kakaru ari* 色にかかるあり、空にかかるあり): Or "some hanging in the sky"; reading *kū* 空 as "emptiness" (rather than "sky") here, in contrast to "form" (*shiki* 色).

23 **River of Heaven** (*Tenga* 天河): A term for the Milky Way.

four great rivers (*shi daika* 四大河): Usually given as the Gaṅgā, Sindhu, Śītā, and Vākṣu, sometimes identified with the modern Ganges, Indus, Syr Darya, and Amu Darya, respectively.

Heatless Lake (*Munetchi* 無熱池): A Chinese translation of the Sanskrit Anavatapta (*Anokuudatsu* 阿耨達; "unheated"); identified with Lake Manasarovar, in western Tibet, and traditionally thought to be the source of the four great rivers.

24 **Uttarakuru** (*Hokkuro* 北倶盧): The continent to the north of Mount Sumeru in Buddhist cosmology. See Supplementary Notes, s.v. "Four Continents."

four Anavatapta Lakes (*shi Anokudatchi* 四阿耨達池): The source of this claim is unknown. Dōgen has here used the transliteration of the Sanskrit name for the "Heatless Lake" mentioned just above; perhaps representing a confusion with the tradition that this lake was the source of the four rivers.

25 **Ground is not necessarily soil** (*chi wa kanarazushimo do ni arazu* 地はかならずしも土にあらず): The translation of the term *chi* (or *ji*) 地 as "ground" obscures the fact that Dōgen is turning here to his comments on "the whole earth" (*daichi* 大地). He expands the term to include its use as "ground," both in the material and metaphorical senses.

26 **soil ground** (*doji* 土地); **mind ground** (*shinji* 心地); **jeweled ground** (*hōji* 寶地): Three examples of the semantic range of the term *ji* 地: "soil ground" is an overly literal translation for a compound expression meaning "land" (as in "tract of land"); "mind

128   DŌGEN'S *SHŌBŌGENZŌ* VOLUME I

"ground."[27] And there must be worlds in which emptiness represents the ground.[28]

Of the sun, moon, and stars, what is seen by humans and devas must not be the same; what is seen by the various types of beings must not be the same. Such being the case, what is seen by one mind is equivalent.[29]

These are "mind." Can we take them as internal? Can we take them as external? Can we take them as coming? Can we take them as going? When they are born, do they add one iota, or do they not add it? When they die, do they remove one dust mote, or do they not remove it? Where are we to put this birth and death, and the view of birth and death? Up till now has been merely one moment or two moments of mind.[30] "One moment or two moments" is one "mountains, rivers, and the whole earth," is two "mountains, rivers, and the whole earth." Since these "mountains, rivers, and the whole earth" are neither existent nor nonexistent, they are neither large nor small, neither attained nor unattained, neither known nor unknown, neither penetrated nor unpenetrated; nor do they change with awakening or not awakening.

[04:7] {1:47}

かくのごとくの心、みづから學道することを慣習するを、心學道といふと決定信受すべし。この信受、それ大小・有無にあらず。いまの知家非家捨家出家の學道、それ大小の量にあらず、遠近の量にあらず。鼻祖鼻末

---

ground" is a common Buddhist term for the fundamental nature of the mind; "jeweled ground" is a geological feature commonly attributed to the lands ruled over by buddhas.

27   **Although they are of myriad types, they must not lack "ground"** (*banpan nari to iutomo, chi nakaru bekarazu* 萬般なりといふとも、地なかるべからず): A somewhat problematic sentence, taken here to mean that, although the sense of "ground" [in the preceding examples] may be different, each example includes the notion of ground.

28   **there must be worlds in which emptiness represents the ground** (*kū o chii to seru sekai mo aru beki nari* 空を地とせる世界もあるべきなり): Again, reading *kū* 空 as "emptiness," in parallel to the previous concluding remark on mountains. This sentence could also be read, "there are worlds in which the sky represents the ground."

29   **what is seen by one mind is equivalent** (*isshin no shoken, kore issei naru nari* 一心の所見、これ一齊なるなり): A sentence subject to various interpretations, the senses of both *isshin* 一心 ("one mind) and *issei* 一齊 ("equivalent") here being uncertain. Some would take the sentence to mean that "the one mind" (*isshin* 一心) sees all things as equal. In the context here, perhaps a more likely reading would take "one mind" as "each instance of mind," or "any given mind," making the point to be that what each type of being sees is consistent within that type.

30   **Up till now has been merely one moment or two moments of mind** (*kōrai wa tada kore shin no ichinen ninen nari* 向來はただこれ心の一念二念なり): "Up till now" (*kōrai* 向來) should probably be taken as "in our discussion up till now." Here and in the following sentence, *ichinen ninen* 一念二念 ("one moment or two moments") can also be understood as "one thought or two thoughts."

4. Studying the Way with Body and Mind *Shinjin gakudō* 身心學道   129

にあまる、向上向下にあまる。展事あり、七尺八尺なり。投機あり、爲自
爲他なり。恁麽なる、すなはち學道なり。學道は恁麽なるがゆえに、牆壁
瓦礫これ心なり。さらに三界唯心にあらず、法界唯心にあらず、牆壁瓦礫
なり。咸通年前につくり、咸通年後にやぶる。挖泥帶水なり、無繩自縛な
り。玉をひくちからあり、水にいる能あり。とくる日あり、くだくるとき
あり、極微にきはまるときあり。露柱と同參せず、燈籠と交肩せず。かく
のごとくなるゆえに、赤脚走して學道するなり、たれか著眼看せん、翻筋
斗して學道するなり、おのおの隨他去あり。このとき、壁落これ十方を學
せしむ、無門これ四面を學せしむ。

We should firmly believe that such minds themselves becoming accustomed to studying the way is called "the mind studying the way." This belief is not [a matter of] large or small, existent or nonexistent. Studying the way here — which, *knowing the home is not a home, abandons home and leaves home* — is not an amount large or small, not an amount far or near.[31] It exceeds first founder and final follower; it exceeds ascending or descending.[32] There is divulging the matter: it is seven feet or eight feet; there is achieving accord: it is for oneself and for the other.[33]

---

31 **knowing the home is not a home, abandons home and leaves home** (*chi ke hi ke shake shukke* 知家非家捨家出家): Variation on a standard trope in Buddhist literature describing the process by which one "leaves home" (*shukke* 出家) to enter the order (see, e.g., *Mohesengqi lü* 摩訶僧祇律, T.1425.22:227c7-8). Dōgen's version here (repeated in "Shōbōgenzō hotsu bodai shin" 正法眼藏發菩提心) does not seem to correspond exactly to any extant text; more common versions give "believing that one's home is not a home, abandons home and leaves home" (*shin ke hi ke shake shukke* 信家非家捨家出家) or "believing that one's home is not a home, leaves home and studies the way" (*shin ke hi ke shukke gakudō* 信家非家出家學道). Dōgen's "knowing the home is not a home" (*chi ke hi ke* 知家非家) may reflect the *Mohe zhiguan* 摩訶止觀 at T.1911.46:96a20.

32 **first founder and final follower** (*biso bimatsu* 鼻祖鼻末): A loose translation of an unusual expression found also in "Shōbōgenzō busshō" 正法眼藏佛性, here perhaps suggesting the beginning and end of one's Buddhist training. The first element, *biso* 鼻祖, is a common term denoting "founder" or "the first person to do something." Literally translated, it means "ancestor from the nose," thought to reflect an early Chinese belief that the nose is the first part of a creature to take shape in the womb. *Bimatsu* 鼻末 (literally, "the tip of the nose") does not occur by itself but only in combination with *biso*.

ascending or descending (*kōjō kōge* 向上向下): A term also meaning simply "above and below" but used, as perhaps here, to indicate the two phases of the bodhisattva path: "ascending" toward one's own liberation, and "descending" into the world for the sake of sentient beings.

33 **divulging the matter** (*tenji* 展事); **achieving accord** (*tōki* 投機): These two terms regularly occur together in Chan literature, the former used for expressions of what one really thinks; the latter, for expressions that accord with one's interlocutor.

seven feet or eight feet (*shichi shaku hachi shaku* 七尺八尺): Dōgen may have in mind here a conversation between Chan Masters Xuansha Shibei 玄沙師備 (835-908) and Xuefeng Yicun 雪峰義存 (822-908), which he records in his *shinji Shōbōgenzō* 眞字正法眼藏 (DZZ.5:158, case 60), and discusses in "Shōbōgenzō juki" 正法眼藏授記 (DZZ.1:249ff); see Supplementary Notes, s.v. "Seven feet or eight feet."

130 DŌGEN'S *SHŌBŌGENZŌ* VOLUME I

Being like this is studying the way. Because studying the way is like this, "fences, walls, tiles, and pebbles" are mind.[34] It is not furthermore the three realms are only mind; it is not the dharma realm is only mind: it is "fences, walls, tiles, and pebbles."[35] "Before the Xiantong years," it builds them; "after the Xiantong years," it breaks them.[36] It is *dragged through the mud and drenched with water;* it is *binding oneself without a rope.*[37] It has the power to take in a jade; it has the ability to enter the water.[38] There are days when it dissolves; there are times when it shatters; there are times when it is ultimately reduced to atoms. It does not study

---

34 **"fences, walls, tiles, and pebbles"** (*shō heki ga ryaku* 牆壁瓦礫): A set expression for the world of things; see Supplementary Notes. Its identification with the mind is treated below, section 10.

35 **the three realms are only mind** (*sangai yui shin* 三界唯心); **the dharma realm is only mind** (*hokkai yui shin* 法界唯心): For the former phrase, see above, Note 7; the latter, less common phrase does not occur elsewhere in the *Shōbōgenzō*. In this sentence and those that follow here, while no grammatical subject is expressed, the translation assumes the antecedent of "it" is "studying the way."

36 **"Before the Xiantong years"** (*Kantsū nen zen* 咸通年前); **"after the Xiantong years"** (*Kantsū nen go* 咸通年後): Allusion to a saying of Shushan Kuangren 疏匡仁 (837-909) (see, e.g., *Liandeng huiyao* 聯燈會要, ZZ.136:802a14-15), recorded in Dōgen's *shinji Shōbōgenzō* 眞字正法眼藏 (DZZ. 5:270, case 285):

老僧咸通年已前、會法身邊事。咸通年已後、會法身向上事。

Before the Xiantong years, this old monk understood what's in the vicinity of the dharma body; after the Xiantong years, I understood what's beyond the dharma body.

The Xiantong 咸通 era of the Tang dynasty corresponds the years 860-874.

it builds them (*tsukuri* つくり); **it breaks them** (*yaburu* やぶる): Neither the subjects nor the objects of these two verbs is expressed. The translation takes the sense to be that "studying the way" first posits a mind of "fences, walls, tiles, and pebbles" ("what's in the vicinity of the dharma body") and then transcends this ("what's beyond the dharma body").

37 **dragged through the mud and drenched with water** (*dadei taisui* 挖泥帶水): An idiomatic expression for being "sullied" by words and concepts; see Supplementary Notes, s.v. "Dragged through the mud and drenched with water."

binding oneself without a rope (*mujō jibaku* 無繩自縛): A common expression for the state of ignorance, though in the context here, like the preceding phrase, it may refer to the master's "binding" himself to the work of teaching.

38 **take in a jade** (*tama o hiku* 玉をひく): Japanese expression likely reflecting the Chinese idiom *paozhuan yinyu* 抛甎引玉 ("to toss out a tile and take in a jade"); in literary usage, a polite way to ask another for a capping verse for your poem; used in Chan for the give and take between interlocutors. See Supplementary Notes, s.v. "Tossing out a tile and taking in a jade."

enter the water (*mizu ni iru* 水にいる): Thought to allude to a story in the *Nirvāṇa Sūtra* of a wise man who "enters the water" and retrieves a jewel that had been dropped in a lake. (See *Da banniepan jing* 大般涅槃經, T.375.12:617c3-10.) The sūtra goes on to compare the jewel to its doctrine that nirvāṇa is "permanence, bliss, selfhood, and purity" (*jō raku ga jō* 常樂我淨).

4. Studying the Way with Body and Mind *Shinjin gakudō* 身心學道   131

together with the pillars; it does not rub shoulders with the lanterns.[39] Because it is like this, it is studying the way while running barefoot.[40] Who looks at it? It is studying the way while doing flips.[41] Each one "goes along with it."[42] At this time, the walls and fences let it study the ten directions; the lack of gates lets it study the four sides.[43]

[04:8] {1:48}

發菩提心は、あるひは生死にしてこれをうることあり、あるひは涅槃にしてこれをうることあり、あるひは生死・涅槃のほかにしてこれをうることあり。ところをまつにあらざれども、發心のところにさへられざるあり。境發にあらず、智發にあらず、菩提心發なり、發菩提心なり。發菩提心は、有にあらず無にあらず、善にあらず惡にあらず、無記にあらず。報地によりて緣起するにあらず、天有情はさだめてうべからざるにあらず。ただまさに時節とともに發菩提心するなり、依にかかはれざるがゆえに。發菩提心の正當恁麼時には、法界ことごとく發菩提心なり。依を轉ずるに相似なりといへども、依にしらるるにあらず。共出一隻手なり、自出一隻手なり、異類中行なり。地獄・餓鬼・畜生・修羅等のなかにしても發菩提心するなり。

---

39   **study together with the pillars** (*rochū to dōsan* 露柱と同參); **rub shoulders with the lanterns** (*tōrō to kōken* 燈籠と交肩): The "pillars and lanterns" of monastic halls are regularly used in Chan texts in reference to inanimate objects in the immediate surroundings; see Supplementary Notes. The point here is presumably that the mind that studies the way, while it may be defined as "fences, walls, tiles, and pebbles," is not the same as inanimate objects.

40   **running barefoot** (*shakkyakusō* 赤脚走): A phrase, not repeated elsewhere in the *Shōbōgenzō*, perhaps expressing total commitment.

41   **doing flips** (*honkinto* 翻筋斗): An expression, occurring several times in the *Shōbōgenzō*, expressing vigorous energy.

42   **"goes along with it"** (*zui ta ko* 隨他去): From a saying of Dasui Fazhen 大隋法眞 (834-919) that "this" (*zhege* 這箇) "goes along with it" when the chiliocosm is destroyed at the end of the kalpa; see *shinji Shōbōgenzō* 眞字正法眼藏 (DZZ.5:138, case 24); Supplementary Notes, s.v. "Goes along with it."

43   **the walls and fences let it study the ten directions; the lack of gates lets it study the four sides** (*hekiraku kore jippō o gaku seshimu, mumon kore shimen o gaku seshimu* 壁落これ十方を學せしむ、無門これ四面を學せしむ): From a saying by Guanxi Zhixian 灌溪志閑 (d. 895): see, e.g., *Liandeng huiyao* 聯燈會要, ZZ.136:830a13; *Biyan lu* 碧巖錄, T.2003.48:192b10:

十方無壁落、四面亦無門。

The ten directions have no walls or fences; the four sides also have no gates.

132   DŌGEN'S *SHŌBŌGENZŌ* VOLUME I

Bringing forth the mind of bodhi — there is attaining it in birth and death; there is attaining it in nirvāṇa; there is attaining it elsewhere than in birth and death or nirvāṇa. It does not depend on the place; yet bringing forth the mind is not impeded by the place.[44] It is not that sense objects bring it forth; it is not that wisdom brings it forth: it is the mind of bodhi bringing it forth; it is bringing forth the mind of bodhi. Bringing forth the mind of bodhi is not existent, it is not nonexistent; it is not good, it is not evil, it is not neutral. It is not that it arises from conditions depending on one's land of recompense; it is not the case that heavenly beings definitely cannot attain it.[45] We simply bring forth the mind of bodhi in accordance with the time; for it has nothing to do with secondary recompense.[46] At the very moment one brings forth the mind of bodhi, the dharma realm in its entirety brings forth the mind of bodhi. Although it may seem as if one is transforming the secondary recompense, it is not known to the secondary recompense. It is "*together, extending a single hand*"; it is oneself, extending a single hand; it is "*moving among different types.*"[47] Even among those in the hells, hungry ghosts, beasts, *aśura*, and the like, there is the bringing forth of the mind of bodhi.

---

44   **bringing forth the mind is not impeded by the place** (*hosshin no tokoro ni saerarezaru ari* 發心のところにさへられざるあり): The translation takes *ari* here as *nari*; otherwise, perhaps "there are [instances in which] bringing forth the mind is not impeded by the place."

45   **land of recompense** (*hōchi* 報地; or *hōji*): I.e., the realm into which one is born as recompense for past actions.

heavenly beings (*ten ujō* 天有情): Literally, "sentient beings of the heavens"; i.e., the devas, who are often thought of as incapable of producing the aspiration for bodhi.

46   **secondary recompense** (*e* 依): Abbreviation for *ehō* 依報, a standard term for the circumstances into which one is born as recompense for past actions; in contrast to the "primary recompense" (*shōhō* 正報) of one's psychophysical organism. See Supplementary Notes, s.v. "Secondary and primary recompense."

47   **"together, extending a single hand"** (*gu shutsu isseki shu* 共出一隻手): Presumably here, the person and the secondary recompense together. Perhaps reflecting the words of Luoshan Daoxian 羅道閑 (dates unknown), in a story recorded in Dōgen's *shinji Shōbō-genzō* 眞字正法眼藏 (DZZ.5:174, case 97): A monk asked Luoshan how much he should pay to have a stūpa built. Luoshan said,

若將三文錢與匠人、和尚此生決定不得塔。若將兩文錢與匠人、和尚與匠人共出一隻手。若將一文錢與匠人、帶累匠人眉鬚墮落。

If you offer the artisan three cash, the Reverend will definitely not get a stūpa in this lifetime. If you offer the artisan two cash, the Reverend and the artisan will together extend a single hand. If you offer the artisan one cash, you'll so perplex him that the artisan's eyebrows and beard will fall off.

"moving among different types" (*irui chū gyō nari* 異類中行なり): A fixed expression that denotes rebirth in any of the six paths other than the human, especially that of animals; usually used to describe the salvific activities of the bodhisattvas. Its use is especially associated with Nanchuan Puyuan 南泉普願 (748-835) (see, e.g., *Zongmen*

4. Studying the Way with Body and Mind *Shinjin gakudō* 身心學道   133

[04:9]

赤心片片といふは、片片なるはみな赤心なり。一片・兩片にあらず、片片なるなり。荷葉團團團似鏡、菱角尖尖尖似錐。かがみに似たりといふとも片片なり、錐に似たりといふとも片片なり。

"Bare mind in pieces" means that what is "in pieces" is all the "bare mind."[48] It is not one piece or two pieces: it is "in pieces."

The leaves of the lotus are round, round, round like a mirror;
The horns of the water caltrop are sharp, sharp, sharp like an awl.[49]

Though one may say it is "like a mirror," it is "in pieces"; though one may say it is "like an awl," it is "in pieces."

[04:10]

古佛心といふは、むかし僧ありて大證國師にとふ、いかにあらんかこれ古佛心。ときに國師いはく、牆壁瓦礫。

"Old buddha mind": Long ago, there was a monk who asked the National Teacher Dazheng, "What is the old buddha mind?" Whereupon, the National Teacher said, "Fences, walls, tiles, and pebbles."[50]

[04:11]

しかあればしるべし、古佛心は牆壁瓦礫にあらず、牆壁瓦礫を古佛心といふにあらず。古佛心、それかくのごとく學するなり。

Thus, we should understand that the "old buddha mind" is not "fences, walls, tiles, and pebbles"; "fences, walls, tiles, and pebbles" are not called the "old buddha mind." "Old buddha mind" — this is how it is studied.

---

tongyao ji 宗門統要集, ZTS.1:148a14; quoted in *shinji Shōbōgenzō* 眞字正法眼藏, DZZ.5:154, case 57). See Supplementary Notes, s.v. "Move among different types." The grammatical subject here is not clear; given the context, likely "the bringing forth of (or the one who brings forth) the mind of bodhi."

48 **"Bare mind in pieces"** (*sekishin henpen* 赤心片片): A common expression in Chan texts, often understood as a sincere mind in every matter; see Supplementary Notes, s.v. "Bare mind in pieces." Dōgen here begins his discussion of the three Chan phrases on mind that he introduced above, in section 4.

49 **The leaves of the lotus are round, round, round like a mirror; the horns of the water caltrop are sharp, sharp, sharp like an awl** (*kayō dandan dan i kyō, ryōkaku sen sen sen i sui* 荷葉團團團似鏡、菱角尖尖尖似錐): Quotation of a popular Chan saying, attributed to Jiashan Shanhui 夾善會 (805-881) (see, e.g., *Liandeng huiyao* 聯燈會要, ZZ.136:774b4-5).

50 **"old buddha mind"** (*kobutsushin* 古佛心): Second of the phrases on mind introduced in section 4.

National Teacher Dazheng (*Daishō kokushi* 大證國師): I.e., Nanyang Huizhong 南陽慧忠 (d. 775), disciple of the Sixth Ancestor. For his saying here, see Supplementary Notes, s.v. "Fences, walls, tiles, and pebbles." Dōgen discusses this exchange in his "Shōbōgenzō kobutsushin" 正法眼藏古佛心 (DZZ.1:89).

134 DŌGEN'S *SHŌBŌGENZŌ* VOLUME I

[04:12] {1:49}

平常心といふは、此界・他界といはず、平常心なり。昔日はこのところよりさり、今日はこのところよりきたる。さるときは漫天さり、きたるときは盡地きたる、これ平常心なり。平常心、この屋裡に開門す、千門萬戸一時開閉なるゆえに平常なり。いまこの蓋天蓋地は、おぼえざることばのごとし、噴地の一聲のごとし。語等なり、心等なり、法等なり。壽行生滅の、刹那に生滅するあれども、最後身よりさきはかつてしらず。しらざれども、發心すれば、かならず菩提の道にすすむなり。すでにこのところあり、さらにあやしむべきにあらず。すでにあやしむことあり、すなはち平常なり。

"Ordinary mind": it is the ordinary mind without reference to this world or other worlds.[51] Yesterday leaves from this place; today comes from this place. When it leaves, the whole of heaven leaves; when it comes, all the earth comes. This is "ordinary mind." The ordinary mind opens the gates to the interior of the house. Since a thousand gates, ten thousand doors, open and close simultaneously, it is "ordinary."[52] This covering of heaven and covering of earth is like words not remembered, like the sound of a sneeze.[53] The words are equal, the minds are equal, the dharmas are equal.[54] While the arising and ceasing throughout our lives arise and cease

---

51 **"Ordinary mind"** (*byōjō shin* 平常心): The third of the three phrases on mind introduced in section 4. The expression "the ordinary mind" is perhaps best known in the saying, "The ordinary mind is the way" (*byōjō shin ze dō* 平常心是道), attributed to Nanquan Puyuan 南泉普願; see Supplementary Notes, s.v. "Ordinary mind is the way."

this world or other worlds (*shikai takai* 此界他界): Terms of ambiguous referent. Depending on context, *shikai* 此界 ("this world") can indicate (a) the Sahā world (*shaba sekai* 娑婆世界), the world of Buddha Śākyamuni; or (b) the human realm (*ningen* 人間), as opposed to other realms of saṃsāra. Similarly, *takai* 他界 ("other worlds") can refer to (a) other buddha lands, or (b) other realms of saṃsāra; it can also be translated in the singular, as a reference (much like the English "the other world") to (c) the world of the dead, of spirits, etc.

52 **a thousand gates, ten thousand doors** (*senmon banko* 千門萬戸): A fairly common expression for the multiplicity of "entrances" to the dharma; their "opening and closing" here may reflect a question of Yungai Zhiyuan 雲蓋志元 (dates unknown) at *Jingde chuandeng lu* 景德傳燈錄 (T.2076.51:321a8-9):

萬戸俱閉即不問。萬戸俱開時如何。

"I don't ask about when the myriad doors all close, but how about when the myriad doors all open?"

53 **covering of heaven and covering of earth** (*gaiten gaichi* 蓋天蓋地): I.e., the entire expanse of heaven and earth; roughly synonymous with the previous "whole of heaven" (*manten* 漫天) and "all the earth" (*jinchi* 盡地).

like words not remembered, like the sound of a sneeze (*oboezaru kotoba no gotoshi, funchi no issei no gotoshi* おぼえざることばのごとし、噴地の一聲のごとし): Perhaps best taken to mean sounds unintelligible to the hearer.

54 **The words are equal, the minds are equal, the dharmas are equal** (*gotō nari, shintō nari, hōtō nari* 語等なり、心等なり、法等なり): Perhaps a variation on the four

4. Studying the Way with Body and Mind *Shinjin gakudō* 身心學道   135

each *kṣaṇa*, we will never know this before our final body.[55] Nevertheless, because we bring forth the mind [of bodhi], we inevitably progress on the way of bodhi. We already have this place; we should not harbor any further doubts. We do already harbor doubts; this is "ordinary."

* * * * *

[04:13]

身學道といふは、身にて學道するなり、赤肉團の學道なり。身は學道より
きたり、學道よりきたれるは、ともに身なり。盡十方界是箇眞實人體
なり、生死去來眞實人體なり。この身體をめぐらして、十惡をはなれ、八
戒をたもち、三寶に歸依して、捨家出家する、眞實の學道なり。このゆえ
に、眞實人體といふ。後學かならず目然見の外道に同ずることなかれ。

"Body studying the way" means to study the way with the body, it is the study of the way of the lump of red meat.[56] The body comes from studying the way, and whatever comes from studying the way is "body."[57] It is *"all the worlds in the ten directions are this true human body"*; it is *"birth and death, coming and going, are the true human body."*[58] Turning this body and leaving the ten evils, keeping the eight precepts, and taking refuge in the three treasures, to *"abandon the home and leave the home"* — this is the true study of the way.[59] Thus, it is called the "true human

---

ways in which buddhas are said to be the same according to the *Laṅkāvatāra Sūtra* (*Dasheng ru lengqie jing* 大乘入楞伽經, T.672.16:608b02): sameness of title (*ji byōdō* 字平等), sameness of speech (*go byōdō* 語平等), sameness of body (*shin byōdō* 身平等), sameness of dharma (*hō byōdō* 法平等). Most readers, however, take Dōgen's sense to be here that words, minds, and dharmas are all equivalent — i.e., match each other and the "covering of heaven and covering of earth." (See, e.g., *Shōbōgenzō keiteki* 正法眼藏啓迪 3:314.)

55 *kṣaṇa* (*setsuna* 刹那): Transliteration of the Sanskrit for "instant."

final body (*saigo shin* 最後身): I.e., our final rebirth on the bodhisattva path to bodhi.

56 **lump of red meat** (*shaku nikudan* 赤肉團): A common expression for the physical body.

57 **The body comes from studying the way** (*shin wa gakudō yori kitari* 身は學道より
きたり): Perhaps expressing a common Buddhist conviction that our fortunate birth as humans reflects the karma of spiritual practice in past lives.

58 **"all the worlds in the ten directions are this true human body"** (*jin jippō kai ze ko shinjitsu nintai* 盡十方界是箇眞實人體): Words attributed to Xuansha Shibei 玄沙師備; see Dōgen's *shinji Shōbōgenzō* 眞字正法眼藏, DZZ.5:196, case 131; and Supplementary Notes, s.v. "True human body."

"birth and death, coming and going, are the true human body" (*shōji korai shinjitsu nintai* 生死去來眞實人體): Likely reflecting the words of Yuanwu Keqin 圓悟克勤 (1063-1135); see Supplementary Notes, s.v. "True human body."

59 **ten evils** (*jūaku* 十惡): (1) killing, (2) stealing, (3) sexual misconduct, (4) lying, (5) frivolous speech, (6) insult, (7) slander, (8) coveting, (9) anger, and (10) false views.

136　　DŌGEN'S *SHŌBŌGENZŌ* VOLUME I

body." Later students, never be like those of the other path that holds the view of spontaneous occurrence.[60]

[04:14]

百丈大智禪師のいはく、若執本清淨・本解脱自是佛、自是禪道解者、即属自然外道。

Chan Master Dazhi of Baizhang said, "*One who clings to the understanding that you are inherently pure and inherently liberated, that you are naturally a buddha and naturally on the way of Chan, belongs to the other path of spontaneous occurrence.*"[61]

[04:15] {1:50}

これら閑家の破具にあらず、學道の積功累德なり。踍跳して玲瓏八面なり、脱落して如藤倚樹なり。或現此身得度而爲説法なり、或現他身得度而爲説法なり、或不現此身得度而爲説法なり、或不現他身得度而爲説法なり、乃至不爲説法なり。

These are not the broken furniture of a vacant house; they are the accumulation of the merit and amassing of the virtue of studying the way.[62] He springs up, and it is crystal clear on all eight sides; he sloughs off, and it is "like vines clinging to a tree."[63] *He manifests this body, attains deliverance, and preaches the dharma to them; or he manifests another*

---

eight precepts (*hakkai* 八戒): A set of precepts followed by the laity on specific days of the month: (1) not to kill, (2) not to steal, (3) not to engage in sexual misconduct, (4) not to lie, (5) not to drink alcohol, (6) not to indulge in adornments or entertainments, (7) not to sleep on fine beds, and (8) not to eat after noon.

60　**other path that holds the view of spontaneous occurrence** (*jinen ken no gedō* 自然見の外道): I.e., non-Buddhist religious teachings (like the so-called Cārvākas, often criticized in Indian Buddhist literature) that claim events occur of their own accord or accidentally, not by reason of prior cause.

61　**Chan Master Dazhi of Baizhang** (*Hyakujō Daichi zenji* 百丈大智禪師): I.e, Baizhang Huaihai 百丈懷海 (749-814). His remark can be found at *Guzunsu yulu* 古尊宿語録, ZZ.118:173b15-16.

62　**These are not the broken furniture of a vacant house** (*korera kanka no hagu ni arazu* これら閑家の破具にあらず): The antecedent of *korera* これら ("these") is not certain; in the context, likely Baizhang's words.

63　**He springs up, and it is crystal clear on all eight sides** (*botchō shite reirō hachimen nari* 踍跳して玲瓏八面なり): The unusual term *botchō* 踍跳 (translated here "springs up") seems akin to the more common *chōshutsu* 跳出 ("to jump out," "to jump beyond") — i.e., "to escape" or "to transcend." The grammatical subject here is unstated; the translation takes it as the speaker, Baizhang. *Reirō hachimen* 玲瓏八面 is a variant of "the eight sides are crystal clear" (*hachimen reirō* 八面玲瓏), a common term for perfect clarity; see Supplementary Notes, s.v. "Crystal clear on all eight sides."

he sloughs off, and it is "like vines relying on a tree" (*datsuraku shite nyo tō i ju nari* 脱落して如藤倚樹なり): See Supplementary Notes, s.v. "Slough off," and "Like vines relying on a tree." The phrase "like the wisteria clinging to the tree" comes from a saying

4. Studying the Way with Body and Mind *Shinjin gakudō* 身心學道   137

*body, attains deliverance, and preaches the dharma to them; or he does
not manifest this body, attains deliverance, and preaches the dharma to
them; or he does not manifest another body, attains deliverance, and
preaches the dharma to them; and so forth, till we come to, he does not
preach the dharma to them.*[64]

[04:16]

しかあるに、棄身するところに揚聲止響することあり、捨命するところに
斷腸得髓することあり。たとひ威音王よりさきに發足學道すれども、なほ
これみづからが兒孫として增長するなり。

Still, where he discards his body, there is *"raising one's voice to stop
the echo"*; where he abandons his life, there is *cutting one's guts and getting the marrow.*[65] Even those who set out to study the way before King

---

attributed to Weishan Lingyou 潙山靈祐 (771-853), recorded at *shinji Shōbōgenzō* 眞字
正法眼藏, DZZ.5:208, case 157.

64 He manifests this body, attains deliverance, and preaches the dharma to them
(*waku gen shishin tokudo ni i seppō* 或現此身得度而爲説法): Dōgen here shifts to Chinese, in playful variation on the famous passage in the *Lotus Sūtra* describing the thirty-three manifestations of Bodhisattva Avalokiteśvara. The passage (at *Miaofa lianhua
jing* 妙法蓮華經, T.262.9:57a23ff) begins:

佛告無盡意菩薩、善男子、若有國土衆生應以佛身得度者、觀世音菩薩即現佛身
而爲説法。

The Buddha said to Bodhisattva Akṣayamati, "Good man, if there are living beings
in the land who ought to attain deliverance by a buddha body, then Bodhisattva
Avalokiteśvara manifests a buddha body and preaches the dharma to them."

65 Still, where he discards his body, there is "raising one's voice to stop the echo"
(*shika aru ni, kishin suru tokoro ni yōshō shigo suru koto ari* しかあるに、棄身すると
ころに揚聲止響することあり): Continuing to take Baizhang as the unexpressed subject. "Raising one's voice to stop an echo" (*yōshō shigo* 揚聲止響) is an expression
found in words attributed to the sixth-century Layman Xiang (*Xiang jushi* 向居士); see
Jingde chuandeng lu 景德傳燈錄, T.2076.51:221b13-16:

影由形起、響逐聲來。弄影勞形、不識形爲影本。揚聲止響、不知聲是響根。除
煩惱而趣涅槃、喻去形而覓影。離衆生而求佛果。喻默聲而求響。

The shadow arises from the shape; the echo comes from the voice. To play with the
shadow to work on the shape is not to recognize that the shape is the basis of the
shadow. To raise one's voice to stop the echo is not to realize that the voice is the root
of the echo. To eliminate the afflictions to hurry to nirvāṇa is like getting rid of the
shape and looking for its shadow. To separate from living beings and seek the fruit
of buddhahood is like silencing the voice and seeking its echo.

The expression in the original is clearly critical of a confusion of cause and effect, but
some would give Dōgen's use of it in this context a positive interpretation; see, e.g.,
Shōbōgenzō keiteki 正法眼藏啓迪 3:324.

cutting one's guts and getting the marrow (*danchō tokuzui* 斷腸得髓): The second
element here alludes to the well-known story of Bodhidharma's having said of his disciple Huike 慧可 that he had "got his marrow" (*tokuzui* 得髓). See Supplementary Notes,
s.v. "Skin, flesh, bones, and marrow." The term *danchō* 斷腸, translated literally here

138 DŌGEN'S *SHŌBŌGENZŌ* VOLUME I

Majestic Voice, he fosters as his own descendants.[66]

[04:17]

盡十方世界といふは、十方面ともに盡界なり。東西南北四維上下を、十方といふ。かの表裏縦横の究盡なる時節を思量すべし。思量するといふは、人體はたとひ自他に罣礙せらるといふとも、盡十方なりと諦觀し決定するなり。これ未曾聞をきくなり。方等なるゆえに、界等なるゆえに。人體は四大五蘊なり、大塵ともに凡夫の究盡するところにあらず、聖者の參究するところなり。又、一塵に十方を諦觀すべし、十方は一塵に囊括するにあらず。あるひは一塵に僧堂・佛殿を建立し、あるひは僧堂・佛殿に、盡界を建立せり。これより建立せり、建立、これよりなれり。恁麼の道理、すなはち盡十方界眞實人體なり。自然・天然の邪見をならふべからず。界量にあらざれば廣狭にあらず。盡十方界は、八萬四千の説法蘊なり、八萬四千の三昧なり、八萬四千の陀羅尼なり。八萬四千の説法蘊、これ轉法輪なるがゆえに、法輪の轉處は、互界なり、互時なり。方域なきにあらず、眞實人體なり。いまのなんぢ、いまのわれ、盡十方界眞實人體なる人なり。これらを蹉過することなく學道するなり。たとひ三大阿僧祇劫、十三大阿僧祇劫、無量阿僧祇劫までも、捨身・受身しもてゆく、かならず學道の時節なる、進歩退歩學道なり。禮拜問訊する、すなはち動止威儀なり。枯木を畫圖し、死灰を磨甎す、しばらくの間斷あらず。暦日は短促なりといへども、學道は幽遠なり。捨家出家せる風流、たとひ蕭然なりとも、樵夫に混同することなかれ。活計たとひ競頭すとも、佃戸に一齊なるにあらず。迷悟・善惡の論に比することなかれ、邪正・眞僞の際にとどむることなかれ。

"All the worlds in the ten directions" means that the ten directions are "all the worlds."[67] East, west, south, and north, the four ordinal points, and up and down, are called the "ten directions." We should think about the time when their surface and interior, length and breadth, are exhaustively investigated.[68] To "think about" means to perceive clearly and be

---

as "cutting one's guts," has the common meaning, "to be in great pain." As others have suggested, it may be that it should be replaced here by the more common *danpi* 斷臂 ("cutting the arm"), in reference to the famous legend that Huike cut off his arm in order to become Bodhidharma's disciple. See Supplementary Notes, s.v. "Cut off an arm."

66   **before King Majestic Voice** (*Ion'ō yori saki ni* 威音王よりさきに): A common expression, occurring often in Dōgen's writing and other Zen texts, used to suggest the primordial past or a state prior to any differentiation; see Supplementary Notes, s.v. "Before King Majestic Voice."

67   **"All the worlds in the ten directions"** (*jin jippō sekai* 盡十方世界): Dōgen here turns to a discussion of the expression, introduced above (section 13), "all the worlds in the ten directions are this true human body" (*jin jippō kai ze ko shinjitsu nintai* 盡十方界是箇眞實人體).

68   **the time when their surface and interior, length and breadth, are exhaustively investigated** (*kano hyōri jūo no gūjin naru jisetsu* かの表裏縦横の究盡なる時節): The translation obscures the fact that Dōgen is playing on the adjective *jin* 盡 in the phrase *jinkai* 盡界 ("all the worlds"), shifting its sense from the quantitative "all" to the qualitative "exhaustive" (as in "exhaustively investigated"; *gūjin* 究盡.), and treating it as

4. Studying the Way with Body and Mind *Shinjin gakudō* 身心學道 139

certain that, though "the human body" may be obstructed by self and other, it is "all the ten directions." This is hearing something never heard before; for the directions are the same, for the worlds are the same.[69] "The human body" is "the four elements and five aggregates."[70] The elements and the dusts are not something exhaustively investigated by common people; they are what is investigated by the sages.[71] Moreover, we should clearly perceive the ten directions in a single dust mote. It is not that the ten directions are bundled up in a single dust mote. Sometimes, we construct a saṃgha hall or a buddha hall in a single dust mote; sometimes we construct all the worlds in a saṃgha hall or buddha hall. They have been constructed from this; the construction has come about from this.[72]

Such a principle is *the true human body of all the worlds in the ten directions.* We should not learn the false view that things arise spontaneously or occur naturally. Since there is no measure of the worlds, they are not wide or narrow. "All the worlds in the ten directions" are the aggregate of eighty-four thousand dharmas, are the eighty-four thousand samādhis, are the eighty-four thousand *dhāraṇīs.*[73] Because the aggregate of the eighty-four thousand dharmas is turning the wheel of the dharma, where the dharma wheel turns spans the worlds, spans time. It is not without location; it is the "true human body." The present you and the present I are the humans that are *the true human body of all the worlds in the ten directions.* We study the way without ever missing

---

modifying "the ten directions," rather than "the worlds."

69 **for the directions are the same, for the worlds are the same** (*hōtō naru yue ni, kaitō naru yue ni* 方等なるゆえに、界等なるゆえに): Recalling this usage above, section 12; typically taken here to mean that the directions and the worlds are equal.

70 **"The human body" is "the four elements and five aggregates"** (*nintai wa shidai goun nari* 人體は四大五蘊なり): Presumably, reflecting the words of Xuansha Shibei 玄沙師備 cited above, Note 58. See Supplementary Notes, s.v. "Four elements and five aggregates."

71 **the elements and the dusts are not something exhaustively investigated by common people** (*dai jin tomo ni bonbu no gūjin suru tokoro ni arazu* 大塵ともに凡夫の究盡するところにあらず): "Dusts" here refers to the objects of the six senses; the literal translation seeks to convey something of the play with the term here in the following expression "single dust mote" (*ichijin* 一塵). See Supplementary Notes, s.v. "Dust."

72 **They have been constructed from this** (*kore yori konryū seri* これより建立せり): The grammatical subject is unexpressed and the antecedent of "this" (*kore* これ) is open to interpretation.

73 **aggregate of eighty-four thousand dharmas** (*hachiman shisen no seppōun* 八萬四千の説法蘊): I.e., the entire body of the buddddhist teachings. "Eighty-four thousand" (*hachiman shisen* 八萬四千) is a standard expression for a great number.

140 DŌGEN'S *SHŌBŌGENZŌ* VOLUME I

these.[74] Whether for three great *asaṃkhyeya-kalpas*, for thirteen great *asaṃkhyeya-kalpas*, for incalculable *asaṃkhyeya-kalpas*, the continued casting aside a body and receiving a body are invariably a study of the way, stepping forward and stepping back, that is the time of studying the way.[75] Paying obeisance and making inquiries is deportment in motion and rest.[76] One depicts the dried-up tree and polishes the tile of dead ashes, without the slightest interruption.[77] Though the passing days are short and pressing, the study of the way is deep and distant. Though the style of one who abandons home and leaves home is lonely, do not confuse it with that of the woodcutter. Though his way of life is a struggle, it is not the same as that of the tenant farmer. Do not compare them in discussions of delusion and awakening, good and evil; do not stay within the limits of false and true, real and spurious.

[04:18] {1:51}
生死去來眞實人體といふは、いはゆる生死は凡夫の流轉なりといへども、大聖の所脱なり。超凡越聖せん、これを眞實體とするのみにあらず。これに二種・七種のしなあれど 、究盡するに、面面みな生死なるゆえに、恐怖すべきにあらず。ゆえいかんとなれば、いまだ生をすてざれども、いま

---

74 **We study the way without ever missing these** (*korera o shaka suru koto naku gakudō suru nari* これらを蹉過することなく學道するなり): The antecedent of "these" (*korera* これら) is unclear; perhaps, "all the worlds in the ten directions."

75 **three great *asaṃkhyeya-kalpas*** (*san dai asōgi kō* 三大阿僧祇劫): "Three great incalculable æons," a standard measure of the time required to attain buddhahood on the bodhisattva path.

casting aside a body and receiving a body (*shashin jushin* 捨身受身): I.e., dying and being reborn.

study of the way, stepping forward and stepping back, that is the time of studying the way (*gakudō no jisetsu naru, shinpo taiho gakudō* 學道の時節なる、進歩退歩學道): An awkward phrase, likely meaning that the time of studying the way is made up of the ongoing practice of "stepping forward and stepping back" (*shinpo taiho* 進歩退歩), an expression that can refer to ordinary activities or, more specifically, to movement forward and back; see Supplementary Notes, s.v. "Stepping forward and stepping back."

76 **Paying obeisance and making inquiries** (*raihai monjin* 禮拜問訊): In Zen practice, to "make inquiries" (*monjin* 問訊) refers to a formal bow of greeting, with hands together.

77 **One depicts the dried-up tree and polishes the tile of dead ashes** (*koboku o gazu shi, shikai o masen su* 枯木を畫圖し、死灰を磨甎す): An odd mixing of Chan expressions, presumably in ironic reference to Zen training. The idiom "dried-up trees and dead ashes" (*koboku shikai* 枯木死灰) is a metaphor typically used, often pejoratively, in reference to meditation; hence, "depicting the dried-up tree" suggests depicting meditation practice. See Supplementary Notes, s.v. "Dried-up tree." "Polishing a tile" (*masen* 磨甎) alludes to the famous story, often cited in the *Shōbōgenzō*, of Nanyue Huairang's 南嶽懷讓 description of the futility of trying to make a buddha by sitting in meditation as "polishing a tile to make a mirror" (*shinji Shōbōgenzō* 眞字正法眼藏, DZZ.5:128, case 8); see Supplementary Notes, s.v. "Nanyue polishes a tile."

4. Studying the Way with Body and Mind *Shinjin gakudō* 身心學道　　141

すでに死をみる。いまだ死をすてざれども、いますでに生をみる。生は死
を罣礙するにあらず、死は生を罣礙するにあらず。生死ともに凡夫のしる
ところにあらず。生は栢樹子のごとし、死は鐵漢のごとし。栢樹はたとひ
栢樹に礙せらるとも、生はいまだ死に礙せられざるがゆえに學道なり。生
は一枚にあらず、死は兩疋にあらず。死の生に相對するなし、生の死に相
待するなし。

"Birth and death, coming and going, are the true human body": while "birth and death" here may refer to the drifting about of the common person, it is what is discarded by the great sages.[78] While one may *transcend the commoner and surpass the sage*, not only does this represent the true body, but in this, while there are twofold and sevenfold types, when exhaustively investigated, we should not fear them, for each and every one of them is birth and death.[79] When we ask why, even though we have not abandoned birth, we already now see death; though we have not abandoned death, we already now see birth. Birth does not obstruct death; death does not obstruct birth. Birth and death are not what is understood by the common people. Birth is like the cypress tree; death is like the iron man: although the cypress tree is obstructed by the cypress

---

78　**"Birth and death, coming and going, are the true human body"** (*shōji korai shinjitsu nintai* 生死去來眞實人體): See above, Note 58, for the source. The term *shōji* 生死 can indicate both "birth and death" and "life and death"; for consistency's sake, the translation here will stick to the former, even when, as might sometimes be the case in this passage, the latter would seem more natural.

drifting about of the common person (*bonbu no ruten* 凡夫の流轉): I.e., the process of rebirth experienced by the ordinary human. The "great sages," or "great nobles" (*daishō* 大聖) are the advanced Buddhist adepts.

79　**transcend the commoner and surpass the sage** (*chōbon osshō* 超凡越聖): I.e., to go beyond the stages of the Buddhist spiritual path; a common expression in Zen literature. The point of this sentence is that even those who transcend the most advanced spiritual adepts share the true human body of birth and death, coming and going.

twofold and sevenfold types (*nishu shichishu no shina* 二種七種のしな): I.e., (a) a standard Buddhist twofold classification of rebirth into (1) the reincarnation of sentient beings according to their karma, known as "delimited birth and death" (*bundan shōji* 分段生死; S. *pariccheda-jarā-maraṇa*), and (2) the incarnations of advanced bodhisattvas according to their salvific purposes, known as "transformational birth and death" (*henyaku shōji* 變易生死; S. *parinamiki-jarā-maraṇa*); and (b) a sevenfold classification, perhaps of the sort found, for example, in the *Zhiguan fuxing zhuan hongjue* 止觀輔行傳弘決 (T.1912.46:358a21-25), by the Tiantai author Zhanran 湛然 (711-782): (1) "delimited birth and death" (*bundan shoji* 分段生死); (2) "birth and death drifting" (*ryūrai shoji* 流來生死), the beginning of ignorance; (3) "birth and death of resistance" (*hanshutsu shoji* 反出生死), turning away from delusion; (4) "birth and death of expedients" (*hōben shoji* 方便生死), entering the nirvāṇa of the two vehicles; (5) "birth and death and causes and conditions" (*innen shoji* 因緣生死), above the first bodhisattva stage; (6) "birth and death with remainder" (*ugo shōji* 有後生死), the tenth bodhisattva stage; (7) "birth and death without remainder" (*mugo shōji* 無後生死), the vajra mind.

142　　　　DŌGEN'S *SHŌBŌGENZŌ* VOLUME I

tree, because birth is not obstructed by death, it is studying the way.[80] Birth is not one thing; death is not a second thing.[81] Death is not opposed to birth; birth is not relative to death.

[04:19] {1:52}
圜悟禪師いわく、生也全機現、死也全機現、闇塞大虚空、赤心常片片。

　　Chan Master Yuanwu said,

Alive, the manifestation of the full function;
Dead, the manifestation of the full function.
Filling the whole of empty space,
The bare mind, always in pieces.[82]

80　**Birth is like the cypress tree; death is like the iron man** (*shō wa hakujushi no gotoshi, shi wa tekkan no gotoshi* 生は栢樹子のごとし、死は鐵漢のごとし): Why Dōgen chose these two particular similes for birth and death is not clear, and no source in which they are meaningfully juxtaposed has been identified. While in popular discourse, the cypress was associated with longevity or eternal life and the man of iron was a symbol of manliness, we do not know that Dōgen had such connotations in mind. In Zen texts, the cypress tree is best known from a famous saying of Zhaozhou Congshen 趙州從諗 (778-897); see Supplementary Notes, s.v. "Cypress tree at the front of the garden." "The man of iron" (*tekkan* 鐵漢) appears regularly in Zen texts and in the *Shōbōgenzō* for the solid practitioner; see Supplementary Notes, s.v. "Man of iron."

although the cypress tree is obstructed by the cypress tree, because birth is not obstructed by death, it is studying the way (*hakuju wa tatoi hakuju ni ge serarutomo, shō wa imada shi ni ge serarezaru ga yue ni gakudō nari* 栢樹はたとひ栢樹に礙せらるとも、生はいまだ死に礙せられざるがゆえに學道なり): The antecedent of "it" in the translation is not clear; indeed, the sentence could be read, "they [i.e., birth and death] are the study of the way." The pattern "A is obstructed by A" is very common in Dōgen's writing, seemingly used in the sense "A is just A," "A is completely A." The point here, then, would seem to be that, in the study of the way, birth is just birth and death is just death.

81　**Birth is not one thing; death is not a second thing** (*shō wa ichimai ni arazu, shi wa ryōhitsu ni arazu* 生は一枚にあらず、死は兩疋にあらず): Or, perhaps, "birth is not one sheet; death is not two head." The translation ignores the playful numerical counters *mai* 枚, used for flat objects, and *hitsu* (or *hiki*) 疋, used for horses (and lengths of cloth).

82　**Chan Master Yuanwu** (*Engo zenji* 圜悟禪師): I.e., Yuanwu Keqin 圜悟克勤 (1063–1135). His words here represent the first two and last two phrases of a verse comment in eight phrases that he wrote on a conversation involving Daowu Yuanzhi 道悟圓智 (769–835) and the latter's dharma heir Jianyuan Zhongxing 漸源仲興 (dates unknown). For the conversation and Yuanwu's entire verse, see Supplementary Notes, s.v. "Manifestation of the full function."

Alive, the manifestation of the full function; Dead, the manifestation of the full function (*shō ya zenki gen, shi ya zenki gen* 生也全機現、死也全機現): The translation here and below of *shō* 生 and *shi* 死 as "alive" and "dead" respectively (rather than "birth" and "death") reflects the fact that, in the original text, Yuanwu is commenting on a conversation over whether a corpse is alive or dead. In which sense Dōgen took the terms in his comments below is unclear.

4. Studying the Way with Body and Mind *Shinjin gakudō* 身心學道　143

[04:20]

この道著、しづかに功夫點撿すべし。圜悟禪師かつて恁麼いふといへども、なおいまだ生死の全機にあまれることをしらず。去來を參學するに、去に生死あり、來に生死あり。生に去來あり、死に去來あり。去來は、盡十方界を兩翼三翼として飛去飛來す、盡十方界を三足五足として進歩退歩するなり。生死を頭尾として、盡十方界眞實人體は、よく翻身回腦するなり。翻身回腦するに、如一錢大なり、似微塵裡なり。平坦坦地、それ壁立千仞なり。壁立千仞處、それ平坦坦地なり。このゆえに、南洲・北洲の面目あり、これを撿して學道す。非想非非想の骨髓あり、これを抗して學道するのみなり。

We should quietly make concentrated effort to examine these words. Chan Master Yuanwu, though he may have spoken like this, does not yet understand that birth and death have exceeded "full function."[83] In studying "coming and going," there is birth and death in "going"; there is birth and death in "coming." There is coming and going in "birth"; there is coming and going in "death." With all the worlds in the ten directions as its two wings or its three wings, coming and going goes flying away and comes flying back; with all the worlds in the ten directions as its three feet or its five feet, it steps forward and steps back. With birth and death as its head and tail, *the true human body of all the worlds in the ten directions* flips its body and spins its brain.[84] When it flips its body and spins its brain, it is the size of a coin, it is like the interior of an infinitesimal dust mote. "Level and flat, it's a wall rising a thousand fathoms; where the wall rises a thousand fathoms, it's level and flat."[85] Therefore, it has the faces of the Southern Continent and Northern Continent; we study the way by examining them.[86] It has the bones and mar-

---

83　**birth and death have exceeded "full function"** (*shōji no zenki ni amareru* 生死の全機にあまれる): Or "'alive' and 'dead' are more than 'full function.'"

84　**flips its body and spins its brain** (*honshin kainō* 翻身回腦): Two expressions for spiritual transformation — the former quite common; the latter rather unusual.

85　**"Level and flat, it's a wall rising a thousand fathoms"** (*heitantanchi, sore heki ryū sen jin nari* 平坦坦地、それ壁立千仞なり): Again, quoting (with slight variation) Yuanwu Keqin 圜悟克勤, at *Yuanwu Foguo chanshi yulu* 圜悟佛果禪師語錄, T.1997.47:797c1213:

平坦坦處、壁立千仞。壁立千仞處、平坦坦。

Where it's level and flat, a wall rises a thousand fathoms; where the wall rises a thousand fathoms, it's level and flat.

The Chinese *jin* 仞 ("fathom"; also written 仭) was a linear measure, used chiefly for vertical distances, ranging in value from 4 to 8 feet (*chi* 尺).

86　**faces of the Southern Continent and Northern Continent** (*Nanshū Hokushū no menmoku* 南洲北洲の面目): I.e, the continents of Jambudvīpa (*Enbudai* 閻浮提) and Uttarakuru (*Kurushū* 倶盧洲), to the south and north respectively of the central Mount Sumeru according to Buddhist cosmology. See Supplementary Notes, s.v. "Four Continents."

row of neither conception nor nonconception; we simply study the way by raising them.[87]

正法眼藏身心學道第四
Treasury of the True Dharma Eye
Studying the Way with Body and Mind
Number 4

[Ryūmonji MS:]

爾時仁治三年壬寅重陽日、在于寶林寺示衆
Presented to the assembly at Hōrin Monastery; the day of double yang, senior water year of the tiger, the third year of Ninji [4 October 1242][88]

永享二年正月書
Copied in the first month of the second year of Eikyō [25 January-22 February 1430][89]

[Tōunji MS:]

仁治癸卯仲春初二日書寫。懷奘
Copied on the second day of mid-spring, the junior water year of the rabbit, Ninji [22 February 1243]. Ejō[90]

嘉慶三年正月廿六日、在永平寺衆寮奉書寫之。宗吾
Copied this as a memorial offering in the common quarters at Eihei Monastery; twenty-sixth day, first month, third year of Kakyō [22 February 1389]. Sōgo[91]

---

87 **neither conception nor nonconception** (*hisō hi hisō* 非想非非想): I.e., the highest state in the three realms of saṃsāra; the last of the four formless concentrations (*shi mushiki jō* 四無色定; S. *ārūpya-samāpatti*).

88 The Tōunji 洞雲寺 MS shares an identical colophon.

double yang (*chōyō* 重陽): The ninth day of the ninth month of the lunar calendar; the date of the Chinese Chongyang 重陽 festival — also known as *denggao* 登高 ("scaling the heights") and, in Japan, as *kiku no hi* 菊の日 ("chrysanthemum day").

89 Copyist unknown.

90 **mid-spring** (*chūshun* 仲春): The second month of the lunar calendar.

junior water year of the rabbit, Ninji (*Ninji kibō* 仁治癸卯): The tenth stem-fourth branch year of the sexagenary calendar would have been the fourth year of the Ninji era, changed during that year to the Kangen 寬元 era.

91 **Sōgo** 宋吾: 1343-1406, ninth abbot of Eiheiji.

TREASURY OF THE TRUE DHARMA EYE
NUMBER 5

This Mind Itself Is the Buddha
Soku shin ze butsu
即心是佛

This Mind Itself Is the Buddha

Soku shin ze butsu

INTRODUCTION

This relatively short work occurs as number 5 in both the sixty- and seventy-five-chapter compilations of the *Shōbōgenzō* and as number 6 in the Honzan edition. It was written at Kōshōji in the summer of 1239, some three years after the founding of the monastery and near the beginning of its author's serious work on the *kana Shōbōgenzō*. The doctrinal theme of the text stands out from Dōgen's other work dated to 1239 ("Jūundō shiki" 重雲堂式, "Senjō" 洗淨, "Senmen" 洗面), all of which tend to focus on monastic practice.

The title phrase, "this mind itself is the buddha" (or "this very mind is the buddha"), is a well-known saying in Zen literature, usually associated with the famous eighth-century master Mazu Daoyi 馬祖道一. Dōgen opens his essay with a lament that so many Zen students misunderstand the saying, thinking that "the mind" here refers to the consciousness present in all forms of awareness. Such a view, he identifies as the non-Buddhist understanding of the brahman Śreṇika, who argues in the *Nirvāṇa Sūtra* for a self that migrates from body to body.

For his part, Dōgen prefers a Zen saying that the mind is "the mountains, rivers, and the whole earth; the sun, moon, and stars." Yet, lest we think that he is talking simply of a cosmic buddha consciousness, he reminds us that the mind of the buddhas is also the mind of undefiled aspiration, practice, and verification of bodhi. Finally, in a rather surprising turn, he ends by collapsing all the buddhas into Buddha Śākyamuni, who is "this mind itself is the buddha."

正法眼藏第五

Treasury of the True Dharma Eye
Number 5

即心是佛

This Mind Itself Is the Buddha

[05:1] {1:53}

佛佛祖祖、いまだまぬかれず保任しきたれるは、即心是佛のみなり。しか
あるを、西天には即心是佛なし、震旦にはじめてきけり。學者おほくあや
まるによりて、將錯就錯せず。將錯就錯せざるゆえに、おほく外道に零落
す。

What buddha after buddha and ancestor after ancestor have maintained without fail is just *"this mind itself is the buddha."*[1] However, *"this mind itself is the buddha"* did not exist in Sindh in the West; it was first heard in Cīnasthāna.[2] Since many students misunderstand it, they do not *make a mistake of a mistake*; and because they do not *make a mistake of a mistake,* many drop into other paths.[3]

[05:2]

いはゆる即心の話をききて、癡人おもはくは、衆生の慮知念覺の未發菩提
心なるを、すなはち佛とすとおもへり。これはかつて正師にあはざるによ
りてなり。

---

1 **"this mind itself is the buddha"** (*soku shin ze butsu* 即心是佛): Or "this very mind is the buddha." A very common phrase in Chan literature, associated especially with Mazu Daoyi 馬祖道一 (709-788); see Supplementary Notes.

2 **"this mind itself is the buddha" did not exist in Sindh in the West; it was first heard in Cīnasthāna** (*Saiten ni wa soku shin ze butsu nashi, Shintan ni hajimete kikeri* 西天には即心是佛なし、震旦にはじめてきけり): Dōgen uses here a Chinese transliteration (*Shintan* 震旦) of a Sanskrit term for China. The claim seems to be that it was the Chinese who first gave voice to what the buddhas and ancestors of India had "maintained" (*hōnin* 保任) without expressing. While the particular phrase, "this mind itself is the buddha," does seem first to occur in China, there is Indian precedent for the equation of the mind and the buddha; see Supplementary Notes, s.v. "This mind itself is the buddha."

3 **make a mistake of a mistake** (*shōshaku jushaku* 將錯就錯): An idiom, found in Zen texts, meaning "to recognize one's mistake as such," "to turn a mistake to one's advantage," or "to make one mistake after another"; see Supplementary Notes, s.v. "Make a mistake of a mistake."

other paths (*gedō* 外道): I.e., [the views of] non-Buddhist religions.

148　　　　　　　　DŌGEN'S *SHŌBŌGENZŌ* VOLUME I

Hearing the words "this mind itself," the foolish think that the thinking and perceiving of living beings, not yet having brought forth the mind of bodhi, is taken as "the buddha."[4] This is because they have never met a true master.

[05:3]

外道のたぐひとなるといふは、西天竺國に外道あり、先尼となづく。かれが見處のいはくは、大道はわれらがいまの身にあり、そのていたらくは、たやすくしりぬべし。いはゆる、苦樂をわきまへ、冷煖を自知し、痛癢を了知す。萬物にさへられず、諸境にかかはれず。物は去來し、境は生滅すれども、靈知はつねにありて不變なり。この靈知、ひろく周遍せり。凡聖含靈の隔異なし。そのなかに、しばらく妄法の空華ありといへども、一念相應の智慧あらはれぬれば、物も亡じ、境も滅しぬれば、靈知本性ひとり了了として鎭常なり。たとひ身相は破れぬれども、靈知はやぶれずしていづるなり。たとへば人舍の失火にやくるに、舍主いでてさるがごとし。昭昭靈靈としてある、これを覺者・智者の性といふ。これをほとけともいひ、さとりとも稱す。自他おなじく具足し、迷悟ともに通達せり。萬法・諸境ともかくもあれ、靈知は境とともならず、物とおなじからず、歴劫に常住なり。いま現在せる諸境も、靈知の所在によらば、眞實といひぬべし。本性より緣起せるゆゑには實法なり。たとひしかありとも、靈知のごとくに常住ならず、存沒するがゆゑに。明暗にかかはれず、靈知するがゆゑに。これを靈知といふ。また眞我と稱し、覺元といひ、本性と稱し、本體と稱す。かくのごとくの本性をさとるを、常住にかへりぬるといひ、歸眞の大士といふ。これよりのちは、さらに生死に流轉せず、不生不滅の性海に證入するなり。このほかは眞實にあらず。この性あらはさざるほど、三界・六道は競起する、といふなり。これすなはち先尼外道が見なり。

To say that they join other paths refers to one such follower of an other path in the Land of Sindhu in the West whose name was Śreṇika.[5] His viewpoint was that the great way is in our present body, and that its true state is easily knowable.[6] It distinguishes pleasure and pain, knows of

---

4　**thinking and perceiving** (*ryo chi nen kaku* 慮知念覺): A loose translation of terms for cognitive functions not commonly found as a set in Buddhist literature but appearing several times in the *Shōbōgenzō*, where they seem to stand collectively for the ordinary operations of consciousness. The translation takes them as two compound expressions (the first of which does occur elsewhere in the *Shōbōgenzō* in reference to the thinking mind); as individual terms, they might be rendered "considering, knowing, thinking, and perceiving." See Supplementary Notes.

not yet having brought forth the mind of bodhi (*mihotsu bodai shin* 未發菩提心): I.e., without the bodhisattva's aspiration for buddhahood, or "thought of bodhi" (*bodai shin* 菩提心; S. *bodhi-citta*); see Supplementary Notes, s.v. "Bring forth the mind."

5　**Śreṇika** (*Senni* 先尼): Tentative reconstruction of the Chinese *Xianni* 先尼, the name of a brahman appearing in the *Nirvāṇa Sūtra* (*Da banniepan jing* 大般涅槃經, T.374.12:594a14-596b10), who argues for a transcendental self that transmigrates from body to body.

6　**the great way is in our present body** (*daidō wa warera ga ima no mi ni ari* 大道はわれらがいまの身にあり): The term *daidō* 大道 (rendered here "great way") may also

5. This Mind Itself Is the Buddha *Soku shin ze butsu* 即心是佛   149

itself cold and heat, recognizes pains and itches. It is unimpeded by the myriad phenomena and unassociated with its objects. Although things come and go, and its objects arise and cease, the spiritual knowing always exists and is unchanging.[7] This spiritual knowing extends everywhere; there is no division among commoners, sages, and all the animate.[8] Within it, there may temporarily be the sky flowers of false dharmas, but when the wisdom of a single thought's correspondence appears, when things die out and its objects cease, the original nature of spiritual knowing alone is clear and constant.[9] Though the corporeal form may break down, the spiritual knowing departs intact. It is just as the owner of a house departs when the house is destroyed by fire.[10] Its existence is

---

(and, here, perhaps better) be understood as "great awakening," taking the glyph *dō* 道 in its use for Sanskrit *bodhi*).

7 **spiritual knowing** (*reichi* 靈知): Or, perhaps, "numinous awareness." The term is not used in the *Nirvāṇa Sūtra* account of Śreṇika's views but is quite common in Chinese Buddhist texts, including those of Chan, where it typically denotes sentience, or the awareness present in every conscious mental state.

8 **commoners, sages, and all the animate** (*bonshō ganrei* 凡聖含靈): An expression, occurring several times in the *Shōbōgenzō*, for all sentient beings, including ordinary humans and advanced Buddhist adepts; best known from a line of verse by the ninth-century lay figure Zhang Zhuo 張拙 (dates unknown), quoted in "Shōbōgenzō kūge" 正法眼藏空華:

> 光明寂照遍河沙。凡聖含靈共我家。
> The radiance shines silent through [worlds like] the Ganges sands;
> Commoners, sages, all the animate, together are my family.

"The animate" renders *ganrei* 含靈 ("beings endowed with spirit"), a translation that loses the syntactic continuity here with *reichi* 靈知 ("spiritual knowing").

9 **sky flowers of false dharmas** (*mōbō no kūge* 妄法の空華): I.e., illusions. "Sky flowers" (*kūge* 空華) is a standard Buddhist expression for spots appearing as a result of visual impairment; see Supplementary Notes, s.v. "Clouded eyes and sky flowers." Note, however, that below Dōgen reports that the objects (*shokyō* 諸境) of spiritual knowing are held to be real (*shinjitsu* 眞實), insofar as they are said to arise from that knowing.

the wisdom of a single thought's correspondence (*ichinen sōō no chie* 一念相應の智慧): A fixed expression for a state in which one is (a) cognizant of the truth and/or (b) in full accord with one's true nature.

the original nature of spiritual knowing (*reichi honshō* 靈知本性): In his description of Śreṇika's view, Dōgen seems to be treating "original nature" (*honshō* 本性) as synonymous with "spiritual knowing" (*reichi* 靈知). The former term was sometimes used in China to render the Sanskrit *prakṛti*, a term of art in Sāṃkhya philosophy for the primordial substance from which the world evolves; but, in that philosophy, the world is merely the unconscious object of experience, distinct from the transcendental subject (S. *puruṣa*).

10 **just as the owner of a house departs when the house is destroyed by fire** (*tatoeba ninsha no shikka ni yakuru ni, shashu idete saru ga gotoshi* たとへば人舍の失火にやくるに、舍主いでてさるがごとし): A simile drawn from Śreṇika's account of his position in the sūtra (*Da banniepan jing* 大般涅槃經, T.374.12:594a28-b1).

luminous and spiritual, and it is said to be "the nature of the awakened and the wise." It is spoken of as "buddha" and called "awakening." It endows equally self and other; it penetrates both delusion and awakening. The myriad dharmas and various objects be as they may, the spiritual knowing does not accompany its objects, is not the same as things; it constantly abides across the kalpas. The objects existing in the present, based on the presence of the spiritual knowing, should also be spoken of as real: because they arise conditionally from the original nature, they are real dharmas. Nevertheless, they are not constantly abiding like the spiritual knowing, for they exist and vanish. It is unrelated to light and darkness, because it knows spiritually. This is called "spiritual knowing."[11] Again it is designated "the true self"; it is called "the source of awakening"; it is designated "the original nature"; it is designated "the original substance." One who awakens to this kind of original nature is said to have "returned to constant abiding" and is called a "great one returned to the true." Thereafter, without further drifting about in birth and death, one enters verification of the ocean of the nature that neither arises nor ceases. Anything other than this is not the true. It is said that, to the extent that this nature has not been manifested, the three realms and six paths arise in profusion.[12] This, then, is the view of the other path of Śreṇika.

* * * * *

[05:4] {1:54}
大唐國大證國師慧忠和尚問僧、從何方來。僧曰、南方來。師曰、南方有何知識。僧曰、知識頗多。師曰、如何示人。僧曰、彼方知識、直下示學人即心是佛。佛是覺義、汝今悉具見聞覺知之性。此性善能揚眉瞬目、去來運用。徧於身中、捉頭頭知、捉脚脚知、故名正徧知。離此之外、更無別佛。此身即有生滅、心性無始以來、未曾生滅。身生滅者、如龍換骨、似蛇脱皮人出故宅。即身是無常、其性常也。南方所説大約如此。師曰、若然者、與彼先尼外道、無有差別。彼云、我此身中有一神性、此性能知痛癢、身壞之時、神即出去。如舍被燒舍主出去。舍即無常、舍主常矣。審如此者、邪正莫辨、孰爲是乎。吾比遊方、多見此色。近尤盛矣。聚却三五百衆、目視雲漢云、是南方宗旨。把他壇經改換、添糅鄙譚、削除聖意、惑亂後徒、豈成言教。苦哉、吾宗喪矣。若以見聞覺知、是爲佛性者、淨名不應云法離見聞覺知、若行見聞覺知、是則見聞覺知非求法也.

---

11 **It is unrelated to light and darkness, because it knows spiritually. This is called "spiritual knowing."** (*meian ni kakawarezu, reichi suru ga yue ni. Kore o reichi to iu* 明暗にかかはれず、靈知するがゆえに。これを靈知といふ): The translation here follows Kawamura's punctuation. The passage might better be parsed, "Because, unrelated to light and darkness, it knows spiritually, this is called 'spiritual knowing.'"

12 **three realms and six paths** (*sangai rokudō* 三界・六道): The three levels of existence and the six stations of rebirth in saṃsāra; see Supplementary Notes, s.v. "Three realms," and "Six paths."

5. This Mind Itself Is the Buddha *Soku shin ze butsu* 即心是佛 151

Reverend Huizhong, National Teacher Dazheng, of the Land of the Great Tang, asked a monk, "Where have you come from?"[13]

The monk said, "I came from the south."

The Master said, "What wise friends are there in the south?"[14]

The monk said, "There is a great number of wise friends."

The Master asked, "How do they instruct people?"

The monk said, "The wise friends there instruct their students straight away that this mind itself is the buddha. [They say,]

"Buddha" means "awakened." You are all already endowed with a nature that sees, hears, perceives, and knows.[15] *This nature enables you to raise your eyebrows and blink your eyes, to come and go and make use of things.*[16] *It pervades your body: when you poke your head, your head knows it; when you poke your foot, your foot knows it. Therefore, it is called "correct pervasive knowing."*[17] *Apart from this, there is no other buddha. This body is subject to arising and ceasing, but since the beginningless past, the nature of the mind has never arisen or ceased. The arising and ceasing of the body are like the dragon changing its*

---

13   **Reverend Huizhong, National Teacher Dazheng, of the Land of the Great Tang** (*Daitō koku Daishō kokushi Echū oshō* 大唐國大證國師慧忠和尚): I.e., Nanyang Huizhong 南陽慧忠 (d. 775), disciple of the Sixth Ancestor and the subject of a number of famous kōans. The conversation quoted here occurs in the *Jingde chuandeng lu* 景德傳燈錄, T.2076.51:437c17-438a6.

14   **"What wise friends are there in the south?"** (*nanpō u ka chishiki* 南方有何知識): "Wise friends" (*chishiki* 知識) is a standard term for a Buddhist teacher. Dazheng lived in the north, at the capital, Chang'an.

15   **"Buddha" means "awakened." You are all already endowed with a nature that sees, hears, perceives, and knows** (*butsu ze kaku gi, nyo kon shitsu gu ken mon kaku chi shi shō* 佛是覺義、汝今悉具見聞覺知之性). The translation obscures the recurrence of the term *kaku* 覺 here, rendered first as "awakened" and then as "perceives." The expression "sees, hears, perceives, and knows" (*ken mon kaku chi* 見聞覺知) is a standard fixed set, standing for the operations of the six consciousnesses.

16   **raise your eyebrows and blink your eyes** (*yōbi shunmoku* 揚眉瞬目): A set phrase used in Chan texts to represent the ordinary actions of human life, often, as here, seen as expressions of the buddha nature; occurs several times in the *Shōbōgenzō*. See Supplementary Notes, s.v. "Raise the eyebrows and blink the eyes."

17   **Therefore, it is called "correct pervasive knowing"** (*ko myō shōhenchi* 故名正遍知): The translation seeks to preserve the word play in the original, which here provides its teaching of the pervasiveness of consciousness throughout the body as an etymology for the term *shōhenchi* 正遍知, one Chinese rendering of the buddhas' epithet "perfectly awakened one" (S. *samyak-sambuddha*).

152 DŌGEN'S *SHŌBŌGENZŌ* VOLUME I

bones, resemble the snake shedding its skin or the person leaving an old house.[18] *That body is impermanent, while the nature is permanent.*

"What they say in the south is roughly like this."

The Master said, *"If this is so, then there's no difference from that other path of Śreṇika. They say, "Within this body of mine, there is a spirit nature.*[19] *This nature knows pain and itching. When the body disintegrates, the spirit departs, like the owner of a house departs when the house burns. The house is impermanent, but the owner is permanent."*

When we examine it, something like this fails to distinguish between true and false. Who would take it as right? When I was wandering about some time ago, I often encountered this type. These days, they're particularly flourishing. They gather assemblies of three to five hundred and, gazing up at the Milky Way, tell them, "This is the message of the South."[20] They revise the *Platform Sūtra*, mixing in vulgar tales and erasing the sage's intent, misguiding and confusing later followers.[21] How could it represent the oral instruction?[22] How painful that our tradition is so ruined! If we take seeing, hearing, perceiving, and knowing as the buddha nature, Vimalakīrti would not have said, "The dharma is apart from seeing, hearing, perceiving, and knowing.[23] If we're engaged in seeing, hearing,

---

18 **like the dragon changing its bones** (*nyo ryū kan kotsu* 如龍換骨): Based on the belief that a dragon "changes" its bones as it outgrows them.

19 **"Within this body of mine, there is a spirit nature"** (*ga shi shin chū u ichi shinshō* 我此身中有一神性): Judging from its description here, we can probably take the term "spirit" (*shin* 神) here as more or less synonymous with the "spiritual knowing" (*reichi* 靈知) used by Dōgen above.

20 **gazing up at the Milky Way** (*mokushi unkan* 目視雲漢): A fixed expression, typically for an idle or vacant state.

"This is the message of the South" (*ze nanpō shūshi* 是南方宗旨): Likely here a reference, not merely to southern China, but to the so-called Southern school, whose members claimed descent from Huizhung's master, the Sixth Ancestor, Huineng 慧能.

21 **the *Platform Sūtra*** (*Dankyō* 壇經): I.e., the *Platform Sūtra of the Sixth Ancestor* (*Liuzu tan jing* 六祖壇經, T.2007) the text purporting to record the teachings of Huineng. The work, originating in the second half of the eighth century, underwent much revision over the centuries. In his "Shōbōgenzō shizen biku" 正法眼藏四禪比丘, Dōgen also dismisses the text current in his time as not the teachings of the Sixth Ancestor.

erasing the sage's intent (*sakujo shōi* 削除聖意): I.e., eliminating the Sixth Ancestor's teachings.

22 **How could it represent the oral instruction?** (*ki jō gonkyō* 豈成言教): Presumably, here again, the authentic teachings of the Sixth Ancestor.

23 **Vimalakīrti** (*Jōmyō* 淨名): From Kumārajīva's translation of the *Vimalakīrti Sūtra* (*Yuima kyō* 維摩經, T.475.14:546a23-25). The first sentence of the quotation here is a variant of the extant sūtra version..

5. This Mind Itself Is the Buddha *Soku shin ze butsu* 即心是佛　153

perceiving, and knowing, this is seeing, hearing, perceiving, and knowing; it is not seeking the dharma."

[05:5] {1:56}

大證國師は、曹溪古佛の上足なり、天上・人間の大善知識なり。國師のし
めす宗旨をあきらめて、參學の龜鑑とすべし。先尼外道が見處、しりてし
たがふことなかれ。

National Teacher Dacheng was a superior disciple of the Old Buddha of Caoxi; he was a great wise friend both in the heavens and among humans.[24] We should clarify the essential point presented by the National Teacher and make it the model for our study.[25] Knowing it as the viewpoint of the other path of Śreṇika, do not adopt it.

[05:6]

近代は大宋國に諸山の主人とあるやから、國師のごとくなるはあるべから
ず。むかしより國師にひとしかるべき知識、いまだかつて出世せず。しか
あるに、世人あやまりておもはく、臨濟・德山も國師にひとしかるべし、
と。かくのごとくのやからのみおほし。あはれむべし、明眼の師なきこ
と。

In recent times among those fellows who serve as the heads of the various mountains in the Land of the Great Song, there could be none like the National Teacher.[26] Since long ago, no wise friend to equal the National Teacher has appeared in the world. However, people of the world mistakenly believe that Linji and Deshan must also be the equal of the National Teacher.[27] There are so many types like this. How deplorable that there are no clear-eyed teachers.

24　**the Old Buddha of Caoxi** (*Sōkei kobutsu* 曹溪古佛): I.e., the Sixth Ancestor, Huineng 慧能 of Caoxi 曹溪.

a great wise friend both in the heavens and among humans (*tenjō ningen no dai zen-chishiki nari* 天上人間の大善知識なり): Allusion to the tradition, mentioned elsewhere in the *Shōbōgenzō*, that Huizhong was teacher, on earth, to the emperors of China and, in the heavens, to Indra, king of the devas.

25　**model for our study** (*sangaku no kikan* 參學の龜鑑): "Model" here loosely translates the term "tortoise mirror" (*kikan* 龜鑑), something that provides a "pattern" for behavior, as cracks in a heated tortoise shell were used by diviners in ancient China.

26　**various mountains** (*shozan* 諸山): Also read *shosan*. A term for the major Buddhist monasteries.

27　**Linji and Deshan** (*Rinzai Tokusan* 臨濟德山): I.e., Linji Yixuan 臨濟義玄 (d. 866), founder of the Linji 臨濟 lineage; and his contemporary Deshan Xuanjian 德山宣鑑 (780-865). These two figures are singled out for criticism elsewhere in the *Shōbōgenzō*.

154   DŌGEN'S *SHŌBŌGENZŌ* VOLUME I

[05:7]

いはゆる佛祖の保任する即心是佛は、外道・二乗のゆめにもみるところに
あらず。唯佛祖與佛祖のみ即心是佛しきたり、究盡しきたる。聞著あり、
行取あり、證著あり。

"*This mind itself is the buddha*" maintained by the buddhas and ancestors is something the other paths or the two vehicles have not seen even
in their dreams. *Only buddhas and ancestors with buddhas and ancestors*
alone have been doing "*this mind itself is the buddha,*" have been exhaustively investigating it.[28] They have the hearing of it; they have the
practice of it; they have the verification of it.

[05:8]

佛、百草を拈却しきたり、打失しきたる。しかあれども、丈六の金身に説
似せず。即、公案あり、見成を相待せず、敗壊を廻避せず。是、三界あ
り、退出にあらず、唯心にあらず。心、牆壁あり、いまだ泥水せず、いま
だ造作せず。あるひは即心是佛を參究し、心即佛是を參究し、佛即是心を
參究し、即心佛是を參究し、是佛心即を參究す。かくのごとくの參究、ま
さしく即心是佛、これを擧して即心是佛に正傳するなり。かくのごとく正
傳して今日にいたれり。

"The buddha": It has been taking away, has been losing, the hundred
grasses.[29] Nevertheless, we do not describe it as the sixteen-foot golden
body.[30] "Itself": There is a kōan; it does not depend on realization; it does

---

28 **Only buddhas and ancestors with buddhas and ancestors alone have been doing
"this mind itself is the buddha"** (*yui busso yo busso nomi soku shin ze butsu shikitari*
唯佛祖與佛祖のみ即心是佛しきたり): Dōgen here creates the novel predicate "to do
this mind itself is the buddha" (*soku shin ze butsu su* 即心是佛す). The expression "only
buddhas and ancestors with buddhas and ancestors" recalls a passage in Kumārajīva's
translation of the *Lotus Sūtra* occurring often in the *Shōbōgenzō*; see Supplementary
Notes, s.v. "Only buddhas with buddhas can exhaustively investigate the real marks of
the dharmas."

29   **"The buddha"** (*butsu* 佛): Dōgen here begins a set of short comments on each of
the four words in the expression "this mind itself is the buddha." The translation treats
each of the words as the topic, rather than the grammatical subject of the comment that
follows. Dōgen's order here rearranges the expression to "the buddha itself is the mind."
It has been taking away, has been losing, the hundred grasses (*hyakusō o nenkyaku
shikitari, dashitsu shikitaru* 百草を拈却しきたり、打失しきたる): "The hundred grasses" (*hyakusō* 百草) is a common term for the manifold phenomena of the world. The
point here may be that the term "buddha" seems to have set aside the phenomenal world.

30 **we do not describe it as the sixteen-foot golden body** (*jōroku no konjin ni setsuji
sezu* 丈六の金身に説似せず): Or, perhaps, "we do not describe them [i.e. the hundred
grasses] as the sixteen-foot golden body"; a standard reference to the body (or the standing image) of a buddha. The association here with "the hundred grasses" may reflect the
well-known Chan saying, referred to several times in the *Shōbōgenzō*, "to use one blade
of grass as a sixteen-foot golden body"; see Supplementary Notes, s.v. "One blade of
grass."

5. This Mind Itself Is the Buddha *Soku shin ze butsu* 即心是佛 155

not escape destruction.[31] "Is": There are the three realms.[32] It is not that they are withdrawn; it is not that they are only mind.[33] "Mind": There are fences and walls.[34] They never [consist of] mud and water; they are never constructed.[35]

We investigate "*this mind itself is the buddha*," or we investigate "*itself this mind the buddha is*," investigate "*the buddha itself is this mind*," investigate "*this mind itself the buddha is*," investigate "is the buddha this mind itself."[36] This kind of investigation is truly "*this mind itself is the buddha*"; it takes this up and directly transmits it to "*this mind itself is the buddha.*"[37] Directly transmitted in this way, it has come down to the present day.

---

31 **"Itself"** (*soku* 即): A particle expressing identity or immediacy: "precisely this," "this very," "just then," etc.

There is a kōan; it does not depend on realization (*kōan ari, genjō o sōtai sezu* 公案あり、見成を相待せず): From the well-known "realized kōan" (or "settled case"; *genjō kōan* 見成公案; more commonly written 現成公案). See Supplementary Notes, s.v. "Realized kōan."

32 **"Is": There are the three realms** (*ze, sangai ari* 是、三界あり): For the "three realms," see above, Note 12.

33 **It is not that they are withdrawn; it is not that they are only mind** (*taishutsu ni arazu, yui shin ni arazu* 退出にあらず、唯心にあらず): The translation takes the unexpressed subject of both phrases as "the three realms"; but the sense of the former phrase is uncertain and might better be understood as "one does not withdraw from them (i.e., enter nirvāṇa)." The latter phrase recalls the common claim that "the three realms are only mind" (*sangai yui shin* 三界唯心); see Supplementary Notes.

34 **"Mind": There are fences and walls** (*shin shō heki ari* 心牆壁あり): Invoking the famous Chan saying, usually associated with the above-cited Nanyang Huizhong 南陽慧忠, that the buddha mind is "fences, walls, tiles, and pebbles" (*shō heki ga ryaku* 牆壁瓦礫), to which Dōgen will refer below. See Supplementary Notes, s.v. "Fences, walls, tiles, and pebbles."

35 **They never [consist of] mud and water** (*imada deisui sezu* いまだ泥水せず): Seemingly a reference to the material of the walls, but perhaps also invoking the common Chan use of "mud and water" for the "dirty" work of teaching Buddhism in the world; see Supplementary Notes, s.v. "Dragged through the mud and drenched with water." The novel use of *deisui* 泥水 as a predicate also occurs in "Shōbōgenzō ango" 正法眼藏安居.

36 **or we investigate "itself this mind the buddha is"** (*shin soku butsu ze* 心即佛是): The translation here and in the following three phrases struggles to express Dōgen's four variations on the syntax of the saying, despite the grotesque linguistic consequences. Most interpreters take the point of this exercise to be that each of the four words in the saying is equal to the others.

37 **This kind of investigation is truly "this mind itself is the buddha"; it takes this up and directly transmits it to "this mind itself is the buddha"** (*kaku no gotoku no sankyū, masashiku soku shin ze butsu, kore o ko shite sokushin ze butsu ni shōden suru nari* かくのごとくの参究、まさしく即心是佛、これを擧して即心是佛に正傳するな

156
DŌGEN'S *SHŌBŌGENZŌ* VOLUME I

[05:9] {1:57}

いはゆる正傳しきたれる心といふは、一心一切法、一切法一心なり。この
ゆえに古人いはく、若人識得心、大地無寸土。しるべし、心を識得すると
き、蓋天撲落し、帀地裂破す。あるひは心を識得すれば、大地さらにあつ
さ三寸をます。

The mind said to have been "directly transmitted" means "*one mind is
all dharmas, all dharmas are one mind.*"[38] Therefore, an ancient has said,
"*If a person knows the mind, there isn't an inch of ground on the whole
earth.*"[39] We should know that, when we know the mind, *the whole of
heaven crashes down and the entire earth is rent asunder.*[40] Or, when one
knows the mind, the whole earth gets three inches thicker.

[05:10]

古德云、作麼生是妙淨明心、山河大地・日月星辰。

A virtuous one of old has said, "What is the wondrous, pure, clear
mind? The mountains, rivers, and the whole earth, the sun, moon, and
stars."[41]

[05:11]

あきらかにしりぬ、心とは山河大地なり、日月星辰なり。しかあれども、
この道取するところ、すすめば不足あり、しりぞくればあまれり。山河大
地心は、山河大地のみなり、さらに、波浪なし、風煙なし。日月星辰心

り): A tentative translation of a sentence subject to varied readings. The sense seems to
be that the expression "this mind itself is the buddha" is "directly transmitted" when it is
subjected to "this kind of investigation."

38 **"one mind is all dharmas, all dharmas are one mind"** (*isshin issai hō, issai
hō isshin* 一心一切法、一切法一心): In his "Shōbōgenzō tsuki" 正法眼藏都機, Dōgen
repeats this sentence as the saying of "an old buddha" (*kobutsu* 古佛). While similar
passages do appear in earlier texts, the actual source of Dōgen's version has not been
identified.

39 **an ancient has said** (*kojin iwaku* 古人いわく): Though often attributed to Chan-
gling Shouzhou 長靈守卓 (1065-1123), in fact, this saying occurs frequently in Chan
literature and can already be found attributed to "an ancient" at *Jingde chuandeng lu*
景德傳燈錄, T.2076.51:464a26. The expression "there isn't an inch of ground on the
whole earth" (*daichi mu sun do* 大地無寸土) or variants thereof occurs several times in
the *Shōbōgenzō*.

40 **the entire earth is rent asunder** (*sōchi reppa* 帀地裂破): More commonly written
sōchi 匝地. Dōgen reuses this image, together with the "inch of ground" mentioned
above, in his "Shōbōgenzō ango" 正法眼藏安居: when the summer retreat is dissolved,
"it rends asunder the entire earth, without an inch of ground remaining" (*sōchi o reppa
su, nokoreru sundo arazu* 帀地を裂破す、のこれる寸土あらず).

41 **A virtuous one of old** (*kotoku* 古德): I.e., Weishan Lingyou 潙山靈祐 (771-853).
The quotation reworks a conversation between Lingyou and his disciple Yangshan Huiji
仰山慧寂 (803-887) recorded in Dōgen's *shinji Shōbōgenzō* 眞字正法眼藏 (DZZ.5:212,
case 168); see Supplementary Notes, s.v. "Sun, moon, and stars."

5. This Mind Itself Is the Buddha *Soku shin ze butsu* 即心是佛   157

は、日月星辰のみなり、さらに、きりなし、かすみなし。生死去來心は、
生死去來のみなり、さらに、迷なし、悟なし。牆壁瓦礫心は、牆壁瓦礫
のみなり、さらに、泥なし、水なし。四大五蘊心は、四大五蘊のみなり、
さらに、馬なし、猿なし。椅子拂子心ま、椅子拂子のみなり、さらに、竹
なし、木なし。かくのごとくなるがゆえに、即心是佛、不染汚即心是佛な
り、諸佛、不染汚諸佛なり。

It is clearly understood that "the mind" is "the mountains, rivers, and
the whole earth," is "the sun, moon, and stars." Although this is so, in
what is said here, if you advance, it is not enough, if you step back, it is
too much.[42] The mind of "mountains, rivers, and the whole earth" is just
mountains, rivers, and the whole earth: there are no additional waves and
billows, no winds and vapors.[43] The mind of "sun, moon, and stars" is
just sun, moon, and stars: there is no additional fog, no mist.[44] The mind
of "birth and death, coming and going," is just birth and death, coming
and going: there is no additional delusion, no awakening.[45] The mind of
"fences, walls, tiles, and pebbles" is just fences, walls, tiles, and pebbles:
there is no additional mud, no water [46] The mind of the four elements and
five aggregates is just the four elements and five aggregates: there are no
additional horses, no monkeys.[47] The mind of the chair and the whisk is

---

42   **if you advance, it is not enough, if you step back, it is too much** (*susumeba fu-
soku ari, shirizokureba amareri* すすめば不足あり、しりぞくればあまれり): Perhaps
meaning that this saying at once falls short of what might be said and says more than
what should be said. See Supplementary Notes, s.v. "Stepping forward and stepping
back."

43   **no additional waves and billows, no winds and vapors** (*sara ni harō nashi, fūen
nashi* さらに波浪なし、風煙なし): Dōgen begins here excluding a set of terms used
to qualify or affect the mind. The mind, for example, is regularly likened to water, and
meditators are told to still the "waves" of the mind, and to protect themselves from
"winds and vapors."

44   **no additional fog, no mist** (*sara ni kiri nashi, kasumi nashi* さらにきりなし、かす
みなし): As in the common simile of the mind likened to the sun (or moon) behind the
"fog" (*kiri* きり) and "mist" (*kasumi* かすみ) of ignorance.

45   **The mind of "birth and death, coming and going"** (*shōji korai shin* 生死去來心):
I.e., the mind subject to the vicissitudes of rebirth.

46   **The mind of "fences, walls, tiles, and pebbles"** (*shō heki ga ryaku shin* 牆壁瓦礫
心): See Note 34, above.

no additional mud, no water (*sara ni dei nashi, sui nashi* さらに泥なし、水なし): See
Note 35, above.

47   **four elements and five aggregates** (*shidai goun* 四大五蘊): I.e., the four primary
forms of matter (S. *mahābhūta*) — earth, water, fire, and wind — of which the physical
world is composed; and the five "heaps" (S. *skandha*) — form, sensation, perception,
formations, and consciousness — into which the psychophysical organism can be analyzed. See Supplementary Notes, s.v. "Four elements and five aggregates."

no additional horses, no monkeys (*sara ni ba nashi, en nashi* さらに馬なし、猿なし):
From the common use of wild horses and forest monkeys as metaphors for the restless

158 DŌGEN'S *SHŌBŌGENZŌ* VOLUME I

just the chair and the whisk: there is no additional bamboo, no wood.[48] Since it is like this, *"this mind itself is the buddha" is an undefiled "mind itself is the buddha." The buddhas are undefiled buddhas.*[49]

[05:12] {1:58}

しかあればすなはち、即心是佛とは、發心・修行・菩提・涅槃の諸佛なり。いまだ發心・修行・菩提・涅槃せざるは、即心是佛にあらず。たとひ一刹那に發心修證するも、即心是佛なり、たとひ一極微中に發心修證するも、即心是佛なり、たとひ無量劫に發心修證するも、即心是佛なり、たとひ一念中に發心修證するも、即心是佛なり、たとひ半拳裏に發心修證するも、即心是佛なり。しかあるを、長劫に修行作佛するは即心是佛にあらず、といふは、即心是佛をいまだ見ざるなり、いまだしらざるなり、いまだ學せざるなり。即心是佛を開演する正師を見ざるなり。

Such being the case, *"this mind itself is the buddha"* means the buddhas who bring forth the mind [of bodhi], practice, attain bodhi, and enter nirvāṇa. Those who have not brought forth the mind, practiced, attained bodhi, and entered nirvāṇa are not [what is referred to by] *"this mind itself is the buddha."* Even if we bring forth the mind and practice and verify for a single *kṣana*, it is *"this mind itself is the buddha"*; even if we bring forth the mind and practice and verify within one atom, it is *"this mind itself is the buddha"*; even if we bring forth the mind and practice and verify for innumerable kalpas, it is *"this mind itself is the buddha"*; even if we bring forth the mind and practice and verify within a single thought, it is *"this mind itself is the buddha"*; even if we bring forth the mind and practice and verify in half a fist, it is *"this mind itself is the buddha."* However, those who say that to practice over long kalpas to become a buddha is not *"this mind itself is the buddha"* have not yet seen *"this mind itself is the*

---

mind, as in the familiar expression "the will is a horse; the mind, a monkey" (*iba shin'en* 意馬心猿).

48 **The mind of the chair and the whisk** (*isu hossu shin* 椅子拂子心): An unusual combination, the Zen master's "whisk" (*hossu* 拂子) usually being paired with his "staff" (*shujō* 拄杖); the "chair" (*isu* 椅子) here belongs, rather, with the following "bamboo" and "wood." See Supplementary Notes, s.v. "Whisk," "Staff."

no additional bamboo, no wood (*sara ni chiku nashi, boku nashi* さらに竹なし、木なし): Likely reflecting the conversation between Luohan Guichen 羅漢桂琛 (867-928) and his master, Xuansha Shibei 玄沙師備 (835-908), about whether to understand "the three realms are only one mind" (*sangai yui isshin* 三界唯一心) as a "chair" or as "bamboo and wood." Recorded in Dōgen's *shinji Shōbōgenzō* 眞字正法眼藏 (DZZ.5:186, case 112); see Supplementary Notes, s.v. "Chairs, bamboo, and wood."

49 **undefiled "mind itself is the buddha"** (*fuzenna soku shin ze butsu* 不染汚即心是佛): Recalls the conversation, alluded to throughout the *Shōbōgenzō*, between the Sixth Ancestor and his disciple Nanyue Huairang 南嶽懷讓 (677-744), to the effect that buddhas and ancestors are "not defiled" (*fuzenna* 不染汚) by Buddhist practice and verification. Recorded at *shinji Shōbōgenzō* 眞字正法眼藏, DZZ.5:178, case 101; see Supplementary Notes, s.v. "What thing is it that comes like this?"

5. This Mind Itself Is the Buddha *Soku shin ze butsu* 即心是佛 159

buddha," not yet understood it, not yet studied it. They have not seen a true master who expounds "*this mind itself is the buddha.*"

[05:13]

いはゆる諸佛とは、釋迦牟尼佛なり。釋迦牟尼佛、これ即心是佛なり。過去・現在・未來の諸佛、ともにほとけとなるときは、かならず釋迦牟尼佛となるなり。これ即心是佛なり。

"The buddhas" here means Buddha Śākyamuni. Buddha Śākyamuni — this is "this mind itself is the buddha." When any of the buddhas of past, present, and future become buddhas, they invariably become Buddha Śākyamuni. This is "this mind itself is the buddha."

正法眼藏即心是佛第五
Treasury of the True Dharma Eye
This Mind Itself Is the Buddha
Number 5

[Ryūmonji MS:]

爾時延應元年五月二十五日、在雍州宇治郡觀音導利興聖寶林寺示衆
Presented to the assembly, at the Kannon Dōri Kōshō Hōrin Monastery, Uji District, Yōshū; twenty-fifth day, fifth month, first year of En'ō [28 June 1239][50]

[Tōunji MS:]

于時寛元三年乙巳七月十二日在越州吉田縣大佛寺侍者寮書寫之。懷奘
Copied this in the acolyte's quarters, Daibutsu Monastery, Yoshida District, Esshū; twelfth day, seventh month of the junior wood year of the snake, the third year of Kangen [15 August 1245]. Ejō

嘉慶三年正月廿八日奉書寫、宗吾
Copied as a memorial offering, twenty-eighth day, first month, third year of Kakyō [24 February 1389]. Sōgo[51]

---

50 The Tōunji 洞雲寺 MS shares an identical colophon.

51 **Sōgo** 宗吾: 1343-1406, ninth abbot of Eiheiji.

TREASURY OF THE TRUE DHARMA EYE

NUMBER 6

Deportment of the Practicing Buddha
Gyōbutsu iigi

行佛威儀

Deportment of the Practicing Buddha

Gyōbutsu iigi

INTRODUCTION

This work, one of the longer texts in the *Shōbōgenzō*, was composed at Kōshōji in November of 1241, around the same time as the "Busshō" 佛性 chapter. It appears as number 6 in both the sixty- and seventy-five-chapter compilations of the *Shōbōgenzō* and as number 23 in the Honzan edition.

The title of this essay is an unusual expression, not encountered elsewhere in Buddhist literature. The phrase *gyōbutsu iigi* 行佛威儀 (also read *gyōbutsu igi*) could well be parsed "to practice the deportment of a buddha"; but it is clear from his opening words that Dōgen wants us to take *gyōbutsu* as a "practicing buddha," in contrast to other notions of "buddha." Buddhas are those who practice buddhahood, who engage in (to use the language of one of Dōgen's favorite Zen dialogues) the "nondefiling practice and verification" of a buddha.

Such deportment is not limited to humans or gods, or even to sentient beings: as we read on, we find it is the practice of heaven and earth, of coming and going in birth and death, of Tuṣita heaven, where the future Buddha Maitreya dwells, of the pure land of Sukhāvatī, where Buddha Amitābha preaches. Finally, Dōgen borrows from the ninth-century Chan masters Xuefeng Yicun 雪峰義存 and Xuansha Shibei 玄沙師備 to depict the deportment of the practicing buddha as buddhas preaching in the midst of flames, flames preaching while the buddhas stand and listen.

正法眼藏第六

Treasury of the True Dharma Eye
Number 6

行佛威儀

Deportment of the Practicing Buddha

[06:1] {1:59}

諸佛かならず威儀を行足す、これ行佛なり。行佛それ報佛にあらず、化佛
にあらず。自性身佛にあらず、他性身佛にあらず。始覺・本覺にあらず、
性覺・無覺にあらず。如是等佛、たえて行佛に齊肩することうべからず。
しるべし、諸佛の佛道にある、覺をまたざるなり。佛向上の道に行履を通
達せること、唯行佛のみなり。自性佛等、夢也未見在なるところなり。

The buddhas always fully practice deportment; this is the practicing
buddha.[1] The practicing buddha is not the buddha of recompense, not the
buddha of transformation, not the buddha of the body of self-nature, not
the buddha of the body of other-nature.[2] It is neither initial awakening nor

---

1 **Deportment of the Practicing Buddha** (*gyōbutsu iigi* 行佛威儀): Also read *gyōbutsu*
igi. In ordinary parlance, the term *iigi* 威儀 ("deportment"; more commonly read *igi*)
refers to "dignified demeanor," proper decorum and etiquette; in Buddhism, it is used
especially for the four deportments (*shi iigi* 四威儀; S. *īryāpatha*) of walking, standing,
sitting, and reclining (*gyōjūzaga* 行住坐臥) (as well as for the donning of formal vest-
ments). See Supplementary Notes, s.v. "Deportment." The term *gyōbutsu* 行佛 ("practicing buddha") is not a standard Buddhist technical term, though it may reflect the common distinction between "buddhahood in (or through) practice" (*gyōbusshō* 行佛性), as
opposed to "buddhahood in principle" (*ribusshō* 理佛性). The four-glyph expression,
gyōbutsu iigi 行佛威儀, is not common and does not occur elsewhere in Dōgen's writing.

fully practice (*gyōsoku* 行足): An unusual verb not occurring elsewhere in the *Shōbō-*
genzō, with *soku* 足 understood as "complete," as in the standard epithet of a buddha
"perfected in wisdom and conduct" (*myōgyōsoku* 明行足) that Dōgen will use below.
Some would derive the term from the phrase, "eye of wisdom, foot of practice" (*chimoku*
gyōsoku 智目行足).

2 **the buddha of recompense** (*hōbutsu* 報佛): I.e., a buddha in his "enjoyment body,"
or "reward body" (*hōshin* 報身; S. *saṃbhoga-kāya*), the glorified body of a buddha resulting from his practices on the bodhisattva path.

the buddha of transformation (*kebutsu* 化佛): I.e., a buddha in the body he manifests to
teach among sentient beings (*keshin* 化身 or *ōjin* 應身; S. *nirmāṇa-kāya*).

the buddha of the body of self-nature (*jishōshin butsu* 自性身佛); **the buddha of the
body of other-nature** (*tashōshin butsu* 他性身佛): The former expression is a technical
term for the dharma body (*hosshin* 法身; S. *dharma-kāya*) as it is in itself (S. *svabhāvi-*
ka), rendered below in this section as "buddha of self-nature" (*jishō butsu* 自性佛); the
latter expression is Dōgen's playful neologism.

164   DŌGEN'S *SHŌBŌGENZŌ* VOLUME I

original awakening; neither awakening by nature nor non-awakening.[3] Such buddhas as these can never be of equal stature with the practicing buddha. We should recognize that the buddhas are on the way of the buddhas; they do not await awakening.[4] Only the practicing buddha has penetrated the conduct on the way beyond the buddha.[5] It is something that *the buddha of self-nature and the rest have never seen even in their dreams.*

[06:2]

この行佛は、頭頭に威儀現成するゆえに、身前に威儀現成す、道前に化機漏泄すること、亙時なり、亙方なり、亙佛なり、亙行なり。行佛にあらざれば、佛縛・法縛いまだ解脱せず、佛魔・法魔に薫類せらるるなり。

    For this practicing buddha, since his deportment appears in each thing, his deportment appears before his body; his teaching spills out before his words, spanning the times, spanning the directions, spanning the buddhas, spanning the practices.[6] Those who are not practicing buddhas are

---

3 **initial awakening** (*shikaku* 始覺); **original awakening** (*hongaku* 本覺): Terms widely used in East Asian Buddhism to distinguish respectively the bodhi acquired upon completion of the bodhisattva path and the bodhi inherent in the buddha nature.

awakening by nature (*shōkaku* 性覺): A term, roughly synonymous with the more common *hongaku* 本覺, for innate awakening; occurs in the *Śuraṅgama-sūtra* (*Shoulengyan jing* 首楞嚴經, T.945.19:120a3).

non-awakening (*mukaku* 無覺): An expression ordinarily meaning both "unawakened" and "unconscious," it is used in reference both to insentience and to a mental state free from ordinary perception, as in Zen sayings such as "the awakening of non-awakening — this is called the true awakening" (*mukaku shi kaku ze myō shinkaku* 無覺之覺是名眞覺), or "right awakening is without awakening; true emptiness is not empty" (*shōkaku mukaku shinkū fukū* 正覺無覺眞空不空).

4 **the buddhas are on the way of the buddhas; they do not await awakening** (*shobutsu no butsudō ni aru, kaku o matazaru nari* 諸佛の佛道にある、覺をまたざるなり): The exact sense is unclear. Buddhas, of course, are by definition awakened and thus would not be expected to "await awakening"; perhaps the point is that their being on the way of the buddhas is not dependent on their awakening (but, rather, on their practice).

5 **the way beyond the buddha** (*butsu kōjō no dō* 佛向上の道): "Beyond the buddha" (*butsu kōjō* 佛向上) is a common expression in Zen texts and Dōgen's writings, see Supplementary Notes, s.v. "Beyond the buddha."

6 **his deportment appears before his body** (*shinzen ni iigi genjō su* 身前に威儀現成す); **his teaching spills out before his words** (*dōzen ni keki rōei suru* 道前に化機漏泄する): Parallel phrases perhaps meaning that both the physical acts and the verbal instructions of the practicing buddha express truths, "before," or "beyond" the buddha. "Before the body" (*shinzen* 身前) can carry the sense "before birth in this life"; here, perhaps, before the buddha manifests a body. "Teachings" here is a loose translation of *keki* 化機, usually interpreted as "to convert (*ke* 化) an audience according to its capacities (*ki* 機)"; the only instance of the term in the *Shōbōgenzō*.

6. Deportment of the Practicing Buddha *Gyōbutsu iigi* 行佛威儀 165

not yet liberated from the bonds of the buddha, the bonds of the dharma; they are grouped with buddha demons and dharma demons.[7]

[06:3]

佛縛といふは、菩提を菩提と知見解會する、即知見、即解會に即縛せられぬるなり。一念を經歷するに、なほいまだ解脱の期を期せず、いたづらに錯解す。菩提をすなはち菩提なりと見解せん、これ菩提相應の知見なるべし、たれかこれを邪見といはん。想憶す、これすなはち無繩自縛なり。縛縛綿綿として樹倒藤枯にあらず、いたづらに佛邊の窠窟に活計せるのみなり。法身のやまふをしらず、報身の窮をしらず。

"Bonds of the buddha" means precisely to be bound by the very knowledge, the very understanding that knows and understands bodhi as bodhi. We pass through each moment of thought without expectation of a time of liberation, vainly given over to our mistaken understandings. To understand bodhi as bodhi must be the knowledge that accords with bodhi. Who would call this a false view?[8] So we imagine, and this is precisely *to bind ourselves without a rope.*[9] Bound and bound, on and on: it is not *"the tree falling and the vines withering"*; it is just vainly making our living in burrows in the vicinity of the buddha.[10] We do not realize that the dharma body is sick; we do not realize that the recompense body is distressed.[11]

---

7 **the bonds of the buddha, the bonds of the dharma** (*butsubaku hōbaku* 佛縛法縛): Likely indicating here intellectual and emotional attachment to the categories of "buddha" and "dharma." The subsequent parallel phrase "buddha demons and dharma demons" (*butsuma hōma* 佛魔法魔) presumably designates the groups of those bound to these same categories.

8 **Who would call this a false view?** (*tare ka kore o jaken to iwan* たれかこれを邪見といはん): This and the preceding sentence represent the rejoinder to Dōgen's claim here.

9 **bind ourselves without a rope** (*mujō jibaku* 無繩自縛): A common expression, especially in Zen texts, for the state in which one is imprisoned by one's own ideas.

10 **"the tree falling and the vines withering"** (*jutō tōko* 樹倒藤枯): A metaphor for the end of ignorance; from the question posed by Shushan Kuangren 疏山匡仁 (837-909) to Weishan Lingyou 潙山靈祐 (771-853) (quoted in Dōgen's *shinji Shōbōgenzō* 眞字正法眼藏, DZZ.5:208, case 157); see Supplementary Notes, s.v. "Like vines relying on a tree."

just vainly making our living in burrows in the vicinity of the buddha (*itazura ni buppen no kakutsu ni kakkei seru nomi* いたづらに佛邊の窠窟に活計せるのみ): The "burrow" (*kakutsu* 窠窟) is a common metaphor for circumscribed views. The "vicinity (or 'confines') of the buddha" (*buppen* 佛邊) appears with some frequency in Zen texts, often in a dismissive sense, as in "to fall into the vicinity of the buddha" (*raku buppen* 落佛邊) or "what is in the vicinity of the buddha" (*buppen ji* 佛邊事) — as opposed to "what lies beyond the buddha" (*butsu kōjō ji* 佛向上事). See Supplementary Notes, s.v. "Beyond the buddha."

11 **dharma body is sick** (*hosshin no yamau* 法身のやまふ); **recompense body is distressed** (*hōshin no kyū* 報身の窮) Dōgen is playing here in Japanese with the Zen

166 DŌGEN'S *SHŌBŌGENZŌ* VOLUME I

[06:4] {1:60}

教家・經師・論師等の、佛道を遠聞せる、なほしいはく、即於法性、起法性見、即是無明。この教家のいはくは、法性に法性の見おこるに、法性の縛をいはず、さらに無明の縛をかさぬ。法性の縛あることをしらず。あはれむべしといへども、無明縛のかさなれるをしれるは、發菩提心の種子となりぬべし。いま行佛、かつてかくのごとくの縛に縛せられざるなり。

Even the sūtra masters and treatise masters of the teaching houses, who have heard the way of the buddhas from afar, say that *to produce a view of the dharma nature within the dharma nature is ignorance.*[12] What these teaching houses say is not that the occurrence of a view of the dharma nature in the dharma nature is the bondage of dharma nature; they go on to add the bondage of "ignorance." They do not know that there is a bondage of dharma nature. While this is to be pitied, that they know [enough] to add the bondage of ignorance should [at least] become a seed for their bringing forth the mind of bodhi. The practicing buddha here has never been bound by this kind of bondage.

[06:5]

かるがゆえに、我本行菩薩道、所成壽命、今猶未盡、復倍上數なり。しるべし、菩薩の壽命、いまに連綿とあるにあらず、佛壽命の、過去に布遍せるにあらず。いまいふ上數は、全所成なり。いひきたる今猶は、全壽命なり。我本行、たとひ萬里一條鐵なりとも、百年抛却任縱横なり。

Therefore, *"the lifespan attained by my original practice of the bodhisattva path is even now still not exhausted; it is twice the above number."*[13]

---

expression "the dharma body is sick" (*hosshin byō* 法身病) — as in the saying, "when the dharma body is sick, the form body is troubled" (*hosshin byō shikishin fuan* 法身病色身不安) (see, e.g., *Xutang heshang yulu* 虛堂和尚語錄, T.2000.47:996c17).

12 **the sūtra masters and treatise masters of the teaching houses** (*kyōke kyōshi ronshi* 教家・經師・論師): I.e., scholars in Buddhist traditions that emphasize scriptural study. In Song-dynasty China, some Buddhist monasteries were categorized as "Teachings" (*jiao* 教), "Chan" (*chan* 禪), or "Vinaya" (*lü* 律) facilities, which meant that their abbots had to belong to those respective lineages; in this classification, the abbots of the teaching monasteries belonged to the Tiantai 天台 lineage. Kawamura's punctuation here treats *kyōke* 教家 as parallel to *kyōshi* 經師 and *ronshi* 論師, to be understood, then, as "specialists in the teachings"; the translation supplies the genitive, based on Dōgen's use elsewhere of *kyōke no ronshi* 教家の論師 and *kyōke no kōshi* 教家の講師).

to produce a view of the dharma nature within the dharma nature is ignorance (*soku o hosshō, ki hosshō ken, soku ze mumyō* 即於法性、起法性見、即是無明): Dōgen switches here to Chinese, as if quoting a text; but no exact source has been identified. Some would take the adverbial *soku o* 即於, translated here "within," in the sense "with regard to." The "dharma nature" (*hosshō* 法性) is a standard technical term for ultimate reality; in this context, Dōgen may be thinking of it as synonymous with the "dharma body" (*hosshin* 法身) of the buddha.

13 **"the lifespan attained by my original practice of the bodhisattva path"** (*ga hongyō bosatsu dō, shojō jumyō* 我本行菩薩道、所成壽命): A line from the *Lotus Sūtra*

6. Deportment of the Practicing Buddha *Gyōbutsu iigi* 行佛威儀 167

We should understand that this does not mean that the Bodhisattva's lifespan continues up to the present; it does not mean that the Buddha's lifespan spreads back into the past: the "above number" spoken of here is the entirety of [what was] "attained"; the "even now" spoken of is the entirety of "the lifespan." While "my original practice" is "*one strip of iron for ten thousand miles*," it is "*one hundred years cast aside, abandoning myself to freedom.*"[14]

[06:6]

しかあればすなはち、修證は無にあらず、修證は有にあらず、修證は染汚にあらず。無佛・無人の處在に百千萬ありといへども、行佛を染汚せず。ゆえに行佛の修證に染汚せられざるなり。修證の不染汚なるにはあらず、この不染汚、それ不無なり。

Thus, it is not that it lacks practice and verification; it is not that it has practice and verification; it is not that practice and verification are defiling.[15] Although there may be a hundred, a thousand, a myriad in the places without buddhas and without humans, they do not defile the practicing buddha.[16] Therefore, the practicing buddha is not defiled by practice and verification. It is not that practice and verification are not defiling; it is that this "not defiled" is "not lacking."

(*Miaofa lianhua jing* 妙法蓮華經, T.262.9:42c22-23), in which Buddha Śākyamuni reveals that the time since he attained buddhahood has been "incalculable, limitless hundreds of thousands of myriads of millions of *nayutas* of kalpas." This is "the above number" of which he says here his remaining lifespan will be twice as long.

14 "**one strip of iron for ten thousand miles**" (*banri ichijō tetsu* 萬里一條鐵): A common Zen idiom for the ultimate unity of the myriad phenomena; here, perhaps, especially the unity of practice through time. See Supplementary Notes, s.v. "One strip of iron."

"**one hundred years cast aside, abandoning myself to freedom**" (*hyakunen hōkyaku nin jūō* 百年抛却任縱橫): From the *Caoan ge* 草庵歌 of Shitou Xiqian 石頭希遷 (700-790); see Supplementary Note, s.v. "*Reverend Shitou's Song of the Thatched Hut.*"

15 **it is not that it lacks practice and verification** (*shushō wa mu ni arazu* 修證は無にあらず): Dōgen turns here to a discussion of one of his favorite sources on practice, a conversation between the Sixth Ancestor and his disciple Nanyue Huairang 南嶽懷讓 (677-744) that he records in his *shinji shōbōgenzō* 眞字正法眼藏 (DZZ.5:178, case 101) and frequently cites in the *Shōbōgenzō*; see Supplementary Notes, s.v. "What thing is it that comes like this?"

16 **a hundred, a thousand, a myriad** (*hyaku sen man* 百千萬): I.e., instances of practice and verification.

places without buddhas and without humans (*mubutsu munin no shozai* 無佛・無人の處在): Perhaps reflecting a line in the *Zhengdao ge* 證道歌 (T.2014.48:396c3), attributed to the early Chan figure Yongjia Xuanjue 永嘉玄覺 (d. 723):

了了見無一物。亦無人亦無佛。

Perfectly clear, not a thing to be seen;
Neither humans nor buddhas.

168　　DŌGEN'S *SHŌBŌGENZŌ* VOLUME I

[06:7] {1:61}

曹溪いはく、祇此不染汚、是諸佛之所護念、汝亦如是、吾亦如是、乃至西天諸祖亦如是。

Caoxi said, "Just this 'not defiled' is what the buddhas bear in mind. You're also like this; I'm also like this; the ancestors of Sindh in the West are also like this."[17]

[06:8]

しかあればすなはち、汝亦如是のゆえに諸佛なり、吾亦如是のゆえに諸佛なり。まことにわれにあらず、なんぢにあらず。この不染汚に、如吾是吾、諸佛所護念、これ行佛威儀なり、如汝是汝、諸佛所護念、これ行佛威儀なり。吾亦のゆえに師勝なり、汝亦のゆえに資強なり、師勝資強、これ行佛の明行足なり。しるべし、是諸佛之所護念と、吾亦なり、汝亦なり、曹溪古佛の道得、たとひわれにあらずとも、なんぢにあらざらんや。行佛之所護念、行佛之所通達、それかくのごとし。

Therefore, since "*you're also like this*," [you] are "the buddhas"; since "*I'm also like this*," [I] am the "the buddhas." Truly, it is not you; it is not I. In this "*not defiled*," "*this*" *I that is* "*like*" *I is* "*what the buddhas bear in mind*" — this is the deportment of the practicing buddha; "*this*" *you that is* "*like*" *you is* "*what the buddhas bear in mind*" — this is the deportment of the practicing buddha.[18] Because "*I'm also*," the master is superior; because "*you're also*," the disciple is strong. That *the master is superior and the disciple strong* — this is the practicing buddha, perfected in wisdom and conduct.[19] We should realize that "*this is what the buddhas bear in mind*" means "*I'm also*," "*you're also*." In the saying of the Old Buddha of Caoxi, even if it is not I, how could it not be you?[20]

17　**Caoxi said** (*Sōkei iwaku* 曹溪いはく): Quoting the Sixth Ancestor's concluding words in his dialogue with Huairang 懷讓 given just above, Note 15.

18　**this I that is like I** (*nyo go ze go* 如吾是吾); **this you that is like you** (*nyo nyo ze nyo* 如汝是汝): A tentative translation of a phrase that could be parsed in various ways — e.g., "like I is this I; like you is this you," etc. Dōgen is here playing with terms in the Sixth Ancestor's statement, "You're also like this; I'm also like this" (*nyo yaku nyo ze, go yaku nyo ze* 汝亦如是、吾亦如是), splitting the predicate "like this" into "like I (or you)" and "this I (or you)." It is possible to take the former ("like I") to represent "the I (or you) that is such" (i.e., universal); and the latter ("this I"), "the I (or you) that is this" (i.e., particular), suggesting that the practicing buddha bears in mind you and me as we really are.

19　**the master is superior and the disciple strong** (*shishō shikyō* 師勝資強): Also read *shishō shigō*. A fixed phrase in Zen texts, occurring twice in the *Shōbōgenzō*, for a capable teacher and able student.

perfected in wisdom and conduct (*myōgyōsoku* 明行足): S. *Vidyā-caraṇa-saṃpanna*, one of the traditional ten epithets of a buddha.

20　**even if it is not I, how could it not be you?** (*tatoi ware ni arazutomo, nanji ni arazaran ya* たとひわれにあらずとも、なんぢにあらざらんや): Perhaps meaning,

6. Deportment of the Practicing Buddha *Gyōbutsu iigi* 行佛威儀

What the practicing buddha "bears in mind," what the practicing buddha penetrates is like this.

[06:9]

かるがゆえにしりぬ、修證は性相・本末等にあらず。行佛の去就、これ果然として佛を行ぜしむるに、佛すなはち行ぜしむ。ここに爲法捨身あり、爲身捨法あり、不惜身命あり、但惜身命あり。法のために法をすつるのみにあらず、心のために法をすつる威儀あり。捨は無量なること、わするべからず。佛量を拈來して、大道を測量し、度量すべからず。佛量は一隅なり、たとへば華開のごとし。心量を擧來して威儀を摸索すべからず、擬議すべからず。心量は一面なり、たとへば世界のごとし。一莖草量、あきらかに佛祖心量なり。これ行佛の蹤跡を認ぜる一片なり。一心量たとひ無量佛量を包含せりと見徹すとも、行佛の容止動靜を量せんと擬するには、もとより過量の面目あり。過量の行履なるがゆえに、即不中なり、使不得なり、量不及なり。

Therefore, we know that practice and verification are not nature and mark, root and branch, and the like.[21] While it is the conduct of the practicing buddha that, in the end, causes the practice of the buddha, it is the buddha himself who causes the practice.[22] Here, there is *discarding the body for the sake of the dharma*; there is *discarding the dharma for the sake of the body*.[23] There is *not begrudging body and life*; there is *simply*

"even if the Sixth Ancestor had not claimed that he was 'like this,' he would still have said it of Nanyue."

21 **practice and verification are not nature and mark, root and branch, and the like** (*shushō wa shōsō honmatsu tō ni arazu* 修證は性相・本末等にあらず): Presumably, meaning that the relationship between "practice" (*shu* 修) and "verification" (*shō* 證) is not like that between such standard pairs expressing the essential nature and phenomenal appearance. Though obscured by the translation, the wording here is suggestive of the famous line in the *Lotus Sūtra* (*Miaofa lianhua jing* 妙法蓮華經, T.262.9:5c11-13), from which the Tiantai tradition derives its characteristic teaching of the "ten suchnesses" (*jū nyoze* 十如是); see Supplementary Notes, s.v. "Only buddhas with buddhas can exhaustively investigate the real marks of the dharmas."

22 **While it is the conduct of the practicing buddha that, in the end, causes the practice of the buddha, it is the buddha himself who causes the practice** (*gyōbutsu no kyoshū, kore kanen toshite butsu o gyōzeshimuru ni, butsu sunawachi gyōzeshimu* 行佛の去就、これ果然として佛を行ぜしむるに、佛すなはち行ぜしむ): The sense of this somewhat problematic sentence is probably that the buddha and the practice entail each other. Dōgen is reflecting on the fact that the expression *gyōbutsu* 行佛 can be parsed as both "practicing buddha" and "practice of buddhahood." The term *kyoshū* 去就 ("departing and approaching") has the sense of "behavior," "conduct," etc. The translation takes the particle *ni* に here as a concessive.

23 **discarding the body for the sake of the dharma** (*ihō shashin* 爲法捨身); **discarding the dharma for the sake of the body** (*ishin shahō* 爲身捨法): The former phrase is a standard Buddhist expression that also can be rendered "sacrificing oneself for the sake of the dharma"; the latter phrase is Dōgen's variation on it. A similar pattern occurs in the "Shōbōgenzō jishō zanmai" 正法眼藏自證三昧: "They discard the body for the sake

170 DŌGEN'S *SHŌBŌGENZŌ* VOLUME I

begrudging body and life.[24] Not only does he discard the dharma for the sake of the dharma; there is deportment in which he discards the dharma for the sake of the mind.[25]

We should not forget that his discardings are without measure.[26] We should not take up the measure of the buddha to calculate, to gauge the great way: the measure of the buddha is one corner, like "a flower opens"; we should not take up the measure of the mind to grope for, to consider deportment: the measure of the mind is one face, like "the world."[27] The measure of "one blade of grass" is clearly the measure of the mind of the buddhas and ancestors.[28] This is one piece where we recognize the traces of the practicing buddha. Even if we see clearly that the measure of the one mind contains the measure of the immeasurable buddha, when we think to measure the bearing and behavior of the practicing buddha, he has from the beginning a face beyond measure. Because it is conduct

---

of the dharma" (*ihō shashin* 爲法捨身); "they seek the dharma for the sake of the body" (*ishin guhō* 爲身求法).

24 **not begrudging body and life** (*fushaku shinmyō* 不惜身命); **simply begrudging body and life** (*tanshaku shinmyō* 但惜身命): Or "not begrudging one's life"; "simply begrudging one's life." Again, the former phrase is a standard Buddhist expression for the willingness to sacrifice for the dharma (or for others); the latter is Dōgen's variation, perhaps meaning to preserve oneself for the dharma.

25 **discards the dharma for the sake of the mind** (*shin no tame ni hō o sutsuru* 心のため に法をすつる): Dōgen has here shifted to a Japanese variant of his earlier "discarding the dharma for the sake of the body."

26 **without measure** (*muryō* 無量): Dōgen begins here an extended treatment of the glyph 量 ("measure"), which can have such senses as "amount," "quantity," "size," "extent," "dimension," etc.

27 **measure of the buddha** (*butsuryō* 佛量): A term that appears several times in Dōgen's writings, sometimes seemingly in the sense "the thinking of a buddha" (*butsu no shiryō* 佛の思量). Dōgen's play with the term throughout this section suggests that he is using *ryō* 量 in its primary sense of "size." See Supplementary Notes, s.v. "Measure of the buddha."

to calculate, to gauge (*sokuryō shi, takuryō su* 測量し、度量す): The translation masks the repetition of the glyph *ryō* 量 in these two terms for measurement.

"a flower opens" (*ke kai* 華開); **"the world"** (*sekai* 世界): From the final line of the dharma transmission verse attributed to Bodhidharma's master, Prajñātāra. See Supplementary Notes, s.v. "A flower opens, and the world arises."

measure of the mind (*shinryō* 心量): A term used in reference to the various types of consciousness and as an equivalent of "mind only" (*yuishin* 唯心; S. *citta-mātra*); here, likely meaning "extent of the mind." See Supplementary Notes, s.v. "Measure of the buddha."

28 **measure of "one blade of grass"** (*ikkyō sō ryō* 一莖草量): Likely reflecting the well-known Zen saying, alluded to elsewhere in the *Shōbōgenzō*, that equates a single blade of grass with the sixteen-foot body of a buddha; see Supplementary Notes, s.v. "One blade of grass," "Measure of the buddha."

6. Deportment of the Practicing Buddha *Gyōbutsu iigi* 行佛威儀　　171

beyond measure, it is "wouldn't hit it"; it is *impossible to use it*; it is *the measure cannot reach it.*[29]

[06:10] {1:62}

しばらく行佛威儀に一究あり。即佛即自と恁麼來せるに、吾亦・汝亦の威儀、それ唯我能にかかはれりといふとも、すなはち十方佛然の脱落、この同條のみにあらず。

There is one investigation of the deportment of the practicing buddha [that we should pursue here] for a bit. In "coming like this," as this very buddha, this very self, while the deportment of "I'm also" and "you're also" may involve "I alone" am able, the immediate sloughing off of "the buddhas of the ten directions are so" is not merely the same.[30]

[06:11]

かるがゆえに古佛云、體取那邊事、却來這裏行履。

Therefore, an old buddha has said, "*Personally experience what's over there and bring it back to your conduct here.*"[31]

---

29 **"wouldn't hit it"** (*soku fuchū* 即不口): From the response of Nanyue Huairang 南嶽懷讓 to the Sixth Ancestor's question, "What is it that comes like this?": "To say it's like any thing wouldn't hit it." See above, Note 15.

it is impossible to use it; it is the measure cannot reach it (*shi futoku nari, ryō fugyū nari* 使不得なり、量不及なり): Two expressions frequently found in Buddhist texts, the latter often in the sense "thinking (*shiryō* 思量) cannot reach it."

30 **"In coming like this"** (*inmo rai seru ni* 恁麼來せるに): From the Sixth Ancestor's question to Nanyue: "What thing is it that comes like this?"

"I'm also" and "you're also" (*go yaku nyo yaku* 吾亦・汝亦): From the Sixth Ancestor's response to Nanyue: "Just this 'nondefilement' is what the buddhas bear in mind. You're also like this, I'm also like this, and all the ancestors of Sindh in the West are also like this."

"I alone" am able (*yui ga nō* 唯我能); **"the buddhas of the ten directions are so"** (*jippō butsu nen* 十方佛然): Variation on a verse in the *Lotus Sūtra* (*Miaofa lianhua jing* 妙法蓮華經, T.262.9:6a20), in which Buddha Śākyamuni says,

唯我知是相、十方佛亦然。
I alone know its marks; as do the buddhas of the ten directions.

not merely the same (*kono dōjō nomi ni arazu* この同條のみにあらず): Probably meaning, "not simply the same as 'I alone.'" Though "sloughing off" (*datsuraku* 脱落) would appear to be the grammatical subject here, the logic of the sentence becomes clearer if we take it as a predicate nominative, with "deportment" (*iigi* 威儀) as the subject: i.e., insofar as deportment includes all the buddhas, it sloughs off, and is therefore not the same as, "I alone." See Supplementary Notes, s.v. "Slough off" and "Deportment."

31 **an old buddha has said** (*kobutsu iwaku* 古佛いはく): Versions of this saying occur in several sources. The closest to Dōgen's version would seem to be that found, attributed to "an ancient," in a lecture by Yunju Daoying 雲居道膺 (d. 902), *Liandeng huiyao* 聯燈會要, ZZ.136:797a12.

172 DŌGEN'S *SHŌBŌGENZŌ* VOLUME I

[06:12]
すでに恁麼保任するに、諸法・諸身・諸行・諸佛、これ親切なり。この行・法・身・佛、おのおの承當に罣礙あるのみなり。承當に罣礙あるがゆえに、承當に脱落あるのみなり。眼礙の明明百草頭なる、不見一法、不見一物と動著することなかれ。這法に若至なり、那法に若至なり。拈來拈去、出入同門に行履する、徧界不曾藏なるがゆえに、世尊の密語・密證・密行・密附等あるなり。

When it has been maintained like this, the dharmas, the bodies, the practices, and the buddhas are intimate.[32] Each of these practices, dharmas, bodies, and buddhas is simply obstructed by what it accedes to.[33] Because it is obstructed by what it accedes to, it simply sloughs off what it accedes to.[34] The eye obstruction is "perfectly clear, the tips of the hun-

32 **When it has been maintained like this** (*sude ni inmo hōnin suru ni* すでに恁麼保任するに): I.e., "when it has been understood in this way." The object of "maintained" (*hōnin* 保任) is unexpressed; perhaps best taken as the "the deportment of the practicing buddha" under "one investigation" here. The antecedent of "like this" (*inmo* 恁麼) is most likely the saying of the "old buddha" just preceding.

the dharmas, the bodies, the practices, and the buddhas are intimate (*shohō shoshin shogyō shobutsu, kore shinsetsu nari* 諸法・諸身・諸行・諸佛、これ親切なり): The "intimacy" (*shinsetsu* 親切) here might refer to the relation between this list and what is "maintained in this way," or the one maintaining it; perhaps more likely, it indicates the unity of the four members of the list. How we are to understand this list is uncertain. The last two members, "practices" (*shogyō* 諸行) and "buddhas" (*shobutsu* 諸佛) seem derived from "the practicing buddha" (*gyōbutsu* 行佛); the first two, "dharmas" (*shohō* 諸法) and "bodies" (*shoshin* 諸身) suggest the "dharma body" (*hosshin* 法身) of the buddha, but they may well reflect the earlier discussion (section 9, above) of "discarding the body (*shin* 身) for the sake of the dharma (*hō* 法)."

33 **Each of these practices, dharmas, bodies, and buddhas** (*kono gyō hō shin butsu* この行・法・身・佛): Dōgen has here rearranged the order of his list; the resulting sequence could be parsed variously: e.g., "the practicing dharma body buddha," "the buddha that practices the dharma body," etc.

simply obstructed by what it accedes to (*jōtō ni keige aru nomi* 承當に罣礙あるのみ): An obscure phrase, more literally reading, "there is simply an obstruction in accession," that has been taken to mean "each has its own identity," "each is wholly itself." (See, e.g., *Shōbōgenzō keiteki* 正法眼藏啓迪 2:362-363). The term *jōtō* 承當 has the sense "to succeed [to a position]," "to accept," "to make one's own." Dōgen regularly uses the term *keige* 罣礙 ("obstruction"), in the sense "to define," "to identify."

34 **it simply sloughs off what it accedes to** (*jōtō ni datsuraku aru nomi* 承當に脱落あるのみ): Likely meaning that, to the extent that the practices, dharmas, bodies, and buddhas are wholly themselves, they transcend their limited identity as themselves — a familiar logic in Dōgen's writings. For the use of "slough off" (*datsuraku* 脱落), see Supplementary Notes, s.v. "Slough off."

A possible paraphrase of this difficult passage might read something like this:

When the deportment of the practicing buddha is understood in terms of the saying of the old buddha (i.e., as putting into practice the experience of awakening), the body and the dharma (of the saying, "discarding the body for the sake of the dharma") and

6. Deportment of the Practicing Buddha *Gyōbutsu iigi* 行佛威儀   173

dred grasses"; do not be moved by "*not seeing a single dharma,*" "*not seeing a single thing*": it is "if it arrives" in this dharma; it is "if it arrives" in that dharma.[35] Since the conduct of *bringing them and taking them away, in and out through the same gate,* is "*in the realms everywhere, it has never been hidden,*" there are the secret words, secret verification, secret practice, secret bequest, and the like, of the World-Honored One.[36]

---

the practice and the buddha (of the term "practicing buddha") are all one. They are all just what they are; but, for that very reason, they are beyond their individuality.

35 **The eye obstruction is "perfectly clear, the tips of the hundred grasses"** (*genge no meimei hyakusōtō naru* 眼礙の明明百草頭なる): I.e., the myriad phenomena are obvious to the eye. The odd expression "eye obstruction" (*genge* 眼礙) may here be echoing the preceding use of "obstruction" (*keige* 罣礙) in the sense of "identity" — i.e., "the eye as it is." At the same time, the diction is reminiscent of a saying of Fayan Wenyi 法眼文益 (885-958) recorded in the *shinji Shōbōgenzō* 眞字正法眼藏 (DZZ.5:186, case 111); see Supplementary Notes, s.v. "Obstructed by the eye." The expression "perfectly clear, the tips of the hundred grasses," which appears elsewhere in the *Shōbōgenzō*, is usually associated with a story of the Layman Pang Yun 龐蘊居士 (740?-808) that Dōgen records in his *shinji Shōbōgenzō* 眞字正法眼藏 (DZZ.5:168, case 88); see Supplementary Notes.

"not seeing a single dharma," "not seeing a single thing" (*fuken ippō, fuken ichimotsu* 不見一法、不見一物): The former phrase is best known from the *Zhengdao ge* 證道歌 (T.2014.48:396c11-12):

不見一法即如來。

Not seeing a single dharma — this is a tathāgata.

The latter phrase occurs with some frequency, as, e.g., in the *Shaoshi liumen* 少室六門 (T.2009.4:370b26-27):

不見一物、名爲見道。不行一物、名爲行道。

Not seeing a single thing is called seeing the way; not practicing a single thing is called practicing the way.

it is "if it arrives" in this dharma; it is "if it arrives" in that dharma (*shahō ni nyaku shi nari, nahō ni nyaku shi nari* 這法に若至なり、那法に若至なり): The odd "if it arrives" (*nyaku shi* 若至) can probably be understood here simply as "it arrives." What it is that arrives and what it means to arrive are subject to interpretation. One reading might take "the perfect clarity of the hundred grasses" as the subject: i.e., such clarity (or, perhaps, the "obstructed" vision that perceives it) "arrives" (is present) in every phenomenon (dharma). Alternatively, given the allusion in the preceding sentence to the saying, "Not seeing a single dharma — this is a tathāgata," the sense may be that the practicing buddha arrives in every phenomenon (dharma). Such a reading might help to explain the use of the problematic "if it arrives" (*nyaku shi* 若至) here, inspired by a saying quoted in the "Shōbōgenzō busshō" 正法眼藏佛性:

時節若至佛性現前。

If the time arrives, the buddha nature appears.

36 **bringing them and taking them away** (*nenrai nenko* 拈來拈去): The verbs *nenrai* 拈來 and *nenko* 拈去 can mean both to "bring" and "take away," respectively, and also to "take up" and "leave off" a topic for discussion. The object of these verbs is unexpressed; the translation takes them as "this dharma" and "that dharma," but it might also be taken as what "arrives" in these dharmas.

174　　DŌGEN'S *SHŌBŌGENZŌ* VOLUME I

[06:13]

出門便是草、入門便是草、萬里無寸草也。入之一字、出之一字、這頭也不用得、那頭也不用得なり。いまの把捉は放行をまたざれども、これ夢幻空華なり。たれかこれを夢幻空華と將錯就錯せん。進歩也錯、退歩也錯、一歩也錯、兩歩也錯なるがゆえに錯錯なり。天地懸隔するがゆえに至道無難なり。威儀儀威、大道體寛と究竟すべし。

"*Once you exit the gate, it's grass*"; *once you enter the gate, it's grass: they are* "*not an inch of grass for ten thousand miles.*"[37] "*The word 'en-*

---

in and out through the same gate (*shutsunyū dōmon* 出入同門): A fixed expression, a variant of which occurs below (section 26), in the line, "going in and out of the same gate without meeting each other" (*dōmon shutsunyū no fusōhō* 同門出入の不相逢). Here, likely an intimation of the gate metaphor introduced in the next section.

"in the realms everywhere, it has never been hidden" (*henkai fu zō zō* 徧界不曾藏): A popular saying attributed to Chan Master Shishuang Qingzhu 石霜慶諸 (807-888) found in the *shinji Shōbōgenzō* 眞字正法眼藏, DZZ.5:157-158, case 58; see Supplementary Notes.

secret words, secret verification, secret practice, secret bequest, and the like, of the World-Honored One (*seson no mitsugo misshō mitsugyō mippu* 世尊の密語密證密行密附): Or, perhaps, "of the world-honored ones." The consistent rendering of *mitsu* 密 as "secret" misrepresents the semantic range of the term in this list; a more natural version might read "secret words, intimate verification, strict practice, and personal bequest." A similar list appears in "Shōbōgenzō mitsugo" 正法眼藏密語, where Dōgen discusses the saying involving Yunju Daoying 雲居道膺 alluded to here (see, e.g., *Jingde chuandeng lu* 景德傳燈錄, T.2076.51:335c1-2):

> 問曰、世尊有密語迦葉不覆藏。如何是世尊密語。

> [An official] asked, "The World-Honored One has secret words; for Kāśyapa, they are not concealed. What are the secret words of the World-Honored One?"

37　**"Once you exit the gate, it's grass"; once you enter the gate, it's grass: they are "not an inch of grass for ten thousand miles"** (*shutsu mon ben ze sō, nyū mon ben ze sō, banri musun sō ya* 出門便是草、入門便是草、萬里無寸草也): From an anecdote involving Dongshan Liangjie 洞山良价 (807-869) and Shishuang Qingzhu 石霜慶諸, a version of which is recorded in Dōgen's *shinji Shōbōgenzō* 眞字正法眼藏 (DZZ.5:166, case 82):

> 洞山夏末示衆曰、初秋夏末、直須向萬里無寸草處去。衆無語。僧舉似石霜。霜曰、何不道出門便是草。

> At the end of the summer [retreat], Dongshan addressed the assembly saying, "It's the beginning of autumn, and the summer [retreat] is at its end. You should head for the place where there's not an inch of grass for ten thousand miles." The assembly was silent.

> A monk raised this with Shishuang. Shuang said, "Why not say, 'Once you exit the gate, it's grass'?"

See Supplementary Notes, s.v. "Not an inch of grass for ten thousand miles." The sentence, "Once you enter the gate, it's grass," represents Dōgen's contribution. He has also added the Chinese copula marker *ya* 也 after Shishuang's statement; the translation takes it as indicating that the statement defines the first two phrases here, in parallel with what seems the function of the Japanese copula *nari* なり in the following sentence.

6. Deportment of the Practicing Buddha *Gyōbutsu iigi* 行佛威儀   175

ter,'" *the word "exit"* — they are *"of no use" here, " of no use" there.*[38]
The "grasping" here, even without the "letting go" — this is "dreams,
phantoms, sky flowers."[39] Who would *make a mistake of the mistake* of
treating this as "dreams, phantoms, sky flowers?"[40] *A step forward is a
mistake; a step back is a mistake; one step is a mistake; two steps are a
mistake.* So it is, "Mistake! Mistake!"[41] Since *"the gap is like that between
heaven and earth," "the supreme way isn't hard."*[42] We should fulfill de-

---

38 **"The word 'enter,'" the word "exit" — they are "of no use" here, "of no use"
there** (*nyūsshi ichiji, shusshi ichiji, shatō ya fuyōtoku, natō ya fuyōtoku nari* 入之一
字、出之一字、這頭也不用得、那頭也不用得なり): Based on a conversation between
Yangshan Huiji 仰山慧寂 (803-887) and the magistrate Lu Xisheng 陸希聲 (d. 895),
appearing as case 139 in the *shinji Shōbōgenzō* 眞字正法眼藏 (DZZ.5:200); see Supplementary Notes, s.v. "The one word 'enter.'"

39 **The "grasping" here, even without the "letting go" — this is "dreams, phantoms, sky flowers"** (*ima no hasoku wa hōgyō o matazaredomo, kore mu gen kūge nari*
いまの把捉は放行をまたざれども、これ夢幻空華なり): The glyphs *mu gen* 夢幻,
rendered here "dreams, phantoms," are often read as a compound term referring to the
objects of the dreaming consciousness. Dōgen's sentence alludes to the *Xinxin ming* 信
心銘, attributed to the Third Ancestor, Sengcan 僧璨 (d. 606), which will be quoted again
just below; see T.2010.48:376c19-21:

> 一切二邊、妄自斟酌。夢幻空華、何勞把捉。得失是非、一時放却。
> All the dualities,
> The deluded serve themselves.
> Dreams, phantoms, sky flowers —
> Why bother to grasp them?
> Gain and loss, right and wrong —
> Let go of them all at once.

40 **make a mistake of the mistake** (*shōshaku jushaku* 將錯就錯): An idiom, found
in Zen texts, meaning "to recognize one's mistake as a mistake," "to turn a mistake to
one's advantage," or "to make one mistake after another"; see Supplementary Notes, s.v.
"Make a mistake of a mistake." Perhaps the sense of this awkward sentence is simply,
"who would call dreams, phantoms, and sky flowers 'dreams, phantoms, and sky flowers'?"

41 **"Mistake! Mistake!"** (*shaku shaku* 錯錯): Or "Wrong! Wrong!" A common retort
of Zen masters, sometimes used in ironic praise. The preceding sentence is given in
Chinese, apparently of Dōgen's own construction.

42 **Since "the gap is like that between heaven and earth," "the supreme way isn't
hard"** (*tenchi kenkyaku suru ga yue ni shiidō bunan nari* 天地懸隔するがゆえに至道
無難なり): From the opening lines of the *Xinxin ming* 信心銘 (T.2010.48:37620-21):

> 至道無難、唯嫌揀擇。但莫憎愛、洞然明白。毫釐有差、天地懸隔。
> The supreme way isn't hard:
> Just dislike picking and choosing.
> If we simply do not hate or love,
> All will be open and clear.
> Where there's a hair's breadth of distinction
> The gap is like that between heaven and earth.

176 DŌGEN'S *SHŌBŌGENZŌ* VOLUME I

portment and comportment as "*the great way, its substance is vast.*"[43]

[06:14] {1:63}

しるべし、出生合道出なり、入死合道入なり。その頭正尾正に、玉轉珠回
の威儀現前するなり。佛威儀の一隅を遣有するは、盡乾坤大地なり、盡生
死去來なり、塵刹なり、蓮華なり。これ塵刹・蓮華おのおの一隅なり。學
人おほくおもはく、盡乾坤といふは、この南瞻部州をいふならんと擬せら
れ、又この一四州をいふならんと擬せられ、ただ又神丹一國おもひにかか
り、日本一國おもひにめぐるがごとし。又、盡大地といふも、ただ三千大
千世界とおもふがごとし、わづかに一州一縣をおもひにかくるがごとし。
盡大地・盡乾坤の言句を參學せんこと、三次五次もおもひめぐらすべし、
ひろきにこそはとてやみぬることなかれ。この得道は、極大同小、極小同
大の超佛越祖なるなり。大の有にあらざる、小の有にあらざる、疑著に似
たりといへども、威儀行佛なり。佛佛祖祖の道趣する盡乾坤の威儀、盡大
地の威儀、ともに不曾藏を徧界と參學すべし。徧界不曾藏なるのみにはあ
らざるなり。これ行佛一中の威儀なり。

We should realize that, *when we emerge at birth, we emerge in accord
with the way; when we enter into death, we enter in accord with the
way.* True from head to tail, it is the manifestation of the deportment
of a jewel turning, a pearl spinning.[44] What provides one corner of the
deportment of the buddha is the whole earth of all heaven and earth, is
the entire birth and death, coming and going, is *kṣetra* like dust motes,
is lotus [lands].[45] These *kṣetra* like dust motes and lotus [lands] are each

---

43 **We should fulfill deportment and comportment as "the great way, its substance
is vast"** (*iigi gii, daidō tai kan to kukyō su beshi* 威儀儀威、大道體寬と究竟すべし):
"The great way, its substance is vast" (*daidō tai kan* 大道體寬) is another line from the
Xinxin ming 信心銘 (T.2010.48:376c11):

大道體寬、無易無難。

The great way, its substance is vast;
With nothing easy, nothing hard.

"Deportment and comportment" represents an attempt to capture something of Dōgen's
play here with *iigi* 威儀 and its reverse *gii* 儀威 (which might be rendered "dignified
demeanor and demeanor dignified"); see Supplementary Notes, s.v. "Deportment."

44 **True from head to tail** (*zushin bishin* 頭正尾正): Also read *zushō bishō* or *tōshō
bishō*. A fixed expression in Zen literature appearing often in the *Shōbōgenzō*. While
typically taken as "true at the beginning and true at the end," Dōgen seems often to use
it in the sense simply of "from start to finish."

a jewel turning, a pearl spinning (*gyoku ten shu kai* 玉轉珠回): Common metaphors
in Zen texts for unimpeded movement; akin to the expression "a pearl running round a
tray" (*isshu sōban* 一珠走盤).

45 **the whole earth of all heaven and earth** (*jin kenkon daichi* 盡乾坤大地): A fixed
expression in Zen texts for the whole of the universe.

***kṣetra* like dust motes** (*jinsetsu* 塵刹); **lotus [lands]** (*renge* 蓮華): The former term can
indicate (a) "lands as numerous as motes of dust" or (b) "dusty lands" (i.e., "this world"
or the "secular world"); see Supplementary Notes, s.v. "Dust." The latter term is likely
here an abbreviation of *renge koku* 蓮華國, used in reference to buddha lands.

6. Deportment of the Practicing Buddha *Gyōbutsu iigi* 行佛威儀　　177

one corner. Students often think "all heaven and earth" must refer to the Southern Continent of Jambudvīpa; or they think it must mean these four continents as a whole.[46] Or, again, they seem to imagine that it is simply the one Land of Cīnasthāna, or they call to mind the one Land of Japan.[47] Or again, they seem to think that "all the whole earth" also means just the trichiliocosm, or they seem to imagine it means merely one province or one district.[48]

When we study the terms "all the whole earth" or "all heaven and earth," we should think them over three to five times; do not take them simply as meaning "vast" and let it go at that. This gaining the way is something *transcending the buddhas and surpassing the ancestors*, where *"the extremely large is the same as the small," "the extremely small is the same as the large."*[49] That the large is not existent, that the small is not existent, might seem doubtful, but it is the practicing buddha of

---

46　**the Southern Continent of Jambudvīpa** (*Nan Senbu shū* 南瞻部州); **these four continents as a whole** (*kono ichi shishū* この一四州): Reference to the geography of the traditional Buddhist account of a single world system, with Mount Sumeru at the center, surrounded by four continents — of which our own is the southern continent of Jambudvīpa ("Rose Apple Island"). See Supplementary Notes, s.v. "Four Continents."

47　**the one Land of Cīnasthāna** (*Shintan ichikoku* 神丹一國): I.e., "China," represented here by a Sanskrit name transliterated by the Chinese *Shendan* 神丹.

48　**trichiliocosm** (*sanzen daisen sekai* 三千大千世界): Or the "threefold, great thousandfold world system"; i.e., a "great chiliocosm," defined as three chiliocosms, or one billion Mount Sumeru world systems.

49　**This gaining of the way** (*kono tokudō* この得道): Here, likely has the sense, "such an understanding."

transcending the buddhas and surpassing the ancestors (*chōbutsu osso* 超佛越祖): A stock expression, occurring several times in the *Shōbōgenzō*, used in reference to going beyond awakening; especially associated with Yunmen Wenyan 雲門文偃 (864-949). See, e.g., *Yunmen Kuangzheng chanshi guanglu* 雲門匡眞禪師廣錄, T.1988.47:548b5-6:

> 時有僧問、如何是超佛越祖之談。師云餬餅。
> At the time, there was a monk who asked, "What is the talk that transcends the buddhas and surpasses the ancestors?"
> The Master said, "A sesame cake."

"the extremely large is the same as the small," "the extremely small is the same as the large" (*gokudai dō shō, gokushō dō dai* 極大同小、極小同大): Again, lines from the *Xinxin ming* 信心銘 (T.2010.48:377a5-6):

> 極小同大、妄絕境界。極大同小、不見邊表。
> The extremely small is the same as the large;
> The boundaries forgotten.
> The extremely large is the same as the small;
> The sides unseen.

178 DŌGEN'S *SHŌBŌGENZŌ* VOLUME I

deportment.[50] We should study as "the realms everywhere" that the deportment of all heaven and earth, the deportment of all the earth, spoken of by buddha after buddha and ancestor after ancestor "has never been hidden."[51] It is not just that "*in the realms everywhere, it has never been hidden*": this is but one deportment of the practicing buddha.[52]

[06:15]

佛道を説著するに、胎生・化生等は佛道の行履なるといへども、いまだ濕生・卵生等を道取せず。いはんやこの胎・卵・濕・化生のほかに、なほ生あること、夢也未見在なり。いかにいはんや胎・卵・濕・化生のほかに、胎・卵・濕・化生あることを見聞覺知せんや。いま佛佛祖祖の大道には、胎・卵・濕・化生のほかの胎・卵・濕・化あること、不曾藏に正傳せり、親密に正傳せり。この道得、きかず・ならはず・しらず・あきらめざらんは、なにの黨類なりとかせん。すでに四生はきくところなり、死はいくばくかある。四生には四死あるべきか、又、三死二死あるべきか、又、五死六死、千死萬死あるべきか。この道理、わづかに疑著せんも、參學の分なり。

In talking about the way of the buddhas, while some may say that birth from the womb or birth through transformation are conduct on the way of the buddhas, they do not say this of birth from moisture or birth from an egg.[53] Not to mention that *they have never seen even in the dreams* that there are other births besides womb, egg, moisture, and transformation. Still less have they seen, heard, perceived, or known that there are births of womb, egg, moisture, and transformation besides births of

---

50   **it is the practicing buddha of deportment** (*iigi gyōbutsu nari* 威儀行佛なり): Dōgen has here reversed the two terms in the expression "deportment of the practicing buddha" (*gyōbutsu iigi* 行佛威儀); how to parse the result is subject to disagreement. The translation takes the sense to be that "it (the seemingly doubtful nonexistence of large and small) is the practicing buddha as deportment." It is also possible to read "the deportment (in which there is no large or small) is the practicing buddha"; or even "it (the seemingly doubtful nonexistence of large and small) is deportment practicing buddhahood."

51   **We should study as "the realms everywhere"** (*henkai to sangaku su beshi* 徧界と參學すべし): The translation struggles to preserve the awkward grammar of this play with Shishuang's saying, "in the realms everywhere, it has never been hidden " (*henkai fu zō zō* 徧界不曾藏) (see above, Note 36).

spoken of by buddha after buddha and ancestor after ancestor (*butsubutsu soso no dōshu suru* 佛佛祖祖の道趣する): The unusual verb *dōshu* 道趣 is taken here as a variant of the familiar *dōshu* 道取 ("to say").

52   **This is but one deportment of the practicing buddha** (*kore gyōbutsu itchū no iigi nari* これ行佛一中の威儀なり): A tentative translation; it is also possible to read *gyōbutsu itchū* 行佛一中 as "the unity of the practice and the buddha," or as "the practicing buddhas as a whole."

53   **birth from the womb or birth through transformation** (*taishō keshō* 胎生化生); **birth from moisture or birth from an egg** (*shisshō ranshō* 濕生卵生): The four ways in which beings are born in saṃsāra; see Supplementary Notes, s.v. "Four births."

6. Deportment of the Practicing Buddha *Gyōbutsu iigi* 行佛威儀 179

womb, egg, moisture, and transformation. In this great way of buddha after buddha and ancestor after ancestor, the fact that there are womb, egg, moisture, and transformation besides births of womb, egg, moisture, and transformation has been authentically transmitted without ever being hidden, has been directly transmitted in intimacy. What bunch is it that would not hear, would not study, would not understand and would not clarify these words? The four births are something we've heard of, but how many deaths are there? With four births, should there be four deaths? Or should there be three deaths, or two deaths? Or should there be five deaths or six deaths, or a thousand deaths or ten thousand deaths? Even to have slight doubts about this reasoning is a part of our study.

[06:16] {1:64}

しばらく功夫すべし、この四生衆類のなかに、生はありて死なきものあるべしや。又、死のみ單傳にして、生を單傳せざるありや。單生單死の類の有無、かならず參學すべし。わづかに無生の言句をききてあきらむることなく、身心の功夫をさしおくがごとくするものあり。これ愚鈍のはなはだしきなり。信・法・頓・漸の論にもおよばざる畜類といひぬべし。ゆえいかんとなれば、たとひ無生ときくといふとも、この道得の意旨作麼生なるべし。さらに無佛・無道・無心・無滅なるべしや、無無生なるべしや、無法界・無法性なるべしや、無死なるべしやと功夫せず。いたづらに水草の但念なるがゆえなり。

Let us work at this for a while. Among the types of these four births, will there be any with only birth and no death? Or are there some who uniquely transmit only death and do not uniquely transmit birth? We should definitely study whether or not there are types with solely birth or solely death. There are those who have barely heard the term "no birth" and, without clarifying it, seem to set aside the concentrated effort of body and mind.[54] This is stupidity in the extreme. They should be called a type of beast that does not reach the level of discussions even of faith or dharma, sudden or gradual.[55] Why? It must be that, they hear "no birth," but *what is the meaning* of these words? Going further, they do not make concentrated effort [to consider] whether it should be "no buddha," "no way," "no mind," "no extinction"; whether it should be "no no birth"; whether it should be "no dharma realm," "no dharma nature";

---

54 **"no birth"** (*mushō* 無生): Or "unborn," a term used in reference to the "non-arising" (S. *anutpāda*) of phenomena, as well as to nirvāṇa as the cessation of birth and death.

55 **faith or dharma, sudden or gradual** (*shinbō tonzen* 信法頓漸): The former disjunction refers to two approaches to advancement on the Buddhist path: following faith (*zuishin gyō* 隨信行; S. *śraddhānusāra*) and following [practice of] the dharma (*zuihō gyō* 隨法行; S. *dharmānusāra*); the latter disjunction likely refers to the classic Chan discussions of whether practice and its fruit are sudden (*ton* 頓) or gradual (*zen* 漸).

180 DŌGEN'S *SHŌBŌGENZŌ* VOLUME I

whether it should be "no death." This is because they pointlessly "think only of water and grass."[56]

[06:17]

しるべし、生死は佛道の行履なり、生死は佛家の調度なり。使也要使なり、明也明得なり。ゆえに諸佛は、この通塞に明明なり、この要使に得得なり。この生死の際にくらからん、たれかなんぢをなんぢといはん、たれかなんぢを了生達死漢といはん。生死にしづめりときくべからず、生死にありとしるべからず。生死を生死なりと信受すべからず、不會すべからず、不知すべからず。

We should understand that birth and death are the conduct of the way of the buddhas, birth and death are the implements of the house of the buddhas. *In using them, they must use them; in clarifying them, they can clarify them.*[57] Hence, the buddhas are perfectly clear about their passage and blockage, are fully able to use what they must.[58] If you are unclear about this realm of birth and death, who can say that you are you? Who can say that you are *one who has comprehended birth and mastered death*?[59] We should not hear that we are sunk in birth and death; we should not think that we exist in birth and death.[60] We should not be-

---

56 **This is because they pointlessly "think only of water and grass"** (*itazura ni sui sō no tan nen naru ga yue nari* いたづらに水草の但念なるがゆえなり): I.e., are like dumb beasts of burden; allusion to a description of animals such as camels and donkeys in the *Lotus Sūtra* (*Miaofa lianhua jing* 妙法蓮華經, T.262.9:15c7-8):

但念水草、餘無所知

They think only of water and grass and know of nothing else.

57 **In using them, they must use them; in clarifying them, they can clarify them** (*shi ya yō shi nari, myō ya myōtoku nari* 使也要使なり、明也明得なり): A tentative translation of a sentence variously interpreted. Dōgen shifts into Chinese syntax here, as if quoting a saying, but no source has been identified. The translation assumes that the unexpressed subject here is "the buddhas."

58 **are perfectly clear about their passage and blockage, are fully able to use what they must** (*kono tsūsoku ni myōmyō nari, kono yōshi ni tokutoku nari* この通塞に明明なり、この要使に得得なり): Dōgen plays here with the predicate "able to clarify" (*myōtoku* 明得) in the previous sentence, split here into *myōmyō* 明明 (rendered "perfectly clear") and *tokutoku* 得得 ("fully able"). "Passage and blockage" here translates *tsūsoku* 通塞, a term that has the idiomatic sense of "things going well or not," what we might call "the vicissitudes of circumstance."

59 **comprehended birth and mastered death** (*ryōshō tasshi* 了生達死): A fixed expression for the realized practitioner.

60 **We should not hear that we are sunk in birth and death** (*shoji ni shizumeri to kiku bekarazu* 生死にしづめりときくべからず): I.e., we should not accept the common metaphor of saṃsāra as an ocean of suffering. Here and in the following sentences, the translation reads the negative verbal suffix *bekarazu* べからず as indicating obligation (rather than supposition or potential).

6. Deportment of the Practicing Buddha *Gyōbutsu iigi* 行佛威儀 181

lieve in birth and death as birth and death. Nor should we not understand them; nor should we not know them.[61]

[06:18]

あるいはいふ、ただ人道のみに諸佛出世す、さらに餘方・餘道には出現せずとおもへり。いふがごとくならば、佛在のところ、みな人道なるべきか。これは人佛の唯我獨尊の道得なり。さらに天佛もあるべし、佛佛もあるべきなり。諸佛は唯人間のみに出現すといはんは、佛祖の闇奥にいらざるなり。

Some say the buddhas appear in the world only in the human path and think that they do not appear in other quarters and other paths.[62] If it were as they say, would every place where the buddhas are be a human path? This is the saying "*I alone am honored*" of a human buddha.[63] There must also be deva buddhas; there must also be buddha buddhas. One who says that the buddhas only appear among humans has not entered the inner sanctum of the buddhas and ancestors.

* * * * *

[06:19] {1:65}

祖宗いはく、釋迦牟尼佛、自從迦葉佛所傳正法、往兜率天、化兜率陀天、于今有在。

The ancestors say, "*Buddha Śākyamuni, after receiving the true dharma from Buddha Kāśyapa, went to Tuṣita Heaven and taught the devas of Tuṣita. He remains there still.*"[64]

61 **Nor should we not understand them; nor should we not know them** (*fue su bekarazu, fuchi su bekarazu* 不會すべからず、不知すべからず): Perhaps, meaning that we should not simply take birth and death as something beyond understanding and unknowable.

62 **buddhas appear in the world only in the human path** (*tada nindō nomi ni shobutsu shusse su* ただ人道のみに諸佛出世す): Presumably, meaning that the buddhas only take human form, the "human path" (*nindō* 人道; S. *mānuṣya-gati* being rebirth as a human being. The traditional account of the buddhas, of course, assumes that the bodhisattva in his final incarnation will descend from Tuṣita Heaven into the womb of a woman of the *kṣatriya* class on the continent of Jambudvīpa. See Supplementary Notes, s.v. "Four Continents."

63 **"I alone am honored"** (*yui ga doku son* 唯我獨尊): Words attributed to Buddha Śākyamuni as a newborn baby; see Supplementary Notes, s.v. "I alone am honored."

64 **The ancestors say** (*soshū iwaku* 祖宗いはく): Or "an ancestor has said." The saying is given in Chinese, as if a quotation, but a source has not been identified.

Buddha Kāśyapa (*Kashō butsu* 迦葉佛): I.e., the sixth of the seven buddhas of the past, just preceding Buddha Śākyamuni; see Supplementary Notes, s.v. "Seven buddhas."

Tuṣita (*Tosotsu* 兜率, *Tosotsuda* 兜率陀): Fourth of the six heavens of the realm of desire (*yokukai* 欲界), from which the bodhisattva descends to the human realm in his last incarnation.

182 DŌGEN'S *SHŌBŌGENZŌ* VOLUME I

[06:20]

まことにしるべし、人間の釋迦は、このとき滅度現の化をしけりといへど
も、上天の釋迦は、于今有在にして化天するものなり。學人しるべし、人
間の釋迦の千變萬化の道著あり、行取あり、説著あるは、人間一隅の放
光現瑞なり。おろかに、上天の釋迦その化さらに千品萬門ならん、しら
ざるべからず。佛佛正傳する大道の、斷絶を超越し、無始無終を脱落せる
宗旨、ひとり佛道のみに正傳せり。自餘の諸類、しらず、きかざる功徳な
り。行佛の設化するところには、四生にあらざる衆生あり、天上・人間・
法界等にあらざるところあるべし。行佛の威儀を覩見せんとき、天上・人
間のまなこをもちいることなかれ、天上・人間の情量をもちいるべから
ず、これを擧して測量せんと擬することなかれ。十聖三賢なほこれをしら
ず、あきらめず、いはんや人中天上の測量のおよぶことあらんや。人量短
小なるには、識智も短小なり、壽命短促なるには、思慮も短促なり。いか
にしてか行佛の威儀を測量せん。

Truly we should realize that, although the Śākyamuni among humans
has at this time spread the teaching of his appearance of extinction, the
Śākyamuni in the heavens "*remains there still,*" teaching the devas.[65]
Students should realize that the fact that Śākyamuni among humans has
a thousand changes and a myriad transformations of speech, practice,
and preaching is his *radiating his light and manifesting his auspicious
signs* in just the one corner among humans.[66] We should not stupidly
fail to realize that the teachings of Śākyamuni of the heavens are also
of a thousand types and myriad gates. The essential point — that the
great way directly transmitted through buddha after buddha transcends
severance and sloughs off beginninglessness and endlessness — has
only been directly transmitted in the way of the buddhas; it is a virtue
unknown, unheard of by other types.[67] Where the practicing buddha provides his teachings, there are living beings other than the four births;
there must be places other than the heavens, among humans, the dharma
realm, and so on. When you would look at the deportment of the practicing buddha, do not use the eyes of devas or humans. You should not

---

65 **the teaching of his appearance of extinction** (*metsudo gen no ke* 滅度現の化):
Likely recalling the claim of the *Lotus Sūtra* (see, e.g., *Miaofa lianhua jing* 妙法蓮華經,
T.262.9:42c23-24) that Buddha Śākyamuni makes a show of entering nirvāṇa merely as
a device for teaching his followers.

66 **a thousand changes and a myriad transformations** (*senpen banka* 千變萬化);
radiating his light and manifesting his auspicious signs (*hōkō genzui* 放光現瑞): Two
fixed phrases found throughout Buddhist texts and appearing elsewhere in the *Shōbōgenzō*.

67 **transcends severance and sloughs off beginninglessness and endlessness**
(*danzetsu o chōotsu shi, mushi mushū o datsuraku seru* 斷絶を超越し、無始無終を脱
落せる): I.e., [the great way] is neither cut off (by reason of Śākyamuni's extinction?)
nor eternal (by reason of his continued presence in Tuṣita?). For the use of "slough off"
(*datsuraku* 脱落), see Supplementary Notes, s.v. "Slough off."

6. Deportment of the Practicing Buddha *Gyōbutsu iigi* 行佛威儀 183

use the sentiments of devas or humans. Do not think to take up these to calculate it.[68] Even the ten sages and three worthies do not know, have not heard of this; how much less could the calculations of humans and devas reach it?[69] As the dimension of humans is short and small, their cognition is short and small; as their lifespan is short and cramped, their thinking is short and cramped. How could they calculate the deportment of the practicing buddha?

[06:21] {1:66}

しかあればすなはち、ただ人間を舉して佛法とし、人法を舉して佛法を局量せる家門、かれこれともに佛子と許可することなかれ、これただ業報の衆生なり。いまだ身心の聞法あるにあらず、いまだ行道せる身心なし。從法生にあらず、從法滅にあらず、從法見にあらず、從法聞にあらず、從法行住坐臥にあらず。かくのごとくの儻類、かつて法の潤益なし。行佛は本覺を愛せず、始覺を愛せず、無覺にあらず、有覺にあらずといふ、すなはちこの道理なり。

Thus, do not acknowledge as children of the Buddha those houses that treat the buddha dharma simply as human, or that reduce the buddha dharma to the human dharma: they are just living beings as the recompense of karma.[70] Their bodies and minds have still never heard the dharma; they still lack a body and mind that practices the way. They are not born in accordance with dharma; they are not extinguished in accordance with dharma; they do not see in accordance with dharma; they do not hear in accordance with dharma; they do not walk, stand, sit, or recline in accordance with dharma. The bunch like this has never enjoyed the nourishment of dharma. This is the principle behind our saying that the practicing buddha does not love original awakening, does not love initial awakening, is not non-awakening, is not awakening.[71]

---

68   **Do not think to take up these to calculate it** (*kore o koshite sokuryō sen to gisuru koto nakare* これを舉して測量せんと擬ることなかれ): I.e., do not try to use the eyes or the sentiments of humans or devas to measure the deportment of the practicing buddha.

69   **ten sages and three worthies** (*jisshō sanken* 十聖三賢): I.e., the advanced bodhisattvas on the ten ārya (*shō* 聖) stages of the path and the three *bhadra* (*ken* 賢) levels preceding them. Also written *sanken jisshō* 三賢十聖, as below, section 27.

70   **children of the Buddha** (*busshi* 佛子): I.e., Buddhists; the progenitor imagined here is no doubt Buddha Śākyamuni, often depicted as the father of his followers — especially, perhaps, of the bodhisattvas among his followers, who sometimes describe themselves as members of the "buddha clan" (S. *buddha-gotra*).

houses (*kamon* 家門): I.e., schools of Buddhism.

71   **This is the principle behind our saying** (*iu, sunawachi kono dōri nari* いふ、すなはちこの道理なり): Reference to the opening section of the essay. The antecedent of "this" would seem to be the principle that one cannot understand Buddhism through merely human categories — as further explained below.

184 DŌGEN'S *SHŌBŌGENZŌ* VOLUME I

[06:22]

いま凡夫の活計する有念無念・有覺無覺・始覺本覺等、ひとへに凡夫の活計なり、佛佛相承せるところにあらず。凡夫の有念と諸佛の有念と、はるかにことなり、比擬することなかれ。凡夫の本覺と活計すると、諸佛の本覺と證せると、天地懸隔なり、比論の所及にあらず。十聖三賢の活計、なほ諸佛の道におよばず。いたづらなる算砂の凡夫、いかでかはかることあらん。しかあるを、わづかに凡夫・外道の本末の邪見を活計して、諸佛の境界とおもへるやからおほし。諸佛いはく、此輩罪根深重なり、可憐憫者なり。深重の罪根たとひ無端なりとも、此輩の深重擔なり。この深重擔、しばらく放行して著眼看すべし、把定して自己を礙すといふとも、起首にあらず。

The thought and non-thought, awakening and non-awakening, initial awakening and original awakening, and so on, here with which common people are occupied, are solely the occupation of the common people, not what has been inherited by buddha after buddha.[72] The "thought" of the common people is very different from the "thought" of the buddhas; do not compare them. The "original awakening" that occupies the common people and the "original awakening" verified by the buddhas are like the gap between heaven and earth; they are not comparable. Even the occupations of the ten sages and three worthies do not approach the way of the buddhas; how could common people, vainly counting sand, ever take its measure?[73] Nevertheless, there are many of the type that, merely occupying themselves with the false views of root and branch held by the common people and other paths, think this to be the realm of the buddhas.[74] The buddhas say, *"The evil roots of this group are deep*

---

is not non-awakening, is not awakening (*mukaku ni arazu, ukaku ni arazu* 無覺にあらず、有覺にあらず): Or "is not lacking awakening, is not having awakening"; here and below, the translation seeks to maintain a consistent rendering of these terms, even when, as here, the result seems less than felicitous.

72 **thought and non-thought** (*unen munen* 有念無念): Or, "having thought and lacking thought." The term *munen* 無念 ("no-thought") is much discussed in the literature of Chan.

with which common people are occupied (*ima bonbu no kakkei suru* いま凡夫の活計する): "Commoners" (*bonbu* 凡夫, or *bonpu*; S. *pṛthagjana*) are those not yet advanced on the Buddhist path, in contrast to "the sage" (or "noble"; *shō* 聖; S. ārya). "Occupied" (and the subsequent "occupation") translates *kakkei* 活計, a common term for one's "livelihood," or "way of life"; here, perhaps, "to be taken up with," "given over to."

73 **counting sand** (*sansha* 算砂): A common pejorative for the study of the details of doctrine; see Supplementary Notes, s.v. "Counting sand."

74 **the false views of root and branch held by the common people and other paths** (*bonbu gedō no honmatsu no jaken* 凡夫外道の本末の邪見): "Root and branch" (*honmatsu* 本末) is a metaphor common throughout Chinese writing for "beginning and end," "originary and derivative," "fundamental and secondary," etc.; here, perhaps applied to the relationship between "original" (*hon* 本) and "initial" (*shi* 始) awakening. "Other paths" translates *gedō* 外道, a standard reference to non-Buddhist religions (S. *tīrthika*).

6. Deportment of the Practicing Buddha *Gyōbutsu iigi* 行佛威儀 185

and grievous"; they are "ones to be pit ed."[75] The "deep, grievous," "evil roots" may be beginningless, but they are the deep, grievous burden of "this group." They should let go of this deep, grievous burden for a while and look at it. Though in holding it fast they may obstruct themselves, this is not its onset.[76]

[06:23]

いま行佛威儀の無礙なる、ほとけに礙せらるるに、挖泥滞水の活路を通達しきたるゆえに無罣礙なり。上天にしては化天す、人間にしては化人す。華開の功徳あり、世界起の功徳あり、かつて間隙なきものなり。このゆえに、自他に迴脱あり、往來に獨拔あり。即往兜率天なり、即來兜率天なり、即即兜率天なり。即往安樂なり、即來安樂なり、即即安樂なり。即迴脱兜率なり、即迴脱安樂なり。即打破百雑砕安樂兜率なり、即把定放行安樂兜率なり。一口呑盡なり。

The deportment of the practicing buddha here is unobstructed: it is without obstructions because, while being obstructed by the buddha, it has penetrated the life-saving path on which one is *dragged through the mud and drenched with water*.[77] In the heavens, it teaches the devas; among humans, it teaches humans. It has the virtue of "a flower opens"; it has the virtue of "the world arises"; it is without the slightest gap.[78] Therefore, it is far off and free from self and other; it is alone and removed in going and coming.[79] It is *"going directly to Tuṣita Heaven"*;

---

75 **The buddhas say** (*shobutsu iwaku* 諸佛いはく): The first phrase is from the *Lotus Sūtra* (*Miaofa lianhua jing* 妙法蓮華經, T.262.9:7a9); the second, from the *Śūraṃgama Sūtra* (*Shoulengyan jing* 首楞嚴經, T.945.19:145b28-29).

76 **Though in holding it fast they may obstruct themselves, this is not its onset** (*hajō shite jiko o gi su to iutomo, kishu ni arazu* 把定して自己を礙すといふとも、起首にあらず): A sentence subject to various interpretations, perhaps meaning something like, "holding fast to [this burden] may be what defines them, but it is not the origin [of the burden]." Dōgen often uses the verb *ge su* 礙す ("to obstruct") in the sense "to identify," "to define"; see, e.g., the opening sentence of the following section.

77 **dragged through the mud and drenched with water** (*dadei taisui* 挖泥滞水): A common idiom referring to the Zen master's "getting his hands dirty," as we might say, in the teaching of his students; see Supplementary Notes.

78 **"a flower opens"** (*ke kai* 華開); **"the world arises"** (*sekai ki* 世界起): See above, Note 27.

it is without the slightest gap (*katsute kangeki naki mono nari* かつて間隙なきものなり): Presumably, meaning with no gap between the "flower opening" and the "world arising."

79 **it is far off and free from self and other; it is alone and removed in going and coming** (*jita ni keidatsu ari, ōrai ni dokubatsu ari* 自他に迴脱あり、往來に獨拔あり): A loose translation: *keidatsu dokubatsu* 迴脱獨拔 (also read *kyōdatsu* and written 迥脱), meaning something like "distantly liberated, extricated in solitude," comes from a saying of Yunju Daoying 雲居道膺 (*Liandeng huiyao* 聯燈會要, ZZ.136:797a8):

一言迴脱獨拔當時、言語不要多、多即無用處。

When a single word is distantly liberated, extricated in solitude, one doesn't need many words; many are useless.

186 DŌGEN'S *SHŌBŌGENZŌ* VOLUME I

it is *coming directly from Tuṣita Heaven*; it is *directly Tuṣita Heaven itself*.[80] It is "*going directly to Sukhāvatī*"; it is *coming directly from Sukhāvatī*; it is *directly Sukhāvatī itself*.[81] It is *directly far off and free from Tuṣita*; it is directly *far off and free from Sukhāvatī*. It is *directly smashing Sukhāvatī and Tuṣita into a hundred fragments*; it is *directly holding fast and letting go of Sukhāvatī and Tuṣita*.[82] It is *swallowing them up in a single gulp*.[83]

[06:24] {1:67}
しるべし、安樂兜率といふは、淨土・天堂ともに輪廻することの同般なるとなり。行履なるは、淨土・天堂おなじく行履なり。大悟なれば、おなじく大悟なり。大迷なれば、おなじく大迷なり。これしばらく行佛の鞋裏の動指なり。あるときは一道の放屁聲なり、放屎香なり。鼻孔あるは齅得す、耳處・身處・行履處あるに聽取するなり。又、得吾皮肉骨髓するときあり、さらに行得に他よりえざるものなり。

80 **"going directly to Tuṣita Heaven"** (*soku ō Tosotsuten* 即往兜率天): From a line in the *Lotus Sūtra* (*Miaofa lianhua jing* 妙法蓮華經, T.262.9:61c8-10):

若有人受持讀誦解其義趣、是人命終爲千佛授手、令不恐怖不墮惡趣、即往兜率天上彌勒菩薩所。

If there is a person who receives and keeps, reads and recites, and interprets the meaning [of the *Lotus Sūtra*], at the end of this person's life, a thousand buddhas will offer their hands to him, causing him to be without fear, and, without falling into the evil destinies, he will go directly to the place of Bodhisattva Maitreya in Tuṣita Heaven.

The subsequent comings and goings and the rest here are Dōgen's variations on the theme.

81 **"going directly to Sukhāvatī"** (*soku ō Anraku* 即往安樂): The name of Buddha Amitābha's Pure Land in the west. Again, from the *Lotus Sūtra* (*Miaofa lianhua jing* 妙法蓮華經, T.262.9:54b29-c2):

若如來滅後後五百歲中、若有女人、聞是經典如説修行、於此命終、即往安樂世界阿彌陀佛大菩薩衆圍繞住處。

If, after the extinction of the Tathāgata, in the final five hundred years, if there is a woman who hears this scripture and practices according to its teachings, then at the end of this life, she will go directly to the world of Sukhāvatī, to the place where Buddha Amitābha dwells surrounded by his assembly of bodhisattvas.

82 **"a hundred fragments"** (*hyaku zassui* 百雜碎): Perhaps an allusion to the saying of Xuansha Shibei 玄沙師備 (835-908) discussed in *Shōbōgenzō kokyō* 正法眼藏古鏡. When asked by his teacher, Xuefeng Yicun 雪峰義存 (822-908), what happens when a bright mirror comes in front of a bright mirror, Xuansha replied, "A hundred fragments." For a somewhat different version of this anecdote and the meanings of the idiom, see Supplementary Notes, s.v. "A hundred fragments."

83 **swallowing them up in a single gulp** (*ikku donjin* 一口吞盡): Perhaps alluding to the famous saying, attributed in Chan texts to Nanyue Huisi 南嶽慧思 (515-577), that he had "swallowed up the buddhas of the three times in a single gulp" (*sanshi jufo bei wo yikou tunjin* 三世諸佛被我一口吞盡) (see, e.g., *Liandeng huiyao* 聯燈會要, ZZ.136:925b5-7).

6. Deportment of the Practicing Buddha *Gyōbutsu iigi* 行佛威儀　　187

We should realize, in speaking of Sukhāvatī and Tuṣita, that revolving [in rebirth] is the same in both the pure land and the heavenly mansion.[84] In regard to conduct, the conduct is the same in the pure land and the heavenly mansion; when it comes to great awakening, great awakening is the same; when it comes to great delusion, great delusion is the same. These are, for the moment, toes wiggling in the sandals of the practicing buddha.[85] Sometimes, they are the single sound of a fart; sometimes, the smell of a shit. Those with noses can smell them; if they have the sphere of ear, sphere of body, and sphere of conduct, they can hear them.[86] Again, there are times when they've *gotten my skin, flesh, bones, and marrow*; it is something never gotten except as attained in practice.[87]

[06:25]

了生達死の大道、すでに豁達するに、ふるくよりの道取あり、大聖は生死を心にまかす、生死を身にまかす、生死を道にまかす、生死を生死にまかす。この宗旨あらはるる、古今の時あらずといへども、行佛の威儀、忽爾として行盡するなり、道環として生死身心の宗旨、すみやかに辨肯するなり。行盡・明盡、これ強爲の爲にあらず、迷頭認影に大似なり、回光返照に一如なり。その明上又明の明は、行佛に彌綸なり、これ行取に一任せり。この任任の道理、すべからく心を參究すべきなり。その參究の兀爾は、萬回これ心の明白なり、三界ただ心の大隔なりと知及し會取す。この知及・會取、さらに萬法なりといへども、自己の家郷を行取せり、當人の活計を便是なり。

Where the great way that *comprehends birth and masters death* is broadly mastered, there is a saying from the past: "The great sages en-

---

84　**the pure land and the heavenly mansion** (*jōdo tendō* 淨土天堂): I.e., the pure land of Sukhāvatī and the heaven of Tuṣita. Dōgen's claim that rebirth is the same in the two is somewhat problematic. While Tuṣita is a realm of devas, one of the paths of rebirth within saṃsāra, Sukhāvatī was popularly imagined as somehow outside rebirth in saṃsāra and technically defined as a place of advanced bodhisattvas, purified of their karma and able to choose their future incarnations.

85　**These are, for the moment, toes wiggling in the sandals of the practicing buddha** (*kore shibaraku gyōbutsu no airi no dōshi nari* これしばらく行佛の鞋裏の動指なり): The translation assumes the antecedent of *kore* これ ("these") is the "conduct," "awakening," and "delusion" of the previous sentence.

86　**sphere of ear, sphere of body, and sphere of conduct** (*nisho shinsho anrisho* 耳處・身處・行履處): Dōgen here uses the Buddhist technical terms for the auditory and tactile sense spheres; the anomalous "conduct sphere" (*anrisho* 行履處), though common enough in Chan texts, does not occur elsewhere in the *Shōbōgenzō*.

87　**gotten my skin, flesh, bones, and marrow** (*toku go hi niku kotsu zui* 得吾皮肉骨髓): From the famous story of Bodhidharma's testing of four disciples, to whom he said of each in turn that he (or, in one case, she) had gotten his skin, flesh, bones, and marrow. Dōgen records the story in his *shinji Shōbōgenzō* 眞字正法眼藏 (DZZ.5:230, case 201) and alludes to it very often in the *Shōbōgenzō*; see Supplementary Notes, s.v. "Skin, flesh, bones, and marrow."

188 DŌGEN'S *SHŌBŌGENZŌ* VOLUME I

trust birth and death to the mind, entrust birth and death to the body, entrust birth and death to the way, entrust birth and death to birth and death."[88] Although the appearance of this essential point may not be in the time of past and present, the deportment of the practicing buddha fully practices it in an instant and immediately confirms the essential point of the body and mind of birth and death as the circling of the way.[89] Fully practicing it, fully clarifying it — this is not a forced act: it is "just like *doubting your head and accepting its reflection*"; it is the same as *turning the light around and shining it back*.[90] Its clarity of the clarity beyond clarity permeates the practicing buddha; it is completely entrusted to the practice.[91] For the principle of this entrustment after entrustment, we should surely investigate the mind.[92] The fixed state of that investigation recognizes and understands that the myriad turnings are the clarity of the mind, that the three realms are just great divisions of the mind.[93] This

---

88   **saying from the past** (*furuku yori no dōshu* ふるくよりの道取): The saying is given in Japanese; no source has been identified.

89   **Although the appearance of this essential point may not be in the time of past and present** (*kono shūshi arawaruru, kokon no toki ni arazu to iedomo* この宗旨あらはるる、古今の時にあらずといへども): On the face of it, this seems to suggest that the saying itself is ahistorical, but presumably the point is that the meaning of the saying points beyond the historical.

the essential point of the body and mind of birth and death as the circling of the way (*dōkan toshite shōji shinjin no shūshi* 道環として生死身心の宗旨): Perhaps meaning something like, "the meaning of our lives as ongoing spiritual practice." The term *dōkan* 道環 occurs several times in the *Shōbōgenzō*, most notably in the opening lines of "Shōbōgenzō gyōji" 正法眼藏行持, where it is defined as continuous sustained practice (*gyōji* 行持) on the Buddhist path. The words *shōji shinjin* 生死身心, rendered here "body and mind of birth and death," might also be read "birth and death and body and mind." See Supplementary Notes, s.v. "Body and mind."

90   **"just like doubting your head and accepting its reflection"** (*meitō nin'yō ni daiji nari* 迷頭認影に大似なり): I.e., like Yajñadatta, who thought that his own reflection in the mirror was the face of a trickster spirit; see Supplementary Notes, s.v. "Doubting your head and accepting its reflection." Although the expression would seem to indicate a deluded state, Dōgen seems here to be giving it a positive valance.

turning the light around and shining it back (*ekō henshō* 回光返照): A common idiom in Zen texts used in reference to Buddhist practice as the study of the self, rather than of the external world; see Supplementary Notes, s.v. "Turn the light around and shine it back." Taken together with the preceding simile, the point here may be that the full practice and clarification of the essential point is merely a matter of Buddhist study and meditation.

91   **permeates the practicing buddha** (*gyōbutsu ni mirin nari* 行佛に彌綸なり): Or, perhaps, "is fully contained within the practicing buddha."

92   **the principle of this entrustment after entrustment** (*kono ninnin no dōri* この任任の道理): Presumably, a reference to the "entrustments" in the "saying from the past."

93   **The fixed state of that investigation** (*sono sankyū no gotsuji* その參究の兀爾): The

6. Deportment of the Practicing Buddha *Gyōbutsu iigi* 行佛威儀   189

recognizing and understanding, while they may further be the myriad dharmas, put into practice one's own home town and represent precisely that person's occupation.[94]

[06:26] {1:68}

しかあれば、句中取則し、言外求巧する、再三撈摝、それ把定にあまれる把定あり、放行にあまる放行あり。その功夫は、いかなるかこれ生、いかなるかこれ死、いかなるかこれ身心、いかなるかこれ與奪、いかなるかこれ任違。それ同門出入の不相逢なるか、一著落在に藏身露角なるか。大慮而解なるか、老思而知なるか。一顆明珠なるか、一大藏教なるか。一條拄杖なるか、一枚面目なるか。三十年後なるか、一念萬年なるか。子細に撿點し、撿點を子細にすべし。撿點の子細にあたりて、滿眼聞聲、滿耳見色、さらに沙門一隻眼の開明なるに、不是目前法なり、不是目前事なり。雍容の破顏あり、瞬目あり。これ行佛の威儀の暫爾なり。被物牽にあらず、不牽物なり。緣起の無生・無作にあらず、本性・法性にあらず。住法位にあらず、本有然にあらず。如是を是するのみにあらず、ただ威儀行佛なるのみなり。

Therefore, in "*taking the norm from within the text*" and *seeking the art outside the words*, "*scooping them up two or three times*," there is holding them fast that is more than holding them fast, there is letting them go that is more than letting them go.[95] That concentrated effort is

---

term *gotsuji* 兀爾 is best known from the line in the *Xinxin ming* 信心銘 (*Jingde chuandeng lu* 景德傳燈錄, T.2010.48:376c23): "Fixedly, forgetting objects" (*wuer wangyuan* 兀爾妄緣); akin to *gotsugotsu* 兀兀 ("fixedly"); *gotsuza* 兀坐 ("fixed sitting"). See Supplementary Notes, s.v. "Sit fixedly."

that the myriad turnings are the clarity of the mind, that the three realms are just great divisions of the mind (*bankai kore shin no meibyaku nari, sangai tada shin no daikaku nari to* 萬回これ心の明白なり、三界ただ心の大隔なりと): The "myriad turnings" (*bankai* 萬回) presumably refers to "turning the light" (*ekō* 回光) just above. The latter clause seems to reflect the common expression "the three realms are only mind" (*sangai yui shin* 三界唯心); see Supplementary Notes, s.v. "The three realms are only mind."

94   **while they may further be the myriad dharmas** (*sara ni manbō nari to iedomo* さらに萬法なりといへども): Presumably, meaning, "although recognizing and understanding are themselves events of the phenomenal world."

represent precisely that person's occupation (*tōnin no kakkei o benze nari* 當人の活計を便是なり): An attempt to render the odd use here of *benze* 便是 ("precisely so," "exactly") as a transitive verb; the only such use in the *Shōbōgenzō*. "That person's occupation" (*tōnin no kakkei* 當人の活計) indicates the way of life of the one engaged in the practice of recognizing and understanding.

95   **"taking the norm from within the text" and seeking the art outside the words** (*kuchū shusoku shi, gonge gukō suru* 句中取則し、言外求巧する): The "art" (*kō* 巧) here should probably be taken as the skillful expedients (*kōben* 巧便) of Buddhist teaching. Likely a variation on the saying of Dayu Shouzhi 大愚守芝 quoted above, Note 89:

言中取則、句裏明機。

Take the norm from within the words and clarify the point inside the text.

190　DŌGEN'S *SHŌBŌGENZŌ* VOLUME I

[asking]: What is birth? What is death? What are body and mind? What are giving and taking away? What are entrusting and opposing?[96] Is this going in and out of the same gate without meeting each other?[97] Is it *hiding the body and showing the horns* where the move has fallen?[98] Is it *"reflect much and you will understand"*? Is it *"think long and you will*

In his "Shōbōgenzō zazen shin" 正法眼藏坐禪箴, Dōgen quotes with approval a saying attributed to Luopu Yuan'an 洛浦元安 (834–898) in Wansong Xingxiu's 萬松行秀 (1166–1246) commentary on case 41 of the *Congrong lu* 從容錄 (T.2004.48:254a25-26):

> 直須旨外明宗、莫向言中取則。
> Clarify the meaning apart from the sense;
> Don't take the norm from within the words.

See Supplementary Notes, s.v. "Clarify the meaning apart from the sense; don't take the norm from within the words."

"scooping them up two or three times" (*saisan rōroku* 再三撈摝): Reflecting a verse found in the *Shi xuantan* 十玄談, by Tong'an Changcha 同安常察 (dates unknown); see Supplementary Notes, s.v. "Scoop up two or three times."

there is holding them fast that is more than holding them fast (*sore hajō ni amareru hajō ari* それ把定にあまれる把定あり): The terms *hajō* 把定 ("holding fast") here and *hōgyō* 放行 ("letting go") in the following clause are typically used in reference to a master's treatment of his student; in our context, however, the object would seem to be the "norm" (*soku* 則) and "art" (*kō* 巧) being "scooped up" (*rōroku* 撈摝) — a usage echoing the practicing buddha's treatment of Sukhāvatī and Tuṣita in section 23, above.

96　**giving and taking away** (*yodatsu* 與奪); **entrusting and opposing** (*nin'i* 任違): Again, terms that may be used to describe a master's teaching methods; here, more likely used in the sense, to "accept or reject," "affirm or deny," the object of investigation. The latter term, not found elsewhere in the *Shōbōgenzō*, recalls the saying on "entrustment" (*nin* 任) in section 25, above.

97　**going in and out of the same gate without meeting each other** (*dōmon shutsunyū no fusōhō* 同門出入の不相逢): After a fixed expression in Zen literature (see, e.g., the use by Tianyi Yihuai 天衣義懷 [993-1064], *Liandeng huiyao* 聯燈會要, ZZ.136:909a12). Here, perhaps used in reference to the preceding dualities (birth and death, body and mind, etc.), as discrete poles in a shared field of meaning.

98　**hiding the body and showing the horns where the move has fallen** (*ichijaku rakuzai ni zōshin rokaku* 一著落在に藏身露角): The unusual expression "hiding the body and showing the horns" (*zōshin rokaku* 藏身露角) combines two more common idioms used in the sense "to avoid saying what one really thinks": "to hide the body and show the shadow" (*zōshin roei* 藏身露影); "to hide the head and show the horns" (*zōtō rokaku* 藏頭露角).

where the move has fallen (*ichijaku rakuzai ni* 一著落在に): The translation tries to make some sense in English of what is in the original a fragment of a fixed expression, based on board games, often found in Chan texts: "miss one move and [play] falls to the opponent" (*fangguo yizhao laozai dier* 放過一著落在第二). Readers often take *ichijaku rakuzai* 一著落在 as meaning "one move having been made" or simply "one move."

6. Deportment of the Practicing Buddha *Gyōbutsu iigi* 行佛威儀 191

know"?[99] Is it "one bright pearl"?[100] Is it one great treasury of the teachings?[101] Is it one staff? Is it one face? Is it after thirty years?[102] Is it *ten thousand years in one moment of thought*?[103] We should examine this in detail and detail our examination. When we detail our examination, *the full eye hears the sound, the full ear sees the form*; and, further, when "the single eye of the *śramaṇa*" is open, it is "*not a dharma before one's eyes*"; it is "*not a thing before one's eyes*."[104] There is the calm breaking into a smile; there is the blinking of the eyes: these are moments in the

---

99 **"reflect much and you will understand"** (*dairyo ni ge* 大慮而解); **"think long and you will know"** (*rōshi ni chi* 老思而知): Variation on a Chinese saying, "think and you will know; reflect and you will understand" (*si er zhi lü er jie* 思而知慮而解), often criticized in Chan texts: so, e.g., the *Zongjing lu* 宗鏡錄 (T.2016.48:580a16):

思而知慮而解。是鬼家活計。

Think and you will know; reflect and you will understand: this is the business of demons.

100 **"one bright pearl"** (*ikka myōju* 一顆明珠): An expression attributed in Zen literature to both Dongshan Liangjie 洞山良价 (807–869) and Xuansha Shibei 玄沙師備 (835-908). Dōgen includes Xuansha's saying in his *shinji Shōbōgenzō* 眞字正法眼藏, DZZ.5:132, case 15) and discusses it at length in "Shōbōgenzō ikka myōju" 正法眼藏一顆明珠; see Supplementary Notes, s.v. "One bright pearl."

101 **one great treasury of the teachings** (*ichi daizō kyō* 一大藏教): I.e., the recorded teachings of the Buddha; here, perhaps, in contrast to the preceding "one bright pearl" of "the worlds in the ten directions." See Supplementary Notes, s.v. "One great treasury of the teachings."

102 **after thirty years** (*sanjū nen go* 三十年後): A fixed expression for training, based on the convention that it takes thirty years to master Zen.

103 **ten thousand years in one moment of thought** (*ichinen bannen* 一念萬年): A common expression in Zen literature for eternity in each moment.

104 **the full eye hears the sound, the full ear sees the form** (*mangen monshō, manni kenshiki* 滿眼聞聲、滿耳見色): The English "full" here seeks to preserve the ambiguity of *mangen* 滿眼 and *manni* 滿耳, which could be read in the senses both that the eye and ears are filled and that they are complete, or whole; elsewhere, the two terms are regularly found together in the sense "fill the eye" and "fill the ear," respectively. The use of synesthesia seen here occurs several times in the *Shōbōgenzō*.

"the single eye of the *śramaṇa*" (*shamon isseki gen* 沙門一隻眼): Also read *isseki gan*. From the saying, cited elsewhere in the *Shōbōgenzō*, of the ninth-century Chan figure Changsha Jingcen (dates unknown); see Supplementary Notes, s.v. "All the worlds in the ten directions are the single eye of the *śramaṇa*."

"not a dharma before one's eyes" (*fuze mokuzen hō* 不是目前法); **"not a thing before one's eyes"** (*fuze mokuzen ji* 不是目前事): Two expressions taken from Chinese Chan texts. For the latter, see, e.g., *Yuanwu Foguo chanshi yulu* 圓悟佛果禪師語錄 (T.1997.47:756a25); the former is associated especially with Jiashan Shanhui 夾山善會 (805-881) (see, e.g., *Jingde chuandeng lu* 景德傳燈錄, T.2076.51:324a9-10):

目前無法意在目前。他不是目前法。

The meaning of there being no dharma before your eyes is right before one's eyes; nothing else is the dharma before one's eyes.

192 DŌGEN'S *SHŌBŌGENZŌ* VOLUME I

deportment of the practicing buddha.[105] It is not pulled by things; it does not pull things.[106] It is not the non-arising or non-production of conditioned arising; it is not the original nature or dharma nature.[107] It is not "abiding in its dharma position."[108] It is not original being as such.[109] It is not just affirming what is like this: it is nothing but the practicing buddha of deportment.[110]

[06:27]

しかあればすなはち、爲法爲身の消息、よく心にまかす。脱生脱死の威儀、しばらくほとけに一任せり。ゆえに道取あり、萬法唯心、三界唯心。さらに向上に道得するに、唯心の道得あり、いはゆる牆壁瓦礫なり。唯心にあらざるがゆえに、牆壁瓦礫にあらず。これ行佛の威儀なる、任心任法、爲法爲身の道理なり。さらに始覺・本覺等の所及にあらず、いはんや外道二乘・三賢十聖の所及ならんや。この威儀、ただこれ面面の不會なり、枚枚の不會なり。たとひ活鱍鱍地も條條藂なり。一條鐵か、兩頭動か。一條鐵は長短にあらず、兩頭動は自他にあらず。この展事・投機のちから、功夫をうるに、威掩萬法なり、眼高一世なり。收放をさへざる光明あり、僧堂・佛殿・廚庫・山門。さらに收放にあらざる光明あり、僧堂・佛殿・廚庫・山門なり。さらに十方通のまなこあり、大地全收のまなこあ

---

105 **There is the calm breaking into a smile; there is the blinking of the eyes** (*yōyō no hagan ari, shunmoku ari* 雍容の破顔あり、瞬目あり): Reference to (one version of) the famous story of Buddha Śākyamuni and the First Ancestor, Mahākāśyapa, on Vulture Peak; when the Buddha held up a flower and blinked, the Ancestor smiled. Recorded in Dōgen's *shinji Shōbōgenzō* 眞字正法眼藏 (DZZ.5:258, case 253). See Supplementary Notes, s.v. "Breaking into a smile," and "Holding up a flower and blinking the eyes."

106 **It is not pulled by things; it does not pull things** (*hi motsu ken ni arazu, fuken motsu nari* 被物牽にあらず、不牽物なり): "Pulled" here probably in the sense, "to induce an effect"; hence, "it is not caused nor does it cause." The unexpressed subject is undoubtedly "the deportment of the practicing buddha."

107 **the non-arising or non-production of conditioned arising** (*engi no mushō musa* 緣起の無生無作): Probably reference to the common claim of Mahāyāna teachings that all conditioned dharmas are "empty" of ultimate reality and, therefore, do not really arise or function as causes.

original nature or dharma nature (*honshō hosshō* 本性法性): Two common terms for the fundamental reality of phenomena.

108 **"abiding in its dharma position"** (*jū hōi* 住法位): Invoking a line in the *Lotus Sūtra* that can be read, "the dharmas abide in their dharma positions"; see Supplementary Notes, s.v. "Dharmas abide in their dharma positions."

109 **original being as such** (*hon'unen* 本有然): A somewhat unusual term, not encountered elsewhere in the *Shōbōgenzō*, probably to be taken as equivalent to the more familiar *hon'u* 本有 ("original, or fundamental, being").

110 **affirming what is like this** (*nyoze o ze suru* 如是を是する): "Like this" (*nyoze* 如是) could refer here simply to the above list of rejected items or to a more abstract notion of "thusness" or "suchness."

practicing buddha of deportment (*iigi gyōbutsu nari* 威儀行佛なり): For this expression, see above, Note 50.

6. Deportment of the Practicing Buddha *Gyōbutsu iigi* 行佛威儀　　193

り。心のまへあり、心のうしろあり。かくのごとくの眼・耳・鼻・舌・
身・意、光明功徳の熾然なるゆえに、不知有を保任せる三世諸佛あり、却
知有を投機せる狸奴・白牯あり。この巴鼻あり、この眼睛あるは、法の行
佛をとき、法の行佛をゆるすなり。

Therefore, the circumstances of "*for the sake of the dharma and for the sake of the body*" are entrusted to the mind; the deportment that *sloughs off birth and sloughs off death* has long been completely entrusted to the buddha.[111] Hence, there are the sayings, "*the myriad dharmas are only mind,*" "*the three realms are only mind.*"[112] To say something further beyond this, there is a saying on "*only mind*": "*fences, walls, tiles, and pebbles.*"[113] Since it is not "*only mind,*" it is not "*fences, walls, tiles, and pebbles.*"[114] This is the principle of *entrusting to the mind and entrusting to the dharma,* and "*for the sake of the dharma, for the sake of body,*" that are the deportment of the practicing buddha. This is certainly not a place reached by initial awakening or original awakening; how much less could it be a place reached by followers of other paths, or the two vehicles, or the three worthies and ten sages? This deportment is just not understanding one after another, not understanding again and again.[115]

111　**"for the sake of the dharma and for the sake of the body"** (*ihō ishin* 爲法爲身): Presumably referring back to the earlier statement (section 9) that the deportment of the practicing buddha consists in "discarding the body for the sake of the dharma" and "discarding the dharma for the sake of the body."

entrusted to the mind (*shin ni makasu* 心にまかす); **completely entrusted to the buddha** (*hotoke ni ichinin seri* ほとけに一任せり): recalling the discussion of "entrusting" (*nin* 任) in section 25, above.

112　**"the myriad dharmas are only mind," "the three realms are only mind"** (*manbō yui shin, sangai yui shin* 萬法唯心、三界唯心): While these two phrases do occur separately in Buddhist texts, the fact that Dōgen puts them together here suggests that he may have been thinking of the very common expression "the three realms are only mind, the myriad dharmas are only consciousness" (*sangai yui shin manbō yui shiki* 三界唯心萬法唯識). See Supplementary Notes, s.v. "The three realms are only mind."

113　**"fences, walls, tiles, and pebbles"** (*shō heki ga ryaku* 牆壁瓦礫): A well-known expression in Zen texts first attributed to Nanyang Huizhong 南陽慧忠 (d. 775); see Supplementary Notes, s.v. "Fences, walls, tiles, and pebbles." Dōgen discusses this expression in his "Shōbōgenzō kobutsushin" 正法眼藏古佛心.

114　**Since it is not "only mind," it is not "fences, walls, tiles, and pebbles"** (*yui shin ni arazaru yue ni, shō heki ga ryaku ni arazu* 唯心にあらざるゆえに、牆壁瓦礫にあらず): The grammatical subjects of these two clauses are unexpressed. The translation takes the sense to be, "just as the mind is not only mind, so fences, walls, tiles and pebbles are not merely fences, walls, tiles, and pebbles."

115　**not understanding one after another, not understanding again and again** (*menmen no fue nari, maimai no fue nari* 面面の不會なり、枚枚の不會なり): "One after another" and "again and again" render the repetitions of two numerical counters, *men* 面 ("face") and *mai* 枚 ("sheet"), respectively, of ambiguous referent. The verb *fue* 不會

194 DŌGEN'S *SHŌBŌGENZŌ* VOLUME I

Even while being brisk and lively, it is each one so.[116] Is it one strip of iron? Is it "both move"?[117] The one strip of iron is not long or short; "both move" is not self or other. When one gets the power, the concentrated effort, that *divulges the matter and achieves accord, one's authority covers the myriad dharmas, one's eye is as high as the whole world.*[118] It has a radiance that does not interfere with taking in and letting go: "saṃgha hall, buddha hall, kitchen, and mountain gate."[119] Further, it has a radiance that is neither taking in nor letting go: "saṃgha hall, buddha hall, kitchen, and mountain gate." Further, there is an eye that penetrates the

---

("not understand") occurs often in the *Shōbōgenzō*, in the senses both of a failing and a virtue — the latter being the obvious sense here.

116 **brisk and lively** (*kappatsupatchi* 活鱍鱍地): A loose translation of a Chinese idiom expressing the quick, powerful movements of a jumping fish; see Supplementary Notes, s.v. "Brisk and lively." While the glyph *di* 地 in the Chinese suggests an adverbial construction, Dōgen tends to use the phrase as a nominal.

each one so (*jōjō nii* 條條聻): I.e., "purely individual instances"; an unusual expression also occurring in the version of "Henzan" 遍參 included in the sixty-chapter *Shōbōgenzō*.

117 **one strip of iron** (*ichijō tetsu* 一條鐵): A common Chan idiom for the unity of phenomena, as in the saying, "one strip of iron for ten thousand miles" (*banri ichijō tetsu* 萬里一條鐵); see above, Note 14.

"both move" (*ryōtō dō* 兩頭動): From a question posed to Changsha Jingcen 長沙景岑 (see, e.g., *Liandeng huiyao* 聯燈會要, ZZ.136:538a13-14):

竺尚書問、蚯蚓斬爲兩段、兩頭俱動。未審佛性在阿那箇頭。師曰、莫妄想。

The minister Chu asked, "When you cut a worm in two pieces, both of them move. I don't understand, in which one is the buddha nature?"

The Master said, "Don't have deluded ideas."

Dōgen discusses this conversation in his "Shōbōgenzō busshō" 正法眼藏佛性.

118 **"divulges the matter and achieves accord"** (*tenji tōki* 展事投機): A fixed idiom, common in Chan texts, used especially for the relationship between master and disciple; see Supplementary Notes, s.v. "Divulging the matter and achieving accord."

one's authority covers the myriad dharmas (*i en manbō* 威掩萬法): Seemingly, a fixed phrase in Chinese, though the precedent for it is unidentified.

one's eye is as high as the whole world (*gen kō isse* 眼高一世): Taking *isse* 一世 as *issekai* 一世界; another fixed phrase in Chinese appearing several times in the Chan canon.

119 **It has a radiance that does not interfere with taking in and letting go** (*shūhō o saezaru kōmyō ari* 收放をさへざる光明あり): The term *shūhō* 收放 usually refers to "grasping and releasing"; here, it may suggest the absorption and emission of light. The term *kōmyō* 光明 ("radiance") is regularly used in reference to the nimbus surrounding the body of a buddha, often taken as a symbol of the buddha's wisdom.

"saṃgha hall, buddha hall, kitchen, and mountain gate" (*sōdō butsuden zuku sanmon* 僧堂佛殿廚庫山門): Recalling a definition of "radiance" attributed to Yunmen Wenyan 雲門文偃 (864-949), quoted at *shinji Shōbōgenzō* 眞字正法眼藏, DZZ.5:166, case 81; see Supplementary Notes, s.v. "Saṃgha hall, buddha hall, kitchen, and mountain gate."

6. Deportment of the Practicing Buddha *Gyōbutsu iigi* 行佛威儀 195

ten directions; there is an eye that completely takes in the whole earth.[120] There is before the mind; there is behind the mind.[121] Since such eyes, ears, nose, tongue, body, and mind are aflame with the virtue of the radiance, there are the "buddhas of the three times," who have maintained "*I don't know they exist*"; there are the "cats and white oxen," who have accorded with "*on the other hand, I know they exist.*"[122] Having this nose grip, having this eye, is the dharma preaching the practicing buddha, is the dharma acknowledging the practicing buddha.[123]

* * * * *

120 **completely takes in the whole earth** (*daichi zenshū* 大地全収): A common phrase in Zen literature, associated especially with Yunmen Wenyan 雲門文偃 (see, e.g., *Yunmen Kuangzheng chanshi guanglu* 雲門匡眞禪師廣錄, T.1988.47:547a23-24):

一塵纔起大地全收。

When a single mote barely arises, the whole earth is completely included.

Dōgen's sentence here may reflect words attributed to Fushan Fayuan 浮山法遠 (991–1067) at *Liandeng huiyao* 聯燈會要, ZZ.136:640a9:

一隻眼。大地全該。十方通暢。

The one eye: the whole earth is entirely contained; the ten directions are penetrated.

121 **There is before the mind; there is behind the mind** (*shin no mae ari, shin no ushiro ari* 心のまへあり、心のうしろあり): The sense of "before" (*mae*) and "behind" (*ushiro*) could be either spatial or temporal: i.e., "[The eye (or the radiance?)] is both in front of and in back of the mind"; or "the mind has a before and after" (i.e., the mind exists in moment after moment).

122 **"buddhas of the three times"** (*sanze shobutsu* 三世諸佛); **"cats and white oxen"** (*rinu byakko* 狸奴白牯): From a saying of Nanquan Puyuan 南泉普願 (748-835) quoted in the *shinji Shōbōgenzō* 眞字正法眼藏 (DZZ.5:272,case 293):

三世諸佛不知有、狸奴白牯却知有。

The buddhas of the three times, I don't know they exist; cats and white oxen, on the other hand, I know they exist.

See Supplementary Notes, s.v. "Buddhas of the three times, I don't know they exist; cats and white oxen, on the other hand, I know they exist."

123 **Having this nose grip, having this eye** (*kono habi ari, kono ganzei aru wa* この巴鼻あり、この眼睛あるは): The term *habi* 巴鼻 ("to grasp by the nose") refers to the nose ring used to lead cattle — hence, a "hold" or "handle" on something; here presumably playing on Nanchuan's "white cows." See Supplementary Notes, s.v. "Nose." The "eye" (*ganzei* 眼睛) is standard metaphor for spiritual insight, here no doubt reflecting the "eye as high as the whole world." See Supplementary Notes, s.v. "Eye."

the dharma preaching the practicing buddha (*hō no gyōbutsu o toki* 法の行佛をとき): Here and in the following clause, reading *no* の as the subject marker (reading it as the genitive particle would yield, "Having this nose grip, having this eye, is preaching the practicing buddha of the dharma, is acknowledging the practicing buddha of the dharma.") The odd "dharma preaching the practicing buddha" no doubt serves as a foretaste of the words of Yuanwu in section 30, below: "The dharma preaches the buddhas" (*hō setsu butsu* 法説佛).

196 DŌGEN'S *SHŌBŌGENZŌ* VOLUME I

[06:28] {1:69}

雪峰山眞覺大師、示衆云、三世諸佛、在火焰裏、轉大法輪。

Great Master Zhenjue of Mount Xuefeng addressed the assembly saying, "The buddhas of the three times are in the flames, turning the great dharma wheel."[124]

[06:29]

玄沙院宗一大師曰、火焰爲三世諸佛説法、三世諸佛立地聽。

Great Master Zongyi of the Xuansha Cloister said, "The flames preach the dharma for the buddhas of the three times, and the buddhas of the three times stand and listen."[125]

[06:30]

圜悟禪師云、將謂猴白、更有猴黑。互換投機、神出鬼没。烈焰互天佛説法、互天烈焰法説佛。風前剪斷葛藤窠、一言勘破維摩詰。

Chan Master Yuanwu said,[126]
Here we thought it was the Marquise White,
But then there's also the Marquis Black.[127]
They have an exchange and reach an accord;
The spirit appears, and the demon vanishes.
Blazing flames throughout the heavens; the buddhas preach the dharma;
Throughout the heavens blazing flames; the dharma preaches the buddhas.

---

124 **Great Master Zhenjue of Mount Xuefeng** (*Seppōzan Shinkaku daishi* 雪峰山眞覺大師): I.e., Xuefeng Yicun 雪峰義存. His words here are thought to have been given as a lecture on the occasion known as *kailu* 開爐 ("opening the braziers"), when the monastic stoves are set out for the winter. See *Yuanwu Foguo chanshi yulu* 圓悟佛果禪師語錄 (T.1997.47:802b26-27); *shinji Shōbōgenzō* 眞字正法眼藏 (DZZ.5:270, case 287).

125 **Great Master Zongyi of Xuansha Cloister** (*Genshain Sōitsu daishi* 玄沙院宗一大師): I.e., Chan Master Xuansha Shibei 玄沙師備, disciple of Xuefeng 雪峰. His words are attached to Xuefeng's saying in both the *Yuanwu Foguo chanshi yulu* 圓悟佛果禪師語錄 (T.1997.47:802b27-28) and the *shinji Shōbōgenzō* 眞字正法眼藏 (DZZ.5:270, case 287).

"the buddhas of the three times stand and listen" (*sanze shobutsu ritchi chō* 三世諸佛立地聽): A common expression in Song Chan texts. "To stand and listen" (*ritchi chō* 立地聽) refers to the practice of the audience standing during a formal dharma talk.

126 **Chan Master Yuanwu** (*Engo zenji* 圓悟禪師): I.e., Yuanwu Keqin 圓悟克勤 (1063-1135). His words here continue the passage in *Yuanwu Foguo chanshi yulu* 圓悟佛果禪師語錄 (T.1997.47:802b29-c2).

127 **the Marquise White** (*Kōhaku* 猴白); **the Marquis Black** (*Kōkoku* 猴黑): Two legendary thieves of the Min 閩, known for their cunning. The sobriquets "marquis" and "marquise" represent a play on the homophonic *hou* 猴 ("monkey") and *hou* 侯 ("marquis," "lord"). Here, presumably, denoting Xuefeng and Xuansha.

6. Deportment of the Practicing Buddha *Gyōbutsu iigi* 行佛威儀   197

Before the wind, they cut through the nest of tangled vines;
With a single word, they see through Vimalakīrti.[128]

[06:31]

いま三世諸佛といふは、一切諸佛なり。行佛はすなはち三世諸佛なり。十
方諸佛、ともに三世にあらざるなし。佛道は三世をとくに、かくのごとく
説盡するなり。いま行佛をたづぬるに、すなはち三世諸佛なり。たとひ知
有なりといへども、たとひ不知有なりといへども、かならず三世諸佛なる
行佛なり。

The "buddhas of the three times" mentioned here are all the buddhas.
The practicing buddha is the "buddhas of the three times." There are no
buddhas of the ten directions that are not the three times.[129] When the
way of the buddhas explains the three times, it gives an exhaustive explanation like this. When we now inquire into the practicing buddha, this
is also "the buddhas of the three times." Whether we *"know they exist"*
or we *"don't know they exist,"* they are invariably the practicing buddha
who is "the buddhas of the three times."[130]

[06:32] {1:70}

しかあるに、三位の古佛、おなじく三世諸佛を道得するに、かくのごとく
の道あり。しばらく雪峰のいふ三世諸佛、在火焰裏、轉大法輪といふ、こ
の道理ならふべし。三世諸佛の轉法輪の道場は、かならず火焰裏なるべ
し。火焰裏かならず佛道場なるべし。經師・論師きくべからず、外道・二
乗しるべからず。しるべし、諸佛の火焰は諸類の火焰なるべからず。又、
諸類は火焰あるかなきかとも照顧すべし。三世諸佛の在火焰裏の化儀な
らふべし。火焰裏に處在するときは、火焰と諸佛と親切なるか、轉疏なる
か。依正一如なるか、依報・正報あるか、依正同條なるか、依正同隔なる
か。轉大法輪は、轉自・轉機あるべし。展事・投機なり、轉法・法轉ある
べし。すでに轉法輪といふ、たとひ盡大地これ盡火焰なりとも、轉火輪の

---

128 **Before the wind, they cut through the nest of tangled vines** (*fūzen sendan kattō
ka* 風前剪斷葛藤窠): The translation here and in the following line takes the subject to
be Xuefeng and Xuansha, whose words Yuanwu is praising. "The nest of tangled vines"
(*kattō ka* 葛藤窠) is a common metaphor for the entanglement of words; see Supplementary Notes, s.v. "Tangled vines."

With a single word, they see through Vimalakīrti (*ichigon kanpa Yuimakitsu* 一言
勘破維摩詰): Allusion to the famous silence of Bodhisattva Vimalakīrti, praised in the
Vimalakīrti Sūtra as the final statement on the "nondual dharma."

129   **There are no buddhas of the ten directions that are not the three times** (*jippō shobutsu, tomo ni sanze ni arazaru nashi* 十方諸佛、ともに三世にあらざるなし):
Though this claim could be taken to mean that all buddhas everywhere exist throughout
all three periods (of past, present, and future), more likely Dōgen means here simply that
all buddhas exist in the three times.

130 **Whether we "know they exist" or we "don't know they exist"** (*tatoi chi u nari to
iedomo, tatoi fuchi u nari to iedomo* たとひ知有なりといへども、たとひ不知有なり
といへども): Recalling Naquan's words on cats and oxen introduced above, section 27.

法輪あるべし、轉諸佛の法輪あるべし、轉法輪の法輪あるべし、轉三世の
法輪あるべし。

Still, when the three old buddhas speak alike of the buddhas of the three times, they have words like these.[131] We should study for a while the reasons for Xuefeng's saying, "*The buddhas of the three times are in the flames, turning the great dharma wheel.*" The practice place where the buddhas of the three times turn the dharma wheel is invariably "in the flames"; "in the flames" is invariably the practice place of the buddhas.[132] The sūtra masters and treatise masters cannot hear of this; followers of other paths and the two vehicles cannot know it. We should realize that "the flames" of the buddhas are not the flames of other types. Again, we should reflect on whether other types have "flames" or not. We should study the forms of teaching by "the buddhas of the three times" "in the flames." When they are located "in the flames," are the flames and the buddhas intimate? Are they estranged? Are their secondary and primary recompense one and the same?[133] Do they have secondary and primary recompense? Is their secondary and primary recompense something shared? Is their secondary and primary recompense something separated? In "turning the great dharma wheel," there should be turning the self and turning the opportunity.[134] It is divulging the matter and achieving an accord. There should be turning the dharma and the dharma turning. He has said, "turning the dharma wheel."[135] Even if all the whole earth is entirely flames, there should be a dharma wheel that turns the flame wheel;

---

131   **the three old buddhas** (*san'i no kobutsu* 三位の古佛): I.e., Xuefeng, Xuansha, and Yuanwu. Dōgen often uses the term "old buddha" in reference to distinguished Chan masters of the past (see Supplementary Notes, s.v. "Old buddha"); here, of course, it plays on the "buddhas of the three times."

132   **practice place** (*dōjō* 道場): A term used in reference to the site, under the bodhi tree, of Buddha Śākyamuni's awakening, as well as, more generally, to sites of Buddhist practice.

133   **secondary and primary recompense** (*eshō* 依正): A standard Buddhist term for the results of past karma; see Supplementary Notes, s.v. "Secondary and primary recompense." Dōgen seems to be asking here not only about the nature of the flames as the buddhas' environment but also about the karmic recompense of the flames themselves, as if they are also living beings; in this, he seems to be presupposing Xuansha's remark that the flames are also teaching the buddhas.

134   **turning the self and turning the opportunity** (*tenji tenki* 轉自轉機): An unusual combination not encountered elsewhere in Dōgen's writings. The term *tenki* 轉機 ("turning the opportunity") ordinarily refers to "a turning point," "a shift of fortune or circumstance"; but here, the graph *ki* 機 may indicate (as it often does in other contexts) the student — i.e., the audience for the "turning of the dharma wheel" (as opposed to the "self" that turns it).

135   **He has said, "turning the dharma wheel"** (*sude ten hōrin to iu* すでに轉法輪と いふ): The unexpressed subject is most likely Xuefeng.

6. Deportment of the Practicing Buddha *Gyōbutsu iigi* 行佛威儀 199

there should be a dharma wheel that turns the buddhas; there should be a dharma wheel that turns the dharma wheel. There should be a dharma wheel that turns the three times.

[06:33]

しかあればすなはち、火焰は諸佛の轉大法輪の大道場なり。これを界量・時量・人量・凡聖量等をもて測量するは、あたらざるなり。これらの量に量せられざれば、すなはち三世諸佛、在火焰裏、轉大法輪なり。すでに三世諸佛といふ、これ量を超越せるなり。三世諸佛轉法輪の道場なるがゆえに、火焰あるなり、火焰あるがゆえに、諸佛の道場あるなり。

Therefore, the flames are the great practice place in which the buddhas turn the great dharma wheel. It is not fitting to calculate it by a measure of worlds, a measure of times, a measure of humans, a measure of the common person or sage, and so on.[136] Because it is not measured by these measures, "*the buddhas of the three times are in the flames, turning the great dharma wheel.*" Since he says, "the buddhas of the three times," they transcend measure. Because it is the practice place at which *the buddhas of the three times turn the dharma wheel*, it has flames; because it has flames, there is the practice place of the buddhas.

[06:34] {1:71}

玄沙いはく、火焰の、三世諸佛のために説法するに、三世諸佛は立地聽法す。この道をききて、玄沙の道は雪峰の道よりも道得是なりといふ、かならずしもしかあらざるなり。しるべし、雪峰の道は玄沙の道と別なり。いはゆる雪峰は、三世諸佛の轉大法輪の處在を道取し、玄沙は、三世諸佛の聽法を道取するなり。雪峰の道、まさしく轉法を道取すれども、轉法の處在、かならずしも聽法・不聽法を論ずるにあらず。しかあれば、轉法にかならず聽法あるべしときこえず。又、三世諸佛、爲火焰説法といはず、三世諸佛、爲三世諸佛、轉大法輪といはず、火焰爲火焰、轉大法輪といはざる宗旨あるべし。轉法輪といひ、轉大法輪といふ、その別あるか。轉法輪は説法にあらず、説法かならずしも爲他あらんや。しかあれば、雪峰の道の、道取すべき道を道取しつくさざる道にあらず。

Xuansha says that, when the flames preach the dharma for "the buddhas of the three times," "the buddhas of the three times" "stand and listen" to the dharma. To say upon hearing this that Xuansha's saying has said it better than Xuefeng's saying is not necessarily correct. We should realize that Xuefeng's saying is different from Xuansha's saying: Xuefeng is speaking of the location in which "the buddhas of the three times" "turn the great dharma wheel"; Xuansha is speaking of "the buddhas of the three times" listening to the dharma. Although, to be sure, Xuefeng's saying speaks of "turning the dharma," at the location where the dharma is turned, he does not discuss the issue of "listening"

---

136 **It** (*kore* これ): Or "them." The translation takes the antecedent here to be "the great practice place"; it might as well be taken as "the flames."

DŌGEN'S *SHŌBŌGENZŌ* VOLUME I

to the dharma or not listening to the dharma. Hence, we do not hear him say that, when there is "turning the dharma," there must always be "listening" to the dharma. Again, there must be an essential point in the fact that he does not say that "*the buddhas of the three times*" *preach the dharma for the flames*, that "*the buddhas of the three times*" "*turn the great dharma wheel*" for "*the buddhas the three times*," that "*the flames*" "*turn the great dharma wheel*" for "*the flames*." Is there a distinction between "turning the dharma wheel" and "turning the great dharma wheel?" "Turning the dharma wheel" is not "preaching the dharma"; must "preaching the dharma" necessarily involve "to" another?[137] Therefore, Xuefeng's saying is not a saying that has failed to say what should be said.

[06:35]
雪峰の在火焰裏、轉大法輪、かならず委悉に參學すべし。玄沙の道に混亂することなかれ。雪峰の道を通ずるは、佛威儀を威儀するなり。火焰の三世諸佛を在裏せしむる、一無盡法界・二無盡法界の周遍のみにあらず、一微塵・二微塵の通達のみにあらず。轉大法輪を量として、大小・廣狭の量に擬することなかれ。轉大法輪は、爲自・爲他にあらず、爲説爲聽にあらず。

We should definitely study in detail Xuefeng's "*in the flames, turning the great dharma wheel*"; do not confuse it with Xuansha's saying. To penetrate Xuefeng's saying is to practice the deportment of the deportment of the buddha. "The flames" causing "the buddhas of the three times" to "be in" them does not extend throughout only one inexhaustible dharma realm or two inexhaustable dharma realms, does not penetrate merely one infinitesimal dust mote or two infinitesimal dust motes. Do not take "turning the great dharma wheel" as a measure and liken it to the measures of big and small, broad and narrow. "Turning the great dharma wheel" is not for oneself or for another, not for preaching or for listening.

[06:36]
玄沙の道に、火焰爲三世諸佛説法、三世諸佛立地聽といふ。これは火焰たとひ爲三世諸佛説法すとも、いまだ轉法輪すといはず、また三世諸佛の、法輪を轉ずといはず。三世諸佛は立地聽すとも、三世諸佛の法輪、いかでか火焰これを轉ずることあらん。爲三世諸佛説法する火焰、又轉大法輪すやいなや。玄沙もいまだいはず、轉法輪はこのときなり、と。轉法輪なし、といはず。しかあれども、想料すらくは、玄沙おろかに轉法輪は説法

---

137 **"Turning the dharma wheel" is not "preaching the dharma"; must "preaching the dharma" necessarily involve "to" another?** (*ten hōrin wa seppō ni arazu, seppō kanarazushimo ita aranya* 轉法輪は説法にあらず、説法かならずしも爲他あらんや): Unlike Xuansha, Xuefeng speaks merely of "turning the great dharma wheel," without reference to "preaching the dharma" to someone.

6. Deportment of the Practicing Buddha *Gyōbutsu iigi* 行佛威儀　　201

輪ならんと會取せるか。もししかあらば、なほ雪峰の道にくらし。火焰の
三世諸佛のために説法のとき、三世諸佛立地聽法す、とはしれりといへど
も、火焰轉法輪のところに、火焰立地聽法す、としらず。火焰轉法輪のと
ころに、火焰同轉法輪す、といはず。三世諸佛の聽法は、諸佛の法なり、
他よりかうぶらしむるにあらず。火焰を法と認ずることなかれ、火焰を佛
と認ずることなかれ、火焰を火焰と認ずることなかれ。まことに師資の
道、なほざりなるべからず。將謂赤鬚胡のみならんや、さらにこれ胡鬚赤
なり。

Xuansha's saying is, "*the flames preach the dharma for the buddhas
of the three times, and the buddhas of the three times stand and listen.*"
Here, although the flames may "*preach the dharma for the buddhas of
the three times,*" he still does not say that they "turn the dharma wheel,"
nor does he say that "the buddhas of the three times" "turn the dharma wheel."[138] Although "the buddhas of the three times" may "stand
and listen," how could "the flames" turn the dharma wheel of "the buddhas of the three times"? Do "the flames" that "preach the dharma for
the buddhas of the three times" also "turn the great dharma wheel" or
not? Xuansha has also not said that this is the time when they "turn the
dharma wheel."[139] Neither does he say there is no turning of the dharma
wheel. Still, what I wonder is, has Xuansha foolishly understood "turning the dharma wheel" to be "preaching the dharma wheel?" If so, he is
still in the dark about Xuefeng's saying. He may know that, when "the
flames preach the dharma for the buddhas of the three times, the buddhas
of the three times stand and listen" to the dharma; but he does not know
that where "the flames" turn the dharma wheel, "the flames" "stand and
listen to the dharma." He does not say that, where the flames turn the
dharma wheel, "the flames" turn the dharma wheel together.[140] "The
dharma" heard by "the buddhas of the three times" is the dharma of the
buddhas; it is not received from another. Do not recognize "the flames"
as "the dharma"; do not recognize "the flames" as "the buddhas"; do not
recognize "the flames" as "the flames." Surely, the sayings of master
and disciple are not to be taken casually. How could it only be "*here I*

138　**nor does he say that "the buddhas of the three times" "turn the dharma wheel"**
(*mata sanze shobutsu no, hōrin o tenzu to iwazu* また三世諸佛の、法輪を轉ずといは
ず): The translation follows Kawamura's punctuation here; without it, the English would
read, "nor does he say that they 'turn the dharma wheel' of 'the buddhas of the three
times.'"

139　**this is the time when they "turn the dharma wheel"** (*ten hōrin wa kono toki nari*
轉法輪はこのときなり): The antecedent of "this" is unclear; it could be the time when
the buddhas "stand and listen" or the time when the flames "preach the dharma."

140　**"the flames" turn the dharma wheel together** (*kaen dō ten hōrin su* 火焰同轉法
輪す): The exact sense is unclear; perhaps "the flames and their turning of the dharma
wheel are the same."

thought he was a red-bearded foreigner"? It is also "the foreigner's beard is red."[141]

[06:37] {1:72}

玄沙の道、かくのごとくなりといへども、參學の力量とすべきところあり。いはゆる經師・論師の大乘・小乘の局量の性相にかかはれず、佛佛祖祖正傳せる性相を參學すべし。いはゆる三世諸佛の聽法なり、これ大小乘の性相にあらざるところなり。諸佛は機緣に逗ずる説法ありとのみしりて、諸佛聽法すとしらず、諸佛修行すといはず、諸佛成佛すといはず。いま玄沙の道には、すでに三世諸佛立地聽法といふ、諸佛聽法する性相あり。かならずしも能説をすぐれたりとし、能聽是法者を劣なりといふことなかれ。説者尊なれば聽者も尊なり。

Although Xuansha's saying is like this, it has something that should be powerful for our study. That is, we should study the nature and marks directly transmitted by buddha after buddha and ancestor after ancestor — which have nothing to do with the restricted nature and marks of the Great Vehicle and Small Vehicle of the sūtra masters and treatise masters: i.e., that the buddhas of the three times listen to the dharma. This is something absent in the nature and marks of the Great and Small Vehicles. They know only that the buddhas preach the dharma that accords with the capacities of their audience; they do not know that the buddhas listen to the dharma. They do not say that the buddhas practice; they do not say that the buddhas attain buddhahood. In Xuansha's saying here, where he has said "*the buddhas of the three times stand there and listen*" to *the dharma*, we have the nature and marks of the buddhas listening to the dharma. Do not say that the preacher is always superior and "the one who can hear this dharma" is inferior.[142] When the one who preaches is to be honored, the one who listens is also to be honored.

[06:38] {1:73}

釋迦牟尼佛のいわく、若説此經、則爲見我、爲一人説、是則爲難。

Buddha Śākyamuni said, *"If one preaches this scripture, one will thereby see me. To preach it even to one person — this will be difficult."*[143]

141　**How could it only be "here I thought he was a red-bearded foreigner"? It is also "the foreigner's beard is red"** (*shōi shakushu ko nomi naranya, sara ni kore koshu shaku nari* 將謂赤鬚胡のみならんや、さらにこれ胡鬚赤なり): "The red-bearded foreigner" and "the foreigner's beard is red" are used as we might say "six of one, a half-dozen of the other" — i.e., a distinction without a difference. From the saying of Baizhang Huaihai 百丈懷海 (749-814), to his disciple Huangbo Xiyun 黄檗希運 (dates unknown) (see, e.g., *Zongmen tongyao ji* 宗門統要集, ZTS.1:58c4-5; *shinji Shōbōgenzō* 眞字正法眼藏, DZZ.5:178, case 102).

142　**"the one who can hear this dharma"** (*nōchō ze hō sha* 能聽是法者): A phrase borrowed from the *Lotus Sūtra* (*Miaofa lianhua jing* 妙法蓮華經, T.262.9:10a27).

143　**Buddha Śākyamuni** (*Shakamuni butsu* 釋迦牟尼佛): Two fragments from the

6. Deportment of the Practicing Buddha *Gyōbutsu iigi* 行佛威儀   203

[06:39]

しかあれば、能説法は見釋迦牟尼佛なり、則爲見我は釋迦牟尼佛なるがゆえに。

Thus, preaching the dharma is seeing Buddha Śākyamuni, for "*will thereby see me*" is Buddha Śākyamuni.[144]

[06:40]

又いはく、於我滅後、聽受此經、問其義趣、是則爲難。

He also said, "*After my extinction, to hear this scripture and ask about its meaning — this will be difficult.*"[145]

[06:41]

しるべし、聽受者もおなじくこれ爲難なり、勝劣あるにあらず。立地聽これ最尊なる諸佛なりといふとも、立地聽法あるべきなり、立地聽法これ三世諸佛なるがゆえに。諸佛は果上なり、因中の聽法をいふにあらず、すでに三世諸佛とあるがゆえに。しるべし、三世諸佛は火焰の説法を立地聽して諸佛なり。一道の化儀、たどるべきにあらず。たどらんとするに、箭鋒相拄せり。火焰は決定して三世諸佛のために説法す。赤心片片として鐵樹華開世界香なるなり。且道すらくは、火焰の説法を立地聽しもてゆくに、畢竟じて現成箇什麼。いはゆるは智勝于師なるべし、智等于師なるべし。師資の闃奥に參究して、三世諸佛なるなり。

We should realize that this is equally "difficult" for the listener as well: there is no superiority or inferiority.[146] The ones who "stand and listen" may be the buddhas, the most honored, but they must have "standing and listening" to the dharma; for "standing and listening" to the dharma is "the buddhas of the three times."[147] The buddhas are at the stage of ef-

---

Lotus Sūtra, run together as if a single passage:

(a) *Miaofa lianhua jing* 妙法蓮華經, T.262.9:34a14-15:

若説此經、則爲見我、多寶如來、及諸化佛。

If one preaches this scripture, one will thereby see me, Tathāgata Prabhūtaratna, and the transformation buddhas.

(b) *Miaofa lianhua jing* 妙法蓮華經, T.262.9:34b1-2:

我滅度後、若持此經、爲一人説、是則爲難。

After my extinction, to keep this scripture and preach it even to one person — this will be difficult.

144 **for "will thereby see me" is Buddha Śākyamuni** (*soku i ken ga wa Shakamuni butsu naru ga yue ni* 則爲見我は釋迦牟尼佛なるがゆえに): I.e., "for the 'me' that 'will thereby be seen' is Buddha Śākyamuni."

145 **He also said** (*mata iwaku* 又いはく): From the same passage in the *Lotus Sūtra* (*Miaofa lianhua jing* 妙法蓮華經, T.262.9:34b5-6).

146 **there is no superiority or inferiority** (*shōretsu aru ni arazu* 勝劣あるにあらず): I.e., between the preacher and the audience of the sūtra.

147 **for "standing and listening" to the dharma is "the buddhas of the three times"**

204 DŌGEN'S *SHŌBŌGENZŌ* VOLUME I

fect; this is not talking about listening to the dharma at the stage of cause; for they are represented as already "the buddhas of the three times."[148] We should realize that "the buddhas of the three times" are buddhas by "standing and listening" to the dharma preached by "the flames." The forms of their teaching of the one way cannot be traced; when we try to trace them, the arrow heads oppose each other.[149] "The flames" definitely preach the dharma for "the buddhas of the three times." Their bare mind in pieces, *on the iron tree a flower blooms and the world is fragrant.*[150] So tell me, when they keep "standing and listening" to "the flames" preach the dharma, in the end, *what appears?* It should be *wisdom exceeding the master's*; it should be *wisdom equal to the master's.*[151] It is "the buddhas of the three times," investigating the inner sanctum of master and disciple.

(*ritchi chōhō kore sanze shobutsu naru ga yue ni* 立地聽法これ三世諸佛なるがゆえ に): Perhaps to be understood "those who 'stand and listen' to the dharma are 'buddhas of the three times.'"

148 **the stage of effect** (*kajō* 果上); **the stage of cause** (*inchū* 因中): Reference to the cause and effect stages of practice on the Buddhist path. The buddhas have, by definition, already achieved the ultimate effect of the practice and, therefore, do not listen to the dharma in order to advance on the bodhisattva path.

149 **the arrow heads oppose each other** (*senpō sōshu seri* 箭鋒相拄せり): A common idiom in Chan texts for the meeting of masters, from the story in the *Liezi* 列子 (Tang wen pian 湯問篇, KR.5c0124.005.14a) of the master archer and his disciple, both so skilled that, when they fought a duel, their arrows met in midair. Exactly what the two arrow heads represent here is unclear — perhaps the "flames" and the "buddhas."

150 **bare mind in pieces, on the iron tree a flower blooms and the world is fragrant** (*sekishin henpen toshite tetsuju kekai sekai kō naru nari* 赤心片片として鐵樹華開世 界香なるなり): "The bare mind in pieces" (*sekishin henpen* 赤心片片) is a common expression in Chan texts, most often understood as a sincere mind in every matter; see Supplementary Notes, s.v. "Bare mind in pieces." "On the iron tree a flower blooms and the world is fragrant" (*tetsuju kekai sekai kō* 鐵樹華開世界香) represents a clever over-lapping of two Chan expressions: "a flower blooms on an iron tree" (*tetsuju kekai* 鐵樹華 開), used to express life in the seemingly lifeless; and "in a single night a flower blooms and the world is fragrant" (*ichiya kekai sekai kō* 一夜華開世界香), used in reference to the experience of awakening (see, e.g., *Dahui Pujue chanshi yulu* 大慧普覺禪師語錄, T.1008A.47:811c3-4).

151 **wisdom exceeding the master's** (*chi shō u shi* 智勝于師); **wisdom equal to the master's** (*chi tō u shi* 智等于師): Although given in Chinese, as if quoting a text, a source is not known; perhaps merely rephrasing the common Chan saying, "A view equal to the master's reduces the master's virtue by half; only a view exceeding the mas-ter's is worthy of his transmission" (*jian yu shi qi, jian shi ban de, jian guo yu shi, fang kan chuanshou* 見與師齊減師半德見過於師方堪傳授).

6. Deportment of the Practicing Buddha *Gyōbutsu iigi* 行佛威儀   205

[06:42]

圜悟いはくの、猴白と將謂する、さらに猴黒をさへざる互換の投機、それ
神出鬼没なり。これは、玄沙と同條出すれども、玄沙に同條入せざる一路
もあるべしといへども、火焰の諸佛なるか、諸佛を火焰とせるか。黒白互
換のこころ、玄沙の神鬼に出没すといへども、雪峰の聲色、いまだ黒白の
際にのこらず。しかもかくのごとくなりといへども、玄沙に道是あり、道
不是あり、雪峰に道拈あり、道放あることをしるべし。

The one of whom Yuanwu says "we thought" it was "the Marquise
White" has a further "accord" in an "exchange" that does not interfere
with "the Marquis Black"; this is "*the spirit appearing and the demon
vanishing.*" This comes out of the same line as Xuansha; but, while it
may also have a route that does not go into the same line as Xuansha,
[the question remains,] are his "flames" the buddhas?[152] Has he taken the
buddhas as the "flames"? The point of the "exchange" between "Black
and White" may be the "appearing and vanishing" of Xuansha's "spirits
and demons," but the voice and form of Xuefeng still do not remain in
the confines of "Black and White."[153] Still, however this may be, we
should recognize that Xuansha has words that are right and words that
are wrong; and Xuefeng has words to take up and words to let go.[154]

[06:43] {1:74}

いま、圜悟さらに玄沙に同ぜず、雪峰に同ぜざる道あり。いはゆる烈焰互
天は、ほとけ、法をとくなり、互天烈焰は、法、ほとけをとくなり。この
道は、眞箇これ晩進の光明なり。たとひ烈焰にくらしといふとも、互天に
おほはれば、われその分あり、他この分あり。互天のおほふところ、すで
にこれ烈焰なり。這箇をきらふて用那頭は作麼生なるのみなり。

Now, Yuanwu has a further saying here that is not the same as Xuansha nor the same as Xuefeng: i.e., that "blazing flames throughout the

---

152   **This comes out of the same line as Xuansha; but, while it may also have a
route that does not go into the same line as Xuansha** (*kore wa Gensha to dōjō shutsu
suredomo, Gensha ni dōjō nyū sezaru ichiro mo aru beshi to iedomo* これは玄沙と同條
出すれども、玄沙に同條入せざる一路もあるべしといへども): Probably to be under-
stood, "Yuanwu's view tends to accord with that of Xuansha; it may also depart from
that view, but . . . ." The sense of the counter *jō* 條 here is unclear; the translation takes
it as a "line" (of text or thought), but it may also be a play on the metaphor of Yuanwu's
"route" (*ichiro* 一路).

153   **the voice and form of Xuefeng still do not remain in the confines of "Black and
White"** (*Seppō no shōshiki, imada kokubyaku no sai ni nokorazu* 雪峰の聲色、いまだ
黒白の際にのこらず): I.e., Yuanwu's use of "Marquise White" and "Marquis Black" in
reference to Xuefeng and Xuansha does not capture Xuefeng's saying.

154   **Xuefeng has words to take up and words to let go** (*Seppō ni dō nen ari, dō hō
aru* 雪峰に道拈あり、道放ある): A tentative translation, taking the unusual expressions
dōnen 道拈 and *dōhō* 道放 to parallel the more common *dōze* 道是 ("words that are
right") and *dōfuze* 道不是 ("words that are wrong").

206   DŌGEN'S *SHŌBŌGENZŌ* VOLUME I

heavens" are the buddha preaching the dharma; "throughout the heavens blazing flames" are the dharma preaching the buddha. This saying is truly a light for latecomers.[155] Even if we are in the dark about the "blazing flames," since we are covered by "the heavens throughout," we have a part in it, and others have a part in it. Wherever "the heavens throughout" cover, this is surely "blazing flames." Using that while hating this — it is just, *what's the point?*[156]

[06:44]
よろこぶべし、この皮袋子、うまれたるところは去聖方遠なり、いけるいまは去聖時遠なりといへども、亙天の化道なほきこゆるにあへり。いはゆる、ほとけ、法をとくことは、きくところなりといへども、法、ほとけをとくことは、いくかさなりの不知をかわづらひこし。

We should rejoice that this bag of skin, though where it was born may be *far removed from the place of the Sage*, and where it now lives may be *far removed from the time of the Sage*, has still been able to hear the guidance of "the heavens throughout."[157] That is, that the buddhas preach the dharma may be something we have heard, but that the dharma preaches the buddhas — how profoundly have we suffered ignorance of it?

[06:45]
しかあればすなはち、三世の諸佛は、三世に法にとかれ、三世の諸法は、三世に佛にとかるるなり。葛藤窠の、風前に剪斷する亙天のみあり。一言は、かくるることなく勘破しきたる、維摩詰をも非維摩詰をも。しかあればすなはち、法説佛なり、法行佛なり、法證佛なり、佛説法なり、佛行佛なり、佛作佛なり。かくのごとくなる、ともに行佛の威儀なり。亙天亙地、亙古亙今にも、得者不輕微、明者不賤用なり。

Therefore, the buddhas of the three times are preached by the dharma in the three times, and the dharmas of the three times are preached by the buddhas in the three times. There is only "the heavens throughout," where "before the wind," the "the nest of tangled vines" has been "cut

---

155   **a light for latecomers** (*banshin no kōmyō* 晩進の光明): I.e., a beacon for later students.

156   **Using that while hating this — it is just, what's the point?** (*shako o kiraute yō natō wa somosan naru nomi nari* 這箇をきらふて用那頭は作麼生なるのみなり): Perhaps meaning that it does not make sense to prefer "throughout the heavens" to the "blazing flames."

157   **far removed from the place of the Sage** (*ko shō hō on* 去聖方遠); **far removed from the time of the Sage** (*ko shō ji on* 去聖時遠): I.e., at a great distance in time and space from Buddha Śākyamuni. The latter phrase seems the more common in Buddhist literature, though neither occurs elsewhere in the *Shōbōgenzō*.

6. Deportment of the Practicing Buddha *Gyōbutsu iigi* 行佛威儀 207

through."[158] "A single word" has obviously "seen through" them — both "Vimalakīrti" and not Vimalakīrti.[159] Therefore, the dharma preaches the buddhas, the dharma practices the buddhas, the dharma verifies the buddhas. The buddhas preach the dharma, the buddhas practice the buddhas, the buddhas become buddhas. Such, in all, is the deportment of the practicing buddha. "Throughout the heavens," throughout the earth, throughout the past, throughout the present, *the one who gets it does not treat it lightly; the one who clarifies it, does not use it cheaply.*"[160]

{1:75}

正法眼藏行佛威儀第六
Treasury of the True Dharma Eye
Deportment of the Practicing Buddha
Number 6

[Ryūmonji MS:]

仁治二年辛丑十月中旬、記于觀音導利興聖寶林寺。沙門道元
Recorded at Kannon Dōri Kōshō Hōrin Monastery; middle third of the tenth month of the junior metal year of the ox, the second year of Ninji [November 1241]. The Śramaṇa Dōgen[161]

---

158 **"the heavens throughout," where "before the wind," the "the nest of tangled vines" has been "cut through"** (*kattō ka no, fūzen ni sendan suru gōten* 葛藤窠の、風前に剪斷する亙天): Taking *sendan suru* 剪斷する as a passive; reading in the more obvious active voice would yield the odd, "the heavens throughout that the nest of tangled vines cuts through before the wind." For "tangled vines" (*kattō* 葛藤), see Supplementary Notes. Here and in the following sentence, Dōgen is commenting on the final lines of Yuanwu's verse, quoted above, section 3C:

風前剪斷葛藤窠、一言勘破維摩詰。
Before the wind, they cut through the nest of tangled vines;
With a single word, they see through Vimalakīrti.

159 **both "Vimalakīrti" and not Vimalakīrti** (*Yuimakitsu o mo hi Yuimakitsu o mo* 維摩詰をも非維摩詰をも): Presumably, both Vimalakīrti and others, though whether Dōgen may have anyone particular in mind here is unclear.

160 **"the one who gets it does not treat it lightly; the one who clarifies it, does not use it cheaply"** (*tokusha fukeibi, myōsha fusen'yō* 得者不輕微、明者不賤用): A saying, quoted here in Chinese, of Yunju Daoying 雲居道膺 (*Liandeng huiyao* 聯燈會要, ZZ.136:797a5).

161 The sixty-chapter *Shōbōgenzō* lacks a colophon for this chapter.

TREASURY OF THE TRUE DHARMA EYE

NUMBER 7

One Bright Pearl
Ikka myōju

一顆明珠

One Bright Pearl

Ikka myōju

INTRODUCTION

This chapter, written at Kōshōji in the early summer of 1238, marks the beginning of Dōgen's serious work on the *Shōbōgenzō* texts. It occurs as number 7 in both the sixty- and seventy-five-chapter compilations and as number 4 in the Honzan edition.

"One Bright Pearl" is devoted entirely to a single saying of the Tang-dynasty monk Xuansha Shibei 玄沙師備 (835-908): "All the worlds in the ten directions are one bright pearl." The pearl has a rich metaphorical life in Buddhist literature: as the luminous consciousness on the floor of the ocean of mind, as the wish-fulfilling jewel held by the dragon, as the perfect self rolling freely round the bowl of the world. Here, everything everywhere is such a pearl. Hence, Dōgen can say toward the end of his essay that merely to know this is itself the bright pearl, even to doubt this is the bright pearl.

正法眼藏第七

Treasury of the True Dharma Eye
Number 7

一顆明珠

One Bright Pearl

[07:1] {1:76}

娑婆世界大宋國、福州玄沙山院宗一大師、法諱師備、俗姓者謝なり。在家
のそのかみ釣魚を愛し、舟を南臺江にうかべて、もろもろのつり人になら
ひけり。不釣自上の金鱗を不待にもありけん。唐の感通のはじめ、たちま
ちに出塵をねがふ。舟をすてて山にいる、そのとし三十歳になりけり。浮
世のあやうきをさとり、佛道の高貴をしりぬ。つひに雪峰山にのぼりて、
眞覺大師に參じて、晝夜に辨道す。

Great Master Zongyi of Mount Xuansha Cloister, in Fuzhou, Land of the
Great Song, in the Sahā world: his dharma name was Shibei; his lay surname
was Xie.[1] As a householder, he loved fishing and went out in a boat on the
Nantai River with the fishermen.[2] It seems he did not wait for the golden-
scaled one that rises of itself without being caught.[3] At the beginning

---

1 **Great Master Zongyi of Mount Xuansha Cloister, in Fuzhou, Land of the Great
Song, in the Sahā world** (*Shaba sekai Daisōkoku, Fukushū Genshasan'in Sōitsu daishi*
娑婆世界大宋國、福州玄沙山院宗一大師): I.e., Xuansha Shibei 玄沙師備 (835-908).
"The Sahā World" (*Shaba sekai* 娑婆世界; S. *sahā-loka-dhātu*) is our world, "the realm
to be endured," in which Buddha Śākyamuni teaches. Fuzhou 福州 is in present-day
Fujian.

2 **As a householder, he loved fishing** (*zaike no sonokami chōgyo o ai shi* 在家のその
かみ釣魚を愛し): The biographical description in this section seems to be drawn from
Xuansha's notice in the *Jingde chuandeng lu* 景德傳燈錄 (T.2076.51:343c25-26). Dōgen discusses Xuansha's own reference to his fishing in the "Henzan" 遍參 chapter of
the *Shōbōgenzō*.

Nantai River (*Nandai kō* 南臺江) is the name given to the Min River 閩江 at the point
where it runs beneath Mount Diaotai 釣臺山 in Fujian.

3 **golden-scaled one that rises of itself without being caught** (*fuchō jijō no konrin* 不
釣自上の金鱗): The mysterious golden-scaled fish is a common topic of Chan conversations. "To rise of itself without being caught" (*fuchō jijō* 不釣自上) may reflect the words
of Dōgen's teacher, Tiantong Rujing 天童如淨 (1162-1227) (*Rujing heshang yulu* 如淨
和尚語錄, T.2002A.48:127a17):

> 盡大地人不釣自上
> People of all the whole earth rise of themselves without being caught.

Dōgen uses the same image, "rising of itself before being caught" (*michō sen jō* 未釣先
上), in his discussion of Xuansha in "Shōbōgenzō henzan" 正法眼藏遍參.

of the Xiantong era of the Tang, he suddenly felt the desire to leave the dusty world.[4] Abandoning his boat, he entered the mountains.[5] He was thirty years of age. He understood the perils of the floating world and knew the great worth of the way of the buddhas. Eventually, he climbed Mount Xuefeng and, studying with Great Master Zhenjue, pursued the way day and night.[6]

[07:2]

あるとき、あまねく諸方を参徹せんため、嚢をたづさへて出嶺するちなみに、脚指を石に築著して流血し痛楚するに、忽然として猛省していはく、是身非有、痛自何來。すなはち雪峰にかへる。

One time, in order widely to study [under masters] in all quarters, he was leaving the ridge with his bag in his hand when he stubbed his toe on a rock.[7] Bleeding and in pain, he suddenly reflected earnestly, saying, "*If this body doesn't really exist, where does the pain come from?*" Thereupon, he returned to Xuefeng.

[07:3]

雪峰とふ、那箇是備頭陀。玄沙いはく、終不敢誑於人。

Xuefeng asked, "*What is this Bei Dhūta?*"

Xuansha said, "*I would never fool anyone.*"[8]

[07:4] {1:77}

このことばを、雪峰ことに愛していはく、たれかこのことばをもたざらん、たれかこのことばを道得せん。

These words, Xuefeng especially liked and said, "Who does not possess these words? Yet who could say these words?"[9]

4　**Xiantong era of the Tang** (*Tō no kantsū* 唐の感通): The Xiantong era covers the years 860-875.

5　**he entered the mountains** (*yama ni iru* 山にいる): Japanese equivalent of a Chinese expression (*rushan* 入山) regularly used for joining a monastic community.

6　**Great Master Zhenjue** (*Shinkaku daishi* 眞覺大師): I.e., Xuefeng Yicun 雪峰義存 (822-908). Mount Xuefeng (*Seppōzan* 雪峰山) is located near Fuzhou in present-day Fujian.

7　**One time, in order widely to study [under masters] in all quarters** (*aru toki, amaneku shohō o santetsu sen tame* あるとき、あまねく諸方を参徹せんため): This anecdote represents a Japanese retelling of a passage appearing in the *Liandeng huiyao* 聯燈會要 (ZZ.136:818b3-6) and other sources.

8　**"What is this Bei Dhūta?"** (*nako ze Bi zuda* 那箇是備頭陀): The Chinese *toutuo* (J. *zuda* 頭陀) transliterates Sanskrit *dhūta*, used in reference to the practice of austerities. According to his biography, Xuansha earned this sobriquet for his strict practice. Xuefeng is expressing surprise at Xuansha's comings and goings. Some readers take Xuansha's response here as a passive: "I would never be deceived by anyone."

9　**"Who does not possess these words?"** (*tare ka kono kotoba o motazaran* たれかこ

7. One Bright Pearl *Ikka myōju* 一顆明珠 213

[07:5]

雪峰さらにとふ、備頭陀、なんぞ遍参せざる。師いはく、達磨不來東土、
二祖不往西天。といふに、雪峰ことにほめき。

Xuefeng further asked, "Bei Dhūta, why don't you go on extensive study?"[10]

The Master said, "*Dharma didn't come to the Land of the East; the Second Ancestor didn't go to Sindh in the West.*"[11]

When he said this, Xuefeng praised him even more.

[07:6]

ひごろは、つりする人にてあれば、もろもろの經書、ゆめにもかつていま
だ見ざりけれども、こころざしのあさからぬをさきとすれば、かたへにこ
ゆる志氣あらはれけり。雪峰も衆のなかにすぐれたりとおもひて、門下の
角立なりとほめき。ころもは、ぬのをもちい、ひとつをかへざりければ、
ももつづりにつづれりけり。はだへには、紙衣をもちいけり。艾草をもき
けり。雪峰に參ずるほかは、自餘の知識をとぶらはざりけり。しかあれど
も、まさに師の法を嗣するちから辦取せりき。

Since he had always been a fisherman, [Xuansha] had never seen books even in his dreams; yet because he made depth of commitment his priority, he displayed a determination beyond that of his peers. Xuefeng, too, thought that he stood out in his assembly and praised him as pre-eminent among his followers. For his robe, he used plant fibers and, since he did not change it for another, he patched and re-patched it. Against his skin, he used a paper garment or wore mugwort fiber. Apart from studying with Xuefeng, he visited no other wise friends. And yet he certainly acquired the authority to inherit the dharma of his master.

[07:7]

つひにみちをえてのち、人にしめすにいはく、盡十方世界、是一箇明珠。

After he eventually attained the way, in instructing people he would say, "*All the worlds in the ten directions are one bright pearl.*"

* * * * *

のことばをもたざらん): Xuefeng's words, given here in Japanese, do not appear in the standard accounts of this episode, and Dōgen's source for them is uncertain.

10 **Xuefeng further asked** (*Seppō sara ni tou* 雪峰さらにとふ): A continuation of the preceding quotation (from ZZ.136:818b6-8).

11 **"Dharma"** (*Daruma* 達磨): I.e., Bodhidharma, said to have brought the Zen lineage from India ("Sindh in the West"; *Saiten* 西天) to China ("the Land of the East"; *Tōdo* 東土) and to have transmitted it there to the Second Ancestor, Huike 慧可.

214 DŌGEN'S *SHŌBŌGENZŌ* VOLUME I

[07:8]

ときに、僧問、承和尚有言、盡十方世界、是一顆明珠。學人如何會得。
師曰、盡十方世界、是一顆明珠、用會作麼。師、來日却問其僧、盡十方
世界、是一顆明珠、汝作麼生會。僧曰、盡十方世界、是一顆明珠、用會作
麼。師曰、知汝向黑山鬼窟裏作活計。

Once, a monk asked him, "I've heard that you say, 'All the worlds in
the ten directions are one bright pearl.' How is your student to understand it?"[12]

The Master said, "All the worlds in the ten directions are one bright
pearl. What's the use of understanding it?"

The next day the Master in his turn asked the monk, "All the worlds in
the ten directions are one bright pearl. How do you understand it?"

The monk said, "All the worlds in the ten directions are one bright
pearl. What's the use of understanding it?"

The Master said, "Now I know that you make your living inside the
ghost cave at the Black Mountains."[13]

[07:9] {1:78}

いま道取する盡十方世界、是一顆明珠、はじめて玄沙にあり。その宗旨
は、盡十方世界は、廣大にあらず、微小にあらず、方圓にあらず、中正に
あらず、活鱍鱍にあらず、露廻廻にあらず。さらに、生死去來にあらざる
ゆえに生死去來なり。恁麼のゆえに、昔日曾此去にして而今從此來なり。
究辨するに、たれか片片なりと見徹するあらん、たれか兀兀なりと撿舉す
るあらん。

The words spoken here, "All the worlds in the ten directions are one
bright pearl," originate with Xuansha. Their essential point is that "all
the worlds in the ten directions" are not vast, are not minute, are not
square or round, are not centered and upright, are not brisk and lively,
are not everywhere exposed.[14] Furthermore, because they are not birth
and death, coming and going, they are birth and death, coming and go-

---

12   **Once, a monk asked him** (*toki ni, sō mon* ときに、僧問): Dōgen here switches into
Chinese to quote the following conversation, which can be found, e.g., at *Jingde chuandeng
lu* 景德傳燈錄 (T.2076.51:346c16-21), as well as in Dōgen's *shinji Shōbōgenzō* 眞字正法
眼藏 (DZZ.5:132, case 15). See Supplementary Notes, s.v. "One bright pearl."

13   **the ghost cave at the Black Mountains** (*Kokusan kikutsu* 黑山鬼窟): A common
image in Zen literature for the confines of fixed intellectual or spiritual positions; see
Supplementary Notes, s.v. "Ghost cave."

14   **brisk and lively** (*kappatsupatsu* 活鱍鱍): A loose rendering of a common Chinese
idiom expressing the quick, powerful movements of a fish.

everywhere exposed (*rokaikai* 露廻廻, also read *roe'e* or *rokeikei* and written 露迴迴 or
露回回) can mean either "clearly visible" or "visible far and wide."

7. One Bright Pearl *Ikka myōju* 一顆明珠　　　　215

ing.[15] This being so, *"Once, in the past, he left from this"; now, he comes through this.*[16] When we exhaustively examine them, who would discern that they are in pieces? Who would propose that they are firmly fixed?[17]

[07:10]

盡十方といふは、逐物爲己、逐己爲物の未休なり。情生智隔を隔と道取する、これ回頭換面なり、展事投機なり。逐己爲物のゆえに、未休なる盡十方なり。機先の道理なるゆえに、機要の管得にあまれることあり。

"All the worlds in the ten directions" means that *pursuing things as the self and pursuing the self as a thing* are without rest.[18] To call *"when feelings arise and wisdom is blocked"* a *"blockage"* — this is *turning the head and changing the face*; it is *divulging the matter and achieving accord.*[19] Because they are *"pursuing things as the self,"* they are *"all ten*

15　**birth and death, coming and going** (*shōji korai* 生死去來): An expression appearing often in Zen texts and in the *Shōbōgenzō* for the process of reincarnation, as in the saying used several times by Dōgen, "birth and death, coming and going, are the true human body" (*shōji korai shinjitsu nintai* 生死去來眞實人體). See Supplementary Notes, s.v. "True human body."

16　**"Once, in the past, he left from this"; now, he comes through this** (*sekijitsu zō shi ko ni shite, nikon jū shi rai nari* 昔日曾此去にして、而今從此來なり): Dōgen here mixes Japanese and Chinese syntax in a sentence likely reflecting the words of Rujing 如淨 (*Rujing hoshang yulu* 如淨和尚語錄, T.2002A.48:126a12-13). In his second tenure as abbot of Jingci Monastery 淨慈寺, pointing to the gate of the monastery (and referring to himself by his monastery name), Rujing said,

昔日淨慈曾此去。淨慈從此又還來。

Once, in the past, Jingci left from this;
Once again, Jingci has come back through this.

Dōgen's own sentence here may represent an explanation of why he has said that "all the worlds" both do and do not "come and go": i.e., because they are "all the worlds," all the "coming and going" takes place within them.

17　**in pieces** (*henpen* 片片); **firmly fixed** (*gotsugotsu* 兀兀): The former is a common term seen perhaps most often in the expression "the bare mind in pieces" (*sekishin henpen* 赤心片片); see Supplementary Notes, s.v. "Bare mind in pieces." The latter is a term associated especially with both the posture and mental state of seated meditation; see Supplementary Notes, s.v. "Sit fixedly."

18　**pursuing things as the self and pursuing the self as a thing** (*chiku motsu i ko, chiku ko i motsu* 逐物爲己、逐己爲物): Dōgen here switches to Chinese, as if quoting a saying, but there is no known source; possibly reflecting a common saying found in the Chan corpus (see, e.g., the words of Jingqing Daofu 鏡清道怤 [864-937], *Jingde chuandeng lu* 景德傳燈錄, T.2076.51:349c13-14; *shinji Shōbōgenzō* 眞字正法眼藏, DZZ.5:270, case 286):

衆生顛倒、迷己逐物。

Living beings are perverse: losing sight of themselves, they pursue things.

19　**"when feelings arise and wisdom is blocked"** (*jōshō chikyaku* 情生智隔): After the saying discussed in a conversation between an unnamed monk and Baoci Zangxu 報慈藏嶼 (dates unknown), (*Liandeng huiyao* 聯燈會要, ZZ.136:853b8-9):

216 DŌGEN'S *SHŌBŌGENZŌ* VOLUME I

directions" "without rest." Because they are a principle before their functioning, they can exceed our control of the essence of their functioning.[20]

[07:11]

是一顆珠は、いまだ名にあらざれども道得なり。これを名に認じきたること あり。一顆珠は直須萬年なり、亙古未了なるに亙今到來なり。身今あ り、心今ありといへども、明珠なり。彼此の草木にあらず、乾坤の山河に あらず、明珠なり。

"This one pearl," though not a name, is a saying, and this has sometimes been recognized as a name.[21] "One pearl" is *it would surely take ten thousand years*."[22] It is "the past throughout is not yet over when the present throughout has already arrived."[23] While there is a present of the

---

僧問、承古有言、情生智隔、想變體殊。只如情未生時如何。師云、隔。

A monk asked, "I've heard the ancients had a saying, 'When feelings arise, wisdom is blocked; when thoughts change, the substance is isolated.' How about when feelings have not yet arisen?"

The Master said, "Blocked."

turning the head and changing the face (*kaitō kanmen* 回頭換面): Also read *uitō kanmen*. A common expression in Zen literature interpreted along various different lines; here, perhaps, conveying the inseparability or interdependence of wisdom and its blockage. See Supplementary Notes, s.v. "Turning the head and changing the face."

divulging the matter and achieving accord (*tenji tōki* 展事投機): Two terms regularly occurring together in Zen literature, the former used for expressions of what one really thinks; the latter, for matching the understanding of one's interlocutor (often the master); see Supplementary Notes, s.v. "Divulging the matter and achieving accord."

20 **Because they are a principle before their functioning, they can exceed our control of the essence of their functioning** (*kisen no dōri naru yue ni, kiyō no kantoku ni amareru koto ari* 機先の道理なるゆえに、機要の管得にあまれることあり): Perhaps meaning that, because "all the worlds in the ten directions" precede their phenomenal activity, their essential nature cannot be fully understood through that activity. The translation strains to preserve the lexical parallel between *kisen* 機先 ("prior to their function") and *kiyō* 機要 ("essence of their function").

21 **"This one pearl," though not a name, is a saying** (*ze ikka ju wa, imada na ni arazaredomo dōtoku nari* 是一顆珠は、いまだ名にあらざれども道得なり): Reading the copula *ze* 是 of Xuansha's "is one pearl" as the pronoun "this" (*kono* この). The sense of "name" (*na* 名) here is uncertain; perhaps the point is that "one pearl" is not a technical term, but its use in this saying has led to its treatment as such.

22 **"it would surely take ten thousand years"** (*jikishu bannen* 直須萬年): Reflecting a saying attributed to Shishuang Chingzhu 石霜慶諸 (807-888) appearing elsewhere in the *Shōbōgenzō* and recorded in the *shinji Shōbōgenzō* 眞字正法眼藏 (DZZ.5:166, case 85); see Supplementary Notes, s.v. "It would surely take ten thousand years."

23 **"the past throughout is not yet over when the present throughout has already arrived"** (*gōko miryō naru ni gōkon tōrai* 亙古未了なるに亙今到來): From the expression "throughout the past and throughout the present" (*gōko gōkon* 亙古亙今), a common idiom for extension through all history.

7. One Bright Pearl *Ikka myōju* 一顆明珠　　　217

body and a present of the mind, they are the "bright pearl."[24] It is not the grasses and trees of here and there; it is not the mountains and rivers of heaven and earth: it is the "bright pearl."[25]

[07:12] {1:79}

學人如何會得。この道取は、たとひ僧の弄業識に相似せりとも、大用現是大軌則なり。すすみて一尺水、一尺波を突兀ならしむべし。いはゆる一丈珠、一丈明なり。

"*How is your student to understand it?*" This saying, though it resembles the monk's playing with karmic consciousness, is "*the manifestation of the great function*" *is the great rule*.[26] Going further, "one foot of water" should thrust up one foot of wave: that is, ten feet of pearl is ten feet of bright.[27]

[07:13]

いはゆるの道得を道取するに、玄沙の道は、盡十方世界、是一顆明珠、用會作麼なり。この道取は、佛は佛に嗣し、祖は祖に嗣す、玄沙は玄沙に嗣する道得なり。嗣せざらんと廻避せんに、廻避のところなかるべきにあらざれども、しばらく灼然廻避するも、道取生あるは、現前の蓋時節なり。

In making his statement, Xuansha's words are, "*All the worlds in the ten directions are one bright pearl. What's the use of understanding it?*" This saying is a statement that buddhas inherit from buddhas, ancestors inherit from ancestors, Xuansha inherits from Xuansha. When he tries to avoid inheriting it, although it is not that it could not be avoided, even if

---

24　**there is a present of the body and a present of the mind** (*shinkon ari, shinkon ari* 身今あり、心今あり): Perhaps merely a playful way of saying "the present body and mind," this could also be parsed, "the body exists in the present; the mind exists in the present."

25　**it is the "bright pearl"** (*myōju nari* 明珠なり): The subject is not expressed; the translation takes it as "this one pearl."

26　**playing with karmic consciousness** (*rō gosshiki* 弄業識): A common expression in Zen literature for being caught up in deluded thoughts; see Supplementary Notes, s.v. "Karmic consciousness."

"manifestation of the great function" is the great rule (*daiyū gen ze dai kisoku* 大用現是大軌則): Perhaps suggesting that the monk's seemingly routine question is expressing "the great function." A reversal of the set phrase, the "manifestation of the great function does not abide in rules"; see Supplementary Notes, s.v. "Manifestation of the great function."

27　**"one foot of water" should thrust up one foot of wave** (*isshaku sui, isshaku ha o totsugotsu narashimu beshi* 一尺水、一尺波を突兀ならしむべし): Perhaps suggesting that the monk's question, while shallow, is complete. This and the following clause are likely playing on a line of verse found in the *Hongzhi chanshi guanglu* 宏智禪師廣錄 (T.2001.48:19a25):

一尺水一丈波。

One foot of water and ten feet of wave.

218 DŌGEN'S *SHŌBŌGENZŌ* VOLUME I

for the moment he does clearly avoid it, this saying is present in all time right before us.[28]

[07:14]

玄沙、來日問其僧、盡十方世界、是一顆明珠、汝作麼生會。

The next day Xuansha asked the monk, "All the worlds in the ten directions are one bright pearl. How do you understand it?"

[07:15]

これは道取す、昨日説定法なる、今日二枚をかりて出氣す。今日説不定法なり、推倒昨日點頭笑なり。

This says, *"Yesterday, I preached a fixed dharma"*; today, I'm borrowing the pair to exhale.[29] It is, *"Today, I'm preaching an indeterminate dharma"*; it is, *overturning yesterday, I'm nodding and laughing.*[30]

---

28 **this saying is present in all time right before us** (*dōshushō aru wa, genzen no gaijisetsu nari* 道取生あるは、現前の蓋時節なり): A tentative translation of a sentence difficult to interpret. Perhaps the sense is that, while Xuansha might have spoken otherwise (and thus "avoided inheriting" the saying), the saying itself is always before us. The expression *dōshushō* 道取生 (also read *dōshusei*) should be taken simply as "saying," the graph *shō* 生 functioning here as an emphatic colloquial suffix. The unusual expression *gaijisetsu* 蓋時節, translated here as "all time," is likely constructed after terms like *gaiten* 蓋天 ("the whole of heaven") or *gaichi* 蓋地 ("all of earth").

29 **"Yesterday, I preached a fixed dharma"** (*sakujitsu setsu jōhō* 昨日説定法); **"Today, I'm preaching an indeterminate dharma"** (*konnichi setsu fujōhō* 今日説不定法): After words attributed to Buddha Śākyamuni in the *Liandeng huiyao* 聯燈會要 (ZZ.136:443b9-11):

世尊因外道問、昨日説何法。云説定法。外道云、今日説何法、云説不定法。外道云、昨日説定法。今日何故説不定法。云昨日定。今日不定。

The World-Honored One was once asked by a follower of an other path, "What dharma did you preach yesterday?"
He said, "I preached a fixed dharma."
The follower said, "What dharma do you preach today?"
He said, "I'm preaching an indeterminate dharma."
The follower said, "Yesterday, you preached a fixed dharma. Why are you preaching an indeterminate dharma today?"
He said, "Yesterday was fixed. Today is not fixed."

I'm borrowing the pair to exhale (*nimai o karite shukki su* 二枚をかりて出氣す): "The pair" (*nimai* 二枚) here likely refers to the lips and "exhale" (*shukki* 出氣), to speaking. The construction parallels the expression, found in the "Shōbōgenzō shinjin gakudō" 正法眼藏身心學道, "to borrow the nostrils of the buddhas and ancestors and exhale through them" (*busso no bikū o karite shukki seshime* 佛祖の鼻孔をかりて出氣せしめ); see Supplementary Notes, s.v. "Nose."

30 **I'm nodding and laughing** (*tentō shō* 點頭笑): A common fixed idiom, more often in reverse order, "laughing and nodding" (*shō tentō* 笑點頭).

7. One Bright Pearl   *Ikka myōju*   一顆明珠   219

[07:16]

僧曰、盡十方世界、是一顆明珠、用會作麼。

The monk said, "All the worlds in the ten directions are one bright pearl. What's the use of understanding it?"

[07:17]

いふべし、騎賊馬逐賊なり。古佛爲汝説するには、異類中行なり。しばらく回光返照すべし、幾箇枚の用會作麼かある。試道するには、乳餅七枚、菜餅五枚なりといへども、湘之南、潭之北の教行なり。

We should say this is *riding the bandit's horse to chase the bandit.*[31] When the old buddha preaches for your sake, *"he moves among different types."*[32] You should for a bit *turn the light around and shine it back:* how many instances are there of *"what's the use of understanding it"*?[33] To try to say something, while it might be *seven milk cakes and five vegetable cakes,* would be a teaching and practice *"south of Xiang and north of Tan."*[34]

---

31   **riding the bandit's horse to chase the bandit** (*ki zokuba chiku zoku* 騎賊馬逐賊): A common idiom (occurring with various verbs for "pursue") for turning a statement back on the interlocutor.

32   **When the old buddha preaches for your sake, "he moves among different types"** (*kobutsu i nyo setsu suru ni wa, irui chū gyō nari* 古佛爲汝説するには、異類中行なり): The translation takes "you" (*nyo* 汝) here to refer to the monk in the story and, though the comments could be read otherwise, treats this entire section as Dōgen's direct address to him. "He moves among different types" (*irui chū gyō* 異類中行) is a fixed expression, occurring often in Dōgen's writings, typically used to indicate the salvific activities of the buddhas and bodhisattvas among the various forms of living beings; see Supplementary Notes, s.v. "Move among different types."

33   **turn the light around and shine it back** (*ekō henshō* 回光返照): A common idiom in Zen texts used in reference to Buddhist practice as the study of the self, rather than of the external world; see Supplementary Notes.

34   **seven milk cakes and five vegetable cakes** (*nyūbyō shichimai, saibyō gomai* 乳餅七枚、菜餅五枚): Perhaps suggesting "standard fare," "humble food." Possibly reflecting a line in the *Rujing hoshang yulu* 如淨和尚語録, T.2002A.48:125a22-23:

齋時三枚乳餅、七枚菜餅。

At the noon meal, three milk cakes and seven vegetable cakes.

"south of Xiang and north of Tan" (*Sō shi nan, Tan shi hoku* 湘之南、潭之北): From a verse by Yingzhen 應眞 (dates unknown), on Huizhong's seamless stūpa (*Jingde chuandeng lu* 景德傳燈錄, T.2076.51:245a12):

湘之南潭之北、中有黄金充一國。

South of Xiang and north of Tan:
Between, there's gold to fill a kingdom.

There are diverse views of the exact geographical locations of "south of Xiang" and "north of Tan" (place names most often said to refer to Xiangzhou 湘州 and Tanzhou 潭州 in present-day Hunan Province), but the sense is generally held to be "anywhere." On such a reading, Dōgen's point here would seem to be that, although the monk's question may seem prosaic, it has universal significance.

220 DŌGEN'S *SHŌBŌGENZŌ* VOLUME I

[07:18]

玄沙曰、知汝向黑山鬼窟裏作活計。

Xuansha said, "Now I know that you make your living inside the ghost cave at the Black Mountains."

[07:19]

しるべし、日面月面は往古よりいまだ不換なり。日面は日面とともに共出す、月面は月面とともに共出するゆえに、若六月道正是時、不可道我姓熱なり。

We should understand that, since ancient times, the face of the sun and the face of the moon have never been switched. The face of the sun emerges together with the face of the sun; the face of the moon emerges together with the face of the moon.[35] Hence, *"If I say in the sixth month that it's just this time, you shouldn't say that my surname is 'Hot.'"*[36]

[07:20] {1:80}

しかあればすなはち、この明珠の有如無始は、無端なり。盡十方世界一顆明珠なり、両顆三顆といはず。全身これ一隻の正法眼なり、全身これ眞實體なり、全身これ一句なり、全身これ光明なり、全身これ全心なり。全身のとき、全身の罣礙なし、圓陀陀地なり、轉轆轆なり。明珠の功德、かくのごとく見成なるゆえに、いまの見色聞聲の觀音・彌勒あり、現身説法の古佛・新佛あり。

---

35 **The face of the sun emerges together with the face of the sun** (*nichimen wa nichimen to tomo ni gūshutsu su* 日面は日面とともに共出す): I.e., the sun is just the sun (and the moon, just the moon). "Sun face" (*nichimen* 日面) and "moon face" (*gachimen* 月面) may also allude to two buddhas of those names given in the *Foming jing* 佛名經, or to a famous saying by Mazu Daoyi 馬祖道一 (709-788); see Supplementary Notes, s.v. "Sun face, moon face." Here, no doubt, the reference is to Xuansha and the monk: Xuansha's question is his question; the monk's question is the monk's question.

36 **"If I say in the sixth month that it's just this time, you shouldn't say that my surname is 'Hot'"** (*nyaku rokugetsu dō shō ze ji, fuka dō ga shō netsu* 若六月道正是時、不可道我姓熱): The words of Yaoshan Weiyan 藥山惟儼 (751-834), found in a story recorded at *Jiatai pudeng lu* 嘉泰普燈錄 (ZZ.137:110b10-13):

昔日有官人問藥山、和尚何姓。藥山云、正是時。官人罔措。下至知事處問云、適來問長老何姓。答道正是時。的當是姓箇甚麼。知事云、只是姓韓。藥山聞云、若六月道正是時、不可道我姓熱也。

Once, there was an official who asked Yaoshan, "What is the Reverend's surname?" Yaoshan said, "Just this time."
The official, not knowing what to make of it, went and asked a steward, "Just now, when I asked the Elder his surname, he said, 'Just this time.' Really, what is this surname?"
The steward said, "It's just that his surname is Han 韓 [homophonous with *han* 寒 ('cold')]."
Hearing about this, Yaoshan said, "If I say in the sixth month that it's just this time, you shouldn't say my surname is Re 熱 ['hot']."

7. One Bright Pearl *Ikka myōju* 一顆明珠   221

Thus, the suchness and beginninglessness of this bright pearl is limitless.[37] It is the one bright pearl of all the worlds in the ten directions; it is not described as "two" or "three." Its whole body is a single true dharma eye; its whole body is the true body; its whole body is a single phrase; its whole body is radiance; its whole body is the whole mind.[38] When it is the whole body, it is not obstructed by the whole body.[39] It is round, round; it rolls round and round.[40] Since the virtues of the bright pearl appear like this, there are the present Avalokiteśvara and Maitreya, seeing forms and hearing sounds, there are old buddhas and new buddhas, manifesting their bodies and preaching the dharma.[41]

---

37 **the suchness and beginninglessness of this bright pearl is limitless** (*kono myōju no u nyo mushi wa, mutan nari* この明珠の有如無始は、無端なり): A tentative translation. The unusual phrase *unyo mushi* 有如無始 (rendered here "suchness and beginninglessness") could be read "having such beginninglessness"; that Dōgen takes the four glyphs as two pairs is suggested by their recurrence in reverse order (*mushi unyo* 無始有如) at *Eihei kōroku* 永平廣錄 (DZZ.3:44, no. 67). The term *mutan* 無端 ("without limit") can mean both "without origin" and "without reason."

38 **a single true dharma eye** (*isseki no shōbō gen* 一隻の正法眼): Perhaps recalling the words of the ninth-century figure Changsha Jingcen 長沙景岑 (dates unknown); see Supplementary Notes, s.v. "All the worlds in the ten directions are the single eye of the śramaṇa."

true body (*shinjitsu tai* 眞實體): Perhaps recalling Xuansha's own words (e.g., at *shinji Shōbōgenzō* 眞字正法眼藏, DZZ.5:196, case 131):

盡十方界是箇眞實人體。

All the worlds in the ten directions are this true human body.

See Supplementary Notes, s.v. "True human body."

radiance (*kōmyō* 光明): A term regularly used for the nimbus surrounding the body of a buddha.

39 **not obstructed by the whole body** (*zenshin no keige nashi* 全身の罣礙なし): Literally, "there is no obstruction of the whole body," perhaps meaning that it is not limited to, or by, its totality.

40 **It is round, round; it rolls round and round** (*en dadachi nari, ten rokuroku nari* 圓陀陀地なり、轉轆轆なり): Loose translation of two idiomatic expressions with the repetitive sounds *dada* and *rokuroku*, the former expressing perfect roundness, the latter free rotation.

41 **the present Avalokiteśvara and Maitreya, seeing forms and hearing sounds** (*ima no kenshiki monshō no Kannon Miroku ari* いまの見色聞聲の觀音・彌勒あり): A characterization of these two bodhisattvas perhaps inspired by the fact that the former's name means "perceiver of sound (i.e., the voices of his supplicants)."

manifesting their bodies and preaching the dharma (*genshin seppō* 現身説法): Recalling a famous passage in the *Pumen* 普門 chapter of the *Lotus Sūtra*; see Supplementary Notes, s.v. "Manifesting a body to preach the dharma."

[07:21]

正當恁麼時、あるひは虚空にかかり、衣裏にかかる、あるひは頷下にをさめ、髻中にをさむる、みな盡十方世界一顆明珠なり。ころものうらにかかるを樣子とせり、おもてにかけんと道取することなかれ。髻中・頷下にかかるを樣子とせり、髻表・頷表に弄せんと擬することなかれ。酔酒の時節にたまをあたふる親友あり、親友にはかならずたまをあたふべし。たまをかけらるる時節、かならず酔酒するなり。既是恁麼は、盡十方界にてある一顆明珠なり。

At this very moment, hanging in empty space or hanging inside a garment, tucked under the chin or tucked in the topknot — these are all the one bright pearl of all the worlds in the ten directions.[42] To be hanging inside your garment represents the standard; do not say, "Let's hang it outside." To be in the topknot or under the chin represents the standard; do not think to play with them in front of the topknot or in front of the chin. There is a close friend who gives a jewel when one is drunk; he always gives the jewel to his close friend. When the jewel is hung, he is always drunk. "*Since you are such*" is the one bright pearl of all the worlds in the ten directions.[43]

[07:22]

しかあればすなはち、轉・不轉のおもてをかへゆくににたれども、すなはち明珠なり。まさに、たまはかくありけるとしる、すなはちこれ明珠なり。明珠は、かくのごとくきこゆる聲色あり。既得恁麼なるには、われは明珠にはあらじとたどらるるは、たまにはあらじとうたがはざるべきなり。たどり、うたがひ、取舍する作・無作も、ただしばらく小量の見なり、さらに小量に相似ならしむるのみなり。

Therefore, although it seems to change its appearance as it spins or does not spin, it is the bright pearl. To know that there truly is a pearl like this — this itself is the bright pearl. The bright pearl has sound and

---

42 **hanging in empty space** (*kokū ni kakari* 虚空にかかり): Perhaps an allusion to the scene in the *Pusa yingluo jing* 菩薩瓔珞經 (T.656.16:1b24-25), in which priceless gems illumine the space above the Buddha and his assembly.

hanging inside a garment (*eri ni kakaru* 衣裏にかかる): Reference to the famous parable in the *Lotus Sūtra*, in which a friend sews a priceless gem into the lining of the garment of a man in a drunken sleep; see Supplementary Notes, s.v. "Jewel in the robe."

tucked under the chin (*ganka ni osame* 頷下にをさめ): Allusion to the black dragon of Chinese lore that holds a gem beneath its chin (see, e.g., *Zhuangzi* 莊子, Lie Yukou 列御寇, KR.5c0126.032.9a).

tucked in the topknot (*keichū ni osamuru* 髻中にをさむる): Reference to the *Lotus Sūtra* metaphor of the sūtra as the jewel in the king's topknot; see Supplementary Notes, s.v. "Jewel in the topknot."

43 **"Since you are such"** (*ki ze inmo* 既是恁麼): Likely an allusion, repeated below, to the famous saying attributed to Yunju Daoying 雲居道膺 (d. 902); see Supplementary Notes, s.v. "Such a person."

7. One Bright Pearl *Ikka myōju* 一顆明珠

form that is perceived like this. When they "have got such," those who confusedly think, "we are not the bright pearl," should be without doubts about not being the pearl.[44] The actions and non-actions of being confused and doubting, accepting and rejecting — these are just temporary small views; going further, they are just making it resemble something small.[45]

[07:23] {1:81}

愛せざらんや、明珠かくのごとくの彩光きはまりなきなり。彩彩光光の片片條條は、盡十方界の功德なり、たれかこれを攙奪せん、行市に博をなぐる人あらず、六道の因果に不落・有落をわづらふことなかれ。不昧本來の頭正尾正なる、明珠は面目なり、明珠は眼睛なり。

Can you not but love it? The colorful lights like this of the bright pearl are boundless. Each bit and each ray of each color and each light is a virtue of all the worlds in the ten directions. Who could seize them? In the market, there is no one who would toss out a tile.[46] Do not worry about falling or not falling into the cause and effect of the six paths.[47] Our not

---

44 **"have got such"** (*ki toku inmo* 既得恁麼): Variation on Yunju's verse cited above, Note 43.

45 **going further, they are just making it resemble something small** (*sara ni shōryō ni sōji narashimuru nomi nari* さらに小量に相似ならしむるのみなり): The object of the causative here is unstated; presumably, "the bright pearl."

46 **Who could seize them? In the market, there is no one who would toss out a tile** (*tare ka kore o zandatsu sen, kōshi ni kawara o naguru hito arazu* たれかこれを攙奪せん、行市に博をなぐる人あらず): Taking the verb *zandatsu* 攙奪 here in the sense "to take by force" (or, perhaps, "to have one's way with"); in his immediately following reference to the "market" (*kōshi* 行市), Dōgen seems to be recalling the phrase, occurring several times in the *Shōbōgenzō*, "to dominate the market" (*zandatsu kōshi* 攙奪行市; perhaps in the sense "to control prices") — as in the saying of Xuansha Shibei 玄沙師備 recorded in Dōgen's *shinji Shōbōgenzō* 眞字正法眼藏 (DZZ.5:146, case 38); see Supplementary Notes, s.v. "Dominate the market." "Toss out a tile" translates Dōgen's Japanese rendering of a Chinese expression from the idiom, "to toss out a tile and take in a jade" (*hōsen ingyoku* 抛甎引玉), in literary usage, a polite way to ask another for a capping verse for your poem, and by extension, as typically in Zen dialogues, to get back more than you offered. See Supplementary Notes, s.v. "Tossing out a tile and taking in a jade."

47 **falling or not falling into the cause and effect of the six paths** (*rokudō no inga ni furaku uraku o wazurau koto nakare* 六道の因果に不落有落をわづらふことなかれ): Allusion to the famous tale of Baizhang Huaihai 百丈懷海 (749-814) and the teacher who was reborn as a fox for saying that the person of great practice "does not fall into cause and effect" (*furaku inga* 不落因果). (See, e.g., *Liandeng huiyao* 聯燈會要, ZZ.136:495a9-b2; *shinji Shōbōgenzō* 眞字正法眼藏, DZZ.5:178, case 102).

six paths (*rokudō* 六道): I.e., the six states of rebirth in saṃsāra; see Supplementary Notes, s.v. "Six paths."

224 DŌGEN'S *SHŌBŌGENZŌ* VOLUME I

being in the dark about the fundamental is true from head to tail; the bright pearl is its face; the bright pearl is its eye.[48]

[07:24]

しかあれども、われもなんぢも、いかなるかこれ明珠、いかなるかこれ明珠にあらざるとしらざる百思・百不思は、明明の草料をむすびきたれども、玄沙の法道によりて、明珠なりける身心の様子をも、きき、しり、あきらめつれば、心これわたくしにあらず、起滅をたれとしてか、明珠なり、明珠にあらざる、と取舎にわづらはん。たとひたどりわづらふも、明珠にあらぬにあらず。明珠にあらぬがありておこさせける行にも念にもにてはあらざれば、ただまさに黑山鬼窟の進歩退歩、これ一顆明珠なるのみなり。

Nevertheless, while neither you nor I knows what is the bright pearl and what is not the bright pearl, a hundred thinkings and a hundred not-thinkings have bundled the perfectly clear fodder.[49] But, thanks to the dharma words of Xuansha, we have heard about and clarified the status of body and mind as the bright pearl; therefore, the mind is not our own, and exactly as whom its arising and ceasing is the bright pearl or is not the bright pearl — the taking and rejecting of this might well worry us.[50] Even being confused and worrying is not not the bright pearl. Since there exists neither action nor thought brought about by what is not the bright pearl, stepping forward and stepping back in the ghost cave at the Black Mountains — this is nothing but one bright pearl.[51]

---

48 **Our not being in the dark about the fundamental is true from head to tail** (*fumai honrai no zushin bishin naru* 不昧本來の頭正尾正なる): A tentative translation of a difficult clause subject to varied readings. The English here takes the phrase *fumai honrai* 不昧本來 as a verb-object expression, playing on Baizhang's opinion in the fox story that the person of great practice is "not in the dark about cause and effect" (*fumai inga* 不昧因果); the phrase might also be read "the fundamental that is not in the dark."

49 **a hundred thinkings and a hundred not-thinkings have bundled the perfectly clear fodder** (*hyaku shi hyaku fushi wa, meimei no sōryō o musubikitaredomo* 百思・百不思は、明明の草料をむすびきたれども): A complicated play with the expression "perfectly clear, the tips of the hundred grasses" (see Supplementary Notes) — as well as, perhaps, with the expression "thinking of not-thinking" (*shiryō ko fushiryō tei* 思量箇不思量底); see Supplementary Notes, s.v "Yaoshan's not thinking." Dōgen has here replaced *sōtō* 草頭 ("tips of the grasses") with *sōryō* 草料 ("fodder"), a term regularly used for the subject of Zen discussion, somewhat as we might say "food for thought."

50 **exactly as whom its arising and ceasing is the bright pearl or is not the bright pearl — the taking and rejecting of this might well worry us** (*kimetsu o tare toshite ka myōju nari, myōju ni arazaru to shusha ni wazurawan* 起滅をたれとしてか、明珠なり、明珠にあらざる、と取舎にわづらはん): I.e., if the mind is not our own, we might well wonder whose mind is being identified with the bright pearl.

51 **stepping forward and stepping back** (*shinpo taiho* 進歩退歩): A term appearing several times in the *Shōbōgenzō*; it can indicate movement forward and back but also all activities, motion and rest, etc.; see Supplementary Notes, s.v. "Stepping forward and stepping back."

7. One Bright Pearl *Ikka myōju* 一顆明珠

正法眼藏一顆明珠第七

Treasury of the True Dharma Eye
One Bright Pearl
Number 7

[Tōunji MS:][52]

爾時嘉禎四年四月十八日、在雍州宇治縣觀音導利興聖寶林寺示衆

*Presented to the assembly at Kannon Dōri Kōshō Hōrin Monastery, Uji
District, Yōshū; eighteenth day, fourth month, fourth year of Katei
[2 June 1238]*

寬元元年癸卯閏七月二十三日、書寫于越州吉田郡志比莊吉峰寺院主房。
侍者比丘懷奘

*Copied at the residence of the head of cloister, Kippō Monastery, Shihi
Estate, Yoshida District, Esshū; twenty-third day, intercalary seventh
month of the junior water year of the rabbit, the first year of Kangen
[8 September 1243].
The acolyte, Bhikṣu Ejō*

嘉慶三年二月三日、在永平寺衆寮奉書寫之。宗吾

*Copied this as a memorial offering in the common quarters of Eihei
Monastery; third day, second month, third year of Kakyō
[1 March 1389].
Sōgo[53]*

---

52 The MSS of the seventy-five-chapter compilation lack colophons for this chapter.

53 **Sōgo** 宗吾: 1343-1406, ninth abbot of Eiheiji.

TREASURY OF THE TRUE DHARMA EYE
NUMBER 8

The Mind Cannot Be Got
Shin fukatoku
心不可得

The Mind Cannot Be Got

Shin fukatoku

INTRODUCTION

According to its colophon, this brief essay was composed during the summer retreat of 1241, at Kōshōji, on the southern outskirts of the capital at Heiankyō (modern Kyoto). The actual date of composition, however, is subject to some doubt. The chapter occurs as number 8 in the seventy-five-chapter compilation of the *Shōbōgenzō* but is not included in the sixty-chapter compilation; instead, it is preserved as title number 4 in fascicle 1 of the so-called *Himitsu* collection of twenty-eight *Shōbōgenzō* texts. In the Honzan edition, where it appears as number 18, it is followed by another chapter of the same name (typically referred to as the "Go Shin fukatoku" 後心不可得, or the "latter" text) that was also preserved in the *Himitsu* collection, as number 3 of fascicle 1. This second version of the "Shin fukatoku" (translated below, in Volume 7, as Supplementary Text 4) bears a colophon identical with the one found in our text here, but the content is rather different.

The first half of this second work is quite similar to our text, while the second half represents material found in the "Tashin tsū" 他心通 chapter, a work of 1245 recorded as number 73 in the seventy-five-chapter compilation. It has been suggested that the "Go Shin fukatoku" was composed first, in 1241, as indicated in its colophon; while our text represents a later revision, perhaps dating from around the time that the "Tashin tsū" was written.

"The Mind Cannot Be Got" represents Dōgen's comments on a single kōan, the famous story of the old woman selling cakes who defeated the monk Deshan Xuanjian 德山宣鑑, a leading scholar of the *Diamond Sūtra*. The Zen tradition valued this story because the victory of the old woman over the scholar monk nicely dramatized the tradition's dismissal of book learning and church hierarchy. For his part, however, Dōgen seems disappointed by the quality of the exchange between the monk and the old woman: Deshan, he says, is quite pathetic; and for that very reason, he is unable to test the depth of the old woman's understanding. Thus, Dōgen wonders what she might have to say if she were really challenged and offers his own suggestions on how the conversation between the two could be improved.

正法眼藏第八
Treasury of the True Dharma Eye
Number 8
心不可得
The Mind Cannot Be Got

[08:1] {1:82}

釋迦牟尼佛言、過去心不可得、現在心不可得、未來心不可得。

Buddha Śākyamuni said, "The past mind cannot be got; the present mind cannot be got; the future mind cannot be got."[1]

[08:2]

これ佛祖の參究なり。不可得裏に過去・現在・未來の窟籠を剜來せり。しかあれども、自家の窟籠をもちいきたれり。いはゆる自家といふは、心不可得なり。而今の思量分別は、心不可得なり。使得十二時の渾身、これ心不可得なり。佛祖の入室よりこのかた、心不可得を會取す。いまだ佛祖の入室あらざれば、心不可得の問取なし、道著なし、見聞せざるなり。經師・論師のやから、聲聞・緣覺のたぐひ、夢也未見在なり。その驗、ちかきにあり。

This is the investigation of the buddhas and ancestors. Within "cannot be got," they have scooped out the holes of "past," "present," and "future."[2] Nevertheless, they have been using holes of their own house.[3] "Their own" here means "the mind cannot be got." The present thinking and discrimination is "the mind cannot be got"; the whole body that "employs the twelve times" is "the mind cannot be got."[4] Once one en-

---

1 **Buddha Śākyamuni** (*Shakamuni butsu* 釋迦牟尼佛): Quoting the *Diamond Sūtra* (*Jingang bore boluomi jing* 金剛般若波羅蜜經, T.235.8:751b27-28).

2 **they have scooped out the holes of "past," "present," and "future"** (*kako genzai mirai no kutsurō o enrai seri* 過去・現在・未來の窟籠を剜來せり): The grammatical subject here is unexpressed; the translation takes it as "the buddhas and ancestors," but it might as well be understood as "Buddha Śākyamuni" or "this [saying]."

3 **holes of their own house** (*jike no kutsurō* 自家の窟籠): Presumably, meaning something like, "the categories [of past, present, and future] as understood by the buddhas and ancestors."

4 **the whole body that "employs the twelve times"** (*shitoku jūni ji no konjin* 使得十二時の渾身): The "whole body" (*konjin* 渾身; also read *konshin*) is a common expression in Dōgen's writings for one's entire being. The notion of "employing the twelve times" (into which the twenty-four hours of the day were traditionally divided) occurs frequently in the *Shōbōgenzō*; it comes from a popular saying attributed to the famous Tang-dynasty Chan master Zhaozhou Congshen 趙州從諗 (778-897); see Supplementary Notes, s.v. "Employ the twelve times."

230 DŌGEN'S *SHŌBŌGENZŌ* VOLUME I

ters the rooms of the buddhas and ancestors, one understands "the mind cannot be got"; one who has yet to enter the rooms of the buddhas and ancestors does not question, or speak of, or see and hear, "the mind cannot be got." Fellows like the sūtra masters and treatise masters, types like the *śrāvakas* and *pratyeka-buddhas*, have never seen this even in *their dreams*. The signs of this are near at hand.[5]

[08:3]

いはゆる德山宣鑑禪師、そのかみ金剛般若經をあきらめたりと自稱す、あるひは周金剛王と自稱す。ことに青龍疏をよくせりと稱す。さらに十二擔の書籍を撰集せり、齊肩の講者なきがごとし。しかあれども、文字法師の末流なり。あるとき、南方に嫡嫡相承の無上の佛法あることをききて、いきどほりにたへず、經書をたづさへて山河をわたりゆく。ちなみに龍潭の信禪師の會にあへり。かの會に投ぜんとおもむく、中路に歇息せり。ときに老婆子きたりあひて、路側に歇息せり。

Chan Master Xuanjian of Deshan used to claim that he had clarified the *Diamond Prajñā Sūtra* and to style himself "Zhou, King of the Diamond."[6] He especially claimed mastery of the *Qinglong Commentary*.[7] He further compiled twelve piculs of books and seemed without peer as a lecturer.[8] Nevertheless, he represents a late line of dharma masters of letters.[9] Once, upon hearing that, in the south, there existed an

---

5 **The signs of this are near at hand** (*sono ken, chikaki ni ari* その驗、ちかきにあり): A reference to the story of Deshan that Dōgen is about to relate.

6 **Chan Master Xuanjian of Deshan** (*Tokusan Senkan zenji* 德山宣鑑禪師): Deshan Xuanjian 德山宣鑑 (or 宣鑒, 780-865), disciple of Longtan Chongxin 龍潭崇信; his biography can be found at *Song gaoseng zhuan* 宋高僧傳 (T.2061.50:778b21); *Jingde chuandeng lu* 景德傳燈錄 (T.2076.51:317b13). The version of the famous story of Deshan and the old woman selling cakes that Dōgen tells in Japanese here does not seem to accord exactly with any extant source; for other versions, see, e.g., *Liandeng huiyao* 聯燈會要, ZZ.136:755b1-12; *Biyan lu* 碧巖錄, T.2003.48:143b23-c8.

Diamond Prajñā Sūtra (*Kongō hannya kyō* 金剛般若經): I.e., Kumārajīva's translation of the *Vajracchedikā-prajñā-pāramitā-sūtra* (*Jingang bore boluomi jing* 金剛般若波羅蜜經, T.235).

"Zhou, King of the Diamond" (*Shū kongō ō* 周金剛王): After Deshan's lay surname, Zhou 周.

7 *Qinglong Commentary* (*Seiryū sho* 青龍疏): Identified as the *Yuzhu Jingang bore boluomi jing xuanyan* 御注金剛般若波羅蜜經宣演 (T.2733), said to have been written at the request of the Tang Emperor Xuanzong 宣宗 by Daoyin of Qinglongsi 青龍寺道氤 (668-740).

8 **twelve piculs of books** (*jūni tan no shojaku* 十二擔の書籍): The picul (*dan* 擔) is a unit of weight equal to 100 *jin* 斤 ("catty"); traditionally defined as what could be carried by a shoulder pole, it is often reckoned at 50 (or sometimes 60) kilograms, the exact weight varying with time and place.

9 **late line of dharma masters of letters** (*monji* [also read *moji*] *hōshi no matsuryū* 文字法師の末流): I.e., a descendant of those Buddhist teachers who simply study texts; a dismissive expression not occurring elsewhere in the *Shōbōgenzō*.

8. The Mind Cannot Be Got *Shin fukatoku* 心不可得   231

unsurpassed buddha dharma inherited by successor after successor, he was overcome by indignation; and, packing his books, he crossed mountains and rivers, eventually to encounter the community of Chan Master Xin of Longtan.[10] As he was headed to join this community, he paused for a rest on the road. An old woman came along and rested by the side of the road.

[08:4] {1:83}

ときに鑑講師とふ、なんぢはこれなに人ぞ。婆子いはく、われは賣餅の老婆子なり。德山いはく、わがためにもちひをうるべし。婆子いはく、和尚、もちひをかふてなにかせん。德山いはく、もちひをかふて點心にすべし。婆子いはく、和尚の、そこばくたづさへてあるは、それなにものぞ。德山いはく、なんぢきかずや、われはこれ周金剛王なり。金剛經に長ぜり、通達せずといふところなし。わがいまたづさへたるは、金剛經の解釋なり。

Lecturer Jian said, "Who are you?"

The old woman said, "I'm an old woman selling cakes."

Deshan said, "Sell me a cake."

The old woman said, "Why is the Reverend buying a cake?"

Deshan said, "I'm buying the cake for a refreshment."[11]

The old woman said, "What is that load the Reverend is carrying?"

Deshan said, "Haven't you heard? I'm Zhou, King of the *Diamond*. I'm an expert on the *Diamond Sūtra*. There's nothing [in it] I haven't penetrated. What I'm carrying here are commentaries on the *Diamond Sūtra*."

[08:5]

かくいふをききて、婆子いはく、老婆に一問あり、和尚これをゆるすやいなや。德山いはく、われいまゆるす、なんぢこころにまかせてとふべし。婆子いはく、われかつて金剛經をきくにいはく、過去心不可得、現在心不可得、未來心不可得。いまいづれの心をか、もちひをしていかに點ぜんとかする。和尚もし道得ならんには、もちひをうるべし。和尚もし道不得ならんには、もちひをうるべからず。

Hearing him speak thus, the old woman said, "This old woman has a question. Does the Reverend grant it?"

Deshan said, "Granted. Feel free to ask."

---

10 **Chan Master Xin of Longtan** (*Ryūtan no Shin zenji* 龍潭の信禪師): I.e., Longtan Chongxin 龍潭崇信 (dates unknown), a disciple of Tianhuang Daowu 天皇道悟 (748-807), in the lineage of Qingyuan Xingsi 青原行思.

11 **"I'm buying the cake for a refreshment"** (*mochii o kaute tenjin ni su beshi* もちひをかふて點心にすべし): The translation "refreshment" for *tenjin* (Mandarin *dianxin*, known in the West by the Cantonese *dimsum*) obscures the old lady's subsequent play on the word that is the key to the story. She takes it, not as the common noun for a light snack, but as a verb-object construction meaning something like "to spark the heart," or "to refresh the mind."

The old woman said, "I once heard it said in the *Diamond Sūtra*, '*The past mind cannot be got; the present mind cannot be got; the future mind cannot be got.*' Now, which mind will you refresh with the cake?[12] If the Reverend can answer, I'll sell you the cake; if the Reverend can't answer, I won't sell you the cake."

[08:6]

徳山、ときに茫然として、祗對すべきところをおぼえざりき。婆子、すなはち拂袖していでぬ。つひにもちひを徳山にうらず。

Deshan was at a loss and could not think of how to respond. The old woman thereupon shook out her sleeves and left.[13] She never sold Deshan the cake.

[08:7]

うらむべし、數百軸の釋主、數十年の講者、わづかに弊婆の一問をうるに、たちまちに負處に墮して、祗對におよばざること。正師をみると、正師に嗣承せると、正法をきけると、いまだ正法をきかず、正師をみざると、はるかにことなるによりてかくのごとし。徳山、このときはじめていはく、畫にかけるもちひ、うえをやむるにあたはず、と。いまは龍潭に嗣法すと稱す。

What a pity. A commentator of several hundred fascicles, a lecturer of several tens of years, gets but a single question from a tired, worn-out old woman and is immediately defeated, without so much as a response. This happens because of the great difference between one who has met a true master, who has inherited from a true master, who has heard the true dharma, and one who has not yet heard the true dharma nor met a true master. At this time, Deshan first said, "A painted cake can't satisfy hunger."[14] Now, it is said he inherited the dharma from Longtan.[15]

12　**"Now, which mind will you refresh with the cake?"** (*ima izure no shin o ka, mochii o shite ika ni ten zen to ka suru* いまいづれの心をか、もちひをしていかに點ぜんとかする): Or, more literally, "which mind now, and in what way, will you try to refresh with the cake?"

13　**shook out her sleeves and left** (*hosshū shite idenu* 拂袖していでぬ): A rude gesture of dismissal; Japanese rendering of such common Chinese phrases as *fu xiou erh chu* 拂袖而出, *fu xiou bian chu* 拂袖便出, etc.

14　**"A painted cake can't satisfy hunger"** (*e ni kakeru mochii ue o yamuru ni atawazu* 畫にかけるもちひゑをやむるにあたはず): Japanese version of a famous saying in the biographies of Xiangyan Zhixian 香嚴智閑 (d. 898) (see Supplementary Notes, s.v. "A painted cake can't satisfy hunger"); it is not elsewhere associated with Deshan.

15　**Now, it is said he inherited the dharma from Longtan** (*ima wa Ryūtan ni shihō su to shōsu* いまは龍潭に嗣法すと稱す): The translation follows Kawamura's section break, but this apparent non-sequiter might as well be read with the following section — i.e., "Now, it is said he inherited the dharma, but at the time of this story . . . ."

8. The Mind Cannot Be Got *Shin fukatoku* 心不可得　233

[08:8] {1:84}

つらつらこの婆子と徳山と相見する因縁をおもへば、徳山のむかしあきら
めざることは、いまきこゆるところなり。龍潭をみしよりのちも、なほ婆
子を怕却しつべし。なほこれ參學の晩進なり、超證の古佛にあらず。婆子
そのとき徳山を杜口せしむとも、實にその人なること、いまださだめがた
し。そのゆえは、心不可得のことばをききては、心、うべからず、心、あ
るべからず、とのみおもひて、かくのごとくとふ。徳山もし丈夫なりせ
ば、婆子を勘破するちからあらまし。すでに勘破せましかば、婆子まこと
にその人なる道理もあらはるべし。徳山いまだ徳山ならざれば、婆子その
人なることもいまだあらはれず。

If we think carefully about this episode of the encounter between the
old woman and Deshan, it is obvious that at that time Deshan had not
clarified [the dharma]. He was probably still afraid of the old lady even
after he met Longtan. He was still a late-comer to study, not an old buddha transcending verification. Although, at the time, the old woman shut
Deshan's mouth, it is still difficult to decide whether she was really that
person.[16] This is because, having heard the words "the mind cannot be
got," she was thinking only that the mind cannot be got, the mind does
not exist, when she asked as she did. If Deshan had been a man, he
would have had the strength to see through the old woman; and, once
he had seen through her, the truth of whether she was really that person
would have appeared.[17] Since Deshan was not yet Deshan, whether the
old woman was that person also remains unclear.

[08:9]

現在大宋國にある雲衲霞袂、いたづらに徳山の對不得をわらひ、婆子が靈
利なることをほむるは、いとはかなかるべし、おろかなるなり。そのゆえ
は、いま婆子を疑著する、ゆえなきにあらず。いはゆるそのちなみ、徳
山、道不得ならんに、婆子なんぞ徳山にむかふていはざる、和尚いま道
不得なり、さらに老婆にとふべし、老婆かへりて和尚のためにいふべし。
かくのごとくいひて、徳山の問をえて、徳山にむかふていふこと道是なら
ば、婆子まことにその人なりといふこと、あらはるべし。問著たとひあり
とも、いまだ道處あらず。むかしよりいまだ一語をも道著せざるを、その
人といふこと、いまだあらず。いたづらなる自稱の始終、その益なき、徳
山のむかしにてみるべし。いまだ道處なきものをゆるすべからざること、
婆子にてしるべし。

Today, in the Land of the Great Song, those robed in clouds and sleeved
in mist foolishly laugh at Deshan's inability to answer and praise the old

---

16　**that person** (*sono hito* その人): An expression occurring several times in the *Shōbōgenzō* in the sense, "a real person," "a person with real understanding."

17　**a man** (*jōbu* 丈夫): I.e., "a real man"; a common Chinese expression for the manly male;
a term also used in Buddhist texts for "person" (S. *puruṣa, pudgala*, etc.).

234 DŌGEN'S *SHŌBŌGENZŌ* VOLUME I

woman as being spiritually acute; this is quite insubstantial and stupid.[18] The reason is that we are not without reasons to doubt the old woman: when Deshan was unable to say anything, why did not the old woman say to him, "Since the Reverend is unable to say anything, ask this old woman, and the old woman will answer for you." Having said this, if what she replied to Deshan's question had been words that were right, that she really was that person would be clear. [As it is,] while she may have a question, she does not yet have anything to say. From ancient times, no one has been considered that person who has yet to make a statement of a single word. That vain boasts from beginning to end are without profit, we should see from Deshan's past; that we should not acknowledge one who does not yet have anything to say, we should know from the old woman.

[08:10] {1:85}

こころみに德山にかはりていふべし、婆子まさしく恁麼問著せんに、德山すなはち婆子にむかひていふべし、恁麼則爾莫與吾賣餅。もし德山かくのごとくいはましかば、伶利の參學ならん。

Let us try speaking for Deshan. As soon as the old woman asked him this question, Deshan should have said to her, "*In that case, don't sell me the cake.*" If Deshan had said this, it would have been a sharp study.[19]

[08:11]

婆子、もし德山とはん、現在心不可得、過去心不可得、未來心不可得、いまもちひをしていづれの心をか點ぜんとかする。かくのごとくとはんに、婆子、すなはち德山にむかふていふべし、和尚はただ、もちひの、心を點ずべからずとのみしりて、心の、もちひを點ずることをしらず、心の、心を點ずることをもしらず。

Suppose Deshan had asked the old woman, "*The past mind cannot be got; the present mind cannot be got; the future mind cannot be got. Which mind will you refresh with the cake?*" Being asked this, the old woman should have said to Deshan, "Reverend, you only know that the cake can't refresh the mind. You don't know that the mind refreshes the cake; you don't know that the mind refreshes the mind."

18　**robed in clouds and sleeved in mist** (*unnō kabei* 雲衲霞袂): Combining two literary references to the monk, the former seemingly somewhat more common than the latter; occurs several times in the *Shōbōgenzō*.

spiritually acute (*reiri* 靈利): A term of approbation for a wise student, fairly common in Chan literature.

19　**sharp study** (*reiri no sangaku* 伶利の參學): I.e., a "perspicacious understanding." The term *reiri* 伶利 (also written 怜悧) is not common in Dōgen's writing; it is virtually synonymous with the term *reiri* 靈利 ("spiritually acute"), appearing just above.

8. The Mind Cannot Be Got *Shin fukatoku* 心不可得 235

[08:12]

恁麼いはんに、德山さだめて擬議すべし。當恁麼時、もちひ三枚を拈じて
德山に度與すべし。德山とらんと擬せんとき、婆子いふべし、過去心不可
得、現在心不可得、未來心不可得。もし又、德山展手擬取せずば、一餅
を拈じて德山をうちていふべし、無魂屍子、爾莫茫然。かくのごとくい
はんに、德山いふことあらばよし、いふことなからんには、婆子さらに德
山のためにいふべし。ただ拂袖してさる、そでのなかに蜂ありともおぼえ
ず。德山も、われはいふことあたはず、老婆わがためにいふべし、ともい
はず。しかあれば、いふべきをいはざるのみにあらず、とふべきをもとは
ず。あはれむべし、婆子・德山、過去心・未來心、問著・道著、未來心不
可得なるのみなり。

If she had said this, Deshan would surely have paused to consider it.
At that moment, she should have taken up three cakes and given them to
Deshan. When Deshan went to take them, the old woman should have
said, "*The past mind cannot be got; the present mind cannot be got; the
future mind cannot be got.*" Or, if Deshan did not open his hand to take
them, she should have taken up a cake and hit him with it, saying, "*You
lifeless corpse. Don't be at such a loss.*" Thus addressed, if Deshan had
something to say, fine; if he had nothing to say, the old woman should
have said something for him. But she just shook out her sleeves and left,
though I doubt she had a bee in her sleeve.[20] And Deshan does not say,
"I have nothing to say; old woman, you should say something for me."
In this way, not only does he not say what he should say, he does not ask
what he should ask. It is pathetic: *the "old woman" and "Deshan," "past
mind" and "future mind," "questions" and "statements"* — these are just
"the future mind cannot be got."[21]

---

20 **though I doubt she had a bee in her sleeve** (*sode no naka ni hachi ari tomo oboezu*
そでのなかに蜂ありともおぼえず): Sometimes said to be an allusion to the Chinese
story of the Phaedra-like stepmother of the paragon of filial piety Yin Boqi 尹伯奇: her
affections spurned by her stepson, in anger she places a bee in her robe in order to trick
him into trying to remove it for her, whereupon she accuses him of making improper
advances. If indeed Dōgen had this story in mind here, perhaps his playful remark might
mean "I doubt she had any ulterior motive in this."

21 **the "old woman" and "Deshan," "past mind" and "future mind," "questions"
and "statements" — these are just "the future mind cannot be got"** (*basu Tokusan,
kako shin mirai shin, monjaku dōjaku, miraishin fukatoku naru nomi nari* 婆子・德山、
過去心・未來心、問著・道著、未來心不可得なるのみなり): A tentative reading, fol-
lowing Kawamura's punctuation, of a sentence in mixed Chinese-Japanese syntax difficult to parse and variously interpreted. However exactly it is to be read, generally taken
to mean that the dialogue between Deshan and the old woman never gets at the issue.

236 DŌGEN'S *SHŌBŌGENZŌ* VOLUME I

[08:13] {1:86}

およそ德山、それよりのちも、させる發明ありともみえず、ただあらあら
しき造次のみなり。ひさしく龍潭にとぶらひせば、頭角觸折することもあ
らまし、頷珠を正傳する時節にもあはまし。わづかに吹滅紙燭をみる、傳
燈に不足なり。

Even after that, we do not see that Deshan had any clarification; he
just engaged in rough hasty acts.[22] Had he long attended on Longtan, the
horns on his head might have been broken off, and he might have had
occasion to transmit directly the jewel at the chin.[23] But all we see is the
paper lantern blown out, not enough to transmit the flame.[24]

[08:14]

しかあれば、參學の雲水、かならず勤學なるべし、容易にせしは不是な
り、勤學なりしは佛祖なり。おほよそ心不可得とは、畫餅一枚を買弄し
て、一口に咬著嚼盡するをいふ。

Thus, monks who study this should always be diligent in their study:
those who have taken it easy are not right; those who have been diligent in
their study are buddhas and ancestors. In sum, "the mind cannot be got"
means to buy a single painted cake and chew it up in a single mouthful.

---

22   **rough hasty acts** (*araarashiki zōji* あらあらしき造次): Possibly a reference to
Deshan's reputation for teaching through "thirty blows."

23   **the horns on his head might have been broken off** (*zukaku sokusetsu suru koto
mo aramashi* 頭角觸折することもあらまし): Likely meaning that he might have lost
some of his pretentions. The term *zukaku* 頭角 ("horn on the head"), normally used in
reference to great promise, can also carry the sense of something impossible, unnecessary, or worthless.

the jewel at the chin (*ganju* 頷珠): The jewel beneath the chin of the black dragon
(*riryū* 驪龍); here, no doubt, the wisdom of Longtan 龍潭 (whose name means "dragon
depths").

24   **the paper lantern blown out** (*suimetsu shishoku* 吹滅紙燭): The story of Deshan's
awakening when his paper lantern was blown out is well known in Chan literature (see,
e.g., Dahui Zonggao's 大慧宗杲 *Zhengfayanzang* 正法眼藏, ZZ.118:114a11-14; *Biyan
lu* 碧巖錄, T.2003.48:143c11-14). Here is the version recorded in Dōgen's *shinji Shōbōgenzō* 眞字正法眼藏 (D.5:180, case 104):

> 至夜入室、侍立更深。潭曰、子何不下。師遂珍重、掲簾而去。見外面黑、却回
> 云、外面黑。潭乃點紙燭度與。師方接次、潭便吹滅。師於是忽然大悟便禮拜。

> At evening, he [i.e., Deshan 德山] entered his [i.e., Longtan's 龍潭] room, where
> he waited in attendance till deep [into the night]. Tan said, "Why don't you retire?"
> The Master [Deshan] thereupon paid his respects, raised the screen and left. When he
> saw that it was dark outside, he came back and said, "It's dark outside."
> Tan then lit a paper lantern and offered it to him. Just as the Master took it, Tan blew
> it out. At this, the Master suddenly had a great awakening and bowed.

transmit the flame (*dentō* 傳燈): I.e., inherit the dharma from his teacher; playing here
on the story of the paper lantern.

8. The Mind Cannot Be Got *Shin fukatoku* 心不可得

正法眼藏心不可得第八
Treasury of the True Dharma Eye
The Mind Cannot Be Got
Number 8

[Ryūmonji MS:]

爾時仁治二年辛丑夏安居于雍州宇治郡觀音導利興聖寶林寺示衆

Presented to the assembly at Kannon Dōri Kōshō Hōrin Monastery, Uji District, Yōshū; summer retreat of the junior metal year of the ox, the second year of Ninji [28 May-28 August 1241]

TREASURY OF THE TRUE DHARMA EYE

NUMBER 9

The Old Buddha Mind
Kobutsushin

古佛心

The Old Buddha Mind

Kobutsushin

INTRODUCTION

"The Old Buddha Mind" ("Kobutsushin," also sometimes read "Kobusshin") is number 9 in the sixty- and seventy-five-chapter compilations of the *Shōbōgenzō* and number 44 in the Honzan edition. According to its colophon, it was delivered in the fourth month of 1243, at Rokuharamitsuji 六波羅蜜寺, the neighborhood in the eastern quarter of Heiankyō in which was located the Rokuhara Tandai 六波羅探題, the headquarters in the capital of the new warrior administration recently established in Kamakura. It is thought that Dōgen was invited to teach there by his chief patron in the administration, Hatano Yoshishige 波多野義重, who maintained a residence in the neighborhood. Several months before he delivered "The Old Buddha Mind," Dōgen had taught the "Zenki" 全機 chapter at this place. These two texts are among the shortest in the *Shōbōgenzō*, perhaps a reflection of the attention span of an audience that may have included Hatano's warrior colleagues. They are also among the last teachings Dōgen would deliver in the capital: three months after producing the "Kobutsushin," he was on his way to Hatano's home district of Echizen, where he would subsequently establish his community at Eiheiji.

The title theme of this essay is a common expression in Zen texts. The word combines two senses: "the mind of the old buddhas" (i.e., the buddhas [or prominent Zen masters] of the past), and "the old buddha mind" (i.e., the timeless mind of a buddha). Dōgen's use of the term, here and elsewhere in the *Shōbōgenzō*, draws on both these senses.

Our text is divided into two sections — the first dealing with the term "old buddha" (*kobutsu* 古佛); the second, with the title theme itself. In the former section, Dōgen is at pains to distinguish his sense of "old buddha" from that in common use in the broader Buddhist community, where it typically refers to the seven buddhas of the past ending with Śākyamuni. Dōgen introduces here a characteristic Zen use of the term in reference to the ancestors of the tradition and argues (to a Japanese audience for which these would have been somewhat novel claims) that

9. The Old Buddha Mind *Kobutsushin* 古佛心 241

all the great masters of the tradition should be understood as buddhas, that there can be more than one such buddha in the world at the same time, and that such buddhas are not merely past but occur throughout (and beyond) history. He then goes on to cite and comment on several examples of Zen usage of "old buddha."

The second section of the text turns to the title theme. Here, the discussion focuses especially on the famous saying, by the Sixth Ancestor's disciple Nanyang Huizhong 南陽慧忠 (d. 775), that the old buddha mind is "fences, walls, tiles, and pebbles." In his comments, Dōgen plays freely with the expression "old buddha mind," resolving it into the "old buddha" that expresses himself as the world, the "old mind" that enacts and verifies the buddha, the "mind buddha" that is always old, and even the curious "buddha old" (*sic*) that makes the mind. He then goes on to warn us not to take the "fences, walls, tiles, and pebbles" of this saying for granted but to study what they really are. Finally, after brief comments on the saying by the Tang-dynasty figure Jianyuan Zhongxing 漸源仲興 that the "old buddha mind" means "the world collapses in ruins," Dōgen returns to his opening theme to remind us that the old buddha mind occurs both before and after the seven buddhas, and (lest we think we have understood it) that the old buddha mind is "sloughed off" before the old buddha mind.

正法眼藏第九
Treasury of the True Dharma Eye
Number 9

古佛心
The Old Buddha Mind

[09:1] {1:87}

祖宗の嗣法するところ、七佛より曹溪にいたるまで四十祖なり、曹溪より七佛にいたるまで四十佛なり。七佛ともに向上向下の功徳あるがゆえに、曹溪にいたり七佛にいたる。曹溪に向上向下の功徳あるがゆえに、七佛より正傳し、曹溪より正傳し、後佛に正傳す。ただ前後のみにあらず、釋迦牟尼佛のとき十方諸佛あり。青原のとき南嶽あり、南嶽のとき青原あり、乃至石頭のとき江西あり。あひ罣礙せざるは、不礙にあらざるべし。かくのごとくの功徳あること、參究すべきなり。

The inheritance of the dharma of the ancestors is forty ancestors from the seven buddhas through Caoxi; it is forty buddhas from Caoxi through the seven buddhas.[1] Since the seven buddhas all have the virtues of both ascent and descent, [the succession] reaches Caoxi; it reaches the seven buddhas.[2] Since Caoxi has the virtue of both ascent and descent, [the lineage] is directly transmitted from the seven buddhas, is directly transmitted from Caoxi, is directly transmitted to later buddhas.[3] It is

---

1 **forty ancestors from the seven buddhas through Caoxi; it is forty buddhas from Caoxi through the seven buddhas** (*shichi butsu yori Sōkei ni itaru made shijisso nari, Sōkei yori shichi butsu ni itaru made shijūbutsu nari* 七佛より曹溪にいたるまで四十祖なり、曹溪より七佛にいたるまで四十佛なり): "Caoxi" is the Sixth Ancestor, Huineng of Caoxi 曹溪慧能. The list of forty consists of the seven buddhas of the past (see Supplementary Notes, s.v. "Seven buddhas"), the twenty-seven ancestors of India, from Mahākāśyapa through Prajñātāra, and the six ancestors of China, from Bodhidharma through Huineng. In his "Shōbōgenzō shisho" 正法眼藏嗣書 (1241) and again in "Shōbōgenzō butsudō" 正法眼藏佛道 (1243), Dōgen attributes this statement to Huineng himself.

2 **the virtues of both ascent and descent** (*kōjō kōge no kudoku* 向上向下の功徳): Or, perhaps, "the virtues above and below." As spiritual virtues, the words *kōjō* and *kōge* typically refer to "ascent" to personal liberation and "descent" into the world for the sake of saving sentient beings — not, as here, movement "up" and "down" the generations of the Zen lineage. It may be that Dōgen means simply that each of the seven buddhas shares the virtues of those in the lineage "above" and "below" him.

3 **is directly transmitted to later buddhas** (*gobutsu ni shōden su* 後佛に正傳す): This could mean simply that the dharma succession continues after the Sixth Ancestor to later generations, or it could be, and often is, read "directly transmitted to the later buddha" — i.e., the future Buddha Maitreya.

9. The Old Buddha Mind *Kobutsushin* 古佛心   243

not only a matter of before and after: at the time of Buddha Śākyamuni,
there were the buddhas of the ten directions; at the time of Qingyuan,
there was Nanyue; at the time of Nanyue, there was Qingyuan.[4] And so
on down to, at the time of Shitou, there was Jiangxi.[5] That they do not
obstruct each other does not mean that they are unobstructed.[6] The fact
that they have such a virtue is something to be investigated.

[09:2]

向來の四十位の佛祖、ともにこれ古佛なりといへども、心あり、身あり、
光明あり、國土あり、過去久矣あり、未曾過去あり。たとひ未曾過去なり
とも、たとひ過去久矣なりとも、おなじくこれ古佛の功德なるべし。古佛
の道を參學するは、古佛の道を證するなり。代代の古佛なり。いはゆる古
佛は、新古の古に一齊なりといへども、さらに古今を超出せり、古今に正
直なり。

Though we say of these forty buddhas and ancestors above that they
are all old buddhas, each has a mind, has a body, has a radiance, has
a land; has "passed long ago," has never passed.[7] Whether it be never
passed or "passed long ago," these are equally virtues of the old bud-

---

4 **Qingyuan** (*Seigen* 青原); **Nanyue** (*Nangaku* 南嶽): I.e., Qingyuan Xingsi 青原行思
(d. 740) and Nanyue Huairang 南嶽懷讓 (677-744), regarded as the two leading disciples of the Sixth Ancestor.

5 **Shitou** (*Sekitō* 石頭); **Jiangxi** (*Kōzei* 江西): I.e., Shitou Xiqian 石頭希遷 (700-
790) and Mazu Daoyi 馬祖道一 (709-788), most prominent disciples of Qingyuan and
Nanyue respectively.

6 **That they do not obstruct each other does not mean that they are unobstructed**
(*ai keige sezaru wa, fuge ni arazaru beshi* あひ里礙せざるは、不礙にあらざるべし):
Some commentaries explain this difficult sentence by resort to two senses of the term
"obstruction": from the relative perspective, the buddhas do not obstruct each other because they are distinct; from the absolute perspective, they obstruct each other because
they are one. At issue here is the question of how, contrary to traditional buddhology, two
buddhas can coexist in the same buddha field.

7 **has a radiance, has a land** (*kōmyō ari, kokudo ari* 光明あり、國土あり): Reference
to classical attributes of a buddha: the radiant nimbus surrounding his body and the buddha "field" (S. *kṣetra*) over which he presides.

has "passed long ago," has never passed (*kako kyūi ari, mizō kako ari* 過去久矣あり、
未曾過去あり): The first phrase, more literally, "has a passing long ago," reflects the
well-known words of Nanyang Huizhong 南陽慧忠 (d. 775) recorded in Dōgen's *shinji
Shōbōgenzō* 眞字正法眼藏 (D.5:234, case 210):

南陽忠國師、因僧問、如何是本身盧舍那。師曰、與我過淨瓶來。僧將淨瓶到。
師曰、却安旧處著。僧復問、如何是本身盧舍那。師曰、古佛過去久矣。

The National Teacher Nanyang Zhong was asked by a monk, "What is Vairocana as
the original body?"
The Master said, "Would you pass me that flask."
The monk brought him the flask. The Master said, "Would you put it back."
The monk asked again, "What is Vairocana as the original body?"
The Master said, "The old buddhas passed long ago."

244 DŌGEN'S *SHŌBŌGENZŌ* VOLUME I

dhas. To study the way of the old buddhas is to verify the way of the old buddhas; it is old buddhas in generation after generation. The old buddhas, though they may have the same "old" as in "new and old," go beyond past and present, they are straightforward in past and present.[8]

* * * * *

[09:3] {1:88}
先師いわく、與宏智古佛相見。

My former master said, "*We meet Old Buddha Hongzhi.*"[9]

[09:4]
はかりしりぬ、天童の屋裏に古佛あり、古佛の屋裏に天童あることを。

Thus, we can deduce that there are old buddhas within the house of Tiantong, there is Tiantong within the house of the old buddhas.

* * * * *

[09:5]
圜悟禪師いわく、稽首曹溪眞古佛。

Chan Master Yuanwu said, "*I make prostrations to the true Old Buddha of Caoxi.*"[10]

[09:6]
しるべし、釋迦牟尼佛より第三十三世は、これ古佛なりと稽首すべきなり。圜悟禪師に古佛の莊嚴光明あるゆゑに、古佛と相見しきたるに、恁麼の禮拜あり。しかあればすなはち、曹溪の頭正尾正を草料して、古佛はか

---

8   **they are straightforward in past and present** (*kokon ni shōjiki nari* 古今に正直なり): Perhaps meaning something like, "they run straight through history."

9   **My former master** (*senshi* 先師): Reference to Dōgen's Chinese master, Tiantong Rujing 天童如淨 (1162-1227), who served as the 31st abbot of Tiantongshan 天童山 in the final years of his life. "The Old Buddha Hongzhi" refers to Hongzhi Zhengjue 宏智正覺 (1091-1157), prominent Caodong figure and former abbot of Tiantongshan 天童山. (For the use of "old buddha" as an epithet, see Supplementary Notes, s.v. "Old buddha.") The words appear in the *Rujing heshang yulu* 如淨和尚語錄 (T.2002A.48:127a25-26):

正當恁麼、且與宏智古佛相見。擧拂子云、相見已了。

"At just such a time, we meet the Old Buddha Hongzhi." He raised his whisk and said, "Have you met him?"

10   **Chan Master Yuanwu** (*Engo Zenji* 圜悟禪師): Yuanwu Keqin 圜悟克勤 (1063–1135), in a verse on "The Great Master, the Sixth Ancestor," *Yuanwu Foguo chanshi yulu* 圓悟佛果禪師語錄, T.1997.47:807b8. "Caoxi" 曹溪 is a reference to the location of the Sixth Ancestor's monastery.

9. The Old Buddha Mind *Kobutsushin* 古佛心 245

くのことくの巴鼻なることをしるべきなり。この巴鼻あるは、これ古佛な
り。

Thus, we know that we are to make prostrations recognizing that the thirty-third generation after Buddha Śākyamuni is an old buddha.[11] Because Chan Master Yuanwu has the adornments and radiance of an old buddha, when he has met an old buddha, he bows to him thus. This being the case, with Caoxi's truth from head to tail as our fodder, we should know that an old buddha is this kind of nose grip.[12] To have this nose grip is to be an old buddha.

* * * * *

[09:7]

疏山いわく、大庾嶺頭有古佛、放光射到此間。

Shushan said, *"There's an old buddha atop Dayu Peak. He emits a light that reaches here."*[13]

[09:8]

しるべし、疏山すでに古佛と相見すといふことを。ほかに參尋すべから
ず、古佛の有處は、大庾嶺頭なり。古佛にあらざる自己は、古佛の出處を
しるべからず。古佛の在處をしるは、古佛なるべし。

Thus, we know that Shushan has surely met the old buddha. One should not seek him elsewhere: the old buddha's location is "atop Dayu Peak." One who is not himself an old buddha cannot know where an old buddha appears. To know an old buddha's location is to be an old buddha.

* * * * *

---

11 **thirty-third generation after Buddha Śākyamuni** (*Shakamuni butsu yori dai sanjūsan se* 釋迦牟尼佛より第三十三世): I.e., the Sixth Ancestor, who represented the thirty-third generation in the lineage of Zen ancestors.

12 **Caoxi's truth from head to tail as our fodder** (*Sōkei no zushin bishin o sōryō shite* 曹溪の頭正尾正を草料して): Dōgen is here playing with the spiritual "adornments and radiance" (*shōgon kōmyō* 莊嚴光明) of the buddha's body, treating them in terms related to livestock: "true from head to tail" (*zushin bishin* 頭正尾正) is a fixed expression appearing often in Dōgen's writings; "fodder" (*sōryō* 草料), or "feed," often refers to what we might call the "food for thought" given by a master to a disciple; "nose grip" (or "nose hold"; *habi* 巴鼻) refers to the ring in the nose of cattle and suggests having a "hold" or "handle" on something (see Supplementary Notes, s.v. "Nose").

13 **Shushan** (*Sozan* 疏山): Chan figure Shushan Guangren 疏山光仁 (837-909), expressing his appreciation of the words of Lushan Daoxian 廬山道閑 (dates unknown), who was living on Dayu Peak 大庾嶺, in southern Jiangxi. (From a story recorded in Dōgen's *shinji Shōbōgenzō* 眞字正法眼藏, DZZ.5:174-75, case 97.)

246　　　　　　　DŌGEN'S *SHŌBŌGENZŌ* VOLUME I

[09:9]

雪峰いわく、趙州古佛。

Xuefeng said, "*Zhaozhou is an old buddha*."[14]

[09:10]

しるべし、趙州たとひ古佛なりとも、雪峰もし古佛の力量を分奉せられざ
らんは、古佛に奉覲する骨法を了達しがたからん。いまの行履は、古佛の
加被によりて古佛に參學するには、不答話の功夫あり。いはゆる雪峰老
漢、大丈夫なり。古佛の家風および古佛の威儀は、古佛にあらざるには相
似ならず、一等ならざるなり。しかあれば、趙州の初・中・後善を參學し
て、古佛の壽量を參學すべし。

We should know that, while Zhaozhou may be an old buddha, if Xuefeng were not allotted the power of an old buddha, it would have been
hard for him to master the forms of an audience with an old buddha.[15]
His conduct here is empowered by the old buddha, and therefore, in
studying with the old buddha, he has the concentrated effort that "does
not give answers."[16] This old man Xuefeng was a great person.[17] The
house style of an old buddha and the deportment of an old buddha are
not similar to those who are not old buddhas; they are not equivalent.
Therefore, studying Zhaozhou's "good in the beginning, middle, and
end," we should study the lifespan of the old buddha.[18]

14　**Xuefeng** (*Seppō* 雪峰): I.e., Xuefeng Yicun 雪峰義存 (822-908), in praise of
Zhaozhou Congshen 趙州從諗 (778-897); a remark found in Xuefeng's recorded sayings (*Xuefeng yulu* 雪峰語錄, ZZ.119:964b16) and other texts; Dōgen records it in his
shinji Shōbōgenzō 眞字正法眼藏 (DZZ.5:268, case 283). See Supplementary Notes, s.v.
"Old buddha."

15　**forms of an audience** (*bugon suru koppō* 奉覲する骨法): Taking *koppō* 骨法 in the
sense of "correct ritual procedures" (*sahō* 作法); the term might also be read as "essen-
tials" or "fundamentals." The only occurrence of this term in the *Shōbōgenzō*.

16　**the concentrated effort that "does not give answers"** (*futōwa no kufū* 不答話の
功夫): Allusion to the story cited in Note 14, above, in which it is said that, after recognizing Zhaozhou as an old buddha, Xuefeng no longer gave answers.

17　**old man Xuefeng was a great person** (*Seppō rōkan daijōbu nari* 雪峰老漢大丈
夫なり): "Old man" (*rōkan* 老漢) is a common form of familiar reference to a teacher,
often applied to Xuefeng; "great person" (*daijōbu* 大丈夫), a term used to translate the
Sanskrit *mahāpuruṣa*, one of the epithets of a buddha, is regularly applied to a person of
extraordinary ability.

18　**Zhaozhou's "good in the beginning, middle, and end"** (*Jōshū no sho chū go zen*
趙州の初・中・後善): Dōgen is playing here with a standard form of praise for the
teachings of a buddha, said to be "good at the beginning, middle, and end"; see Supplementary Notes, s.v. "Good in the beginning, middle, and end."

the lifespan of the old buddha (*kobutsu no juryō* 古佛の壽量): Dōgen here evokes
Chapter 16 of the *Lotus Sūtra*, in which Śākyamuni famously reveals the true, and truly
enormous, extent of his lifespan.

9. The Old Buddha Mind *Kobutsushin* 古佛心   247

* * * * *

[09:11] {1:89}

西京光宅寺大證國師は、曹溪の法嗣なり。人帝・天帝おなじく恭敬尊重す
るところなり。まことに神丹國に見聞まれなるところなり。四代の帝師な
るのみにあらず、皇帝てづからみづから車をひきて參内せしむ。いはんや
また帝釋宮の請をえて、はるかに上天す。諸天衆のなかにして、帝釋のた
めに説法す。

National Teacher Dazheng, of Guangzhai Monastery in the Western
Capital, was the dharma heir of Caoxi.[19] He was revered and honored
by the human lord and the deva lord alike, truly something rarely experienced in the Land of Cīnasthāna.[20] Not only was he teacher to four
generations of emperors, but the emperor himself brought him into the
palace in a cart pulled by his own hands.[21] Not to mention that, receiving
an invitation to Lord Śakra's palace, he ascended far into heaven, where
in the assembly of devas, he preached the dharma for Lord Śakra.[22]

[09:12]

國師、因僧問、如何是古佛心。師云、牆壁瓦礫。

*The National Teacher was once asked by a monk, "What is the old
buddha mind?"*

The Teacher said, "Fences, walls, tiles, and pebbles."[23]

---

19 **National Teacher Dazheng** (*Daishō kokusai* 大證國師): I.e., Nanyang Huizhong 南
陽慧忠, about whom there are several legends of the sort reflected here. Dōgen turns here
to two sayings on "the old buddha mind."

20 **the human lord and the deva lord** (*nintei tentei* 人帝・天帝): I.e., the emperors of
China and Indra, king of the devas.

21 **teacher to four generations of emperors** (*shidai no teishi* 四代の帝師): The source
of this claim is unclear; Huizhong's biography at *Jingde chuandeng lu* 景德傳燈錄,
T.2076.51:244a-245a, mentions only the emperors Suzong 肅宗 (r. 756-762) and Dai-
zong 代宗 (r. 762-779). If not simply an error, perhaps the claim is only that Huizhong
was an imperial teacher who lived during the reigns of four emperors. Huizhong's date
of birth is uncertain; but, if he lived at least into his mid-sixties, he would have been
alive during the reigns of the emperors Ruizong 睿宗 (684-690, 710-712) and his successor, Xuanzong 玄宗 (712-756). The claim that the Emperor pulled Huizhong's cart
into the palace seems an improvement on the tradition that, in 761, Huizhong was invited to lecture at the imperial palace and so impressed the Emperor Suzong that the
latter personally mounted Huizhong's cart to see him off. (See, e.g., *Biyan lu* 碧巖錄,
T.2003.48:158a9-11.)

22 **Lord Śakra's palace** (*Taishaku gū* 帝釋宮) This tradition of Huizhong's audience
with the deva sovereign Indra is mentioned at *Biyan lu* 碧巖錄, T.2003.48:158a13.

23 **"Fences, walls, tiles, and pebbles"** (*shō heki ga ryaku* 牆壁瓦礫): Variants of this
conversation occur in several texts; see Supplementary Notes, s.v. "Fences, walls, tiles,
and pebbles."

248 DŌGEN'S *SHŌBŌGENZŌ* VOLUME I

[09:13]

いはゆる問處は、這頭得恁麼といひ、那頭得恁麼といふなり。この道得を
擧して、問處とせるなり。この問處、ひろく古今の道得となれり。

The question here is saying, "*this side gets such,*" is saying "*that side gets such.*"[24] He took up this saying and made it a question, and this question became a saying widely known in past and present.[25]

[09:14]

このゆえに、華開の萬木百草、これ古佛の道得なり、古佛の問處なり。世
界起の九山八海、これ古佛の日面・月面なり、古佛の皮肉骨髓なり。さら
に又、古心の行佛なるあるべし、古心の證佛なるあるべし、古心の作佛な
るあるべし、佛古の爲心なるあるべし。古心といふは、心古なるがゆえな
り。心佛はかならず古なるべきがゆえに、古心は、椅子・竹木なり。盡大
地覓一箇會佛法人不可得なり、和尚喚這箇作甚麼なり。いまの時節因緣、
および塵刹・虚空、ともに古心にあらずといふことなし。古心を保任す
る、古佛を保任する、一面目にして兩頭保任なり、兩頭畫圖なり。

Therefore, the myriad trees and hundred grasses of "a flower opens" are a statement of the old buddha, are a question of the old buddha; the nine mountains and eight oceans of "the world arises" are the sun face and moon face of the old buddha, are the skin, flesh, bones, and marrow of the old buddha.[26] Going further, there should also be the old mind that is practicing the buddha; there should be the old mind that is verifying

---

24 **"this side gets such"** (*shatō toku inmo* 這頭得恁麼); **"that side gets such"** (*natō toku inmo* 那頭得恁麼): Dōgen here shifts to colloquial Chinese, which might be read more naturally, "it's like this here; it's like this there." The translation strains to preserve the expression *toku inmo* 得恁麼 ("get such"), often encountered in Zen texts in casual reference to spiritual attainment — as in the well-known saying attributed to the ninth-century master Yunju Daoying 雲居道膺 (d. 902); see Supplementary Notes, s.v. "Such a person." To what "here" (*shatō* 這頭) and "there" (*natō* 那頭) refer is up for interpretation. Given that, in what follows here, Dōgen wants to read the monk's question as a statement, it is possible that they refer to the two sides of the copula (*ze* 是) in the statement: "'what' (*ikan* 如何) is like this; 'the old buddha mind' (*kobutsushin* 古佛心) is like this."

25 **He took up this saying and made it a question** (*kono dōtoku o koshite, monsho to seru nari* この道得を擧して、問處とせるなり): The grammatical subject here is unexpressed; the translation takes it as the "monk," understanding Dōgen's comment here to represent a play with the monk's question: He posed the statement, "'What' is the old buddha mind" as the question, "What is the old buddha mind?"

26 **the myriad trees and hundred grasses** (*manboku hyakusō* 萬木百草): Both *manboku* 萬木 (also read *banboku*) and *hyakusō* 百草 are regularly used in reference to all the things in the phenomenal world.

"a flower opens'" (*ke kai* 華開); **"the world arises"** (*sekai ki* 世界起): From the final line of the dharma transmission verse attributed to Bodhidharma's master, Prajñātāra. See Supplementary Notes, s.v. "A flower opens, and the world arises."

the nine mountains and eight oceans (*kusen hakkai* 九山八海): I.e., the topographic features of the world surrounding Mount Sumeru in Buddhist cosmology.

9. The Old Buddha Mind *Kobutsushin* 古佛心 249

the buddha; there should be the old mind that is becoming the buddha; there should be the buddha old that is making the mind.[27] We say "the old mind" because mind is old. Because the "mind buddha" must always be old, the old mind is "a chair," "bamboo and wood."[28] It is *I can't find a single person anywhere on all the whole earth who understands the buddha dharma*"; it is "*Reverend, what do you call this?*" Whether it be these conditions of the time, or *kṣetra* like dust motes, or empty space, it cannot be said that any are not the old mind.[29] To maintain the old

---

the sun face and moon face (*nichimen gachimen* 日面・月面): The terms may be taken either as referring to the sun and moon, or as allusion to two buddhas given in the *Foming jing* 佛名經, or to a famous saying by Mazu Daoyi 馬祖道一 (709-788); see Supplementary Notes, s.v. "Sun face, moon face."

skin, flesh, bones, and marrow (*hi niku kotsu zui* 皮肉骨髓): An expression commonly used by Dōgen for the essence or truth or entirety of something or someone, as handed down in the Zen tradition; see Supplementary Notes, s.v. "Skin, flesh, bones, and marrow."

27 **old mind that is practicing the buddha** (*koshin no gyōbutsu naru* 古心の行佛なる); **old mind that is verifying the buddha** (*koshin no shōbutsu naru* 古心の證佛なる): Or "old mind that is a practicing buddha"; "old mind that is a verifying (or verified?) buddha."

old mind that is becoming the buddha (*koshin no sabutsu naru* 古心の作佛なる): Or "old mind that is making a buddha."

the buddha old that is making the mind (*butko no ishin naru* 佛古の爲心なる): The awkward translation seeks to preserve Dōgen's play with the three terms, "old," "buddha," and "mind." A sentence as odd in the original as it is in English, perhaps meaning something like "the antiquity of its buddhahood is what constitutes the mind." Though masked by the translation, the following sentence repeats this reversal of noun and adjective; it might be read "We say 'old mind' because it is 'mind old.'"

28 **the "mind buddha" must always be old** (*shinbutsu wa kanarazu ko naru beki* 心佛はかならず古なるべき): The awkward English translation assumes that Dōgen is continuing his play with the syntax of "old buddha mind" here. The phrase could also be read, "The mind and the buddha must always be old."

the old mind is "a chair," "bamboo and wood" (*koshin wa, isu chikuboku nari* 古心は、椅子・竹木なり): Here, and in the next sentence, Dōgen is alluding to a discussion between Luohan Guichen 羅漢桂琛 (867-928) and Xuansha Shibei 玄沙師備 (835-908) about whether to understand "the three realms are only one mind" (*sangai yui isshin* 三界唯一心) as a "chair" or as "bamboo and wood." The episode is recorded in the *shinji Shōbōgenzō* 眞字正法眼藏 (DZZ.5:186, case 112) and discussed in the "Sangai yuishin" 三界唯心 chapter of the *Shōbōgenzō*. See Supplementary Notes, s.v. "Chairs, bamboo, and wood."

29 **conditions of the time** (*jisetsu innen* 時節因縁): Or "the time and conditions"; an expression occurring often in Zen texts, typically in the sense "the actual circumstances of the particular occasion." For examples of usage and a discussion of the possible source of the saying in the *Nirvāṇa Sūtra* (*Da banniepan jing* 大般涅槃經), see Supplementary Notes, s.v. "If you wish to know the meaning of 'buddha nature,' you should observe the conditions of the time."

250 DŌGEN'S *SHŌBŌGENZŌ* VOLUME I

mind, to maintain the old buddha, is maintaining two heads, depicting two heads, with a single face.[30]

[09:15] {1:90}

師いはく、牆壁瓦礫。

The Master said, *"Fences, walls, tiles, and pebbles."*

[09:16]

いはゆる宗旨は、牆壁瓦礫にむかひて道取する一進あり、牆壁瓦礫なり。道出する一途あり、牆壁瓦礫の牆壁瓦礫の許裏に道著する一退あり。これらの道取の現成するところの圓成十成に、千仞萬仞の壁立せり、市地市天の牆立あり。一片半片の瓦蓋あり、乃大乃小の礫尖あり。かくのごとくあるは、ただ心のみにあらず、すなはちこれ身なり、乃至依正なるべし。

The essential point here is that there is one advance that speaks to "fences, walls, tiles, and pebbles": it is "fences, walls, tiles, and pebbles." There is one way to speak out. There is one retreat in which the "fences, walls, tiles, and pebbles" speak within the "fences, walls, tiles, and pebbles."[31] In the fullness and completion of what these sayings express are "walls" built to a thousand fathoms, a myriad fathoms; "fences" built to encircle the earth and encircle the heavens; "tile" coverings of one piece or half a piece; "pebbles" pointed large and small.[32] What is like this is not only the mind; it is the body, it is right down to the secondary and primary recompense of karma.[33]

---

kṣetra **like dust motes** (*jinsetsu* 塵刹): I.e., "fields" (S. *kṣetra*), or "lands," numerous as motes of dust; see Supplementary Notes, s.v. "Dust."

30 **maintaining two heads, depicting two heads, with a single face** (*ichi menmoku nishite ryōtō hōnin nari, ryōtō gazu nari* 一面目にして兩頭保任なり、兩頭畫圖なり): I.e., "the old mind" and "the old buddha" amount to the same thing. The term *ryōtō* 兩頭 might more naturally be taken simply as "both"; the translation "two heads" seeks to preserve what is presumably a play with "single face" (*ichi menmoku* 一面目).

31 **one advance** (*isshin* 一進); **one way** (*itto* 一途); **one retreat** (*ittai* 一退): Dōgen is here playing with terms expressing motion forward and back along a path (or out from and back toward the subject), as well as three terms for speech (*dōshu* 道取, *dōshutsu* 道出, *dōjaku* 道著). The phrase "one way to speak out" is a tentative translation for an unusual expression, in which Dōgen seems to be offering the verb *dōshutsu* 道出 in a play against the colloquial predicate marker *shu* 取 ("to take in") in *dōshu* 道取; it could also be understood as "one road beyond speech."

32 **"walls" built to a thousand fathoms, a myriad fathoms** (*senjin banjin no hekiryū* 千仞萬仞の壁立): "Fathom" here translates *jin* 仞, a measurement of length of about eight *shaku* 尺, or "feet"; sometimes defined as the arm span of an adult male. In this sentence, Dōgen goes through each of the four objects given in Huizhong's answer.

33 **it is right down to the secondary and primary recompense of karma** (*naishi eshō naru beshi* 乃至依正なるべし): I.e., down to and including the environment into which one is born (*ehō* 依報) and the psychophysical makeup of the individual (*shōbō* 正報),

9. The Old Buddha Mind *Kobutsushin* 古佛心 251

[09:17]

しかあれば、作麼生是牆壁瓦礫と問取すべし、道取すべし。答話せんには、古佛心と答取すべし。かくのごとく保任して、さらに參究すべし。いはゆる牆壁は、いかなるべきぞ、なにをか牆壁といふ、いまいかなる形段をか具足せる、と審細に參究すへし。造作より牆壁を出現せしむるか、牆壁より造作を出現せしむるか。造作か、造作にあらざるか。有情なりとやせん、無情なりや。現前すや、不現前なりや。かくのごとく功夫參學して、たとひ天上・人間にもあれ、此土・他界の出現なりとも、古佛心は牆壁瓦礫なり、さらに一塵の出頭して染汚する、いまだあらざるなり。

Thus, we should ask, we should say, "*What are fences, walls, tiles, and pebbles?*" In answering, we should answer, "old buddha mind." Maintaining it in this way, we should go on to investigate it. We should investigate in detail just what these fences and walls are, what it is we call "fences and walls," with what shape they have now been endowed. Are fences and walls made to appear from construction?[34] Is construction made to appear from fences and walls? Are they a construction? Are they not a construction? Are they sentient? Are they insentient? Are they immediately apparent? Are they not immediately apparent? Making concentrated effort and studying them in this way, [we should understand that] whether among the devas or humans, whether an appearance in this land or other worlds, the old buddha mind is "fences, walls, tiles, and pebbles." Nor has a single dust mote ever emerged to defile it.[35]

* * * * *

both seen as the consequences of one's previous deeds; see Supplementary Notes, s.v. "Secondary and primary recompense."

34 **Are fences and walls made to appear from construction?** (*zōsa yori shōheki o shutsugen seshimuru ka* 造作より牆壁を出現せしむるか): The term *zōsa* 造作 ("construction") here may be taken either in the mundane sense, "built by human labor," or in the more metaphysical sense, "fabricated by the mind."

35 **Nor has a single dust mote ever emerged to defile it** (*sara ni ichijin no shuttō shite zenna suru, imada arazaru nari* さらに一塵の出頭して染汚する、いまだあらざるなり): Probably reflecting the Chinese idiom, "unstained by a single dust mote" (*yi chen bu ran* 一塵不染), usually used in reference to an uncorrupted official.

252 DŌGEN'S *SHŌBŌGENZŌ* VOLUME I

[09:18]

漸源仲興大師、因僧問、如何是古佛心。師云、世界崩壊。僧云、爲甚麼世
界崩壊。師云、寧無我身。

> Once, Great Master Jianyuan Zhongxing was asked by a monk, "What
> is the old buddha mind?"[36]
> The Master answered, "The world collapses."
> The monk asked, "Why does the world collapse?"
> The Master answered, "How could it be without me?"[37]

[09:19] {1:91}

いはゆる世界は、十方みな佛世界なり、非佛世界いまだあらざるなり。崩
壊の形段は、この盡十方界に參學すべし、自己に學することなかれ。自己
に參學せざるゆえに、崩壊の正當恁麼時は、一條兩條、三四五條なるがゆ
えに無盡條なり。かの條條、それ寧無我身なり。我身は寧無なり。而今を
自惜して、我身を古佛心ならしめざることなかれ。

The "world" here means that the ten directions are all the buddha
world; there is no non-buddha world. The shape of its "collapse" should
be studied throughout all these worlds in the ten directions; do not study
it in the self. Because we do not study it in the self, this very moment
of the collapse is one instance, two instances, three, four, five instances;
and hence it is inexhaustible instances. Each of those instances is "*how
could it be without me?*" "Me" is "how could it be without?" Do not
begrudge the present and fail to make "me" the old buddha mind.[38]

* * * * *

[09:20]

まことに七佛以前に古佛心壁豎す、七佛以後に古佛心才生す、諸佛以前に
古佛心華開す、諸佛以後に古佛心結果す、古佛心以前に古佛心脱落なり。

Truly, before the seven buddhas, the old buddha mind is already erect-
ed; after the seven buddhas, the old buddha mind is just born. Before the
buddhas, the old buddha mind opens its flower; after the buddhas, the

---

36 **Great Master Jianyuan Zhongxing** (*Zengen Chūkō daishi* 漸源仲興大師): Dates
unknown, a disciple of Daowu Yuanzhi 道吾圓智 (769-835). This conversation appears
at *Jingde chuandeng lu* 景德傳燈録, T.2076.51:289a12-13.

37 **"How could it be without me?"** (*nei mu gashin* 寧無我身): Or "without my body."
A tentative translation of a sentence variously understood, here taking the glyph *nei* 寧
in the sense, "how could?"; others prefer to take it as "preferably" and read the sentence,
"Better without me (or without my body)." Some readers take Zhongxing's mysterious
statement to mean that, when the world collapses, the self remains; others, that when the
world collapses, there is no self.

38 **Do not begrudge the present** (*nikon o jishaku shite* 而今を自惜して): "The present" here is not entirely clear; presumably, the "me" of the present saying.

9. The Old Buddha Mind *Kobutsushin* 古佛心 253

old buddha mind forms its fruit.[39] Before the old buddha mind, the old buddha mind is sloughed off.[40]

正法眼藏古佛心第九

Treasury of the True Dharma Eye
The Old Buddha Mind
Number 9

[Ryūmonji MS:]

爾時寛元元年癸卯四月二十九日、在六波羅蜜寺示衆

Presented to the assembly at Rokuharamitsuji; twentieth day, fourth month of the junior water year of the rabbit, the first year of Kangen [19 May 1243][41]

[Tōunji MS:]

寛元二年甲辰五月十二日、在越州吉峰庵下侍司書寫之。懷弉

Copied in the acolyte's office, Kippō Hermitage, Esshū; twelfth day, fifth month of the senior wood year of the dragon, the second year Kangen [18 June 1244]. Ejō

嘉慶三年二月六日奉書寫之。宗吾

Copied this as a memorial offering, sixth day, second month, third year of Kakyō [4 March 1389]. Sōgo[42]

---

39 **the old buddha mind opens its flower** (*kobusshin kekai su* 古佛心華開す); **the old buddha mind forms its fruit** (*kobusshin kekka su* 古佛心結果す): Or, "the flower of the old buddha mind opens; the old buddha mind bears fruit." Evocative of the final lines of the transmission verse of the First Ancestor, Bodhidharma (*Jingde chuandeng lu* 景德傳燈錄, T.2076.51:219c17-18):

吾本來茲土、傳法救迷情。一華開五葉、結果自然成。

I originally came to this land
To transmit the dharma and save deluded beings.
A single flower opens five petals;
The fruit forms, ripening naturally of itself.

For more on this verse, see Supplementary Notes s.v. "A single flower opens five petals."

40 **the old buddha mind is sloughed off** (*kobusshin datsuraku nari* 古佛心脱落なり): Reminiscent of the famous expression, "body and mind sloughed off" (*shinjin datsuraku* 身心脱落) occurring several times in the *Shōbōgenzō*; see Supplementary Notes, s.v. "Body and mind sloughed off."

41 The Tōunji 洞雲寺 MS shares an identical colophon.

42 **Sōgo** 宋吾: 1343-1406, ninth abbot of Eiheiji.

TREASURY OF THE TRUE DHARMA EYE

NUMBER 10

Great Awakening
Daigo

大悟

Great Awakening

Daigo

INTRODUCTION

This relatively short essay represents number 10 in the sixty- and seventy-five-chapter compilations of the *Shōbōgenzō*; it occurs as number 26 in the Honzan edition. According to its colophons, it was first presented in the early spring of 1242, when Dōgen was living at Kōshōji, his monastery just south of the capital, and then re-presented in the spring of 1244, after its author had taken up residence at Kippōji, in Echizen. A variant version of the work (translated below as Variant Text 6) discovered at Shinpukuji 真福寺, in Nagoya, while lacking a colophon, may well preserve the original 1242 draft.

The title word, *daigo* 大悟, is found throughout Buddhist literature for deep insight into, or profound understanding of, the Buddhist teachings. Often the word is associated with a transformative spiritual experience that overcomes delusion and reveals a truth; thus, many Zen stories end with the student experiencing a "great awakening" to the point of the master's teaching. But, as is so often the case, Dōgen has his own sense of the word — a sense in which, as he says in his opening lines, great awakening "springs beyond the buddhas and ancestors."

For Dōgen here, "great awakening" is not merely a state of knowledge that overcomes delusion, let alone a momentary leap of insight; it seems rather to be a basic condition, or fundamental way of being, that is shared, not only by buddhas and deluded beings, but by all things — by "earth, water, fire, wind, and space," by "pillars and lanterns," by the "Snowy Mountains," by "the trees and rocks." Such great awakening, he says, "is without origin"; it "fills the ditches and clogs the gullies" of our world.

正法眼藏第十
Treasury of the True Dharma Eye
Number 10
大悟
Great Awakening

[10:1] {1:92}

佛佛の大道、つたはれて綿密なり、祗祖の功業、あらはれて平展なり。このゆえに、大悟現成し、不悟至道し、省悟弄悟し、失悟放行す。これ佛祖家常なり。擧拈する使得十二時あり、抛却する被使十二時あり。さらにこの關棙子を跳出する弄泥團もあり、弄精魂もあり。大悟より佛祖かならず恁麼現成する參學を究竟すといへども、大悟の渾悟を佛祖とせるにはあらず、佛祖の渾佛祖を渾大悟なりとにはあらざるなり。佛祖は大悟の邊際を跳出し、大悟は佛祖より向上に跳出する面目なり。

The great way of buddha after buddha, in its transmission, is detailed and thorough; the meritorious deeds of ancestor after ancestor, in their manifestation, are open and expansive. Therefore, great awakening is realized; and arriving at the way without awakening, observing awakening and playing with awakening, losing awakening and letting it go — these are everyday matters among the buddhas and ancestors.[1] They have "employing the twelve times" they take up; they have "being

---

1 **great awakening** (*daigo* 大悟): A term found throughout Buddhist literature for insight into the Buddhist teachings; "deep understanding," or "full apprehension"; may be, but is not necessarily, used synonymously with other terms for spiritual knowledge, such as *bodai* 菩提, *kaku* 覺, etc. To maintain lexical continuity in the translation, we will use the awkward "greatly to awaken" for the verbal form.

observing awakening and playing with awakening (*shōgo rōgo* 省悟弄悟): The term *shōgo* 省悟 (also read *seigo*; "reflecting and understanding") is a common compound expression for "awakening," but Dōgen seems to be using it here as a verb-object construction paralleling *rōgo* 弄悟 ("playing with awakening") and *shitsugo* 失悟 ("losing awakening") — hence, the rather forced translation, "observing awakening."

losing awakening and letting it go (*shitsugo hōgyō* 失悟放行): The expression *hōgyō* 放行 is regularly used in Chan texts for giving free rein to someone. Note that the order of these phrases here suggests a spiritual progression in the realization of great awakening, from unawakened, through awakening, the enjoyment of awakening, and the abandonment, or transcendence, of awakening.

everyday matters among the buddhas and ancestors (*busso kajō* 佛祖家常): The expression contains a clever "turning word" (*kakekotoba* 掛け詞), *ka* (or *ke* 家, "house"), that suggests both *busso ke* 佛祖家, "house of the buddhas and ancestors," and *kajō* 家常, the "daily fare of the household."

258 DŌGEN'S *SHŌBŌGENZŌ* VOLUME I

employed by the twelve times" they throw away.[2] And, going further, they also have the playing with the mud ball and playing with the spirit that spring forth from this pivot.[3] From great awakening, the buddhas and ancestors always thoroughly investigate the study that appears like this; however, it is not the case that the full awakening of the great awakening represents the buddhas and ancestors; nor is it the case that the full buddhas and ancestors of the buddhas and ancestors represent the full great awakening: the buddhas and ancestors spring forth from the boundaries of great awakening; great awakening is a face that springs forth beyond the buddhas and ancestors.

[10:2]

しかあるに、人根に多般あり。いはく、生知。これは生じて生を透脱するなり。いはゆるは、生の初・中・後際に體究なり。いはく、學而知。これは學して自己を究竟す。いはゆるは、學の皮肉骨髓を體究するなり。いはく、佛知者あり。これは生知にあらず、學知にあらず。自他の際を超越して、遮裏に無端なり、自他知に無拘なり。いはく、無師知者あり。善知識によらず、經卷によらず、性によらず、相によらず、自を撥轉せず、他を回互せざれども、露堂堂なり。これらの數般、ひとつを利と認し、ふたつを鈍と認ぜざるなり。多般ともに多般の功業を現成するなり。

Still, human faculties are of many types.[4] There are "those who know at birth": they transcend birth at birth; that is, theirs is the personal inves-

---

2 **"employing the twelve times"** (*shitoku jūni ji* 使得十二時); **"being employed by the twelve times"** (*hishi jūni ji* 被使十二時): The expression "to employ the twelve times" (into which the twenty-four hours of the day were traditionally divided) occurs frequently in the *Shōbōgenzō*; it comes from a popular saying attributed to the famous Tang-dynasty Chan master Zhaozhou Congshen 趙州從諗 (778-897); see Supplementary Notes, s.v. "Employ the twelve times."

3 **playing with the mud ball** (*rō deidan* 弄泥團); **playing with the spirit** (*rō zeikon* 弄精魂): Two expressions common in Zen literature; both typically have a pejorative connotation and are no doubt used here in an ironic sense. "A guy who plays around with a mud ball" (*rō deidan kan* 弄泥團漢) is a common expression in the literature for someone who wastes his time "fiddling around" with meaningless thoughts or activities. "To play with the spirit" occurs often in the literature for a distracted, or "possessed," state of mind. In his "Shōbōgenzō udonge" 正法眼藏優曇華 (DZZ.2:171), Dōgen gives a much more positive interpretation, as "just sitting, sloughing off body and mind" (*shikan taza datsuraku shinjin* 祇管打坐脱落身心); see Supplementary Notes, s.v. "Just sit" and "Body and mind sloughed off."

spring forth from this pivot (*kono kanreisu o chōshutsu suru* この關捩子を跳出する): See Supplementary Notes, s.v., "Pivot." "To spring forth" (or "jump out"; *chōshutsu* 跳出) is one of Dōgen's favorite expressions for "getting free from," or "transcending."

4 **human faculties are of many types** (*ninkon ni tahan ari* 人根に多般あり): The list of four types that Dōgen discusses here seems to be of his own design and does not appear elsewhere in the Buddhist literature. In his "Shōbōgenzō kokū" 正法眼藏虚空, he gives a similar but slightly different list; see Supplementary Notes, s.v. "Knowledge at birth."

10. Great Awakening *Daigo* 大悟   259

tigation of the beginning, middle, and end of birth.[5] There are "those who know from study": they study and thoroughly investigate themselves; that is, they personally investigate the skin, flesh, bones, and marrow of study.[6] There are those with buddha knowledge.[7] This is not knowledge at birth or knowledge from study. Transcending the boundaries of self and other, it is here without reason; it is unconcerned with the knowledge of self and other.[8] There are those who know without a teacher.[9] Without relying on wise friends, without relying on sūtra scrolls, without relying on nature, without relying on characteristics, without turning about the

---

5   **"those who know at birth"** (*shōchi* 生知): This and the following type are taken from the *Lunyu* 論語 16 (KR.1h0005.008.16b-17a), in a passage Dōgen quotes in his "Shōbōgenzō shizen biku" 正法眼藏四禪比丘; see Supplementary Notes, s.v. "Knowledge at birth." Dōgen's interpretation of *shōchi* 生知 here is of course a playful departure from the language of the *Lunyu*, in that it reads the expression as "knowledge of birth" (as opposed to "knowledge at birth"). It is worth bearing in mind that the element *shō* 生 (translated "birth") also has the meanings "life," "to live," "living being" — meanings that may be in play in Dōgen's discussion below.

6   **"those who know from study"** (*gaku ni chi* 學而知): The second of the *Lunyu* types, though Dōgen does not suggest a hierarchy here. His first definition of this type of knowledge reminds us of his famous remark, in the "Shōbōgenzō genjō kōan" 正法眼藏現成公案 (DZZ.1:3), that "to study the way of the buddhas is to study the self" (*butsudō o narau wa jiko o narau nari* 佛道をならふは自己をならふなり). His second definition here again shifts the sense from "knowledge *from* studying" to "knowledge *of* the true nature ('skin, flesh, bones, and marrow') of study."

personally investigate the skin, flesh, bones, and marrow of study (*gaku no hi niku kotsu zui o taikyū suru* 學の皮肉骨髓を體究する): The translation of *taikyū* 體究 as "personally investigate" masks the corporeal connotation of the glyph *tai* 體 ("body") with which Dōgen may be playing here. The expression "skin, flesh, bones, and marrow" (*hi niku kotsu zui* 皮肉骨髓) occurs very often throughout the *Shōbōgenzō*, typically, as here, indicating the essence or truth or entirety of something or someone. From the famous story of Bodhidharma's testing of four disciples, to whom he said of each in turn that he (or, in one case, she) had got his skin, flesh, bones, and marrow. Recorded in the *shinji Shōbōgenzō* 眞字正法眼藏, DZZ.5:230, case 201; see Supplementary Notes, s.v. "Skin, flesh, bones, and marrow."

7 **those with buddha knowledge** (*butchisha* 佛知者): Likely a variation on the more common *butchi* 佛智 (S. *buddha-jñāna*), the knowledge of a buddha, in scholastic writing, often defined as omniscience, the "knowledge of all forms" (*issaishuchi* 一切種智; S. *sarvākāra-jñatā*).

8 **here without reason** (*shari ni mutan* 遮裏に無端): Taking the term *mutan* 無端 here in its common use as "for no [apparent] reason," "without [good] reason"; it is also possible to take it as "without limits" or "without beginning."

unconcerned with the knowledge of self and other (*jitachi ni mukō nari* 自他知に無拘なり): The term *mukō* 無拘 ("unconcerned with") here might also be understood in the sense "unconstrained by."

9 **those who know without a teacher** (*mushichisha* 無師知者): Likely a variant of the more common *mushichi* 無師智, a standard characterization of the knowledge of a buddha; "knowledge untaught" (S. *anupadiṣṭa-jñāna*).

260 DŌGEN'S *SHŌBŌGENZŌ* VOLUME I

self or interacting with the other, they are nevertheless exposed and imposing.[10] It is not that, of these several sorts, one is recognized as sharp and another is recognized as dull: the many sorts all manifest many sorts of meritorious deeds.

[10:3] {1:93}

しかあれば、いづれの情・無情か生知にあらざらんと參學すべし。生知あれば生悟あり、生證明あり、生修行あり。しかあれば、佛祖すでに調御丈夫なる、これを生悟と稱しきたれり。悟を拈來せる生なるがゆえにかくのごとし。參飽大悟する生悟なるべし。拈悟の學なるがゆえにかくのごとし。

Therefore, we should study which sentient or insentient being is not one of those who "know at birth." If they have knowledge at birth, they have awakening at birth; they have verification at birth; they have practice at birth. Therefore, since the buddhas and ancestors are tamers of persons, they have been called "awakened at birth."[11] This is so because theirs is a birth that has taken up awakening; it is an awakening at birth that studies its fill and greatly awakens.[12] This is so because it is a study that takes up awakening.

---

10 **wise friends** (*chishiki* 知識); **sūtra scrolls** (*kyōkan* 經卷): From the fixed expression, occurring often in Dōgen's writing, "whether from a wise friend, whether from a sūtra scroll"; see Supplementary Notes.

nature (*shō* 性); **characteristics** (*sō* 相): A standard Buddhist dichotomy between what a thing is in itself and its phenomenal "marks" (S. *lakṣana*).

without turning about the self (*ji o hatten sezu* 自を撥轉せず): Perhaps meaning "without working to transform themselves." *Hatten* 撥轉 is a term that can also mean "to lead [someone] about," "to handle or manage [someone]" (as a master with a student).

exposed and imposing (*rō dōdō* 露堂堂): A common Zen expression for the bearing of the realized practitioner.

11 **tamers of persons** (*chōgo jōbu* 調御丈夫): One of the standard epithets of a buddha, from his role as one who trains people; S. *puruṣa-damya-sārathi*.

they have been called "awakened at birth" (*kore o shōgo to shōshikitareri* これを生悟と稱しきたれり): "Awakened at birth" is not, in fact, a standard epithet of the buddhas, nor is it clear why such an epithet would follow from their status as "tamers of persons." It may be that Dōgen is shifting the sense of *shō* 生 here from "birth" to "life" or "living"; or, as he seems to be saying in the next lines, the buddhas and ancestors are "born to" "take up awakening" — i.e., live for the study and expression of awakening. Such a formulation would seem to break down the distinction between "knowledge at birth" and "knowledge from study."

12 **studies its fill** (*sanpō* 參飽): I.e., is fully trained; an expression, occurring several times in the *Shōbōgenzō*, suggesting a state in which one is "satiated" or "surfeited" with Buddhist study.

10. Great Awakening *Daigo* 大悟   261

[10:4]

しかあればすなはち、三界を拈じて大悟す、百草を拈じて大悟す、四大を
拈じて大悟す、佛祖を拈じて大悟す、公案を拈じて大悟す。みなともに大
悟を拈來して、さらに大悟するなり。その正當恁麼時は而今なり。

Therefore, they take up the three realms and greatly awaken; they take
up the hundred grasses and greatly awaken; they take up the four elements and greatly awaken; they take up the buddhas and ancestors and
greatly awaken; they take up a kōan and greatly awaken.[13] In every case,
they are taking up the great awakening and further awakening greatly.
This very moment that they do so is the present.

* * * * *

[10:5]

臨濟院慧照大師云、大唐國裏、覓一人不悟者難得。

*Great Master Huizhao of the Linji Cloister said, "In the Land of the
Great Tang, it's hard to find a single person who's unawakened."*[14]

[10:6]

いま慧照大師の道取するところ、正脈しきたれる皮肉骨髓なり、不是ある
べからず。大唐國裏といふは、自己眼睛裏なり。盡界にかかはれず、塵刹
にとどまらず。遮裏に不悟者の一人をもとむるに難得なり。自己の昨自己
も不悟者にあらず、他己の今自己も不悟者にあらず。山人・水人の古今、
もとめて不悟を要するにいまだえざるべし。學人かくのごとく臨濟の道を
參學せん、虚度光陰なるべからず。

What Great Master Huizhao says here is "the skin, flesh, bones, and
marrow" passed down through the main artery; it could not be false.[15]

---

13   **three realms** (*sangai* 三界): I.e, the threefold world system of saṃsāra; see Supplementary Notes, s.v. "Three realms."

hundred grasses (*hyakusō* 百草): A term regularly used in Zen texts for the myriad
phenomena of the world.

four elements (*shidai* 四大): Earth, water, fire, and wind; see Supplementary Notes, s.v.
"Four elements and five aggregates."

14   **Great Master Huizhao of the Linji Cloister** (*Rinzaiin Eshō daishi* 臨濟院慧照
大師): I.e., Linji Yixuan 臨濟義玄 (d. 866), famous founder of the Linji 臨濟 lineage
of Chan. The source of Dōgen's version of his saying is unknown; a similar saying that
does not mention the term "awakening" is attributed to Linji at *Liandeng huiyao* 聯燈會
要, ZZ.136:301b12:

打破大唐國、覓箇不會人難得。

You can bust up the whole Land of the Great Tang, and it's hard to find anyone who
doesn't understand.

15   **passed down through the main artery** (*shōmyaku shikitareru* 正脈しきたれる):
I.e., the essence of Bodhidharma's teaching transmitted in the orthodox line of the ancestors. The translation of *shōmyaku* 正脈 as "main artery" (here in an unusual verbal

262 DŌGEN'S *SHŌBŌGENZŌ* VOLUME I

"In the Land of the Great Tang" means "in one's own eye": it is not concerned with all the worlds; it is not confined to *kṣetra* like dust motes.[16] Here, it is hard to find a single person "who's unawakened."[17] Yesterday's self of one's own is not one "who's unawakened"; today's self of another is not one "who's unawakened."[18] Searching through the past and present of the people of the mountains and the people of the waters, the unawakened cannot be found.[19] Students who study Linji's saying in this way will not "*pass their years and months in vain.*"[20]

[10:7] {1:94}

しかもかくのごとくなりといへども、さらに祖宗の懷業を參學すべし。いはく、しばらく臨濟に問すべし、不悟者難得のみをしりて、悟者難得をしらずば、未足爲是なり、不悟者難得をも參究せるといひがたし。たとひ一人の不悟者をもとむるには難得なりとも、半人の不悟者ありて面目雍容、巍巍堂堂なる、相見しきたるやいまだしや。たとひ大唐國裏に一人の不悟者をもとむるに難得なるを、究竟とすることなかれ。一人・半人のなかに、兩三箇の大唐國をもとめこころみるべし。難得なりや、難得にあらずや。この眼目をそなへんとき、參飽の佛祖なりとゆるすべし。

While this may be so, we should nevertheless go on to study the cherished deeds of the ancestors.[21] That is, we should question Linji for a bit.

---

form) tries to retain something of Dōgen's play with the physiological metaphor of "skin, flesh, bones, and marrow."

16   **all the worlds** (*jinkai* 盡界); ***kṣetra* like dust motes** (*jinsetsu* 塵刹): Two terms for what we might call the entire cosmos. The former represents an abbreviation of "all the worlds in the ten directions" (*jin jippō kai* 盡十方界); the latter refers to an incalculable number of "fields" (S. *kṣetra*), or "lands." See Supplementary Notes, s.v. "Dust."

17   **Here, it is hard to find a single person "who's unawakened"** (*shari ni fugosha no hitori o motomuru ni nantoku nari* 遮裏に不悟者の一人をもとむるに難得なり): Dōgen here simply translates Linji's remark into Japanese, substituting "here" (*shari ni* 遮裏に; i.e., "in one's own eye") for the original "in the Land of the Great Tang."

18   **Yesterday's self of one's own** (*jiko no saku jiko* 自己の昨自己); **today's self of another** (*tako no kon jiko* 他己の今自己): Unusual expressions suggesting, "the self, either of past or present, either one's own or another's."

19   **the past and present of the people of the mountains and the people of the waters** (*sanjin suijin no kokon* 山人・水人の古今): I.e., the history of the general populace; the somewhat unusual expression *sanjin suijin* 山人水人 ("mountain people, water people") is no doubt a variant of the ancient practice of dividing the populace into those who live in the mountains (*yamado* 山人) and those who live by the sea (*ama* 海人).

20   **"pass their years and months in vain"** (*ko do kōin* 虛度光陰): A phrase well known from the *Cantong qi* 參同契, of Shitou Xiqian 石頭希遷 (700-791) (*Jingde chuandeng lu* 景德傳燈錄, T.2076.51:459b20-21). The term *kōin* 光陰 (literally, "light and shade") refers to the sun and moon; variously understood as "years and months," "days and months," and "days and nights."

21   **cherished deeds of the ancestors** (*soshū no egō* 祖宗の懷業): Or, perhaps, the "inner acts" [i.e., thinking] of the ancestors."

10. Great Awakening *Daigo* 大悟

To know only that *"it's hard to find someone who's unawakened,"* without knowing that *it's hard to find someone who's awakened, is to take as right what is not enough.*[22] It is hard to say that you have fully investigated even *"it's hard to find someone who's unawakened."* Although it may be hard to find a single person who is unawakened, there is half a person who is unawakened, his countenance calm, solemn and imposing — have you seen him or not?[23] Do not think that your difficulty in finding a single person who is unawakened in the "Land of the Great Tang" is the ultimate. You should try to find two or three Lands of the Great Tang within a single person or half a person. Are they hard to find or not hard to find? When you are equipped with this eye, I will accept you as a buddha and ancestor who has studied his fill.

* * * * *

[10:8]

京兆華嚴寺寶智大師〈嗣洞山、諱休靜〉、因僧問、大悟底人却迷時如何。師云、破鏡不重照、落華難上樹。

Great Master Baozhi of Huayan Monastery in Jingzhao (heir to Dongshan, called Xiujing) was once asked by a monk, "What about when the person of great awakening reverts to delusion?"[24]

The Master said, "The broken mirror doesn't reflect again; the fallen flower can't climb the tree."

---

22 **take as right what is not enough** (*misoku i ze* 未足爲是): Dōgen shifts to Chinese syntax here. Some texts read here *misoku i soku* 未足爲足 ("to take as enough what is not enough"). This is not the only place in the *Shōbōgenzō* in which Dōgen is critical of Linji.

23 **his countenance calm, solemn and imposing** (*menmoku yōyō gigi dōdō* 面目雍容巍巍堂堂): Adjectives typically describing an awakened person, especially a buddha.

24 **Great Master Baozhi of the Huayan Monastery in Jingzhao (heir to Dongshan, called Xiujing)** (*Keichō Kegonji Hōchi daishi [shi Tōzan ki Kyūjō]* 京兆華嚴寺寶智大師[嗣洞山諱休靜]): I.e., Huayan Xiujing 華嚴休靜 (dates unknown), disciple of Dongshan Liangjie 洞山良价 (807-869). Great Master Baoji is his posthumous title. His monastery, Huayansi 華嚴寺, was to the south of the Tang capital at Chang'an. Slightly variant versions of Xiujing's conversation with the monk are recorded in several sources; see, e.g., *Jingde chuandeng lu* 景德傳燈錄, T.2076.51:338a17-18:

問、大悟底人爲什麼却迷。師曰、破鏡不重照、落華難上枝。

[Someone] asked, "How does the person of great awakening revert to delusion?"
The master said, "The broken mirror doesn't reflect again; the fallen flower can't climb up to the branch."

264 DŌGEN'S *SHŌBŌGENZŌ* VOLUME I

[10:9]

いまの問處は、問處なりといへども示衆のごとし。華嚴の會にあらざれば開演せず、洞山の嫡子にあらざれば加被すべからず。まことにこれ參飽佛祖の方席なるべし。

This question may be a question, but it is like a presentation to the assembly.[25] If not in the community of Huayan, it would not have been expounded; if not by a legitimate heir of Dongshan, it could not have been bestowed.[26] Truly this must be the proper seat of buddhas and ancestors who have studied their fill.[27]

[10:10]

いはゆる大悟底人は、もとより大悟なりとにはあらず、餘外に大悟してたくはふるにあらず。大悟は、公界におけるを、末上の老年に相見するにあらず。自己より強爲して牽挽出來するにあらざれども、かならず大悟するなり。不迷なるを大悟とするにあらず、大悟の種草のために、はじめて迷者とならんと擬すべきにもあらず。大悟人さらに大悟す、大迷人さらに大悟す。大悟人あるがごとく、大悟佛あり、大悟地水火風空あり、大悟露柱燈籠あり。いまは大悟底人と問取するなり。大悟底人却迷時如何の問取、まことに問取すべきを問取するなり。華嚴きらはず、叢席に慕古す、佛祖の勳業なるべきなり。

The "person of great awakening" does not mean someone with great awakening from the beginning; it is not someone who stores up a great awakening from somewhere else. Great awakening is not something that, though present in the public realm, one only encounters at last in old age.[28] It is not something one forcibly pulls out of oneself. Nevertheless, one invariably greatly awakens. It is not that great awakening is not being deluded: we need not suppose that, in order to be the seedling for great awakening, we ought first become deluded.[29] The person of great

---

25 **presentation to the assembly** (*jishu* 示衆): I.e., formal instruction of a master.

26 **the community of Huayan** (*Kegon no e* 華嚴の會): I.e., in the community of Huayan Xiujing 華嚴休靜.

27 **this must be the proper seat of buddhas and ancestors who have studied their fill** (*kore sanpō busso no hōseki naru beshi* これ參飽佛祖の方席なるべし): "Proper seat" renders *hōseki* 方席, taking it as "correct dharma seat" (*hōseki* 法席) — i.e., an authentic place of instruction; here, no doubt, a reference to the Huayan community.

28 **public realm** (*kugai* 公界): The reference could be to the world at large or to the common areas of the monastery (where the monks engage in formal training); see Supplementary Notes, s.v. "Public realm."

at last in old age (*matsujō no rōnen* 末上の老年): Or, perhaps, "first in old age." The term *matsujō* 末上 appears elsewhere in the *Shōbōgenzō* in both the sense "last," as well as in its usual sense, "first."

29 **the seedling for great awakening** (*daigo no shusō no tame ni* 大悟の種草のため に): The use of "seedling" here (rather than "seed") doubtless reflects the practice of wet rice planting.

10. Great Awakening *Daigo* 大悟   265

awakening goes on greatly to awaken; the person of great delusion goes on greatly to awaken. Just as there is the person of great awakening, there is the buddha of great awakening; there are the earth, water, fire, wind, and space of great awakening, there are the pillars and lanterns of great awakening.[30] Here they are being questioned as the "person of great awakening." The question, *"What about when the person of great awakening reverts to delusion?"* is truly asking what should be asked. Huayan does not reject it: he emulates the ancients in the monastic seat.[31] His is the meritorious deed of a buddha and ancestor.

[10:11] {1:95}

しばらく功夫すべし、大悟底人の却迷は、不悟底人と一等なるべしや、大悟底人却迷の時節は、大悟を拈來して迷を造作するか、他那裏より迷を拈來して、大悟を蓋覆して却迷するか、また大悟底人は一人にして、大悟をやぶらずといへども、さらに却迷を參ずるか、また大悟底人の却迷といふは、さらに一枚の大悟を拈來するを却迷とするか、と、かたがた參究すべきなり。また、大悟也一隻手なり、却迷也一隻手なるか。いかやうにても、大悟底人の却迷ありと聽取するを、參來の究徹なりとしるべし。却迷を親曾ならしむる大悟ありとしるべきなり。

We should work at this a bit. Is the "reversion to delusion" of "the person of great awakening" the equivalent of an unawakened person? When *the person of great awakening reverts to delusion*, does he take up great awakening and create delusion? Does he revert to delusion by taking up delusion from over there and covering over great awakening? Again, does the person of great awakening, although remaining themself without destroying great awakening, go on to study "reverting to delusion"?[32] Or does the "reverting to delusion" of the person of great awakening refer to taking up a further great awakening as "reverting to delusion"? We should investigate it in these various ways. Again, is great awakening one hand and reverting to delusion the other hand?

---

30   **earth, water, fire, wind, and space** (*chi sui ka fū kū* 地水火風空): I.e., the five elements (*godai* 五大), a list, popular especially in esoteric Buddhism, that adds space to the set of four given in Note 13, above.

pillars and lanterns (*rochū tōrō* 露柱燈籠): I.e., the free-standing columns and the lanterns of monastic buildings; regularly used in Zen texts for the immediate surroundings of the inanimate phenomenal world (or of the monks' environment). See Supplementary Notes, s.v. "Pillars and lanterns."

31   **he emulates the ancients in the monastic seat** (*sōseki ni boko su* 叢席に慕古す): I.e., his response is worthy of the old masters of the Zen tradition.

32   **remaining themself without destroying great awakening** (*ichinin ni shite daigo o yaburazu* 一人にして大悟をやぶらず): I.e., remaining fundamentally unchanged as a person of great awakening.

go on to study "reverting to delusion" (*sara ni kyakumei o san zu* さらに却迷を參ず): Taking the verb *san* 參 here in the sense *sangaku* 參學, "to study."

266 DŌGEN'S *SHŌBŌGENZŌ* VOLUME I

However we take it, we should recognize that hearing that the person of great awakening reverts to delusion is the complete mastery of our study. We should recognize that there is a great awakening that makes reverting to delusion a personal experience.[33]

[10:12]
しかあれば、認賊爲子を却迷とするにあらず、認子爲賊を却迷とするにあらず。大悟は認賊爲賊なるべし、却迷は認子爲子なり。多處添些子を大悟とす、少處減些子これ却迷なり。しかあれば、却迷者を摸著して、把定了に大悟底人に相逢すべし。而今の自己、これ却迷なるか、不迷なるか、撿點將來すべし。これを參見佛祖とす。

Therefore, *seeing a thief as your child* does not represent "reverting to delusion"; *seeing your child as a thief* does not represent "reverting to delusion."[34] Great awakening is to *see the thief as a thief;* reverting to delusion is to *see the child as your child. Adding a bit where there is a lot* is great awakening; *reducing a bit where there is little* is reverting to delusion.[35] Therefore, when you grope for the one who reverts to delusion and have got him held fast, you will encounter the person of great

---

33 **makes reverting to delusion a personal experience** (*kyakumei o shinzō narashimu* 却迷を親曾ならしむ): A loose translation of the unusual term *shinzō* 親曾, an adverbial expression, meaning something like "personally in the past," regularly used by Dōgen to indicate an intimate relationship. This use likely reflects a verse by Dōgen's teacher, Tiantong Rujing 天童如淨 (1162-1227), that he quotes more than once in the *Shōbōgenzō*. Here is the version given in the "Shōbōgenzō kenbutsu" 正法眼藏見佛 (DZZ.2:107):

> 先師天童古佛舉、波斯匿王問賓頭盧尊者、承聞尊者親見佛來是否。尊者以手策起眉毛示之。先師頌云、策起眉毛答問端、親曾見佛不相瞞、至今應供四天下、春在梅梢帶雪寒。

> My former master, the Old Buddha of Tiantong, brought up [the following]:
> King Prasenajit asked the worthy Piṇḍola, "I've heard that the worthy has personally seen the Buddha. Is this true?"
> The worthy brushed up his [famously long] eyebrows with his hand to show it.
> In a verse, my former master said,

>> He brushed up his eyebrows, and his answer was obvious;
>> He'd personally once seen the Buddha; he doesn't deceive.
>> Worthy of offerings even now, throughout the four continents.
>> Spring is on the twigs of the plum, cold in their girdle of snow.

34 **seeing a thief as your child** (*nin zoku i shi* 認賊爲子): A common Zen expression used to describe an egregious misunderstanding; usually traced to the *Shoulengyan jing* 首楞嚴經 (*Śuraṅgama-sūtra*), T.945.19:108c21. The following, "seeing your child as a thief," represents Dōgen's variation on the phrase.

35 **Adding a bit where there is a lot** (*tasho ten shasu* 多處添些子); **reducing a bit where there is little** (*shōsho gen shasu* 少處減些子): Common expressions, typically occurring together in Zen texts, though not found elsewhere in the *Shōbōgenzō*. In the context here, perhaps suggesting that addition and subtraction do not fundamentally affect great awakening and reverting to delusion.

10. Great Awakening *Daigo* 大悟

awakening. Is the self at this time reverting to delusion? Is it undeluded? You should examine this and bring it forward.[36] This is to meet with a buddha and ancestor.[37]

[10:13] {1:96}

師云、破鏡不重照、落華難上樹。この示衆は、破鏡の正當恁麼時を道取するなり。しかあるを、未破鏡の時節にこころをつかはして、しかも破鏡のことばを參學するは不是なり。いま華嚴道の破鏡不重照、落華難上樹の宗旨は、大悟底人不重照といひ、大悟底人難上樹といひて、大悟底人さらに却迷せずと道取する、と會取しつべし。しかあれども、恁麼の參學にあらず。人のおもふがごとくならば、大悟底人家常如何とら問取すべし。これを答話せんに、有却迷時とらいはん。而今の因緣、しかにはあらず。大悟底人却迷時如何と問取するがゆえに、正當却迷時を未審するなり。恁麼時節の道取現成は、破鏡不重照なり、落華難上樹なり。落華のまさしく落華なるときは、百尺の竿頭に昇晉するとも、なほこれ落華なり。破鏡の正當破鏡なるゆえに、そこばくの活計見戾すれども、おなじくこれ不重照の照なるべし。破鏡と道取し落華と道取する宗旨を拈來して、大悟底人却迷時の時節を參取すべきなり。

The Master said, "*The broken mirror doesn't reflect again; the fallen flower can't climb the tree.*" This instruction to the assembly speaks of the very moment of "the broken mirror." Thus, to study the words "broken mirror" while having in mind the time when the mirror was not yet broken is not right. The essential point of this saying by Huayan — "*the broken mirror doesn't reflect again; the fallen flower can't climb the tree*" — has likely been understood as saying, "*the person of great awakening doesn't reflect again,*" saying "*the person of great awakening can't climb the tree,*" saying that the person of great awakening does not once again revert to delusion. However, it is not a study like this. If it were as people have thought, he would be asking something like, "*How about the everyday life of the person of great awakening?*"[38] And in answering, one would say something like, "*There are times when he reverts to delusion.*" The present episode is not like this. Since he asks, "What about when the person of great awakening reverts to delusion?"

---

36 **examine this and bring it forward** (*kenten shōrai su* 撿點將來す): The term *kenten* 撿點 ("examine"; also written 檢點) occurs elsewhere in the *Shōbōgenzō*; seemingly synonymous with *tenken* 點撿, "to investigate in detail." *Shōrai* 將來 ("to bring") here probably has the sense "to bring up," "introduce into [the discussion]."

37 **This is to meet with a buddha and ancestor** (*kore o sanken busso to su* これを參見佛祖とす): The verb *sanken* 參見 refers especially to seeing, paying a visit to, or studying under, a teacher. The "buddha and ancestor" here may be taken either as Huayan Xiujing 華嚴休靜 or as a generic reference to the masters of the tradition.

38 **would be asking something like** (*to ra monshu su beshi* とら問取すべし): Taking the plural marker *ra* ら here as giving a somewhat vague quality to what is being asked. Similarly, below, "say something like" (*to ra iwan* とらいはん).

268 DŌGEN'S *SHŌBŌGENZŌ* VOLUME I

he is still uncertain about the very moment of "reverting to delusion."[39] The saying that appears at such a time is, "*the broken mirror doesn't reflect again*"; "*the fallen flower can't climb the tree*."[40] When the fallen flower is truly a fallen flower, even if it climbs beyond a hundred-foot pole, it is still "the fallen flower."[41] Since "the broken mirror" is precisely a broken mirror, however many ways of life it expresses, they will all be reflections that "don't reflect again."[42] Taking up the essential point of his saying "broken mirror" and saying "fallen flower," we should inquire into the time "*when the person of great awakening reverts to delusion*."

[10:14]
これは、大悟は作佛のごとし、却迷は衆生のごとし、還作衆生といひ、從本垂迹とらいふがごとく學すべきにはあらざるなり。かれは、大覺をやぶりて衆生となるがごとくいふ、これは、大悟やぶるるといはず、大悟うせぬるといはず、迷きたるといはざるなり。かれらにひとしむべからず。まことに大悟無端なり、却迷無端なり。大悟を罣礙する迷あらず、大悟三枚を拈來して、小迷半枚をつくるなり。ここをもて、雪山の雪山のために大悟するあり、木石は木石をかりて大悟す。諸佛の大悟は、衆生のために大悟す、衆生の大悟は、諸佛の大悟を大悟す、前後にかかはれざるべし。而今の大悟は、自己にあらず、他己にあらず、きたるにあらざれども、填溝塞壑なり、さるにあらざれども切忌隨他覓なり。なにとしてか恁麼なる。いはゆる隨他去なり。

It is not that we should study this as if "great awakening" were like becoming a buddha, "reverting to delusion" were like living beings, and it is saying, "*again becoming a living being*," or saying something like, "*leaving traces from the original*."[43] That seems to say he destroys his

---

39 **he is still uncertain** (*mishin su* 未審す): Or, "he is inquiring." Dōgen here treats as a transitive verb an expression, meaning something like, "I don't yet fully understand," regularly used by Zen students to request further instruction from a teacher.

40 **The saying that appears at such a time** (*inmo jisetsu no dōshu genjō* 恁麼時節の道取現成): The antecedent of "such a time" (*inmo jisetsu* 恁麼時節) here could be taken either as the moment of "reverting to delusion" or as the moment in the dialogue when the monk asks his question.

41 **even if it climbs beyond a hundred-foot pole** (*hyakushaku no kantō ni shōshin suru tomo* 百尺の竿頭に昇晋するとも): From a common expression in Zen literature for going beyond the extreme limit of spiritual practice, as in "proceed one step beyond the tip of a hundred-foot pole" (*hyakushaku kantō shin ippo* 百尺竿頭進一歩). Dōgen's Japanese version suggests that he read *tō* 頭 here as a nominal suffix, rather than as "tip."

42 **however many ways of life it expresses** (*sokobaku no kakkei genjō suredomo* そこばくの活計見成すれども): The term *kakkei* 活計 ("way of life," "livelihood," or "pursuit") is regularly used in reference to the Zen master's activities.

43 **It is not that we should study this** (*kore wa . . . gaku su beki ni wa arazaru nari* これは . . . 學すべきにはあらざるなり): The translation treats the final negative verb as applying to the entire passage. Some readers would break the passage, to read, "In this, great awakening is like making a buddha, reverting to delusion is like living beings. We

10. Great Awakening *Daigo* 大悟 269

great awakening to become a living being; this is not saying that he destroys great awakening, is not saying that he loses great awakening, is not saying that delusion has come.[44] We should not identify it with those. Truly, great awakening is without origin; reverting to delusion is without origin.[45] There is no delusion that obstructs great awakening; taking up three pieces of great awakening, we make a half piece of slight delusion. With this, there are Snowy Mountains having a great awakening because of the Snowy Mountains; the trees and rocks have a great awakening by dint of trees and rocks.[46] The great awakening of the buddhas has a great awakening because of living beings; the great awakening of living beings has a great awakening to the great awakening of the buddhas.[47] This has nothing to do with before or after. The present great awakening is not self, is not other. It has not come; yet it *fills the ditches and clogs the gullies*.[48] It has not gone; yet "seeking it from another is strictly

---

should not study that this is saying 'again becoming a living being,' or saying something like 'leaving traces from the original.'"

"again becoming a living being" (*gen sa shujō* 還作衆生); **"leaving traces from the original"** (*jū hon sui jaku* 從本垂迹): Two fixed phrases for discussion of the relationship between a buddha and his phenomenal body: the former expresses the notion that the buddha returns to saṃsāra from nirvāṇa; the latter reflects the view that a buddha manifests a phenomenal body from his transcendental dharma body — the so-called *honji suijaku* 本地垂迹 ("original ground and manifest traces") theory quite popular in the Japanese Tendai Buddhism of Dōgen's day.

44 **That seems to say ... this is not saying** (*kare wa ... gotoku iu, kore wa ... to iwazu* かれは . . . ごとくいふ、これは . . . といはず): Taking the antecedent of the pronoun *kare* かれ ("that") to be the mistaken views just mentioned, and *kore* これ ("this") to refer to the correct interpretation of the saying given above.

45 **without origin** (*mutan* 無端): Or "without reason." See above, Note 8.

46 **Snowy Mountains** (*Sessen* 雪山); **trees and rocks** (*kiseki* 木石): The juxtaposition of "Snowy Mountains" (*Sessen* 雪山) with "trees and rocks" (*bokuseki* 木石) suggests an allusion to the famous story, invoked elsewhere in the *Shōbōgenzō*, of the prior life of Śākyamuni as the so-called "boy of the Snowy Mountains [i.e., Himalayas]" (*Sessen dōji* 雪山童子), who wrote the *Verse of Impermanence* (*Mujō ge* 無常偈) on trees and rocks; see Supplementary Notes, s.v. "Whether on trees or on rocks." At the same time, the use of the glyphs *bokuseki* 木石 for "trees and rocks" (or "wood and stone"), rather than the story's *nyaku ju nyaku seki* 若樹若石, suggests Dōgen may simply have had in mind here the natural, inanimate world.

47 **has a great awakening because of living beings** (*shujō no tame ni daigo su* 衆生のために大悟す): It is also possible to read this phrase, "has the great awakening for the sake of living beings."

48 **it fills the ditches and clogs the gullies** (*ten kō soku gaku* 填溝塞壑): I.e., it is ubiquitous; see Supplementary Notes, s.v. "Fill the ditches and clog the gullies."

270 DŌGEN'S *SHŌBŌGENZŌ* VOLUME I

prohibited."[49] Why is this so? As it is said, "It goes along with it."[50]

* * * * *

[10:15] {1:97}

京兆米胡和尚、令僧問仰山、今時人、還假悟否。仰山云、悟即不無、爭奈
落第二頭何。僧廻舉似米胡。胡深肯之。

*Reverend Mihu of Jingzhao had a monk ask Yangshan, "People of the
present time, do they also avail themselves of awakening?"*[51]

*Yangshan said, "It's not that they lack awakening, but how can they
help falling into the second rate?"*

*The monk returned and presented this to Mihu. Mihu deeply assented
to it.*

[10:16]

いはくの今時は、人人の而今なり。令我念過去未來現在いく千萬なりと
も、今時なり、而今なり。人の分上は、かならず今時なり。あるひは眼睛
を今時とせるあり、あるひは鼻孔を今時とせるあり。

The "present time" spoken of here is every person's present moment. *The
pasts, futures, and presents that "you make me recall"* may be thousands,
myriads, but they are "the present time," the present moment.[52] A person's

---

49 **"seeking it from another is strictly prohibited"** (*sekki zui ta myaku* 切忌隨他覓):
From a verse by Dongshan Liangjie 洞山良价 after his great awakening, upon seeing
his reflection in the water (*Jingde chuandeng lu* 景德傳燈錄, T.2076.51:321c21). The
translations here and in the final sentence of this section mask the play on the phrase *zui
ta* 隨他 ("to follow another").

50 **"goes along with it"** (*zui ta ko* 隨他去): From a saying of Dasui Fazhen 大隋法眞
(834-919), recorded in the *shinji Shōbōgenzō* 眞字正法眼藏 (DZZ.5:138, case 24), that
"this" (*shako* 這箇) "goes along with it" when the chiliocosm is destroyed at the end of
the kalpa; see Supplementary Notes.

51 **Reverend Mihu of Jingzhao** (*Keichō Beiko oshō* 京兆米胡和尚): A disciple of
Weishan Lingyou 潙山靈祐 (771-853), also known simply as Reverend Mi 米和
尚, dates unknown. This story appears in various sources; see, e.g., *Hongzhi chanshi guanglu* 宏智禪師廣錄 (T.2001.48:24a21-23); *Jingde chuandeng lu* 景德傳燈錄
(T.2076.51:285c20-22); *shinji Shōbōgenzō* 眞字正法眼藏 (DZZ.5:128, case 7). Yangshan 仰山 is Yangshan Huiji 仰山慧寂 (803-887), also a disciple of Weishan.

52 **The pasts, futures, and presents that "you make me recall"** (*ryō ga nen kako
mirai genzai* 令我念過去未來現在): Reflecting a line from a verse spoken by Ānanda in
the *Lotus Sūtra* (*Miaofa lianhua jing* 妙法蓮華經, T.262.9:30a1213):

世尊甚希有、令我念過去、無量諸佛法、如今日所聞。

The World-Honored One, how very rare,
To make me recall past
Incalculable buddha dharmas,
As if I were hearing them today.

10. Great Awakening *Daigo* 大悟 271

status is invariably "the present time."[53] Or we could take their eyes as "the present time"; or we could take their nose as "the present time."

[10:17]

還假悟否。この道をしづかに參究して、胸襟にも換却すべし、頂顇にも換却すべし。近日大宋國禿子等いはく、悟道是本期。かくのごとくいひて、いたづらに待悟す。しかあれども、佛祖の光明にてらされざるがごとし。ただ眞善知識に參取すべきを、懶墮にして蹉過するなり。古佛の出世にも度脱せざりぬべし。

"Do they also avail themselves of awakening?" Quietly investigating these words, you should switch them for your breast; you should switch them for the crown of your head.[54] Recently, shavelings in the Land of the Great Song say, *"Awakening to the way is the basic expectation."* So saying, they vainly await awakening.[55] Nevertheless, they seem not to be illumined by the radiance of the buddhas and ancestors. Given over to laziness, they miss the fact that they should just study with a true wise friend. Even during the appearance in the world of the old buddhas, they would probably not have been liberated.[56]

[10:18] {1:98}

いまの還假悟否の道取は、さとりなしといはず、ありといはず、きたるといはず、かるやいなやといふ。今時人のさとりはいかにしてさとれるぞ、と道取せんがごとし。たとへば、さとりをう、といはば、ひごろはなかりつるかとおぼゆ。さとりきたれり、といはば、ひごろはそのさとりいづれのところにありけるぞ、とおぼゆ。さとりとなれり、といはば、さとり、はじめありとおぼゆ。かくのごとくいはず、かくのことくならずといへども、さとりのありやうをいふときに、さとりをかるやとはいふなり。

---

53 **A person's status** (*nin no bunjō* 人の分上): Following Kawamura's text; other editions give *ninnin no bunjō* 人人の分上 ("people's status"). The term *bunjō* 分上 ("status") occurs frequently in the *Shōbōgenzō*; it is generally taken to mean "one's natural lot or disposition."

54 **you should switch them for your breast; you should switch them for the crown of your head** (*kyōkin ni mo kankyaku su beshi, chōnei ni mo kankyaku su beshi* 胸襟にも換却すべし、頂顇にも換却すべし): I.e., make them your own. Perhaps reflecting the saying, alluded to elsewhere in the *Shōbōgenzō*, "to switch the soapberry seeds [of the Buddhist rosary] for your eyes" (*shō mokukansu kankyoku ni ganzei* 將木槵子換却爾眼睛) (see, e.g., *Yunmen yulu* 雲門語錄, T.1988.47:544a12). See Supplementary Notes, s.v. "Crown of the head."

55 **they vainly await awakening** (*itazura ni taigo su* いたづらに待悟す): A criticism of those who hold that awakening is the final goal of Buddhist practice, after which practice is abandoned. The term *taigo* 待悟 ("await awakening") is not used in the *Shōbōgenzō* apart from the two versions of this "Daigo" 大悟 chapter, but Dōgen does mention it in his *Eihei kōroku* 永平廣錄. See Supplementary Notes, s.v. "Await awakening."

56 **the appearance in the world of the old buddhas** (*kobutsu no shusse* 古佛の出世): The referent of "old buddhas" (*kobutsu* 古佛) here is unclear: it could refer to the seven buddhas of the past or to any of the Chan masters for whom Dōgen uses the term as an honorific; see Supplementary Notes, s.v. "Old buddha."

The words *"do they also avail themselves of awakening?"* do not say that they do not have awakening; they do not say that they have awakening; they do not say that awakening comes: they say "do they avail themselves of it, or not?" It is like asking, "How has the awakening of people nowadays been awakened?" For example, if we say that they "get awakening," we wonder whether for some time they did not have it. If we say that "awakening has come," we wonder where it was until now. If we say they have "become awakened," we imagine that awakening was already there. He does not say it like this; it is not like this. Yet, when he speaks of how awakening is, he says, "do they avail themselves of it?"

[10:19]

しかあるを、さとりといふには、いはる。しかあれども、第二頭へおつるぞいかにかすべき、といひつれば、第二頭もさとりなり、といふなり。第二頭といふは、さとりになりぬる、といひや、さとりをう、といひや、さとりきたれり、といはんがごとし。なりぬ、といふも、きたれり、といふも、さとりなりといふなり。しかあれば、第二頭におつることをいたみながら、第二頭をなからしむるがごとし。さとりのなれらん第二頭は、またまことの第二頭なりともおぼゆ。しかあれば、たとひ第二頭なりとも、たとひ百千頭なりとも、さとりなるべし。第二頭あれば、これよりかみに第一頭のあるをのこせるにはあらぬなり。たとへば、昨日のわれをわれとすれども、昨日はけふを第二人といはんがごとし。而今のさとり、昨日にあらずといはず、いまはじめたるにあらず、かくのごとく参取するなり。しかあれば、大悟頭黑なり、大悟頭白なり。

Nevertheless, we can speak of awakening. However, since he has said, "What about their falling into the second rate?" he is saying that "the second rate" is also awakening.[57] "The second rate" is like saying, "became awakened," or "get awakening," or "awakening has come." He is saying that "became" or "has come" are also awakening. Therefore, while lamenting the fall into "the second rate," it seems he eliminates "the second rate." One may also think that "the second rate" that awakening becomes is the real second rate. Therefore, though it be second rate, though it be a hundred or a thousand rate, it must still be awakening. It is not that, since there is a second rate, it exists where some prior first rate is left behind. This would be, for example, like saying that, while we take ourselves yesterday to be ourselves, yesterday's [self] takes today's as a second person. The present awakening, we do not say

---

57 **we can speak of awakening. However** (*satori to iu ni wa iwaru shikaaredomo* さとりといふにはいはるしかあれども): A tentative translation of a disputed text; other versions read here only *satori to iu wa* さとりといふは ("regarding 'awakening'").

"What about their falling into the second rate?" (*dainitō e otsuru zo ikan ni ka su beki* 第二頭へおつるぞにかすべき): Dōgen here gives his Japanese reading of Yangshan's Chinese question, *zhengnai luo diertou he* 爭奈落第二頭何, translated above as "How can they help falling into the second rate?"

10. Great Awakening *Daigo* 大悟 273

is not yesterday's; it has not begun now. This is how we study it. Therefore, great awakening's head is black; great awakening's head is white.[58]

正法眼藏大悟第十

Treasury of the True Dharma Eye
Great Awakening
Number 10

[Ryūmonji MS:]

爾時仁治三年壬寅春正月二十八日、住觀音導利院興聖寶林寺示衆

*Presented to the assembly while residing at Kannon Dōri Cloister,
Kōshō Hōrin Monastery; twenty-eighth day, first month, spring of the
senior water year of the tiger, the third year of Ninji [1 March 1242]*

而今寛元二年甲辰春正月二十七日、駐錫越宇吉峰古寺而書示於人天大衆

*Written and presented to the great assembly of humans and devas at the
old monastery of Kippō, in Etsuu, where I rested my staff; twenty-seventh day, first month, spring of the senior wood year of the dragon, the
second year of Kangen [7 March 1244]*[59]

[Tōunji MS:]

同二年甲辰春三月二十日、侍越宇吉峰精舍堂奥次書寫之。懷奘

*Copied this while serving as acolyte in the inner sanctum of Kippō Vi-
hāra, Etsuu; twentieth day, third month, spring of the senior wood year
of the dragon, the second year of the same era [28 April 1244]. Ejō*[60]

嘉慶三年二月七日奉書寫之。宗吾

*Copied this as a memorial offering, seventh day, second month, third
year of Kakyō [5 March 1389]. Sōgo*[61]

---

58 **great awakening's head is black; great awakening's head is white** (*daigo tō koku
nari. daigo tō haku nari* 大悟頭黑なり、大悟頭白なり): Likely inspired by the remark
of Mazu Daoyi 馬祖道一 (709-788) about his two disciples Xitang Zhizang 西堂智藏
(735-814) and Baizhang Huaihai 百丈懷海 (749-814) (e.g., at *Jingde chuandeng lu* 景德
傳燈錄, T.2076.51:252a29):
藏頭白海頭黑。
Zang's head is white; Hai's head is black.

59 The Tōunji 洞雲寺 MS shares these two colophons.

60 Ejō's colophon is also attested in the Rurikōji 瑠璃光寺 MS in 83 chapters.

61 **Sōgo** 宋吾: 1343-1406, ninth abbot of Eiheiji.

TREASURY OF THE TRUE DHARMA EYE
NUMBER 11

Principles of Seated Meditation
Zazen gi
坐禪儀

Principles of Seated Meditation

Zazen gi

INTRODUCTION

This brief work is said to have been composed in the eleventh month of 1243, at Kippōji, the monastery in Echizen (modern Fukui Prefecture) to which its author had moved in the summer of the same year. It occurs as number 11 in both the seventy-five and sixty-chapter compilations of the *Shōbōgenzō* and as number 58 in the Honzan edition.

The "Principles of Seated Meditation" is rather different in character from most of the texts of the *Shōbōgenzō*: it is not an essay commenting on themes in the Chinese Chan literature but rather, as its title suggests, a set of instructions for the practice of zazen. Thus, it shares much with Dōgen's more famous treatment of meditation, the *Fukan zazen gi* 普勧坐禪儀, as well as with his account of zazen given in the *Bendō hō* 辦道法, both of which were likely composed in the years following his move to Echizen.

The title, *zazen gi* 坐禪儀 (Chinese, *zuochan yi*, which might also be rendered "procedures" or "rites of seated meditation"), was used for a genre of practical manuals on Chan meditation in China. The best-known example of this genre in the Southern Song when Dōgen visited there was the *Zuochan yi* 坐禪儀 included in the *Chanyuan qinggui* 禪苑清規 (*Rules of Purity for Chan Monasteries*), a monastic code composed in 1103 by Changlu Zongze 長蘆宗賾. Dōgen borrowed heavily from this work in composing his own meditation instructions. Yet he was also critical of Zongze's understanding of Zen and went on to introduce into his instructions several crucial passages alluding to the sayings of other Chinese masters.

The most important innovations in our text are thought to reflect the account of meditation presented in the "Zazen shin" 坐禪箴. This *Shōbōgenzō* chapter, composed in 1242, discusses two kōans on zazen known as "Nanyue polishes a tile" and "Yaoshan's not thinking," both of which appear here in the "Zazen gi." Although, in the "Zazen shin," Dōgen gives more attention to the former story, it is the latter that stands out in our text. Here, as in the *Fukan zazen gi*, "Yaoshan's not thinking" is given as the very content of zazen, what Dōgen calls in both texts "the art" of the practice. Consequently, this passage has become central to the interpretation of Dōgen's meditation teaching and has received much attention in Sōtō commentary.

正法眼藏第十一
Treasury of the True Dharma Eye
Number 11
坐禪儀
Principles of Seated Meditation

[11:1] {1:100}

參禪は坐禪なり。坐禪は靜處よろし。坐蓐あつくしくべし。風煙をいらし
むることなかれ、雨露をもらしむることなかれ、容身の地を護持すべし。
かつて金剛のうへに坐し、盤石のうへに坐する蹤跡あり、かれらみな草を
あつくしきて坐せしなり。坐處あきらかなるべし、晝夜くらからざれ。冬
暖夏涼をその術とせり。

Studying Zen is seated meditation.[1] For seated meditation, one should
have a quiet place.[2] Spread a thick sitting mat. Do not let in drafts or
vapors; do not admit rain or dew.[3] You should secure and maintain the
place you use.[4] There are traces from the past of those who sat on a *vajra*
[throne] or sat on a rock; they all spread a thick layer of grass to sit on.[5]
The place where you sit should be bright; it should not be dark either day
or night. The technique is to keep it warm in winter and cool in summer.

---

1 **Studying Zen is seated meditation** (*sanzen wa zazen nari* 參禪は坐禪なり): The
term *sanzen* 參禪 refers to training in the Zen form of Buddhism. The common term *zazen* 坐禪 ("seated dhyāna" or "seated meditation"), though often associated in particular
with the Zen tradition, is widely used in East Asian Buddhist texts for the practice of
meditation; it has no exact equivalent in the Sanskrit.

2 **a quiet place** (*jōsho* 靜處): In traditional meditation literature, the term is defined as a
mountain fastness, an isolated forest retreat, or a pure monastery (see, e.g., *Xiuxi zhiguan
zuochan fayao* 修習止觀坐禪法要, T.1915.46:463b9-14).

3 **drafts or vapors** (*fūen* 風煙): A similar warning against drafts during meditation
appears among the teachings attributed to Dōgen's master, Tiantong Rujing 天童如淨
(1162-1227), in Dōgen's *Hōkyō ki* 寶慶記 (DZZ.7:26, number 23).

4 **You should secure and maintain the place you use** (*yōshin no ji o goji su beshi*
容身の地を護持すべし): More literally, "the place that accommodates you"; likely, an
admonishment to take care of the place where you regularly practice seated meditation.

5 ***vajra*** (*kongō* 金剛); **grass** (*kusa* 草): The reference to those who spread grass and sat
on a *vajra* recalls the legend of the Buddha's awakening under the bodhi tree, according
to which, at the time of Śākyamuni's attainment of buddhahood, a jewel-encrusted throne,
known as the *vajra* ("diamond," or "adamantine") seat, arose from the earth beneath the
tree. The Buddha is supposed to have been offered by the god Indra a sacred grass to
spread on the seat, in accordance with the practice of all the past buddhas. The practice of
meditation on a rock appears in several descriptions of Zen monks who practiced outdoors.

278   DŌGEN'S *SHŌBŌGENZŌ* VOLUME I

[11:2]

諸縁を放捨し、萬事を休息すべし。善也不思量なり、惡也不思量なり。心意識にあらず、念想観にあらず。作佛を圖することなかれ、坐臥を脱落すべし。飲食を節量すべし、光陰を護惜すべし。頭燃をはらふがごとく坐禪をこのむべし。黄梅山の五祖、ことなるいとなみなし、唯務坐禪のみなり。

"Cast aside the various involvements and discontinue the myriad affairs."[6] *Good is not thought of; evil is not thought of.*[7] It is not mind, mentation, or consciousness; it is not thoughts, ideas, or perceptions.[8] Do not figure to make a buddha; slough off sitting or reclining.[9] You should be moderate in food and drink.[10] Hold dear the passing years and

---

6 **"Cast aside the various involvements and discontinue the myriad affairs"** (*shoen o hōsha shi, banji o kyūsoku su beshi* 諸縁を放捨し、萬事を休息すべし): Japanese version of an expression likely taken from the *Zuochan yi* 坐禪儀 of Changlu Zongze 長蘆宗賾 (dates unknown) (Kagamishima Genryū 鏡島元隆, *Yakuchū Zennen shingi* 訳注禪苑清規, p. 279): *fangshe zhuyuan, xiuxi wanshi* 放捨諸緣、休息萬事. (The *Taishō* [T.2025.48:1183a5-6] and *Zokuzōkyō* [ZZ.111:920a8-9] printings of the text have slightly variant versions.) Similar advice to the contemplative to avoid worldly entanglements occurs in many meditation texts. The *Xiuxi zhiguan zuochan fayao* 修習止觀坐禪法要 (T.1915.46:463b14-19), for example, recommends avoiding four sorts of activities (*yuanwu* 緣務): occupational pursuits, social intercourse with the laity, arts and sciences, and scholarship.

7 **Good is not thought of; evil is not thought of** (*zen ya fu shiryō nari, aku ya fushiryō nari* 善也不思量なり、惡也不思量なり): Variation on a passage in Zongze's *Zuochan yi* 坐禪儀 (Kagamishima, 281):

一切善惡都莫思量
Do not think of any good or evil.

The expression comes from a popular saying attributed to the Sixth Ancestor, Huineng 慧能 (*Jingde chuandeng lu* 景德傳燈錄, T.2076.51:236a20); probably first appearing in the *Nanyang heshang tan yu* 南陽和尚壇語 of Heze Shenhui 荷澤神會 (668-760) (Hu Shih 胡適, *Shenhui heshang yiji* 神會和尚遺集, 236).

8 **It is not mind, mentation, or consciousness; it is not thoughts, ideas, or perceptions** (*shin i shiki ni arazu, nen sō kan ni arazu* 心意識にあらず、念想観にあらず): The idiom "mind, mentation, and consciousness" (*shin i shiki* 心意識, in scholastic writing representing the Sanskrit *citta, manas,* and *vijñāna* respectively) is regularly used in Zen texts as equivalent to "thought" (*nen* 念). The expression "thoughts, ideas, and perceptions" (*nen sō kan* 念想観) is rather less common and somewhat ambiguous: it likely refers here to discriminative cognition (S. *vikalpa*), but it can also represent various Buddhist contemplative exercises.

9 **Do not figure to make a buddha** (*sabutsu o zu suru koto nakare* 作佛を圖することなかれ): From a conversation between Nanyue Huairang 南嶽懷讓 (677-744) and Mazu Daoyi 馬祖道一 (709-788), recorded it Dōgen's *shinji Shōbōgenzō* 眞字正法眼藏 (DZZ.5:128, case 8); Dōgen often refers to this story and comments on it at length in his "Shōbōgenzō zazen shin" 正法眼藏坐禪箴. See Supplementary Notes, s.v. "Nanyue polishes a tile."

10 **be moderate in food and drink** (*onjiki o setsuryō su beshi* 飲食を節量すべし): Variation on a passage in the *Zuochan yi* 坐禪儀 (Kagamishima, 279).

11. Principles of Seated Meditation *Zazen gi* 坐禪儀   279

months, and take to seated meditation as though brushing a fire from
your head. The Fifth Ancestor on Mount Huangmei worked only at seated meditation, without any other occupation.[11]

[11:3]

坐禪の時、袈裟をかくべし、蒲團をしくべし。蒲團は全跏にしくにはあらず、跏趺の半よりはうしろにしくなり。しかあれば、累足のしたは坐蓐にあたれり、脊骨のしたは蒲團にてあるなり。これ佛佛祖祖の坐禪のとき坐する法なり。

During seated meditation, you should wear the *kāṣāya*.[12] Put down a
cushion.[13] The cushion is not placed completely under your crossed legs
but only under the rear half, so that the sitting mat is beneath the folded
legs and the cushion beneath the spine. This is the way that buddha after
buddha and ancestor after ancestor have sat during seated meditation.

[11:4] {1:101}

あるひは半跏趺坐し、あるひは結跏趺坐す。結跏趺坐は、右の足を左のももものうへにおく、左の足を右のももものうへにおく。足のさき、おのおのもとひとしくすべし、參差なることをえざれ。半跏趺坐は、ただ左の足を右のももものうへにおくのみなり。

Assume either the semi-cross-legged or fully cross-legged sitting posture.[14] For the fully cross-legged sitting posture, place your right foot on

---

11 **The Fifth Ancestor on Mount Huangmei** (*Ōbaisan no goso* 黄悔山の五祖): Reference to Daman Hongren 大滿弘忍 (602-675). The description here may reflect a passage
in the notice on Hongren's follower Shenxiu 神秀 (d. 706) in the *Jingde chuandeng lu* 景
德傳燈錄 (T.2076.51:231b15), where Hongren is said to have "made seated meditation
his work."

12 **you should wear the *kāṣāya*** (*kesa o kaku beshi* 袈裟をかくべし): The *kāṣāya* is the
outer robe worn by the monk especially during services. Note that Dōgen's reference to
this clerical garb makes it clear that the zazen instruction of the text is directed to those
who have taken orders.

13 **Put down a cushion** (*futon o shiku beshi* 蒲團をしくべし): The *futon* (in modern
usage, *zafu* 坐蒲) placed on top of the meditation mat is still a standard feature of Sōtō
zazen practice. The *Zazen yōjin ki* 坐禪用心記 of Keizan Jōkin 瑩山紹瑾 (1264-1325),
which also emphasizes the need for such a cushion, gives its diameter as one *shaku* 尺,
two *sun* 寸 (roughly fourteen inches) (SSZ.*Shūgen* 宗源 2:426b). Despite Dōgen's final
remark here, the use of such a combination of cushion and mat does not seem to have
been a universal practice. The *Zuochan yi* 坐禪儀 (Kagamishima, 279), for example,
recommends simply spreading a single mat, a practice still commonly encountered in
East Asian meditation halls.

14 **Assume either the semi-cross-legged or fully cross-legged sitting posture** (*aruiwa hankafu za shi, aruiwa kekkafu za su* あるひは半跏趺坐し、あるひは結跏趺坐す):
Dōgen's directions here follow the recommendation of the *Zuochan yi* 坐禪儀 (Kagamishima, 279), but there is considerable difference of opinion within the Buddhist tradition on how to arrange the legs during meditation. The posture described here, with the
left leg crossed over the right, is sometimes called the *gōma* 降魔 ("demon quelling")

280 DŌGEN'S *SHŌBŌGENZŌ* VOLUME I

your left thigh and your left foot on your right thigh. The toes should be even with the thighs, not out of alignment. For the semi-cross-legged sitting posture, simply place your left foot on your right thigh.

[11:5]

衣衫を寛繫して、齊整ならしむべし。右手を左の足のうへにおく、左手を右手のうへにおく。ふたつのおほゆびさきあひささふ。兩手かくのごとくして、身にちかづけておくなり。ふたつのおほゆびのさしあはせたるさきを、ほぞに對しておくべし。

Loosen your upper robe and arrange it properly. Place your right hand on your left foot and your left hand on your right hand. Put the tips of your thumbs together. With your hands in this position, place them against your body, so that the joined thumb tips are aligned with your navel.[15]

[11:6]

正身端坐すべし。ひだりへそばだち、みぎへかたぶき、まへにくぐまり、うしろへあほのくことなかれ。かならず耳と肩と對し、鼻と臍と對すべし。舌はかみの腭にかくべし。息は鼻より通すべし。くちびる・歯あひつくべし。目は開すべし、不張・不微なるべし。

Straighten your body and sit erect. Do not lean to the left or right; do not bend forward or back. The ears should always be aligned with the shoulders, and the nose aligned with the navel. The tongue should be placed against the front of the palate.[16] The breath should pass through

---

position; the opposite form, in which the right leg is crossed over the left (the so-called *kichijō* 吉祥, or "auspicious" posture), is probably the more common in iconography and in many practice traditions. Though Dōgen's style is sometimes considered standard for the Zen school, both forms can be found in the school's literature. Similar disagreements over whether the left or the right should be on top can be found in descriptions of the semi-cross-legged posture and in the placement of the hands. In the *Hōkyō ki* 寶慶記 (DZZ.7:42, number 36), Dōgen reports that his teacher, Tiantong Rujing 天童如淨, held that the position of the legs might be reversed if they become painful after long sitting.

In his *Fukan zazen gi* 普勸坐禪儀 (DZZ.5:6), Dōgen follows the *Zuochan yi* 坐禪儀 in recommending at this point that the practitioner stretch the body up and swing it back and forth to the left and the right. Keizan's *Zazen yōjin ki* 坐禪用心記 (SSZ.*Shūgen* 宗原 2:427a) explains that one should swing the body from side to side seven or eight times, gradually reducing the length of the arc, an exercise still widely followed in Sōtō practice.

15   This and the following paragraph largely follow the text of the *Zuochan yi* 坐禪儀 (Kagamishima, 279), although Dōgen has added the information on aligning the hands with the navel.

16   **The tongue should be placed against the front of the palate** (*shita wa kami no agito ni kaku beshi* 舌はかみの腭にかくべし): In the *Hōkyō ki* 寶慶記 (DZZ.7:42, number 36), Rujing advises Dōgen that one may either press the tongue against the palate or the front teeth.

11. Principles of Seated Meditation *Zazen gi* 坐禪儀

the nose. The lips and teeth should be closed. The eyes should be open, neither too widely nor too narrowly.[17]

[11:7]

かくのごとく身心をととのへて、欠氣一息あるべし。兀兀と坐定して、思量箇不思量底なり、不思量底如何思量. これ非思量なり。これすなはち坐禪の法術なり。坐禪は習禪にはあらず、大安樂の法門なり、不染汚の修證なり。

Having thus regulated body and mind, take a breath and exhale fully. Sitting fixedly, it is *"thinking of not thinking." "How do you think of not*

---

17 **The eyes should be open** (*me wa kai su beshi* 目は開すべし): The recommendation here to keep the eyes open during zazen follows the advice of the *Zuochan yi* 坐禪儀 (Kagamishima, 279), whose author goes on to argue for this practice, citing the precedent of past meditation adepts and quoting his own teacher, Chan Master Fayun Faxiu 法雲法秀 (1027-1090), who criticized the practice of meditation with the eyes closed as "the ghost cave of the Black Mountains" (*heishan gueiku* 黑山鬼窟). Not only, he says, does the opening of the eyes ward off drowsiness, but it can serve to enhance the power of samādhi (Kagamishima, 279). Other Buddhist accounts of meditation, however, sometimes favor closing the eyes completely. In the *Hōkyō ki* 寶慶記 (DZZ.7:42, number 36), Rujing 如淨 says that, while experienced meditators, not susceptible to drowsiness, may sit with eyes closed, beginners should keep them open.

282 DŌGEN'S *SHŌBŌGENZŌ* VOLUME I

thinking?" It is "nonthinking."[18] "This is the art of seated meditation."[19] Seated meditation is not the practice of dhyāna.[20] It is the dharma gate of

---

18 **Sitting fixedly, it is "thinking of not thinking." "How do you think of not thinking?" It is "nonthinking"** (*gotsugotsu to zajō shite, shiryō ko fushiryō tei nari, fushiryō tei ikan shiryō, kore hi shiryō nari* 兀兀と坐定して、思量箇不思量底なり、不思量底如何思量、これ非思量なり): The expression *gotsugotsu* 兀兀, translated here as "fixedly," is a Chinese idiom indicating something "massive and immovable" (also "towering"); regularly used for a state of fixed concentration (and sometimes for a state of obliviousness). See Supplementary Notes, s.v. "Sit fixedly."

This passage is taken from the kōan known as "Yaoshan's not thinking" (*Yakusan fushiryō tei* 藥山不思量底), which appears several times in Dōgen's writings. The story is found in a number of Zen sources, as well as in Dōgen's *shinji Shōbōgenzō* 眞字正法眼藏 (DZZ.5:196, case 129); see Supplementary Notes, s.v. "Yaoshan's not thinking."

Here is the version of the story on which Dōgen comments at the opening of his "Shōbōgenzō zazen shin" 正法眼藏坐禪箴 (DZZ.1:103).

> 藥山弘道大師坐次、有僧問、兀兀地思量什麼。師云、思量箇不思量底。僧曰、不思量底、如何思量。師云、非思量。

> Once, when the Great Master Hongdao of Yaoshan was sitting [in meditation], a monk asked him, "What are you thinking of, [sitting there] so fixedly?"
> The Master answered, "I'm thinking of not thinking."
> The monk asked, "How do you think of not thinking?"
> The Master answered, "Nonthinking."

The use of Yaoshan's words here to describe the practice of zazen accords with the vulgate text of Dōgen's *Fukan zazen gi* 普勸坐禪儀 (DZZ.5:6), but the earlier, autograph text of the *Fukan zazen gi* (DZZ.5:11) uses instead a quotation from the *Zuochan yi* 坐禪儀 (Kagamishima, 281):

> 念起即覺、覺之即失。久久妄緣、自成一片。

> Whenever a thought occurs, be aware of it; as soon as you are aware of it, it will vanish. If you remain for a long period forgetful of objects, you will naturally become unified.

19 **"This is the art of seated meditation"** (*kore sunawachi zazen no hōjutsu nari* これすなはち坐禪の法術なり): Japanese variation of a line from the *Zuochan yi* 坐禪儀 (Kagamishima, 281):

> 此坐禪之要術也。

> This is the essential art of seated meditation.

20 **Seated meditation is not the practice of dhyāna** (*zazen wa shūzen ni wa arazu* 坐禪は習禪にはあらず): Likely an allusion to a passage in the *Linjian lu* 林間錄 (ZZ.148:590b7-12), in which the author, Juefan Huihong 覺範慧洪 (1071-1128), criticizes the association of Bodhidharma's famous nine years of sitting before a wall at Shaolin 少林 with the practice of dhyāna — a practice he dismisses as "dried-up trees and dead ashes" (*koboku shikai* 枯木死灰). Dōgen quotes the passage at length in his "Shōbōgenzō gyōji" 正法眼藏行持, part 2. See Supplementary Notes, s.v. "Dried-up tree," and "Practitioner of dhyāna."

11. Principles of Seated Meditation *Zazen gi* 坐禪儀 283

great ease and joy.[21] It is nondefiling practice and verification.[22]

正法眼藏坐禪儀第十一
Treasury of the True Dharma Eye
Principles of Seated Meditation
Number 11

[Ryūmonji MS:]

爾時寬元元年癸卯冬十一、在越州吉田縣吉峰精舍示衆

*Presented to the assembly at Kippō Vihāra, Yoshida District, Esshū;
eleventh [month], winter of the junior water year of the rabbit, the first
year of Kangen [13 December 1243-11 January 1244]* [23]

{1:102}

[Fumon'in MS:]

同二年甲辰正月廿日、書寫之在越州吉峰庵侍者寮

*Copied this at the attendant's quarters, Kippō Hermitage, Esshū; twen-
tieth day, first month of the senior wood year of the dragon, the second
year of the same [era] [29 February 1244]* [24]

---

21 **dharma gate of great ease and joy** (*dai anraku no hōmon* 大安樂の法門): A phrase,
reflecting the *Zuochan yi* 坐禪儀 (Kagamishima, 281), that evokes the Sukhavihāra chapter of the *Lotus Sūtra*, in which it is said that the bodhisattva's life of ease and joy (S. *sukha*)
consists in always enjoying seated meditation (S. *pratisaṃlayana*), retiring from the world
to practice control of his mind (*Miaofa lianhua jing* 妙法蓮華經, T.262.9:37b10). Dōgen
gives this claim a more concrete sense in his "Bendōwa" 辦道話 (DZZ.2:470), where he
uses it as a justification of the superiority of the seated posture itself.

22 **nondefiling practice and verification** (*fu zenna no shushō* 不染汚の修證): One of
Dōgen's favorite expressions, from a conversation between the Sixth Ancestor, Huineng
慧能 and his disciple Nanyue Huairang 南嶽懷讓; it is recorded in the *shinji Shōbōgenzō*
眞字正法眼藏 (DZZ.5:178, case 101) and referred to often in the *Shōbōgenzō*. See Supplementary Notes, s.v. "What thing is it that comes like this?"

23 The Fumon'in 普門院 MS shares an identical colophon.

24 The Tōunji 洞雲寺 MS lacks a colophon by Ejō; it is supplied in Kawamura's edition
from the Fumon'in 普門院 MS of the sixty-chapter *Shōbōgenzō*, belonging to Myōshōji
妙昌寺 (Aichi Prefecture), a copy completed in 1751.

TREASURY OF THE TRUE DHARMA EYE

NUMBER 12

Needle of Seated Meditation
Zazen shin
坐禪箴

Needle of Seated Meditation

Zazen shin

INTRODUCTION

This essay, number 12 in the seventy-five-chapter *Shōbōgenzō* and number 27 in the Honzan edition, does not occur elsewhere in the early compilations, nor do any of the early manuscripts provide a colophon for the work. Nevertheless, internal evidence dates the composition to the spring of 1242, when its author was residing at Kōshōji, on the southern outskirts of the capital at Heiankyō. A colophon of the Honzan edition states that the work was subsequently presented to the monastic assembly in the winter of 1243-1244 at Kippōji, the monastery where Dōgen taught following his move to Echizen Province in the summer of 1243; but the similarity of this colophon to that of the "Zazen gi" 坐禪儀 chapter casts doubt on its reliability.

The "Zazen shin" represents one the most important texts for the study of Dōgen's views on Zen meditation. It is divided into three major sections. The first is devoted to the famous kōan known as "thinking of not thinking," a saying of the early eighth-century master Yaoshan Weiyan 藥山惟儼. Although the discussion of it here is very brief, this kōan is central to the Sōtō understanding of Dōgen's meditation; for it appears as a description of (or perhaps prescription for) the practice in his *Fukan zazen gi* 普勸坐禪儀, a manual recognized by the school as the chief source for its style of meditation teaching. This section concludes with a sharp criticism of those in Chinese Chan who do not understand seated meditation.

In his second section, Dōgen turns to another famous story, known as "Nanyue polishes a tile," in which the eighth-century master Nanyue Huairang 南嶽懷讓 likens his disciple Mazu Daoyi's 馬祖道一 attempt to "make a Buddha" by sitting in meditation to someone's trying to make a mirror by polishing a clay tile or trying to drive an ox cart by whipping the cart. On the face of it, the story would seem to be a criticism — often in fact seen in the sayings of the masters — of the view that meditation practice is central to Zen soteriology. But Dōgen's commentary here goes through the story to bring out in each line of the dialogue his own vision of a higher understanding of the practice.

12. Needle of Seated Meditation *Zazen shin* 坐禪箴 287

The final section of the essay opens with a return to its author's lament over the benighted Chan understanding of seated meditation. After dismissing most of the literature on the practice, he introduces with high praise the verse from which our essay takes its name: the "Needle of Seated Meditation" (*Zuochan zhen* 坐禪箴) by Hongzhi Zhengjue 宏智正覺, most famous master in the recent history of Dōgen's Caodong lineage and former head of the monastery at Mt. Tiantong 天童山 where Dōgen had studied in China. After commenting on the lines of Hongzhi's piece, Dōgen offers in closing his own version of the poem.

正法眼藏第十二
Treasury of the True Dharma Eye
Number 12
坐禪箴
Needle of Seated Meditation

[12:1] {1:103}

藥山弘道大師坐次、有僧問、兀兀地思量什麼。師云、思量箇不思量底。僧
曰、不思量底、如何思量。師云、非思量。

> *Once, when Great Master Hongdao of Yaoshan was sitting, a monk asked him, "What are you thinking [sitting there] so fixedly?"*[1]
>
> *The Master answered, "I'm thinking of not thinking."*
>
> *The monk asked, "How do you think of not thinking?"*
>
> *The Master answered, "Nonthinking."*[2]

[12:2]

大師の道、かくのごとくなるを證して、兀坐を參學すべし。兀坐正傳すべ
し。兀坐の、佛道につたはれる參究なり。兀兀地の思量、ひとりにあらず

---

1 **Great Master Hongdao of Yaoshan** (*Yakusan Kudō daishi* 藥山弘道大師): The posthumous title of Yaoshan Weiyan 藥山惟儼 (751-834). See Supplementary Notes, s.v. "Yaoshan's not thinking." This dialogue appears in a number of Chan sources: see, e.g., *Jingde chuandeng lu* 景德傳燈錄 (T.2076.51:311c26-28); *Liandeng huiyao* 聯燈會要 (ZZ.136:740b13-14), *shinji Shōbōgenzō* 眞字正法眼藏 (DZZ.5:196, case 129). The passage is one of the prime sources for Dōgen's meditation teachings: it forms the core of his description of zazen in his (vulgate) *Fukan zazen gi* 普勸坐禪儀 (DZZ.5:6), "Shōbōgenzō zazen gi" 正法眼藏坐禪儀, and *Bendō hō* 辦道法 (DZZ.6:40), and is cited several times in the *Shōbōgenzō* and *Eihei kōroku* 永平廣錄 (e.g., DZZ.3:238, no. 373; DZZ.4:104, no. 524).

[sitting there] so fixedly (*gotsugotsuchi* 兀兀地): The Chinese idiom (*wuwu* 兀兀) suggests something "massive and immovable" (also "towering") and is regularly used for a state of fixed concentration (and sometimes for a state of obliviousness), in which use it is synonymous with *gotsuza* 兀坐; see Supplementary Notes, s.v. "Sit fixedly." The translation "fixedly" here and below attempts to preserve the original adverbial sense of the form *gotsugotsuchi*, which Dōgen will treat in his commentary as a noun (perhaps indicating something like "the activity of being in a massively fixed state").

2 **"not thinking"** (*ko fushiryō tei* 箇不思量底); **"Nonthinking"** (*hi shiryō* 非思量): The translation follows the usual Sōtō interpretation of these famous expressions, which treats them both as mental states. Yaoshan's first answer might also be rendered, "I'm thinking the unthinkable" (*fu ka shiryō* 不可思量), and his final remark could be read, "It isn't thinking."

12. Needle of Seated Meditation *Zazen shin* 坐禪箴　289

といへども、薬山の道は其一なり。いはゆる思量箇不思量底なり。思量の
皮肉骨髄なるあり、不思量の皮肉骨髄なるあり。

Verifying that such are the words of the Great Master, we should study
fixed sitting; we should directly transmit fixed sitting.[3] This is the investigation of fixed sitting transmitted in the way of the buddhas. Although
he is not alone in "thinking [while sitting] fixedly," Yaoshan's words are
the first: he is "*thinking of not thinking.*"[4] [These words] have what is the
very skin, flesh, bones, and marrow of "thinking," the very skin, flesh,
bones, and marrow of "not thinking "[5]

[12:3]
僧のいふ、不思量底如何思量、まことに不思量底たとひふるくとも、さら
にこれ如何思量なり。兀兀地に思量なからんや、兀兀地の向上、なにによ
りてか通せざる。賤近の愚にあらずば、兀兀地を問著する力量あるべし、
思量あるべし。

"The monk asked, '*How do you think of not thinking?*'" Indeed,
though "not thinking" may be old, going further, this is "*how do you
think?*"[6] Could there be no "thinking" in "sitting fixedly"? How could

---

3　**we should study fixed sitting** (*gotsuza o sangaku su beshi* 兀坐を參學すべし): The
term *gotsuza* 兀坐, translated here as "fixed sitting," is virtually synonymous with the
expression *gotsugotsu* 兀兀 on which Dōgen is commenting; see Supplementary Notes,
s.v. "Sit fixedly."

4　**Although he is not alone in "thinking [while sitting] fixedly," Yaoshan's words
are the first** (*gotsugotsuchi no shiryō, hitori ni arazu to iedomo, yakusan no dō wa sore
ichi nari* 兀兀地の思量、ひとりにあらずといへども、薬山の道は其一なり): Perhaps
best interpreted to mean that, while the practice of thinking in zazen is the common her-
itage of the buddhas and ancestors, Yaoshan's words are the best expression of it, or the
first to describe it as "thinking of not thinking."

5　**[These words] have what is the very skin, flesh, bones, and marrow of "thinking," the very skin, flesh, bones, and marrow of "not thinking"** (*shiryō no hi niku
kotsu zui naru ari, fushiryō no hi niku kotsu zui naru ari* 思量の皮肉骨髄なるあり、
不思量の皮肉骨髄なるあり): Or, perhaps, "[Yaoshan] has . . . ." Likely meaning that
Yaoshan has fully expressed the meaning of both "thinking" and "not thinking." "Skin,
flesh, bones, and marrow" (*hi niku kotsu zui* 皮肉骨髄) is an expression, occurring very
often throughout the *Shōbōgenzō*, indicating the essence or truth or entirety of something
or someone; see Supplementary Notes, s.v. "Skin, flesh, bones, and marrow."

6　**Indeed, though "not thinking" may be old, going further, this is "how do you
think?"** (*makoto ni fushiryōtei tatoi furukutomo, sara ni kore ikan shiryō nari* まこと
に不思量底たとひふるくとも、さらにこれ如何思量なり): Most commentators take
"old" (*furuku* ふるく) here to mean "well known," "familiar" (e.g., *Shōbōgenzō keiteki*
正法眼藏啓迪 2:523). The antecedent of "this" (*kore* これ) here is unclear; the most
common reading identifies it as "not thinking" (e.g., *Shōbōgenzō keiteki* 正法眼藏啓
迪 2:523) and thus understands the second clause to be identifying "not thinking" with
"how do you think?" (*ikan shiryō* 如何思量).

290   DŌGEN'S *SHŌBŌGENZŌ* VOLUME I

it not pass beyond "sitting fixedly"?[7] If we are not the sort of fool that "despises the near," we ought to have the strength, ought to have the "thinking," to question "sitting fixedly."[8]

[12:4] {1:104}

大師いはく、非思量。いはゆる非思量を使用すること玲瓏なりといへども、不思量底を思量するには、かならず非思量をもちいるなり。非思量にたれあり、たれ、我を保任す。兀兀地たとひ我なりとも、思量のみにあらず、兀兀地を挙頭するなり。兀兀地たとひ兀兀地なりとも、兀兀地いかでか兀兀地を思量せん。

"The Master answered, 'Nonthinking.'" Although the employment of "nonthinking" is crystal clear, when we "think of not thinking," we always use "nonthinking." There is someone in "nonthinking," and [this] someone maintains us.[9] Although it may be we who are "sitting fixedly," "sitting fixedly" is not merely "thinking": it presents "sitting fixedly."[10] Although "sitting fixedly" is "sitting fixedly," how could "sitting fixedly" "think" of "sitting fixedly"?[11]

7   **How could it not pass beyond "sitting fixedly?"** (*gotsugotsuchi no kōjō, nani ni yorite ka tsū zezaru* 兀兀地の向上、なきによりてか通ぜざる): A tentative translation of a sentence variously interpreted. The grammatical subject here is unexpressed; given the context, this translation interprets it as the "thinking" of the previous sentence. On such a reading, then, Dōgen is asserting that the thinking present in zazen must also be operating outside of zazen. Whether he would also hold that our ordinary thinking outside of zazen is the thinking present in zazen is another matter.

8   **the sort of fool that "despises the near"** (*sengon no gu* 賤近の愚): From the old Chinese saying, "The ordinary person values the distant (*gui yuan* 貴遠) and despises the near (*jian jin* 賤近)." Dōgen will allude to this saying again below, section 10.

we ought to have the strength, ought to have the "thinking," to question "sitting fixedly" (*gotsugotsuchi o monjaku suru rikiryō aru beshi, shiryō aru beshi* 兀兀地を問著する力量あるべし、思量あるべし): Here, as below in the text, the translation loses Dōgen's play on the element *ryō* 量 ("measure") in the expressions *shiryō* 思量 ("thinking") and *rikiryō* 力量 ("strength").

9   **There is someone in "nonthinking," and [this] someone maintains us** (*hishiryō ni tare ari, tare, ware o hōnin su* 非思量にたれあり、たれ、我を保任す): Some interpreters follow the *Shōbōgenzō shō* 正法眼藏抄 (SCZ.4:74) here in associating the mysterious "someone" (*tare* たれ) with "thinking" and "not thinking," and "us" (*ware* 我) with "nonthinking"; thus, "thinking" and "not thinking" maintain "nonthinking."

10   **it presents "sitting fixedly"** (*gotsugotsuchi o kotō suru* 兀兀地を挙頭する): An odd locution, perhaps meaning "sitting fixedly presents itself" — i.e., is just "sitting fixedly." The glyph *tō* 頭 ("head") here is best read as the nominalizing suffix.

11   This section is one of the more obscure arguments in the text. A possible paraphrase might look something like the following:

Although nonthinking is an awakened activity, free from all obstructions to knowledge (as in the Zen expression, "all eight sides are crystal clear"), it is a distinct act of cognition, with its own agent (the awakened "someone" who is present in all our cognitive states). But the activity of nonthinking in meditation ("sitting fixedly") is not merely

12. Needle of Seated Meditation *Zazen shin* 坐禪箴   291

[12:5]

しかあればすなはち、兀兀地は佛量にあらず、法量にあらず、悟量にあらず、會量にあらざるなり。藥山かくのごとく單傳すること、すでに釋迦牟尼佛より直下三十六代なり。藥山より向上をたづぬるに、三十六代に釋迦牟尼佛あり。かくのごとく正傳せる、すでに思量箇不思量底あり。

Therefore, "sitting fixedly" is not the measure of the buddha, not the measure of the dharma, not the measure of awakening, not the measure of understanding.[12] Such unique transmission by Yaoshan represents the thirty-sixth generation directly from Buddha Śākyamuni: if we trace beyond Yaoshan thirty-six generations, we come to Buddha Śākyamuni.[13] And in what was thus directly transmitted, there was already "*thinking of not thinking.*"

[12:6]

しかあるに、近年おろかなる杜撰いはく、功夫坐禪、得胸襟無事了、便是平穩地也。この見解、なほ小乘の學者におよばず、人天乘よりも劣なり、いかでか學佛法の漢といはん。見在大宋國に、恁麼の功夫人おほし、祖道の荒蕪かなしむべし。

Recently, however, some stupid illiterates say, "*Once the breast is without concerns, the concentrated effort at seated meditation is a state of peace and calm.*"[14] This view does not reach that of the scholars of the

---

a matter of cognitive states ("thinking"): it is the act of meditation itself ("it presents sitting fixedly"). When it is just the act itself ("sitting fixedly" is "sitting fixedly"), it is not thinking even of itself.

12   **measure of the buddha** (*butsuryō* 佛量); **measure of the dharma** (*hōryō* 法量); **measure of awakening** (*goryō* 悟量); **measure of understanding** (*eryō* 會量): As above (Note 8), Dōgen is here again playing with the glyph *ryō* 量 ("measure") in *shiryō* 思量 ("thinking"), here, perhaps, to be taken as "to be measured by"; See Supplementary Notes, s.v. "Measure of the buddha."

13   **Such unique transmission by Yaoshan** (*Yakusan kaku no gotoku tanden suru koto* 藥山かくのごとく單傳すること): "Unique transmission" (*tanden* 單傳) is commonly used in Zen to describe the transmission of the dharma from master to disciple. Though the term suggests (and in some cases is used to indicate) a lineage in which there is only one legitimate representative, or "ancestor," in each generation, it regularly appears in contexts where the element *tan* 單 is better understood as "direct," "pure," "simple," etc. **the thirty-sixth generation directly from Buddha Śākyamuni** (*Shakamuni butsu yori jikige sanjūroku dai* 釋迦牟尼佛より直下三十六代): I.e., twenty-seven generations of Indian ancestors before Bodhidharma and nine generations of masters in China. Yaoshan was a disciple of Shitou Xiqian 石頭希遷 (700-790), in the third generation after the Sixth Ancestor, Huineng 慧能.

14   **illiterates** (*zusan* [or *zuzan*] 杜撰): Literally, "Du composition," used in pejorative reference to a literary work that, like those of Du 杜, is ignorant of classical precedents. (Du is most often identified as the Song-dynasty poet Du Mo 杜默; for alternative theories, see M.14477.122.) Dōgen regularly uses the term to refer to those in the Chan lineage who are ignorant of the tradition.

292 DŌGEN'S *SHŌBŌGENZŌ* VOLUME I

Small Vehicle; it is inferior even to the Vehicle of Humans and Devas.[15] How could one [who holds such a view] be called a man who studies the buddha dharma? At present, there are many such practitioners in the Land of the Great Song; it is lamentable that the path of the ancestors is overgrown.

[12:7]
又一類の漢あり、坐禪辨道は、これ初心晩學の要機なり、かならずしも佛祖の行履にあらず、行亦禪、坐亦禪、語黙動靜體安然なり、ただいまの功夫のみにかかはることなかれ。臨濟の餘流と稱するともがら、おほくこの見解なり。佛法の正命つたはれることおろそかなるによりて、恁麼道するなり。なにかこれ初心、いづれか初心にあらざる、初心いづれのところにかおく。

Then there is another type [that holds] that to pursue the way in seated meditation is a function essential for the beginner's mind and late student, but it is not necessarily the conduct of the buddhas and ancestors.[16] "*Walking is Zen, sitting is Zen; in speech or silence, motion or rest, the substance is at ease.*"[17] Do not adhere solely to the present concentrated

---

"**Once the breast is without concerns, the concentrated effort at seated meditation is a state of peace and calm**" (*kufū zazen, toku kyōkin buji ryō, ben ze heionchi ya* 功夫坐禪、得胸襟無事了、便是平穩地也): The translation follows the usual reading of this passage, which could also be read, "Once one attains [the state in which] the breast is without concerns through concentrated effort at seated meditation, this is peace and tranquility." Dōgen here shifts into Chinese, as if quoting a text; but the passage has not been identified as a direct citation from any known source. A similar sentiment appears in the letters of Dahui Zonggao 大慧宗杲 (1089-1163) ("Da Fu shumi dier shu" 答富樞密第二書, *Dahui yulu* 大慧語錄, T.1998A.47:921c29-a1), where he criticizes those who make concentrated effort (*gongfu* 功夫) in a quiet place:

乍得胸中無事、便認著以爲究竟安楽、殊不知似石圧草。

"If they happen to achieve a state in which the breast is without concerns, they think it is the ultimate ease and joy; they don't realize it is simply like a stone pressing down grass."

15 **Vehicle of Humans and Devas** (*ninten jō* 人天乘): Buddhist teachings and practices appropriate for, or directed toward rebirth as, a human or deva. In Dōgen's usage, probably equivalent to the teachings of humans and devas (*ninten kyō* 人天教), the lowest in the schema of the five teachings (*gokyō* 五教) popularized by Guifeng Zongmi 圭峰宗密 (780-841). In his account, this teaching emphasizes the laws of karma and encourages the keeping of the precepts (to ensure rebirth as a human or a deva in one of the heavens of the desire realm (*yokkai* 欲界; S. *kāma-loka*) and practice of the four dhyānas (*shizen* 四禪) and four formless absorptions (*shi mushiki jō* 四無色定; S. *ārūpya-samāpatti*) (for rebirth in the form and formless realms [*shikikai* 色界, S. *rūpa-loka*; *mushikikai* 無色界, S. *ārūpya-loka*]). (See, e.g., *Yuanren lun* 原人論, T.1886.45:707ff.)

16 **beginner's mind and late student** (*shoshin bangaku* 初心晩學): An expression occurring often in the *Shōbōgenzō* for the inexperienced practitioner; see Supplementary Notes, s.v. "Beginner's mind."

17 "**Walking is Zen, sitting is Zen; in speech or silence, motion or rest, the sub-**

12. Needle of Seated Meditation *Zazen shin* 坐禪箴 293

effort. This view is common among those calling themselves a branch of Linji. It is because of a deficiency in the transmission of the correct life of the buddha dharma that they say this.[18] What is the beginner's mind? Where is there no beginner's mind? Where do we leave the beginner's mind?

[12:8] {1:105}

しるべし、學道のさだまれる參究には、坐禪辦道するなり。その榜樣の宗旨は、作佛をもとめざる行佛あり。行佛さらに作佛にあらざるがゆえに、公案見成なり。身佛さらに作佛にあらず、籬籠打破すれば、坐佛さらに作佛をさへず。正當恁麼のとき、千古萬古、ともにもとよりほとけにいり、魔にいるちからあり、進歩退歩、したしく溝にみち、壑にみつ量あるなり。

We should realize that, in the established [means of] investigation for studying the way, one pursues the way in seated meditation. The essential point that is the model for this [investigation] is that there is a practice of a buddha that does not seek to "make a buddha."[19] Since the practice of a buddha is not further to make a buddha, it is the realization of the kōan.[20] The embodied buddha does not further make a buddha; when the nets and cages are broken, a seated buddha does not further interfere with making a buddha.[21] At this very time — "from a thousand

---

stance is at ease" (*gyō yaku zen, za yaku zen, go moku dō jō tai annen* 行亦禪、坐亦禪、語默動靜體安然): From the *Zhengdao ge* 證道歌 (T.2014.48:396a10-11), attributed to the early eighth-century figure Yongjia Xuanjue 永嘉玄覺.

18 **correct life** (*shōmyō* 正命): A term usually indicating "right livelihood" (S. *samyag-ājīva*), one of the practices of the traditional Buddhist eightfold path, but sometimes occurring in Dōgen's writings in a sense in which the element *myō* 命 is taken to suggest the "lifeblood" or "vital artery" (*meimyaku* 命脈) of the lineage; often interpreted as "the rightly transmitted life of wisdom" (*shōden emyō* 正傳慧命).

19 **practice of a buddha that does not seek to "make a buddha"** (*sabutsu o motomezaru gyōbutsu* 作佛をもとめざる行佛): In the term *sabutsu* 作佛 ("make [or become] a buddha"), Dōgen is here introducing the topic of the conversation between Mazu Daoyi 馬祖道一 (709-788) and Nanyue Huairang 南嶽懷讓 (677-744) that he will explore below. As in that conversation, this passage is playing with a set of parallel compounds, the first member of which may function as either a verb or an adjective: *sabutsu* 作佛: "to make a buddha," "a made buddha"; *gyōbutsu* 行佛: "to practice [as a] buddha," "a practicing buddha"; *shinbutsu* 身佛: "to embody a buddha," "an embodied buddha"; and *zabutsu* 坐佛: "to sit [as a] buddha," "a seated buddha."

20 **realization of the kōan** (*kōan genjō* 公案見成): Or "the case is settled" (more often written 公案現成). An expression (or its reverse, "a settled case" [*genjō kōan* 現成公案]) occurring often in Zen texts and in Dōgen's writing. See Supplementary Notes, s.v. "Realized kōan."

21 **nets and cages are broken** (*rarō taha* 籬籠打破): The term "nets and cages" occurs very commonly in Chan literature as a metaphor for spiritual or intellectual "traps" or "snares"; see Supplementary Notes, s.v. "Nets and cages."

294 DŌGEN'S *SHŌBŌGENZŌ* VOLUME I

ages past, ten thousand ages past"— they both have the power from the beginning to enter into buddha and enter into Māra.[22] Stepping forward and stepping back, their measure "fills the ditches and fills the gullies."[23]

---

22 **"from a thousand ages past, ten thousand ages past"** (*senko banko* 千古萬古): Together with the phrase below, "fills the ditches, fills the gullies" (*mizo ni michi, tani ni mitsu* 溝にみち、壑にみつ), likely reflects the words of Yuanwu Keqin 圜悟克勤 (1063-1135) (see, e.g., *Biyan lu* 碧巖錄, T.2003.48:156c10):

千古萬古、黑漫漫。填溝塞壑、無人會。

From a thousand ages past, ten thousand ages past;
The blackness is everywhere.
It fills the ditches and clogs the gullies;
No one understands it.

they both (*tomo ni* ともに): The grammatical subject is unstated, and the sense of the adverbial *tomo ni* ("together," "both") here is unclear. The translation assumes that it refers to a plural subject (presumably, the "seated buddha" and the "making of a buddha"; a somewhat grammatically more awkward reading might take it as referring to the verbs "enter into buddha and enter into Māra" — on which reading, the subject here might well be understood as "we" or "one."

enter into buddha and enter into Māra (*hoteke ni iri, ma ni iru* ほとけにいり、魔にいる): Māra, the Evil One (S. *Māra-pāpīyān*) appears often in Buddhist literature as the deva who seeks to keep beings in saṃsāra. "To enter into Māra" is used in Zen texts to express the spiritual freedom of advanced practice, as in the saying, "You can enter into buddha (*nyūbutsu* 入佛), but you can't enter into Māra (*nyūma* 入魔). (See, e.g., Dahui Zonggao's 大慧宗杲 *Zongmen wuku* 宗門武庫, T.1998B.47:950a15.)

23 **Stepping forward and stepping back** (*shinpo taiho* 進步退步): An expression appearing several times in the *Shōbōgenzō*; it can indicate both activities in general and movement forward and back; see Supplementary Notes, s.v. "Stepping forward and stepping back."

"fills the ditches and fills the gullies" (*mizo ni michi, tani ni mitsu* 溝にみち、壑にみつ): I.e., is everywhere. A Japanese version of the expression *tenkō sokugaku* 填溝塞壑, "to fill the ditches and clog the gullies," said of the bodies of those who have died of starvation along the roadside; regularly used in Chan texts in the sense, "extends or pervades everywhere." See Supplementary Notes, s.v. "Fill the ditches and clog the gullies."

A variant version of this important passage occurs in the text of the "Butsu kōjō ji" 佛向上事 chapter preserved in the twenty-eight-text *Shōbōgenzō* collection (DZZ.2:572), where it serves to describe what Dōgen calls there "studying with the body."

佛道をならふに、しばらく二の樣子あり。いはゆる、こころしてならひ、身てならふなり。身してならふ、といふは、坐禪辦道するところに、作佛をもとめざる行佛あり。公案見成するに、身佛もとより作仏にあらず。羅籠ひさしくやぶれぬれば、坐佛さらに作佛をさへず。かくのごとく、身してならふとき、千古萬古、とこしなへにほとけにいり、魔にいるちからあり。進步退步に、溝にみち壑にみつ、ひかりをあらしむる、これを父母未生以前の面目といはざらめやは。

In studying the way of the buddhas, there are provisionally two types: studying with the mind and studying with the body. "Studying with the body" means that, where the way is pursued in seated meditation, there is the practice of a buddha that does not seek to make a buddha. In the realization of the kōan, from the beginning, the

12. Needle of Seated Meditation *Zazen shin* 坐禪箴 295

* * * * *

[12:9]

江西大寂禪師、ちなみに南嶽大慧禪師に參學するに、密受心印よりこのか
た、つねに坐禪す。南嶽、あるとき大寂のところにゆきてとふ、大德、坐
禪圖箇什麼。

When Chan Master Daji of Jiangxi was studying with Chan Master
Dahui of Nanyue, after intimately receiving the mind seal, he always
sat in meditation.[24] Once, Nanyue went to Daji and said, "*Most Virtuous
One, what are you figuring to do, sitting there in meditation?*"

[12:10]

この間、しづかに功夫參究すべし。そのゆえは、坐禪より向上にあるべき
圖のあるか、坐禪より格外に圖すべき道のいまだしきか、すべて圖すべか
らざるか、當時坐禪せるに、いかなる圖か現成すると問著するか、審細に
功夫すべし。彫龍を愛するより、すすみて眞龍を愛すべし、彫龍・眞龍と
もに雲雨の能あること、學習すべし。遠を貴することなかれ、遠を賤する
ことなかれ、遠に慣熟なるべし。近を賤することなかれ、近を貴すること
なかれ、近に慣熟なるべし。目をかろくすることなかれ、目をおもくする
ことなかれ、耳をおもくすることなかれ、耳をかろくすることなかれ、耳
目をして聰明ならしむべし。

We should quietly make concentrated effort at the investigation of this
question. Is its point that he has some "figuring" that must be beyond
"seated meditation"? Does he not yet have a way that should be "figured" outside of "seated meditation"? Should he not "figure" at all? Or
does it ask what kind of "figuring" occurred at the time he was practicing

---

embodied buddha is not making a buddha. When "the nets and cages" are long broken, a seated buddha does not interfere with making a buddha. When we study with
the body like this, "from a thousand ages, ten thousand ages past," from eternity, we
have the power to "enter into buddha and enter into Māra." In stepping forward and
stepping back, we display a light that "fills the ditches, fills the gullies." How could
this not be called our "face before our father and mother were born"?

24 **Chan Master Daji of Jiangxi** (*Kōzei Daijaku zenji* 江西大寂禪師); **Chan Master
Dahui of Nanyue** (*Nangaku Daie zenji* 南嶽大慧禪師): I.e., Mazu Daoyi 馬祖道一 and
his teacher, Nanyue Huairang 南嶽懷讓, respectively. Their famous conversation, on
which Dōgen will provide a line-by-line commentary below, is found at *Jingde chuandeng lu* 景德傳燈錄, T.2076.51:240c18-28; Dōgen recorded it in his *shinji Shōbōgenzō*
眞字正法眼藏 (DZZ.5:128-130, case 8) and gave a Japanese retelling in his "Shōbōgenzō kokyō" 正法眼藏古鏡. See Supplementary Notes, s.v. "Nanyue polishes a tile."

mind seal (*shin'in* 心印): A common term for the "seal of approval" of the transmission
of the "buddha mind" (*busshin* 佛心). This element of the story, which places the conversation at a time after Mazu had already received his master's certification, does not occur
in the *Jingde chuandeng lu* 景德傳燈錄 version; it is found in the *shinji Shōbōgenzō* 眞字
正法眼藏 account, which seems to reflect elements from Mazu's biography in the *Jingde
chuandeng lu* 景德傳燈錄 (T.2076.51:245c26f).

296 DŌGEN'S *SHŌBŌGENZŌ* VOLUME I

"seated meditation"? We should make concentrated effort to examine this in detail. Rather than love the carved dragon, we should go on to love the real dragon.[25] We should learn that both the carved and the real dragons have the ability [to produce] clouds and rain. Do not "value the distant"; do not despise the distant; become completely familiar with the distant.[26] Do not "despise the near"; do not value the near; become completely familiar with the near. Do not "take the eyes lightly"; do not give weight to the eyes.[27] Do not "give weight to the ears"; do not take the ears lightly. We should make our eyes and ears clear and sharp.

[12:11] {1:106}

江西いはく、圖作佛。

Jiangxi said, "*I'm figuring to make a buddha.*"

[12:12]

この道、あきらめ達すべし。作佛と道取するは、いかにあるべきぞ。ほとけに作佛せらるるを作佛と道取するか、ほとけを作佛するを作佛と道取するか、ほとけの一面出・兩面出するを作佛と道取するか。圖作佛は脱落にして、脱落なる圖作佛か。作佛たとひ萬般なりとも、この圖に葛藤しもてゆくを圖作佛と道取するか。

We should clarify and penetrate these words. What could he mean by saying "make a buddha"? Is he saying that "make a buddha" is being made a buddha by the buddha? Is he saying that "make a buddha" is making a buddha of a buddha? Is he saying that "make a buddha" is one or two faces of a buddha emerging? Is it that "figuring to make a buddha" is sloughing off, and it is a sloughed off "figuring to make a buddha"?[28] Or is he saying that, while there are ten thousand ways to "make a buddha," "figuring to make a buddha" is becoming entangled in this "figuring"?[29]

25   **love the carved dragon** (*chōryū o ai suru* 彫龍を愛する): Allusion to the ancient Chinese story of the Duke of She 楚葉公, who loved the image of the dragon but was terrified of the real thing; the *locus classicus* is *Xinxu* 新序, Zashi 雜事 5 (KR3a0008.005.14a).

26   **Do not "value the distant"** (*en o ki suru koto nakare* 遠を貴することなかれ): See above, Note 8.

27   **Do not "take the eyes lightly"** (*me o karoku suru koto nakare* 目をかろくすることなかれ): Allusion to the Chinese saying, "To give weight to the ears and take the eyes lightly is the constant failing of the common person" (*zhong er qing mu su zhi heng bi* 重耳輕目俗之恆弊).

28   **sloughing off** (*datsuraku* 脱落): Reminscent of Dōgen's famous term for awakening, "sloughing off body and mind" (*shinjin datsuraku* 身心脱落); see Supplementary Notes, s.v. "Slough off" and "Body and mind sloughed off." Here, however, it may also be that it is "figuring to make a buddha" that is itself "sloughed off."

29   **becoming entangled in this "figuring"** (*kono zu ni kattō shi moteyuku* この圖に

12. Needle of Seated Meditation *Zazen shin* 坐禪箴　　297

[12:13]

しるべし、大寂の道は、坐禪かならず圖作佛なり、坐禪かならず作佛の圖なり。圖は作佛より前なるべし、作佛より後なるべし、作佛の正當恁麼時なるべし。且問すらくは、この一圖、いくそばくの作佛を葛藤すとかせん。この葛藤、さらに葛藤をまつふべし。このとき、盡作佛の條條なる、葛藤かならず盡作佛の端的なる、みなともに條條の圖なり。一圖を廻避すべからず。一圖を廻避するときは、喪身失命するなり。喪身失命するとき、一圖の葛藤なり。

It should be recognized that Daji's words mean that "seated meditation" is always "figuring to make a buddha," that "seated meditation" is always the "figuring" that is "making a buddha." This "figuring" must be prior to "making a buddha"; it must be subsequent to "making a buddha"; it must be at the very moment of "making a buddha." Now what I ask is this: How many [ways of] "making a buddha" does this one "figuring" entangle? This entanglement should further intertwine with entanglement.[30] At this point, the entanglements that are individual instances of the entirety of "making a buddha" are invariably the reality of the entirety of "making a buddha" and are all instances of "figuring."[31] We cannot avoid a single "figuring": when we avoid a single "figuring," we *forfeit our bodies and lose our lives*; when we *forfeit our bodies and lose our lives*, this is entanglement in the single "figuring."[32]

葛藤しもてゆく): "Entangled" loosely renders Dōgen's verbal form of "arrowroot and wisteria" (*kattō* 葛藤; elsewhere, rendered "tangled vines"); see Supplementary Notes, s.v. "Tangled vines." Zen texts regularly use the term in reference to the spiritual entanglements of conceptual thought and language, but here and elsewhere Dōgen also uses it in a more positive sense close to "intertwining" (for example, of master and disciple).

30　**This entanglement should further intertwine with entanglement** (*kono kattō, sara ni kattō o matsuu beshi* この葛藤、さらに葛藤をまつふべし): Probably reflecting the saying of Dōgen's master, Tiantong Rujing 天童如淨 (1162-1227), that "the bottle gourd vine entwines the bottle gourd"; see Supplementary Notes, s.v. "The bottle gourd vine entwines the bottle gourd."

31　**entanglements that are individual instances of the entirety of "making a buddha"** (*jin sabutsu no jōjō naru, kattō* 盡作佛の條條なる、葛藤): A tentative translation of a difficult sentence, disregarding the punctuation following *jōjō naru* 條條なる in Kawamura's text.

32　**We cannot avoid a single "figuring"** (*ichizu o kaihi subekarazu* 一圖を廻避すべからず): Taking the modal *beshi* here as expressing possibility, rather than the deontic "should."

forfeit our bodies and lose our lives (*sōshin shitsumyō* 喪身失命): A fixed expression for dying; perhaps best known from the famous problem, recorded in Dōgen's *shinji Shōbōgenzō* 眞字正法眼藏 (DZZ.5:254, case 243), of the man hanging by his teeth over a thousand-foot cliff who is asked the meaning of Bodhidharma's arrival from the west: "If he opens his mouth to answer, he forfeits his body and loses his life." See Supplementary Notes, s.v. "Forfeit one's body and lose one's life." Dōgen will re-introduce the expression below, section 43.

298 DŌGEN'S *SHŌBŌGENZŌ* VOLUME I

[12:14]

南嶽、ときに一甎をとりて、石上にあててとぐ。大寂つひにとふにいは
く、師作什麼。

At this point, Nanyue took up a tile and began to rub it on a stone. At
length, Daji asked, *"Master, what are you making?"*

[12:15]

まことに、たれかこれを磨甎とみざらん、たれかこれを磨甎とみん。しか
あれども、磨甎は、かくのごとく作什麼と問せられきたるなり。作什麼な
るは、かならず磨甎なり。此土・他界、ことなりといへども、磨甎、いま
だやまざる宗旨あるべし。自己の所見を自己の所見と決定せざるのみにあ
らず、萬般の作業に參學すべき宗旨あることを一定するなり。しるべし、
佛をみるに佛をしらず、會せざるがごとく、水をみるをもしらず、山をみ
るをもしらざるなり。眼前の法、さらに通路あるべからずと倉卒なるは、
佛學にあらざるなり。

Who could fail to see that he was "polishing a tile"? Who could see
that he was "polishing a tile"? Still, "polishing a tile" has been questioned in this way: "What are you making?" This "what are you making?" is itself always "polishing a tile." This land and other worlds may
differ, but the essential point of "polishing a tile" never ceases.[33] It is
not only that we do not decide that what we see is what we see; it is that
we are firmly convinced that there is an essential point to be studied in
all the ten thousand activities. We should know that, just as we may see
buddhas without knowing or understanding them, so we may see waters
and yet not know waters, may see mountains and yet not know mountains. The precipitate assumption that the phenomena before one's eyes
offer no further passage [for understanding] is not Buddhist study.

[12:16] {1:107}

南嶽いはく、磨作鏡。

Nanyue said, *"I'm polishing this to make a mirror."*

---

33 **This land and other worlds** (*shido takai* 此土・他界): Terms of ambiguous referent. Depending on context, *shido* 此土 ("this land") can indicate (a) the Sahā world
(*shaba sekai* 娑婆世界), the world of Buddha Śākyamuni; (b) the human realm (*ningen*
人間), as opposed to other realms of saṃsāra; or (c) China (or East Asia), as opposed to
India. Similarly, *takai* 他界 ("other worlds") can refer to (a) other buddha lands, or (b)
other realms of saṃsāra; it can also be translated in the singular, as a reference (much
like the English "the other world") to (c) the world of the dead, of spirits, etc.

12. Needle of Seated Meditation *Zazen shin* 坐禪箴 299

[12:17]

この道旨、あきらむべし。磨作鏡は、道理かならずあり、見成の公案あり、虚設なるべからず。甎はたとひ甎なりとも、鏡はたとひ鏡なりとも、磨の道理を力究するに、許多の榜様あることをしるべし。古鏡も明鏡も、磨甎より作鏡をうるなるべし。もし諸鏡は磨甎よりきたるとしらざれば、佛祖の道得なし、佛祖の開口なし、佛祖の出氣を見聞せず。

We should clarify the meaning of these words. There is definitely a principle in his "*polishing this to make a mirror*": there is the realized kōan; this is no mere empty contrivance. A tile may be a tile and a mirror, a mirror, but when we exert ourselves in rigorously investigating the principle of "polishing," we shall find there are many models: the old mirror and the bright mirror — these are mirrors made through "polishing a tile."[34] If we do not realize that these mirrors come from "polishing a tile," then the buddhas and ancestors have nothing to say; they do not open their mouths, and we do not perceive them exhaling.

[12:18]

大寂いはく、磨甎豈得成鏡耶。

Daji said, "*How can you produce a mirror by polishing a tile?*"

[12:19]

まことに磨甎の鐵漢なる、他の力量をからざれども、磨甎は成鏡にあらず。成鏡たとひ響なりとも、すみやかなるべし。

Indeed, though [the one who is] "polishing a tile" be a man of iron, who does not borrow the power of another, "polishing a tile" is not "producing a mirror."[35] Even if it is "producing a mirror," it must be quick about it.[36]

---

34 **the old mirror and the bright mirror** (*kokyō mo meikyō mo* 古鏡も明鏡も): Venerable symbols for the buddha nature, or buddha mind, which is by definition unproduced and by standard Chan account quite unaffected by polishing; see Supplementary Notes, s.v. "Old mirror," "Bright mirror." The many "models" (*bōyō* 榜様) here, may refer to kōans in which these mirrors occur, of which there are a goodly number.

35 **a man of iron** (*tekkan* 鐵漢): A common Chan term, occurring frequently in Dōgen's writings, for the solid practitioner; see Supplementary Notes, s.v., "Man of iron." "To borrow the power of another" (*ta no rikiryō o karu* 他の力量をかる) may suggest the Buddhist teachings of "other power" (*tariki* 他力), which offer birth in the land of Sukhāvatī through faith in Buddha Amitābha.

36 **it must be quick about it** (*sumiyaka naru beshi* すみやかなるべし): Likely an allusion to the venerable Zen tradition of "sudden practice and sudden awakening" (*tonshu tongo* 頓修頓悟), or, as Dōgen might say, the "intertwining" of practice and verification.

300   DŌGEN'S *SHŌBŌGENZŌ* VOLUME I

[12:20]

南嶽いはく、坐禪豈得作佛耶。

Nanyue replied, "*How can you make a buddha by sitting in meditation?*"

[12:21]

あきらかにしりぬ、坐禪の、作佛をまつにあらざる道理あり、作佛の、坐禪にかかはれざる宗旨かくれず。

This is clearly understood: there is a principle that seated meditation does not await "making a buddha"; there is nothing obscure about the essential message that "making a buddha" is not connected with seated meditation.

[12:22] {1:108}

大寂いはく、如何即是。

Daji asked, "*So, what is right?*"[37]

[12:23]

いまの道取、ひとすぢに這頭の問著に相似せりといへども、那頭の即是をも問著するなり。たとへば、親友の、親友に相見する時節をしるべし。われに親友なるは、かれに親友なり。如何・即是、すなはち一時の出現なり。

While these words may resemble a simple question about this, they are also asking about that "is right."[38] We should understand the occasion, for example, when one friend meets another: the fact that he is my friend means that I am his friend. [Similarly, the meanings here of] "What" and "is right" emerge simultaneously.[39]

---

37   **"So, what is right?"** (*ikan sokuze* 如何即是): Or, more colloquially, "So, what should I do?" The translation tries to capture at least some of Dōgen's play below with the two parts of the question, the interrogative "what" (*ikan* 如何) and the predicate "is right" (*soku ze* 即是), which in other semantic contexts would function as an emphatic copula ("is precisely").

38   **While these words may resemble a simple question about this, they are also asking about that "is right"** (*ima no dōshu, hitosuji ni shatō no monjaku ni sōji seri to iedomo, natō no sokuze o mo monjaku suru nari* いまの道取、ひとすぢに這頭の問著に相似せりといへども、那頭の即是をも問著するなり): Probably meaning that Mazu's question may seem to be asking merely about "this" (*shatō* 這頭) practical matter of what to do to make a buddha, but we can also read it as asking about "that" (*natō* 那頭) ultimate "rightness," or identity (*sokuze* 即是), of "making a buddha."

39   **"What" and "is right" emerge simultaneously** (*ikan sokuze, sunawachi ichiji no shutsugen nari* 如何・即是、すなはち一時の出現なり): More literally, "'what is right' is a simultaneous emergence." Presumably meaning that, like the relationship between two friends, the interrogative "what" (*ikan* 如何) and what "is right" (*sokuze* 即是) are interdependent.

12. Needle of Seated Meditation *Zazen shin* 坐禪箴   301

[12:24]

南嶽いはく、如人駕車、車若不行、打車即是、打牛即是。

Nanyue replied, "*When someone's driving a cart, if the cart doesn't go, is beating the cart right, or is beating the ox right?*"[40]

[12:25]

しばらく、車若不行といふは、いかならんかこれ車行、いかならんかこれ車不行。たとへば、水流は車行なるか、水不流は車行なるか。流は水の不行といつべし、水の行は流にあらざるもあるべきなり。しかあれば、車若不行の道を參究せんには、不行ありとも參ずべし、不行なしとも參ずべし、時なるべきがゆえに。若不行の道、ひとへに不行と道取せるにあらず。打車即是、打牛即是といふ、打車もあり、打牛もあるべきか。打車と打牛と、ひとしかるべきか、ひとしからざるべきか。世間に打車の法なし、凡夫に打車の法なくとも、佛道に打車の法あることをしりぬ、參學の眼目なり。たとひ打車の法あることを學すとも、打牛と一等なるべからず、審細に功夫すべし。打牛の法、たとひよのつねにありとも、佛道の打牛は、さらにたづね參學すべし。水牯牛を打牛するか、鐵牛を打牛するか、泥牛を打牛するか。鞭打なるべきか、盡界打なるべきか、盡心打なるべきか、打迸髓なるべきか、拳頭打なるべきか。拳打拳あるべし、牛打牛あるべし。

For the moment, [let us consider,] when he says, "*if the cart doesn't go,*" what is the "cart going" or the "cart not going"? For example, is water flowing the cart going, or is water not flowing the cart going?[41] We might say that flowing is the water's not going, and there should also be [cases where] water's going is not its flowing. Therefore, when we investigate the words, "*if the cart doesn't go,*" we should study that there is "not going,"

---

40 **"is beating the cart right, or is beating the ox right?"** (*tasha sokuze, tagyū sokuze* 打車即是、打牛即是): Or more colloquially, "should one beat the cart or beat the ox?" Nanyue's example of the cart and ox reflects a story found in the *Da zhuangyan jing lun* 大莊嚴經論 (T.201.4:266a15-b2), in which a *bhikṣuṇī*, coming upon a brahmanical ascetic engaged in the *pañca-tapas,* or "five fires" (*gonetsu* 五熱; the yogic ordeal of sitting in the sun surrounded by four fires), criticizes him for broiling the wrong thing. When the ascetic asks in anger, "What should I broil?" the *bhikṣuṇī* replies,

汝若欲知可炙處者、汝但炙汝瞋恚之心。若能炙心是名眞炙。如牛駕車、車若不行乃須策牛不須打車。身猶如車、心如彼牛。

If you wish to know what you should broil, you should broil your mind of anger. If you can broil the mind, this is called true broiling. It is like the ox that pulls the cart: if the cart doesn't go, you should whip the ox, not beat the cart. The body is like the cart; the mind is like the ox.

41 **is water flowing the cart going, or is water not flowing the cart going?** (*sui ryū wa sha kō naru ka, sui furyū wa sha kō naru ka* 水流は車行なるか、水不流は車行なるか): The notion of water's not flowing is best known from the line attributed to Fu Dashi 傅大士 (497-569); see Supplementary Notes, s.v. "Water doesn't flow."

302   DŌGEN'S *SHŌBŌGENZŌ* VOLUME I

and we should study that there is no "not going"; for they must be in time.[42] The words "*if it doesn't go*" do not mean simply that it does not go.

"*Is beating the cart right, or is beating the ox right?*" Does this mean that there should be "beating the cart" as well as "beating the ox"? Are "beating the cart" and "beating the ox" the same or not the same? In the mundane world, there is no method of beating the cart; but, though the common people have no such method, we know that on the way of the buddhas there is a method of beating the cart; it is the eye of study. Even though we study that there is a method of beating the cart, we should give concentrated effort to examining in detail that this is not the same as beating the ox.[43] And even though the method of beating the ox is common in the world, we should go on to sudy the "ox-beating" on the way of the buddhas. Do we "ox-beat" the water buffalo?[44] Or "ox-beat" the iron bull?[45] Or "ox-beat" the clay ox?[46] Should it be the whip beat-

---

42 **for they must be in time** (*toki naru beki ga yue ni* 時なるべきがゆえに): The grammatical subject is unexpressed; the translation takes it to be the preceding "not going" and "no not going." This cryptic remark is subject to various interpretations. It may mean simply that sometimes there is going and sometimes not. A more philosophical reading might be that Dōgen is expressing the seeming paradox of the Buddhist teachings on the momentariness of dharmas (i.e., phenomena): dharmas, as they say, "abide in their own positions" in time; hence, they do not "go" through time, even as the things we experience move and change.

43 **method of beating the cart** (*tasha no hō* 打車の法): Most often interpreted to refer to the physical practice of seated meditation, in contrast to the mental process of "making a buddha" ("beating the ox"). The distinction here is perhaps akin to that made in the "Shōbōgenzō shinjin gakudō" 正法眼藏身心學道, where Dōgen speaks of "studying with the mind" (*shin o mote gaku shi* 心をもて學し) and "studying with the body" (*shin o mote gaku su* 身をもて學す).

44 **"ox-beat" the water buffalo** (*suikogyū o dagyū suru* 水牯牛を打牛する): Note that the English "ox," "buffalo," and the following "bull" all translate the same glyph, *gyū* 牛, used for bovines. The odd English verb "to ox-beat" seeks to retain something of Dōgen's playful use in this passage of the verb-object compound "beat the ox" as a transitive verb with its own object. Water buffalo often appear in Zen lore; see Supplementary Notes, s.v. "Water buffalo."

45 **iron bull** (*tetsugyū* 鐵牛): The iron bull is also common in Zen literature; see Supplementary Notes. s.v. "Iron bull."

46 **clay ox** (*deigyū* 泥牛): Clay oxen were used in ancient China as ritual offerings at the beginning of the new year. Because they were whipped as part of an agricultural rite, the term can connote the deluded, discriminating mind. A particularly famous instance of the term occurs in the records of Dongshan Liangjie 洞山良价 (807-869): Dongshan asked the master Tanzhou Longshan 潭州龍山 (dates unknown) why he was living on Longshan; the Master answered (*Jingde chuandeng lu* 景德傳燈錄, T.2076.51:263a28-29; see also *Ruizhou Dongshan Liangjie chanshi yulu* 瑞州洞山良价禪師語錄, T.1986B.47:521a11-12):

師云、我見兩箇泥牛鬪入海、直至如今無消息。

12. Needle of Seated Meditation *Zazen shin* 坐禪箴 303

ing? Should it be all the worlds beating? Should it be the whole mind beating?[47] Should it be beating out the marrow?[48] Should it be the fist beating? There should be the fist beating the fist; there should be the ox beating the ox.

[12:26] {1:109}

大寂無對なる、いたづらに蹉過すべからず。抛甎引玉あり、回頭換面あり。この無對、さらに攙奪すべからず。

That "*Daji had no reply*," we should not carelessly overlook. There is *tossing out a tile and taking in a jade*;[49] there is *turning the head and changing the face*.[50] We definitely should not seize this "no reply."[51]

[12:27]

南嶽、またしめしていはく、汝爲學坐禪、爲學坐佛。

Nanyue went on, "*Are you studying seated meditation, or are you studying seated buddha?*"[52]

"I saw two clay oxen fighting till they fell in the ocean, and since then there's been no report of them."

47 **whole mind** (*jinshin* 盡心): In common parlance, a term for "wholehearted effort." The translation loses the semantic parallel with the preceding "all the worlds" (*jinkai* 盡界).

48 **beating out the marrow** (*tahei zui* 打迸髓) A tentative translation. Dōgen is clearly playing with the colloquial verbal marker *ta* 打 ("to beat"), but commentarial opinion on the interpretation of the predicate *hei* 迸 here is widely divided. The translation follows perhaps the most common reading, that suggested by the *Shōbōgenzō monge* 正法眼藏聞解 (SCZ.4.118): to beat till one's very marrow gushes forth. The *Shōbōgenzō shō* 正法眼藏抄 (SCZ.4.118) prefers the odd "to beat with the marrow."

49 **tossing out a tile and taking in a jade** (*hōsen ingyoku* 抛甎引玉): I.e., getting back more than you give; see Supplementary Notes, s.v. "Tossing out a tile and taking in a jade." The sense here could be either that Mazu's silence is the "jade" response to Nanyue's "tile" question, or that Mazu's silence is itself a statement that seeks a response."

50 **turning the head and changing the face** (*kaitō kanmen* 回頭換面): A common expression in Chan literature interpreted variously. Here, perhaps, expressing the inseparability or interdependence of Nanyue's question and Mazu's silence. See Supplementary Notes, s.v. "Turning the head and changing the face."

51 **We definitely should not seize this "no reply"** (*kono mutai, sara ni zandatsu su bekarazu* この無對、さらに攙奪すべからず): The English "seize" here renders *zandatsu* 攙奪, a term meaning "to take by force" or "to take control over" — as in the expression occurring several times in the *Shōbōgenzō*, "to dominate the market" (*zandatsu kōshi* 攙奪行市), used in reference to arbitrary behavior; here, then, perhaps, "by no means should we treat this silence arbitrarily."

52 **"Are you studying seated meditation, or are you studying seated buddha?"** (*nyo i gaku zazen, i gaku zabutsu* 汝爲學坐禪、爲學坐佛): The translation follows the normal reading of the Chinese. Like other traditional readers, Kawamura prefers to parse this phrase in accordance with Dōgen's interpretation of it below:

304　　DŌGEN'S *SHŌBŌGENZŌ* VOLUME I

[12:28]

この道取を參究して、まさに祖宗の要機を辨取すべし。いはゆる學坐禪の
端的いかなりとしらざるに、學坐佛としりぬ。正嫡の兒孫にあらずより
は、いかでか學坐禪の學坐佛なると道取せん。まことにしるべし、初心の
坐禪は最初の坐禪なり、最初の坐禪は最初の坐佛なり。

Investigating these words, we should distinguish the essential function
of the ancestors. Without knowing what "studying seated meditation"
really is, we do know here that it is "studying seated buddha." Who but
a scion of direct descent could say that "studying seated meditation" is
"studying seated buddha"? We should know indeed that the beginner's
"seated meditation" is the beginning "seated meditation," and the beginning "seated meditation" is the beginning "seated buddha."

[12:29]

坐禪を道取するにいはく、若學坐禪、禪非坐臥。

In speaking of "seated meditation," he said, "*If you're studying seated
meditation, meditation is not sitting or reclining.*"

[12:30]

いまいふところは、坐禪は坐禪なり、坐臥にあらず。坐臥にあらずと單傳
するよりこのかた、無限の坐臥は自己なり。なんぞ親疏の命脈をたづね
ん、いかでか迷悟を論ぜん、たれか智斷をもとめん。

The point of what he says here is that "seated meditation" is "seated
meditation"; it is not "sitting or reclining." Ever since the fact that it is
not "sitting or reclining" is uniquely transmitted to us, our unlimited "sitting or reclining" is our own self.[53] Why should we inquire about close or
distant vital arteries?[54] How could we discuss delusion and awakening?
Who would seek wisdom and eradication?[55]

汝、坐禪を學ばんとせば、爲れ坐佛を學するなり。
Should you seek to study seated meditation, this is to study seated buddha.

53　**Ever since the fact that it is not "sitting or reclining" is uniquely transmitted to
us, our unlimited "sitting or reclining" is our own self** (*zaga ni arazu to tanden suru
yori kono kata, mugen no zaga wa jiko nari* 坐臥にあらずと單傳するよりこのかた、
無限の坐臥は自己なり): Perhaps, meaning something like, "Once we know that seated
meditation is not a matter of sitting, we become true, unlimited sitters."

54　**close or distant vital arteries** (*shinso no meimyaku* 親疏の命脈): Perhaps best
interpreted as referring here to the relationship between our activities of sitting and reclining, on the one hand, and seated meditation on the other. The term *meimyaku* 命脈
("vital artery") occurs often in the *Shōbōgenzō*, in the senses both of the "lifeblood" and
the "bloodline" (especially of the Zen tradition).

55　**wisdom and eradication** (*chidan* 智斷): The attainment of bodhi and the elimination
of the defilements (*bonnō* 煩惱; S. *kleśa*), the two goals of Buddhist spiritual training.

12. Needle of Seated Meditation *Zazen shin* 坐禪箴 305

[12:31]

南嶽いはく、若學坐佛、佛非定相。

Nanyue said, "*If you're studying seated buddha, buddha is no fixed mark.*"[56]

[12:32]

いはゆる道取を道取せんには、恁麼なり。坐佛の、一佛二佛のごとくなるは、非定相を莊嚴とせるによりてなり。いま佛非定相と道取するは、佛相を道取するなり。非定相佛なるがゆえに、坐佛さらに廻避しがたきなり。しかあればすなはち、佛非定相の莊嚴なるゆえに、若學坐禪すなはち坐佛なり。たれか無住法におきて、ほとけにあらずと取捨し、ほとけなりと取捨せん。取捨、さきより脱落せるによりて坐佛なるなり。

Such is the way to say what is to be said. The reason that the "seated buddha" is like one or two buddhas is that he adorns himself with "*no fixed mark.*"[57] Saying here that "*buddha is no fixed mark*" is describing the mark of a buddha. Since he is a buddha of "no fixed mark," the "seated buddha" is very hard to avoid. Therefore, since it is adorned with this [mark of] "*buddha is no fixed mark,*" "*if you're studying seated meditation,*" you are a "seated buddha." "In a nonabiding dharma," who would "grasp or reject" anything as not the buddha?[58] Who would "grasp or reject" it as the buddha? It is because long ago it sloughed off "grasping and rejecting" that it is a "seated buddha."

---

56 **"no fixed mark"** (*hijōsō* 非定相): Or, more colloquially, "not a fixed form." The translation here tries to preserve the technical sense of *sō* 相, the auspicious "marks" (S. *lakṣana*) of a buddha's body, with which Dōgen will play in his comments. The discussion of these marks draws on the famous teaching in the *Diamond Sūtra* (e.g., at *Jingang bore boluomi jing* 金剛般若波羅蜜經, T.235.8:750a20-23) that the true mark of a buddha is no mark, because he transcends all phenomenal characteristics. The translation of *jō* 定 as "fixed" loses the play on a term used in the Buddhist lexicon for "meditation" (from *samādhi*: "to hold [the mind] steady"); hence, the secondary sense here, "buddha is not marked by meditation."

57 **the "seated buddha" is like one or two buddhas** (*zabutsu no ichi butsu ni butsu no gotoku naru* 坐佛の、一佛二佛のごとくなる): Presumably meaning that [because he has no fixed form] the seated buddha can appear as one or another buddha.

58 **"In a nonabiding dharma," who would "grasp or reject" anything as not the buddha?** (*tare ka mujūhō ni okite, hotoke ni arazu to shusha shi* たれか無住法におきて、ほとけにあらずと取捨し): Dōgen is here introducing material from Nanyue's answer to Mazu that he does not bother to quote (*Jingde chuandeng lu* 景德傳燈錄, T.2076.51:240c26-27):

於無住法不應取捨。

In a nonabiding dharma, there should be no grasping or rejecting.

306 DŌGEN'S *SHŌBŌGENZŌ* VOLUME I

[12:33] {1:110}

南嶽いはく、汝若坐佛、即是殺佛。

Nanyue said, "*If you're a seated buddha, this is killing buddha.*"

[12:34]

いはゆるさらに坐佛を參究するに、殺佛の功德あり。坐佛の正當恁麼時
は、殺佛なり。殺佛の相好光明は、たづねんとするに、かならず坐佛なる
べし。殺の言、たとひ凡夫のことばにひとしくとも、ひとへに凡夫と同す
べからず。又坐佛の殺佛なるは、有什麼形段と參究すべし。佛功德すでに
殺佛あるを拈擧して、われらが殺人・未殺人をも參學すべし。

This means that, when we further investigate "seated buddha," it has
the virtue of "killing buddha." At the very moment that we are a "seated
buddha" we are "killing buddha." When we seek them, the marks and
signs and radiance of "killing buddha" are always a "seated buddha."[59]
Although the word "kill" here is identical with that used by common
people, it is not the same. Moreover, we must investigate in what shape
it is that a "seated buddha" is "killing buddha." Taking up the fact that
the virtues of a buddha definitely include "killing buddha," we should
also study whether we are killers or not yet killers.

[12:35]

若執坐相、非達其理。

"*If you grasp the mark of sitting, this is not reaching its principle.*"

[12:36]

いはゆる執坐相とは、坐相を捨し、坐相を觸するなり。この道理は、すで
に坐佛するには、不執坐相なることえざるなり。不執坐相なることえざる
がゆゑに、執坐相はたとひ玲瓏なりとも、非達其理なるべし。恁麼の功夫
を脱落身心といふ。いまだかつて坐せざるものに、この道のあるにあら
ず。打坐時にあり、打坐人にあり、打坐佛にあり、學坐佛にあり。ただ、
人の坐臥する坐の、この打坐佛なるにあらず。人坐の、おのづから坐佛・
佛坐に相似なりといへども、人作佛あり、作佛人あるがごとし。作佛人あ
りといへども、一切人は作佛にあらず、ほとけは一切人にあらず、一切佛
は一切人のみにあらざるがゆゑに、人、かならず佛にあらず、佛、かなら
ず人にあらず。坐佛もかくのごとし。

To "grasp the mark of sitting" here means to "reject the mark of sitting" and to touch "the mark of sitting." The principle of this is that, in

---

59 **marks and signs and radiance of "killing buddha"** (*setsubutsu no sōgō kōmyō* 殺
佛の相好光明): I.e., the thirty-two marks (*sō* 相; S. *lakṣana*) and eighty auspicious signs
(*kō* 好; S. *vyañjana*) and the radiant nimbus (*kōmyō* 光明) characteristic of the body of a
buddha. Dōgen is here playing on the compound *setsubutsu* 殺佛, shifting its sense from
a verb-object construction ("killing a buddha") to an adjective-noun form ("a killing
buddha"). The notion of killing a buddha is best known from the saying attributed to
Linji Yixuan 臨濟義玄 (d. 866); see Supplementary Notes, s.v. "Kill the buddha."

12. Needle of Seated Meditation *Zazen shin* 坐禪箴 307

being a "seated buddha," we cannot fail to "grasp the mark of sitting."
Since we cannot fail to "grasp the mark of sitting," though our "grasping
the mark of sitting" is crystal clear, we are "not reaching its principle."
Such concentrated effort is called "sloughing off body and mind."

Those who have never sat do not have these words: they belong to
the time of sitting and the sitting human, to the sitting buddha and the
study of the seated buddha.[60] The sitting of the human's mere sitting and
reclining is not that of this sitting buddha.[61] Although the human's sitting
may naturally resemble a seated buddha, or a buddha's sitting, it is like
there being buddhas made by humans, or humans who make buddhas:
there may be humans who make buddhas, but not all humans make buddhas, and buddhas are not all humans. Since all buddhas are not simply
all humans, a human is by no means a buddha, and a buddha is by no
means a human.[62] The seated buddha is also like this.

* * * * *

[12:37] {1:111}

南嶽・江西の師勝資強、かくのごとし。坐佛の、作佛を證する、江西これ
なり。作佛のために坐佛をしめす、南嶽これなり。南嶽の會に恁麼の功夫
あり、藥山の會に向來の道取あり。しるべし、佛佛祖祖の要機とせるは、
これ坐佛なりといふことを。すでに佛佛祖祖とあるは、この要機を使用せ
り。いまだしきは夢也未見在なるのみたり。おほよそ西天・東地に佛法つ
たはるるといふは、かならず坐佛のつたはるるなり。それ要機なるにより
てなり。佛法つたはれざるには、坐禪つたはれず、嫡嫡相承せるは、この
坐禪の宗旨のみなり。この宗旨、いまだ單傳せざるは、佛祖にあらざるな
り。この一法、あきらめざれば、萬法あきらめざるなり、萬行あきらめざ
るなり。法法あきらめざらんは、明眼といふべからず、得道にあらず、い

---

60 **Those who have never sat do not have these words** (*imada katsute za sezaru mono
ni, kono dō no aru ni arazu* いまだかつて坐セざるものに、この道のあるにあらず):
I.e., this could not have been said by those who have never engaged in seated meditation.
The antecedent of "these words" (*kono dō* この道) may be Nanyue's final line: "If you
grasp the mark of sitting, this is not reaching its principle." Alternatively, Dōgen may
well be referring here to the entire discussion on which he has been commenting.

sitting human (*taza nin* 打坐人): Though here and below in this paragraph, the glyph
nin 人 could be rendered "person" or "people" (*hito*), Dōgen is clearly contrasting buddhas with human beings (*ningen* 人間).

61 **The sitting of the human's mere sitting and reclining** (*tada, nin no zaga suru za*
ただ、人の坐臥する坐): I.e., our ordinary acts of sitting.

62 **a human is by no means a buddha, and a buddha is by no mean a human** (*nin,
kanarazu butsu ni arazu, butsu, kanarazu nin ni arazu* 人、かならず佛にあらず、佛、か
ならず人にあらず): Or, perhaps, "humans are not necessarily buddhas, and buddhas are
not necessarily humans." The stronger denial assumes that "human" here refers to ordinary
humans, who may sit but "have never sat."

308 DŌGEN'S *SHŌBŌGENZŌ* VOLUME I

かでか佛祖の今古ならん。ここをもて、佛祖かならず坐禪を單傳すると一
定すべし。

In this way are Nanyue and Jiangxi [a case of] "*the master is superior and the disciple strong.*"[63] The one who verifies that a "seated buddha" is "making a buddha" is Jiangxi; the one who shows the "seated buddha" for "making a buddha" is Nanyue. There was such concentrated effort in the community of Nanyue and words like the above in the community of Yaoshan.

We should know that what buddha after buddha and ancestor after ancestor have taken as their essential function is the "seated buddha." Those who are among buddha after buddha and ancestor after ancestor have employed this essential function; those who are not yet have *never seen it even in their dreams*. In general, to say that the buddha dharma has been transmitted from Sindh in the West to the Land of the East necessarily implies the transmission of the "seated buddha," for that is its essential function. Where the buddha dharma is not transmitted, neither is seated meditation. What has been inherited by successor after successor is just this essential point of seated meditation; those who do not participate in the unique transmission of this essential point are not buddhas or ancestors. When they are not clear about this one dharma, they are not clear about the myriad dharmas, they are not clear about the myriad practices. Without being clear about each of the dharmas, they cannot be said to have a clear eye. They have not gained the way; how could they represent the present or past of the buddhas and ancestors? By this, then, we should be firmly convinced that the buddhas and ancestors always uniquely transmit seated meditation.

[12:38]

佛祖の光明に照臨せらるるといふは、この坐禪を功夫參究するなり。おろ
かなるともがらは、佛光明をあやまりて、日月の光明のごとく、珠火の光
耀のごとくあらんずると、おもふ。日月光耀は、わづかに六道輪廻の業相
なり、さらに佛光明に比すべからず。佛光明といふは、一句を受持聽聞
し、一法を保任護持し、坐禪を單傳するなり。光明にてらさるるにおよば
されば、この保任なし、この信受なきなり。

To be illumined by the radiance of the buddhas and ancestors means to concentrate one's efforts in the investigation of this seated meditation. Some fools, misunderstanding the radiance of the buddha, think it must be like the radiance of the sun or moon or the light from a pearl or fire.[64]

---

63 **"the master is superior and the disciple strong"** (*shishō shikyō* 師勝資強): Also read *shishō shigō*. A fixed phrase in Zen texts, occurring twice in the *Shōbōgenzō*, for a capable teacher and able student.

64 **radiance of the buddha** (*butsu kōmyō* 佛光明): The nimbus, or aureola, said to emanate from the body of a buddha, often taken as symbol of the effulgence of his perfect wis-

12. Needle of Seated Meditation *Zazen shin* 坐禪箴 309

But the light of the sun and moon is nothing but a mark of karma within transmigration in the six paths; it is not to be compared with the radiance of the buddha.[65] The radiance of the buddha means receiving and hearing a single line, maintaining and protecting a single dharma, participating in the unique transmission of seated meditation. So long as we have not been illumined by the radiance, we lack this maintaining, we lack this faithfully receiving.

[12:39] {1:112}

しかあればすなはち、古來なりといへども、坐禪を坐禪なりとしれるすくなし。いま現在大宋國の諸山に、甲刹の主人とあるもの、坐禪をしらず、學せざるおほし。あきらめしれるありといへども、すくなし。諸寺にもとより坐禪の時節さだまれり。住持より諸僧、ともに坐禪するを本分の事とせり。學者を勸誘するにも、坐禪をすすむ。しかあれども、しれる住持人はまれなり。このゆゑに、古來より近代にいたるまで、坐禪銘を記せる老宿一兩位あり、坐禪儀を撰せる老宿一兩位あり、坐禪箴を記せる老宿一兩位あるなかに、坐禪銘、ともにとるべきところなし、坐禪儀、いまだその行履にくらし。坐禪をしらず、坐禪を單傳せざるともがらの記せるところなり。景德傳燈錄にある坐禪箴、および嘉泰普燈錄にあるところの坐禪銘等なり。

This being the case, from ancient times there have been few who understood seated meditation as seated meditation. And at present, at the various mountains of the Land of the Great Song, many of those who are heads of the principal monasteries do not understand, and do not study, seated meditation.[66] There may be those who have clearly understood it but not many. Of course, the monasteries have fixed periods for seated meditation; the monks, from the abbot down, take seated meditation as their basic task; and, in leading their students, they encourage seated meditation. Nevertheless, the abbots who understand it are rare. For this reason, although from ancient times to the present there have been one or two elders who have written an "Inscription on Seated Meditation," one

---

dom that illumines the world. In his "Shōbōgenzō kōmyō" 正法眼藏光明, devoted to this image, Dōgen identifies such radiance with the spiritual tradition of Bodhidharma and, as here, criticizes those who think of it as visible light. In this, he may have had in mind the mystical visualization of the buddha's radiance (*bukkō zanmai* 佛光三昧) popularized in Dōgen's day by the Japanese Kegon 華嚴 master Myōe Kōben 明慧高辨 (1173-1232).

65 **mark of karma within transmigration in the six paths** (*rokudō rinne no gōsō* 六道輪廻の業相): I.e., an expression of karma in the mundane world of the six states of rebirth; see Supplementary Notes, s.v. "Six paths."

66 **various mountains of the Land of the Great Song** (*Daisōkoku no shozan* 大宋國の諸山): I.e., the major Buddhist monasteries of Song-dynasty China.

principal monasteries (*kassetsu* 甲刹): I.e. the larger, more famous public institutions, known as "monasteries of the ten directions" (*jippō setsu* 十方刹); a rather unusual term, not occurring elsewhere in the *Shōbōgenzō*.

310 DŌGEN'S *SHŌBŌGENZŌ* VOLUME I

or two elders who have composed a "Principles of Seated Meditation," one or two elders who have written a "Needle of Seated Meditation," among them there is nothing worth taking from any "Inscription on Seated Meditation," and the "Principles of Seated Meditation" are ignorant of its conduct. They were written by those who do not understand, do not participate in, its unique transmission. Such are the *Needle of Seated Meditation* in the *Jingde Record of the Transmission of the Flame* and the *Inscription on Seated Meditation* in the *Jiatai Record of the Universal Flame*.[67]

[12:40]
あはれむべし、十方の叢林に經歴して一生をすごすといへども、一坐の功夫あらざることを。打坐すでになんぢにあらず、功夫さらにおのれと相見せざることを。これ坐禪の、おのが身心をきらふにあらず、眞箇の功夫をこころざさず、倉卒に迷醉せるによりてなり。かれらが所集は、ただ還源返本の樣子なり、いたづらに息慮凝寂の經營なり。觀練薫修の階級におよばず、十地・等覺の見解におよばず、いかでか佛佛祖祖の坐禪を單傳せん。宋朝の錄者、あやまりて錄せるなり、晩學、すててみるべからず。

What a pity that, though they may have spent their entire lives passing among the groves of the ten directions, they lack the concentrated effort of a single sitting — that sitting has never been you, and concentrated effort never meets you.[68] This is not because seated meditation rejects

---

67 *Needle of Seated Meditation* in the *Jingde Record of the Transmission of the Flame* (*Keitoku dentō roku ni aru Zazen shin* 景德傳燈錄にある坐禪箴): The *Jingde chuandeng lu* 景德傳燈錄, compiled in 1004, includes a *Zuochan zhen* 坐禪箴 by Wuyun Heshang 五雲和尚 (i.e., Wuyun Zhifeng 五雲志逢, 909-985) (T.2076.51:459c23-460a13).

Inscription on Seated Meditation in the *Jiatai Record of the Universal Flame* (*Katai futō roku ni aru tokoro no Zazen mei* 嘉泰普燈錄にあるところの坐禪銘): The *Jiatai pudeng lu* 嘉泰普燈錄, compiled in 1204, records a *Zuochan ming* 坐禪銘 by Longmen Foyan Yuan chanshi 龍門佛眼遠禪師 (i.e., Foyan Qingyuan 佛眼清遠, 1067-1120) (ZZ.137:427b2-16). Elsewhere, Dōgen also singles out for criticism the *Zuochan yi* 坐禪儀 of the Song-dynasty figure Changlu Zongze 長蘆宗賾 (dates unknown) (see the so-called "Fukan zazengi senjutsu yurai" 普勸坐禪儀撰述由來, DZZ.5:2).

68 **they may have spent their entire lives passing among the groves of the ten directions** (*jippō no sōrin ni kyōryaki shite isshō o sugosu* 十方の叢林に經歴して一生をすごす): I.e., one may have a lifelong career serving as abbot at major monasteries throughout China. Though not explicit, the reference would seem to be to the authors of the texts mentioned in the previous section. The translation here of *isshō* 一生 as "entire life" (rather than "single life") loses its artful balance with *ichiza* 一坐 ("single sitting") in the following clause.

sitting has never been you, and concentrated effort never meets you (*taza sude ni nanji ni arazu, kufū sara ni onore to shōken sezaru* 打坐すでになんぢにあらず、功夫さらにおのれと相見せざる): A tentative translation of an awkward passage, in which Dōgen rudely addresses his authors in the second person. Some take the point to be simply that they never properly sit and hence do not engage in true practice; some would prefer to read the second clause to mean that, in their practice, they never encounter

12. Needle of Seated Meditation *Zazen shin* 坐禪箴　　311

their bodies and minds but because they do not aspire to the true concentrated effort and are precipitately given over to their delusion. What
they have collected is nothing but models for *reverting to the source and
returning to the origin*, vain programs for *suspending considerations and
congealing in tranquility*.[69] They do not approach the stages of observation, exercise, infusion, and cultivation, or the understandings of the ten
stages and virtual awakening; how, then, could they represent the unique
transmission of the seated meditation of buddha after buddha and ancestor after ancestor?[70] The chroniclers of the Song court were mistaken to
record them, and later students should cast them aside and not read them.

[12:41] {1:113}
坐禪箴は、大宋國慶元府太白名山天童景德寺、宏智禪師正覺和尚の撰せる
のみ佛祖なり、坐禪箴なり、道得是なり。ひとり法界の表裏に光明なり、
古今の佛祖に佛祖なり。前佛後佛、この箴に箴せられもてゆき、今祖古
祖、この箴より現成するなり。かの坐禪箴は、すなはちこれなり。

Among the *Needles of Seated Meditation*, only that composed by
Reverend Zhengjue, Chan Master Hongzhi of the Jingde Monastery at
Tiantong, Renowned Mount Taibai, in the Prefecture of Qingyuan in
the Land of the Great Song, is by a buddha and ancestor, is a "needle of
seated meditation," has said it right.[71] It alone is a radiance throughout

---

themselves. Note that here and in the following sentence Dōgen has personified Zen
practice as a conscious agent that encounters and chooses us.

69　**reverting to the source and returning to the origin** (*gengen henpon* 還源返本):
More often in reverse order, *henpon gengen* 返本還源; an expression of Daoist origin
that found its way into Chinese Buddhist texts (see, e.g., *Xu gaoseng zhuan* 續高僧
傳, T.260.50:556c12-13). Both phrases suggest a model of spiritual practice, especially
meditation, as the process of recovering the original mind. Perhaps best known as the
title of the ninth of Kuoan's 廓庵 famous "Verses on the Ten Oxherding Pictures" (*Shi
niu tu song* 十牛圖頌); see Supplementary Notes, s.v. "Water buffalo."

suspending considerations and congealing in tranquility (*sokuryo gyōjaku* 息慮凝
寂): Two expressions suggesting calm transic states free from all thinking; a similar
expression, "suspending considerations and forgetting objects" (*xi lü wang yuan* 息慮忘
緣), appears in Wuyun's *Zuochan zhen* (T.2076.51:459c27), though the text itself also
warns against attachment to the cultivation of samādhi.

70　**observation, exercise, infusion, and cultivation** (*kan ren kun ju* 觀練薰修): A set
of terms, taken from the *Dazhidu lun* 大智度論, used especially in Tiantai 天台 systems for the stages of the "undefiled" (*muro* 無漏; S. *anāsrava*), or "transmundane"
(*shusseken* 出世間; S. *lokottara*), meditations (see, e.g., the *Fahua xuanyi* 妙法玄義,
T.1716.33:719b10-720a4).

ten stages and virtual awakening (*jitchi tōgaku* 十地・等覺): The final phases of the
bodhisattva path according to the fifty-two stage system popular in East Asian texts: the
ten "grounds" (S. *bhūmi*) and the penultimate state, just preceding, but virtually equivalent to, buddhahood.

71　**Reverend Zhengjue, Chan Master Hongzhi** (*Wanshi zenji Shōgaku oshō* 宏智禪師

312 DŌGEN'S *SHŌBŌGENZŌ* VOLUME I

the surface and interior of the dharma realm, is by a buddha and ancestor among the buddhas and ancestors of past and present. Prior buddhas and later buddhas have been probed by this *Needle*; present ancestors and past ancestors appear from this *Needle*.[72] Here is that *Needle of Seated Meditation*.[73]

* * * * *

[12:42]

坐禪箴

勅諡宏智禪師正覺撰

佛佛要機、祖祖機要'。不觸事而知、不對緣而照。不觸事而知、其知自微。不對緣而照、其照自妙。其知自微、曾無分別之思。其照自妙、曾無毫忽之兆。曾無分別之思、其知無偶而奇。曾無毫忽之兆、其照無取而了。水清徹底兮、魚行遲遲。空闊莫涯兮、鳥飛杳杳。

Needle of Seated Meditation

by Zhengjue, by imperial designation Chan Master Hongzhi

Essential function of buddha after buddha,
Functioning essence of ancestor after ancestor.
Knowing without touching things,
Illumining without facing objects.
Knowing without touching things,
The knowing inherently subtle.
Illumining without facing objects,
The illumining inherently mysterious.
The knowing inherently subtle,
Ever without discriminatory thought.
The illumining inherently mysterious,
Ever without a hair's breadth of sign.
Ever without discriminatory thought,
The knowing is rare without peer.
Ever without a hair's breadth of sign,

正覺和尚): Hongzhi Zhengjue 宏智正覺 (1091-1157), a leading figure of the Caodong 曹洞 lineage and former abbot of the Jingdesi 景德寺, where Dōgen studied with the Caodong master Tiantong Rujing 天童如淨. Zhengjue received his title, Zhengjue Chanshi 宏智禪師 ("Chan Master Spacious Wisdom") from the Song Emperor Gaozong 高宗 (r. 1127-1162).

72 **probed by this *Needle*** (*kono shin ni shin serare moteyuki* この箴に箴せられもてゆき): Playing on the sense of *shin* 箴 ("needle") as "admonition."

73 ***Needle of Seated Meditation*** (*Zazen shin* 坐禪箴): Hongzhi's *Zuochan zhen* appears in the *Hongzhi chanshi guanglu* 宏智禪師廣錄 (T.2001.48:98a29-b5).

12. Needle of Seated Meditation *Zazen shin* 坐禪箴 313

The illumining comprehends without grasping.
The water is clear right through to the bottom;
A fish goes lazily along.
The sky is vast without horizon;
A bird flies far far away.

[12:43]
いはゆる坐禪箴の箴は、大用現前なり、聲色向上威儀なり、父母未生前の
節目なり。莫謗佛祖好なり、未免喪身失命なり、頭長三尺頸長二寸なり。

The "needle" in this *Needle of Seated Meditation* is the manifestation
of the great function;[74] it is the "deportment beyond sound and form";[75]
it is the juncture *before your father and mother were born;*[76] it is *you'd
better not slander the buddhas and ancestors;*[77] it is *you can't help for-*

---

74 **manifestation of the great function** (*daiyū genzen* 大用現前): Dōgen begins here a
series of references to familiar expressions in Zen literature. "The great function" (*daiyū* 大
用; also read *daiyō*) is used especially for the actions of the Zen master; see Supplementary
Notes, s.v. "Manifestation of the great function."

75 **"deportment beyond sound and form"** (*shōshiki kōjō iigi* 聲色向上威儀): Variation on a phrase best known from a verse by Xiangyan Zhixian 香嚴智閑 recorded in
Dōgen's *shinji Shōbōgenzō* 眞字正法眼藏 (DZZ.5:134, case 17) and invoked elsewhere
in Dōgen's writings (see also *Liandeng huiyao* 聯燈會要, ZZ.136:566a8):

處處無蹤跡、聲色外威儀。
No traces wherever I go;
Deportment beyond sound and form.

See Supplementary Notes, s.v. "Deportment."

76 **before your father and mother were born** (*bumo mishō zen* 父母未生前): A common
expression in Zen literature; see Supplementary Notes, s.v. "Before your father and mother
were born." Given its proximity here to Zhixian's "deportment beyond sound and form,"
Dōgen may have had in mind the challenge to Zhixian by his master, Weishan Lingyou 潙
山靈祐 (771-853), that he try saying something "from the time before his father and mother were born" (*bumo mishō ji* 父母未生時) (*Liandeng huiyao* 聯燈會要, ZZ.136:565b15).
For a slightly different version of that encounter, in which Weishan asks Zhixian to say
something about "the time before you emerged from the womb" (*nyo mishutsu hōtai* 汝未
出胞胎), see Supplementary Notes, s.v. "A painted cake can't satisfy hunger."

77 **you'd better not slander the buddhas and ancestors** (*maku bō busso kō* 莫謗佛祖
好): Perhaps a variation on a remark of Guangxiao Huijue 光孝慧覺 (dates unknown) in
reference to his master, Zhaozhou Congshen 趙州從諗 (778-897) (*Liandeng huiyao* 聯
燈會要, ZZ.136:557a13-16):

師到崇壽。法眼問、近離甚處。師云、趙州。眼云、承聞趙州有柏樹子話、是
否。師云無。法眼云、往來皆謂、僧問如何是祖師西來意。州云、庭前柏樹子。
上座何得言無。師云、先師實無此語。和尚莫謗先師好。
The Master [Huijue] went to Chongshou [Cloister]. [The abbot] Fayan [Wenyi]
asked, "Where are you coming from?"
The Master said, "Zhaozhou."
Yan said, "I hear Zhaozhou has a saying about a cypress tree. Right?"

314   DŌGEN'S *SHŌBŌGENZŌ* VOLUME I

feiting your body and losing your life;[78] *it is a head of three feet and neck of two inches.*[79]

[12:44] {1:114}

佛佛要機。

"*Essential function of buddha after buddha.*"

[12:45]

佛佛はかならず佛佛を要機とせる、その要機現成せり、これ坐禪なり。

Buddha after buddha always takes "buddha after buddha" as the "essential function"; the manifestation of that "essential function" is "seated meditation."

[12:46]

祖祖機要。

"*Functioning essence of ancestor after ancestor.*"

[12:47]

先師無此語なり、この道理、これ祖祖なり。法傳・衣傳あり。おほよそ回頭換面の面面、これ佛佛の要機なり。換面回頭の頭頭、これ祖祖の機要なり。

"*My former master had no such words*" — this principle is "ancestor after ancestor."[80] They have the transmission of the dharma, the transmission of the robe.[81] In sum, face after face of "*turning the head and*

The Master said, "No."

Fayan said, "Everyone says that, when a monk asked the intention of the Ancestral Master's coming from the west, Zhou said, 'The cypress tree at the front of the garden.' How can the Senior Seat say, 'No.'"

The Master said, "My former master really had no such words. The Reverend had better not slander my former master."

78 **can't help forfeiting your body and losing your life** (*mimen sōshin shitsumyō* 未免喪身失命): See above, Note 32; here perhaps reflecting the words of Baofu Congzhan 保福從展 (d. 928) (*Liandeng huiyao* 聯燈會要, ZZ.136:835a17-18):

此事如擊石火、似閃電光。搆得搆不得、未免喪身失命。

This matter is like a spark from a flint, like a flash of lightening. Whether you get it or you don't get it, you can't help forfeiting your body and losing your life.

79 **a head of three feet and neck of two inches** (*zuchō sanjaku keichō nisun* 頭長三尺頸長二寸): Also written *keitan nisun* 頸短二寸. A saying attributed to Dongshan Liangjie 洞山良价 (807–869) in a number of Zen texts. The reference is to the physiognomy of an ox; see Supplementary Notes, s.v. "A head of three feet and a neck of two inches."

80 **"My former master had no such words"** (*senshi mu shi go* 先師無此語): Variation on the words of Guangxiao Huijue 光孝慧覺; see above, Note 77.

81 **the transmission of the dharma, the transmission of the robe** (*hōden eden* 法傳・衣傳): Reference to the bequest of the teaching and robe of Bodhidharma that marks the Zen ancestral lineage.

12. Needle of Seated Meditation *Zazen shin* 坐禪箴   315

changing the face" is the "*essential function of buddha after buddha*";
head after head of "*changing the face and turning the head*" is "*the functioning essence of ancestor after ancestor.*"

[12:48]
不觸事而知。

"*Knowing without touching things,*"

[12:49]
知は、覺知にあらず、覺知は小量なり。了知の知にあらず、了知は造作な
り。かるがゆえに、知は不觸事なり、不觸事は知なり。遍知と度量すべか
らず、自知と局量すべからず。その不觸事といふは、明頭來明頭打、暗頭
來暗頭打なり、坐破孃生皮なり。

"Knowing" is not perception: perception is of small measure. Recognition is not "knowing": recognition is constructed.[82] Therefore, this
"knowing" is "not touching things," and "not touching things" is "knowing." We should not gauge it as pervasive knowledge; we should not
reduce it to self-knowledge. This "not touching things" is "*When the
bright comes, the bright does it; when the dark comes, the dark does it.*"[83]
It is *sitting and breaking the skin born of mother.*[84]

[12:50]
不對緣而照。

"*Illumining without facing objects.*"

---

82   **perception** (*kakuchi* 覺知); **recognition** (*ryōchi* 了知): Although these two terms are
used in various senses, the translations take the former here as awareness of the data of
the six senses, the latter as "comprehension," or "understanding," of what is perceived
— the two phases of the epistemological process in much Buddhist explanation.

83   **"When the bright comes, the bright does it; when the dark comes, the dark
does it"** (*meitō rai meitō ta, antō rai antō ta* 明頭來明頭打、暗頭來暗頭打): A tentative
rendering of a vexed saying attributed to the Chan monk Puhua 普化 (dates unknown),
quoted in Dōgen's *shinji Shōbōgenzō* 眞字正法眼藏 (DZZ.5:136-138, case 22); see Supplementary Notes.

84   **sitting and breaking the skin born of mother** (*zaha jō shō hi* 坐破孃生皮): An
unusual expression not found elsewhere in Dōgen's writings. "The skin born of mother"
may be a truncated form of "the skin bag born of mother" (*jō shō hitaisu* 孃生皮袋子)
— i.e., this body; for the meaning of the metaphor and other examples of its usage, see
Supplementary Notes, s.v. "Bag of skin." In colloquial usage, the verb *zaha* 坐破 might
be read simply as "breaking" (reading *za* as in *zadan* 坐斷); the translation here treats it
in parallel with the common "sitting and breaking the meditation cushion" (*zaha futon*
坐破蒲團).

316 DŌGEN'S *SHŌBŌGENZŌ* VOLUME I

[12:51]

この照は、照了の照にあらず、靈照にあらず、不對緣を照とす。照の、緣
と化せざるあり、緣、これ照なるがゆえに。不對といふは、遍界不曾藏な
り、破界不出頭なり。微なり、妙なり、回互・不回互なり。

This "illumining" is not the "illumining" of "luminous comprehension" or of "spiritual illumination"; he takes "without facing objects"
as "illumining." "Illumining" does not change into the "object," for the
"object" itself is "illumining." "Without facing" means, "*in the realms
everywhere, it has never been hidden*"; *it does not emerge when you
break up the realms.*[85] It is "subtle"; it is "mysterious"; it is "*interacting
without interacting.*"[86]

[12:52]

其知自微、曾無分別之思。

"*The knowing inherently subtle,
Ever without discriminatory thought.*"

[12:53]

思の、知なる、かならずしも他力をからず。其知は形なり、形は山河な
り。この山河は微なり、この微は妙なり、使用するに活鱍鱍なり。龍を作
するに、禹門の内外にかかはれず。いまの一知わづかに使用するは、盡界
山河を拈來し、盡力して知するなり。山河の親切にわが知なくば、一知半
解あるべからず。分別思量の、おそく來到するとなげくべからず、已曾分
別なる佛佛、すでに現成しきたれり。曾無は已曾なり、已曾は現成なり。
しかあればすなはち、曾無分別は、不逢一人なり。

That "thought" is itself "knowing" is not necessarily dependent on the
power of the other: "its knowing" is its shape, and its shape is the mountains and rivers.[87] These mountains and rivers are "subtle"; this "subtle-
ty" is "mysterious." When we put it to use, it is brisk and lively.[88] When

---

85 **"in the realms everywhere, it has never been hidden"** (*henkai fu zō zō* 遍界不
曾藏): A popular saying attributed to Chan Master Shishuang Qingzhu 石霜慶諸 (807-
888); found in the *shinji Shōbōgenzō* 眞字正法眼藏 (DZZ.5:157-158, case 58). See Supplementary Notes.

it does not emerge when you break up the realms (*hakai fu shuttō* 破界不出頭): Probably meaning, "even if you break apart the entire world, you still can't find it." Though
the phrase is in Chinese like the other quotations and allusions in these comments, no
particular source has been identified.

86 **"interacting without interacting"** (*ego fuego* 回互・不回互): A phrase from the
Cantong qi 參同契, of Shitou Xiqian 石頭希遷, *Jingde chuandeng lu* 景德傳燈錄,
T.2076.51:459b10; usually interpreted to mean that [subject and object] are both inde-
pendent and interdependent.

87 **the power of the other** (*tariki* 他力): Probably to be understood here as the object
of the thought.

88 **brisk and lively** (*kappatsupatsu* 活鱍鱍): A loose translation of a Chinese idiom ex-

12. Needle of Seated Meditation *Zazen shin* 坐禪箴 317

we become a dragon, it does not matter whether we are inside or outside of the Yu Gate.[89] To put this single "knowing" to the slightest use is to take up the mountains and rivers of all the worlds and "know" them with all one's power. Without our "knowing" intimately the mountains and rivers, we cannot have a single knowledge and a half understanding.[90] We should not lament that "discriminatory" thinking comes later: every buddha who has previously discriminated has already appeared.[91] "Ever without" is "previously"; "previously" is "appeared." Therefore, "ever without discrimination" is "*you don't meet a single person.*"[92]

[12:54] {1:115}
其照自妙、曾無毫忽之兆。

"The illumining inherently mysterious,
Ever without a hair's breadth of sign."

[12:55]
毫忽といふは、盡界なり。しかあるに、自妙なり、自照なり。このゆえ
に、いまだ將來せざるがごとし。目をあやしむことなかれ、耳を信ずべか

---

pressing the quick, powerful movements of a fish; see Supplementary Notes, s.v. "Brisk and lively."

89   **Yu Gate** (*Umon* 禹門): I.e., Longmen (in present-day Shansi Province), the rapids on the Yellow River beyond which the climbing carp is said to change into a dragon; here, likely taken as a metaphor for the point of awakening.

90   **a single knowledge and a half understanding** (*itchi hange* 一知半解): A set phrase for little or shallow knowledge.

91   **every buddha who has previously discriminated** (*izō funbetsu naru butsubutsu* 已曾分別なる佛佛): This passage is particularly murky, and the translation here loses something of Dōgen's play on Hongzhi's line, "Ever without discriminatory thought" (*sō mu funbetsu shi shi* 曾無分別之思). He appears to be reading the line as something like, "thought never discriminating," against which he balances his own "buddhas previously discriminating." While the term *funbetsu* 分別 ("discrimination") typically carries a negative connotation, as in Hongzhi's line, Dōgen seems here to be using it in reference to the buddha's power to discern things as they really are. On this reading, the argument of this section might look something like the following:

> The "subtle knowing" of the buddhas clearly discriminates all phenomena (the "mountains and rivers"). We should not think that this (higher) "discriminatory thinking" is something for which we must wait; it has "already appeared" in each mind's inherent power of discrimination ("every buddha who has previously discriminated"). Zhengjue's "ever without [discriminatory thought]" here refers to this inherent power, which "appears" even in ordinary perception. The spiritual practice of one who understands this is free to travel Dongshan's "path of the bird" (where "you don't meet a single person").

92   **"you don't meet a single person"** (*fuhō ichinin* 不逢一人): The words of Dongshan Liangjie 洞山良价, when asked to define his "path of the bird" (*chōdō* 鳥道); see Supplementary Notes, s.v. "Dongshan's three roads." Dōgen will draw again below on other lines of this conversation.

318　DŌGEN'S *SHŌBŌGENZŌ* VOLUME I

らず。直須旨外明宗、莫向言中取則なるは照なり。このゆえに無偶なり、
このゆえに無取なり。これを奇なりと住持しきたり、了なりと保任しきた
るに、我却疑著なり。

"A hair's breadth" here means all the worlds. Yet it is "inherently mysterious"; it is inherently "illumining." Therefore, it is as if it has never been brought out.[93] The eyes are not to be doubted; we should not trust the ears. *"Clarify the meaning apart from the sense; don't take the norm from within the words"* — this is "illumining."[94] Therefore, it is "without peer"; therefore, it is "without grasping."[95] This has been upheld as "rare" and maintained as "comprehending," but *I still have my doubts about it.*[96]

[12:56]

水清徹底分、魚行遲遲。

"*The water is clear right through to the bottom;*
A fish goes lazily along."

[12:57]

水清といふは、空にかかれる水は清水に不徹底なり。いはんや器界に泓澄
する水清の水にあらず、邊際に涯岸なき、これを徹底の清水とす。魚もし
この水をゆくは、行なきにあらず。行はいく萬程となくすすむといへど

93　**it is as if it has never been brought out** (*imada shōrai sezaru ga gotoshi* いまだ將
來せざるがごとし): Possibly reflecting the topic of case 57 of Hongzhi's *Congrong lu*
從容錄 (T.2004.48:263a24):

一物不將來時如何。

How about when not a single thing has been brought out?

94　**"Clarify the meaning apart from the sense; don't take the norm from within the
words"** (*jikishu shigai myō shū, maku kō gonchū shu soku* 直須旨外明宗、莫向言中取
則): A saying attributed to Luopu Yuan'an 洛浦元安 (834–898) in Wansong Xingxiu's
萬松行秀 (1166–1246) commentary on case 41 of the *Congrong Hermitage Record*
(*Congrong lu* 從容錄, T.2004.48:254a25-26). See Supplementary Notes, s.v. "Clarify
the meaning apart from the sense; don't take the norm from within the words."

95　**"without peer"** (*mugu* 無偶); **"without grasping"** (*mushu* 無取): Dōgen here introduces terms from the fourth quatrain of Hongzhi's verse that he does not bother to
repeat in full:

曾無分別之思、其知無偶而奇。曾無毫忽之兆、其照無取而了。

Ever without discriminatory thought,
The knowing is rare without peer.
Ever without a hair's breadth of sign,
The illumining comprehends without grasping.

96　**"without peer"** (*mugū* 無偶); **"rare"** (*ki* 奇): The translation masks the play in
Hongzhi's verse on "odd" (*ki* 奇) and "even" (*gū* 偶) numbers; hence the additional
sense, "its knowing is singular, not dual."

I still have my doubts about it (*ga kyaku gijaku* 我却疑著): Dōgen switches here to
Chinese. His doubts may be taken in the sense, "there is more to this than meets the eye."

12. Needle of Seated Meditation *Zazen shin* 坐禪箴   319

も、不測なり、不窮なり。はかる岸なし、うかむ空なし、しづむそこなき
がゆえに、測度するたれなし。測度を論ぜんとすれば、徹底の清水のみな
り。坐禪の功德、かの魚行のごとし、千程萬程、たれか卜度せん。徹底の
行程は、擧體の不行鳥道なり。

"The water is clear" means that the water that rests in space does not
get "right through to the bottom" of "clear water"; still less is that which
forms clear, deep pools in the vessel world the "water" of "the water
is clear."[97] Having no shore as its boundary — this is what is meant by
"clear water" "right through to the bottom." If a "fish" goes through this
"water," it is not that it does not "go"; yet, however many myriads the
degree of its progress, its "going" is incalculable, inexhaustible. There is
no shoreline by which it is gauged; there is no sky to which it floats, nor
bottom to which it sinks. And, therefore, there is no one who can take its
measure. If we try to discuss its measure, it is only "clear water" "right
through to the bottom." The virtue of seated meditation is like the "fish
going": who can calculate its degree in thousands or tens of thousands?
The degree of the "going" "right through to the bottom" is the body as a
whole does not "go" on "the path of the bird."[98]

[12:58] {1:116}
空闊莫涯兮、鳥飛杳杳。

"*The sky is vast, without horizon;
A bird flies far far away.*"

[12:59]
空闊といふは、天にかかれるにあらず、天にかかれる空は、闊空にあら
ず、いはんや彼此に普遍なるは闊空にあらず、隱顯に表裏なき、これを闊
空といふ。とり、もしこの空をとぶは、飛空の一法なり。飛空の行履、は
かるべきにあらず。飛空は盡界なり、盡界飛空なるゆえに。この飛、いく
そばくといふことしらずといへども、卜度のほかの道取を道取するに、杳
杳と道取するなり。直須足下無糸去なり。空の飛去するとき、鳥も飛去す
るなり。鳥の飛去するに、空も飛去するなり。飛去を參究する道取にいは
く、只在這裏なり。これ兀兀地の箴なり。いく萬程か只在這裏をきほひい
ふ。

---

97 **the water that rests in space does not get "right through to the bottom" of "clear
water"** (*kū ni kakareru mizu wa seisui ni futettei nari* 空にかかれる水は清水に不徹底
なり): Dōgen is taking advantage here of the term *tettei* 徹底 in Hongzhi's verse, which
conveys both a literal and a figurative sense of "getting to the bottom" of something. By
"the water that rests in space," Dōgen is likely thinking of the primary element water,
understood in Buddhist cosmology as resting on the wheel of space (*kūrin* 空輪).

the vessel world (*kikai* 器界; S. *bhājana-loka*): The natural world, seen as the container
of sentient beings.

98 **the body as a whole does not "go" on "the path of the bird"** (*kotai no fukō chōdō*
擧體の不行鳥道): Variation on Dongshan's remark that the original face "does not go on
the path of the bird." See above, Note 92.

320 DŌGEN'S *SHŌBŌGENZŌ* VOLUME I

"The sky is vast" does not refer to what hangs in the heavens: the "sky" that hangs in the heavens is not the "vast sky"; still less is that which extends everywhere here and there the "vast sky." Without surface or interior either hidden or manifest — this is what is meant by the "vast sky." When the "bird" flies this sky, it is the single dharma of "flying" the "sky." This conduct of "flying" the "sky" is not to be measured: "flying" the "sky" is all the worlds; for it is *all the worlds* "flying" *the* "sky." Although we do not know how far this "flying" goes, to express what is beyond our calculations, we call it "far far away." It is "*you should go without a string at your feet.*"[99] When the "sky" flies off, the "bird" flies off; when the "bird" flies off, the "sky" flies off. In an expression of the investigation of this flying off, it is said, "*they're right here.*"[100] This is the needle of sitting fixedly. How many myriad degrees vie to express "*they're right here*"?

[12:60]

宏智禪師の坐禪箴、かくのごとし。諸代の老宿のなかに、いまだいまのごとくの坐禪箴あらず。諸方の臭皮袋、もしこの坐禪箴のごとく道取せしめんに、一生・二生のちからをつくすとも、道取せんことうべからざるなり。いま諸方にみえず、ひとりこの箴のみあるなり。

Such, then, is the *Needle of Seated Meditation* of Chan Master Hongzhi. Among the elders throughout the generations, there has never been another "Needle of Seated Meditation" like this one. If the stinking skin bags throughout all quarters were to attempt to express a "Needle of Seated Meditation" like this one, they could not do so though they exhaust the efforts of a lifetime or two.[101] This is the only "Needle" in any quarter; there is no other to be found.

---

99 **"you should go without a string at your feet"** (*jikishu sokka mu shi ko* 直須足下無糸去): From Dongshan's explanation of how one is to follow his "path of the bird"; see above, Note 92. Perhaps reflecting the simile that training the mind to concentrate is like training a bird to sit on your shoulder by tying a string to its foot.

100 **"they're right here"** (*shi zai shari* 只在這裏): From a conversation between the Tang-dynasty masters Baizhang Huaihai 百丈懷海 (749-814) and Mazu Daoyi 馬祖道一 over a passing flock of wild geese. (See, e.g., *Zongmen tongyao ji* 宗門統要集, ZTS.1:56d2-6; *shinji Shōbōgenzō* 眞字正法眼藏, DZZ.5:218, case 182.) When Mazu asked where the birds were going, Baizhang said they had flown away. Mazu twisted Baizhang's nose and said,

又道飛過去、元來只在這裏。

"You say they've flown away, but they've been right here all along."

101 **stinking skin bags** (*shū hitai* 臭皮袋): A common term for the body, especially of humans; often used by Dōgen in reference to Chan monks. For the meaning of the metaphor and other examples of its usage, see Supplementary Notes, s.v. "Bag of skin."

12. Needle of Seated Meditation *Zazen shin* 坐禪箴   321

[12:61]

先師上堂のとき、よのつねにいはく、宏智古佛、なり。自餘の漢を恁麼い
ふこと、すべてなかりき。知人の眼目あらんとき、佛祖をも知音すべきな
り。まことにしりぬ、洞山に佛祖あることを。いま、宏智禪師よりのち八
十餘年なり。かの坐禪箴をみて、この坐禪箴を撰す。いま仁治三年壬寅三
月十八日なり。今年より紹興二十七年十月八日にいたるまで、前後を算數
するに、わづかに八十五年なり。いま撰する坐禪箴、これなり。

In his convocations, my former master always said, "Old Buddha
Hongzhi."[102] He never said this about any other person. When one has
the eye to know a person, he will also know the music of the buddhas
and ancestors.[103] Truly, we know that there are buddhas and ancestors
under Dongshan.[104] Now, some eighty years and more since Chan Master Hongzhi, reading his *Needle of Seated Meditation*, I compose this
Needle of Seated Meditation. It is now the eighteenth day of the third
month of the senior water year of the tiger, the third year of Ninji; if we
calculate back from this year to the eighth day of the tenth month in the
twenty-seventh year of Shaoxing, there are just eighty-five years.[105] The
Needle of Seated Meditation I now compose is as follows.

---

102   **convocations** (*jōdō* 上堂): I.e., formal addresses in the dharma hall to the assembled community.

my former master (*senshi* 先師): I.e., Tiantong Rujing 天童如淨.

"Old Buddha Hongzhi" (*Wanshi kobutsu* 宏智古佛): Dōgen repeats this claim in his
"Shōbōgenzō ō saku sendaba" 正法眼藏王索仙陀婆; in the context there, it seems clear
that he had in mind in particular a remark recorded in the *Rujing heshang yulu* 如淨和
尚語錄 (T.2002A.48:127a25). Hongzhi, of course, had been the most famous abbot of
Rujing's Tiantong 天童 Monastery.

103   **know the music of the buddhas and ancestors** (*busso o mo chi in su beki* 佛祖
をも知音すべき): The translation tries to preserve the etymological sense of this expression meaning "to know another's true heart," "to be a true friend"; from the ancient
Chinese story of Zhong Zi Qi 鍾子期, who is said to have known the state of mind of his
friend Bo Ya 伯牙 from the sound of his music. See Supplementary Notes, s.v. "Knowing
the music."

104   **there are buddhas and ancestors under Dongshan** (*Tōzan ni busso aru* 洞山に
佛祖ある): Hongzhi, like Rujing (and, of course, Dōgen), belonged to the Caodong 曹洞
lineage descended from the Tang-dynasty master Dongshan Liangjie 洞山良价.

105   **It is now the eighteenth day of the third month of the senior water year of the
tiger, the third year of Ninji** (*ima Ninji sannen mizunoe-tora sangatsu jūhachinichi
nari* いま仁治三年壬寅三月十八日なり): I.e., 19 April 1242, in the Gregorian calendar.
"The eighth day of the tenth month in the twenty-seventh year of Shaoxing" (*Shōkō
nijūshichinen jūgatsu yōka* 紹興二十七年十月八日) refers to the date of Honzhi's death,
11 November 1157.

322   DŌGEN'S *SHŌBŌGENZŌ* VOLUME I

[12:62] {1:117}

坐禪箴

佛佛要機、祖祖機要。不思量而現、不回互而成。不思量而現、其現自親。
不回互而成、其成自證。其現自親、曾無染汙。其成自證、曾無正偏。曾無
染汙之親、其親無委而脱落。曾無正偏之證、其證無圖而功夫。水清徹地
分、魚行似魚。空闊透天分、鳥飛如鳥。

Needle of Seated Meditation

Essential function of buddha after buddha,
Functioning essence of ancestor after ancestor.
Present without thinking,
Completed without interacting.[106]
Present without thinking,
The presence is inherently intimate.
Completed without interacting,
The completion is inherently verified.[107]
The presence inherently intimate,
Ever without stain or defilement;
The completion inherently verified,
Ever without upright or inclined.[108]
Intimacy ever without stain or defilement,
The intimacy sloughs off without discarding;

---

106   **Present** (*gen* 現); **Completed** (*jō* 成): The two elements in the compound *genjō* 現成, meaning "realization," "appearance," "manifestation," etc.

without thinking (*fushiryō* 不思量): Recalling Yaoshan's words quoted in the opening section, above:

> 思量箇不思量底。
>
> I'm thinking of not thinking.

without interacting (*fuego* 不回互): Recalling the line from the *Cantong qi* 參同契 evoked above, section 53.

107   **intimate** (*shin* 親); **verified** (*shō* 證): From the common Buddhist term, *shinshō* 親證, "intimate verification (or realization)."

108   **stain or defilement** (*zenna* 染汙): A standard Buddhist compound term for what is spiritually "defiled" (S. *kliṣṭa*); best known in Dōgen's writings from the saying of Nanyue Huairang 南嶽懷讓 (*shinji Shōbōgenzō* 眞字正法眼藏, DZZ.5:178, case 101):

> 修證即不無、染汙即不得
>
> "It's not that it lacks practice and verification, but it can't be defiled by them."

See Supplementary Notes, s.v. "Not defiled."

upright or inclined (*shōhen* 正偏): Terms for "absolute" and "relative," respectively, used in the famous schema of five ranks (*wu wei* 五位) developed especially in the Caodong tradition (on which Hongzhi wrote an appreciative verse: *Hongzhi chanshi guanglu* 宏智禪師廣錄, T.2001.48:99a5ff); see Supplementary Notes, s.v. "Upright or inclined."

12. Needle of Seated Meditation *Zazen shin* 坐禪箴

Verification ever without upright or inclined,
The verification makes effort without figuring.[109]
The water is clear right through the earth;
A fish goes along like a fish.
The sky is vast straight into the heavens,
A bird flies just like a bird.

[12:63]

宏智禪師の坐禪箴、それ道未是にあらざれども、さらにかくのごとく道取すべきなり。おほよそ佛祖の兒孫、かならず坐禪を一大事なりと參學すべし。これ單傳の正印なり。

It is not that the *Needle of Seated Meditation* by Chan Master Hongzhi has not yet said it right, but we can go on to say it like this. Above all, descendants of the buddhas and ancestors should study seated meditation as the one great matter. This is the orthodox seal of the unique transmission.

{1:118}

正法眼藏坐禪箴第十二

Treasury of the True Dharma Eye
Needle of Seated Meditation
Number 12

[Honzan edition:][110]

仁治三年壬寅三月十八日、記興聖寶林寺

Recorded at Kōshō Hōrin Monastery; on the eighteenth day, third month of the senior water year of the tiger, third year of Ninji [19 April 1242]

同四年癸卯冬十一月、在越州吉田縣吉峰精舍示衆

Presented to the assembly at Kippō Vihāra, Yoshida District, Esshū; in the eleventh month, winter of the junior water year of the rabbit, fourth year of the same [era] [13 December 1243-11 January 1244]

---

109 **without figuring** (*muzu* 無圖): No doubt reflecting the conversaton between Nanyue 南嶽 and Mazu 馬祖 on "figuring to make a buddha" (*zu sabutsu* 圖作佛) discussed above in sections 9ff.

110 These colophons are not found in the early MSS of the *Shōbōgenzō*. They are supplied in Kawamura's edition from the Honzan edition. The first colophon here is no doubt based on the date given in section 61 of the text; the second is nearly identical to Dōgen's colophon for the "Zazen gi" 坐禪儀 chapter.

TREASURY OF THE TRUE DHARMA EYE
NUMBER 13

Ocean Seal Samādhi
Kaiin zanmai
海印三昧

Ocean Seal Samādhi

Kaiin zanmai

INTRODUCTION

This chapter of the *Shōbōgenzō* was composed at Dōgen's Kōshōji, in 1242, a year perhaps the most productive in its author's career. It occurs as number 13 in the seventy-five and sixty-chapter compilations and as number 31 in the Honzan edition.

The essay takes its name from a state of concentration, known in Sanskrit sources as the *sāgara-mudrā-samādhi*. In this state, likened to an ocean on which appear images of the forms of all things, it is said that the bodhisattva can see the mental activities of all beings or, more generally, can discern all phenomena (dharmas) in detail. The samādhi is often, though not exclusively, associated with the tradition of the *Avataṃsaka Sūtra*, which is said to have been taught while the Buddha was absorbed in this state.

Dōgen's piece represents a commentary on two texts. The first, which occupies him for some two thirds of his work, is a passage from the *Vimalakīrti Sūtra*, with a comment by the famous Tang-dynasty Chan master Mazu Daoyi 馬祖道一. The sūtra tells how the bodhisattva should regard his body as merely the combination of dharmas arising and ceasing. In his comment, Mazu says that in fact the dharmas occur in each moment without relation to each other, a condition he identifies as the ocean seal samādhi. The second text is a teaching on the ocean by the Tang figure, Caoshan Benji 曹山本寂, one of the founding ancestors of Dōgen's Sōtō lineage.

Dōgen's commentary takes up almost every word in these texts, playing with their interpretation and glossing them with cryptic allusions to the sayings and poems of the Chan masters. In the process, as is often the case in his writings, he seeks at once to lift the language of his texts to a more mysterious metaphysical plane and to ground the metaphysics in the spiritual practice of the buddhas and ancestors of his tradition.

正法眼藏第十三
Treasury of the True Dharma Eye
Number 13
海印三昧
Ocean Seal Samādhi

[13:1] {1:119}

諸佛諸祖とあるに、かならず海印三昧なり。この三昧の游泳に、説時あり、證時あり、行時あり。海上行の功徳、その徹底行あり。これを深深海底行なりと海上行するなり。流浪生死を還源せしめんと願求する、是什麼心行にはあらず。從來の透關破節、もとより諸佛諸祖の面面なりといへども、これ海印三昧の朝宗なり。

To exist as the buddhas and the ancestors do is invariably the ocean seal samādhi.[1] As they swim in this samādhi, they have a time to teach, a time to verify, a time to practice.[2] Among the virtues of their walking on the ocean is a walk that gets to its bottom: it is their walking on the ocean in which they take this as *"walking the floor of the deepest ocean."*[3] Their aspiring to return to the source of our drifting about in birth and death is not a case of *"what are you thinking?"*[4] While, of course, their previous

---

1 **To exist as the buddhas and the ancestors do** (*shobutsu shoso to aru ni* 諸佛諸祖とあるに): Somewhat unusual phrasing, which might also be taken to mean, "where there are those who exist as buddhas and ancestors."

2 **a time to teach, a time to verify, a time to practice** (*setsuji ari, shōji ari, gyōji ari* 説時あり、證時あり、行時あり): Suggesting the phases (in reverse order) of the buddhas' and ancestors' career of practice, awakening, and teaching. The translation of *gyō* 行 here as "practice" masks Dōgen's play with the glyph used in the sense "to go" or "to walk" in the following sentence.

3 **walking on the ocean** (*kaijō kō* 海上行): Dōgen is here playing on Yaoshan's phrase *kaitei kō* ("walking on the bottom of the ocean") that he will quote just below.

walk that gets to its bottom (*tettei kō* 徹底行): Punning on the term *tettei* 徹底 ("thorough," "complete," "exhaustive"; literally, "penetrate to the bottom").

they take this as "walking the floor of the deepest ocean" (*kore o jinjin kaitei kō nari to* これを深深海底行なりと): I.e., the buddhas and ancestors take this walking on the ocean as the saying attributed to Yaoshan Weiyan 藥山惟儼 (751-834) (*Jingde chuandeng lu* 景德傳燈錄, T.2076.51:440c13):

須向高高山頂立、深深海底行。

"We should stand atop the highest peak, walk the floor of the deepest ocean."

4 **"what are you thinking?"** (*ze jūmo shingyō* 是什麼心行): Literally, "what mental act is this?"; a standard Zen retort to an inadequate statement (that also uses the glyph *gyō* 行).

328   DŌGEN'S *SHŌBŌGENZŌ* VOLUME I

acts of passing through the barriers and breaking down the sections were by the individual buddhas and ancestors, they are merged in the ocean seal samādhi.[5]

[13:2]

佛言、但以衆法、合成此身。起時唯法起、滅時唯法滅。此法起時、不言我起、此法滅時、不言我滅。前念後念、念念不相待、前法後法、法法不相對。是即名爲海印三昧。

> The Buddha said,[6]
>
> It is just the dharmas that combine to form this body. When they arise, it is simply the dharmas arising; when they cease, it is simply the dharmas ceasing. When these dharmas arise, they do not state, "I arise"; when these dharmas cease, they do not state, "I cease."
>
> In prior thoughts and subsequent thoughts, the thoughts are not relative to each other; in prior dharmas and subsequent dharmas, the dharmas are not opposed to each other. This is called the "ocean seal samādhi."[7]

---

5 **passing through the barriers and breaking down the sections** (*tōkan hasetsu* 透關破節): To "pass the barrier" is a common Zen expression for understanding, as in the phrase, "the eye that passes through the barrier" (*tōkan gen* 透關眼); elsewhere, Dōgen also uses the variant "to assault the barriers and break down the sections" (*gyakukan hasetsu* 擊關破節).

merged in the ocean seal samādhi (*kaiin zanmai no chōsō* 海印三昧の朝宗): "Merged" represents a loose translation of a term that has the primary sense "to attend court" (i.e., by multiple lords coming together before the emperor) but is regularly used in reference to rivers flowing into the ocean. It is also possible to read this phrase, "they are the merging of the ocean seal samādhi."

6 **The Buddha said** (*butsu gon* 佛言): The attribution to the Buddha here is misleading, since this text is taken, not from the words of the Buddha, but from the teachings of Mazu Daoyi 馬祖道一 (709-788) (see, e.g., *Liandeng huiyao* 聯燈會要, ZZ.136:487a3-6; *Tiansheng guangdeng lu* 天聖廣燈錄, ZZ.135:652a17-b2). The first part of the text represents Mazu's (slightly abbreviated) quotation of the *Vimalakīrti Sūtra* (*Weimo jing* 維摩經, T.475.14:545a), in which Vimalakīrti is instructing Bodhisattva Mañjuśrī on how a sick bodhisattva should regard his body. The second part is Mazu's comment on the sūtra passage.

7 **In prior thoughts and subsequent thoughts** (*zennen gonen* 前念後念): No source for Dōgen's version of Mazu's comment here has been identified. The text in the *Liandeng huiyao* 聯燈會要 (ZZ.136:487a4-6), which is fairly close to other extant versions, reads:

> 前念後念、念念不相待、念念寂滅。喚作海印三昧。攝一切法、如百千異流、同歸大海。
>
> In prior thoughts and subsequent thoughts, when the thoughts are not relative to each other, the thoughts become quiescent. This is called the "ocean seal samādhi." It takes in all the dharmas, just as the hundred thousand different streams all return to the great ocean.

13. Ocean Seal Samādhi: *Kaiin zanmai* 海印三昧   329

[13:3] {1:120}

この佛道、くはしく參學功夫すべし。得道入證は、かならずしも多聞によ
らず、他語によらざるなり。多聞の廣學は、さらに四句に得道し、恒沙の
徧學、つひに一句偈に證入するなり。いはんやいまの道は、本覺を前途に
もとむるにあらず、始覺を證中に拈來するにあらず。おほよそ、本覺等を
現成せしむるは佛祖の功德なりといへども、始覺・本覺等の諸覺を佛祖と
せるにはあらざるなり。

These words of the Buddha, we should make concentrated effort to
study closely. Gaining the way and entering verification do not necessarily depend on much hearing, do not depend on many words.[8] Those
with the broad learning of much hearing will go on to gain the way
through four lines; those with the universal learning equal to the sands
of the Ganges will eventually enter verification through a gāthā of a
single line.[9] Needless to say, then, the present words do not seek original
awakening on the road ahead and do not take up initial awakening within
verification. Generally speaking, while it may be a virtue of the buddhas
and ancestors that they manifest original awakening and so on, it is not
the case that the awakenings of initial awakening, original awakening,
and so on, are taken as the buddhas and ancestors.[10]

---

8 **Gaining the way and entering verification** (*tokudō nisshō* 得道入證): An unusual
phrase not encountered elsewhere in Dōgen's writings. The translation treats *nisshō* 入
證 here and the more familiar *shōnyū* 證入 in the next sentence as synonyms, meaning
"to realize [awakening]."

do not depend on many words (*tago ni yorazu* 他語によらざる): The translation follows those texts that read *tago* 多語 ("many words") here; Kawamura's text would yield
"do not depend on those words" (or "do not depend on others' words").

9 **much hearing** (*tamon* 多聞): I.e., much learning.

four lines (*shiku* 四句): Though a term regularly used to translate the Sanskrit *catuṣkoṭi*
("four propositions," "tetralemma"), here probably indicating a verse of four lines (S.
catuṣ-pādikā-gāthā), in parallel with the following "one-line gāthā" (*ikku ge* 一句偈).
Elsewhere in the *Shōbōgenzō*, Dōgen refers to the famous *Verse of Impermanence*
(*Mujō ge* 無常偈) from the story in the *Nirvāṇa Sūtra* (*Da banniepan jing* 大般涅槃經,
T.374.12:449b8ff), in which Buddha Śākyamuni in a previous life received a four-line
verse from a *rākṣasa* ("hungry demon"):

諸行無常、是生滅法、生滅滅已、寂滅爲樂。
All things are impermanent:
This is the law of arising and ceasing.
When the arising and ceasing have ceased,
Their cessation is ease.

See Supplementary Notes, s.v. "Whether on trees or on rocks."

10 **original awakening** (*hongaku* 本覺); **initial awakening** (*shikaku* 始覺): Terms
widely used in East Asian Buddhism to distinguish respectively the bodhi inherent in the
buddha nature and the bodhi attained at the end of the bodhisattva path.

330   DŌGEN'S *SHŌBŌGENZŌ* VOLUME I

[13:4]

佛言、但以衆法、合成此身。起時唯法起、滅時唯法滅。此法起時、不言我起、此法滅時、不言我滅。前念後念、念念不相待。前法後法、法法不相對。是即名爲海印三昧。

> The Buddha said,[11]
>> It is just the dharmas that combine to form this body. When they arise, it is simply the dharmas arising; when they cease, it is simply the dharmas ceasing. When these dharmas arise, they do not state, "I arise"; when these dharmas cease, they do not state, "I cease."
>
> In prior thoughts and subsequent thoughts, the thoughts are not relative to each other; in prior dharmas and subsequent dharmas, the dharmas are not opposed to each other. This is called the ocean seal samādhi.

[13:5]

いはゆる海印三昧の時節は、すなはち但以衆法の時節なり、但以衆法の道得なり。このときを合成此身といふ。衆法を合成せる一合相、すなはち此身なり。此身を一合相とせるにあらず、衆法合成なり。合成此身を此身と道得せるなり。

The time of the ocean seal samādhi is the time of "*just the dharmas*," is the saying of "*just the dharmas*." This time is called "*combine to form this body*." The single conglomerate that has "combined to form" "the dharmas" is "this body." This does not mean that "this body" is taken as a single conglomerate: "*the dharmas*" "*combine to form*" it. It says that "*combine to form this body*" is "this body."

[13:6]

起時唯法起。この法起、かつて起をのこすにあらず。このゆえに、起は知覺にあらず、知見にあらず、これを不言我起といふ。我起を不言するに、別人は此法起と見聞覺知し、思量分別するにはあらず。さらに向上の相見のとき、まさに相見の落便宜あるなり。

"*When they arise, it is simply the dharmas arising.*" This "dharmas arising" never leaves behind arising.[12] Therefore, its arising is not perception, is not knowledge.[13] This is called "*do not state, 'I arise.'*" When

---

11 **Buddha said** (*butsu gon* 佛言): A repetition of the quotation in section 2; missing from some MS witnesses, especially in the sixty-chapter compilation.

12 **never leaves behind arising** (*katsute ki o nokosu ni arazu* かつて起をのこすにあらず): Perhaps meaning that each instance of arising is complete in itself and does not leave behind some arisen "thing" that could be the object of knowledge.

13 **is not perception, is not knowledge** (*chikaku ni arazu, chiken ni arazu* 知覺にあらず、知見にあらず): Presumably, meaning that we do not perceive, do not know, the dharmas. In fact, in traditional scholastic Buddhist epistemology, the momentary occurrence of the individual dharmas is not directly perceived by consciousness.

13. Ocean Seal Samādhi *Kaiin zanmai* 海印三昧 331

they "do not state" that "I arise," this does not mean that someone else sees, hears, perceives, and knows "these dharmas arising" or discriminates them in thinking. When there is a further encounter beyond, one loses the advantage of the encounter.[14]

[13:7]

起はかならず時節到來なり、時は起なるがゆえに。いかならんかこれ起なる、起也なるべし。すでにこれ時なる起なり、皮肉骨髓を獨露せしめずといふことなし。起すなはち合成の起なるがゆえに、起の此身なる、起の我起なる、但以衆法なり。聲色と見聞するのみにあらず、我起なる衆法なり、不言なる我起なり。不言は不道にはあらず、道得は言得にあらざるがゆえに。起時は此法なり、十二時にあらず。此法は起時なり、三界の競起にあらず。

"Arising" is always when the time comes; for time is arising.[15] What is "arising"? It should be "arisen!"[16] Since this is arising as time, it does not fail to expose the skin, flesh, bones, and marrow.[17] Because arising is the

---

14 **When there is a further encounter beyond, one loses the advantage of the encounter** (*sara ni kōjō no shōken no toki, masa ni shōken no raku bengi aru nari* さらに向上の相見のとき、まさに相見の落便宜あるなり): A tentative translation of a passage variously interpreted. The phrase *kōjō no shōken* 向上の相見, rendered here as "encounter beyond," can be interpreted to mean the experience of dharmas arising without our usual distinction between subject and object. The expression *raku bengi* 落便宜, translated as "lose the advantage," often carries the sense "to be taken advantage of" (in contrast to *toku bengi* 得便宜, "to gain an advantage"); here, it can be interpreted to mean that the sense of encounter between subject and object is lost in the experience of the dharmas arising.

15 **when the time comes** (*jisetsu tōrai* 時節到來): A set expression, used several times in the *Shōbōgenzō*, especially for the present moment.

16 **"arisen!"** (*ki ya* 起也): Likely an allusion to a saying of Caoshan Benji 曹山本寂 (840-901):

> 問、承古有言。未有一人倒地不因地而起。如何是倒。師曰、肯即是。曰、如何是起。師曰、起也。
>
> [Someone] asked, "There's a saying handed down from the ancients, 'No one who has fallen to the earth has ever arisen without depending on the earth.' What is this 'falling'?"
> The Master said, "Consent to it."
> He said, "What is this 'arising'?"
> The Master said, "Arisen!"

This passage occurs in the *Jingde chuandeng lu* 景德傳燈錄 (T.2076.51:336b10-12) just before Caoshan's 曹山 teaching on the ocean that Dōgen will cite below, section 16.

17 **skin, flesh, bones, and marrow** (*hi niku kotsu zui* 皮肉骨髓): An expression, occurring very often throughout the *Shōbōgenzō*, indicating the essence or truth or entirety of something or someone. From the famous story found in the *shinji Shōbōgenzō* 眞字正法眼藏 (DZZ.5:230, case 201), of Bodhidharma's testing of four disciples, to whom he said of each in turn that he (or, in one case, she) had gotten his skin, flesh, bones, and marrow. See Supplementary Notes.

332   DŌGEN'S *SHŌBŌGENZŌ* VOLUME I

arising of "combine to form," arising is "this body"; arising is "I arise";
it is "just the dharmas." It is not simply hearing and seeing sound and
form. It is "the dharmas" that are "I arise"; it is the "I arise" that is "do
not state." "Do not state" is not not saying anything, for a saying is not
a statement.[18] "When they arise" is "these dharmas"; it is not the twelve
times.[19] "These dharmas" are "when they arise"; they are not the profuse
arisings of the three realms.[20]

[13:8] {1:121}
古佛いはく、忽然火起。この起の相待にあらざるを、火起と道取するな
り。

An old buddha said, "*Suddenly, a fire arose.*"[21] The fact that this "arising" is not "relative" is expressed as "a fire arose."[22]

[13:9]
古佛いはく、起滅不停時如何。

An old buddha said, "*When arising and ceasing don't stop, what's it
like?*"[23]

[13:10]
しかあれば、起滅は我我起、我我滅なるに不停なり。この不停の道取、か
れに一任して辨肯すべし。この起滅不停時を、佛祖の命脈として斷續せし

---

18 **"Do not state" is not not saying anything, for a saying is not a statement** (*fugon
wa fudō ni wa arazu, dōtoku wa gontoku ni arazaru ga yue ni* 不言は不道にはあらず、
道得は言得にあらざるがゆえに): Dōgen seems here to be making a distinction be-
tween simply not speaking (*fugon* 不言) and not expressing something meaningful (*fudō*
不道); hence, though it is not stated, "I arise" can be a significant saying (*dōtoku* 道得).

19 **the twelve times** (*jūni ji* 十二時): The twenty-four hours of the day, figured traditionally in two-hour divisions.

20 **three realms** (*sangai* 三界): I.e, the threefold world system of saṃsāra; see Supplementary Notes, s.v. "Three realms."

21 **An old buddha** (*kobutsu* 古佛): From the famous *Lotus Sūtra* parable of the burning
house (*Miaofa lianhua jing* 妙法蓮華經, T.262.9:12b17-18). The use here of the expression "old buddha" (*kobutsu* 古佛) in reference to Buddha Śākyamuni, revealer of the
Lotus Sūtra, is somewhat unusual; see Supplementary Notes, s.v. "Old buddha."

22 **this "arising" is not "relative"** (*kono ki no sōtai ni arazaru* この起の相待にあら
ざる): Here, Dōgen recalls Mazu's saying that prior thoughts and subsequent thoughts
are "not relative" (*fu sōtai* 不相待) to each other.

23 **An old buddha** (*kobutsu* 古佛): From a conversation between Luoshan Daoxian
羅山道閑 (dates unknown) and Yantou Quanhuo 巖頭全豁 (828-887). There are several versions; Dōgen's source is most likely the *Hongzhi chanshi yulu* 宏智禪師語錄
(T.2001.48:22b18-19):

> 羅山問巖頭、起滅不停時如何。頭咄云、是誰起滅。
>
> Luoshan asked Yantou, "When arising and ceasing don't stop, what's it like?"
>
> Yantou shouted, "Who's arising and ceasing?"

13. Ocean Seal Samādhi *Kaiin zanmai* 海印三昧　　333

む。起滅不停時は、是誰起滅なり。是誰起滅は、應以此身得度者なり、即現此身なり、而爲説法なり、過去心不可得なり、汝得吾髓なり、汝得吾骨なり、是誰起滅なるゆえに。

Thus, "arising and ceasing" "don't stop," as I after I arises, and I after I ceases.[24] This saying, "don't stop" — we should give ourselves over to it and confirm it.[25] It causes the severance and continuation of *"when arising and ceasing don't stop"* as the vital artery of the buddhas and ancestors [26] *"When arising and ceasing don't stop"* is *"who's arising and ceasing?"*[27] *"Who's arising and ceasing"* is *"those who can attain deliverance through this body"*; it is *"manifesting this body"*; it is *"preaching the dharma for them."*[28] It is *"the past mind cannot be got"*; it is *"you've gotten my marrow"*; it is *"you've gotten my bones."*[29] For it is *"who's arising and ceasing?"*

---

24 **I after I arises, and I after I ceases** (*ga ga ki, ga ga metsu* 我我起、我我滅): A tentative translation of a cryptic passage, literally "I I arise; I I cease." Depending on how one parses it, the passage could be interpreted to mean, "I arise again and again; I cease again and again," or "Each I arises, each I ceases."

25 **we should give ourselves over to it and confirm it** (*kare ni ichinin shite benkō su beshi* かれに一任して辨肯すべし): Again, a tentative translation of an ambiguous remark, variously interpreted; taken here as meaning that we should master the saying.

26 **It causes the severance and continuation** (*danzoku seshimu* 斷續せしむ): The agent of this causative predicate is unexpressed; *Shōbōgenzō monge* 正法眼藏聞解 (SCZ:4:558) understands it as "arising and ceasing" respectively — i.e., "ceasing" severs and "arising" continues the time in which "arising and ceasing don't stop." It is also possible to take the agent as the "confirmation" (*benkō* 辨肯) of the previous sentence. On this reading, the quality of our study of the words "don't stop" determines whether Luoshan's phrase, "when arising and ceasing don't stop," is severed or continues as the "vital artery" (*meimyaku* 命脈) of the buddhas and ancestors.

27 **"who's arising and ceasing?"** (*ze sui ki metsu* 是誰起滅): From Yantou's 巌頭 response to Luoshan 羅山. See Note 23, above.

28 **"those who can attain deliverance through this body"** (*ō i shi shin toku do sha* 應以此身得度者); **"manifesting this body"** (*soku gen shi shin* 即現此身); **"preaching the dharma for them"** (*ni i seppō* 而爲説法): Three phrases based on the Avalokiteśvara chapter of the *Lotus Sūtra* (*Miaofa lianhua jing* 妙法蓮華經, T.262.9:57a23ff.), in which it said that, to those who can attain deliverance through contact with a particular body (a buddha, a *pratyeka-buddha*, a *śrāvaka*, etc.), Bodhisattva Avalokiteśvara appears as that body and preaches the dharma for them. See Supplementary Notes, s.v. "Manifesting a body to preach the dharma."

29 **"the past mind cannot be got"** (*kako shin fukatoku* 過去心不可得): From the *Diamond Sūtra* (*Jingang jing* 金剛經, T.235.8:751b27).

"you've gotten my marrow" (*nyo toku go zui* 汝得吾髓); **"you've gotten my bones"** (*nyo toku go kotsu* 汝得吾骨): From Bodhidharma's comments to his disciples, introduced above, section 7.

334　　　DŌGEN'S *SHŌBŌGENZŌ* VOLUME I

[13:11]

此法滅時、不言我滅。まさしく不言我滅のときは、これ此法滅時なり。滅は法の滅なり、滅なりといへども法なるべし。法なるゆゑに客塵にあらず、客塵にあらざるゆゑに不染汚なり。ただこの不染汚、すなはち諸佛諸祖なり。汝もかくのごとしといふ、たれか汝にあらざらん、前念・後念あるはみな汝なるべし。吾もかくのごとしといふ、たれか吾にあらざらん、前念・後念はみな吾なるがゆゑに。この滅に多般の手眼を莊嚴せり。いはゆる無上大涅槃なり、いはゆる謂之死なり、いはゆる執爲斷なり、いはゆる爲所住なり。いはゆるかくのごとくの許多手眼、しかしながら滅の功德なり。滅の我なる時節に不言なると、起の我なる時節に不言なるとは、不言の同生ありとも、同死の不言にはあらざるべし。

"When these dharmas cease, they do not state, 'I cease.'" The time when "they do not state, 'I cease,'" is precisely "when the dharmas cease."[30] "Ceasing" is the ceasing of the dharmas; though it is ceasing, it must be the dharmas. Because it is the dharmas, it is not adventitious dust.[31] Because it is not adventitious dust, it is "not defiled."[32] Just this "not defiled" is the "buddhas and ancestors." He says, "You're also like this."[33] Who is not "you"? "Prior thoughts and subsequent thoughts are all "you." He says, "I'm also like this." Who is not "I"? For "prior thoughts and subsequent thoughts" are all "I."

This "ceasing" is adorned with many types of "hands and eyes": it is "the unsurpassed great nirvāṇa"; it is "call it death"; it is "grasp it as annihilation"; it is "treat it as an abode."[34] "So many hands and eyes" such

---

30　**The time when "they do not state, 'I cease,'"** (*fugon ga metsu no toki* 不言我滅のとき): This phrase might also be read, "the time of the 'I cease' that they do not state."

31　**Because it is the dharmas, it is not adventitious dust** (*hō naru yue ni kakujin ni arazu* 法なるゆゑに客塵にあらず): The term *kakujin* 客塵 is used to translate the Sanskrit *āgantuka-kleśa*, the spiritual defilements (*bonnō* 煩惱) understood as extrinsic to consciousness; See Supplementary Notes, s.v. "Dust." Here, it seems to be used in reference to "ceasing": i.e., because ceasing is itself a dharma, it is not something extrinsic to the dharmas that defiles them.

32　**"not defiled"** (*fuzenna* 不染汚): Dōgen begins here a series of allusions to one of his favorite cases in the Chan literature, recorded in his *shinji Shōbōgenzō* 眞字正法眼藏 (DZZ.5:178, case 101), the conversation between the Sixth Ancestor, Huineng 慧能 and his student Nanyue Huairang 南嶽懷讓 (677-744); see Supplementary Notes, s.v. "Not defiled."

33　**He says, "You're also like this"** (*nyo mo kaku no gotoshi to iu* 汝もかくのごとしといふ): The translation of this and the following "He says, 'I'm also like this'" (*go mo kaku no gotoshi to iu* 吾もかくのごとしといふ) assumes that the unspoken subject of "says" is the Sixth Ancestor, whose words are here put into Japanese.

34　**adorned with many types of "hands and eyes"** (*tahan no shugen o shōgon seri* 多般の手眼を莊嚴せり): An allusion to the thousand-armed Bodhisattva Avalokiteśvara, who has an eye in each of his hands. Although here we may take the passage to mean simply that "ceasing" can be understood in many ways, the allusion to Avolokiteśvara's hands and eyes introduces material that Dōgen will develop in the following section.

13. Ocean Seal Samadhi *Kaiin zanmai* 海印三昧 335

as these are in any case the virtue of "ceasing." The "not stating" at the moment when "ceasing" is "I" and the "not stating" at the moment when "arising" is "I" have the same birth of "not stating," but they must not be the "not stating" of the same death.[35]

[13:12] {1:122}

すでに前法の滅なり、後法の滅なり。法の前念なり、法の後念なり。爲法の前後法なり、爲法の前後念なり。不相待は爲法なり、不相對は法爲なり。不相對ならしめ、不相待ならしむるは、八九成の道得なり。滅の四大五蘊を手眼とせる、拈あり收あり。滅の四大五蘊を行程とせる、進歩あり相見あり。このとき、通身是手眼、還是不足なり。遍身是手眼、還是不足なり。おほよそ滅は、佛祖の功德なり。

They are entirely the "ceasing" of the "prior dharmas," the "ceasing" of the "subsequent dharmas."[36] They are the "prior thoughts" of the "dharmas," the "subsequent thoughts" of the "dharmas." They are the "prior and subsequent dharmas" that constitute the "dharmas"; it is the "prior and subsequent thoughts" that constitute the "dharmas."[37] Their being

---

"the unsurpassed great nirvana" (*mujō dai nehan* 無上大涅槃); **"call it death"** (*i shi shi* 謂之死); **"grasp it as annihilation"** (*shū i dan* 執爲斷), **"treat it as an abode"** (*i shojū* 爲所住): Allusions to the verse attributed to Huineng 慧能 at *Jingde chuandeng lu* 景德傳燈錄, T.2076.51:239c21-23:

無上大涅槃、圓明常寂照。凡愚謂之死、外道執爲斷。諸求二乘人、目以無爲作。

The unsurpassed great nirvāṇa,
Perfect and bright, always quietly shining.
The commoners call it death;
The other paths grasp it as annihilation.
Those who seek the two vehicles
Look on it as the unconditioned.

See also the *Platform Sūtra of the Sixth Ancestor* (*Liuzu tan jing* 六祖壇經, T.2008.48:357a24). The source of Dōgen's substitution in the last line of "abode" for "unconditioned" is not clear.

35 **have the same birth of "not stating," but they must not be the "not stating" of the same death** (*fugon no dōshō ari tomo, dōshi no fugon ni wa arazaru beshi* 不言の同生ありとも、同死の不言にはあらざるべし): This obscure sentence is subject to various interpretations. It is usually understood to mean that, whereas the term "not stating" may be the same (*dōshō* 同生) in the cases both of "arising" and "ceasing," it is not the same (*dōshi* 同死) according to whether it applies to "arising" or "ceasing." Some would interpret the second phrase to mean simply that the "ceasing" that is not stated is not the same as death.

36 **They are entirely the "ceasing" of the "prior dharmas"** (*sude ni zenpō no metsu nari* すでに前法の滅なり): Taking the unexpressed subject here to remain the instances of "not stating" of the previous section.

37 **constitute the "dharmas"** (*ihō* 爲法): Tentative translation of an unusual term, not appearing in this sense elsewhere in the *Shōbōgenzō*, taking it here to mean simply "what the dharmas are" or, perhaps, "what makes them dharmas."

336 DŌGEN'S *SHŌBŌGENZŌ* VOLUME I

"not relative" constitutes the "dharmas"; their being "not opposed" is the constitution of the "dharmas."[38]

To make them be "not opposed," to make them be "not relative," is a saying "eight or nine tenths complete."[39] There is a taking up, there is a taking in, that takes as "hands and eyes" the four elements and five aggregates of "ceasing"; there is an advance, there is an encounter, that takes as its course the four elements and five aggregates of "ceasing."[40] At this time, *the body throughout is hands and eyes* is still not enough; *the body everywhere is hands and eyes* is still not enough. In sum, "ceasing" is the virtue of the buddhas and ancestors.

[13:13]

いま不相對と道取あり、不相待と道取あるは、しるべし、起は初・中・後起なり。官不容針、私通車馬なり。滅を初・中・後に相待するにあらず、相對するにあらず。從來の滅處に忽然として起法すとも、滅の起には あらず、法の起なり。法の起なるゆえに、不對待相なり。また、滅と滅と 相待するにあらず、相對するにあらず。滅も初・中・後、滅なり。相逢不 拈出、舉意便知有なり。從來の起處に忽然として滅すとも、起の滅にあら ず、法滅なり。法の滅なるがゆえに、不相對待なり。

That now we have the words, "not opposed," that we have the words, "not relative," means that we should realize that "arising" is "arising" in beginning, middle, and end; it is *officially, you can't insert a needle; privately, you could drive a horse and cart through it.*[41] In beginning, mid-

---

38 **constitution of the "dharmas"** (*hōi* 法爲): A playful reversal of the preceding *ihō* 爲法 ("constitute the dharmas"), perhaps to be understood as "what the dharmas do."

39 **a saying "eight or nine tenths complete"** (*hakku jō no dōtoku* 八九成の道得): I.e., good but not the whole story; see Supplementary Notes, s.v. "Eight or nine tenths complete." Dōgen here turns to the conversation on "hands and eyes" to which he alluded in section 11, a dialogue between Yunyan Tansheng 雲巖曇晟 (782-841) and fellow disciple Daowu Yuanzhi 道吾圓智 (769-835) regarding the thousand-armed, thousand-eyed Bodhisattva Avalokiteśvara (*senju sengen Kannon* 千手千眼觀音). The text, which Dōgen discusses in his "Shōbōgenzō Kannon" 正法眼藏觀音, appears in several Chan sources, as well as Dōgen's *shinji Shōbōgenzo* 眞字正法眼藏 (DZZ.5:182, case 105). See Supplementary Notes, s.v. "His body everywhere is hands and eyes."

40 **There is a taking up, there is a taking in** (*nen ari shū ari* 拈あり收あり): Some would understand the latter verb here as "letting go" or "leaving be."

the four elements and five aggregates (*shidai goun* 四大五蘊): I.e., the four primary forms of matter (S. *mahābhūta*) — earth, water, fire, and wind — of which the physical world is composed; and the five "heaps" (S. *skandha*) — form, sensation, cognition, formations, and consciousness — into which the psychophysical organism can be analyzed. See Supplementary Notes, s.v. "Four elements and five aggregates."

41 **"officially, you can't insert a needle; privately, you could drive a horse and cart through it"** (*kan fuyō shin shi tsū shaba* 官不容針私通車馬): A popular expression in Zen texts, usually taken to mean externally strict but internally open, or strict in principle but flexible in practice.

13. Ocean Seal Samādhi *Kaiin zanmai* 海印三昧 337

dle, and end, it is not "relative" to, is not "opposed" to, "ceasing." Though there is the sudden "arising" of "dharmas" where there had previously been "ceasing," this is not the "arising" of "ceasing"; it is the "arising" of "dharmas." Because it is the "arising" of "dharmas," it is marked by "not opposed" or "relative."[42] Nor are "ceasing" and "ceasing" "relative" or "opposed" to each other. "Ceasing" is "ceasing" at beginning, middle, and end. This is [a case of] "*in meeting, they don't bring it out; but if one thinks about it, one knows it's there.*"[43] Though "ceasing" occurs suddenly where there had previously been "arising," this is not the "ceasing" of "arising"; it is the "ceasing" of the "dharmas." Because it is the "ceasing" of the "dharmas," it is "not opposed or relative."

[13:14] {1:123}
たとひ滅の是即にもあれ、たとひ起の是即にもあれ、但以海印三昧、名爲衆法なり。是即の修證はなきにあらず、只此不染汚、名爲海印三昧なり。

Whether it be the "this is" of "ceasing" or the "this is" of "arising," it is *just the ocean seal samādhi called "the dharmas."*[44] It is not that the practice and verification of "this is" is lacking; it is *just this "not defiled" that is "called the ocean seal samādhi."*[45]

[13:15]
三昧は現成なり、道得なり、背手摸枕子の夜間なり。夜間のかくのごとく背手摸枕子なる、摸枕子は億億萬劫のみにあらず、我於海中、唯常宣説妙法華經なり。不言我起なるがゆえに、我於海中なり。前面も一波纔動萬波隨なる常宣説なり、後面も萬波纔動一波隨の妙法華經なり。たとひ千尺萬尺の糸綸を卷舒せしむとも、うらむらくはこれ直下垂なることを。いはゆ

---

42 **marked by "not opposed" or "relative"** (*futaitai sō* 不對待相): Tentative attempt to capture Dōgen's play with the terms *fusōtai* 不相待 ("not relative") and *fusōtai* 不相對 ("not opposed"), reading the glyph *sō* 相 here in the sense "characterized by."

43 **"in meeting, they don't bring it out; but if one thinks about it, one knows it's there"** (*sōhō funenshutsu, ko i ben chi u* 相逢不拈出、擧意便知有): A popular saying in Zen literature (see, e.g., *Congrong lu* 從容錄, T.2004.48:262b6; *Yuanwu Foguo chanshi yulu* 圓悟佛果禪師語錄, T.1997.47:740c11). Usually interpreted to mean that, while something is not apparent on the surface, if one probes, it will be clear. Some would read the "meeting" (*sōhō* 相逢) here to be the relation between "arising" and "ceasing." Hence, though we cannot "bring out" (i.e., talk about) a "meeting" between the two, if we "think about it" (i.e., question the point), we understand each as it is.

44 **"this is"** (*ze soku* 是即): Dōgen is here playing with the first two words of the last sentence of the Mazu 馬祖 quotation with which he opened this text: "This is called the ocean seal samādhi" (*ze soku myō i kaiin zanmai* 是即名爲海印三昧). The final words of this section complete Mazu's sentence.

45 **It is not that the practice and verification of "this is" is lacking; it is just this "not defiled"** (*ze soku no shushō wa naki ni arazu, shi shi fuzenna* 是即の修證はなきにあらず、只此不染汚): Allusion again to the interchange between Huineng 慧能 and Huairang 懷讓 cited above; see Note 32.

る前面・後面は、我於海面なり、前頭・後頭といはんがごとし、前頭・後頭といふは、頭上安頭なり。海中は有人にあらず、我於海は世人の住處にあらず、聖人の愛處にあらず、我於ひとり海中にあり。これ唯常の宣説なり。この海中は、中間に屬せず、内外に屬せず、鎮常在説法華經なり。東西南北に不居なりといへども、滿舩空載月明歸なり。この實歸は、便歸來なり。たれかこれを滯水の行履なりといはん、ただ佛道の劑限に現成するのみなり。これを印水の印とす。さらに道取す、印空の印なり。さらに道取す、印泥の印なり。印水の印、かならずしも印海の印にはあらず、向上さらに印海の印なるべし。これを海印といひ、水印といひ、泥印といひ、心印といふなり。心印を單傳して、印水し、印泥し、印空するなり。

Samādhi is an occurrence; it is a saying. It is "in the night" when "*the hand gropes for the pillow behind*."[46] The "groping for a pillow" of "*the hand groping for the pillow behind*" "in the night" like this is not merely "*koṭis and koṭis of myriads of kalpas*"; it is "*I, in the ocean, always only preached the Lotus Sūtra of the Wondrous Dharma*."[47] Because they "*do not state, 'I arise,'*" he is "*I, in the ocean*."[48] The former face is the "I always preached" of "*the slightest motion of a single wave and ten thousand waves follow*"; the latter face is the *Lotus Sūtra of the Wondrous Dharma* of "*the slightest motion of ten thousand waves and a single wave follows*."[49] Whether we wind up or let out "a line of a thousand feet" or ten thousand feet, what we regret is that it "goes straight down."

---

46 **"in the night" when "the hand gropes for the pillow behind"** (*hai shu mo chinsu no yakan* 背手摸枕子の夜間): Allusion again to the conversation on the thousand-armed Avalokiteśvara cited above; see Note 39.

47 **"*koṭis and koṭis of myriads of kalpas*"** (*oku oku mangō* 億億萬劫): Allusion to the Sadāparibhūta chapter of the *Lotus Sūtra* (*Miaofa lianhua jing*, T.262.9:51c4-5):

億億萬劫、至不可議、諸佛世尊、時説是經。

"[After] *koṭis and koṭis* of myriads of kalpas, after an inconceivable [period], the buddhas, the world-honored ones, preach this sūtra."

"I, in the ocean, always only preached the *Lotus Sūtra of the Wondrous Dharma*" (*ga o kaichū, yui jō senzetsu myōhō renge kyō* 我於海中、唯常宣説妙法華經): From the Devadatta chapter of the *Lotus Sūtra* (*Miaofa lianhua jing* 妙法蓮華經, T.262.9:35b1213), in which Bodhisattva Mañjuśrī tells how he taught in the palace of the dragon king:

文殊師利言、我於海中、唯常宣説、妙法華經。

Mañjuśrī said, "In the ocean, I always only preached the *Lotus Sūtra of the Wondrous Dharma*."

48 **Because they "do not state, 'I arise,'" he is "I, in the ocean"** (*fugon ga ki naru ga yue ni, ga o kaichū nari* 不言我起なるがゆえに、我於海中なり): I.e., the bodhisattva can say he is in the ocean because the dharmas do not say, "I arise."

49 **former face** (*zenmen* 前面); **latter face** (*gomen* 後面): The modifiers "former" and "latter" here likely refer respectively to the subject and predicate of the preceding clause, "I am in the ocean" — i.e., to the self and its environment. Ordinarily, the terms *zenmen* and *gomen* would be better rendered simply as "former" and "latter" (or "former side" and "latter side"); the translation here and in the following passage struggles to retain

13. Ocean Seal Samādhi *Kaiin zanmai* 海印三昧 339

The "former face" and "latter face" here are *I, on the face of the ocean.*[50] They are like saying the "former head" and the "latter head." The "former head" and the "latter head" are *putting a head on top of your head.*[51]

It is not that "in the ocean" there is someone. "I in the ocean" is not "where the worldly dwell"; it is not "what is loved" by the sages.[52] "I am in" alone "in the ocean." This is the "preaching" of "always only."[53] This "in the ocean" "does not belong to the center"; it does not belong to "inside or outside": it is "*remaining forever,*" "*preaching the Lotus Sūtra.*" Though it is "not in east, west, north or south," it is "*I come home with*

---

something of Dōgen's play on the numeric classifier *men* 面, which has the primary meaning, "face" (also "aspect," "side," "surface").

"the slightest motion of a single wave and ten thousand waves follow" (*ippa zan dō ban ha zui* 一波纔動萬波隨); **"the slightest motion of ten thousand waves and a single wave follows"** (*ban ha zan dō ippa zui* 萬波纔動一波隨): Here, Dōgen is quoting, and then reversing, a line from a charming poem by the Tang figure Chuanzi ("The Boatman") Decheng 船子德誠 (dates unknown) (*Liandeng huiyao* 聯燈會要, ZZ.136:375c6-7), to which he also alludes in the sentence just below:

千尺絲綸直下垂，一波纔動萬波隨. 夜靜水寒魚不食，滿船空載月明歸。
A line of a thousand feet goes straight down.
The slightest motion of a single wave, and ten thousand waves follow.
The evening is still, the water cold; the fish aren't feeding.
I come home with a fully empty boat, laden with moonlight.

The last line here plays with the colloquial Chinese felicitation *manzai er gui* 滿載而歸, "come back fully laden."

50 **I, on the face of the ocean** (*ga o kaimen* 我於海面): Dōgen's variation on Mañjuśrī's "I, in the ocean" (*ga o kaichū* 我於海中).

51 **the "former head" and the "latter head"** (*zentō gotō* 前頭・後頭): Dōgen is here again playing with the numeric classifier *tō*, which has the primary sense "head." "Putting a head on top of your head" (*zujō an zu* 頭上安頭; also read *tōjō an tō*) is a common expression in Chan texts for the mistake of adding something superfluous, of saying something unnecessary, or imagining or seeking something one already has; see Supplementary Notes, s.v. "Putting a head on top of your head."

52 **"where the worldly dwell"** (*sejin no jūsho* 世人の住處); **"what is loved" by the sages** (*shōnin no aisho* 聖人の愛處): Here and below, Dōgen is introducing (and modifying) phrases from the poem *Caoan ge* 草庵歌, by Shitou Xiqian 石頭希遷 (700-790); see Supplementary Notes, s.v. "*Reverend Shitou's Song of the Thatched Hut.*" Dōgen's phrase "what is loved by the sages" here replaces the poem's "what the worldly love" (*sejin aisho* 世人愛處),

53 **"I am in" alone "in the ocean." This is the "preaching" of "always only"** (*ga o hitori kaichū ni ari. kore yui jō no senzetsu nari* 我於ひとり海中にあり。これ唯常の宣説なり): A tentative translation of a grammatically odd passage. Dōgen has here split up the eight Chinese glyphs in his earlier quotation of the *Lotus Sūtra* passage, "in the ocean, I always only preached" (*ga o kaichū yui jō senzetsu* 我於海中唯常宣説), into four compound nouns. The result yields the improbable nominative-locative combination *ga o* (translated by the awkward "I am in") and the curious adverbial-adverbial *yui jō* (rendered by "always only").

340   DŌGEN'S *SHŌBŌGENZŌ* VOLUME I

a fully empty boat, laden with moonlight." This true return is he "*immediately comes back home.*"

Who could call it the conduct of getting drenched with water?[54] It appears only at the limits of the way of the buddhas. [We] take this as the seal that seals the water. Expressing it further, it is the seal that seals the sky; expressing it further, it is the seal that seals the mud.[55] The seal that seals the water is not necessarily the seal that seals the ocean. Beyond this, there must be further the seal that seals the ocean. This is called the "ocean seal," called the "water seal," called the "mud seal," called the "mind seal." Uniquely transmitting the mind seal, [it] seals the water, seals the mud, seals the sky.

* * * * *

[13:16] {1:124}

曹山元證大師、因僧問、承教有言、大海不宿死屍。如何是海。師云、包含萬有。僧云、爲什麼不宿死屍。師云、絕氣者不著。僧云、既是包含萬有、爲什麼絕氣者不著。師云、萬有非其功絕氣。

Great Master Yuanzheng of Caoshan was once asked by a monk, "I've heard of a teaching that says, 'The great ocean does not house a dead body.' What's the 'ocean'?"[56]

---

54 **the conduct of getting drenched with water** (*taisui no anri* 滯水の行履): Taking *tai* 滯 ("to stay," "stagnate") as equivalent to *tai* 帶 (here, "to splash"). The term *taisui* 滯水 is often taken by commentators to mean "staying in the water"; Dōgen's use of the term "mud" (*dei* 泥) just below suggests he has in mind the idiomatic Chinese expression "muddied and drenched" (*tuoni daishui* 拖泥帶水), used in Zen texts (and elsewhere in the *Shōbōgenzō*) for getting "dirty," or "sullied," by the compromises involved in teaching. See Supplementary Notes, s.v. "Dragged through the mud and drenched with water."

55 **seals the water** (*in sui* 印水); **seals the sky** (*in kū* 印空); **seals the mud** (*in dei* 印泥): Dōgen is here introducing the "three seals" found in several Zen texts; see, e.g., "The mind seal of the ancestral masters: one seal seals the sky; one seal seals the water; one seal seals the mud" (*zushi shinyin yiyin yin kong yiyin yin shui yiyin yin ni* 祖師心印一印印空一印印水一印印泥) (*Tiansheng guangdeng lu* 天聖廣燈錄, ZZ.135:769b6). The three are sometimes interpreted as three levels of disciple, sometimes as the three bodies of the buddha. The "mind seal" (*shin'in* 心印) is of course a favored metaphor for the authentication of the transmission of the awakened mind from master to disciple.

56 **The Great Master Yuanzheng of Caoshan** (*Sōzan Genshō Daishi* 曹山元證大師): I.e, Caoshan Benji 曹山本寂, disciple of Dongshan Liangjie 洞山良价 (807-869). The conversation occurs at *Jingde chuandeng lu* 景德傳燈錄, T.2076.51:336b1215; see also *shinji Shōbōgenzō* 眞字正法眼藏, DZZ.5:224, case 194.

"**The great ocean does not house a dead body**" (*taikai fushuku shishi* 大海不宿死屍): A common expression in Buddhist literature. See, e.g., the *Avataṃsaka Sūtra* (*Huayan jing* 華嚴經, T.279.10:422a19-20):

善知識者不受諸惡、譬如大海不宿死屍。

The wise friend does not accept evil, just as the great ocean does not house a dead body.

13. Ocean Seal Samādhi *Kaiin zanmai* 海印三昧　　341

The Master said, "It contains the myriad beings."
The monk said, "Then why doesn't it house a dead body?"
The Master said, "One whose breath has stopped doesn't belong there."[57]
The monk said, "If it contains the myriad beings, why is it that one whose breath has stopped doesn't belong there?"
The Master said, "It's not a virtue of the myriad beings that their breath has stopped."[58]

[13:17]
この曹山は、雲居の兄弟なり。洞山の宗旨、このところに正的なり。いま承教有言といふは、佛祖正教なり。凡聖の教にあらず、附佛法の小教にあらず。

This Caoshan was a brother disciple of Yunju.[59] He gets Dongshan's essential point right on the mark here. This *"I've heard of a teaching that says"* refers to the true teachings of the buddhas and ancestors; it is not the teachings of the common people and sages; it is not the lesser teachings of those who attach themselves to the buddha dharma.[60]

[13:18]
大海不宿死屍。いはゆる大海は、内海・外海等にあらず、八海等にはあらざるべし。これらは學人のうたがふところにあらず。海にあらざるを海と

---

57 **"One whose breath has stopped doesn't belong there"** (*zekkisha fujaku* 絕氣者不著): Reading *jaku* 著 here in the sense *chi* 置 ("to place").

58 **"It's not a virtue of the myriad beings that their breath has stopped"** (*ban'u hi go kō zekki* 萬有非其功絕氣): A tentative translation of a notoriously problematic line, following Kawamura's *kaeriten* 返り点 (*ban'u, sono ku zekki ni arazu* 萬有、其の功絕氣に非ず). Many interpreters favor a reading that would yield something like, "the myriad beings, lacking their virtue, stop breathing" (*ban'u wa sono kō ni arazareba zekki nari* 萬有は其の功に非ざれば絕氣なり). Dōgen's sentence is difficult to interpret because his quotation here (and in his *shinji Shōbōgenzō* 眞字正法眼藏) cuts off Caoshan's answer in mid-sentence, making a predicate of what had been in the original the subject of a second clause (and, indeed, some manuscripts of the *Shōbōgenzō* restore the full version):

師曰、萬有非其功、絕氣有其德。

The Master said, "The myriad beings are without their virtues; those whose breath has stopped have their merits."

Caoshan's original statement seems to be saying that the ocean holds only those beings that are devoid of virtue, whereas the dead body has merit and, hence, does not belong.

59 **brother disciple of Yunju** (*Ungo no hindei* 雲居の兄弟): A reference to Yunju Daoying 雲居道膺 (d. 902), a fellow disciple under Dongshan.

60 **common people and sages** (*bonshō* 凡聖): A standard distinction between two classes of Buddhists: the ordinary, or "common" (S. *pṛthagjana*) type; and the advanced adept, or "noble" (S. *ārya*) type.

those who attach themselves to the buddha dharma (*fu buppō* 附佛法): An expression used for adherents of non-Buddhist religions (*gedō* 外道) within the Buddhist ranks.

342 DŌGEN'S *SHŌBŌGENZŌ* VOLUME I

認ずるのみにあらず、海なるを海と認ずるなり。たとひ海と強爲すとも、大海といふべからざるなり。大海はかならずしも八功徳水の重淵にあらず、大海はかならずしも鹹水等の九淵にあらず。衆法は合成なるべし、大海かならずしも深水のみにてあらんや。このゆえに、いかなるか海と問著するは、大海のいまだ人天にしられざるゆえに、大海を道著するなり。これを問著せん人は、海執を動著せんとするなり。

"The great ocean does not house a dead body." The "great ocean" here is not an inner ocean or outer ocean, not the eight oceans.[61] These are not what the student asks about.[62] He not only recognizes what is not the ocean as the ocean; he recognizes what is the ocean as the ocean. Even if we insist that they are oceans, they cannot be called the "great ocean." The "great ocean" is not necessarily a deep abyss of the water of the eight virtues; the "great ocean" is not necessarily a ninefold abyss of salt water or the like.[63] "The dharmas" must be "combining to form" it; could the "great ocean" necessarily be only deep water?[64] Therefore, his asking, "What's the 'ocean'?" is speaking of the "great ocean" because the "great ocean" is as yet unknown to humans and devas. The person who would ask this question is trying to move his grasp of "ocean."[65]

[13:19] {1:125}

不宿死屍、といふは、不宿は明頭來明頭打、暗頭來暗頭打なるべし。死屍は死灰なり、幾度逢春不變心なり。死屍といふは、すべて人人いまだみざるものなり。このゆえにしらざるなり。

In saying *"it does not house a dead body,"* "not housing" must be, *"When the bright comes, the bright does it; when the dark comes, the dark does it."*[66] "A dead body" is dead ashes; it is *"how many times has*

---

61 **inner ocean or outer ocean** (*naikai gekai* 内海・外海); **eight oceans** (*hakkai* 八海): Likely a reference to the eight oceans surrounding Mount Sumeru in Buddhist cosmology, of which the first is called the "inner ocean" and the remainder, the "outer oceans."

62 **not what the student asks about** (*gakunin no utagau tokoro ni arazu* 學人のうたがふところにあらず): I.e., what the monk in the story is asking about.

63 **water of the eight virtues** (*hachi kudoku sui* 八功徳水): The excellent water said to fill the oceans surrounding Mount Sumeru (and the lakes of the Pure Land of Sukhāvatī); its eight positive qualities are described as sweet, cool, soft, light, pure, odorless, harmless to the throat, and harmless to the stomach.

ninefold abyss (*kyūen* 九淵): A standard Chinese term for deep waters.

64 **"The dharmas" must be "combining to form" it** (*shuhō wa gōjō naru beshi* 衆法は合成なるべし): Recalling the line, "It is just the dharmas that combine to form this body" (*tan i shuhō gōjō shi shin* 但以衆法合成此身) in the quotation of Mazu, above, section 2.

65 **trying to move his grasp of "ocean"** (*kaishū o dōjaku sen to suru* 海執を動著せんとする): I.e., seeks to revise, or "shake up," his understanding of "ocean."

66 **"When the bright comes, the bright does it; when the dark comes, the dark does it"** (*meitō rai meitō ta, antō rai antō ta* 明頭來明頭打、暗頭來暗頭打): A tentative

13. Ocean Seal Samādhi *Kaiin zanmai* 海印三昧　343

it met the spring without changing its mind?"[67] A "dead body" is a thing people have never seen. Therefore, they do not know it.

[13:20]

師云の包含萬有は、海を道著するなり。宗旨の道得するところは、阿誰なる一物の、萬有を包含するとはいはず、包含萬有なり。大海の、萬有を包含するといふにあらず、包含萬有を道著するは大海なるのみなり。なにものとしれるにあらざれども、しばらく萬有なり。佛面祖面と相見することも、しばらく萬有を錯認するなり。包含のときは、たとひ山なりとも、高高峰頭立のみにあらず。たとひ水なりとも、深深海底行のみにあらず。收はかくのごとくなるべし、放はかくのごとくなるべし。佛性海といひ、毗盧藏海といふ、ただこれ萬有なり。海面みえざれども、游泳の行履に疑著することなし。たとへば、多福一叢竹を道取するに、一莖兩莖曲なり、三莖四莖斜なるも、萬有を錯失せしむる行履なりとも、なにとしてかいまだいはざる、千曲萬曲なりと。なにとしてかいはざる、千叢萬叢なりと。一叢の竹、かくのごとくある道理、わすれざるべし。曹山の包含萬有の道著、すなはちなほこれ萬有なり。

The Master's saying "*it contains the myriad beings*" is speaking of the "ocean." What he is saying about the essential point is not that some single thing "contains" the "myriad beings": it is "*containing is the myriad beings.*"[68] He does not mean that the "great ocean" "contains" the "myriad beings." Saying "*it contains the myriad beings*" just means it is the "great ocean." Although we do not know what they are, for now we call them the "myriad beings." Even our encountering the buddha faces and ancestor faces is temporarily misperceiving the "myriad beings." When they are "contained," even mountains are not only "*standing atop the highest peak*"; even water is not only "*walking the floor of the deepest ocean.*"[69]

---

rendering of a vexed saying attributed to the Chan monk Puhua 普化 (dates unknown), quoted in Dōgen's *shinji Shōbōgenzō* 眞字正法眼藏 (DZZ.5:136-138, case 22); see Supplementary Notes.

67　**dead ashes** (*shikai* 死灰): A common expression, used in both positive and pejorative senses, for the mind in trance, as in the idiom, "dried-up trees and dead ashes" (*koboku shikai* 枯木死灰). See Supplementary Notes, s.v. "Dried-up tree."

"how many times has it met the spring without changing its mind?" (*kido hō shun fu hen shin* 幾度逢春不變心): From a verse by Damei Fachang 大梅法常 (752-839) (*Jingde chuandeng lu* 景德傳燈錄, T.2076.51:254c1213):

摧殘枯木倚寒林、幾度逢春不變心。
Broken dried-up tree keeping to the cold forest.
How many times has it met the spring without changing its mind?

68　**"containing is the myriad beings"** (*hōgan ban'u nari* 包含萬有なり): Or, perhaps, "it is the myriad beings contained." Dōgen merely repeats here the four-character phrase translated in the conversation as "it contains the myriad beings."

69　**"standing atop the highest peak"** (*kōkō hō tō ryū* 高高峰頭立); **"walking the floor of the deepest ocean"** (*jinjin kai tei kō* 深深海底行): Variant of the saying by Yaoshan Weiyan 藥山惟儼 cited earlier; see above, Note 3.

344 DŌGEN'S *SHŌBŌGENZŌ* VOLUME I

Taking them in must be like this; letting them go must be like this.[70]

We say, "the ocean of the buddha nature," or we say, "the ocean of the womb of Vairocana"; these are simply the "myriad beings."[71] Though we may not see the face of the ocean, there are no doubts about the conduct of swimming. For example, when he speaks of "Duofu's one grove of bamboo", it is "*one or two stalks are bent*," and it is "*three or four stalks are slanted*"; but, while this is conduct that causes the "myriad beings" to be misunderstood, why does he not say, "a thousand are bent, a myriad are bent"?[72] Why does he not say, "a thousand groves, a myriad groves"? We should not forget the reason why his one grove of bamboo is like this. Caoshan's saying, "*it contains the myriad beings*," is precisely the "myriad beings."

[13:21] {1:126}

僧のいわく、爲什麼絕氣者不著は、あやまりて疑著の面目なりといふとも、是什麼心行なるべし。從來疑著這漢なるときは、從來疑著這漢なるときは、從來疑著這漢に相見するのみなり。什麼處在に爲什麼絕氣者不著なり、爲什麼不宿死屍なり。這頭にすなはち既是包含萬有、爲什麼絕氣者不著なり。しるべし、包含は著にあらず、しるべし、包含は著にあらず、包含は不宿なり。萬有たとひ死屍なりとも、不宿の直須萬年なるべし、不著の這老僧一著子なるべし。

The monk said, "*Why is it that one whose breath has stopped doesn't belong there?*" Although this has the face of a mistaken question, it must be, "*What are you thinking?*"[73] When it is, "*I've always had my doubts*

---

70 **Taking them in must be like this; letting them go must be like this** (*shū wa kaku no gotoku naru beshi, hō wa kaku no gotoku naru beshi* 收はかくのごとくなるべし、放はかくのごとくなるべし): The sense of *shū* 收 ("take in") and *hō* 放 ("let go") here is uncertain; while often meaning "to grasp and release," here, they may refer to taking the myriad beings as a whole or separately.

71 **"ocean of the buddha nature"** (*busshō kai* 佛性海); **"ocean of the womb of Vairocana"** (*Biru zō kai* 毗盧藏海): Two common Buddhist expressions for the *dharma-kāya* (*hosshin* 法身), or all-embracing cosmic body of the buddha.

72 **"Duofu's one grove of bamboo"** (*Tafuku issōchiku* 多福一叢竹): Variation on lines from a dialogue featuring Hangzhou Duofu 杭州多福 (dates unknown) found in several Zen sources; e.g., *Jingde chuandeng lu* 景德傳燈錄, T.2076.51:287c15-17:

僧問、如何是多福一叢竹。師曰、一莖兩莖斜。曰學人不會。師曰。三莖四莖曲。

A monk asked, "What is Duofu's one grove of bamboo?"
The Master answered, "One or two stalks are slanted."
The monk said, "I don't understand."
The Master said, "Three or four stalks are bent."

conduct that causes the "myriad beings" to be misunderstood (*ban'u o shakushitsu seshimuru anri* 萬有を錯失せしむる行履): Perhaps, meaning something like, "a way of speaking that causes us to lose sight of the myriad beings."

73 **"What are you thinking?"** (*ze jūmo shingyō* 是什麼心行): See above, Note 4.

13. Ocean Seal Samādhi *Kaiin zanmai* 海印三昧 345

about this guy," it is just an encounter with "*this guy I've always had my doubts about*."[74] "*Where are we?*" that it is, "*Why is it that one whose breath has stopped doesn't belong there?*" or it is, "*Why doesn't it house a dead body?*"[75] Here, it is, "*If it contains the myriad beings, why is it that one whose breath has stopped doesn't belong there?*" We should realize that "containing" is not "belonging"; containing is "not housing." Even if the "myriad beings" are "dead bodies," "not housing" them must be, "*It would surely take ten thousand years*"; "not belonging" must be, *this old monk makes one move.*[76]

[13:22]

曹山の道すらく、萬有非其功絕氣、いはゆるは、萬有はたとひ絕氣なりとも、たとひ不絕氣なりとも、不著なるべし。死屍たとひ死屍なりとも、萬有に同參する行履あらんがごときは、包含すべし、包含なるべし。萬有なる前程後程、その功あり、これ絕氣にあらず。いはゆる、一盲引衆盲。一盲引衆盲の道理は、さらに一盲引一盲なり、衆盲引衆盲なり。衆盲引衆盲なるとき、包含萬有包含于包含萬有なり。さらにいく大道にも萬有にあらざる、いまだその功夫現成せず、海印三昧なり。

Caoshan said, "*It's not a virtue of the myriad beings that their breath has stopped.*" This means that, whether the "myriad beings" are those whose "breath has stopped" or whose "breath has not stopped," it should be they "don't belong." A "dead body" may be a "dead body," but those who have conduct that studies together with the "myriad beings," should be "contained," should be "containing." The prior states and subsequent states that are the "myriad beings" have their "virtue": it is not that "their breath has stopped." This is *the blind leading the blind.*[77] The principle of *a blind person leading the blind* is, furthermore, *a blind person leading*

74　**"I've always had my doubts about this guy"** (*jūrai gijaku sha kan* 從來疑著這漢); **"this guy I've always had my doubts about"** (*jūrai gijaku sha kan* 從來疑著這漢): Two readings of the same Chinese text, from the remark by Linji 臨濟 (d. 867) in response to the saying by Puhua 普化 quoted above, Note 66.

75　**"Where are we?"** (*jūmo sho zai* 什麼處在): Suggestive of the stock rhetorical question, appearing several times in the *Shōbōgenzō*, "Where are we here that . . . ?" (*shari ze jūo sho zai* 這裏是什麼處在).

76　**"It would surely take ten thousand years"** (*jikishu bannen* 直須萬年): From a saying by Shishuang 石霜 (807-888); see Supplementary Notes, s.v. "It would surely take ten thousand years."

this old monk makes one move (*sha rōsō ichi jakusu* 這老僧一著子): Seemingly, a quote from a Chinese text, though no source has been identified. "One move" (*ichi jakusu* 一著子) is used in reference to moving a piece in a board game; in Chan texts, often a "move" in a dialogue. The translation loses the pun here on the term *jaku* 著, rendered as "belong" in the sentence, "Someone whose breath has stopped doesn't belong there."

77　**the blind leading the blind** (*ichimō in shumō* 一盲引衆盲): A fixed saying in Chinese, more literally, "one blind person leading a group of blind people." In the following sentence, Dōgen plays with the singular and plural here.

346 DŌGEN'S *SHŌBŌGENZŌ* VOLUME I

a blind person, or *the blind leading the blind*. When it is *the blind leading the blind*, it is *"containing the myriad beings" itself containing "containing the myriad beings."* Going further, in however many of the great ways, for those who are not among the "myriad beings," their concentrated efforts have never appeared — this is the "ocean seal samādhi."[78]

正法眼藏海印三昧第十三
Treasury of the True Dharma Eye
Ocean Seal Samādhi
Number 13

[Ryūmonji MS:]

仁治三年壬寅孟夏二十日、記于觀音導利興聖寶林寺
Recorded at Kannon Dōri Kōshō Hōrin Monastery; twentieth day of early summer [fourth month] of the senior water year of the tiger, the third year of Ninji [21 May 1242]

天文丁未二月書焉
Copied second month, junior fire year of the sheep, Tenbun [16] [20 February-21 March 1547][79]

[Tōunji MS:]

仁治三年壬寅孟夏二十日、記于觀音導利興聖寶林寺
Recorded at Kannon Dōri Kōshō Hōrin Monastery; twentieth day of early summer [fourth month] of the senior water year of the tiger, the third year of Ninji [21 May 1242]

寬元元年癸卯、書寫之。懷弉
Copied this, junior water year of the rabbit, the first year of Kangen [1243]. Ejō

---

78 **Going further, in however many of the great ways, for those who are not among the "myriad beings," their concentrated efforts have never appeared — this is the "ocean seal samādhi"** (*sara ni iku daidō ni mo ban'u ni arazaru, imada sono kufū genjō sezu, kaiin zanmai nari* さらにいく大道にも萬有にあらざる、いまだその功夫現成せず、海印三昧なり): A tentative translation of a rather obscure sentence, variously interpreted; taken to mean that the ocean seal samādhi embraces even those not included among the myriad beings contained in the great ocean. The notion here of multiple "great ways" (*daidō* 大道) is unusual in Dōgen's writing and probably should not be read here as a reference to his familiar "great way of the buddhas and ancestors."

79 By Tessō Hōken 喆囪芳賢 (d. 1551), copyist of the Ryūmonji 龍門寺 MS.

TREASURY OF THE TRUE DHARMA EYE
NUMBER 14

Sky Flowers
Kūge
空華

Sky Flowers

Kūge

INTRODUCTION

This chapter was composed in the spring 1243, during Dōgen's last months at Kōshōji. It occurs as number 14 in the sixty- and seventy-five-chapter compilations of the *Shōbōgenzō* and as number 43 in the ninety-five-chapter Honzan edition.

The title of the essay, "sky flowers" (*kūge* 空華; S. *khapuṣpa*), refers to spots appearing in the vision of a diseased eye. It is widely used in Buddhist literature as a metaphor for something empty of substance, only apparently real, lacking objective existence, and so on. Beginning with a verse attributed to Bodhidharma on the "flowering" of the Zen lineage, Dōgen comments here on eight quotations on flowers by representatives of the lineage, from Buddha Śākyamuni to Chan figures of the Song dynasty.

Throughout his comments, Dōgen seeks to transform the sense of "sky flowers" from a symbol of delusion to an expression of the way everything really exists. As he argues at one point, if we take what we see with our ordinary, "clouded" eyes as delusion, then everything will be delusion, and the very notion of delusion will make no sense. Rather, he says, sky flowers are precisely the sūtras of the buddhas, and the sky blossoms scattering in rank profusion are the manifestations of the buddhas.

正法眼藏第十四
Treasury of the True Dharma Eye
Number 14

空華
Sky Flowers

[14:1] {1:127}

高祖道、一華開五葉、結果自然成。

The Eminent Ancestor said,[1]

A single flower opens five petals;
The fruit forms, ripening naturally of itself.[2]

[14:2]

この華開の時節、および光明色相を參學すべし。一華の重は五葉なり、五葉の開は一華なり。一華の道理の通ずるところ、吾本來此土、傳法救迷情なり。光色の尋處は、この參學なるべきなり。結果任儞結果なり、自然成をいふ。自然成といふは、修因感果なり。公界の因あり、公界の果あり、この公界の因果を修し、公界の因果を感ずるなり。自は己なり、己は、必定これ儞なり、四大五蘊をいふ。使得無位眞人のゆえに、われにあらず、たれにあらず。このゆえに、不必なるを自といふなり。然は聽許なり。自然成、すなはち華開結果の時節なり、傳法救迷の時節なり。たとへば、優鉢羅華の開敷の時處は、火裏・火時なるがごとし。鑽火・焰火、みな優鉢羅華の開敷處なり、開敷時なり。もし優鉢羅華の時處にあらざれば、一星

---

1   **Eminent Ancestor** (*kōso* 高祖): Quoting the last two lines of the transmission verse attributed to the First Ancestor, Bodhidharma (*Jingde chuandeng lu* 景德傳燈錄, T.2076.51:219c17-18):

> 吾本來茲土、傳法救迷情。一華開五葉、結果目然成。

I originally came to this land
To transmit the dharma and save deluded beings.
A single flower opens five petals;
The fruit forms, ripening naturally of itself.

For more on this verse, see Supplementary Notes, s.v. "A single flower opens five petals."

2   **A single flower opens five petals** (*ikke kai goyō* 一華開五葉): There are two lines of interpretation of the "five petals" (*goyō* 五葉) in this famous verse: one that takes it as a prediction of the five houses (*goke* 五家) of Chan recognized by the Song-dynasty historians of the school; the other that takes it as foretelling the first five generations of the Chan lineage following Bodhidharma (see Supplementary Notes, s.v. "A single flower opens five petals" for details). In his "Shōbōgenzō baika" 正法眼藏梅華, Dōgen dismisses the latter interpretation, preferring to see "five petals" as a reference to the entire lineage from the seven buddhas of the past up to and including himself.

350 DŌGEN'S *SHŌBŌGENZŌ* VOLUME I

火の出生するなし、一星火の活計なきなり。しるべし、一星火に百千朶の
優鉢羅華ありて、空に開敷し、地に開敷するなり。過去に開敷し、現在に
開敷するなり。火の現時・現處を見聞するは、優鉢羅華を見聞するなり。
優鉢羅華の時處をすごさず見聞すべきなり。

We should study the occasion, as well as the physical mark of radiance, of this "flower opens."[3] The layers of the "single flower" are the "five petals"; the "opening" of the "five petals" is the "single flower." Where the truth of the "single flower" is penetrated, it is *I originally came to this land, to transmit the dharma and save deluded beings.*"[4] Inquiry into the radiance should be this study.

"*The fruit forming is up to your fruit forming*" — this is "ripening of itself."[5] "Ripening of itself" means cultivating the cause and experiencing the fruit.[6] There are causes in the public realm, and there are fruits in the public realm; one cultivates these causes and fruits of the public realm and experiences the causes and fruits of the public realm.[7] "Itself" is oneself; "oneself" is definitely "you"; it is the four elements and the five aggregates.[8] Since *it uses the "true person of no rank,"* it is not self;

---

3 **physical mark of radiance** (*kōmyō shikisō* 光明色相): Reference to the aureole (*kōmyō* 光明) surrounding the body of a buddha, one of the thirty-two marks (*sō* 相; S. *lakṣana*) of a buddha's body; an expression common enough in the Buddhist canon but not occurring elsewhere in the *Shōbōgenzō*.

4 **"I originally came to this land, to transmit the dharma and save deluded beings"** (*go hon rai shido, denbō gu meijō* 吾本來此土、傳法救迷情): The first two lines of Bodhidharma's transmission verse; see above, Note 1.

5 **"The fruit forming is up to your fruit forming"** (*kekka nin ji kekka* 結果任儞結果): I.e., the results are up to you. Dōgen is here commenting on the last line of Bodhidharma's verse, "The fruit forms, ripening naturally of itself" (*kekka jinen jō* 結果自然成), using a remark of Jingshan Hongyin 徑山洪諲 (d. 901) found in the *shinji Shōbōgenzō* 眞字正法眼藏 (DZZ.5:166-168, case 85); see Supplementary Notes, s.v. "It would surely take ten thousand years."

6 **cultivating the cause and experiencing the fruit** (*shuin kanka* 修因感果): A standard Buddhist expression for the cause and effect relationship of karma — that one will reap what one sows.

7 **public realm** (*kugai* 公界): A term regularly used to refer to the common spaces of a monastery shared by the great assembly (*daishu* 大衆); here, however, more likely referring to the objective, or shared, world beyond the private experience of the subject. See Supplementary Notes, s.v. "Public realm."

8 **"Itself" is oneself; "oneself" is definitely "you"** (*ji wa ko nari, ko wa, hitsujō kore ji nari* 自は己なり、己は、必定これ儞なり): Dōgen is here commenting on the glyph *ji* 自 ("itself") in Bodhidharma's phrase "ripening naturally of itself" (*jinen jō* 自然成), identifying it first with the term *jiko* 自己 ("oneself"), and then with the second person pronoun *ji* 儞 in his quotation of Hongyin 洪諲: "The fruit forming is up to your fruit forming" (*kekka nin ji kekka* 結果任儞結果).

14. Sky Flowers *Kūge* 空華　　　351

it is not other; hence, that it is indefinite is called "itself."[9] "Naturally" is consent.[10] "Ripening of itself" is the occasion when the "flower opens" and the "fruit forms"; it is the occasion of "transmit the dharma and save the deluded."

It is like, for example, the fact that the time and place in which the *utpala* flower blooms are within fire at the time of fire.[11] Every flicker and blaze is a place where the *utpala* flower blooms, a time when the *utpala* flower blooms.[12] Where it is not the time and place of the *utpala* flower, there is no birth of a single spark, there is no way of life of a single spark. We should realize that, in a single spark, there are a hundred thousand clusters of *utpala* flowers, which bloom in the sky and bloom on the earth. They bloom in the past; they bloom in the present. To perceive the time when the fire appears, the place where it appears, is to perceive the *utpala* flower. We should perceive them without overlooking the time and place of the *utpala* flower.

---

the four elements and the five aggregates (*shidai goun* 四大五蘊): Standard Buddhist technical terms for the physical and mental constituents of the world; see Supplementary Notes, s.v. "Four elements and five aggregates." Here, as elsewhere, Dōgen seems to be using these terms to refer to what we might call the psychophysical organism, much as he uses the expression "body and mind" (*shinjin* 身心).

9　**Since it uses the "true person of no rank"** (*shitoku mui shinnin no yue ni* 使得無位眞人のゆえに): The grammatical subject is unexpressed; presumably, the "itself" (*ji* 自) of the preceding sentence. The term "true person" (*shinnin* 眞人) first occurs in Chapter 6 of the *Zhuangzi* 莊子 (Dazongshi 大宗師, KR.5c0126.006.1a), to describe the ideal sage of ancient times; "the true person of no rank" (*mui shinnin* 無位眞人) is an expression coined by Linji Yixuan 臨濟義玄 (d. 866). See Supplementary Notes, s.v. "True person of no rank." Dōgen regularly uses the term *shitoku* 使得 in the sense "to make use of," as seen, for example, in the well-known Zen expression "employ the twelve times" (*shitoku jūni ji* 使得十二時), attributed to Zhaozhou Congshen 趙州從諗 (778-897); see Supplementary Notes.

that it is indefinite (*fuhitsu naru* 不必なる): In contrast here to the "definitely" (*hitsujō* 必定) of the preceding sentence. The point would seem to be that the "itself" (*ji* 自) of Bodhidharma's verse is at once the definite person (the "you" of "the four elements and the five aggregates") and the indefinite "true person of no rank."

10　**"Naturally" is consent** (*nen wa chōko nari* 然は聽許なり): Dōgen is here commenting on the glyph *nen* 然 in the adverb *jinen* 自然 (translated here "naturally of itself") and shifting its sense to "so be it," or "so it is." The nature of the "consent," or "approval," in question is unclear; perhaps, affirmation of the "indefiniteness" of what happens "naturally of itself."

11　*utpala* **flower** (*ubarage* 優鉢羅華; also read *upparage*): A flower variously identified, most often taken as a blue lotus or other type of water lily. The image here of the *utpala* blooming in fire derives from a line in the *Shixuan tan* 十玄談 of Tong'an Changcha 同安常察 (dates unknown) that Dōgen will quote below in section 3.

12　**flicker** (*sanka* 鑽火): A loose translation for a term indicating fire generated by a flint or boring tool, here presumably in contrast to a great conflagration.

352 DŌGEN'S *SHŌBŌGENZŌ* VOLUME I

[14:3] {1:128}
古先いはく、優鉢羅華火裏開。しかあれば、優鉢羅華はかならず火裏に開敷するなり。火裏をしらんとおもはば、優鉢羅華開敷のところなり。人見・天見を執して、火裏をならはざるべからず。疑著せんことは、水中に蓮華の生ぜるも疑著しつべし、枝條に諸華あるをも疑著しつべし。又疑著すべくは、器世間の安立も疑著しつべし。しかあれども疑著せず。佛祖にあらざれば、華開世界起をしらず。華開といふは、前三三後三三なり。この員數を具足せんために、森羅をあつめていよよかにせるなり。

An old forebear has said, "*The utpala flower blooms within fire.*"[13] Thus, the *utpala* flower invariably blooms "within fire." If we wish to know about "within fire," it is where the *utpala* flower blooms. We should not cling to the view of humans or the view of devas and fail to learn about "within fire." To doubt this means we should also doubt that lotuses grow in water, and we should also doubt that there are flowers on branches. Again, among things to doubt, we should also doubt that the vessel world is stable; yet we do not have doubts about this.[14] Those who are not buddhas and ancestors do not know about "*a flower opens, and the world arises.*"[15] "A flower opens" means "*three three in front; three three in back.*"[16] In order to be endowed with this number, it has gathered the thicket of things and raised them to towering heights.[17]

[14:4]
この道理を到來せしめて、春秋をはかりしるべし。ただ春秋に華果あるにあらず、有時かならず華果あるなり。華果ともに時節を保任せり、時節ともに華果を保任せり。このゆえに、百草みな華果あり、諸樹みな華果あり。金・銀・銅・鐵・珊瑚・頗梨樹等、みな華果あり。地・水・火・風・空樹、みな華果あり。人樹に華あり、人華に華あり、枯木に華あり。

---

13 **old forebear** (*kosen* 古先): Reference to the tenth-century figure Tong'an Changcha 同案常察, author of the *Shixuan tan* 十玄談, from which this line is taken (see *Jingde chuandeng lu* 景德傳燈錄, T.2076.51:455c10).

14 **vessel world** (*ki seken* 器世間): S. *bhājana-loka*; a standard Buddhist term for the physical environment understood as a receptacle for living beings.

15 **"a flower opens, and the world arises"** (*ke kai sekai ki* 華開世界起): The final line of the dharma transmission verse attributed to Bodhidharma's master, Prajñātāra. See Supplementary Notes, s.v. "A flower opens, and the world arises."

16 **"three three in front; three three in back"** (*zen sansan go sansan* 前三三後三三): Or, perhaps, "three and three of the former; three and three of the latter." From a well-known kōan recorded in Dōgen's *shinji Shōbōgenzō* 眞字正法眼藏 (DZZ.5:194-195, case 127); see Supplementary Notes.

17 **thicket of things** (*shinra* 森羅): A metaphor for the myriad things of the universe, based on the image of a dense growth of trees. The subject of this sentence is unexpressed; the translation takes it as "a flower opens."

raised them to towering heights (*iyoyoka ni seru* いよよかにせる): The word *iyoyoka* いよよか represents an earlier form of *iyoyaka* いよやか ("to tower").

14. Sky Flowers *Kūge* 空華

353

Bringing in this principle, we should understand spring and autumn. It is not just that there are flowers and fruits in spring and autumn: any given time invariably has flowers and fruits.[18] Flowers and fruits all maintain their moments; moments all maintain flowers and fruits. Hence, the hundred grasses all have flowers and fruits; the various trees all have flowers and fruits.[19] The trees of gold, silver, copper, iron, coral, *sphaṭika*, and so on, all have flowers and fruits.[20] The trees of earth, water, fire, wind, and space all have flowers and fruits.[21] The trees of humans have flowers; the flowers of humans have flowers; the dried-up trees have flowers.[22]

[14:5] {1:129}

かくのごとくあるなかに、世尊道、虚空華、なり。しかあるを、少聞小見のともがら、空華の彩光葉華いかなるとしらず、わづかに空華と聞取するのみなり。しるべし、佛道に空華の談あり、外道は空華の談をしらず、いはんや覺了せんや。ただし、諸佛諸祖ひとり、空華・地華の開落をしり、世界華等の開落をしれり、空華・地華・世界華等の經典なりとしれり、これ學佛の規矩なり。佛祖の所乗は空華なるがゆえに、佛世界および諸佛法、すなはちこれ空華なり。

Among such [flowers], the *World-Honored One spoke of "flowers in empty space."*[23] Nonetheless, those of little hearing and small views know nothing of the brilliant leaves and petals of sky flowers and only

---

18 **any given time** (*uji* 有時): Dōgen uses here a term — commonly meaning "at one time," "sometimes," "once upon a time," etc. — famous as the title of his "Shōbōgenzō uji" 正法眼藏有時.

19 **hundred grasses** (*hyakusō* 百草): A term regularly used in Chan texts for the myriad phenomena of the world.

20 **trees of gold, silver, copper, iron, coral, *sphaṭika*, and so on** (*kon gon dō tetsu sango hari ju tō* 金・銀・銅・鐵・珊瑚・頗梨樹等): While the trees in Amitābha's land of Sukhāvatī are said to be of the seven precious substances, the members of this list of six do not seem to correspond to any standard set. The last item, *sphaṭika* (transliterated here as *hari* 頗梨; also written 玻璃), is typically identified as crystal.

21 **trees of earth, water, fire, wind, and space** (*chi sui ka fū kū ju* 地・水・火・風・空樹): Trees of the five elements (*godai* 五大), discussed especially in esoteric Buddhism.

22 **dried-up trees** (*koboku* 枯木): A term appearing often in Chan literature as a metaphor for the seemingly lifeless thing or person, as in the phrase "dried-up trees and dead ashes" (*koboku shikai* 枯木死灰); see Supplementary Notes, s.v. "Dried-up tree."

23 **the World-Honored One spoke of "flowers in empty space"** (*seson dō, kokū ge* 世尊道、虚空華): Or "of empty sky flowers," a term synonymous with "sky flowers" (*kūge* 空華). Dōgen shifts here to Chinese, as if quoting a source; though it is unclear whether he had a specific text in mind, given that he refers just below to "world flowers" and identifies "the buddha worlds" with sky flowers, he may have been thinking here of a line from the *Yuanjue jing* 圓覺經 (T.842.17:915b6):

一切佛世界猶如虚空花。
All the buddha worlds are like flowers in empty space.

354 DŌGEN'S *SHŌBŌGENZŌ* VOLUME I

barely hear of sky flowers.[24] We should understand that the way of the buddhas has talk of sky flowers, while the other paths do not know talk of sky flowers, much less comprehend it. Only the buddhas and ancestors know the blooming and falling of sky flowers and earth flowers, know the blooming and falling of world flowers, and the like, know that the sky flowers, the earth flowers, the world flowers, and the like, are scriptures.[25] This is a standard for the study of Buddhism. Since the vehicle ridden by the buddhas and ancestors is sky flowers, the buddha worlds and the buddha dharmas are sky flowers.[26]

[14:6]

しかあるに、如來道の、翳眼所見は空華、とあるを、傳聞する凡愚おもはくは、翳眼といふは、衆生の顚倒のまなこをいふ、病眼すでに顚倒なるゆえに、淨虚空に空華を見聞するなり、と消息す。この理致を執するによりて、三界・六道、有佛・無佛、みなあらざるをありと妄見する、とおもへり。この迷妄の眼翳もしやみなば、この空華みゆべからず、このゆえに空本無華と道取する、と活計するなり。あはれむべし、かくのごとくのやから、如來道の空華の時節・始終をしらず。諸佛道の翳眼空華の道理、いまだ凡夫・外道の所見にあらざるなり。諸佛如來、この空華を修行して、衣座室をうるなり、得道・得果するなり。拈華し瞬目する、みな翳眼空華の現成する公案なり。正法眼藏涅槃妙心、いまに正傳して斷絶せざるを、翳眼空華といふなり。菩提・涅槃・法身・自性等は、空華の開五葉の兩三葉なり。

Nonetheless, the foolish people who hear that the Tathāgata said sky flowers are what is seen by clouded eyes declare that "clouded eyes" means the perverse eyes of living beings, and that diseased eyes, since they are perverse, perceive sky flowers in pure empty space.[27] Because

---

24 **little hearing and small views** (*shōmon shōken* 少聞少見): I.e., little learning and limited perspectives.

25 **world flowers** (*sekai ge* 世界華): Likely reflecting the phrase, quoted above (section 3), "a flower opens, and the world arises" (*ke kai sekai ki* 華開世界起). See Supplementary Notes, s.v. "A flower opens, and the world arises."

26 **vehicle ridden by the buddhas and ancestors** (*busso no shojō* 佛祖の所乘): Or perhaps simply "what the buddhas and ancestors avail themselves of" — i.e., the subject matter of Buddhist study.

buddha dharmas (*shobuppō* 諸佛法): Probably, "the teachings of the buddhas."

27 **the Tathāgata said sky flowers are what is seen by clouded eyes** (*nyorai dō no, eigen shoken wa kūge* 如來道の、翳眼所見は空華): "Clouded eyes" (*eigen* 翳眼) refers to a medical condition, often identified as cataracts, in which the vision is blurred or, as here, sees spots before the eyes. Dōgen's report of the Tathāgata's words, given in Japanese, does not seem to be a quotation of any particular source but near precedents are found in several sūtras; see Supplementary Notes, s.v. "Clouded eyes and sky flowers."

perverse eyes of living beings (*shujō no tendō no manako* 衆生の顚倒のまなこ): I.e., the distorted view of ordinary people. "Perverse" imperfectly renders *tendō* 顚倒 (S. *viparyasta*), a technical term in Buddhism for perspectives that are "upside down" —

14. Sky Flowers *Kūge* 空華　　　355

they cling to this theory, they think that the three realms and six paths, with a buddha or without a buddha, are all nonexistent things deludedly seen as existent; and that, if this delusional cloudiness of the eye ceases, these sky flowers will not be seen.[2⁸] Hence, they make it their business to say, "*the sky originally has no flowers.*"[29] How pitiful, that such types know nothing of the occasion, from beginning to end, of the sky flower spoken of by the Tathāgata.[30] The principles behind the "clouded eyes" and "sky flowers" spoken of by the buddhas is not something ever seen by common people or followers of other paths. It is by practicing this "sky flower" that the buddhas, the tathāgatas, get their robes, seats, and rooms, gain the way, and gain the fruit.[31] Holding up the flower and blinking the eyes are both the kōan in which the "clouded eye" and "sky flower" are realized.[32] That "the treasury of the true dharma eye, the wondrous mind of nirvāṇa" has been directly transmitted without inter-

i.e., that see things as just the opposite of what they really are. The term appears in the passage from the *Śūraṅgama-sūtra* (*Shoulengyan jing* 首楞嚴經, T.945.19:120c3) that Dōgen quotes below; for the full context, see Supplementary Notes, s.v. "Clouded eyes and sky flowers."

28　**three realms and six paths** (*sangai rokudō* 三界・六道): The levels of existence and the stations of rebirth in saṃsāra; see Supplementary Notes, s.v. "Three realms," and "Six paths."

with a buddha or without a buddha (*ubutsu mubutsu* 有佛・無佛): Translating the most common senses of these terms, used in reference to times or places in which a buddha is or is not present. Some commentators take the two terms here in a more metaphysical sense, as "buddhas that exist" and "buddhas that transcend existence."

29　**"the sky originally has no flowers"** (*kū hon mu ge* 空本無華): A line often used by Chinese Buddhist authors; see, e.g., *Yuanjue jing lüeshu* 圓覺經略疏 (T.1795.39:533c29) by Guifeng Zongmi 圭峰宗密 (780-841); *Zongjing lu* 宗鏡錄 (T.2016.48:670b21) by Yongming Yanshou 永明延壽 (904-975). Although the glyphs vary slightly, the source that Dōgen had in mind was probably the passage from the *Śūraṅgama-sūtra* (*Shoulengyan jing* 首楞嚴經, T.945.19:120c3) that he will quote in the following section. There, Pūrṇa says to the Buddha: "The sky originally has no flowers (*kū gen mu ge* 空元無華); they are falsely seen as arising and disappearing. To see the flowers as vanishing from the sky is already an inverted view; to will them to reappear is real lunacy." For the full context, see Supplementary Notes, s.v. "Clouded eyes and sky flowers."

30　**the occasion, from beginning to end** (*jisetsu shishu* 時節・始終): A phrase that could be interpreted either as "the entire occasion from start to finish" or as "the occasion and its beginning and end" [i.e., the appearance and disappearance of the sky flower].

31　**robes, seats, and rooms** (*e za shitsu* 衣座室): Allusion to a verse in the *Lotus Sūtra*; see Supplementary Notes, s.v. "Robe of the Tathāgata."

32　**Holding up the flower and blinking the eyes** (*nenge shi shunmoku suru* 拈華し瞬目する): Reference to (one version of) the famous story of the first transmission of the "treasury of the true dharma eye" (*shōbōgenzō* 正法眼藏) from Śākyamuni to Mahākāśyapa at an assembly on Vulture Peak; when the Buddha held up a flower and blinked his eyes, the Ancestor smiled slightly. See Supplementary Notes, s.v. "Holding up a flower and blinking the eyes."

356 DŌGEN'S *SHŌBŌGENZŌ* VOLUME I

ruption till now is called "the clouded eye and the sky flower."[33] Bodhi, nirvāṇa, the dharma body, the self-nature, and so on, are two or three petals of the sky flower's "opening five petals."[34]

* * * * *

[14:7]

釋迦牟尼佛言、亦如翳人見空中華、翳病若除華於空滅。

Buddha Śākyamuni said, "Again, it is like the person with clouded vision who sees sky flowers. If the disease of cloudiness is removed, the flowers disappear from the sky."[35]

[14:8] {1:130}

この道著、あきらむる學者いまだあらず。空をしらざるがゆえに空華をしらず、空華をしらざるがゆえに、翳人をしらず、翳人をみず、翳人にあはず、翳人ならざるなり。翳人と相見して、空華をもしり、空華をもみるべし。空華をみてのちに、華於空滅をもみるべきなり。ひとたび空華やみなば、さらにあるべからずとおもふは、小乘の見解なり。空華みえざらんときは、なににてあるべきぞ。ただ空華は所捨となるべしとのみしりて、空華ののちの大事をしらず、空華の種熟脱をしらず。

There have never been students who clarified this statement. Because they do not know the sky, they do not know sky flowers. Because they do not know sky flowers, they do not know "the person with clouded vision," they do not see the person with clouded vision, they do not meet the person with clouded vision, they are not the person with clouded vision. We should meet the person with clouded vision, know the sky flowers, see the sky flowers. After seeing the sky flowers, we should also see

---

kōan in which the "clouded eye" and "sky flower" are realized (*eigen kūge no genjō suru kōan* 翳眼空華の現成する公案): I.e., a case expressing the clouded eye and sky flower. Dōgen invokes here the "realized kōan" (*genjō kōan* 現成公案) that appears so often in his writing; see Supplementary Notes, s.v. "Realized kōan."

33 **"treasury of the true dharma eye, the wondrous mind of nirvāṇa"** (*shōbōgenzō nehan myōshin* 正法眼藏涅槃妙心): Reference to the words of Buddha Śākyamuni describing what he was transmitting on Vulture Peak to the First Ancestor, Mahākāśyapa; the essence of the Buddhist teaching, transmitted through the lineage of the buddhas and ancestors; see Supplementary Notes, s.v. "Treasury of the true dharma eye."

34 **the dharma body, the self-nature** (*hosshin jishō* 法身 · 自性): Or "the self-nature of the dharma body"; the translation follows Kawamura's punctuation. The term *jishō* 自性 refers to the ultimate nature of a thing, what it is in itself.

sky flower's "opening five petals" (*kūge no kai goyō* 空華の開五葉): Recalling Bodhidharma's verse, in section 1, above.

35 **Buddha** Śākyamuni (*Shakamuni butsu* 釋迦牟尼佛): Quoting the *Śūraṅgama-sūtra* (*Shoulengyan jing* 首楞嚴經, T.945.19:120b29-c1). The sūtra text gives the homophonous "cataract" (*ei* 瞖), rather than Dōgen's "clouded" (*ei* 翳); but the glyphs seem interchangeable when the referent is the human eye. For the full context, see Supplementary Notes, s.v. "Clouded eyes and sky flowers."

14. Sky Flowers *Kūge* 空華   357

"the flowers disappear from the sky." To think that, once the sky flowers cease, they should no longer exist is a view of the Small Vehicle.[36] When sky flowers are not to be seen, what would there be? Knowing only that sky flowers are just something to be discarded, we do not know the great matter after sky flowers, do not know the planting, maturing, and dropping off of the sky flower.[37]

[14:9]

いま凡夫の學者おもはくは、陽氣のすめるところ、これ空ならんとおもひ、日月星辰のかかれるところを空ならんとおもへるによりて、假令すらくは、空華といはんは、この清氣のなかに、浮雲のごとくして、飛華の風にふかれて東西し、および昇降するがごとくなる彩色のいできたらんずるを、空華といはんずる、とおもへり。能造・所造の四大、あはせて器世間の諸法、ならびに本覺・本性等を空華といふとは、ことにしらざるなり。又諸法によりて能造の四大等ありとしらず、諸法によりて器世間は住法位なりとしらず、器世間によりて諸法ありとばかり知見するなり。眼翳によりて空華ありとのみ覺了して、空華によりて眼翳あらしむる道理を覺了せざるなり。

Nowadays, commoner students, because they think that the "sky" is where the yang energy resides or think that the "sky" is where the sun, moon, and stars are suspended, think, for example, that, when we say "sky flowers," we mean the appearance of colors like blossoms flying east and west, or up and down, before the wind, like clouds floating in this clear air.[38] They do not really know that the four elements as fabricator and fabricated, as well as the dharmas of the vessel world, along

---

36 **To think that, once the sky flowers cease, they should no longer exist** (*hitotabi kūge yaminaba, sara ni aru bekarazu to omou* ひとたび空華やみなば、さらにあるべからずとおもふ): A view expressed in the passage of the *Śūraṅgama-sūtra* from which Dōgen quoted in the preceding section; see Note 29, above.

37 **great matter** (*daiji* 大事): The ultimate purpose of Buddhism, as understood especially through the passage in the *Lotus Sūtra* where it is defined as leading all beings to buddhahood (*Miaofa lianhua jing* 妙法蓮華經, T.262.9:7a21-28).

planting, maturing, and dropping off (*shu juku datsu* 種熟脱): A horticultural metaphor, used in the literature especially of the Tiantai 天台 tradition, for three stages of Buddhist spiritual development based on the *Lotus Sūtra*: to plant the seed of faith in the sūtra (*geshu* 下種); to develop one's wholesome roots through practice (*jōjaku* 調熟); and to attain liberation for the sake of all beings (*tokudatsu* 得脱).

38 **commoner students** (*bonbu no gakusha* 凡夫の學者): I.e., students of Buddhism who are still among the "common people" (S. *prthagjana*) not yet advanced to the higher, "noble" (S. ārya) stages of the Buddhist path.

where the yang energy resides (*yōki no sumeru tokoro* 陽氣のすめるところ): In accordance with the common understanding of Chinese cosmology that heaven is yang and earth is yin.

for example (*keryō suraku wa* 假令すらくは): Alternatively, one might take this as "what they casually assume."

358   DŌGEN'S *SHŌBŌGENZŌ* VOLUME I

with original awakening, the original nature, and the like, are called "sky flowers."[39] Furthermore, they do not know that the four elements as fabricators, and the rest, exist because of the dharmas; they do not know that the vessel world "abides in its dharma position" because of the dharmas.[40] They hold the view only that the dharmas exist because of the vessel world. Comprehending only that sky flowers exist because of the cloudiness of the eye, they do not comprehend the principle that the cloudiness of the eye is enabled to exist because of the sky flowers.

[14:10] {1:131}

しるべし、佛道の翳人といふは、本覺人なり、妙覺人なり、諸佛人なり、三界人なり、佛向上人なり。おろかに翳を妄法なりとして、このほかに眞法ありと學することなかれ。しかあらんは、少量の見なり。翳華もし妄法ならんは、これを妄法と邪執する能作・所作、みな妄法なるべし。ともに妄法ならんがごときは、道理の成立すべきなし。成立する道理なくば、翳華の妄法なること、しかあるべからざるなり。悟の翳なるには、悟の衆法、ともに翳莊嚴の法なり。迷の翳なるには、迷の衆法、ともに翳莊嚴の法なり。しばらく道取すべし、翳眼平等なれば空華平等なり、翳眼無生なれば空華無生なり、諸法實相なれば翳華實相なり。過・現・來を論ずべからず、初・中・後にかかわれず。生滅に罣礙せざるゆえに、よく生滅をして生滅せしむるなり。空中に生じ、空中に滅す。翳中に生じ、翳中に滅す。華中に生じ、華中に滅す。乃至諸餘の時處も、またまたかくのごとし。

We should realize that the "person with clouded vision" on the way of the buddhas is a person of original awakening, is a person of wondrous awakening, is a person of the buddhas, is a person of the three realms, is

---

39   **four elements as fabricator and fabricated** (*nōzō shozō no shidai* 能造所造の四大): The expression *nōzō shozō* 能造所造 most often refers to the four elements as the "fabricator" and the material world as the "fabricated." Here, the four elements themselves seem to be both fabricator and fabricated, perhaps in the sense that the four elements both produce the material world and are themselves produced from the characteristics of hardness (earth), fluidity (water), heat (fire), and motion (wind).

original awakening, the original nature, and the like (*hongaku honshō tō* 本覺・本性等): The former term refers to the nature of awakening inherent in all beings, in contrast to the "initial awakening" (*shikaku* 始覺) attained as a result of Buddhist practice. The latter term refers to the fundamental reality of something; roughly synonymous with "self-nature" (*jishō* 自性) (seen above, section 6).

dharmas of the vessel world (*ki sekai no shohō* 器世間の諸法): I.e., the phenomena of the physical environment.

40   **the vessel world "abides in its dharma position" because of the dharmas** (*shohō ni yorite ki sekai wa jū hōi nari* 諸法によりて器世間は住法位なり): I.e., the physical world is constant in the sense that it is made up of a series of momentary phenomena. Dōgen here invokes a a line in the *Lotus Sūtra* that can be read, "the dharmas abide in their dharma positions"; see Supplementary Notes, s.v. "Dharmas abide in their dharma positions."

14. Sky Flowers *Kūge* 空華

359

a person beyond the buddha.[41] Do not stupidly study that the cloudiness is delusive dharmas, apart from which there are real dharmas: to do so is a small view. Were clouded flowers to be delusive dharmas, then both the agent and the act of clinging mistakenly to them as delusive dharmas would themselves be delusive dharmas; where both are delusive dharmas, the truth could not be established; and where there is no truth established, it could not be the case that the clouded flowers are delusive dharmas.[42] When our awakening is clouded, the dharmas of our awakening are all dharmas adorned with cloudiness; when our delusion is clouded, the dharmas of our delusion are all dharmas adorned with cloudiness.[43]

For now, we can say that, when clouded eyes are equal, sky flowers are equal; when clouded eyes are unborn, sky flowers are unborn, when it is "the real marks of the dharmas," it is the real marks of sky flowers.[44] We should not make an issue of past, present, or future; it has nothing to do with beginning, middle, or end. Since they are not obstructed by their arising and ceasing, they cause arising and ceasing to arise and cease. They appear in the sky; they disappear in the sky. They arise in

---

41 **person of original awakening** (*hongaku nin* 本覺人); a **person of wondrous awakening** (*myōkaku nin* 妙覺人): A contrasting pair: the person understood as awakened by reason of the buddha nature inherent in consciousness, and the person who has attained the unsurpassed perfect awakening of buddhahood.

person of the buddhas (*shobutsu nin* 諸佛人); **a person of the three realms** (*sangai nin* 三界人): Another contrasting pair: the person who ranks among the buddhas, and the person who belongs to the threefold world of rebirth. See Supplementary Notes, s.v. "Three realms."

person beyond the buddha (*butsu kōjō nin* 佛向上人): A common term in Zen texts for one who, like the awakened Zen master, has transcended the distinction between the human and the buddha; see Supplementary Notes, s.v. "Beyond the buddha."

42 **it could not be the case that the clouded flowers are delusive dharmas** (*eiga no mōbō naru koto, shika aru bekarazaru nari* 翳華の妄法なること、しかあるべからざ るなり*): The argument would seem to be that the claim that all our knowledge is false is incoherent, since (a) we would have no knowledge against which to contrast it, and (b) the claim would apply to the claim itself.

43 **dharmas of our awakening** (*go no shuhō* 悟の衆法); **dharmas of our delusion** (*mei no shuhō* 迷の衆法): I.e., the objects of our awakened consciousness and the objects of our deluded consciousness.

44 **clouded eyes are equal** (*eigen byōdō* 翳眼平等); **clouded eyes are unborn** (*eigen mushō* 翳眼無生); **"the real marks of the dharmas"** (*shohō jissō* 諸法實相): The first two adjectives are common Buddhist descriptions of ultimate reality — that it is without distinctions, and that it does not arise and cease as do the dharmas we ordinarily perceive. The third expression introduces a famous phrase in Chinese Buddhist literature, best known from Kumārajīva's translation of the *Lotus Sūtra*, that Dōgen discusses at length in his "Shōbōgenzō shohō jissō" 正法眼藏諸法實相; see Supplementary Notes, s.v. "Only buddhas with buddhas can exhaustively investigate the real marks of the dharmas."

the clouded vision; they cease in the clouded vision. They arise in the flower; they cease in the flower. And so forth, to every other time and place, in just the same way.

[14:11]

空華を學せんこと、まさに衆品あるべし。瞖眼の所見あり、明眼の所見あり、佛眼の所見あり、祖眼の所見あり、道眼の所見あり、瞎眼の所見あり、三千年の所見あり、八百年の所見あり、百劫の所見あり、無量劫の所見あり。これらともにみな空華をみるといへども、空すでに品品なり、華また重重なり。

Studying sky flowers can be of multiple types: there is what is seen by the clouded eye; there is what is seen by the clear eye; there is what is seen by the buddha eye; there is what is seen by the ancestor eye; there is what is seen by the eye of the way; there is what is seen by the eye of the blind; there is what is seen in three thousand years; there is what is seen in eight hundred years; there is what is seen in a hundred kalpas; there is what is seen in innumerable kalpas.[45] All of these may see sky flowers, but the sky itself is already multiple, and the flowers are various.

[14:12]

まさにしるべし、空は一草なり、この空かならず華さく、百草に華さくがごとし。この道理を道取するとして、如來道は空本無華と道取するなり。本無華なりといへども、今有華なることは、桃・李もかくのごとし、梅・柳もかくのごとし。梅昨無華、梅春有華と道取せんがごとし。しかあれども、時節到來すればすなはち華さく、華時なるべし、華到來なるべし。この華到來の正當恁麼時、みだりなることいまだあらず。梅柳の華は、かならず梅柳にさく。華をみて梅柳をしる、梅柳をみて華をわきまふ。桃李の華、いまだ梅柳にさくことなし。梅柳の華は梅柳にさき、桃李の華は桃李にさくなり。空華の、空にさくも、またまたかくのごとし。さらに餘草にさかず、餘樹にさかざるなり。空華の諸色をみて、空菓の無窮なるを測量するなり。空華の開落をみて、空華の春秋を學すべきなり。空華の春と餘華の春と、ひとしかるべきなり。空華のいろいろなるがごとく、春時もおほかるべし。このゆえに、古今の春秋あるなり。空華は實にあらず、餘華はこれ實なり、と學するは、佛教を見聞せざるものなり。空本無華の説

---

45 **buddha eye** (*butsu gen* 佛眼); ancestor eye (*sogen* 祖眼); **eye of the way** (*dōgen* 道眼): The first term here is a standard Buddhist expression for the wisdom of a buddha, the highest of a commonly encountered set of "five eyes" (*gogen* 五眼); see Supplementary Notes, s.v. "Eye." The "ancestor eye" (*sogen* 祖眼) is no doubt modeled on the "buddha eye" and used especially in reference to the wisdom of the Zen masters. "The eye of the way" (*dōgen* 道眼) is another standard Buddhist term, sometimes listed with the five eyes, for the wisdom especially of the advanced bodhisattva.

eye of the blind (*katsugen* 瞎眼): A term that can also mean "one-eyed."

seen in three thousand years (*sanzen nen no shoken* 三千年の所見): Perhaps an allusion to the *udumbara* flower (*udonge* 優曇華), said to blossom only once every three thousand years.

14. Sky Flowers *Kūge* 空華　　　361

をききて、もとよりなかりつる空華の、いまあると學するは、短慮少見なり。進歩して遠慮あるべし。

We should realize that the "sky" is a single blade of grass, and that flowers bloom in this sky just as flowers bloom in the hundred grasses. As an expression of this principle, the words of the Tathāgata say, "*The sky originally has no flowers.*"[46] Although it "originally has no flowers," that now it has flowers is quite like the peach or the damson, like the plum or the willow.[47] It is like saying, "*the plum yesterday had no flowers, but the plum in spring has flowers.*"[48] Although this is so, when the time arrives, the flowers bloom; it will be the time for flowers, and the flowers will arrive. The very moment when the flowers arrive is never random: the flowers of the plum and the willow invariably bloom on the plum and the willow. Seeing the flowers, we know it is a plum or a willow; seeing the plum or the willow, we distinguish between their flowers. The flowers of the peach or the damson never bloom on the plum or the willow; the flowers of the plum and the willow bloom on the plum and the willow; the flowers of the peach and damson bloom on the peach and damson. The blooming of the sky flowers in the sky is also like this: they do not bloom on other grasses; they do not bloom on other trees.

Seeing the various colors of the sky flowers, we calculate that the sky fruits are unlimited. Seeing the opening and falling of the sky flowers, we can study the spring and autumn of sky flowers. The springtime of sky flowers and the springtime of other flowers should be identical. And just as the sky flowers are varied, so there should be many kinds of springtimes. Therefore, there are the springs and autumns of past and present. Those who study that sky flowers are not real, while other flowers are real, have not seen or heard the teachings of the buddhas. Hearing the

---

46　**"The sky originally has no flowers"** (*kū hon muge* 空本無華): Curiously, Dōgen repeats here as the words of the Buddha the phrase he seems to reject above, section 6, as the words of the foolish. While common enough in other texts, this exact phrase does not seem to occur in any extant sūtra. However, a very similar expression, "the sky from the beginning has no flowers" (*kū gen mu ge* 空元無花) does appear in the *Śūraṅgama-sūtra* (*Shoulengyan jing* 首楞嚴經, T.945.19:120c2), in the passage on the diseased eye cited above, Note 29. Perhaps Dōgen's reference to "the words of the Tathāgata (*Nyorai dō* 如來道) was to the sūtra as a whole, rather than to the speech of the Buddha.

47　**damson** (*ri* 李); **plum** (*bai* 梅): The former (*Prunus insititia*), called *sumomo* in Japanese, is also known as the Damask plum, or plum of Damascus; the latter may refer to several trees of the genus *Prunus*, especially *Prunus mume*, called *ume* in Japanese, or the Chinese plum.

48　**"the plum yesterday had no flowers, but the plum in spring has flowers"** (*bai saku mu ke, baishun u ke* 梅昨無華、梅春有華): Dōgen here shifts to Chinese syntax, though there is no evident Chinese source. The line is sometimes read, "In the yesterday of the plum, there were no flowers; in the spring of the plum, there are flowers."

362 DŌGEN'S *SHŌBŌGENZŌ* VOLUME I

preaching that "*the sky originally has no flowers*," to study that it means the sky flowers that originally did not exist now exist is weak thinking and a small view; we should step forward and think more fully.[49]

[14:13] {1:132}

祖師いはく、華亦不曾生。この宗旨の現成、たとへば華亦不曾生、華亦不曾滅なり、華亦不曾華なり、空亦不曾空の道理なり。華時の前後を胡亂して、有無の戯論あるべからず。華はかならず諸色にそめたるがごとし、諸色かならずしも華にかぎらず。諸時また青・黄・赤・白等のいろあるなり。春は華をひく、華は春をひくものなり。

An ancestral master has said, "*The flowers, too, have never arisen*."[50]

The expression of this essential point is, for example, "*the flowers, too, have never arisen*," and *the flowers, too, have never ceased*; it is *the flowers, too, have never flowered*; it is the truth that *the sky, too, has never sky-ed*.[51] There should be no dispute about their being or non-being, talking nonsense about the before and after of the time of the flowers. Flowers seem always to be imbued with colors, but colors are not always limited to flowers: various times also have their colors, such as blue, yellow, red, and white. Spring draws forth the flowers; flowers draw forth the spring.

* * * * *

[14:14] {1:133}

張拙秀才は、石霜の俗弟子なり。悟道の頌をつくるにいはく、光明寂照遍河沙。

The Refined Talent Zhang Zhuo was a lay disciple of Shishuang.[52] In a

---

49 **weak thinking and a small view** (*tanryo shōken* 短慮少見): Both expressions are a bit unusual. The latter is likely synonymous with the more common *shōken* 小見; the former (literally, "short thought") is the opposite of the common *enryo* 遠慮 (literally, "extended, or long-term, thinking"), translated in the next clause as "think more fully."

50 **An ancestral master** (*soshi* 祖師): From the transmission verse of Bodhidharma's successor, the Second Ancestor, Huike 慧可 (487–593) (*Jingde chuandeng lu* 景德傳燈錄, T.2076.51:220c29):

本來無有種、華亦不曾生。

Originally, there are no seeds;
The flowers, too, have never arisen.

51 **the sky, too, has never sky-ed** (*kū yaku fuzō kū* 空亦不曾空): Or, less playfully, "the sky, too, has never been the sky."

52 **Refined Talent Zhang Zhuo** (*Chō Setsu shūsai* 張拙秀才): "Refined Talent" renders *shūsai* 秀才, a reference to one who has passed the examination for civil service (C. *jinshi* 進士). Zhang Zhuo is a ninth-century lay figure (dates unknown), who left a verse marking his spiritual insight under Chan master Shishuang Qingzhu 石霜慶諸 (807–888). In the following sections, Dōgen will quote and comment on each line of

14. Sky Flowers *Kūge* 空華 363

verse on his awakening to the way, he said, "*The radiance shines silently,
throughout the sands of the Ganges.*"[53]

[14:15]

この光明、あらたに僧堂・佛殿・廚車・山門を現成せり。遍河沙は光明現
成なり、現成光明なり。

This "radiance" reveals anew "*saṃgha hall, buddha hall, kitchen, and
mountain gate.*"[54] "Throughout the sands of the Ganges" is the manifestation of the radiance, is the radiance manifest.

[14:16]

凡聖含靈共我家。凡夫・賢聖なきにあらず、これによりて凡夫・賢聖を謗
することなかれ。

"*Commoners, sages, all the animate — together are my family.*"[55]

It is not that there are no commoners or worthy sages; do not slander
the commoners and worthy sages by this.

[14:17]

一念不生全體現。念念一一なり、これはかならず不生なり。これ全體全現
なり。このゆえに、一念不生と道取す。

"*A single moment of thought unborn, the entire body appears.*"[56]

the verse, beginning here with the first line. Here is the entire verse as recorded in the
Liandeng huiyao 聯燈會要 (ZZ.136:794a11-14):

光明寂照徧河沙。凡聖含靈共我家。一念不生全體現。六根纔動被雲遮。斷除煩
惱重增病。趣向眞如亦是邪。隨順世緣無罣礙。涅槃生死是空華。

The radiance shines silently, throughout the sands of the Ganges.
Commoners, sages, all the animate — together are my family.
A single moment of thought unborn, the entire body appears.
The slightest movement of the six senses, and it's obscured by clouds.
The afflictions cut off and cleared away, the disease only doubles.
Tending toward true suchness — this, too, is a mistake.
Conforming to worldly conditions, there are no obstructions.
Nirvāṇa and birth and death — they're sky flowers.

53 **"sands of the Ganges"** (*gasha* 河沙): Also written *gōgasha* 恆河沙; a standard
metaphor for something too numerous to count; in this case, no doubt, "worlds equal to
the sands of the Ganges."

54 **"saṃgha hall, buddha hall, kitchen, and mountain gate"** (*sōdō butsuden zuku
sanmon* 僧堂・佛殿・廚庫・山門): I.e., the buildings of the monastery, the last of which
is also known as the "triple (or 'threefold') gate" (*sanmon* 三門). Recalling a saying attributed to Yunmen Wenyan 雲門文偃 (864-949) quoted at *shinji Shōbōgenzō* 眞字正法
眼藏, case 81, DZZ.5:166; see Supplementary Notes.

55 **Commoners, sages, all the animate** (*bonshō ganrei* 凡聖含靈): I.e., ordinary humans, spiritual adepts, and all sentient beings.

56 **"A single moment of thought unborn, the entire body appears"** (*ichinen fushō zentai
gen* 一念不生全體現): Or "when a single thought does not occur, the entirety is present."

364 DŌGEN'S *SHŌBŌGENZŌ* VOLUME I

Thought by thought, one by one — this is always "unborn." This is "the entire body" entirely "appearing." Therefore, he says, "a single moment of thought unborn."

[14:18]

六根繞動被雲遮。六根はたとひ眼・耳・鼻・舌・身・意なりとも、かならずしも二三にあらず、前後三三なるべし。動は如須彌山なり、如大地なり、如六根なり、如繞動なり。動すでに如須彌山なるがゆえに、不動また如須彌山なり。たとへば、雲をなし水をなすなり。

"The slightest movement of the six organs, and it's obscured by clouds."

The "six organs" may be eye, ear, nose, tongue, body, and mind, but they are not necessarily two threes; they should be the front and back, three and three.[57] "Movement" is like Mount Sumeru, like the whole earth, like the six sense organs, like "the slightest movement." Since their moving is like Mount Sumeru, their not moving is also like Mount Sumeru.[58] For example, it makes clouds and produces water.

[14:19]

斷除煩惱重增病。從來やまふなきにあらず、佛病・祖病あり。いまの智斷は、やまふをかさね、やまふをます。斷除の正當恁麼時、かならずそれ煩惱なり、同時なり、不同時なり。煩惱かならず斷除の法を帶せるなり。

"The afflictions cut off and cleared away, the disease only doubles."[59]

It is not that we have had no sickness up till now: there is the buddha "disease" and the ancestor "disease." The wisdom and eradication here pile up the sickness, increase the sickness.[60] The very moment of "cut off and cleared away" is always "affliction"; they are simultaneous; they are not simultaneous. "The afflictions" necessarily entail the dharma of "cut off and cleared away."

---

57 **two threes** (*ni san* 二三): I.e., six in number.

Front and back, three and three (*zengo sansan* 前後三三): For the source, see above, Note 16.

58 **Since their moving is like Mount Sumeru** (*dō sude ni nyo Shumisen naru ga yue ni* 動すでに如須彌山なるがゆえに): Mount Sumeru, the mountain at the center of the world in Buddhist cosmology, is often used as a symbol of the unmoving — as when the meditator is told to sit "like Mount Sumeru." The translation assumes the subject is the movement of the six sense organs, but it could also be taken simply as movement in the abstract.

59 **"The afflictions cut off and cleared away"** (*danjo bonnō* 斷除煩惱): I.e., to eradicate the spiritual defilements (S. *kleśa*).

60 **wisdom and eradication** (*chidan* 智斷): Technical terms for the two prime desiderata of the Buddhist path: the wisdom of bodhi and the eradication of the *kleśa* enabling nirvāṇa; here used in reference to the verse's *danjo* 斷除 ("to eradicate," translated here "cut off and cleared away").

14. Sky Flowers *Kūge* 空華

365

[14:20] {1:134}

趣向眞如亦是邪。眞如を背する、これ邪なり。眞如に向する、これ邪なり。眞如は向背なり、向背の各各に、これ眞如なり。たれかしらん、この邪の亦是眞如なることを。

"*Tending toward true suchness — this, too, is a mistake.*"[61]

To turn away from true suchness — this is a "mistake"; to turn toward true suchness — this is a "mistake." True suchness is turning toward and turning away; each and every turning toward and turning away — this is true suchness. Who knows that this "mistake" is "this, too," is suchness.

[14:21]

隨順世緣無罣礙。世緣と世緣と隨順し、隨順と隨順と世緣なり。これを無罣礙といふ。罣礙・不罣礙は、被眼礙に慣習すべきなり。

"*Conforming to worldly conditions, there are no obstructions.*"[62]

"Worldly conditions" and "worldly conditions" "conform"; "conforming" and "conforming" are "worldly conditions." This is called "there are no obstructions." We should get familiar with the fact that obstructing and not obstructing are "obstructed by the eye."[63]

[14:22]

涅槃生死是空華。涅槃といふは、阿耨多羅三藐三菩提なり。佛祖および佛祖の弟子の所住これなり。生死は眞實人體なり。この涅槃・生死は、その法なりといへども、これ空華なり。空華の根莖枝葉・華果光色、ともに空華の華開なり。空華かならず空菓をむすぶ、空種をくだすなり。いま見聞する三界は、空華の五葉開なるゆえに、不如三界、見於三界なり。この諸法實相なり、この諸法華相なり。乃至不測の諸法、ともに空華・空果なり、梅柳・桃李とひとしきなり、と參學すべし。

Nirvāṇa and birth and death — they're sky flowers.

"Nirvāṇa" means *anuttara-samyak-saṃbodhi*.[64] The abode of the buddhas and ancestors, as well as the disciples of the buddhas and ances-

---

61 **"Tending toward true suchness"** (*shu kō shinnyo* 趣向眞如): I.e., seeking to reach the ultimate reality of things, their "suchness," or "thusness" (S. *tathatā*).

62 **Conforming to worldly conditions** (*zuijun se'en* 隨順世緣): I.e., going along with circumstances.

63 **"obstructed by the eye"** (*higen ge* 被眼礙): Likely reflecting a saying of Fayan Wenyi 法眼文益 (885-958) that Dōgen records in his *shinji Shōbōgenzō* 眞字正法眼藏 (DZZ.5:186, case 111); see Supplementary Notes.

64 ***anuttara-samyak-saṃbodhi*** (*anokutara sanmyaku sanbodai* 阿耨多羅三藐三菩提): The unsurpassed, perfect awakening of a buddha.

366 DŌGEN'S *SHŌBŌGENZŌ* VOLUME I

tors, is this. "Birth and death" are "the true human body."[65] Though we say this "nirvāṇa and birth and death" are those dharmas, they are "sky flowers."[66] The "roots, stalks, branches, and leaves, flowers and fruit, lustrous and colored" of the sky flowers are all the blooming of "sky flowers."[67] Sky flowers always produce sky fruit and drop sky seeds. Because the three realms we now perceive are the sky flower's "five petals opening," it is "*he sees the three realms not as the three realms.*"[68] It is these "real marks of the dharmas"; it is these flower marks of the dharmas.[69] And so on, through incalculable dharmas — all of which are sky flowers and sky fruits. We should study that they are the same as the plum, the willow, the peach, and the damson.

* * * * *

[14:23]

大宋國福州芙蓉山靈訓禪師、初參歸宗寺至眞禪師而問、如何是佛。歸宗云、我向汝道、汝還信否。師云、和尚誠言、何敢不信。歸宗云、即汝便是。師曰、如何保任。歸宗云、一翳在眼、空華亂墜。

Chan Master Lingxun of Mount Furong in Fuzhou in the Land of the Great Song, when he first went to consult Chan Master Zhizhen of

---

65 **"Birth and death" are "the true human body"** (*shōji wa shinjitsu nintai* 生死は眞實人體): After the words of Yuanwu Keqin 圓悟克勤 (1063-1135); see Supplementary Notes, s.v. "True human body."

66 **this "nirvāṇa and birth and death" are those dharmas** (*kono nehan shōji wa, sono hō nari* この涅槃・生死は、その法なり): The referent of "those dharmas" (*sono hō* その法) is unclear: perhaps, simply the dharmas of "nirvāṇa and birth and death"; alternatively, the dharmas of "*anuttara-samyak-saṃbodhi*" and "the true human body," respectively.

67 **"roots, stalks, branches, and leaves, flowers and fruit, lustrous and colored"** (*kon kyō shi yō ke ka kō shiki* 根莖枝葉・華果光色): From a verse in the *Lotus Sūtra* describing the varied plants of the world watered by the same rain; see Supplementary Notes.

68 **"he sees the three realms not as the three realms"** (*funyo sangai, ken o sangai* 不如三界、見於三界): Reference to a passage in the *Lotus Sūtra* (*Miaofa lianhua jing* 妙法蓮華經, T.262.9:42c13-15):

如來如實知見三界之相。無有生死若退若出。亦無在世及滅度者。非實非虛非如非異。不如三界見於三界。

The Tathāgata views the marks of the three realms as they really are. There is no birth and death, whether withdrawal or emergence; there is no one remaining in the world or passing into extinction. They are not reality or vanity; they are not thus or different. He sees the three realms not as the three realms.

See Supplementary Notes, s.v. "Three realms."

69 **"real marks of the dharmas"** (*shohō jissō* 諸法實相): See section 10, above.

14. Sky Flowers *Kūge* 空華　　367

Guizong Monastery, asked, "What is a buddha?"[70]

Guizong said, "If I tell you, will you believe it?"

The Master said, "The Reverend's words are sincere, how could I not believe them?"

Guizong said, "You yourself are one."

The Master said, "How can I maintain it?"

Guizong said, "A single cloudiness in the eye; the sky flowers flutter down."

[14:24] {1:135}

いま歸宗道の一翳在眼、空華亂墜は、保任佛の道取なり。しかあればしるべし、翳華の亂墜は、諸佛の現成なり。眼空の華果は、諸佛の保任なり。翳をもて眼を現成せしむ。眼中に空華を現成し、空華中に眼を現成せり。空華在眼、一翳亂墜。一眼在空、衆翳亂墜なるべし。ここをもて、翳也全機現、眼也全機現、空也全機現、華也全機現なり。亂墜は千眼なり、通身眼なり。おほよそ一眼の在時在處、かならず空華あり、眼華あるなり。眼華を空華とはいふ。眼華の道取、かならず開明なり。

Guizong's words here, "*A single cloudiness in the eye; the sky flowers flutter down*," are a saying that "maintains" "a buddha." This being the case, we should realize that the "tumbling down" of the "cloudy" "flowers" is the manifestation of the buddhas. The flowers and fruits of the "eye sky" are the "maintaining" of the buddhas.[71] They use the cloudiness to make the eye manifest. They manifest the sky flowers in the eye; they manifest the eye in the sky flowers. It should be, "*a sky flower in the eye; a single cloudiness flutters down; a single eye in the sky; the multiple cloudinesses flutter down.*" Hence, "*cloudiness,*" "*the manifestation of the full function*"; "*eye,*" "*the manifestation of the full function*"; "*sky,*" "*the manifestation of the full function*"; "*flower,*" "*the manifestation of the full function.*"[72] "Flutter down" is "the thousand

---

70　**Chan Master Lingxun of Mount Furong in Fuzhou in the Land of the Great Song** (*Daisōkoku Fukushū Fuyōzan Reikun zenji* 大宋國福州芙蓉山靈訓禪師): I.e. Furong Linxun 芙蓉靈訓 (dates unknown). This dialogue can be found at *Jingde chuandeng lu* 景德傳燈錄, T.2076.51:280c23-26.

Chan Master Zhizhen of Guizong Monastery (*Kisuji Shishin zenji* 歸宗寺至眞禪師): I.e., Guizong Zhichang 歸宗智常 (dates unknown).

71　**The flowers and fruits of the "eye sky"** (*genkū no keka* 眼空の華果): A play on Guizong's line, "A single cloudiness in the eye; the sky flowers flutter down" (*ichi ei zai gen kūge rantsui* 一翳在眼空華亂墜), suggesting that the Chinese could be parsed, "A single cloudiness in the eye sky, and flowers flutter down."

72　**"cloudiness," "the manifestation of the full function"** (*ei ya zenki gen* 翳也全機現): This and the following three clauses are variations on a verse comment by Yuanwu Keqin 圜悟克勤 (1063–1135) on a converstion involving Daowu Yuanzhi 道悟圓智 (769–835) and his dharma heir Jianyuan Zhongxing 漸源仲興 (dates unknown). When

368　DŌGEN'S *SHŌBŌGENZŌ* VOLUME I

eyes"; it is "eyes throughout the body."[73] In general, in the time and the place of a single eye, invariably there are sky flowers, there are eye flowers. "Eye flowers" means "sky flowers." The words "eye flowers" are always clear.[74]

* * * * *

[14:25]

このゆえに、瑯琊山廣照大師いはく、奇哉十方佛、元是眼中華。欲識眼中華、元是十方佛。欲識十方佛、不是眼中華。欲識眼中華、不是十方佛。於此明得、過在十方佛。若未明得、聲聞作舞、獨覺臨粧。

Therefore, Great Master Guangzhao of Mount Langya said,[75]

Wonderful! The buddhas of the ten directions:
Fundamentally, they are flowers in the eye.
If we wish to know the flowers in the eye,
Fundamentally, they are the buddhas of the ten directions.
If we wish to know the buddhas of the ten directions,
They are not flowers in the eye.
If we wish to know the flowers in the eye,
They are not the buddhas of the ten directions.
If we have clarified this,
The fault lies with the buddhas of the ten directions;
If we haven't clarified it,

Daowu was asked by Jianyuan at a funeral whether what was in the coffin was alive or dead, he replied "I don't say alive; I don't say dead." On this, Yuanwu commented:

生也全機現、死也全機現。

Alive, the manifestation of the full function;
Dead, the manifestation of the full function.

For the conversation and Yuanwu's entire verse comment, see Supplementary Notes, s.v. "Manifestation of the full function."

73　**"Flutter down" is "the thousand eyes"; it is "eyes throughout the body"** (*rantsui wa sengen nari, tsūshingen nari* 亂墜は千眼なり、通身眼なり): Allusion to the thousand hands and eyes of Bodhisattva Avalokiteśvara and the saying, by Daowu Yuanzhi 道吾圓智, that "His body throughout is hands and eyes." Dōgen records the source in his *shinji Shōbōgenzō* 眞字正法眼藏 (DZZ.5:182, case 105) and discusses it at length in his "Shōbōgenzō Kannon" 正法眼藏觀音. See Supplementary Notes, s.v. "His body throughout is hands and eyes."

74　**The words "eye flower" are always clear** (*genge no dōshu, kanarazu kaimei nari* 眼華の道取、かならず開明なり): A tentative translation; some would read the predicate as "necessarily clarifies." In his use here of *kaimei* 開明, Dōgen may be playing on the image of the "clear eye."

75　**Great Master Guangzhao of Mount Langya** (*Rōyasan Kōshō daishi* 瑯琊山廣照大師): I.e., Langya Huijue 瑯琊慧覺 (dates unknown). His verse can be found at *Jianzhong Jingguo xudeng lu* 建中靖國續燈錄 (ZZ.136:79a2-5).

14. Sky Flowers *Kūge* 空華　　369

The *śrāvakas* dance,
And the *pratyeka-buddhas* admire their makeup.

[14:26]

しるべし、十方佛の實ならざるにあらず、もとこれ眼中華なり。十方諸佛
の住位せるところは眼中なり。眼中にあらざれば、諸佛の住處にあらず。
眼中華は、無にあらず有にあらず、空にあらず實にあらず、おのづからこ
れ十方佛なり。いまひとへに十方諸佛と欲識すれば、眼中華にあらず、ひ
とへに眼中華と欲識すれば、十方諸佛にあらざるがごとし。

We should realize that "the buddhas of the ten directions" are not un-
real; fundamentally, they are flowers "in the eye." The position where
the buddhas of the ten directions dwell is "in the eye." If it is not "in the
eye," it is not the dwelling place of the buddhas. "Flowers in the eye"
are not nonexistent, are not existent, are not empty, are not real: just as
they are, they are "the buddhas of the ten directions." Now, if we solely
wish to know the buddhas of the ten directions, they are not "flowers in
the eye"; if we solely wish to know "flowers in the eye," they seem not
to be the buddhas of the ten directions.

[14:27] {1:136}

かくのごとくなるゆえに、明得・未明得、ともに眼中華なり、十方佛な
り。欲識および不是、すなはち現成の奇哉なり、太奇なり。佛佛祖祖の道
取する、空華・地華の宗旨、それ恁麼逞風流なり。空華の名字は、經師・
論師もなほ聞及すとも、地華の命脈は、佛祖にあらざれば見聞の因緣あら
ざるなり。地華の命脈を知及せる佛祖の道取あり。

Because it is like this, both "have clarified" and "haven't clarified" are
"flowers in the eye," are "buddhas of the ten directions." "If we wish
to know" and "they are not" are the "wonderful" manifested; are "most
wonderful!" The essential point of sky flowers and earth flowers spoken by buddha after buddha and ancestor after ancestor is *full of style
like this.*[76] While the term "sky flowers" is something heard even by the
sūtra masters and treatise masters, the vital artery of "earth flowers" is
something there are no conditions to see or hear if one is not a buddha

---

76　**full of style like this** (*inmo tei fūryū* 恁麼逞風流): Also read *ei fūryū* 逞風流; taking
逞 as 盈. A fixed expression appearing elsewhere in the *Shōbōgenzō*, where it reflects a
line of verse by Tiantong Rujing 天童如淨 (1162-1227) (*Rujing chanshi yulu* 如淨禪師
語錄, T.2002A.48:122c18):

放行把住逞風流。

Letting go and holding on, full of style.

370   DŌGEN'S *SHŌBŌGENZŌ* VOLUME I

or ancestor.[77] There is a saying by a buddha and ancestor who knew the vital artery of "earth flowers."[78]

[14:28]

大宋國石門山の慧徹禪師は、梁山下の尊宿なり。ちなみに僧ありてとふ、如何是山中寶。

Chan Master Huiche of Mount Shimen in the Land of the Great Song was a venerable in the line of Liangshan.[79] Once, a monk asked him, *"What is the treasure in the mountain?"*

[14:29]

この問取の宗旨は、たとへば、如何是佛と問取するにおなじ、如何是道と問取するがごとくなり。

The essential point of this question is the same as asking, for example, "What is a buddha?" or like asking, "What is the way?"

[14:30]

師いはく、空華從地發、蓋國買無門。

The Master said, *"Sky flowers arise from the earth. There's no place to buy them in the entire land."*[80]

[14:31]

この道取、ひとへに自餘の道取に準的すべからず。よのつねの諸方は、空華の空華を論ずるには、於空に生してさらに於空に滅するとのみ道取す。從空、しれるなほいまだあらず、いはんや從地としらんや。ただひとり石門のみしれり。從地、といふは、初・中・後つひに從地なり。發は開なり。この正當恁麼のとき、從盡大地發なり、從盡大地開なり。

This saying, we should definitely not equate with other sayings. Ordinary abbots in all quarters, in discussing the sky flowers of "sky flow-

---

77   **vital artery of "earth flowers"** (*chige no meimyaku* 地華の命脈): I.e., transmission of the meaning of "earth flowers." The term *meimyaku* 命脈 ("vital artery") occurs often in the *Shōbōgenzō*, in the senses both of the "lifeblood" and the "bloodline" (especially of the lineage of the buddhas and ancestors).

78   **There is a saying** (*dōshu ari* 道取あり): Dōgen is here introducing the quotation that follows in the next section.

79   **Chan Master Huiche of Mount Shimen in the Land of the Great Song** (*Daisōkoku Sekimonzan no Etetsu zenji* 大宋國石門山の慧徹禪師): I.e. Shimen Huiche 石門慧徹 (early Song, dates unknown). The passage quoted here appears in *Tiansheng guangdeng lu* 天聖廣燈録 (ZZ.135:842b11-12).

in the line of Liangshan (*Ryōzanka* 梁山下): Thought to refer to Liangshan Yuanguan 梁山緣觀 (dates unknown), a disciple of Tong'an Daopi 同安道丕.

80   **"There's no place to buy them in the entire land"** (*gaikoku mai mumon* 蓋國買無門): Taking *mumon* 無門 ("no gate") to suggest no shop that sells "sky flowers"; other readers take it to mean "no way" to buy.

14. Sky Flowers *Kūge* 空華

ers," say only that they appear "in the sky" and disappear "in the sky." They do not know even "from the sky"; how could they know "from the earth?" Only Shimen alone has known it. "From the earth" means beginning, middle, and end are, finally, "from the earth." "To arise" is "to bloom." At this very moment, they arise from all the whole earth; *they bloom from all the whole earth.*

[14:32] {1:137}

盡國買無門は、盡國買はなきにあらず、買無門なり。從地發の空華あり、從華開の盡地あり。しかあればしるべし、空華は地・空ともに開發せしむる宗旨あり。

"*There's no place to buy them in the entire land*" is not that there is no "buying them in the entire land"; it is "to buy no place." There are sky flowers that arise from the earth; there is all the earth that blooms from a flower. Therefore, we should realize that there is an essential point that sky flowers make both the earth and the sky bloom and arise.

正法眼藏空華第十四

Treasury of the True Dharma Eye
Sky Flowers
Number 14

[Ryūmonji MS:]

爾時寛元元年癸卯三月十日、在觀音導利興聖寶林寺示衆
Presented to the assembly at Kannon Dōri Kōshō Hōrin Monastery; tenth day, third month of the junior water year of the rabbit, the first year of Kangen [31 March 1243][81]

[Tōunji MS:]

同二年甲辰正月二十七日、在越宇吉峰寺侍者寮書寫。懷奘
Copied this in the acolyte's quarters, Kippō Monastery, Etsuu; seventeenth day, first month of the senior wood year of the dragon, the second year of the same [era] [7 March 1244]. Ejō

于時永正七年庚午五月廿日、在阿陽桂林精舍丈室中。暮齡七十三用兼謹寫焉
Respectfully copied in the abbot's quarters of Keirin Vihāra, Ayō; twentieth day, fifth month, senior metal year of the horse, the seventh year of Eishō [26 June 1510]. Yōken, an elder of seventy-three[82]

---

81 The Tōunji 洞雲寺 MS shares an identical colophon.

82 **Ayō** 阿陽: I.e., Awa 阿波, present-day Tokushima Prefecture.
Yōken 用兼: I.e., Kinkō Yōken 金岡用兼 (1437–1513?).

Treasury of the True Dharma Eye

Number 15

Radiance
Kōmyō

光明

Radiance

Kōmyō

INTRODUCTION

According to its colophon, this essay, number 15 in the sixty- and seventy-five-chapter *Shōbōgenzō* compilations and number 36 in the Honzan edition, was composed at Kōshōji in the early morning hours of a rainy summer night in 1242. The colophon includes a rare comment: "The plum rains rain on, drip dripping from the eaves. What is this radiance? Gentlemen: We can't help but be seen through by Yunmen's words."

"Radiance" (*kōmyō* 光明) refers to the nimbus held to surround the body of a buddha, often taken as a symbol of the wisdom with which he illumines the world. The question, "What is this radiance?" reflects a saying of the Tang-dynasty Chan master Yunmen Wenyan 雲門文偃, who asked his monks, "What is this radiance that all people have?" Dōgen's essay focuses on this saying and another, by Yunmen's older contemporary, Changsha Jingcen 長沙景岑, that "all the worlds in the ten directions are the radiance of the self." In his comments, he moves the sense of "radiance" beyond the self and the world of these sayings to include the lineage and the practice of his Buddhist tradition.

正法眼藏第十四

Treasury of the True Dharma Eye
Number 15

光明

Radiance

[15:1] {1:138}

大宋國湖南長沙招賢大師、上堂。示衆云、盡十方界、是沙門眼。盡十方界、是沙門家常語。盡十方界、是沙門全身。盡十方界、是自己光明。盡十方界、在自己光明裏。盡十方界、無一人不是自己。

Great Master Zhaoxian of Changsha in Hunan in the Land of the Great Song, in a convocation, addressed the assembly, saying,[1]

All the worlds in the ten directions are the eye of the śramaṇa. All the worlds in the ten directions are the everyday words of the śramaṇa.[2] All the worlds in the ten directions are the entire body of the śramaṇa. All the worlds in the ten directions are the radiance of the self. All the worlds in the ten directions are within the radiance of the self. In all the worlds in the ten directions, there is no one that is not the self.

[15:2]

佛道の參學、かならず勤學すべし、轉疏轉遠なるべからず。これによりて、光明を學得せる作家、まれなるものなり。

---

1 **Great Master Zhaoxian of Changsha** (*Chōsa Shōken daishi* 長沙招賢大師): I.e., the ninth-century figure Changsha Jingcen 長沙景岑 (dates unknown), a disciple of Nanquan Puyuan 南泉普願 (748-835). Changsha 長沙 is a district in Hunan; Zhaoxian dashi 招賢大師 is a posthumous title. A slightly different version of the saying quoted here is found in the *Jingde chuandeng lu* 景德傳燈錄 (T.2076.51:274a1215) and elsewhere; see Supplementary Notes, s.v. "All the worlds in the ten directions are the single eye of the śramaṇa."

2 **All the worlds in the ten directions are the everyday words of the śramaṇa** (*jin jippō kai, ze shamon kajō go* 盡十方界、是沙門家常語): This line, although repeated in the "Shōbōgenzō jippō" 正法眼藏十方, is not found in the extant sources of Changsha's sayings; Dōgen's source for it is unknown.

376
DŌGEN'S *SHŌBŌGENZŌ* VOLUME I

In studying the way of the buddhas, we should always study diligently; we should not get remote and distant from it.[3] According to this, the maestros who have studied "radiance" are rare.[4]

[15:3]

震旦國後漢の孝明皇帝、帝諱は莊なり、廟號は顯宗皇帝とまうす。光武皇帝の第四の御子なり。孝明皇帝の御宇、永平十年戊辰の年、摩騰迦・竺法蘭、はじめて佛教を漢國に傳來す。焚經臺のまへに、道士の邪徒を降伏し、諸佛の神力をあらはす。それよりのち、梁武帝の御宇、普通年中にいたりて、初祖みづから西天より南海廣州に幸す。これ正法眼藏正傳の嫡嗣なり。釋迦牟尼佛より二十八世の法孫なり。ちなみに嵩山少室峰少林寺に掛錫しまします。法を二祖大祖禪師に正傳せりし、これ佛祖光明の親曾なり。それよりさきは、佛祖光明を見聞せるなかりき。いはんや自己の光明をしれるあらんや。たとひその光明は、頂顋より擔來して相逢すといへども、自己の眼睛に參學せず。このゆえに、光明の長短方圓をあきらめず、光明の卷舒斂放をあきらめず。光明の相逢を厭却するゆえに、光明と光明と轉疏轉遠なり。この疏遠たとひ光明なりとも、疏遠に罣礙せらるるなり。

Emperor Xiao Ming of the Later Han in the Land of Cīnasthāna was named Zhuang; his ancestral shrine name was Emperor Xianzong.[5] He was the fourth son of Emperor Guangwu. During the reign of Xiao Ming, in the tenth year of Yongping, senior earth year of the dragon, Mātaṅga and Dharmaratna first transmitted the teachings of the buddhas to the Han Kingdom.[6] Before the platform for burning the sūtras, they subdued

---

3　**get remote and distant** (*tenso ten'on* 轉疏轉遠): An expression best known from the saying of Mazu Daoyi 馬祖道一 (709–788) (*Liandeng huiyao* 聯燈會要, ZZ.136:486b18):

若向外馳求轉疏轉遠。

If you run around seeking it outside, you get more remote and distant from it."

4　**maestros** (*sakke* 作家): Also read *soka*. A term widely used for an author or poet and, in Chan usage, an accomplished master.

5　**Emperor Xiao Ming of the Later Han** (*Gokan no Kō Mei kōtei* 後漢の孝明皇帝): Posthumous name of the Emperor Ming 明 (27-75 CE), second ruler of the Later Han dynasty, whose personal name was Liu Zhuang 劉莊.

Land of Cīnasthāna (*Shintan koku* 震旦國): Dōgen uses here the Chinese transliteration of a Sanskrit term meaning "Land of Chin," a name perhaps derived from the Qin 秦 dynasty that first unified China in 221 BCE. The English word "China" also derives from Qin by way of the Arabic pronunciation of the Sanskrit Cīna.

ancestral shrine name (*byōgō* 廟號): Or "temple name"; the name assigned to the deceased in the ancestral temple of the royal family.

6　**tenth year of Yongping, senior earth year of the dragon** (*Eihei jūnen tsuchinoe-tatsu no toshi* 永平十年戊辰の年): Probably indicating 67 CE, a date often given for the introduction of Buddhism to China. However, the cyclical year *wu chen* 戊辰 corresponds to 68 CE, and some MS witnesses give "eleventh year of Yongping" here.

15. Radiance *Kōmyō* 光明   377

the false followers of the Daoists and displayed the spiritual powers of the buddhas.[7]

Thereafter, during the reign of Emperor Wu of the Liang, in the Futong years, the First Ancestor proceeded from Sindh in the West across the southern seas to Guangdong.[8] He was the legitimate heir to the directly transmitted treasury of the true dharma eye; he was a dharma descendant in the twenty-eighth generation from Buddha Śākyamuni. Thereupon, he hung his staff at the Shaolin Monastery on the Shaoshi Peak of Mount Song.[9] He directly transmitted the dharma to the Second Ancestor, Chan Master Dazu; this was personal familiarity with the radiance of the buddhas and ancestors.[10]

Prior to this, [the Chinese] had not experienced the radiance of the buddhas and ancestors; how much less could they have known the radiance of the self? Though they might have encountered this radiance by bearing it from the crown of the head, they did not study it in the eye of

---

Mātaṅga and Dharmaratna (*Matōgya Jiku Hōran* 摩騰迦・竺法蘭): Two Indian monks, whose names are often reconstructed as Kāśyapa Mātaṅga and Dharmaratna, traditionally said to have undertaken the first translations of Buddhist texts into Chinese.

7 **platform for burning the sūtras** (*bonkyō dai* 焚經臺): Reference to the legend that, in the year 71, Daoists resisting the introduction of Buddhism tested the Buddhist scriptures against their own books by setting both afire at platforms in the imperial palace. The Daoist books were reduced to ashes, while the Buddhist books refused to burn.

displayed the spiritual powers of the buddhas (*shobutsu no jinriki o arawasu* 諸佛の神力をあらはす): Likely reference to the legend that Mātaṅga flew into the air and sat cross-legged in space (See, e.g., *Guang hongming ji* 廣弘明集, T.2103.52:99b11-12).

8 **Emperor Wu of the Liang** (*Ryō Bu tei* 梁武帝): Xiao Yan 蕭衍 (472–549), founder of the Liang dynasty (502-557).

Futong years (*Futsū nenchū* 普通年中): I.e., 520–527.

First Ancestor (*Shoso* 初祖): I.e., Bodhidharma.

9 **hung his staff at the Shaolin Monastery on the Shaoshi Peak of Mount Song** (*Sūzan Shōshippō Shōrinji ni kashaku shimashimasu* 嵩山少室峰少林寺に掛錫しまします): Shaoshi 少室 is the western peak of Songshan 嵩山, in the Dengfeng district 登封縣 of Henan. "To hang one's staff" (*kashaku* 掛錫) is used in reference to a monk's enrolling in or residing at a monastery.

10 **Second Ancestor, Chan Master Dazu** (*Niso Daiso zenji* 二祖大祖禪師): Posthumous title of Huike 慧可 (487–593), successor to Bodhidharma.

personal familiarity with the radiance of the buddhas and ancestors (*busso kōmyō no shinzō* 佛祖光明の親曾): "Personal familiarity" represents a loose translation of the adverbial expression *shinzō* 親曾, appearing several times in the *Shōbōgenzō* in a nominal sense to indicate what is personal or intimate; probably adopted by Dōgen from a line in a poem by his teacher, Rujing: "He once personally saw the Buddha" (*shin zō ken butsu* 親曾見佛).

378 DŌGEN'S *SHŌBŌGENZŌ* VOLUME I

the self.[11] Therefore, they had not clarified whether the radiance is long or short, square or round; they had not clarified whether the radiance is rolled or unrolled, gathered or dispersed. Because they disdained to encounter the radiance, the radiance got remote and distant from radiance. This remote and distant may be radiance, but it is obstructed by remote and distant.[12]

[15:4] {1:139}

轉疏轉遠の臭皮袋おもはくは、佛光も自己光明も、赤・白・青・黄にして、火光・水光のごとく、珠光・玉光のごとく、龍天の光のごとく、日月の光のごとくなるべしと見解す。或從知識し、或從經卷すといへども、光明の言教をきくには、螢光のごとくならんとおもふ、さらに眼睛・頂顋の參學にあらず。漢より隋・唐・宋および而今にいたるまで、かくのごとくの流類おほきのみなり。文字の法師に習學することなかれ、禪師胡亂の説、きくべからず。

The stinking skin bags who are remote and distant hold the view that the light of the buddha and the light of the self are red, white, blue, and yellow, and must be like the light of fire or the light of water, like the light of a pearl or the light of a jewel, like the light of dragons and devas, like the light of sun and moon.[13] *Whether from a wise friend, whether from a sūtra scroll,* upon hearing the teaching of "radiance," to think that it is like the light of the firefly is not the study of the eye or crown.[14]

---

11 **Though they might have encountered this radiance by bearing it from the crown of the head, they did not study it in the eye of the self** (*tatoi sono kōmyō wa, chōnei yori tanrai shite sōhō su to iedomo, jiko no ganzei ni sangaku sezu* たとひその光明は、頂顋より擔來して相逢すといへども、自己の眼睛に參學せず): Both *chōnei* 頂顋 ("crown") and *ganzei* 眼睛 ("eye") are regularly used in reference to one's true identity; see Supplementary Notes, s.v. "Crown of the head," "Eye." (Here, however, the radiance at the "crown of the head" may also allude to the halo that surrounds the head in Buddhist iconography). The sense of this sentence would seem to be that, while the Chinese always had access to the radiance of the self, they had not truly recognized it in themselves.

12 **This remote and distant may be radiance, but it is obstructed by remote and distant** (*kono so'on tatoi kōmyō nari tomo, so'on ni keige seraruru nari* この疏遠たとひ光明なりとも、疏遠に罣礙せらるるなり): Perhaps meaning that, while one can never really get away from radiance, there is still a (radiant) state that is distant from it.

13 **stinking skin bags** (*shū hitai* 臭皮袋): A common term for the body, especially of humans; often used by Dōgen in reference especially to Chan monks. For the meaning of the metaphor and other examples of its usage, see Supplementary Notes, s.v. "Bag of skin."

dragons and devas (*ryūten* 龍天): Presumably, listed here as beings whose bodies can glow.

14 **Whether from a wise friend, whether from a sūtra scroll** (*waku jū chishiki shi, waku jū kyōkan su* 或從知識し、或從經卷す): A fixed expression (here put in verbal form) often used by Dōgen for the two sources of hearing the buddha dharma; see Supplementary Notes.

15. Radiance *Kōmyō* 光明   379

From the Han, through the Sui, Tang, and Song, till the present, there have been many such types. Do not study with the dharma masters of letters.[15] We should not listen to the confused talk of Chan masters.[16]

[15:5]

いはゆる佛祖の光明は、盡十方界なり、盡佛盡祖なり、唯佛與佛なり、佛光なり、光佛なり。佛祖は佛祖を光明とせり、この光明を修證して、作佛し、坐佛し、證佛す。このゆえに、此光照東方萬八千佛土の道著あり。

The "radiance of the buddhas and ancestors" here is "all the worlds in the ten directions"; it is all the buddhas and all the ancestors; it is "*only buddhas with buddhas.*"[17] It is the light of the buddha; it is the buddha of light.[18] The buddhas and ancestors take the buddhas and ancestors as radiance; practicing and verifying this radiance, they make a buddha, sit [as] a buddha, and verify a buddha.[19] Therefore, there is the saying, "*This light illumined a myriad eight thousand buddha lands in the eastern quarter.*"[20]

---

15   **dharma masters of letters** (*monji no hosshi* 文字の法師): I.e., teachers specializing in Buddhist texts.

16   **confused talk of Chan masters** (*zenji uron no setsu* 禪師胡亂の説): The term "Chan master" (J. *Zenji* 禪師) could refer either to "meditation masters" (as opposed to dharma masters) or to members of the Chan lineage.

17   **"only buddhas with buddhas"** (*yui butsu yo butsu* 唯佛與佛): A well-known expression from Kumārajīva's translation of the *Lotus Sūtra*, often invoked in the *Shōbōgenzō*; see Supplementary Notes, s.v. "Only buddhas with buddhas can exhaustively investigate the real marks of the dharmas."

18   **It is the light of the buddha; it is the buddha of light** (*bukkō nari, kōbutsu nari* 佛光なり、光佛なり): Dōgen here simply reverses the two terms "light" (*kō* 光) and "buddha" (*butsu* 佛). He is likely just emphasizing the identification of "buddha" and "radiance," but the "Buddha of Light" can also be used in reference to Amitābha, the buddha of infinite light (Muryōkō butsu 無量光佛).

19   **make a buddha, sit [as] a buddha, and verify a buddha** (*sabutsu shi, zabutsu shi, shōbutsu su* 作佛し、坐佛し、證佛す): Or "become a buddha, practice seated buddhahood, and verify buddhahood." The first two phrases reflect the famous conversation on meditation, often quoted by Dōgen, between Nanyue Huairang 南嶽懷讓 (677-744) and Mazu Daoyi 馬祖道一 (e.g., at *Jingde chuandeng lu* 景德傳燈錄, T.2076.51:240c18ff). When Mazu says he is practicing seated meditation (*zazen* 坐禪) in order to "make a buddha" (*sabutsu* 作佛), Nanyue asks him, "Are you studying seated meditation or are you studying seated buddha (*zabutsu* 坐佛)?" See Supplementary Notes, s.v. "Nanyue polishes a tile." Dōgen comments on this conversation at length in his "Shōbōgenzō zazen shin" 正法眼藏坐禪箴.

20   **"This light illumined a myriad eight thousand buddha lands in the eastern quarter"** (*shi kō shō tōhō manhassen butsudo* 此光照東方萬八千佛土): From the *Lotus Sūtra*, describing the light emitted from between the eyebrows of Buddha Śākyamuni (*Miaofa lianhua jing* 妙法蓮華經, T.262.9:4c6). The English "myriad eight thousand" for "eighteen thousand" (*manhassen* 萬八千) seeks to accommodate Dōgen's play with the number below.

380 DŌGEN'S *SHŌBŌGENZŌ* VOLUME I

[15:6] {1:140}

これ話頭光なり。此光は佛光なり、照東方は東方照なり。東方は彼此の俗論にあらず、法界の中心なり、拳頭の中央なり。東方を罣礙すといへども、光明の八兩なり。此土に東方あり、他土に東方あり、東方に東方ある宗旨を參學すべし。萬八千といふは、萬は半拳頭なり、半即心なり。かならずしも十千にあらず、萬萬・百萬等にあらず。佛土といふは、眼睛裏なり。照東方のことばを見聞して、一條白練去を東方へひきわたせらんがごとくに憶想參學するは、學道にあらず。盡十方界は東方のみなり、東方を盡十方界といふ。このゆえに、盡十方界あるなり。盡十方界と開演する話頭、すなはち萬八千佛土の聞聲するなり。

This is the light of a saying.[21] "This light" is "the light of the buddha"; "illumined the eastern quarter" is the illumination of the eastern quarter.[22] "The eastern quarter" is not a secular discussion of this or that: it is the center of the dharma realm; it is the center of the fist.[23] Though it may restrict the eastern quarter, it is eight tael of radiance.[24] We should study the essential point that there is an eastern quarter in this land, there is an eastern quarter in that land, there is an eastern quarter in the eastern quarter. In "a myriad eight thousand," a "myriad" is half a fist; it is half this mind itself.[25] It is not necessarily ten thousand, nor a myriad

---

21 **light of a saying** (*watō kō* 話頭光): I.e., the light of the Buddha's saying just cited. The term *watō* 話頭, translated here as "a saying," occurs several times in this chapter but only rarely elsewhere in the *Shōbōgenzō*. Dōgen seems to use it simply for the "words" or "sayings" he is discussing.

22 **"illumined the eastern quarter" is the illumination of the eastern quarter** (*shō tōhō wa tōhō shō nari* 照東方は東方照なり): I.e., the Buddha's saying that his light illumined the buddha lands in the eastern direction is a reference to the luminosity of the eastern direction.

23 **secular discussion of this or that** (*hishi no zokuron* 彼此の俗論): Presumably referring to the ordinary understanding of spatial directions.

center of the fist (*kentō no chūō* 拳頭の中央): The "fist" appears often in Zen texts, and in Dōgen's writings, as a synecdoche for the true self or a true master; see Supplementary Notes, s.v. "Fist."

24 **Though it may restrict the eastern quarter, it is eight tael of radiance** (*tōhō o keige su to iedomo, kōmyō no hachi ryō nari* 東方を罣礙すといへども、光明の八兩なり): The first clause should probably be understood, "while the term 'eastern quarter' may define the particular direction of the eastern quarter." A tael (*ryō* 兩) is a Chinese unit of weight, varying throughout history, equal to 1/16th catty (*kin* 斤). It may here be short for "eight tael, half a catty" (*hachi ryō han kin* 八兩半斤), an expression used elsewhere by Dōgen as we might say "six of one, half dozen of the other" — hence, "it is the same radiance."

25 **a myriad is half a fist; it is half this mind itself** (*man wa han kentō nari, han soku shin nari* 萬は半拳頭なり、半即心なり): The expression "this mind itself" (*soku shin* 即心) likely recalls the famous saying, "this mind itself is the buddha" (*soku shin ze butsu* 即心是佛); see Supplementary Notes. Both "fist" (*kentō* 拳頭) and "this mind itself" (*soku shin* 即心) are regularly used to express the true person; see Supplementary

15. Radiance *Kōmyō* 光明 381

myriads, nor a hundred myriads, and so on. The "buddha lands" are in the eye. Hearing the words "illumined worlds in the eastern quarter," to presume or to study that it is like stretching a single piece of white silk to the eastern quarter is not study of the way.[26] "All the worlds in the ten directions" is just "the eastern quarter"; "the eastern quarter" means "all the worlds in the ten directions." Therefore, there are "all the worlds in the ten directions." The saying that proclaims "all the worlds in the ten directions" is heard as "the myriad eight thousand buddha lands."

* * * * *

[15:7]

唐憲宗皇帝は、穆宗・宣宗兩皇帝の帝父なり・敬宗・文宗・武宗三皇帝の祖父なり。佛舍利を拜請して、入内供養のちなみ[に]、夜放光明あり。皇帝大悦し、早朝の群臣、みな賀表をたてまつるにいはく、陛下の聖德・聖感なり。

Emperor Xianzong of the Tang was the imperial father of two emperors, Muzong and Xuanzong; he was the imperial grandfather of three emperors, Jingzong, Wenzong, and Wuzong.[27] Requesting *śarira* of the Buddha, he installed them in the palace and made offerings to them; at night, they emitted a radiance.[28] The Emperor was greatly pleased, and his ministers at morning court all presented congratulatory memorials saying, "It is a sacred response to your majesty's sacred virtue."

[15:8]

ときに一臣あり、韓愈文公なり、字は退之といふ。かつて佛祖の席末に參學しきたれり。文公ひとり賀表せず。憲宗皇帝宣問す、群臣みな賀表をたてまつる、卿なんぞ賀表せざる。文公奏對す、微臣かつて佛書をみるにいはく、佛光は青・黄・赤・白にあらず、いまのはこれ龍神衞護の光明なり。皇帝宣問す、いかにあらんかこれ佛光なる。文公無對なり。

Notes, s.v. "Fist." Here, then, the sense may be that, while "a myriad" may be only a part, it is a part of something that cannot be divided into parts.

26 **a single piece of white silk** (*ichijō hyakuren ko* 一條白練去): A fixed expression in Chan literature, understood as unblemished spiritual practice; best known as the last of "Shishuang's seven tendencies" (*Sekisō shichi ko* 石霜七去) (see, e.g., *Liandeng huiyao* 聯燈會要, ZZ.136:790b10-12). The translation makes no attempt to render the final predicate *qu* 去 ("depart"; here, perhaps something like "inclination") in the Chinese phrase, which Dōgen has retained despite its oddity here.

27 **Xianzong** (Kenshū 憲宗): reigned 805-820; Muzong (Bokushū 穆宗): reigned 820–824; Xuanzong (Senshū 宣宗): reigned 846–859; Jingzong (Keishū 敬宗): reigned 824–826; Wenzong (Bunshū 文宗): reigned 826–840; Wuzong (Bushū 武宗): reigned 840–846.

28 *śarira* **of the Buddha** (*busshari* 佛舍利): I.e., relics of the buddha's physical body, the imperial worship of which was an important feature of Buddhism in the capital during the reign of Emperor Xianzong 憲宗.

382 DŌGEN'S *SHŌBŌGENZŌ* VOLUME I

At that time, there was one minister, Han Yu, or Wen Gong, who was styled Tuizhi.[29] He had once studied at the back seats of the buddhas and ancestors. Wen Gong alone did not present a congratulatory memorial. Emperor Xianzong inquired of him, "The ministers have all presented congratulatory memorials. Why do you, sir, not present a congratulatory memorial?"

Wen Gong respectfully replied, "Your humble minister once read in a Buddhist book that the light of the buddha is not blue, yellow, red, or white. What happened just now was the radiance of the protection of the dragon spirits."[30]

The Emperor inquired, "What is the light of the buddha?"

Wen Gong had no reply.

[15:9] {1:141}
いまこの文公、これ在家の士俗なりといへども、丈夫の志氣あり、回天轉
地の才といひぬべし。かくのごとく參學せん、學道の初心なり。不如是學
は、非道なり。たとひ講經して天華をふらすとも、いまだこの道理にいた
らずば、いたづらの功夫なり。たとひ十聖三賢なりとも、文公と同口の長
舌を保任せんとき、發心なり、修證なり。

This Wen Gong, though he may have been a householder layman, had a manly spirit, a talent to revolve the heavens and turn the earth.[31] To study as he did is the initial thought in the study of the way.[32] *A study not*

---

29 **Han Yu, or Wen Gong** (*Kan Yu Bun Kō* 韓愈文公): I.e., the important government official and scholar Han Yu 韓愈 (768-824), whose posthumous name was Wen Gong 文公 ("Duke Wen"), and whose public name (*ji* 字) was Tuizhi 退之. He famously wrote a memorial to the throne opposing the worship of a finger bone relic of the Buddha; the story told here seems to be a Buddhist response to that incident. Versions of it are recorded in several Chinese texts, as well as Dōgen's *shinji Shōbōgenzō* 眞字正法眼藏 (DZZ.5:214, case 173).

30 **Buddhist book** (*bussho* 佛書): The reference is uncertain. Perhaps a variation on a description in the *Fanwang jing* 梵網經 (T.1484.24:1004b3-4) of the light emitted from the mouths of those reciting the monastic rule:

光光非青黄赤白黒。非色非心。非有非無。非因果法。

The brightness is not blue, yellow, red, white, or black, not form and not mind, not being and not nothing, not dharmas of cause and effect.

31 **householder layman** (*zaike no shizoku* 在家の士俗): The term *shizoku* 士俗 ("gentlemen and commoners") may refer to the classes of society or to officials and the general public.

talent to revolve the heavens and turn the earth (*kaiten tenchi no sai* 回天轉地の才): A combination of two idioms used in reference to one of great power.

32 **initial thought in the study of the way** (*gakudō no shoshin* 學道の初心): "Initial thought" (*shoshin* 初心) refers to the bodhisattva's initial aspiration for awakening (*hosshin* 發心; S. *bodhi-cittotpāda*) or the motivation to begin Buddhist practice. See Supplementary Notes, s.v. "Beginner's mind."

15. Radiance *Kōmyō* 光明 383

like this is not the way.[33] Even if by lecturing on the scriptures, we cause heavenly flowers to fall, if we have not yet reached this truth, it is effort in vain.[34] Even though they be the ten sages and three worthies, when they seek to maintain the long tongue in the same mouth as Wen Gong, this is bringing forth the mind, this is practice and verification.[35]

[15:10]

しかありといへども、韓文公なほ佛書を見聞せざるところあり。いはゆる佛光非青黄赤白等の道、いかにあるべしとか學しきたれる。卿もし青・黄・赤・白をみて佛光にあらずと參學するちからあらば、さらに佛光をみて青・黄・赤・白とすることなかれ。憲宗皇帝、もし佛祖ならんには、かくのごとくの宣問ありぬべし。

Though this may be so, there is something Han Wen Gong has not seen in Buddhist books. His saying, *"the light of the buddha is not blue, yellow, red, or white"* — has he studied what this is? If, sir, you have the power to study that, when you see blue, yellow, red, and white, it is not the light of the buddha, then, when you see the light of the buddha, do not take it as blue, yellow, red, and white. If Emperor Xianzong were a buddha or ancestor, he would have questioned him like this.

---

33 **study not like this** (*funyo ze gaku* 不如是學): Or "not to study like this." Dōgen here shifts to Chinese, using a phrase that recalls a passage in the eight-thousand line *Perfection of Wisdom Sūtra* (*Xiaopin bore boluomi jing* 小品般若波羅蜜經, T.227.8:567b24), in which the Buddha asks Subhūti if the bodhisattva destroys all marks (*xiang* 相); Subhūti replies,

世尊、是菩薩不如是學。
World-Honored One, this bodhisattva does not study like this.

34 **heavenly flowers** (*tenge* 天華): Reference to the trope in Buddhist literature that blossoms fall from the heavens onto those skilled in preaching the dharma.

35 **ten sages and three worthies** (*jisshō sanken* 十聖三賢): Also read *jisshō sangen*. Reference to the traditional path of the bodhisattva: the ten stages, or "grounds" (*chi* 地; S. *bhūmi*), of the "noble" (S. *ārya*) — i.e., those on the advanced levels of the path — and the three types of "worthy" (S. *bhadra*) — i.e., those on the level just preceding the ārya.

when they seek to maintain the long tongue in the same mouth as Wen Gong (*Bun Kō to dōku no chōzetsu o hōnin sen toki* 文公と同口の長舌を保任せんとき): I.e., when they try to speak like Wen Gong. The "long tongue" (*chōzetsu* 長舌) suggests eloquence and evokes the "long, broad tongue" (*kōchōzetsu* 廣長舌), one of the thirty-two marks of the buddha body.

this is bringing forth the mind, this is practice and verification (*hosshin nari, shushō nari* 發心なり、修證なり): I.e., generating the bodhisattva's initial aspiration for buddhahood, his practice, and his realization.

384 DŌGEN'S *SHŌBŌGENZŌ* VOLUME I

[15:11]

しかあれば、明明の光明は百草なり。百草の光明、すでに根茎・枝葉・華
果・光色、いまだ與奪あらず。五道の光明あり、六道の光明あり。這裏是
什麼處在なればか、説光説明する。云何忽生山河大地なるべし。長沙道の
盡十方界、是自己光明の道取を、審細に參學すべきなり。光明自己、盡十
方界を參學すべきなり。

Hence, the perfectly clear radiance is the hundred grasses.[36] The radiance of the hundred grasses — its roots and stems, branches and leaves, flowers and fruits, light and colors are never given or taken away.[37] There is a radiance of the five paths; there a radiance of the six paths.[38] *Where are we here*, that we *talk of light and talk of bright?*[39] It should be, "*how does it suddenly give rise to the mountains, rivers, and the whole earth?*"[40] We should study in detail Changsha's saying, "*All the worlds in the ten directions are the radiance of the self.*" We should study the radiant self is all the worlds in the ten directions.

[15:12]

生死去來は、光明の去來なり、超凡越聖は、光明の藍朱なり、作佛作祖
は、光明の玄黄なり。修證はなきにあらず、光明の染汚なり。草木牆壁・
皮肉骨髓、これ光明の赤白なり。煙霞水石・鳥道玄路、これ光明の廻環な
り。自己の光明を見聞するは、値佛の證驗なり、見佛の證驗なり。盡十方
界は是自己なり、是自己は盡十方界なり。廻避の餘地あるべからず。たと
ひ廻避の地ありとも、これ出身の活路なり。而今の髑髏七尺、すなはち盡
十方界の形なり、象なり。佛道に修證する盡十方界は、髑髏形骸・皮肉骨
髓なり。

---

36 **the perfectly clear radiance is the hundred grasses** (*meimei no kōmyō wa hyakusō nari* 明明の光明は百草なり): "The hundred grasses" (*hyakusō* 百草) is a standard expression for "all phenomena." Playful allusion to a well-known Zen saying cited several times by Dōgen; see Supplementary Notes, s.v. "Perfectly clear, the tips of the hundred grasses."

37 **never given or taken away** (*imada yodatsu arazu* いまだ與奪あらず): Perhaps, meaning that the concrete properties of the phenomenal world are inherent in the radiance.

38 **five paths** (*godō* 五道); **six paths** (*rokudō* 六道): The five or six realms of sentient beings in saṃsāra; See Supplementary Notes, s.v. "Six paths."

39 **Where are we here?** (*shari ze jūmo sho zai* 這裏是什麼處在): Dōgen here shifts to Chinese, in a variant of the question famously put to Linji 臨濟 by the monk Puhua 普化 (dates unknown) (as seen, e.g., at *shinji Shōbōgenzō* 眞字正法眼藏 (DZZ.5:174, case 96):

這裏是什麼所在、説麁説細。
Where are we here, that we're talking of crude and talking of fine?

40 **"how does it suddenly give rise to the mountains, rivers, and the whole earth?"** (*unga kotsu shō senga daichi* 云何忽生山河大地): A standard question in Zen literature, taken from the *Sūraṅgama-sūtra* (*Shoulengyan jing* 首楞嚴經; T.945.19:119c17), where the question concerns how the phenomenal world arises from the pure *tathāgata-garbha*.

15. Radiance *Kōmyō* 光明 385

Birth and death, coming and going, are the coming and going of the radiance; transcending the commoner and surpassing the sage are the indigo and vermilion of the radiance; becoming a buddha and becoming an ancestor are the black and yellow of the radiance.[41] "It's not that it lacks practice and verification" is the "defilement" of the radiance.[42] Grasses and trees, fences and walls, skin, flesh, bones, and marrow — these are the red and white of the radiance.[43] Smoke and mist, water and stone, the path of the bird and the dark road — these are the circling of the radiance.[44] Perceiving the radiance of the self is evidence of meeting the buddha, is evidence of seeing the buddha. "All the worlds in the ten directions" are "this self"; "this self" is "all the worlds in the ten directions."[45] There is no other place of escape; even if there were a place of escape, it would be the life-saving path for leaving the body.[46] The present skull and seven feet are the shape, are the image, of "all the worlds

---

41   **transcending the commoner and surpassing the sage** (*chōbon osshō* 超凡越聖): I.e., going beyond the stages of the Buddhist spiritual path; a common expression in Zen literature.

42   **"It's not that it lacks practice and verification" is the "defilement" of the radiance** (*shushō wa naki ni arazu, kōmyō no zenna nari* 修證はなきにあらず、光明の染汚なり): Dōgen here plays with one of his favorite passages from Chan literature, the conversation between the Sixth Ancestor, Huineng 慧能, and his follower Nanyue Huairang 南嶽懷讓 (see, e.g., *shinji Shōbōgenzō* 眞字正法眼藏, DZZ.5:178, case 101). When Huineng asks whether "the thing that comes like this" is dependent on practice and verification, Huairang responds,

修證即不無、染汚即不得。

It's not that it lacks practice and verification, but it can't be defiled by them.

For the full dialogue, see Supplementary Notes, s.v. "What thing is it that comes like this?"

43   **skin, flesh, bones, and marrow** (*hi niku kotsu zui* 皮肉骨髓): An expression, occurring very often throughout the *Shōbōgenzō*, indicating the essence or truth or entirety of something or someone. From the famous story of Bodhidharma's testing of four disciples, to whom he said of each in turn that he (or, in one case, she) had gotten his skin, flesh, bones, and marrow. See Supplementary Notes.

44   **the path of the bird and the dark road** (*chōdō genro* 鳥道玄路): The first two of "Dongshan's three roads" (*Tōzan sanro* 洞山三路) for teaching people; see Supplementary Notes, s.v. "Dongshan's three roads."

45   **"All the worlds in the ten directions" are "this self"** (*jin jippō kai wa ze jiko nari* 盡十方界は是自己なり): Dōgen here plays with Changsha's words to create the new term "this self" (*ze jiko* 是自己) by reading the Chinese copula "are" (*ze* 是) as the pronoun "this."

46   **the life-saving path for leaving the body** (*shusshin no katsuro* 出身の活路): The term *katsuro* 活路 has the sense "survival route" — i e., the way out of a dangerous situation; the term *shusshin* 出身, while having the colloquial sense "advance one's status," is regularly used in Chan texts for "liberation."

386 DŌGEN'S *SHŌBŌGENZŌ* VOLUME I

in the ten directions."[47] "All the worlds in the ten directions" practiced and verified on the way of the buddhas are the skull and body, the skin, flesh, bones, and marrow.

* * * * *

[15:13] {1:142}
雲門山大慈雲匡眞大師は、如來世尊より三十九世の兒孫なり。法を雪峰眞覺大師に嗣す。佛衆の晚進なりといへども、祖席の英雄なり。たれか雲門山に光明佛の未曾出世と道取せむ。

Great Master Daciyun Kuangzhen of Mount Yunmen was a thirty-ninth-generation descendant of the Tathāgata, the World-Honored One.[48] He succeeded to the dharma of Great Master Zhenjue of Xuefeng.[49] Although he may have been a latecomer to the buddha assembly, he was a hero of the ancestral seat.[50] Who could say that a radiant buddha never appeared in the world on Mount Yunmen?

[15:14]
あるとき、上堂示衆云、人人盡有光明在、看時不見暗昏昏、作麼生是諸人光明在。衆無對。自代云、僧堂・佛殿・廚庫・山門。

At one time, in a convocation, he addressed the assembly, saying, "People all have a radiance, but when they look for it, they can't see it in the dark. What is this radiance that people have?"[51]

The assembly had no answer.

He himself, in their place, said, "The saṃgha hall, buddha hall, kitchen, and mountain gate."[52]

---

47 **skull and seven feet** (*dokuro shichi shaku* 髑髏七尺): I.e., the human body. The term "seven feet" (*shichi shaku* 七尺) used for the human body is based on the ancient value of the Chinese "foot" (*chi* 尺).

48 **Great Master Daciyun Kuangzhen of Mount Yunmen** (*Unmonzan Daijiun Kyōshin daishi* 雲門山大慈雲匡眞大師): I.e., Yunmen Wenyan 雲門文偃 (864–949).

49 **Great Master Zhenjue of Xuefeng** (*Seppō Shinkaku Daishi* 雪峰眞覺大師): I.e., Xuefeng Yicun 雪峰義存 (822–908).

50 **latecomer to the buddha assembly** (*busshu no banshin* 佛衆の晚進): I.e., a latter-day member of the saṃgha.

hero of the ancestral seat (*soseki no eiyū* 祖席の英雄): An expression of high praise for a past master, appearing several times in Dōgen's writings. The "ancestral seat" (*soseki* 祖席) is a common term for the Zen lineage.

51 **At one time** (*aru toki* あるとき): An incident recorded in the *shinji Shōbōgenzō* 眞字正法眼藏 (DZZ.5:166, case 81), probably from the *Yuanwu yulu* 圓悟語錄 (T.1997.47:803a25-27).

52 **"saṃgha hall, buddha hall, kitchen, and mountain gate"** (*sōdō butsuden zuku sanmon* 僧堂・佛殿・廚庫・山門): Four common buildings of a Chan monastery. The

15. Radiance *Kōmyō* 光明 387

[15:15]

いま大師道の人人盡有光明在は、のちに出現すべしといはず、往世にあり
しといはず、傍觀の現成といはず。人人自有光明在と道取するを、あきら
かに聞持すべきなり。百千の雲門をあつめて同參せしめ、一口同音に道取
せしむるなり。人人盡有光明在は、雲門の自搆にあらず、人人の光明みづ
から拈光爲道なり。人人盡有光明とは、渾人自是光明在なり。光明といふ
は、人人なり。光明を拈得して、依報・正報とせり。光明盡有人人在なる
べし、光光自是人人在なり、人人自有人人在なり、光光自有光光在なり、
有有盡有有有在なり、盡盡有有盡盡在なり。

The Great Master's saying here that "*people all have a radiance*" does
not say that it will appear later, does not say that it was in the past, does
not say it occurs to an onlooker. We should clearly hear the saying that
"*people naturally have a radiance.*"[53] It is gathering a hundred thousand
Yunmens and having them study together and say it in unison with a
single voice. That "*people all have a radiance*" is not Yunmen's own
construction: people's radiance itself takes up the light and forms the
words.[54] "*People all have a radiance*" means *the whole person is naturally the radiance.*[55] "Radiance" means "people." They have taken up
the radiance and made it their secondary recompense and primary recompense.[56] It should be "*the radiance all has the people*"; it is "*the lights
naturally are the people*"; it is "*the people naturally have the people*";

---

saṃgha hall is the building in which the registered monks normally meditate, eat, and
sleep; the buddha hall houses the main icon; the mountain gate is the main entrance to a
monastery, also called the "triple gate" (*sanmon* 三門), the homophonous term by which
Dōgen will refer to it in his comments below. See Supplementary Notes, s.v. "Saṃgha
hall, buddha hall, kitchen, and mountain gate."

53 **"people naturally have a radiance"** (*ninnin ji u kōmyō zai* 人人自有光明在): Dōgen has here added "naturally" (*ji* 自) to Xuefeng's statement, a version that does appear
in other texts.

54 **Yunmen's own construction** (*Unmon no jikō* 雲門の自搆): The term *jikō* 自搆 is
rather unusual; the element *kō* 搆 is regularly used in the sense "to take something in,"
hence, "to grasp something"; the translation takes it as equivealent here to the homophonous *kō* 構 ("to build").

takes up the light and forms the words (*nen kō i dō* 拈光爲道): Or, more simply,
"speaks of light."

55 **the whole person** (*konnin* 渾人): An unusual expression, not seen elsewhere in Dōgen's writing; the sense of 渾 here seems akin to its use in *konji* 渾自 ("whole self"), or
the more common *konjin* 渾身 ("whole body"). Given the context, it is tempting to read
it "people as a whole."

56 **secondary recompense and primary recompense** (*ehō shōhō* 依報・正報): Standard Buddhist terms for the two aspects of karmic consequences: respectively, the environment, or circumstances, into which one is born, and the psychophysical makeup of
the person; see Supplementary Notes, s.v. "Secondary and primary recompense."

388 DŌGEN'S *SHŌBŌGENZŌ* VOLUME I

it is "*the lights naturally have the lights*"; it is "*the havings all have the havings*"; it is "*the alls have having the alls.*"[57]

[15:16] {1:143}

しかあればしるべし、人人盡有の光明は、現成の人人なり、光光盡有の人人なり。しばらく雲門にとふ、なんぢなにをよんでか人人とする、なにをよんでか光明とする。

This being so, we should realize that the radiance that "people all have" is the "people" actually appearing, is the "people" the lights "all have."[58] Let us now ask Yunmen, "What do you mean by 'people'? What do you mean by 'radiance'?"

[15:17]

雲門みづからいはく、作麼生是光明在。この問著は、疑殺話頭の光明なり。しかあれども、恁麼道著すれば、人人光光なり。

Yunmen himself says, "*What is this radiance?*"[59] This question is the radiance completely doubting a saying.[60] Nevertheless, when said like this, it is "people" and "lights."[61]

---

57 **It should be "the radiance all has the people"** (*kōmyō jin u ninnin zai naru beshi* 光明盡有人人在なるべし): From this point, Dōgen launches into a series of increasingly odd plays with the vocabulary of Yunmen's saying, culminating in the almost unintelligible "all all have have all all" (*jinjin u u jinjin zai* 盡盡有有盡盡在).

"the lights naturally are the people" (*kōkō ji ze ninnin nari* 光光自是人人在なり): "Lights" here renders *kōkō* 光光, a term normally meaning "formitable," "imposing," etc., but here merely the duplication of the first element in the compound *kōmyō* 光明 ("radiance").

58 **"people" actually appearing** (*genjō no ninnin* 現成の人人); **"people" the lights "all have"** (*kōkō jin u no ninnin* 光光盡有の人人): Continuing the play with Yunmen's words. The former phrase suggests "real people"; the latter represents a variation on the phrase above, "the radiance all has the people."

59 **"What is this radiance?"** (*somosan ze kōmyō zai* 作麼生是光明在): Dōgen here merely repeats Yunmen's question, though it is also possible to read this as a declarative sentence — i.e., "[the question] 'what' is this radiance."

60 **radiance completely doubting a saying** (*gisatsu watō no kōmyō* 疑殺話頭の光明): Seemingly, a variation on the earlier "light of a saying" (*watō kō* 話頭光) (above, section 6): i.e., radiance in the form of questioning the meaning of the saying. The verb *gisatsu* 疑殺 carries the sense, "to question thoroughly," with the element *satsu* 殺 serving as an intensive.

61 **Nevertheless, when said like this, it is "people" and "lights"** (*shika aredomo, inmo dōjaku sureba, ninnin kōkō nari* しかあれども、恁麼道著すれば、人人光光なり): Or, perhaps, "it is 'the 'lights' of 'people.'" A tentative translation of a sentence subject to diverse interpretation. Both the antecedent of "like this" (*inmo* 恁麼) and the grammar of the pattern *ninnin kōkō* 人人光光 ("people lights") are unclear. One possible reading might be something like, "Although Yunmen's question is the radiance of doubting a saying, asking this question is the light of every person."

15. Radiance *Kōmyō* 光明 389

[15:18]

ときに衆無對。たとひ百千の道得ありとも、無對を拈じて道著するなり。
これ佛祖正傳の正法眼藏涅槃妙心なり。

At that time, "*the assembly had no answer.*" Even if they had a hundred thousand sayings, they took up "no answer" to say them.[62] This is "the treasury of the true dharma eye, the wondrous mind of nirvāṇa" directly transmitted by the buddhas and ancestors.[63]

[15:19]

雲門自代云、僧堂・佛殿・廚庫・三門。いま道取する自代は、雲門に自代
するなり、大衆自代するなり、光明に自代するなり、僧堂・佛殿・廚庫・
三門に自代するなり。しかあれども、雲門なにをよむでか僧堂・佛殿・廚
庫・三門とする。大衆および人人をよむで僧堂・佛殿・廚庫・三門とすべ
からず。いくばくの僧堂・佛殿・廚庫・三門かある。雲門なりとやせん、
七佛なりとやせん、四七なりとやせん、二三なりとやせん、拳頭なりとや
せん、鼻孔なりとやせん。いはくの僧堂・佛殿・廚庫・三門、たとひいづ
れの佛祖なりとも、人人をまぬかれざるものなり。このゆえに、人人にあ
らず。しかありしよりこのかた、有佛殿の無佛なるあり、無佛殿の無佛な
るあり。有光佛あり、無光佛あり。無佛光あり、有佛光あり。

Yunmen "*himself, in their place, said, 'The saṃgha hall, buddha hall, kitchen, and triple gate.*'" The "himself in their place" mentioned here is "himself in place" of Yunmen; it is "himself in place" of the great assembly; it is "himself in place" of "radiance"; it is "himself in place" of "the saṃgha hall, buddha hall, kitchen, and triple gate." Still, what did Yunmen call "the saṃgha hall, buddha hall, kitchen, and triple gate"? He should not call the great assembly or "people" "the saṃgha hall, buddha hall, kitchen, and triple gate."[64] How many saṃgha halls, buddha halls, kitchens, and triple gates are there? Shall we say they are Yunmen? Say they are the seven buddhas? Say they are four sevens? Say they are

---

62 **they took up "no answer" to say them** (*mutai o nenjite dōjaku suru nari* 無對を拈じて道著するなり): I.e., they spoke with no answer.

63 **"the treasury of the true dharma eye, the wondrous mind of nirvāṇa"** (*shōbō-genzō nehan myōshin* 正法眼藏涅槃妙心): Reference to the words of Buddha Śākyamuni describing what he was silently transmitting on Vulture Peak to the First Ancestor, Mahākāśyapa; the essence of the Buddhist teaching, transmitted through the lineage of the buddhas and ancestors; see Supplementary Notes, s.v. "Treasury of the true dharma eye."

64 **He should not call the great assembly or "people" "the saṃgha hall, the buddha hall, the kitchen, the triple gate"** (*daishu oyobi ninnin o yomude sōdō butsuden zuku sanmon to su bekarazu* 大衆および人人をよむで僧堂・佛殿・廚庫・三門とすべから
ず): The grammatical subject is unstated and might be taken as "we" or the impersonal "one." The "great assembly" (*daishu* 大衆) refers to the congregation of monastics; here, likely the assembly being addressed by Yunmen. "People" (*ninnin* 人人) are the people said to have a radiance.

390 DŌGEN'S *SHŌBŌGENZŌ* VOLUME I

two threes?[65] Say they are a fist? Say they are a nose?[66] The "saṃgha hall, buddha hall, kitchen, and triple gate" here, whichever buddhas and ancestors they are, do not avoid "people." Therefore, they are not "people."[67] Ever since this was so, there are cases in which there are buddha halls that have no buddha, cases in which there are no buddha halls that have no buddha; there are buddhas that have light, buddhas that have no light, light that has no buddhas, light that has buddhas.[68]

---

65   **seven buddhas** (*shichi butsu* 七佛); **four sevens** (*shi shichi* 四七); **two threes** (*ni san* 二三): Reference to the Zen lineage. "Seven buddhas" refers to the series of seven ancient buddhas culminating in Buddha Śākyamuni (see Supplementary Notes, s.v. "Seven buddhas"). "Four sevens" refers to the twenty-eight Indian ancestors, from Mahākāśyapa to Bodhidharma; "two threes" refers to the first six ancestors in China, from Bodhidharma to Huineng 慧能.

66   **Say they are a fist? Say they are a nose?** (*kentō nari to ya sen, bikū nari to ya sen* 拳頭なりとやせん、鼻孔なりとやせん): Like the "fist," introduced above (Note 25), the "nose" is regularly used as synecdoche for the person, especially for Zen teachers and students. See Supplementary Notes, s.v. "Fist," "Nose."

67   **do not avoid "people." Therefore, they are not "people"** (*ninnin o manukarezaru mono nari. kono yue ni, ninnin ni arazu* 人人をまぬかれざるものなり。このゆえに、人人にあらず): Perhaps meaning that, since they are identified with the "people" who have (or are) the "radiance," they are not merely people.

68   **there are cases in which there are buddha halls that have no buddha** (*u butsuden no mu butsu* 有佛殿の無佛): A tentative translation of a sentence, each of whose clauses might be parsed differently. Dōgen is playing with the verb "to have" (*u* 有), from Yunmen's phrase, "people all have a radiance," and its opposite, "to lack" (*mu* 無) — play complicated by the fact that the two verbs also mean, respectively, "to exist" and "not to exist."

It is sometimes suggested that the sentence reflects an exchange between Guling Shenzan 古靈神贊 (fl. ninth c.) and his ordination teacher recorded in the *Jingde chuandeng lu* 景德傳燈錄; the version of the exchange appearing at T.2076.51:268a12-15 does not seem particularly relevant:

一日因澡身、命師去垢。師乃拊背曰、好所佛殿而佛不聖。其師迴首視之。師曰、佛雖不聖且能放光。

One day, when [his teacher] was bathing, he ordered the Master [Shenzan 神贊] to wash him. The Master rubbed his back and said, "A nice buddha hall, but the buddha isn't sacred."
His teacher turned his head to look at him. The Master said, "The buddha may not be sacred, but it still emits a light."

The influential nineteenth-century *Shōbōgenzō shōten zokuchō* 正法眼藏涉典續貂 (SCZ.5:317) records a variant version, closer to our text here, that may or may not have been known to Dōgen:

師乃撫背曰、好箇佛殿無佛。師囘首視之。師曰、雖無佛且能放光。

The Master rubbed his back and said, "A nice buddha hall with no buddha."
His teacher turned his head to look at him. The Master said, "There may be no buddha, but it still emits a light."

15. Radiance *Kōmyō* 光明 391

* * * * *

[15:20] {1:144}

雪峰山眞覺大師、示衆云、僧堂前、與諸人相見了也。

Great Master Zhenjue of Mount Xuefeng addressed the assembly, saying, "I met everyone in front of the saṃgha hall."[69]

[15:21]

これすなはち、雪峰の通身是眼睛時なり、雪峰の雪峰を覻見する時節なり、僧堂の僧堂と相見するなり。

This is the time when Xuefeng's "body throughout is eyes"; it is the occasion when Xuefeng looks at Xuefeng; it is the saṃgha hall meeting the saṃgha hall.[70]

[15:22]

保福擧問鵝湖、僧堂前且置、什麼處望州亭・烏石嶺相見。鵝湖驟步歸方丈。保福便入僧堂。

Raising this, Baofu asked Ehu, "Setting aside 'in front of the saṃgha hall,' where were the meetings at Wangzhou Pavilion and Wushi Ridge?"[71]

---

69 **Great Master Zhenjue of Mount Xuefeng** (*Seppōzan Shinkaku daishi* 雪峰山眞覺大師): See above, Note 49. This saying can be found in the *Yuanwu yulu* 圜悟語錄 (T.1997.47:802c28-29) and elsewhere. For the version recorded in Dōgen's *shinji Shōbōgenzō* 眞字正法眼藏, see below, Note 71.

"I met everyone" (*yo shonin shōken ryō ya* 與諸人相見了也): Can be understood as "I met all of you."

70 **the time when Xuefeng's "body throughout is eyes"** (*Seppō no tsūshin ze ganzei ji* 雪峰の通身是眼睛時): The expression *tsūshin* 通身, translated here "body throughout," occurs regularly in Dōgen's writings, typically, as no doubt here, alluding to the saying of Daowu Yuanzhi 道吾圓智 (769-835) regarding the thousand-armed, thousand-eyed Bodhisattva Avalokiteśvara (*senju sengen Kannon* 千手千眼觀音) that "his body throughout is hands and eyes" (*tsūshin ze shu gen* 通身是手眼). See Supplementary Notes, s.v. "His body throughout is hands and eyes."

71 **Raising this, Baofu asked Ehu** (*Hofuku kō mon Gako* 保福擧問鵝湖): I.e., Baofu Congzhan 保福從展 (d. 928) and Ehu Zhifu 鵝湖智孚 (dates unknown), two followers of Xuefeng. The anecdote comes from the passage in which Xuefeng said he had met everyone in front of the monks' hall. Here is the version in the *shinji Shōbōgenzō* 眞字正法眼藏 (DZZ.5:272, case 290):

> 雪峰示衆云、望州亭與諸人相見了也、烏石嶺與諸人相見了也、僧堂前與諸人相見了也。後保福擧問鵝湖、僧堂前且置。什麼處是望州亭・烏石嶺相見。鵝湖驟步歸方丈。保福便入僧堂。
>
> Xuefeng addressed the assembly, saying, "I met everyone in front of the saṃgha hall. I met everyone at Wangzhou Pavilion. I met everyone at Wushi Ridge."
>
> Later, raising this, Baofu asked Ehu, "Setting aside 'in front of the saṃgha hall,' where were the meetings at Wangzhou Pavilion and Wushi Ridge?"

392 DŌGEN'S *SHŌBŌGENZŌ* VOLUME I

Ehu ran back to the abbot's quarters. Baofu then entered the saṃgha hall.

[15:23]

いま歸方丈・入僧堂、これ話頭出身なり、相見底の道理なり、相見了也僧
堂なり。

This "back to the abbot's quarters" and "entered the saṃgha hall" —
these are leaving the body of the statement; they are the principle of
"meeting"; *they are the saṃgha hall "met."*[72]

* * * * *

[15:24]

地藏院眞應大師云、典座入庫堂。

*Great Master Zhenying of Dicang Cloister said, "The cook enters the
kitchen."*[73]

[15:25]

この話頭は、七佛已前事なり。

This statement is something prior to the seven buddhas.[74]

正法眼藏光明第十五
Treasury of the True Dharma Eye
Radiance
Number 15

Ehu ran back to the abbot's quarters. Baofu then entered the saṃgha hall.

"Wangzhou Pavilion and Wushi Ridge" (*Bōshū tei Useki rei* 望州亭烏石嶺): The former is a scenic spot at Xuefeng; the latter, probably the mountain of that name in Fujian.

72 **leaving the body of the statement** (*watō shusshin* 話頭出身): A tentative translation of an unusual phrase that might mean that the statement itself "leaves the body," or
that one "leaves the body" from the statement.

the principle of "meeting" (*shōken tei no dōri* 相見底の道理); **the saṃgha hall "met"**
(*shōken ryō ya sōdō* 相見了也僧堂): Dōgen is playing here with Xuefeng's "I met everyone in front of the saṃgha hall." The latter phrase could be interpreted variously: "the
saṃgha hall where he met"; "the saṃgha that was met"; "the saṃgha that itself met."

73 **Great Master Zhenying of Dicang Cloister** (*Jizō in Shin'ō daishi* 地藏院眞應大
師): I.e., Luohan Guichen 羅漢桂琛 (867–928); "Great Master Zhenying" is a posthumous title. The saying is found at *Jingde chuandeng lu* 景德傳燈録, T.2076.51:400a18.

74 **something prior to the seven buddhas** (*shichi butsu izen ji* 七佛已前事): A fixed
idiom for that which precedes even the seven buddhas of the past (for which, see above,
Note 65.)

15. Radiance *Kōmyō* 光明   393

[Ryūmonji MS:]

仁治三年壬寅夏六月二日夜、三更四點、示衆于觀音導利興聖寶林寺

Presented to the assembly at Kannon Dōri Kōshō Hōrin Monastery; fourth strike of the third watch [approximately 1:30 a.m.], night of the second day, sixth month, summer of the senior water year of the tiger, the third year of Ninji [1 July 1242]

于時梅雨霖霖、簷頭滴滴、作麼生是光明在、大家未免雲門道覷破

At the time,
The plum rains rain on,
Drip dripping from the eaves.
What is this radiance?
Gentlemen:
We can't help but be seen through by Yunmen's words.[75]

[Tōunji MS:]

寛元甲辰臘月中三日、在越州大佛寺之侍司書寫之。懷奘

Copied at the acolyte's office of Daibutsu Monastery, Esshū; third day, month of offerings, senior wood year of the dragon, Kangen [14 January 1244]. Ejō

于旹永正七年庚午六月廿一日、於阿陽桂林精舍丈室中用兼。七十三歳寫焉

Copied in the abbot's quarters of Keirin Vihāra, Ayō; twenty-first day, sixth month, senior metal year of the horse, the seventh year of Eishō [26 July 1510]. Yōken, in his seventy-third year[76]

---

75 The Tōunji 洞雲寺 MS shares an identical colophon.

76 **Ayō** 阿陽: I.e., Awa 阿波, present-day Tokushima Prefecture.
Yōken 用兼: I.e., Kinkō Yōken 金岡用兼 (1437–1513?).

The Sōtō Zen Text Project *Shōbōgenzō*

Volume I
The Seventy-five-Chapter Compilation, Part 1

1. The Realized Kōan *Genjō kōan* 現成公案
2. Mahā-prajñā-pāramitā *Maka hannya haramitsu* 摩訶般若波羅蜜
3. Buddha Nature *Busshō* 佛性
4. Studying the Way with Body and Mind *Shinjin gakudō* 身心學道
5. This Mind Itself Is the Buddha *Soku shin ze butsu* 即心是佛
6. Deportment of the Practicing Buddha *Gyōbutsu iigi* 行佛威儀
7. One Bright Pearl *Ikka myōju* 一顆明珠
8. The Mind Cannot Be Got *Shin fukatoku* 心不可得
9. The Old Buddha Mind *Kobutsushin* 古佛心
10. Great Awakening *Daigo* 大悟
11. Principles of Seated Meditation *Zazen gi* 坐禪儀
12. Needle of Seated Meditation *Zazen shin* 坐禪箴
13. Ocean Seal Samādhi *Kaiin zanmai* 海印三昧
14. Sky Flowers *Kūge* 空華
15. Radiance *Kōmyō* 光明

Volume II
The Seventy-five-Chapter Compilation, Part 2

16A. Sustained Practice, Part 1 *Gyōji jō* 行持上
16B. Sustained Practice, Part 2 *Gyōji ge* 行持下
17. Such *Inmo* 恁麼
18. Avalokiteśvara *Kannon* 觀音
19. The Old Mirror *Kokyō* 古鏡
20. Sometimes *Uji* 有時
21. Prediction *Juki* 授記
22. Full Function *Zenki* 全機
23. The Moon *Tsuki* 都機
24. Painted Cake *Gabyō* 畫餅
25. Sound of the Stream, Form of the Mountain *Keisei sanshoku* 谿聲山色
26. Beyond the Buddha *Butsu kōjō ji* 佛向上事
27. Talking of a Dream within a Dream *Muchū setsumu* 夢中説夢
28. Making a Bow and Getting the Marrow *Raihai tokuzui* 禮拜得髓
29. The Mountains and Waters Sūtra *Sansui kyō* 山水經
30. Sūtra Reading *Kankin* 看經

Volume III
The Seventy-five-Chapter Compilation, Part 3

31. Do No Evil *Shoaku makusa* 諸惡莫作
32. Transmitting the Robe *Den'e* 傳衣
33. Sayings *Dōtoku* 道得
34. The Teachings of the Buddhas *Bukkyō* 佛教
35. Spiritual Powers *Jinzū* 神通
36. The Arhat *Arakan* 阿羅漢

37. Spring and Autumn *Shunjū* 春秋
38. Tangled Vines *Kattō* 葛藤
39. The Inheritance Certificate *Shisho* 嗣書
40. The Cypress Tree *Hakujushi* 柏樹子
41. The Three Realms Are Only Mind *Sangai yui shin* 三界唯心
42. Talking of the Mind, Talking of the Nature *Sesshin sesshō* 説心説性
43. The Real Marks of the Dharmas *Shohō jissō* 諸法實相
44. The Way of the Buddhas *Butsudō* 佛道
45. Secret Words *Mitsugo* 密語

Volume IV
The Seventy-five-Chapter Compilation, Part 4

46. The Insentient Preach the Dharma *Mujō seppō* 無情説法
47. Sūtras of the Buddhas *Bukkyō* 佛經
48. Dharma Nature *Hosshō* 法性
49. Dhāraṇī *Darani* 陀羅尼
50. Washing the Face *Senmen* 洗面
51. Face-to-Face Conferral *Menju* 面授
52. Buddhas and Ancestors *Busso* 佛祖
53. Plum Blossoms *Baika* 梅華
54. Washing and Purifying *Senjō* 洗淨
55. The Ten Directions *Jippō* 十方
56. Seeing Buddha *Kenbutsu* 見佛
57. Extensive Study *Henzan* 遍參
58. The Eye *Ganzei* 眼睛
59. Everyday Matters *Kajō* 家常
60. The Thirty-seven Factors of Bodhi *Sanjūshichi hon bodai bunpō* 三十七品菩提分法

Volume V
The Seventy-five-Chapter Compilation, Part 5

61. Song of the Dragon *Ryūgin* 龍吟
62. The Intention of the Ancestral Master's Coming from the West
    Soshi seirai i 祖師西來意
63. Bringing Forth the Mind of Bodhi *Hotsu bodai shin* 發菩提心
64. The Udumbara Blossom *Udonge* 優曇華
65. The Entire Body of the Tathāgata *Nyorai zenshin* 如來全身
66. The King of Samādhis Samādhi *Zanmai ō zanmai* 三昧王三昧
67. Turning the Dharma Wheel *Ten hōrin* 轉法輪
68. Great Practice *Dai shugyō* 大修行
69. The Samādhi of Self Verification *Jishō zanmai* 自證三昧
70. Empty Space *Kokū* 虛空
71. The Pātra Bowl *Hou* 鉢盂
72. The Retreat *Ango* 安居
73. Reading Other Minds *Tashin tsū* 他心通
74. The King Requests Saindhava *Ō saku sendaba* 王索仙陀婆
75. Leaving Home *Shukke* 出家

Volume VI
The Twelve-Chapter Compilation

T1. The Merit of Leaving Home *Shukke kudoku* 出家功德
T2. Receiving the Precepts *Jukai* 受戒
T3. The Merit of the Kāṣāya *Kesa kudoku* 袈裟功德
T4. Bringing Forth the Mind of Bodhi *Hotsu bodai shin* 發菩提心
T5. Offerings to the Buddhas *Kuyō shobutsu* 供養諸佛
T6. Refuge in the Treasures of Buddha, Dharma, and Saṃgha
　Kie buppōsōbō 歸依佛法僧寶
T7. Deep Faith in Cause and Effect *Jinshin inga* 深信因果
T8. Karma of the Three Times *Sanjigō* 三時業
T9. Four Horses *Shime* 四馬
T10. The Bhikṣu of the Fourth Dhyāna *Shizen biku* 四禪比丘
T11. One Hundred Eight Gateways to the Illumination of the Dharma
　Ippyakuhachi hōmyōmon 一百八法明門
T12. The Eight Understandings of the Great Person *Hachi dainin gaku* 八大人覺

Volume VII
Supplementary Chapters, Variant Texts

Supplementary Chapters

S1. Talk on Pursuing the Way *Bendōwa* 辦道話
S2. Procedures for the Hall of Gathered Clouds *Jūundō shiki* 重雲堂式
S3. The *Lotus* Turns the *Lotus* *Hokke ten Hokke* 法華轉法華
S4. The Mind Cannot Be Got *Shin fukatoku* 心不可得
S5. The Four Attractions of the Bodhisattva *Bodaisatta shishōbō* 菩提薩埵四攝法
S6. Instructions to the Administration Cloister *Ji kuin mon* 示庫院文
S7. Only Buddhas with Buddhas *Yui butsu yo butsu* 唯佛與佛
S8. Birth and Death *Shōji* 生死
S9. The Way of the Buddhas *Butsudō* 佛道 (*Dōshin* 道心)

Variant Texts

V1. Talk on Pursuing the Way *Bendōwa* 辦道話
V2. The Inheritance Certificate *Shisho* 嗣書
V3. Beyond the Buddha *Butsu kōjō ji* 佛向上事
V4. Washing the Face *Senmen* 洗面
V5. Extensive Study *Henzan* 遍參
V6. Great Awakening *Daigo* 大悟
V7. Karma of the Three Times *Sanji gō* 三時業

Volume VIII

Introduction
Appendices
Supplementary Notes
Works Cited